The Development of Jury Service in Japan

This book presents a comprehensive account of past and present efforts to introduce the jury system in Japan. Four legal reforms are documented and assessed: the implementation of the bureaucratic and all-judge special jury systems in the 1870s, the introduction of the all-layperson jury in the late 1920s, the transplantation of the Anglo-American-style jury system to Okinawa under the U.S. occupation, and the implementation of the mixed-court lay judge (*saiban'in*) system in 2009. While being primarily interested in the related case studies, the book also discusses the instances when the idea of introducing trial by jury was rejected at different times in Japan's history. Why does legal reform happen? What are the determinants of success and failure of a reform effort? What are the prospects of the *saiban'in* system to function effectively in Japan? This book offers important insights on the questions that lie at the core of the law and society debate and are highly relevant for understanding contemporary Japan and its recent and distant past.

Anna Dobrovolskaia is an independent scholar currently based in Tokyo, Japan. Her main areas of interest include the sociology of law and Japan's legal, political, and cultural history.

"This book is a superb contribution to the field of law and society. It breaks new ground in our understanding of the success and failure of legal transplants, and reveals the political and legal factors that can promote or undermine democratic institutions like trial by jury. All those who are interested in trial by jury and democratic legal reform should read this extraordinary book."

Professor Valerie P. Hans, Cornell Law School, USA

The Development of Jury Service in Japan
A square block in a round hole?

Anna Dobrovolskaia

LONDON AND NEW YORK

First published 2017
by Routledge
2 Park Square, Milton Park, Abingdon, Oxon OX14 4RN

and by Routledge
711 Third Avenue, New York, NY 10017

Routledge is an imprint of the Taylor & Francis Group, an informa business

© 2017 Anna Dobrovolskaia

The right of Anna Dobrovolskaia to be identified as author of this work has been asserted by her in accordance with sections 77 and 78 of the Copyright, Designs and Patents Act 1988.

All rights reserved. No part of this book may be reprinted or reproduced or utilised in any form or by any electronic, mechanical, or other means, now known or hereafter invented, including photocopying and recording, or in any information storage or retrieval system, without permission in writing from the publishers.

Trademark notice: Product or corporate names may be trademarks or registered trademarks, and are used only for identification and explanation without intent to infringe.

British Library Cataloguing in Publication Data
A catalogue record for this book is available from the British Library

Library of Congress Cataloging-in-Publication Data
Names: Dobrovolskaia, Anna, author.
Title: The development of jury service in Japan : a square block in a round hole? / Anna Dobrovolskaia.
Description: New York, NY : Routledge, 2016. | Includes bibliographical references and index.
Identifiers: LCCN 2016012223 (print) | LCCN 2016013531 (ebook) | ISBN 9781472482556 (hardback) | ISBN 9781315615455 (Master) | ISBN 9781317035985 (Web PDF) | ISBN 9781317035978 (ePub) | ISBN 9781317035961 (Mobipocket)
Subjects: LCSH: Jury—Japan.
Classification: LCC KNX1585 .D63 2016 (print) | LCC KNX1585 (ebook) | DDC 347.52/0752—dc23
LC record available at http://lccn.loc.gov/2016012223

ISBN: 978-1-4724-8255-6 (hbk)
ISBN: 978-1-315-61545-5 (ebk)

Typeset in Galliard
by Apex CoVantage, LLC

Contents

Preface viii
List of abbreviations xi
List of illustrations xii

1 **Introduction** 1
   Legal change: contending explanations 9
   Plan of the book 18

2 **The pre-war history of the concept of trial by jury in Japan** 20
   Historical background: the developments in the Japanese legal system in the Meiji *period* 20
   The introduction of the concept of jury service to Japan 26
   *The bureaucratic jury (*sanza*) system* 33
   The Meiji *Constitution: the public debate* 44
   Boissonade's proposal: provisions concerning the jury in the draft of the Code of Criminal Instruction 46
   Evaluating the first attempts to introduce trial by jury in Meiji*-period Japan* 50
   Conclusions 54

3 **The pre-war jury system** 55
   Historical background: the developments in the legal system in the late Meiji, Taishō, *and early* Shōwa *periods* 55
   The background to the drafting of the Jury Act 58
   Drafting and implementation 66
   The Jury Act: a summary 73
   Promotion efforts and implementation 76
   The Japanese jury in action 85
   Amendments and suspension 90
   Evaluating Japan's pre-war experience with jury trials 93
   Conclusions 96

vi *Contents*

4 Attempts to introduce the jury system in Japan's colonial possessions 97
Historical background: Japan and its colonies 97
Taiwan: attempts to introduce the jury system in the Japanese colonial period 100
Karafuto: the jury system on the island during the Japanese colonial period 114
The jury system in colonial Japan: the colonized peoples in Japanese jury courts 121
Evaluating the attempts to introduce the jury system in Taiwan and Karafuto 125
Conclusions 127

5 The occupation years: Attempts to introduce the jury system 129
Historical background: the developments in the legal system in the immediate post-war period 129
The proposals to introduce the jury system in mainland Japan under the Allied occupation 132
The jury system in Okinawa under the U.S. occupation 151
Evaluating Japan's and Okinawa's experiences with jury trials under the occupation 161
Conclusions 165

6 The mixed-court jury (*saiban'in*) system in contemporary Japan 167
Historical background: the developments in the legal system in the post-occupation period 167
The background to the adoption of the Lay Judge Act 176
Drafting and enactment 183
The Lay Judge Act: a summary 188
Preparation for enforcement 191
Public debate 196
Implementation and the first lay judge case 203
The first six years of the functioning of the system 205
*Evaluating Japan's new lay judge (*saiban'in*) system 208*
Conclusions 212

7 Conclusions 214
Why was the jury system introduced (or not introduced) at different times in Japan's history? 214
*What were the determinants of success and failure of Japan's past experiences with the jury system and how does the lay judge (*saiban'in*) system fare with regard to these parameters? 219*
A summary of findings: revisiting the two approaches to analyzing legal change 222

Bibliography 227
Appendix 259
  I *Translated documents: the* Hōritsu Shinbun *articles* 259
    (1) 1928, "Oita District Court: the first jury verdict", Hōritsu Shinbun, *November 3, p. 17* 259
    (2) 1928, "Tokyo's first jury trial: detective intrigue overflowing", Hōritsu Shinbun, *December 30, p. 20* 261
    (3) 1928, "The accused members of the Communist Party to request trial by jury", Hōritsu Shinbun, *December 28, p. 19* 269
    (4) 1930, "Violation of the Jury Act", Hōritsu Shinbun, *March 13, p. 18* 269
  II *Illustrations* 270
Index 279

Preface

In 1871, Kunitake Kume embarked on a journey of observation through the United States and Europe as a member of the Iwakura Embassy – one of the most important Japanese diplomatic journeys for Japan's modernization efforts. Japan had just opened up to the world following 200 years of being a "closed country" (*sakoku*) and pursuing the policy of national isolation from 1630 onward, and was seeking to be reintegrated in the international political order and to reassert itself after signing the "unequal treaties" in 1858. The Iwakura delegation gathered information regarding the culture, technological capabilities as well as the social, economic, and legal structures and institutions of the Western countries that the mission visited. It was Kume's task to compile an account of the impressions of the members of the Embassy upon the conclusion of the trip. Among the institutions that attracted the attention of the Japanese delegation and that are discussed in the documents subsequently prepared by Kume is the institution of jury service.

The jury is commonly defined as a system by which laypersons are assembled on a temporary basis with the goal of determining the absence or presence of guilt on the part of the accused in a trial. In his account of the Iwakura Embassy's journey, Kume describes the jury trial that the members of the Embassy observed on January 22, 1873, in Paris and shares his own views regarding this system:

> This [system] may be regarded as a thoroughly comprehensive system indeed, but difficulties might arise, if one were to try to introduce it to Japan. No one is sufficiently familiar with the study of law in our country to enable them to appear in court as qualified lawyers. If a jury were to be nominated, the members would be terrified of the authorities and do no more than submit tamely to their words. Even if strong-willed and outspoken people were to be selected, they would be ignorant of the principles of the law and would create endless complications with their moralistic arguments, always quarreling amongst themselves and wasting their breath on useless matters.[1]

---

1 K. Kume, 1878, *Tokumei Zenken Taishi Beiō Kairan Jikki* [A True Account of the Ambassador Extraordinary and Plenipotentiary's Journey of Observation through the United States of America and Europe], Tokyo: Hakubunsha, translated in K. Kume (translated by A. Cobbling), 2002, *The Iwakura Embassy, 1871–1873, A True Account of the Ambassador Extraordinary and Plenipotentiary's Journey of Observation through the United States of America and Europe*, Vol. 3, Matsudo: Japan Documents, p. 134.

Kume concludes his discussion of the institution of jury service by cautioning against merely copying the institutions of the West:

> This is just one of numerous examples in which customs in the East and West are very opposite of each other. Learned men should do well to consider the import of this, for unless great care is taken to discard the traces of their origins and adopt only their substance, the introduction of wonderful Western laws and regulations to the East would frequently be like *trying to fit a square block of wood into a round hole*.[2]

Despite Kume's warnings, Japan chose to transplant the institution of jury service on several occasions over the course of history.

This book is a comprehensive history of the institution of jury service in Japan – from the introduction of the notion of trial by laypersons to Japan through Chinese classical texts in the 8th century AD onto the implementation of the mixed-court (*saiban'in*) system in contemporary Japan (the Act Concerning Participation of Lay Judges in Criminal Trials ("Lay Judge Act")), which was passed by the Diet on May 28, 2004, and enforced on May 21, 2009).

Based on the documentation and analysis of the efforts – successful and failed – to introduce the jury system in Japan, this book demonstrates that whenever Japan decided to implement the institution of jury service, it invariably created completely new systems of layperson participation that were different from the models of jury trials functioning in other countries. The book argues that the uniqueness of the jury systems implemented in Japan was the result of the conscious effort on the side of the Japanese government to not merely copy the Western models, but to adjust them to fit in with the pre-existing environment in Japan. It shows that in introducing distinctive models of jury trials at different points in history, Japan adapted the features of the institution of jury service as implemented in the West to ensure that it would function effectively in the legal, social, political, and cultural environment of Japan at those times in its history when reform was initiated and by doing so altered a "square block of wood" to fit into a "round hole".

This book is not the first contribution to focus exclusively on the history of the institution of jury service in Japan. It is the first attempt, however, to focus on the issue of institutional design as carried out by the Japanese government in introducing the jury system.

Throughout this book, all names appear in accordance with the Western tradition, with the family name following the given name.

I would like to gratefully acknowledge the support of the Taiwan Fellowship Program that provided the funding for the research that I conducted in Taiwan and that lies at the core of Chapter 4 of this book. I would also like to thank the Supreme Court of Japan, the Ministry of Justice of Japan, and the members of the We Do Not Need the Lay Judge System Movement Office for kindly permitting the reproduction of the illustrations that appear in this volume and to express my gratitude to Professor Harald Baum and the *Journal of Japanese Law* for kindly permitting the reproduction of the materials that were originally published in the journal.

---

2 Kume, *The Iwakura Embassy, 1871–1873, A True Account of the Ambassador Extraordinary and Plenipotentiary's Journey of Observation through the United States of America and Europe*, Vol. 3, pp. 134–135 (emphasis added).

This book would not have been completed had it not been for the generous help and support of a great number of unique individuals whom I have been fortunate enough to meet, have conversations with, and be inspired by at various stages of my work on the manuscript. I would like to take this opportunity to express my gratitude to Professors Jeremy S. Eades, David Askew, Kent Anderson, Hiroshi Fukurai, and Satoru Shinomiya for their encouragement, to all of the authors whose names appear in the bibliography section of this book for providing me with ample food for thought, to the anonymous reviewers of this manuscript for their insightful comments, to Alison Kirk, Jade Lovitt, Anna Dolan, Marie Louise Roberts, and all the members of the editorial, design, and production teams that have worked on this book for their invaluable suggestions, to my family for always cheering me on, and – last but not least – to Kunitake Kume and Andrew Cobbling who has translated Kume's work into English and to whose ingenious writing I owe the inspiration for writing this book and its title.

Anna Dobrovolskaia

Abbreviations

EEOL	Equal Employment Opportunity Law
GRI	Government of the Ryukyu Islands
JSRC	Judicial System Reform Council
LDP	Liberal Democratic Party of Japan
METI	Ministry of Economy, Trade, and Industry
SCAP	The Supreme Commander for the Allied Powers
USCAR	U.S. Civil Administration of the Ryukyu Islands

Illustrations

1a	The front page of the issue of *Hōritsu Shinbun* (*Legal News*) reporting on the first jury trial in Japan (Ōita District Court)	270
1b	The front page of the issue of *Hōritsu Shinbun* (*Legal News*) reporting on the first jury trial in Tokyo	271
2	The machine used in pre-war Japan to determine who would become candidates for jury service	272
3	A photograph taken during a mock trial held in 1928	273
4	Court clothing	273
5	Photographs taken inside the jury accommodation facility at the Tokyo District Court (1928)	274
6	Drawing names for the first jury panel in Okinawa	275
7	The logo of the lay judge system	275
8	Promotional character *Saiban'inko*	276
9	Posters prepared by the "We Do Not Need the Lay Judge System!" movement	276
10	Promotional character *Saiban'iniranainko*	277

1 Introduction

Why does legal reform happen? Is it triggered by a preceding change in society, as legislators become aware of the necessity to adjust the legal system to a new social reality, or does the law more frequently act as a tool for changing society? Is the discussion of social change at all relevant to the analysis of legal reform, or should law be understood not as the natural outgrowth of a particular society but as an intellectual creation of lawyers that is not socially determined and is therefore easily transferable to other countries? What are the determinants of success and failure of a legal reform? These questions lie at the very core of the ongoing academic debate regarding the origins and nature of law.

Japan's legal system is a good case study for attempting to address each of these questions. First, both the Japanese legal system and society have undergone several radical transformations since the mid-19th century, which implies that a significant amount of relatively recent documentary sources are available for conducting such an enquiry. Second, each of the groundbreaking developments in Japan's legal system involved selective borrowing from foreign jurisdictions. This in turn makes it possible to attempt to evaluate the effectiveness of legal transplants in the Japanese context.[1]

Japan has witnessed three "revolutionary" developments in its legal system and society since the mid-19th century. The first major change coincided with the *Meiji* Restoration of 1868 and resulted in the introduction of the concept of individual rights and the promulgation of a Western-inspired constitution (the *Meiji* Constitution of 1889), through which Japan embraced Continental jurisprudence.[2] Another development was triggered by World War II and the Allied occupation that brought along the democratization of the Japanese society and the drafting and promulgation of a new constitution (the *Shōwa* Constitution) in 1946. At the end of the 20th century, Japan's legal system appeared to be on the verge of yet another radical transformation as the government of Japan displayed a strong willingness to reform the legal system. In July 1999, the Cabinet established the Judicial System Reform Council (JSRC) with the aim of debating and making recommendations regarding

---

1 The question of how to define the effectiveness of legal reform has been the focus of considerable debate in the academic literature. This book follows the definition proposed by Antony Allot, who has argued a legal initiative may be called effective if it realizes the objectives and fulfills the purposes of its implementers (A. Allott, 1981, "The Effectiveness of Law", *Valparaiso University Law Review*, Vol. 15, pp. 229–242, at p. 233).
2 M. Dean (ed.), 2002, *Japanese Legal System*, 2nd edition, London: Cavendish, pp. 55–127; K. Takayanagi, "A Century of Innovation: The Development of Japanese Law", in A. T. Von Mehren (ed.), 1964, *Law in Japan: The Legal Order in a Changing Society*, Cambridge, MA: Harvard University Press, pp. 5–41.

2 Introduction

the possibility of fundamental legal change.[3] In 2000, Research Commissions on the Constitution (*Kenpō Chōsa Kai*) were set up in both houses of the National Diet. Five years later, Special Committees for Research on the Constitution of Japan (*Nihon Koku Kenpō ni kansuru Chōsa Tokubetsu Iinkai*) were established, and on May 14, 2007, the Law Concerning the Procedures of Revising the Constitution of Japan[4] was passed by the Diet, making the amendment of the world's oldest unrevised constitution less distant a prospect.[5] The provisions of the *Meiji* Constitution and the reforms that accompanied its promulgation were heavily influenced by Western thinking;[6] the drafting of the *Shōwa* Constitution of 1946 and subsequent reforms were carried out under the direct control of the Allied occupation forces;[7] and the preparation for the latest round of reforms also involved elements of adopting from other jurisdictions.[8]

Analyzing the judicial system of Japan in its entirety is problematic. Focusing on one aspect of the legal architecture, on the other hand, should make it possible to draw important conclusions with regard to the development of society and law in Japan. This book chooses the past and present efforts to expand lay participation in Japan as its area of focus. While lay participation in the judicial system can take various forms, this study focuses on the institution of jury service.[9]

---

3 The website of the Judicial Reform Council is available online at http://www.kantei.go.jp/foreign/judica_e.html (in English).
4 Nihon Koku Kenpō no Kaisei ni kansuru Hōritsu, Law No. 51 of 2007. Also see Anonymous, 2007, "Japan Must Change Constitution to Change Nation: Abe", *Japan Times*, May 3.
5 P. Brasor, 2015, "Split Clears a Path for Constitutional Revisionists", *Japan Times*, November 21; Anonymous, 2014, "Public Interest Strong in Constitution Debate as Newspapers Asked to Step Up", *Japan Times*, October 19; G. D. Hook and G. McCormack, 2001, *Japan's Contested Constitution: Documents and Analysis*, London: Routledge, p. 2. See generally E. Takemae (ed.), 2001, *Goken, Kaiken Shiron* [A History of the Constitutional Debate: Conservative and Revisionist Perspectives], Tokyo: Shōgakukan; N. Komuro, 2002, *Nihonkoku Kenpō no Mondai Ten* [Constitutional Issues of Japan], Tokyo: Shueisha; T. Nakanishi (ed.), 2000, *Kenpō Kaisei* [Constitutional Revision], Tokyo: Chūokōronshinsha; N. Harima, S. Kinoshita, H. Watanabe, and Y. Wakita (eds), 2002, *Dō Natte Iru?! Nihonkoku Kenpō: Kenpō to Shakai o Kangaeru* [The Constitution of Japan: What Has Become of It?! Thoughts on the Constitution and Society], Kyoto: Hōritsubunkasha.
6 The *Meiji* Constitution provided for a form of constitutional monarchy based on the Prussian model, the provisions regarding the relations between the executive and legislative powers were based on the German model (Takayanagi, "A Century of Innovation", p. 8, and Dean (ed.), *Japanese Legal System*, p. 68). The text of the *Meiji* Constitution is available in C. J. Milhaupt, J. M. Ramseyer, and M. K. Young (eds), 2001, *Japanese Law in Context: Readings in Society, the Economy, and Politics*, Cambridge, MA: Harvard University Asia Center, pp. 607–611. See Chapter 2 for a discussion of the developments in the Japanese legal system in the *Meiji* period.
7 For an overview of the process of drafting the 1946 Constitution see H. Tanaka, "A History of the Constitution of Japan of 1946", in C. J. Milhaupt, J. M. Ramseyer, and M. D. West (eds), 2006, *The Japanese Legal System*, New York: Foundation Press, pp. 191–205; Dean (ed.), *Japanese Legal System*, pp. 445–462. See Chapter 5 for a discussion of the developments in the Japanese legal system in the immediate post-war period.
8 The members of JSRC visited the United States, Germany, France, and the United Kingdom to hold consultations during the process of preparing recommendations (S. Miyazawa, "Summary and Comments on the Recommendations of the Judicial Reform Council (2001)", in M. M. Feeley and S. Miyazawa (eds), 2002, *The Japanese Adversary System in Context: Controversies and Comparisons*, New York: Palgrave Macmillan, pp. 247–252, at p. 248). See Chapter 6 for a discussion of the developments in the Japanese legal system in the post-occupation period and a detailed overview of the activities of the JSRC.
9 Laypersons can participate in the process of administration of justice in various capacities. In contemporary Japan, citizens participate in formal "regular procedures" (*soshō*) as judicial commissioners

Two principal models of jury systems exist in the world: the Anglo-American model and the Continental-European model. The Anglo-American model provides for the formation of an all-layperson jury panel that is composed of six to twelve jurors who are selected at random from the local population, whose task is to make decisions on the questions of fact and to come up with the verdict of guilty or not guilty independently of the judge.[10] The Continental-European model, on the other hand, involves the creation of a mixed-court panel where jurors and professional judges sit together in a single panel and jointly make decisions on the questions of fact and law.[11] Jurors in the Continental-European model (or "lay assessors" as they are sometimes called) are not selected at random from the list of persons eligible to vote to serve on one case only, as is the case in the Anglo-American model of jury trials, but are instead nominated by local authorities to serve a fixed term.[12]

The Anglo-American model of jury trials is also referred to in the literature as the "adversarial jury" system. Indeed, this model of jury trials is used predominantly in countries that have the adversarial system of justice – that is, a system of law that relies on the skills of each advocate representing his or her party's positions and where the judge's role is that of

---

(*shihō iin*), as councilors (*san'yoin*) at the family court, as expert commissioners (*kantei iin*) for the resolution of landlord and tenant disputes, and as conciliation commissioners (*chōtei iin*). See K. Anderson and M. Nolan, 2004, "Lay Participation in the Japanese Justice System: A Few Preliminary Thoughts Regarding the Lay Assessor System (*saiban-in seido*) from Domestic Historical and International Psychological Perspectives", *Vanderbilt Journal of Transnational Law*, Vol. 37, pp. 966–973 (containing an overview of the status of lay participation in contemporary Japan). In addition, laypersons in Japan participate in Prosecutorial Review Commissions (PRC; *Kensatsu Shinsa Kai*). See *id.*, pp. 965–966 (outlining the features of PRC); M. West, 1992, "Prosecution Review Commissions: Japan's Answer to the Problem of Prosecutorial Discretion", *Columbia Law Review*, Vol. 92, pp. 684–724, at pp. 694–714 (discussing the operation of PRC); and H. Fukurai, 2007, "The Rebirth of Japan's Petit Quasi-Jury and Grand Jury Systems: A Cross-National Analysis of Legal Consciousness and the Lay Participatory Experience in Japan and the U.S.", *Cornell International Law Journal*, Vol. 40, pp. 315–354, at pp. 325–327 (outlining the 2004 revisions to the PRC law).

10 See J. Abramson, 1994, *We, the Jury: The Jury System and the Ideals of Democracy*, New York: Basic Books (reviewing the features of the jury system as understood by the adversarial process); W. L. Dwyer, 2002, *In the Hands of the People: The Trial Jury's Origins, Troubles, and Future in American Democracy*, New York: Thomas Dunne Books (discussing the history and features of the jury system in the United States); L. Kiss, 1999, "Reviving the Criminal Jury in Japan", *Law and Contemporary Problems*, Vol. 62, No. 2, pp. 261–283, at pp. 270–271 (summarizing the features of the Anglo-American model of jury trials).

11 N. Osner, A. Quinn, and G. Crown (eds), 1993, *Criminal Justice Systems in Other Jurisdictions*, London: HMSO, pp. 83–104 (discussing the features of the criminal justice and jury systems in France and Germany); R. O. Lempert, 2001, "Citizen Participation in Judicial Decision Making: Juries, Lay Judges and Japan", *Saint Louis-Warsaw Transatlantic Law Journal*, Vol. 127, No. 16, pp. 1–14, at pp. 10–12 (discussing the differences between the mixed-court lay assessor system and the jury system); Kiss, "Reviving the Criminal Jury in Japan", p. 271 (summarizing the features of the Continental-European model of jury trials). Also see Saikō Saibansho [The Supreme Court], "Baishin Sei ya Sanshin Sei to wa Chigau no desu ka" [Is [Japan's *Saiban'in* System] Different from the [Anglo-American] Jury and the [Continental-European] Lay Assessor Systems?], available online at http://www.saibanin.courts.go.jp/qa/c8_2.html (containing a table that summarizes the differences between the Anglo-American and Continental-European jury systems and Japan's new *saiban'in* system (in Japanese)).

12 Osner, Quinn, and Crown (eds), *Criminal Justice Systems in Other Jurisdictions*, pp. 98–99 (discussing the features of the German mixed-court jury system). The French jury is an exception to this rule. While France uses the Continental-European model of jury trials, its jurors are selected by lot from the electoral registers (*id.*, p. 88).

a referee between the defense counsel and the prosecutor.[13] Countries using the adversarial system of justice are the United States, Britain, and several other common law countries.[14] The Anglo-American model of jury trials fits in well with the principles of adversarial justice. After all, this model provides for a jury panel consisting exclusively of laypersons; outsiders who have no connection to the criminal justice system apart from their service as jurors and who consequently lack the incentive to abuse their power are perfectly placed to carry out the role of impartial referees in adversarial trials.

Countries using the inquisitorial system of justice – that is, a legal system where it is the judge rather than the prosecutor and the defense counsel who is the active party – on the other hand, have historically been reluctant to adopt the Anglo-American model of jury trials.[15] Indeed, some features of inquisitorial procedure conflict with elements important to trial by jury as understood by the adversary process.[16] Specifically, under the inquisitorial system, where the judge is the active party, it may be difficult for jurors to arrive at their decisions on questions of fact independently. In addition, the inquisitorial system heavily relies on the expertise of court officials, and professional judges working within the system may be unwilling to allow the result of their work be potentially overturned by a group of laypersons.[17] In view of these elements of inquisitorial procedure, it is not surprising that many countries using this system have chosen to implement the Continental-European model of jury trials, where laypersons and professional judges make decisions together regarding the verdict and sentencing in cases. The role of laypersons on these mixed-court panels is to broaden the perspectives of professional judges and help limit elite bias rather than act as triers of fact expected to reach a rational and impartial verdict independently.[18] The inquisitorial system is generally adopted in civil law countries, such as Germany and France, among others.[19]

The alternative to trial by jury is trial by professional judges alone, and many countries using the adversarial system of justice and those that have the inquisitorial system as a means for dispute resolution have chosen not to introduce jury trials.

---

13 The adversarial system of justice is defined as a "procedural system, such as the Anglo-American legal system, involving active and unhindered parties contesting with each other in order to put forth a case before an independent decision-maker" (B. A. Garner (ed.), 2004, *Black's Law Dictionary*, 8th edition, St. Paul: West Group, p. 58).
14 Common law is defined as a system of law where procedure is "governed by laws and precedents, which, if codified at all, simply organize past experiences" (E. Fairchild and H. R. Dammer, 2001, *Comparative Criminal Justice Systems*, London: Wadsworth, p. 54).
15 Black's Law Dictionary defines the inquisitorial system of justice as a "system of proof-taking used in civil law, whereby the judge conducts the trial, determines what questions to ask, and defines the scope and extent of the inquiry. The system prevails in most Continental Europe, in Japan, and in Central and South America" (Garner (ed.), *Black's Law Dictionary*, p. 809). See G. Walpin, 2003, "America's Adversarial and Jury Systems: More Likely to Do Justice", *Harvard Journal of Law and Public Policy*, Vol. 26, pp. 175–186, at pp. 175–183 (discussing the features of the adversarial and the inquisitorial systems of justice); S. Macaulay, L. M. Friedman, and J. Stookey (eds), 1995, *Law & Society: Readings on the Social Study of Law*, New York: W. W. Norton, pp. 660–661 (contrasting the features of the adversarial and the inquisitorial systems of justice).
16 N. Vidmar, "A Historical and Comparative Perspective on the Common Law Jury", in N. Vidmar (ed.), 2000, *World Jury Systems*, New York: Oxford University Press, pp. 1–52, at p. 15.
17 *Id.*, p. 15.
18 *Id.*, p. 15; F. Stier, 1992, "What Can the American Adversary System Learn from an Inquisitorial System of Justice?", *Judicature*, Vol. 76, pp. 109–111, at p. 109.
19 Civil law is defined as a system of law where procedure is "governed by separate, comprehensive, systematized codes, which are forward-looking, wishing to anticipate all new problems" (Fairchild and Dammer, *Comparative Criminal Justice Systems*, p. 54).

The debate regarding the virtues and vices of citizen participation in the administration of justice is as old as the institution of jury service itself.[20] Opponents of the institution of jury service make several arguments. First, they claim that laypersons are not good at judging, and that making decisions regarding the fate of the accused should be done by professionals who were especially trained for that purpose. Second, they argue that citizens may be biased and irrational in their decision-making. Third, implementing the institution of jury service is costly, as jurors need to be paid for their services.[21]

Proponents of layperson participation, on the other hand, have argued that jurors are actually good at fact-finding despite their lack of professional training. Several studies have found based on the evidence from the United States that in both criminal and civil cases verdicts returned by the jury were in agreement with the judge's verdicts in three-quarters of instances.[22] In addition, the supporters of the jury system have emphasized the fact that jurors – being complete outsiders to the system – are free to return unpopular verdicts, unlike judges who might face government retribution, such as an assignment to an unimportant court.[23] Furthermore, the jury system has been praised for its value as a democratic institution. The institution of jury service allows citizens to directly participate in the administration of justice and therefore serves as a vehicle for citizen empowerment.[24] As the French statesman Alexis de Tocqueville noted in his travels through 19th-century America, the jury system may be viewed as "a political institution . . . [as] one form of the sovereignty of the people".[25] He praised this institution for investing "each citizen with a kind of magistracy" and for making "all feel the duties which they are bound to discharge towards society and the part which they take in its government".[26]

Japan is a civil law country that has witnessed efforts to expand lay participation in court proceedings several times over history.[27] The idea of allowing laypersons to participate in the

---

20 The trial jury's origins go back to ancient Athens. It was there that the mechanism by which the accused was tried by jurors (*dikasts*) was first implemented. Most cases were tried with the participation of 500 jurors. Capital cases, however, were tried before a jury of 1,000 to 1,500 *dikastai*. Socrates was famously sentenced by jurors to death (Abramson, *We, the Jury*, p. 1; R. K. Green, 2002, *Democratic Virtue in the Trial and Death of Socrates: Resistance to Imperialism in Classical Athens*, New York: Peter Lang, pp. 114–115).
21 Lempert, "Citizen Participation in Judicial Decision Making", pp. 2–7 (summarizing the arguments against the jury system); V. P. Hans, 2007, "Introduction: Citizens as Legal Decision Makers: An International Perspective", *Cornell International Law Journal*, Vol. 40, pp. 303–314, at pp. 308–309 (discussing the challenges of citizen participation).
22 H. Kalven Jr. and H. Zeisel, 1986, *The American Jury*, Chicago: University of Chicago Press, p. 56. Also see T. Eisenberg, P. L. Hannaford-Agor, V. P. Hans, N. L. Walters, G. T. Munsterman, S. J. Schwab, and M. T. Wells, 2005, "Judge-Jury Agreement in Criminal Cases: A Partial Replication of Kalven and Zeisel's *The American Jury*", *Journal of Empirical Legal Studies*, Vol. 2, pp. 171–207.
23 Lempert, "Citizen Participation in Judicial Decision Making", p. 8.
24 *Id.*, p. 8.
25 A. de Tocqueville, 1994, *Democracy in America*, New York: David Campbell, p. 283.
26 *Id.*, p. 285. Several relatively recent studies have discussed the link between jury service and other forms of civic engagement. See J. Gastil, E. P. Deess, and P. Weiser, 2002, "Civic Awakening in the Jury Room: A Test of the Connection between Jury Deliberation and Political Participation", *Journal of Politics*, Vol. 64, No. 2, pp. 585–595; J. Gastil and P. Levine (eds), 2005, *The Deliberative Democracy Handbook: Strategies for Effective Civic Engagement in the Twenty-First Century*, San Francisco: Jossey-Bass.
27 While the question of whether Japan's contemporary system of justice can be called inquisitorial or adversarial has remained a subject of debate, there is consensus that in the pre-war period Japan had the inquisitorial system of justice. Black's Law Dictionary gives contemporary Japan as an example of a country that uses the inquisitorial system of justice (Garner (ed.), *Black's Law Dictionary*, p. 809). Some scholars have

adjudication of cases first reached Japan as early as the 8th century AD through Chinese classical texts. The notion of the jury as a legal institution, however, was first introduced to the country in the middle of the 19th century, when Japan turned its attention to learning from the West after a period of seclusion. Japan became familiar with both the Anglo-American and the Continental-European models of jury trials through the documents written by foreign scholars describing the political and legal systems of Western countries and the written accounts of Japanese bureaucrats who were sent abroad to learn about the political and legal institutions of other countries after the *Meiji* Restoration.

The first attempt to introduce the jury system in Japan dates back to the first decade of the *Meiji* period – the early 1870s – when the Ministry of Justice discussed the possibility of implementing trial by laypersons on the experimental basis in cases of extraordinarily complex nature. As the result of deliberations, however, Japan chose to introduce not the layperson jury, but two alternatives: the "bureaucratic jury" (*kan'in baishin* or *sanza*) system (a jury that consisted not of laypersons, but of bureaucrats appointed by the government); and what may be called the "judge-only jury" (a panel consisting of twelve professional judges who deliberated the facts of the case and came up with the verdict). The "bureaucratic jury" system was used in only two civilian trials and in several military tribunals in the 1870s, while the "judge-only jury" was used in one civilian trial that took place in 1879.

The first reform introducing trial by laypersons in Japan was implemented half a century later, in the 1920s – a time associated with the popular movement towards democratization known as "*Taishō* Democracy".[28] Japan's pre-war Jury Act was enacted in 1923 and became operative in 1928. The jury system that was implemented in pre-war Japan had some peculiarities that distinguished it from the systems of lay participation used in other countries at the time. Specifically, the twelve-layperson jury panels in Japan did not yield a verdict of guilty or not guilty, but instead were required to give answers to the questions submitted to them by the judge regarding points of fact. The answers of the jury were not binding on the court, and the judge was given the option of disregarding the jury's responses and calling another jury. The system operated in the *naichi* portion of the Japanese Empire and in the colony of Karafuto.[29] Several proposals aimed at introducing the jury trial system in the colony of Taiwan were discussed in the late 1920s and early 1930s but failed to lead to reform.[30] Japan's pre-war jury system was unpopular among users and was suspended in 1943.

In the post-war era, jury trials took place in Okinawa under the U.S. occupation. The San Francisco Peace Treaty that was signed in 1951 gave the United States the right to exercise "all and any powers of administration, legislation, and jurisdiction over the territory

---

emphasized, however, that Japan's post-war system seems to incorporate the features of both the adversary and the inquisitorial systems (D. H. Foote, "Reflections on Japan's Cooperative Adversary Process", in Feeley and Miyazawa (eds), *The Japanese Adversary System in Context*, p. 29).

28 A popular movement of the *Taishō* period that demanded the establishment of universal suffrage and the suppression of the privileges of the Privy Council (*sumitsuin*), *genrō*, House of Peers, and the army. See generally B. S. Silberman and H. D. Harootunian (eds), 1974, *Japan in Crisis: Essays on Taisho Democracy*, Princeton: Princeton University Press. See Chapter 3 for a discussion of *Taishō* Democracy.

29 *Naichi* literally means "inner lands" and is a word used to refer to the lands constituting Japan proper (R. H. Myers and M. R. Peattie (eds), 1984, *The Japanese Colonial Empire, 1895–1945*, Princeton: Princeton University Press, p. 267).

30 See Chapter 4 for a discussion of these proposals.

and inhabitants" of Japan's Okinawa prefecture,[31] and the occupation forces introduced Anglo-American-style criminal and civil jury systems to the U.S. Civil Administration of the Ryukyu Islands (USCAR) courts in 1963 and 1964, respectively.[32] Procedurally, the jury system in Okinawa closely resembled that in the United States. Jury panels of twelve laypersons deliberated questions of fact, and their verdict of guilty or not guilty was binding. In one respect, however, the Okinawan jury system differed from the system used in the United States: there was no nationality requirement for jury service, so Okinawans and persons of other nationalities who could speak and write English were summoned and served on jury panels. The criminal and civil jury systems functioned in USCAR courts until 1972, when Okinawa reverted to Japan's control.

The most recent effort to expand lay participation in Japan resulted in the drafting of the Act Concerning Participation of Lay Judges in Criminal Trials (the "Lay Judge Act")[33] that was passed by the Diet on May 28, 2004, and enforced on May 21, 2009. The Lay Judge Act provides for the establishment of a new mixed-court jury (*saiban'in*) system where the verdict and sentencing in major crimes is decided by a panel consisting of either three professional judges and six laypersons or one judge and four jurors, depending on the complexity of the case.

The pros and cons of the institution of jury service in general and of the different models of jury trials in particular were actively deliberated at the key junctures of Japan's modern history. Following Japan's first experiments with the institution of jury service in the *Meiji* period, scholar and advisor to the Japanese government Emile Gustave Boissonade de Fontarabie proposed to include the provisions regarding the jury system in his 1879 draft of Japan's Code of Criminal Instruction. While this idea was ultimately rejected by the *Meiji* government, it served to trigger academic debate regarding the virtues and vices of the institution of jury service for the first time in Japan. The process of drafting the Jury Act of 1923 also involved active deliberations among academics regarding the features of trial by jury that Japan should implement. This debate was revived following the suspension of the Jury Act in 1943, when the Allied occupation forces discussed the possibility of reintroducing trial by jury with the Japanese government – a proposal that was never realized – and then again in the 1960s, 1980s, and 1990s when the Japanese people considered introducing the jury system.

Every time Japan chose to implement trial by jury, the features of the system that it introduced were different from those of the models that the country experimented with previously. What strikes an observer as even more remarkable, however, is that whenever Japan decided to introduce the institution of jury service it invariably created completely new systems of layperson participation that were different from the models of jury trials functioning

---

31 The full text of the peace treaty is available in E. O. Reischauer, 1965, *The United States and Japan*, Cambridge, MA: Harvard University Press, pp. 363–378. See R. D. Eldridge, 2001, *The Origins of the Bilateral Okinawa Problem: Okinawa in Postwar US-Japan Relations, 1945–1952*, New York: Garland (discussing the details of post-war planning for Okinawa following the surrender of Japan).
32 Code of Penal Procedure, Civil Administration Ordinance No. 144 of 1955, as amended on 8 March 1963, and United States Civil Administration Criminal Courts, Civil Administration Proclamation No. 8 of 1958, as amended by Civil Administration Proclamation No. 18 of 1963.
33 Saiban'in no Sanka Suru Keiji Saiban ni Kansuru Hōritsu [Act Concerning Participation of Lay Judges in Criminal Trials], Law No. 63 of 2004, translated in K. Anderson and E. Saint, 2005, "Japan's Quasi-Jury (*Saiban'in*) Law: An Annotated Translation of the Act Concerning Participation of Lay Assessors in Criminal Trials", *Asian-Pacific Law & Policy Journal*, Vol. 6, pp. 233–283.

in other countries. The "bureaucratic jury" and the "all-judge jury" systems of the *Meiji* period were Japan's inventions, conceptualized as alternatives to Western jury trials: the jury system used in Okinawa under the U.S. occupation was a modified version of the adversarial Anglo-American model, and both the pre-war jury and the *saiban'in* systems were unique crosses between the Continental mixed-court jury and the Anglo-American common law jury. While the *saiban'in* system as outlined in the Lay Judge Act may be looked upon as essentially a Continental-European jury system that has several unique features, Japan's pre-war jury system may be described as an Anglo-American jury system that had a number of distinctive characteristics. The *saiban'in* is a mixed-court system where judges and laypersons deliberate questions of guilt and sentencing together – a feature that is characteristic of most Continental-European jury systems. Japanese lay judges, however, are selected at random from the list of persons eligible to vote and appointed to adjudicate only one case rather than be nominated by local authorities to serve a fixed term. The pre-war jury system, on the other hand, while being based on the Anglo-American model, differed from its common law adversarial counterpart in that the members of the jury were responsible for answering the questions submitted to them by the judge rather than for coming up with the verdict of guilty or not guilty, and because the judge was given the right to dismiss the opinions of the jury.

This study argues that the uniqueness of the jury systems implemented in Japan was the result of the conscious effort on the side of the Japanese government to not merely copy the Western models, but to adapt them to fit in with the pre-existing environment in Japan. It shows that each attempt to introduce the jury system in Japan differed in terms of how much priority was given to the efforts to adjust the features of either the Continental-European or the Anglo-American model of jury trials that Japan chose to adopt to suit the characteristics of the country's legal system, political situation, traditions, and cultural values. Among the three layperson jury systems that were implemented in Japan, the Okinawan model was least adapted to the local conditions, as it was introduced with the sole purpose of protecting the constitutional right to jury trial of Americans stationed in Okinawa. This study argues that the jury system in Okinawa functioned without any disruption precisely due to the fact that it was introduced only in USCAR courts that carried out trial hearings in a manner that was similar to courts in the United States that have a long tradition of jury trials. The *Shōwa*-period system, on the other hand, appears to have been the most adapted among the three. This study demonstrates that although Japan's pre-war jury system was originally based on the Anglo-American adversarial model of jury trials, the enacted version of the Jury Act of 1923 did not provide for a mere replication of this model. It shows that the unique features of the *Shōwa* period system were added by the legislators in an effort to adjust the adversarial element that was the all-layperson jury system to Japan's inquisitorial and otherwise Continental-European system of criminal procedure and to the political environment of militaristic Japan. This study finds that contrary to the expectations of the legislators, these modifications prevented Japan's pre-war jury system from functioning smoothly and contributed to the subsequent fall in the popularity of jury trials and the suspension of the Jury Act. The *saiban'in* system may arguably be placed between the aforementioned two extremes. This system is based on the Continental-European model of jury trials, but features some elements of adaptation that are neither as negligible as in the case of the jury system in Okinawa nor as drastic as in the case of Japan's pre-war jury system.

The scope of this study makes it possible to analyze the attempts to implement different models of the jury system in one country (the pre-war jury system and the system in occupied Okinawa were based on the Anglo-American all-layperson system, while the *saiban'in* mixed-court jury system introduced in 2009 is modeled on the Continental-European lay assessor system). It also allows for an examination of three cases that differed in terms of the results that they brought along. One may be looked upon as a case of failure (the pre-war jury system); another is an example of successful implementation of the system in the situation of occupation (the jury system in Okinawa). The third model (the *saiban'in* system) is a "case in progress". This study uses the insights that Japan's past experiences with the jury system offer to evaluate the *saiban'in* system's potential to function smoothly in contemporary Japan.[34] Finally, looking at the attempts to introduce the jury system provides insights into the periods that are of definite importance in Japan's history: the *Meiji* period during which Japan turned to the West after a period of isolation, the period of "*Taishō* Democracy" that was followed by the militaristic expansion of the early *Shōwa* era, the period of the U.S. occupation, and contemporary times.

The first objective of this book is to document Japan's experiences with the institution of jury service. The second is to analyze these experiences.

Through examining the reforms aiming to introduce the jury system in Japan, this study attempts to answer two basic questions. First, why was the jury system introduced (or not introduced) at different times in Japan's history? Second, what were the determinants of success and failure of the system to function effectively and how does the *saiban'in* system fare with regard to these parameters?

Before addressing these questions it is important to look at the body of the existing literature on the subject of legal reform – theoretical contributions discussing the origins of law, identifying the triggers of reform, and highlighting the elements that may determine the success or failure of a reform initiative – and Japanese law. This is the goal of the following section.

Legal change: contending explanations

Theories of legal change

It is possible to group existing theories analyzing the process of legal change into three clusters based on their conceptualization of the relationship between law and society.

The first group proceeds from the supposition that law is not the natural outgrowth of a particular society.[35] One of the most influential theories in this group is Alan Watson's

---

34 The notion of "success" when discussing legal reforms – that is, the precise definition of the features of a reform or legal transplant that can be called "successful" – is disputed. It has been argued specifically that the notion of "success" depends on the baseline that one uses for measurement and that this issue is controversial (D. Nelken, "Towards a Sociology of Legal Adaptation", in D. Nelken and J. Feest (eds), 2001, *Adapting Legal Cultures*, Oxford: Hart, pp. 7–55, at pp. 37–39). Hideki Kanda and Curtis J. Milhaupt, in their discussion of successful and failed legal transplants, have argued that success implies "use of the imported legal rule in the same way that it is used in the home country, subject to adaptations to local conditions", and that failure occurs "when the imported rule is ignored by relevant actors in the host country, or the application and enforcement of the rule lead to unintended consequences" (H. Kanda and C. J. Milhaupt, 2003, "Re-examining Legal Transplants: The Director's Fiduciary Duty in Japanese Corporate Law, *American Journal of Comparative Law*, Vol. 51, pp. 887–901, at p. 890), and it is this definition that is presumed in this study.
35 I. Markovits, 2004, "Exporting Law Reform – But Will It Travel?", *Cornell International Law Journal*, Vol. 37, pp. 95–114, at p. 95.

theory of legal transplants.[36] Watson observes that although law "exists in society and for society's needs", legal rules can be easily transplanted from one society to the other.[37] This fact makes Watson conclude that changes in law are not dependent on the forces external to law. Based on an extensive study of Roman law and the instances of transplantation of Roman legal rules throughout Continental Europe, Watson argues that legal change is not dependent on society, but develops as a result of borrowing from other jurisdictions.

On the other side of the spectrum are theories that see law as socially determined. The proponents of this view argue that legal rules change in response to external forces in the society in which they operate, that not only law but also the way in which law is conceptualized by scholars is "historically and culturally conditioned".[38] The supporters of the socio-legal approach agree with Watson that laws may be transplanted from one society to another, but claim that for any legal export to be accepted in a legal culture other than its original one it needs to be fundamentally changed in character in order to accommodate for the differences between the "exporting" and "importing" societies.[39]

The third group that may be placed between the aforementioned two extremes emphasizes the cross-border flows of social norms. The theories belonging to this cluster claim that the fact that legal systems borrow from one another successfully does not imply a weak influence of society on law, but actually does precisely the opposite. The supporters of this view argue that the transferability of law reflects the fact that no society can be completely isolated from interaction with other societies and that this becomes the source of increasing similarities across the globe.[40] L. M. Friedman has argued that legal systems are converging, "drawing closer and closer together" due to the fact that "legal practice is globalizing," and most importantly, because "legal systems reflect the societies in which they are embedded; and these societies are becoming more and more alike."[41]

---

36 A. Watson, 1974, *Legal Transplants: An Approach to Comparative Law*, Edinburgh: Scottish Academic Press; A. Watson, 1977, *Society and Legal Change*, Edinburgh: Scottish Academic Press; A. Watson, 1978, "Comparative Law and Legal Change", *Cambridge Law Journal*, Vol. 37, pp. 313–336; W. Ewald, 1995, "Comparative Jurisprudence (II): The Logic of Legal Transplants", *American Journal of Comparative Law*, Vol. 43, pp. 489–505; Kanda and Milhaupt, "Re-examining Legal Transplants, pp. 887–901; R. Stack, 2000, "Western Law in Japan: The Antimonopoly Law and Other Legal Transplants", *Manitoba Law Journal*, Vol. 27, pp. 391–414; D. Berkowitz, K. Pistor, and J. Richard, 2003, "The Transplant Effect", *American Journal of Comparative Law*, Vol. 51, pp. 163–202; Nelken and Feest (eds), *Adapting Legal Cultures*.
37 Watson, "Comparative Law and Legal Change", p. 313.
38 P. Legrand, 1997, "The Impossibility of 'Legal Transplants'", *Maastricht Journal of European and Comparative Law*, Vol. 4, pp. 111–124, at p. 117.
39 Ewald, "Comparative Jurisprudence (II)", pp. 489–490; Markovits, "Exporting Law Reform – But Will It Travel?", pp. 95–96.
40 L. M. Friedman, "Some Thoughts on the Rule of Law, Legal Culture, and Modernity in Comparative Perspective", in Institute of Comparative Law in Japan (ed.), 1998, *Toward Comparative Law in the 21st Century*, Tokyo: Chuo University Press, pp. 1075–1090; L. M. Friedman, 2002, *Law in America: A Short History*, New York: Modern Library. This approach is frequently linked to the study of globalization. See S. Zifcak (ed.), 2005, *Globalization and the Rule of Law*, London: Routledge; P. S. Berman (ed.), 2005, *The Globalization of International Law*, Aldershot: Ashgate; Y. Dezalay and B. G. Garth (eds), 2002, *Global Prescriptions: The Production, Exportation, and Importation of a New Legal Orthodoxy*, Ann Arbor: University of Michigan Press; L. M. Friedman and R. Pérez-Perdomo, 2003, *Legal Culture in the Age of Globalization: Latin America and Europe*, Stanford: Stanford University Press.
41 Friedman, *Law in America*, pp. 9–10; L. Friedman, "Some Comments on Cotterrell and Legal Transplants", in Nelken and Feest (eds), *Adapting Legal Cultures*, pp. 70–93.

The second group that stipulates that law is socially determined may be subdivided further based on how each theory belonging to this cluster conceptualizes the role that society plays with regard to the creation of law. Some theorists within this group have defined law as "institutionalized custom" and as a means of expressing values and norms that develop naturally in a given society as a result of constant struggle on the part of its members to address and find solutions to the problems in group life. Paul Bohannan has argued that law is custom that is "recreated, by agents of society, in a narrower and recognizable context".[42] Structuralists, on the other hand, view law not as custom but as an inevitable outcome of the transformations in the structure of relationships existing in a society. Émile Durkheim has argued that modern legal systems emerged as an inevitable result of the process of the division of labor.[43] Structuralists claim that an increase in the population and in the density of interaction is one of the factors behind the rise of new legal institutions. Proponents of this view conceptualize legal institutions as a means for coordinating the diverse actions and purposes of people in society.[44] Yet another group of theories assumes what is known as the conflict perspective on law. Theories belonging to this group view law as a device that is used by powerful elites to establish and maintain their dominance over other classes. Conflict theorists conceptualize law as a method of social control and argue that the pattern of legal development in a given society is shaped not only by the efforts of the ruling class to dominate, but also by the efforts of the ruled class to resist domination.[45]

In addition to discussing the nature and origins of law, socio-legal theories offer a variety of explanations with regard to the question of what triggers legal reform. Some scholars in this group have attributed legal change primarily to the activities of rational lawmakers and politicians responding to incentives such as re-election (this perspective is known as the principal-agent theory).[46] The basic argument of principal-agent theorists is that legal change

---

42 P. Bohannan, 1965, "The Differing Realms of the Law", *American Anthropologist*, Vol. 67, pp. 33–42, at p. 34. Also see P. Bohannan, 1967, *Law and Warfare: Studies in the Anthropology of Conflict*, New York: Natural History Press.
43 E. Durkheim, 1933, *The Division of Labor in Society*, New York: Free Press; H. M. Maine, 1986, *Ancient Law: Its Connection with the Early History of Society and Its Relation to Modern Ideas*, New York: Dorset Press.
44 B. Mayhew and R. Levinger, 1976, "Size and Density of Interaction in Human Aggregates", *American Journal of Sociology*, Vol. 82, pp. 86–110; B. Mayhew and R. Levinger, 1976, "On the Emergence of Oligarchy in Human Interaction", *American Journal of Sociology*, Vol. 81, pp. 1017–1049; R. Shwartz and J. Millers, 1964, "Legal Evolution and Societal Complexity", *American Sociological Review*, Vol. 70, pp. 159–169.
45 See Macaulay, Friedman, and Stookey (eds), *Law & Society*, pp. 209–211; R. L. Kiddler, 1983, *Connecting Law and Society: An Introduction to Research and Theory*, Englewood Cliffs, NJ: Prentice-Hall, pp. 83–111; A. Turk, 1976, "Law as a Weapon in Social Conflict", *Social Problems*, Vol. 23, pp. 276–291; C. Sumner, 1979, *Reading Ideologies: An Investigation into the Theory of Ideology and Law*, New York: Pantheon; M. Tushnet, 1972, "Lumber and the Legal Process", *Wisconsin Law Review*, No. 1, pp. 114–132; L. Salamini, "Towards a Sociology of Intellectuals: A Structural Analysis of Gramsci's Marxist Theory", in J. Martin (ed.), 2002, *Antonio Gramsci: Critical Assessments of Leading Political Philosophers(3)*, New York: Routledge, pp. 63–93; C. E. Reasons and R. M. Rich (eds), 1979, *The Sociology of Law: A Conflict Perspective*, Toronto: Butterworth.
46 See A. Downs, 1957, *An Economic Theory of Democracy*, Boston: Addison-Wesley; J. Laffont and D. Martimort, 2002, *The Theory of Incentives: The Principle-Agent Model*, Princeton: Princeton University Press; S. Parsons, 2005, *Rational Choice in Politics: A Critical Introduction*, London: Continuum. For a brief overview of the main arguments of the principle-agent theorists, see E. A. Feldman, 2006, "The Culture of Legal Change: A Case Study of Tobacco Control in Twenty-First Century Japan", *Michigan Journal of International Law*, Vol. 27, pp. 743–821, at p. 744.

is triggered primarily by self-interested actions of politicians whose main aim and concern is to get re-elected. Other influential theories regarding the triggers of reform emphasize the role of government officials[47] and of political entrepreneurs,[48] while Max Weber's conceptualization of the impact of bureaucratic structure on the organization of social life – and through it, on the law – has also remained a prominent explanation of legal change.[49]

A vast body of existing theoretical literature is devoted to identifying the key components that determine the success and failure of a given legal initiative. One factor behind the successful adoption of a legal reform proposal that has been pointed out in the literature is the prestige and power of the "exporter" (if a legal model is "transplanted" from one society to the other), or of the domestic promoter of the reform.[50] Another is interest group politics. The approach to analyzing the potential of a given legal reform to succeed that emphasizes interest group politics proposes to evaluate which parties will benefit from a reform and which are likely to be harmed. It has been argued, for instance, that opposition from various actors in the legal system, such as the Bar Association and the members of the judiciary who may be interested in preserving the status quo, may hinder the implementation of a reform.[51] The scholarly literature has also highlighted the fact that the nature of the advantages that a legal change is likely to bring along is also important to consider when evaluating the prospects of that reform.[52] The proponents of this view argue that one of the most important questions to consider is whether a given reform is likely to produce short-term or long-term benefits. They claim that the presence of short-term results tends to be particularly important in less economically developed states where there is still a significant amount of uncertainty in the society regarding the value of law, and in authoritarian and post-authoritarian states where a society may be fearful of the possibility that the elites might use the law as a tool for repression.[53] The presence and nature of the civil society in the country choosing to implement a legal reform is yet another feature that according to the existing literature requires evaluation, as the ability of reformers to mobilize the civil society may be critical for ensuring the success of any reform proposal.[54] Other factors requiring assessment are economic factors (amounts of foreign direct investments and such indicators as gross domestic product per capita, which may affect the demand for rule of law in a society and the ability of the state to enforce new laws),[55] the nature of the political regime

---

47 J. W. Kingdon, 2001, "A Model of Agenda-Setting, with Applications", *Law Review of Michigan State University Detroit College of Law*, No. 2, pp. 331–339; J. W. Kingdon, 2003, *Agendas, Alternatives, and Public Policies*, New York: Longman.
48 N. Frohlich, J. A. Oppenheimer, and O. R. Young, 1971, *Political Leadership and Collective Goods*, Princeton: Princeton University Press.
49 M. Weber, 1968, *Economy and Society: An Outline of Interpretive Sociology*, New York: Bedminster Press. Also see A. Giddens, 1971, *Capitalism and Modern Social Theory: An Analysis of the Writings of Marx, Durkheim, and Weber*, London: Cambridge University Press.
50 R. Peerenboom, 2006, "What Have We Learned about Law and Development? Describing, Predicting, and Assessing Legal Reforms in China", *Michigan Journal of International Law*, Vol. 27, pp. 823–871, at p. 831. Randall Peerenboom bases this assertion on his analysis of the cases when the United States and the European countries promoted their own models of corporate governance, criminal law, and capital markets to other countries and exercised their influence indirectly through international organizations, development agencies, and through various non-governmental organizations (*id.*, p. 831).
51 *Id.*, p. 832.
52 *Id.*, p. 832.
53 *Id.*, p. 832.
54 *Id.*, p. 832.
55 *Id.*, p. 832.

in the country,[56] the presence of the institutional capacity to implement reforms (most significantly the courts, law schools, the legal profession),[57] and finally, the compatibility of proposed reforms with the institutional culture of the society where the legal initiative will be implemented.[58]

The role that the last component – that is, institutional culture and more broadly, culture in general – plays in the process of legal change has been in the spotlight of academic debate as well. The views proposed in the scholarly literature regarding this question are diverse. Eric A. Feldman, for instance, in his study of tobacco control in contemporary Japan, has emphasized the fact that international norms may serve as an "inspiration for domestic legal change and local culture" and argued that culture gives imported laws a distinctive identity.[59] Randall Peerenboom, on the other hand, concluded his analysis of legal reforms in China by observing that institutional culture is an element that more frequently inhibits reform than inspires it.[60]

While the nature of the effect that a country's culture may have on that country's willingness to implement reforms has been the subject of debate, the fact that culture does influence the public's perception of a reform is arguably beyond dispute. Takao Tanase has claimed that people in any country evaluate laws on their ability to facilitate efficient market transactions as well as on their relative success in promoting good society, and that it is in this process of definition of what is good and what is bad for the society that culture plays an important role.[61] Setsuo Miyazawa has argued that in order to analyze the contribution of culture to the process of legal change it is useful to observe social movements existing in that country, as they "utilize culture strategically, selectively and instrumentally".[62] Miyazawa emphasized that culture plays an important part in the process of framing the proposals that are put forth by the leaders of social movements in order to effectively mobilize potential adherents and to demobilize antagonists.[63]

---

56 *Id.*, p. 833.
57 *Id.*, p. 833.
58 *Id.*, p. 833.
59 Feldman, "The Culture of Legal Change", p. 746; S. Miyazawa, 2006, "How Does Culture Count in Legal Change? A Review with a Proposal from a Social Movement Perspective", *Michigan Journal of International Law*, Vol. 27, pp. 917–931, at pp. 920–923.
60 Peerenboom, "What Have We Learned about Law and Development?", p. 833.
61 T. Tanase, 2006, "Global Markets and the Evolution of Law in China and Japan", *Michigan Journal of International Law*, Vol. 27, pp. 873–893. Also see Miyazawa, "How Does Culture Count in Legal Change?", p. 918.
62 Miyazawa, "How Does Culture Count in Legal Change?", pp. 928–931.
63 *Id.*, p. 930. The thematic classification of the existing literature on the subject of legal reform – classification based on the major questions that each theory addresses – that is proposed and used in this section is, of course, not the only possible method of grouping the existing theoretical perspectives. An alternative method has been proposed by Randall Peerenboom. Peerenboom divides the literature on legal reform into two groups: (1) theories that conceptualize legal reform as a "horizontal" development, and (2) theories that view legal change as a "vertical" development. Peerenboom's "horizontal" reforms imply borrowing of models from other jurisdictions and includes "legal transplants", while "vertical" reforms are initiatives that developed within the society and include top-down (imposed by the government or the elites) efforts and bottom-up (originating from the civil society, the media, and legal academics) reforms. He also proposes to classify legal changes based on how the reform process is initiated ("deductive" versus "inductive" reforms). According to Peerenboom, "deductive" reforms derive "appropriate rules, practices, or institutions from a pre-given set of general principles or models", while an "inductive" approach "identifies a problem, examines the various solutions . . . to identify patterns and general principles, and then tests the principles by applying them in different contexts and observing the results or consequences" (Peerenboom, "What Have We Learned about Law and Development?", pp. 825–830).

Japan's law and legal reform

Scholars have frequently used Japan as an example to illustrate theories of legal change. The literature on Japanese law in both Japanese and English has encompassed almost all of the themes that were mentioned in the preceding section and has made use of both the socio-legal approach and Alan Watson's theory of legal transplants to explain legal change in the country.

The socio-legal approach to the study of Japanese law is exemplified by three main schools of analysis.

The "Japanese exceptionalism" school[64] has emphasized the unique features of Japanese legal consciousness that are deeply rooted in cultural values, arguing that these distinguish Japan's legal system from the rest of the world. Japanese society is frequently described as "vertical", which implies that the relative status of parties determines social relationships, and as one that is characterized by the traditional attitude of "Respect for Officials and Contempt for the People" (*kanson minpi*) – that is, a heightened respect for authority.[65] These cultural attributes of the Japanese society, claim the proponents of the "Japanese exceptionalism" school, have affected the formation of attitudes towards litigation in Japan. For instance, Takeyoshi Kawashima has argued that in a hierarchical society such as Japan's, where the definitions of roles and duties are characterized by harmony, judicial decisions that emphasize conflict between parties and assign moral fault cannot be popular. Instead, claims Kawashima, extra-legal means, such as reconcilement and conciliation, are preferred.[66] The "Japanese exceptionalism" approach was embraced and promoted not only by Japanese scholars. For instance, Steve Lohr in 1982 examined the case of an airplane crash after which none of the passengers' relatives sued the airline company involved and came to the conclusion that Japan's is "a nonadversarial, nonlitigious society", which he attributed to the country's culture of avoiding open confrontation.[67]

The "rational actor" school[68] of analyzing Japanese law, on the other hand, sets aside the cultural factors and proposes to rely instead on the universal rationality of legal actors. For instance, John O. Haley has contested the arguments of "Japanese exceptionalists" by suggesting that Japan's low litigation rates should be attributed not to the culture of avoiding conflict, but to such institutional barriers to litigation as overcrowded courts (lack of judges and, as a result, excessively high caseloads per judge), long trials with recurring hearings spaced at least at one-month intervals, the limited range of remedies available to courts, and lack of enforcement power.[69] A different

---

64 J. O. Haley, 1998, *The Spirit of Japanese Law*, Athens: University of Georgia Press, pp. xv–xvi. It may be argued that the postulates of the "Japanese exceptionalism" school are in congruence with Pierre Legrand's approach to analysis of law (rules necessarily reflect the culture in which they were proposed). Legrand, "The Impossibility of 'Legal Transplants'".
65 Kiss, "Reviving the Criminal Jury in Japan", p. 269.
66 T. Kawashima, "Dispute Resolution in Contemporary Japan", in Von Mehren (ed.), *Law in Japan*, pp. 41–59.
67 S. Lohr, 1982, "Tokyo Air Crash: Why the Japanese Don't Sue", *New York Times*, March 10, reprinted in Milhaupt, Ramseyer, and Young (eds), *Japanese Law in Context*, pp. 108–109.
68 Haley, *The Spirit of Japanese Law*, pp. xv–xvi.
69 J. O. Haley, 1978, "The Myth of the Reluctant Litigant", *Journal of Japanese Studies*, Vol. 4, pp. 362–390. The argument that Japanese law should be treated like the law of any other country is made by Bruce Aronson (see B. Aronson, 2014, "My Keyphrase for Understanding Japanese Law: Japan as a Normal Country . . . with Context", *Michigan State International Law Review*, Vol. 22, No. 3, pp. 816–837).

explanation was offered by J. Mark Ramseyer and Minoru Nakazato in their article "The Rational Litigant: Settlement Amounts and Verdict Rates in Japan".[70] They argue that formal litigation rates in Japan may be low because potential litigants find it easy to agree on how courts would adjudicate their cases. This predictability of Japanese courts, claim the authors, is due to a number of factors, including (1) the absence of juries, (2) the fact that Japanese professional judges are famous for uniformity in their decision-making and often deploy detailed formulae for calculation of victim's damages, and (3) the tendency of judges to explain their views to the parties before the case is closed, thus eliminating the incentive to finish the trial.[71] The notion that it is the institutional barriers that are primarily contributing to the lack of litigiousness on the part of the Japanese people has found its support in subsequent studies. Most notably, Tom Ginsburg and Glenn Hoetker in their study of the impact of the reforms of the law of civil procedure and corporate law, as well as of the attempts to expand the bar carried out in the 1990s, have argued that the attempts on the part of the Japanese government to remove the barriers to litigation in the course of these reforms have served to increase the number of cases taken to court.[72]

The third school of analysis attributes legal change to intervention by elites.[73] Frank Upham, whose work is representative of this school, disagrees with the claims that Japan's is a conflict-free society and argues that the Liberal Democratic Party (LDP) politicians and Ministry of Economy, Trade, and Industry (METI) officials have used legal rules and institutions to "manage and direct conflict and control change at a social level".[74] The issue of the role of the elites in the legal system of Japan has also been addressed by J. Mark Ramseyer. Ramseyer has questioned the nature of judicial independence in Japan by demonstrating that the LDP controlled access to favored posts for judges, thereby manipulating the system to reward those judges that produced decisions favorable to the LDP and to punish those that did not.[75] In a response to Ramseyer's argument, John O. Haley has suggested that the post-war constitution was intentionally designed to achieve a degree of political accountability among judges towards the government and thus contained the element of control over the appointment of Supreme Court justices as well as lower court career judges.[76]

---

70 J. M. Ramseyer and M. Nakazato, 1989, "The Rational Litigant: Settlement Amounts and Verdict Rates in Japan", *Journal of Legal Studies*, Vol. 18, pp. 266–290.

71 In an interesting account of her experiences leading trials, Shunko Muto, a professional judge and instructor at the Legal Research and Training Institute, has argued that the central role of the judge is to make every effort to help the parties achieve a compromise. See S. Muto, 1973, "Concerning Trial Leadership in Civil Litigation: Focusing on the Judge's Inquiry and Compromise", *Law in Japan*, Vol. 12, pp. 23–28. Also see H. Itoh, 1970, "How Judges Think in Japan", *American Journal of Comparative Law*, Vol. 18, pp. 775–804, reprinted in K. Fujikura (ed.), 1996, *Japanese Law and Legal Theory*, Aldershot: Dartmouth, pp. 87–119.

72 T. Ginsburg and G. Hoetker, 2006, "The Unreluctant Litigant? An Empirical Analysis of Japan's Turn to Litigation", *Journal of Legal Studies*, Vol. 35, No. 1, pp. 31–59, at p. 50.

73 F. Upham, 1987, *Law and Social Change in Postwar Japan*, Cambridge: Harvard University Press.

74 *Id.*, p. 1.

75 J. M. Ramseyer, 1993, "Judicial (In)dependence in Japan", *University of Chicago Law School Record*, Vol. 39, pp. 5–11; J. M. Ramseyer and E. B. Rasmusen, 2003, *Measuring Judicial Independence: The Political Economy of Judging in Japan*, Chicago: University of Chicago Press.

76 J. O. Haley, 1995, "Judicial Independence in Japan Revisited", *Law in Japan*, Vol. 25, pp. 1–18.

16 *Introduction*

The contributions of all three aforementioned schools proceed from the supposition that the developments in law reflect the changes that the society in which it operates undergoes. Alan Watson's theory of legal transplants has also been used to analyze the development of Japanese law. For instance, Hideki Kanda and Curtis J. Milhaupt developed an analytical framework for analyzing transplant feasibility and determining the success or failure of a legal transplant based on their study of the introduction of the provision regarding the fiduciary duty of corporate directors in Japan's corporate law (Article 254(3) of the Commercial Code).[77] Luke Nottage has applied Alan Watson's theory of legal transplants in his examination of the emergence of product liability legislation in Japan. Nottage has concluded that Watson's theoretical framework alone is limiting in analyzing Japan's experiences and that the picture is incomplete if the historical evolution of product liability is discussed without reference to the social and economic forces.[78]

Unlike other areas of Japanese law, past and present efforts to implement the jury system in Japan have not yet been sufficiently analyzed from the socio-legal studies perspective and Alan Watson's "legal transplant" approach has not at all been utilized to explain these reforms.

Japan's past and present experiences with the institution of jury service

Why was the jury system in Japan introduced at different junctures in its history? What were the determinants of the success and failure of expanding lay participation in Japan in the past, and how well does the mixed-court *saiban'in* system in Japan fare with regard to these parameters? This study explores two approaches to the analysis of the nature of legal change, one or both of which may have some bearing on these two questions.

Past and present efforts to introduce the jury system in Japan as examples of legal transplants

Alan Watson's conception of legal transplants assumes that law does not reflect the changes in the society in which it operates and that law develops autonomously. From this perspective, the past and present attempts to introduce the jury system in Japan are seen exclusively as borrowings from other jurisdictions. The transplant theory predicts that the jury system would only be successfully implemented if there is a "fit" between the imported rule and the host environment. In the existing literature, "fit" is understood to have at least two components. "Micro-fit" concerns the extent to which an imported rule complements the pre-existing legal infrastructure in the host country, while "macro-fit" is said to imply the degree to which the imported rule complements the pre-existing institutions of the political economy in the host country.[79] The transplant theory states that the degree of motivation and of enthusiasm on the part of law reformers initially responsible for the transplant and on the part of legal actors (courts, attorneys, and government officials) is another critical factor for analyzing the prospects of a law reform.[80]

---

77 Kanda and Milhaupt, "Re-examining Legal Transplants".
78 L. Nottage, "The Still-Birth and Re-birth of Product Liability in Japan", in Nelken and Feest (eds), *Adapting Legal Cultures*, pp. 147–185.
79 Kanda and Milhaupt, "Re-examining Legal Transplants", p. 891.
80 *Id.*, p. 891.

Past and present efforts to introduce the jury system in Japan as the result of interaction between society and law

The socio-legal approach to analyzing legal change assumes that all developments in law reflect the society in which law operates. It proposes to evaluate the success of the implementation of a given reform based on how well it reflects the processes occurring in the society. This perspective predicts that the institution of jury service may only be expected to be introduced at those times in Japan's history when there was a strong demand in the society for the expansion of rights. It holds that the jury system may be expected to function effectively only when the society in which it operates is moving in the direction of democratization and the expansion of rights of citizens, and that the system would stagnate at those times when the society develops in the opposite direction.[81]

The subject matter and the scope of enquiry endow this study with the potential to contribute to the existing literature on Japanese law and legal change.

Methodology and significance of the study

In addressing the two research questions, this study relies on primary and secondary data in Japanese and English. It makes extensive use of declassified and newly discovered government documents and trial records from archives in Okinawa and Tokyo, Japan.[82,83,84]

---

81 While the case may be made that the items that fall under consideration in the literature that is adopting the socio-legal approach may also be included in the "macro-fit" aspect of the legal transplant approach, the author believes that there is value in separating the discussion of the socio-political developments in the country as drivers for reform on the one hand and of the notions of "macro" and "micro" fit on the other. The former is clearly associated with the socio-legal approach to the study of law and the latter is representative of the theoretical perspective that emphasizes the view of law as a self-contained system of logic (for a brief overview of the two approaches to the study of law see, for example, S. E. Barkan, 2009, *Law and Society: An Introduction*, Upper Saddle River, NJ: Prentice-Hall, pp. 7–10).

82 Examples of the contributions to the literature on the subject of the latest attempt to implement the jury system in Japan in English include R. Lempert, 1992, "A Jury for Japan?", *American Journal of Comparative Law*, Vol. 40, pp. 37–71; M. Dean, 1995, "Trial by Jury: A Force for Change in Japan", *International and Comparative Law Quarterly*, Vol. 44, pp. 379–404; Kiss, "Reviving the Criminal Jury in Japan"; Anderson and Nolan, "Lay Participation in the Japanese Justice System", pp. 966–973; Anderson and Saint, "Japan's Quasi-Jury (*Saiban'in*) Law"; K. Anderson and L. Ambler, 2006, "The Slow Birth of Japan's Quasi-Jury System (*Saiban-in Seido*): Interim Report on the Road to Commencement", *Journal of Japanese Law*, Vol. 11, No. 21, pp. 55–80; R. M. Bloom, 2006, "Jury Trials in Japan", *Loyola of Los Angeles International & Comparative Law Review*, Vol. 28, pp. 35–68. The literature in Japanese includes O. Niikura (ed.), 2003, *Saiban'in Seido ga Yatte Kuru: Anata ga Yuzai, Muzai o Kimeru: Shimin Sanka no Saiban* [Jury System Is on Its Way: The "Guilty" or "Non-Guilty" Verdict Will Be Up to You: Trials with Public Participation], Tokyo: Gendaijinbunsha; Y. Tsuchiya, 2009, *Saiban'in Seido to Kokumin: Kokuminteki Kiban wa Kakuritsu Dekiru ka* [The Lay Judge System and the People: Will the Popular Base Be Established?], Tokyo: Kadensha.

83 The existing literature in Japanese on the subject of pre-war jury trials includes T. Mitani, 1980, *Kindai Nihon no Shihōken to Seitō: Baishin Seiritsu no Seiji Shi* [Judicial Power in Modern Japan and Political Parties: The Political History of the Creation of the Jury System], Tokyo: Hanawa Shobō; T. Mitani, 2001, *Seiji Seido toshite no Baishinsei: Kindai Nihon no Shihōken to Seiji* [The Jury System as a Political Institution: The Judiciary and Modern Japanese Politics], Tokyo: University of Tokyo Press; S. Shinomiya, "Nihon ni mo Baishin Seido ga Sonzai Shita" [The Jury System Existed in Japan, Too], in S. Shinomiya (ed.), 1999, *Baishin Tebiki: Hōtei San'yo Nisshi Tsuki* [The Jury Guidebook: Includes Journal of Trial Participation], Tokyo: Gendaijinbunsha, pp. 97–98. The contributions examining the unique experience of Okinawa in Japanese include C. Isa, *Gyakuten: Amerika Shihaika Okinawa no Baishin Saiban*

18 Introduction

This book is a response to the call for the start of academic debate regarding the unique insights that the study of the history of jury trials provides us with that was offered by Dimitri Vanoverbeke in "Juries in the Japanese Legal System: The Continuing Struggle for Citizen Participation and Democracy".[85]

Through its discussion of the history and present of the institution of jury service in Japan, this book aims to shed light on the central questions of the ongoing academic debate regarding the origins and nature of law – that is, why does legal reform happen and what are the determinants of success and failure of a legal initiative?

Plan of the book

This book consists of seven chapters. Chapters 2 through 6 describe and evaluate the attempts – successful and failed – to implement the jury system initiated at different times in Japan's history. The case studies examined in each chapter are grouped in accordance with the historical periods that they belonged to. Chapter 2 discusses Japan's experiences with the institution of jury service in the *Meiji* period (1868–1912). Chapters 3 and 4 cover the developments in the *Taishō* period (1912–1926) and in the section of the *Shōwa* period that preceded the conclusion of World War II (1926–1945). Chapter 5 is concerned with the immediate post-war period and discusses the Allied occupation of mainland Japan (1945–1952) and the U.S. occupation of Okinawa (1951–1972). Finally, Chapter 6 is devoted to the post-occupation developments in mainland Japan (1953–2015). Each of these chapters opens with a brief overview of the historical developments that formed the background to the discussion of the proposals to introduce trial by jury. Each chapter concludes by evaluating these proposals and addressing the two research questions set forth in this chapter.

Chapter 2 discusses the introduction of the concept of jury service to Japan and describes the first attempts to implement jury trials in the *Meiji* period.

Chapter 3 describes the jury system that was introduced in mainland Japan in the pre-war period, discusses the reasons behind the introduction of the Jury Act in 1928 and its suspension in 1943, and examines some of the cases that were tried by jury.

Chapter 4 examines the efforts to extend the right to be tried by jury to the citizens of the colonial possessions of the Japanese Empire. It introduces the proposals to institute jury

---

[Turnaround: A Jury Trial in Okinawa under American Rule], Tokyo: Iwanami Shoten; Japan Federation of Bar Associations (ed.), 1992, *Okinawa no Baishin Saiban: Fukkizen no Okinawa Baishin Sei* [Jury Trials in Okinawa: The Jury System in Okinawa Prior to Its Return to Japan], Tokyo: Takachiho Shobo. The possibility of introducing the all-layperson jury system in contemporary Japan is discussed in S. Nakahara, 2000, *Baishin Sei Fukkatsu no Jōken: Kenpō to Nihon Bunkaron no Shiten kara* [The Conditions [Necessary] for the Revival of the Jury System: From the Perspectives of the Constitution and of the Japanese Cultural Theory], Tokyo: Gendaijinbunsha.

84 Chihiro Isa has compared the *saiban'in* system with the Anglo-American jury system that existed in Okinawa under the U.S. occupation (C. Isa, 2006, *Saiban'in Seido wa Keiji Saiban o Kaeru ka: Baishin Seido o Motomeru Wake* [Will the Lay Judge System Transform Criminal Courts? Reasons for Demanding a Jury System], Tokyo: Gendaijinbunsha). Masahiro Fujita, on the other hand, has contrasted the features of Japan's new *saiban'in* system with those of the pre-war jury system (M. Fujita, 2009, *Shihō e no Shimin Sanka no Kanōsei: Nihon no Baishin Seido, Saiban'in Seido no Jisshōteki Kenkyū* [The Prospects of Citizen Participation in the Justice System of Japan: An Empirical Study of Japan's Jury System and the *Saiban'in* System], Tokyo: Yūhikaku).

85 D. Vanoverbeke, 2015, *Juries in the Japanese Legal System: The Continuing Struggle for Citizen Participation and Democracy*, London: Routledge.

service in Taiwan that did not lead to reform, and analyzes the reasons behind the successful implementation of jury trials in Karafuto, the southern section of the island of Sakhalin.

Chapter 5 looks at the two attempts to implement the jury system in the immediate postwar period – one failed (in occupied mainland Japan) and another successful (in occupied Okinawa).

Chapter 6 is devoted to the most recent effort to introduce the jury system in Japan. It discusses the process of drafting the Lay Judge Act of 2004 and highlights those issues that have been in the spotlight of public debate regarding the introduction of the mixed-court jury system. It describes the first case tried by *saiban'in* and discusses the insights that the first five years of the functioning of the lay judge system provide.

Chapter 7 summarizes the findings of the preceding chapters and concludes this book.

2 The pre-war history of the concept of trial by jury in Japan

This chapter describes the process by which Japan became familiar with the idea of trial by jury and analyzes the first efforts to implement the jury system in the *Meiji* period. It first provides a brief overview of the historical background, focusing on the developments in the Japanese legal system in the *Meiji* period. It then discusses the first documents mentioning the institution of jury service that reached Japan in the 19th century. Subsequent sections describe the features of the "bureaucratic" and the "judge-only" special jury systems used in Japan in the 1870s, outline the points raised in the debate concerning the possibility of adding the provisions regarding jury service to the text of the *Meiji* Constitution, and look at the stipulations about trial by jury included in the 1879 draft of Japan's Code of Criminal Instruction. Japan's first attempts to introduce the jury system in the *Meiji* period are then analyzed, and a conclusion summarizes the chapter's findings.

Historical background: the developments in the Japanese legal system in the *Meiji* period

The pre-war history of the concept of jury service in Japan unfolded within the context of the development of the modern Japanese legal system, the starting point of which can be placed in the second half of the 19th century.[1]

The Charter Oath of Five Articles promulgated by the *Meiji* Emperor on April 6, 1868, laid the foundation for the transformation of feudal Japan into a nation-state with a modern legal system and set forth the main principles for that process.[2] It proclaimed that "deliberative councils" would be "widely established", that "evil customs of the past" would

---

1 According to the classification proposed by Professor Ryosuke Ishii, Japan's legal history may be divided into six periods. The Archaic period (c. 250 BC to AD 603) – a time when law was "of uniquely Japanese origins" – was followed by the Ancient (AD 603–967), the Medieval (967–1467) and the Early Modern (1467–1858) periods, which were all characterized by the heavy influence of Chinese law. The Modern period (1858–1945) was a time when the law of Western nations had the most profound influence on Japanese law. The Contemporary period (1945–) is a period influenced by the Allied occupation of Japan (R. Ishii, 1988, *A History of Political Institutions in Japan*, Tokyo: University of Tokyo Press, p. vii, cited in M. Dean (ed.), 2002, *Japanese Legal System: Text and Materials*, 2nd edition, London: Cavendish, p. 55). For an overview of the history of the concept of jury service in Japan and an alternative analysis of the developments described in this chapter, see Vanoverbeke, *Juries in the Japanese Legal System*. pp. 37–59.
2 Gokajō no Goseimon [The Charter Oath of Five Articles], promulgated on April 6, 1868, translated in M. B. Jansen, 2000, *The Making of Modern Japan*, London: Belknap Press of Harvard University Press, p. 338.

be broken off, and that knowledge would be "sought throughout the world" so as "to strengthen the foundations of imperial rule".[3] The Oath inspired the intellectual leaders of Japan to study Western political ideas and institutions and to travel abroad.[4] It also triggered a wide range of reforms, encompassing the legislative, administrative, and judicial spheres. During the decades that followed the promulgation of the Charter Oath, the feudal fiefs were turned into provinces, the privileges of the *samurai* class were abolished, and the country introduced a central taxation system. The Great Council of State (*Dajōkan*) – the central administrative organ in the *ritsuryō* system of government – was replaced by the Cabinet (*Naikaku*) system of government.[5] By the end of the 19th century, Japan had a Western-inspired constitution, criminal and civil codes, a Parliament (the Imperial Diet), and political parties.

The decision to turn to the West in search of ideas for modernizing the Japanese state and for developing the new legal system was motivated by several factors. First, after 200 years of being a "closed country" (*sakoku*) and pursuing the policy of national isolation from 1630 onward, Japan was seeking to be reintegrated in the international political order and to reassert itself after signing the "unequal treaties" in 1858.[6] The overwhelming military power

---

3 The full text of the charter is as follows: "1) Deliberative Councils shall be widely established and all matters decided by public discussion; 2) All classes, high and low, shall unite in vigorously carrying out the administration of affairs of state; 3) The common people, no less than the civil and military officials, shall each be allowed to pursue his own calling so that there may be no discontent; 4) Evil customs of the past shall be broken off and everything based upon the just laws of Nature; 5) Knowledge shall be sought throughout the world so as to strengthen the foundations of imperial rule" (*id.*, p. 338).

4 S. Hirakawa, "Japan's Turn to the West", in B. T. Wakabayashi (ed.), 1998, *Modern Japanese Thought*, New York: Cambridge University Press, pp. 30–97, at p. 47.

5 *Dajōkan* was the collective name for the Japanese government between 1868 and 1885. It was headed by the Great Minister of State (*Dajō Daijin*), who was assisted by the Minister of the Left (*Sadaijin*) and the Minister of the Right (*Udaijin*). Under their chairmanship the Counselors of State (*Sangi*) discussed and decided important matters. Their decisions were submitted by the Great Minister of State to the Emperor for approval and then issued as decrees of the *Dajōkan*. The *Dajōkan* was abolished in 1885 and replaced by the Cabinet (*Naikaku*) system of government (Edwin O. Reischauer (ed.), 2003, *Japan: An Illustrated Encyclopedia*, Tokyo: Kōdansha, p. 270).

6 From 1630 onwards Japan pursued the policy of national isolation that implied that foreigners were not permitted to enter, while Japanese citizens were not allowed to leave the country. Trade was conducted with China and Holland alone and was limited to the port of Nagasaki. During this period of isolation Japan developed a social, political, and legal order with little outside influence. In 1853, Commodore Matthew Perry arrived on the shores of Japan with eight "black ships" (steamships), displaying the military might of his country. He delivered a letter from U.S. President Fillmore asking for permission for U.S. ships to enter Japanese ports and proposing to establish trading relations between Japan and the United States. Perry succeeded at securing the agreement that Japan would open two of its ports and grant the United States most favored nation status in trade. The Treaty of Kanagawa was signed on March 31, 1854, and was followed by similar treaties with Britain, France, Russia, and Holland (Jansen, *The Making of Modern Japan*, pp. 274–279 (discussing the Perry Mission); C. Tsuzuki, 2000, *The Pursuit of Power in Modern Japan: 1825–1995*, New York: Oxford University Press, pp. 38–42 (discussing the opening of Japan)). The "unequal treaties" were international conventions that Japan concluded between 1854 and 1873 that rendered extraterritorial privileges and fixed conventional tariffs to sixteen Western states (L. G. Perez, 1999, *Japan Comes of Age: Mutsu Munemitsu and the Revision of the Unequal Treaties*, London: Associated University Presses, p. 47; M. R. Auslin, 2004, *Negotiating with Imperialism: The Unequal Treaties and the Culture of Japanese Diplomacy*, Cambridge: Harvard University Press, pp. 11–33 (discussing the "unequal treaties")). The treaties had the following distinctive characteristics: (1) they gave rights and privileges to foreigners in Japan, but not to Japanese citizens abroad; (2) upon conclusion they were to be in force for an indefinite period of time (the treaties contained neither an expiration date nor clauses stipulating the procedure for their termination); (3) the treaties provided for

that the Western nations demonstrated to induce Japan to conclude the "unequal treaties" prompted Japanese politicians to seek "civilization and enlightenment" (*bunmei kaika*) as a means for realizing national unity and for establishing a centralized imperial government capable of effectively renegotiating the treaties. Second, a modern nation-state, defined as a state with a centralized political system under which popular participation is structured through the parliamentary institutions of a constitutional order, had yet to be established in any non-Western country.[7]

Japan's turn to the West following the *Meiji* Restoration did not imply a complete denunciation of the ideas developed during the pre-*Meiji* period. Instead, the post-restoration period involved efforts to balance between reform and continuity. Neither did the westernization of Japan mean that once open to outside influences, Japan merely copied the institutions of the West. Rather than emulate the outward products of Western civilization, Japan sought to understand the inner "spirit" of that civilization,[8] and if it chose to adopt a concept, it invariably strove to adapt it to fit the existing environment in Japan.

These two trends in the development of *Meiji*-period Japan – that is, balancing reform and continuity and adapting Western concepts when adopting them – encompassed the legal reforms carried out in Japan following the *Meiji* Restoration.

Prior to the *Meiji* period, Japanese law was primarily influenced by the Confucian values of Chinese scholarship.[9] The separation of powers in the modern sense did not exist and law was seen as the exercise of bureaucratic function. During the *Tokugawa* period (1600–1867), justice was administered through the officials of the *shogunate* (*bakufu*) based on the guidelines for determining appropriate punishment provided in the "Book of Rules for Public Officials" (*Kujikata Osadamegaki*). This book of rules, drawn up by Shogun Yoshimune Tokugawa in 1742, contained a series of directives addressed to judicial authorities and could only be consulted by the top magistrates (*bugyō*) of the three important *bakufu* courts.[10] National codes as promulgated law did not exist.

The beginning of the *Meiji* period was marked by the movement towards codification. This movement was at first based primarily on Japan's internal sources but was subsequently transformed into a process during which Japan adopted and adapted Western sources of law. The codification movement began without the participation of Western scholars. In

---

customs duties that were set at an artificially low level (Japan was allowed to collect only less than a half of what Western nations collected in customs); and (4) according to the treaties, all citizens of the treaty nations were given extraterritorial privileges that made them immune from Japanese justice (foreigners were allowed to live in settlements that were separated from the Japanese and were in some instances given the right to administer their own regulations and legislation within these settlements (Perez, *Japan Comes of Age*, p. 47)). It has been argued that the fact that foreigners living in Japan were given immunity from Japanese justice was the primary reason behind the sense of shame that came to be associated with the "unequal treaties" on the Japanese side, as the administration of the concept of extraterritoriality implied the inferiority of the Japanese society and culture (*id.*, p. 48).

7 Hirakawa, "Japan's Turn to the West", p. 30.
8 B. T. Wakabayashi, "Introduction", in Wakabayashi (ed.), *Modern Japanese Thought*, pp. 1–29, at p. 4.
9 See generally J. H. Wigmore, 1967–1986, *Law and Justice in Tokugawa Japan: Materials for the History of Japanese Law and Justice under the Tokugawa Shogunate 1603–1867*, Tokyo: University of Tokyo Press; H. Takashio, 2004, *Edo Jidai no Hō to Sono Shūen: Yoshimune to Shigekata to Sadanobu to* [The Law of the Edo Period and Its Surroundings: Yoshimune, Shigekata, and Sadanobu], Tokyo: Kyūko Shoin.
10 Y. Noda, 1976, *Introduction to Japanese Law*, Tokyo: University of Tokyo Press, p. 35.

the second part of this movement, however, European jurists played the central role.[11] The indigenous codification movement included the promulgation of the "Provisional Criminal Code" (*Kari Keiritsu*) in either 1868 or 1869,[12] the "Essences of the New Code" (*Shinritsu Kōryō*) in 1871,[13] and the "Statutes and Substatutes as Amended" (*Kaitei Ritsurei*) in 1873.[14] The first two promulgated codes focused on the adaptation of the pre-existing Japanese and Chinese legal traditions – a move that was arguably natural for Japanese jurists, given their Confucian background and training.[15] The Provisional Criminal Code and the Essences of the New Code, which became Japan's first national criminal law, incorporated the principles of the *Ming* Code of China.[16] The 1873 Statutes and Substatutes as Amended was the first indigenous code that was influenced by the modern criminal law of the West.[17] In the area of civil law, the Great Council of State Decree No. 103 that was shaped by the provisions of the French Civil Code was promulgated in 1875.[18]

The increased contact with the West and the changes that the Japanese society had undergone since the *Meiji* Restoration led the Ministry of Justice, which was established in 1871, to turn its attention towards the West rather than to China's or Japan's pre-*Meiji* decrees in its subsequent codification efforts. Under the leadership of Shinpei Etō,[19] the Ministry sent students to Europe and the United States and translated foreign legislation. Rinshō Mitsukuri first translated the French Criminal Code, and by 1873 the translations of the French Civil Code and of the remaining Napoleonic Codes were completed.[20] In addition, the Ministry invited two French scholars (George Bousquet, who arrived in 1872, and

---

11 The transition from the first to the second phase of the codification movement was a smooth one, with the indigenous codification movement serving as a bridge linking the legal tradition of the pre-*Meiji* period and the reception of European continental jurisprudence that was to follow (Dean (ed.), *Japanese Legal System*, p. 60).
12 The precise date of the promulgation is unknown (P. H. Ch'en, 1981, *The Formation of the Early Meiji Legal Order: The Japanese Code of 1871 and Its Chinese Foundation*, Oxford: Oxford University Press, p. 5).
13 *Id.*, p. 14. The English translation of the "Essences of the New Code" (*Shinritsu Kōryō*) is provided in *id.*, pp. 81–184.
14 *Id.*, p. 20. The Draft of "Statutes and Substatutes as Revised" (*Kōsei Ritsurei Kō*) that was written in 1874 belongs to the first codification movement, but is omitted in the discussion here as it was never promulgated. See *id.*, pp. 23–30.
15 *Id.*, p. xix, pp. 9–10 (discussing the sources that have influenced the "Provisional Criminal Code" (*Kari Keiritsu*)) and p. 17 (discussing the sources that have influenced the "Essences of the New Code" (*Shinritsu Kōryō*)).
16 *Id.*, pp. 9 and 16.
17 The French legal system influenced the "Statutes and Substatutes as Amended" (*id.*, pp. 21–22).
18 K. Takayanagi, "A Century of Innovation: The Development of Japanese Law", in A. T. Von Mehren (ed.), 1964, *Law in Japan: The Legal Order in a Changing Society*, Cambridge, MA: Harvard University Press, pp. 5–41, at p. 25.
19 Shinpei Etō (1834–1874) was a Japanese statesman who served as the Minister of Justice and then became a Counselor of State (*Sangi*) at the *Dajōkan*. Etō authored the "Statutes and Substatutes as Amended" (*Kaitei Ritsurei*). Nichigai Associates, Inc., Editorial Department (ed.), 1996, *Jinbutsu Refarensu Jiten* [Biography Index], Tokyo: Nichigai Associates, p. 381 [hereinafter Biography Index].
20 Noda, *Introduction to Japanese Law*, p. 21; Dean (ed.), *Japanese Legal System*, p. 62. Rinshō Mitsukuri (1846–1897) was a Japanese statesman and translator. He served on the *Genrōin* and later became vice minister of justice (1888–1889). Biography Index, p. 2331. See also Vanoverbeke, *Juries in the Japanese Legal System*, pp. 40–43.

Emile Gustave Boissonade de Fontarabie, who arrived in 1873) and three German jurists (Hermann Roesler, Hermann Techow, and Otto Rudorff) to offer advice and participate in the process of drafting the codes for a modernized Japan.[21]

Gustave Boissonade was central to the compilation of the first Western-inspired modern codes implemented in Japan: the Criminal Code and the Code of Criminal Instruction of 1880.[22] The drafts of the two codes prepared by Boissonade relied on French law, however they were not adopted immediately. They were revised and adapted by the Japanese scholars and members of the Council of Elders (*Genrōin*) – the legislative body that preceded the establishment of Parliament in Japan.[23] Boissonade was also involved in the drafting of the Civil Code.[24] Prior to the assignment of the French jurist to the task of writing the draft of the code, there was discussion of the possibility of adopting the French Civil Code without making any adaptations.[25] It was finally decided, however, that Japan needed to draft its own version of the code, and Boissonade together with Japanese jurists began writing it in 1879.[26] The completed version was influenced by French law and was scheduled for enforcement in 1893, but never became operational. Many scholars and statesmen opposed the code, arguing that this version did not sufficiently take into account Japan's traditional family structures.[27] The controversy regarding the

---

21 The total number of foreigners in *Meiji* government employ is provided in Hirakawa, "Japan's Turn to the West", pp. 65–68. Also see J. Teraoka (ed.), 1981, *Meiji Shoki no Zairyū Gaijin* [Foreigners Residing in Japan in the Early *Meiji* Period], Tokyo: Teraoka Shodō; and Yunesuko Higashi Ajia Bunka Kenkyū Sentā [East Asia Cultural Center for UNESCO], 1975, *Oyatoi Gaikokujin* [Foreigners in Government Employ], Tokyo: Shōgakukan.
22 *Dajōkan* Decree Nos. 36 and 37 of 1880. Emile Gustave Boissonade de Fontarabie (1825–1920) was employed by the Japanese government in the *Meiji* period (1868–1912). He went to Japan in 1873 at the invitation of the Ministry of Justice and remained until 1895. He served as an advisor to the government and as an instructor in the Law School of the Ministry of Justice (Reischauer, *Japan: An Illustrated Encyclopedia*, p. 112).
23 For a summary of the provisions of the Penal Code of 1880, see Takayanagi, "A Century of Innovation", p. 5. The *Genrōin* was a quasi-legislative body of the early *Meiji* period. Established in 1875, the *Genrōin* replaced the *Sain* (Chamber of the Left) and was responsible for reviewing legislation. The *Genrōin* was dissolved in 1890 with the formation of the Imperial Diet (Reischauer, *Japan: An Illustrated Encyclopedia*, p. 450).
24 Takayanagi, "A Century of Innovation", pp. 27–30.
25 Shinpei Etō is said to have ordered Rinsho Mitsukuri to translate the French Civil Code with a view to promulgating it as the "Japanese Civil Code" (*id.*, p. 24).
26 Although Boissonade based his Civil Code on French law, he was determined to make adjustments necessary to ensure that the contents of his draft fitted Japan's environment. He stated the following on the subject of the Civil Code: "Doubtless what Japan adopts should not be French law purely and simply. I want your government to adopt our laws only to the extent that they have been proved good by the experience of three-quarters of a century. I will use every effort to incorporate in the draft the improvements that time has shown necessary and particularly those improvements that other Western jurisdictions have adopted in their wisdom and justified by their experience" (G. Boissonade, 1874, "Ecole de droit de Jedo", *Revue de Législation*, p. 511, cited in English in Noda, *Introduction to Japanese Law*, p. 46).
27 Dean (ed.), *Japanese Legal System*, p. 66. The importance of the Japanese family system is discussed in T. Fukutake, 1989, *The Japanese Social Structure*, Tokyo: University of Tokyo Press, pp. 25–32. Other arguments against the Code included the views that Japan's Civil Code should have been modeled on the German or on the English rather than on the French system (Takayanagi, "A Century of Innovation", pp. 30–31).

Civil Code led to the preparation of the new draft of the Civil Code, this time by three Western-educated Japanese jurists – Kenjirō Ume and Masaaki Tomii, who had both studied in Germany and France, and Nobushige Hozumi, who was educated in Germany and qualified as a barrister in Britain.[28] The new version of the code was based on the German Civil Code but was also influenced by French and English law. Most importantly, it incorporated Japan's traditional customs to a greater extent than Boissonade's version and was enforced in 1898.[29]

Japan's post-restoration Commercial Code, promulgated in 1890, was based on the draft prepared by Hermann Roesler, a German advisor to the *Meiji* government, and incorporated elements of French, German, and English law.[30] While parts of the Commercial Code were put into effect, the main sections were revised by the Drafting Committee. The finalized version of the code came into effect on June 16, 1899.[31]

The Constitution of the Empire of Japan (*Meiji* Constitution) was promulgated in 1889 as a gift of the Emperor to his subjects.[32] It was drafted by a group of Japanese statesmen led by Hirobumi Itō, though Hermann Roesler also provided input and advice.[33] Prior to the drafting of the constitution, Itō visited Europe and studied the Prussian and Austrian Constitutions as well as the works of German jurists Rudolf von Gneist, Albert Mosse, and Lorenz von Stein. According to the *Meiji* Constitution, which remained the fundamental law of the Japanese state for fifty-six years, sovereignty resided in the hereditary monarch, not in the people. The main constitutional bodies under the Emperor were the Ministers of State, the Diet, and the Court of Justice. The constitution provided for an independent judiciary, but the province of the judicial branch was restricted to the trial of civil and criminal cases and did not include administrative matters. While the *Meiji* Constitution was conservative and essentially undemocratic, there is no doubt that its promulgation signaled the transformation of Japan from a feudal state to a modern constitutional monarchy. The constitution was yet another example of Japan's ability to preserve its tradition (the Emperor's divine right to rule) while simultaneously embracing reform (the provisions concerning the new structures of government).[34]

The majority of the developments in the legal system in the *Meiji* period were top-down reforms that resulted from the decisions made by the elites. This does not imply, however, that there were no demands for change in the society. The liberal movement for human rights – the Freedom and People's Rights Movement (*Jiyū Minken Undō*) – began in the 1870s and peaked in the 1880s. Accompanied by peasant protests, this movement became one of the most substantial forms of organized opposition to the government after the failure of the Satsuma Rebellion.[35] It was inspired by Western ideas of liberalism and democracy

---

28 Takayanagi, "A Century of Innovation", p. 30.
29 Dean (ed.), *Japanese Legal System*, p. 66.
30 Takayanagi, "A Century of Innovation", p. 31.
31 Shohō [Commercial Code], Law No. 48 of 1899.
32 Constitution of the Empire of Japan, 1889 (*Meiji* Constitution) [hereinafter Meiji Kenpō], Preamble.
33 The group included Kowashi Inoue, Miyojo Itō, and Kentarō Kaneko (G. Akita, 1976, *Foundations of Constitutional Government in Modern Japan 1868–1900*, Cambridge, MA: Harvard University Press, p. 63).
34 Dean (ed.), *Japanese Legal System*, p. 69.
35 E. K. Tipton, 2002, *Modern Japan: A Social and Political History*, London: Routledge, p. 51; Jansen, *The Making of Modern Japan*, p. 380.

and succeeded at making the government agree to the establishment of a National Assembly before being violently suppressed.[36]

The introduction of the concept of jury service as a legal institution to Japan and the first attempts to implement trial by jury in the *Meiji* period took place against the background of the modernization of Japan and of the westernization of its legal system. Japan's pre-war history of the concept of jury trials was shaped by the same principles that guided the development of Japan's legal system and society in the *Meiji* period – that is, efforts to strike a balance between reform and continuity and the commitment to adapting Western concepts when adopting them.

The introduction of the concept of jury service to Japan

There is no agreement in the historical accounts regarding the precise date when Japan became acquainted with the concept of jury service. Neither is there consensus concerning the question of whether it was the East or the West that provided the first documentary source of information regarding lay participation in the legal system to Japan.

Chinese classical texts

Some authors argue that the spirit behind the concept of jury service was not alien to Chinese classical philosophy.[37] These scholars refer in particular to the following passage from "King Hūi of Liang" by Mencius:

> When all those about you say, – "This man deserves death," don't listen to them. When all your great officers say, – "This man deserves death," don't listen to them. When the people all say, "This man deserves death," then inquire into the case, and when you see that the man deserves death, put him to death. In accordance with this we have the saying, "The people killed him."[38]

The proponents of the view that it was the East that provided the first document describing the idea of layperson participation in justice argue that it was through these words that the Japanese elites first learned about the concept of jury service in the *Nara* and *Heian* periods (AD 710–794 and AD 794–1192, respectively).[39] A noted lawyer and politician of the *Meiji*, *Taishō* and *Shōwa* periods, Fusaaki Uzawa, writing in the 1920s, has for instance

---

36 Noda, *Introduction to Japanese Law*, pp. 49–50; O. Terasaki, 2008, *Jiyū Minken Undō no Kenkyū: Kyūshinteki Jiyū Minken Undōka no Kiseki* [Research on the Liberal Movement for Human Rights: The Tracks of the Radical Activists of the Movement], pp. 3–26 (discussing the political philosophy behind the movement). Some authors have argued that while liberal in appearance, the Freedom and People's Rights movement was driven by the political ambitions of its leaders, former *samurai* who found themselves excluded from power after the *Meiji* restoration (Noda, *Introduction to Japanese Law*, p. 50).
37 F. Uzawa, 1928, "Baishin Hō no Seishin" [The Spirit of the Jury Act], *Hōritsu Shinbun*, May 18, pp. 3–5, at p. 5; K. Ōmori, 1927, "Baishin Seido no Konpongi" [The Fundamentals of the Jury System], *Hōritsu Shinbun*, August 28, pp. 4–6, at p. 6; T. Hanai, 1928, "Baishin Hō Ron" [The Theory [Behind] the Jury Act], *Hōritsu Shinbun*, November 8, pp. 17–20, at p. 17.
38 *King Hūi of Liang* Book I, Part II, Chapter 7, Section 5; Mencius (translated by J. Legge), 1895, *The Works of Mencius*, Oxford: Clarendon Press, available online at http://nothingistic.org/library/mencius/.
39 Uzawa, "Baishin Hō no Seishin" [The Spirit of the Jury Act], p. 5.

claimed that this passage from Mencius affected the actions and philosophy of such Japanese statesmen of the *Tokugawa* period as Shigemune Itakura[40] and Echizennokami Ōoka,[41] who famously argued for the humanization of law and of law enforcement in Japan.[42]

Another Chinese classical text credited as being one of the first sources of information regarding the concept of jury service in Japan is the "Rights of Zhou" (*Zhouli*) – one of the three ancient ritual texts listed among the Classics of Confucianism, compiled in the middle of the 2nd century BC. The authoritative "Japanese Comprehensive Dictionary of Chinese Characters" (*Daikanwa Jiten*), first published in 1959, stated that the jury system (*baishin seido*), which it defined as a system that provided for the participation of either officials other than judicial officials or of laypersons in the process of determining the guilt of the accused, was originally based on the conception mentioned in the section of the "Rights

---

40 Shigemune Itakura (1586–1657) was a feudal lord (*daimyō*) of the early *Edo* period. In 1620, Itakura became the third Kyoto *Shōshidai* – *Shogun*'s deputy in Kyoto – and retained this post until 1654 (Biography Index, p. 204). Itakura was a proponent of the development of impartiality of justice. When approached with a case to adjudicate, he would place a lantern between himself and the speaker and busy himself with making tea, so that he would not let external appearances interfere with his sense of justice (M. Takayanagi and T. Matsudaira, 1962, *Sengoku Jinmei Jiten* [Biographical Dictionary of the Warring States [Period]], Tokyo: Yoshikawa Kōbunkan, pp. 34–40). See generally H. Bolitho, 1974, *Treasures among Men: The Fudai Daimyō in Tokugawa Japan*, New Haven: Yale University Press; J. Murdoch, 1996, *A History of Japan*, London: Routledge; R. P. Porter, 2001, *Japan: The Rise of a Modern Power*, Boston: Adamant Media; Timon Screech, 2006, *Secret Memoirs of the Shoguns: Isaac Titsingh and Japan, 1779–1822*, London: RoutledgeCurzon. The details of Itakura's attitudes to the administration of justice are provided in *Hankanpu* (*Hankanfu*) – a collection of biographies of feudal lords (*Daimyō*) compiled by Arai Hakuseki (1657–1725) in 1702 (A. Hakuseki, 1977, *Arai Hakuseki Zenshū* [The Complete Works of Arai Hakuseki], Vol. 1, Tokyo: Kokusho Kankōkai, pp. 193–199, especially pp. 196–197).

41 Tadasuke (*Echizen no kami*; Lord of the Echizen) Ōoka (1677–1751) was a *samurai* in the service of the Tokugawa shogunate. During the rule of Yoshimune Tokugawa he assumed the role of magistrate (*machi bugyō*) of Edo, and in this capacity carried out the responsibilities of the chief of police and judge before becoming the South Magistrate (*Minami Machi bugyō*) of Edo (Biography Index, p. 413). Ōoka was highly respected as an incorruptible judge. He argued that if a judge "were not acquainted with the living conditions of the common people, his judgment would be corrupt" (*Kajō ni tsūjizareba sabaki wa magaru*). This statement of Ōoka is mentioned in the "Kasshiyawa Chronicles" – a collection of essays about politics, economics, and diplomacy. The "Kasshiyawa Chronicles" describe several cases that Ōoka adjudicated to illustrate his sense of justice. One such case involved a fight between a seven-year-old boy and a five-year-old boy during which the older child tried to take the younger's bamboo stick. During the fight, the stick pierced through the older boy's throat, and the child died. In a suit initiated by the parents of the deceased, Ōoka found that the younger boy was guilty. Instead of sentencing the boy to be beheaded, which was the penalty that the parents of the deceased had requested, however, Ōoka ordered that the boy be sent away to one of the smaller islands together with his nurse and ordered that the residents of the island take good care of the boy, stating that he would prosecute those responsible, if this child fell ill (M. Ōishi, 2006, *Ōoka Tadasuke*, Tokyo: Yoshikawa Kōbunkan, p. 271).

42 Uzawa, "Baishin Hō no Seishin" [The Spirit of the Jury Act], p. 5. Fusaaki Uzawa (1872–1955) represented clients in some of the most famous criminal trials of his time: the High Treason Case (*Taigyaku Jiken*) of 1910; the March 15 incident (*San Ichi Go Jiken*) of 1928 that involved mass arrests of suspected communists; and the Blood-Pledge Corps incident (*Ketsumeidan Jiken*) of 1932, which involved the assassination of the former Finance Minister Inoue Junnosuke and the Director-General of Mitsui Dan Takuma. Uzawa became an elected member of the House of Representatives in 1908 and a member of the House of Peers in 1928. In 1934, Uzawa became the first director of Meiji University (T. Ichinose (ed.), 2004, *Major 20th Century People in Japan: A Biographical Dictionary*, Tokyo: Nichigai Associates, p. 381; M. Ishikawa, 1997, *Uzawa Fusaaki: Sono Shōgai to Tatakai* [Uzawa Fusaaki: His Life and Fights], Tokyo: Ōzorasha).

28 *The concept of trial by jury in Japan*

of Zhou" titled "Office of Autumn".[43] "Office of Autumn" is devoted to the issues related to the administration of justice and postulates that grave crimes should not be adjudicated by judicial officials alone and that in such difficult cases judges should ask for the opinions of subordinates (*gunjin*), advisors (*gunri*), and ordinary citizens of sound sense, especially selected for that purpose.[44]

Documents describing the jury systems functioning in the West

While the concept of layperson participation in the adjudication of cases may have reached Japan as early as the 8th century AD through Chinese classical texts, the notion of the jury as a legal institution was first introduced to the country in the middle of the 19th century through the documents describing the jury systems in Western countries. The first documents describing the jury system used in foreign countries include the accounts written by foreign scholars and those authored by Japanese scholars and bureaucrats based on their experiences abroad.

The first document describing the institution of jury service reached Japan in the 1840s and 1850s, when the Chinese translation of the book written in 1838 by American missionary Elijah Coleman Bridgman,[45] *Brief Account of the United States of America*, was published in Japan.[46] Bridgman included a description of the American court system in his book and mentioned the institution of jury service.[47]

---

43 T. Morohashi, 1976, *Dai Kanwa Jiten* [A Dictionary of *Kanji*], 3rd edition (first published in 1959), Vol. 11, Tokyo: Taishūkan Shoten, p. 838; T. Mitani, 1980, *Kindai Nihon no Shihōken to Seitō: Baishin Seiritsu no Seiji Shi* [Judicial Power in Modern Japan and Political Parties: The Political History of the Creation of the Jury System], Tokyo: Hanawa Shobō, p. 98.

44 The author of this dictionary entry bases his explanation on and cites the interpretation of the text of "The Rights of Zhou" offered by Yi Rang Sun, a specialist in the study of classical Chinese texts, in a commentary written in 1902 (Y. Sun, 1902, *Zhou Li Zheng Ya*, Rui'an: Putong Xuetang). Mitani, *Kindai Nihon no Shihōken to Seitō* [Judicial Power in Modern Japan and Political Parties], p. 98.

45 Elijah Coleman Bridgman (April 22, 1801–November 2, 1861) was the first American Protestant Christian missionary appointed to China. See M. C. Lazich, 2000, *E.C. Bridgman, 1801–1861: America's First Missionary to China*, Lewiston: E. Mellen Press.

46 S. Lin, G. Gi, and A. Masaki, 1854, *Amerika Koku Sōki Wage* [Brief Account of the United States of America], Place of Publication Unknown: Seiki Senhachi. See Lazich, *E.C. Bridgman, 1801–1861*, p. 143. Bridgman's *Brief Account of the United States of America* was first published by the American Board's press in Singapore in 1938. After the First Opium War, this book was published again in Hong Kong in 1844. An updated version was published in Canton in 1846. The fourth and final version was published in 1862 in Shanghai (Lazich, *E.C. Bridgman, 1801–1861*, p. 154). Lawyer and legal historian Takeki Osatake has argued that this document was first published in Japan in 1854 (T. Osatake, 1926, *Meiji Bunka Shi toshite no Nihon Baishin Shi* [The History of Jury in Japan as [Part of] *Meiji* Cultural History], Tokyo: Hōkōdō Shoten, p. 10). Osatake adds that there is the possibility that the introduction of the Chinese translation of Bridgman's account to Japan belonged to a slightly earlier time, pointing out that Bridgman's piece was included in Wei Yuan's "Illustrated Treatise on the Maritime Kingdoms" (*Haiguo Tuzhi*), which was originally published in 1842 (Osatake, *Meiji Bunka Shi toshite no Nihon Baishin Shi* [The History of Jury in Japan as [Part of] *Meiji* Cultural History], p. 10. Also see Mitani, *Kindai Nihon no Shihōken to Seitō* [Judicial Power in Modern Japan and Political Parties], pp. 94–95).

47 Osatake, *Meiji Bunka Shi toshite no Nihon Baishin Shi* [The History of Jury in Japan as [Part of] *Meiji* Cultural History], pp. 10–11. A slightly modified version of Bridgman's account was published in Japan in 1861 under the title of *Renpō Shiryaku* and included additions made by Genpo Mitsukuri (Genpo

The concept of trial by jury in Japan 29

The first English-Japanese dictionary, originally published in 1862 and reprinted in 1869, included an entry concerning the jury system.[48] Unlike Bridgman's account, this dictionary entry did not mention that laypersons could serve on the jury panel and defined the jury as "a person/persons who have the duty to (*yakunin*) and are [bound by] an oath to examine the details of an event".[49] Yet another definition of the jury system was provided in the first French-Japanese dictionary, published in Japan in 1864. This dictionary defined the jury as "a position (*yaku*) of those who have established and are working for a guild (*jurande*)".[50] Neither one of the dictionary definitions featured the word *baishin*, which is the present-day Japanese equivalent of the English word "jury".

The word *baishin* was first used in 1864. It appeared in the Japanese commentary section of an English-language textbook, *Graduated Reading: Comprising a Circle of Knowledge in 200 Lessons*, that was translated by Shunzō Yanagawa.[51] This textbook was authored by James Legge, a noted Scottish sinologist and the first professor of Chinese at Oxford University, when he was serving as a representative of the London Missionary Society in Hong Kong; the book was originally published there.[52] Lesson 146 of the textbook was devoted to trial by jury and specified the following:

> Trial by Jury is an excellent institution of Britain. According to it, twelve of the people attend at the court with the judge, to determine whether prisoners are or are not guilty of crime. It is their business to hear the accusation, to listen to the witnesses, to attend the defense, and to bring in the verdict, upon which the judge passes sentence according to the law.[53]

The word *baishin* was used in the Japanese translation of the first sentence.

Mitsukuri, 1861, *Renpō Shiryaku* [A Brief America History], Edo: Rōkyūkan). This version also featured a description of the twelve-person American-style jury system (Osatake, *Meiji Bunka Shi toshite no Nihon Baishin Shi* [The History of Jury in Japan as [Part of] *Meiji* Cultural History], pp. 11–12). Genpo Mitsukuri (1799–1863) was a physician and scholar of Western learning. Mitsukuri contributed to the translation of the Dutch Code of Civil Procedure (F. B. Verwayen, 1998, "Tokugawa Translations of Dutch Legal Texts", *Monumenta Nipponica*, Vol. 53, No. 3, pp. 335–358, at p. 336). He was also a member of the mission led by Kawaji Toshiakira that negotiated with Russian envoy Putiatin at Nagasaki in 1853 and participated in the talks that led to the conclusion of the Kanagawa Treaty with the United States (Biography Index, p. 2331).

48 T. Hori, 1862, *Eiwa Taiyaku Shūchin Jisho* [A Pocket Dictionary of the English and Japanese Language], Edo: Publisher Unknown; Osatake, *Meiji Bunka Shi toshite no Nihon Baishin Shi* [The History of Jury in Japan as [Part of] *Meiji* Cultural History], p. 13.

49 T. Hori, 1869, *Eiwa Taiyaku Shūchin Jisho* [A Pocket Dictionary of the English and Japanese Language], Edo: Kurataya Seiemon, p. 220, on file with the National Diet Library, Japan.

50 H. Murakami, 1864, *Futsugo Meiyō* [Dictionary of the French Language], Place of publication unknown: Publisher unknown, reproduced in Osatake, *Meiji Bunka Shi toshite no Nihon Baishin Shi* [The History of Jury in Japan as [Part of] *Meiji* Cultural History], p. 14.

51 J. Legge, 1864, *Chikan Keimō* [Circle of Knowledge], Tokyo: Kondo Makoto.

52 James Legge (1815–1897) was a noted Scottish sinologist and first professor of Chinese at Oxford University (1876–1897). Iwanami Shoten Henshūbu [Editorial Department of Iwanami Shoten], 1981, *Seiyōjin Jinmei Jiten* [Reference Guide to Foreign Names], Tokyo: Iwanami Shoten, p. 1704.

53 The reprint of the English and Japanese versions of this section is available in Osatake, *Meiji Bunka Shi toshite no Nihon Baishin Shi* [The History of Jury in Japan as [Part of] *Meiji* Cultural History], pp. 14–15.

The word *baishin* did not immediately become a widely accepted term, however, and in the few years that followed the invention of this new word various other phrases were used to describe the institution of jury service in Japanese. For instance, Yūkichi Fukuzawa chose to use the English words "trial by jury" in his Japanese transcription – *toraiaru bai jūri* – when describing the British judicial system in his "Conditions in the West" (*Seiyō Jijō*), published in 1866. In this piece that became the first systematic account of the structure of Western civilization written by a Japanese person,[54] Fukuzawa explained that the role of the members of the jury in British courts was to be that of an independent observer (*tachiai no mono*).[55]

An alternative way of referring to the institution of jury service was proposed by Shin'ichirō (Mamichi) Tsuda, who chose to call the members of the Dutch jury "decision-makers" (*danshi*) and "those who have pledged" (*seishi*)[56] in his translation of the notes that he took while listening to Simon Vissering's lectures at the University of Leiden, which were first published in 1868.[57]

Baron Hiroyuki Katō relied on the legal lexicon proposed by Tsuda in his own translation of Johann Bluntschli's "Allgemeines Staatsrecht" (General Constitutional Law) that appeared in press in 1871.[58] Like Tsuda, he referred to the members of the jury as "those who have pledged" (*seishi*) in the section discussing the jury system in the United Kingdom.

The first document written based on the actual observation of trials by jury by a Japanese person was "A True Account of the Ambassador Extraordinary and Plenipotentiary's Journey of Observation through the United States of America and Europe", published in 1878 and compiled by Kunitake Kume based on the experiences of the Iwakura Embassy of 1871–1873, one of the most important Japanese diplomatic journeys around the world.[59]

---

54 Hirakawa, "Japan's Turn to the West", p. 60; Y. Fukuzawa, 1866, *Seiyō Jijō* [Conditions in the West], reprinted in K. Gijuku (ed.), *Fukuzawa Yukichi Zenshū* [The Complete Works of Fukuzawa Yukichi], Vol. 1, Tokyo: Iwanami Shoten.
55 Gijuku, *Fukuzawa Yukichi Zenshū* [The Complete Works of Fukuzawa Yukichi], Vol. 1, pp. 357–358; Osatake, *Meiji Bunka Shi toshite no Nihon Baishin Shi* [The History of Jury in Japan as [Part of] *Meiji* Cultural History], p. 17.
56 S. Vissering (translated by S. Tsuda), 1878, *Taisei Koku Hō Ron* [The Jurisprudence of the Western Countries], Tokyo: Tōyōsha, p. 66, cited in Mitani, *Kindai Nihon no Shihōken to Seitō* [Judicial Power in Modern Japan and Political Parties], pp. 100–101; Osatake, *Meiji Bunka Shi toshite no Nihon Baishin Shi* [The History of Jury in Japan as [Part of] *Meiji* Cultural History], p. 18.
57 Mitani, *Kindai Nihon no Shihōken to Seitō* [Judicial Power in Modern Japan and Political Parties], p. 100.
58 J. K. Bluntschli (translated by H. Katō), 1971, *Kokuhō Hanron* [Allgemeines Staatsrecht (General Constitutional Law)] Tokyo: Nihon Hyōronsha; Osatake, *Meiji Bunka Shi toshite no Nihon Baishin Shi* [The History of Jury in Japan as [Part of] *Meiji* Cultural History], p. 19. Johann Kaspar Bluntschli (March 7, 1808–October 21, 1881) was a Swiss jurist and politician (Nichigai Associates, Inc. (ed.), 1999, *Seiyōjin Chōsha Mei Refarensu Jiten* [Reference Guide to Foreign Author Names in Katakana], Tokyo: Nichigai Associates, Inc., p. 190).
59 K. Kume, 1878, *Tokumei Zenken Taishi Beiō Kairan Jikki* [A True Account of the Ambassador Extraordinary and Plenipotentiary's Journey of Observation through the United States of America and Europe], Tokyo: Hakubunsha, translated in Kume *The Iwakura Embassy, 1871–1873*. See generally C. Tsuzuki, 2000, *The Pursuit of Power in Modern Japan: 1825–1995*, New York: Oxford University Press, pp. 64–65 (discussing the Iwakura Embassy); K. Takii, 2003, *Bunmei Shi no Naka no Meiji Kenpō: Kono Kuni no Katachi to Seiyō Taiken* [The *Meiji* Constitution within the History of Civilization: The Shape of this Country and Its Experience of the West], Tokyo: Kōdansha, pp. 20–80 (discussing the Iwakura Embassy).

The concept of trial by jury in Japan 31

Kume described the jury trial that the Japanese delegation observed on January 22, 1873,[60] in Paris:

> Next we visited the Cour d'Assizes [in the Palais de Justice], the supreme court of justice in France. [. . .] We then made our way into the courtroom, where a trial of a woman accused of killing her husband was in progress. Five magistrates sat in a line at the front, with the public prosecutor seated to the left. The witnesses, jury members and defense lawyers occupied seats in separate sections before the magistrates, while the offender made her entrance from the right under an escort of police guards. [. . .] In trials of criminal cases in the West, [. . .] no wrongful accusations can be made as there is a jury which listens and adjudicates, waiting for leave to decide before arriving at a verdict.[61]

In addition to outlining the features of the French jury system, Kume also discussed his own views on the question of whether Japan should introduce this system:

> This [system] may be regarded as a thoroughly comprehensive system indeed, but difficulties might arise, if one were to try to introduce it to Japan. No one is sufficiently familiar with the study of law in our country to enable them to appear in court as qualified lawyers. If a jury were to be nominated, the members would be terrified of the authorities and do no more than submit tamely to their words. Even if strong-willed and outspoken people were to be selected, they would be ignorant of the principles of the law and would create endless complications with their moralistic arguments, always quarreling amongst themselves and wasting their breath on useless matters. As far as witnesses are concerned, none of them would speak the truth, for if the punishment was light, they would only win the animosity of the neighborhood, but if it was severe, they would secure people's everlasting hatred in the land of the dead. [. . .] In Japan, [. . .] while those who voice their thoughts with abandon on [general] matters of principle may win the admiration of the public, it is considered a virtue not to reveal other people's affairs, so disclosing information frankly is regarded with distaste.[62]

Kume concluded his discussion of the institution of jury service by cautioning against merely copying the institutions of the West:

> This is just one of numerous examples in which customs in the East and West are very opposite of each other. Learned men should do well to consider the import of this, for unless great care is taken to discard the traces of their origins and adopt only their substance, the introduction of wonderful Western laws and regulations

---

60 Osatake, *Meiji Bunka Shi toshite no Nihon Baishin Shi* [The History of Jury in Japan as [Part of] *Meiji Cultural History*], pp. 22–23.
61 Kume, *The Iwakura Embassy, 1871–1873*, Vol. 3, p. 133.
62 *Id.*, p. 134.

to the East would frequently be like trying to fit a square block of wood into a round hole.[63]

The Rescripts of the Meiji Emperor

There is evidence that suggests that the first documents discussing the concept of jury service were not unnoticed by the *Meiji* Emperor.[64] The Emperor referred to the idea of public participation in the governance of the state in general and the administration of justice in particular in two Imperial Rescripts. The proponents of the introduction of the jury system in the 20th century subsequently promoted the argument that these Rescripts were in fact referring to the institution of jury service.[65]

The first Rescript was issued on December 7, 1868, and stated the following:

> Rewards and punishments [determined by] the important laws of the country should not be the prerogative of the Emperor alone. Rather, [members from] the whole country should be assembled and should make their decisions in a right and just manner that would not allow any errors [in judgment], however small.[66]

Takuzō Hanai (1868–1931), famous criminal attorney and one of the authors of the draft of the Jury Act of 1923, argued that this statement implied the sovereign's understanding of the importance of lay participation in the judiciary.[67]

The second Rescript was issued on May 2, 1874, on the occasion of the distribution of the "Explanatory Notes for the Parliamentary Constitution and Parliamentary Laws" (*Giin Kenpō oyobi Giin Kisoku Hanrei*).[68] The Rescript proclaimed the following:

> I, the Emperor, promise to the Gods that the principles [contained therein] shall be gradually expanded and supplemented and that the representatives of the people from all over the country shall be summoned and the laws shall be established through public deliberations, thus paving the way for the harmonization between the people of all social standings and for the enhancement of the living conditions of the people, allowing the people to go about their business without worry. I expect that the people shall

---

63 *Id.*, pp. 134–135.
64 The 122nd sovereign (*Tennō*) of Japan. He reigned between 1867 and 1912 (Reischauer, *Japan: An Illustrated Encyclopedia*, p. 946).
65 T. Hanai, "Baishin Hō ni tsuite" [About the Jury Act], in T. Hanai, 1927, *Shōtei Ronsō: Matetsu Jiken o Ronzu Fu Baishin Hō ni tsuite* [Courtroom Notes: A Discussion of the Mantetsu Incident, Includes [Notes on] the Jury Act], Tokyo: Mukenshoya, pp. 1–45, at pp. 4–6.
66 Imperial Rescript, partially reprinted in Hanai, *Shōtei Ronsō* [Courtroom Notes], p. 4; Hanai, "Baishin Hō Ron" [The Theory [Behind] the Jury Act], p. 17.
67 Hanai, "Baishin Hō Ron" [The Theory [Behind] the Jury Act], p. 17.
68 Shūgiin Kenpō Chōsakai Jimukyoku [Office of the Research Commission on the Constitution, House of Representatives], 2003, *Meiji Kenpō to Nihonkoku Kenpō ni kansuru Kisoteki Shiryō* [Fundamental Materials Concerning the *Meiji* Constitution and the Constitution of Japan], Tokyo: Shūgiin Kenpō Chōsakai Jimukyoku, also available online at http://www.shugiin.go.jp/itdb_kenpou.nsf/html/kenpou/shukenshi027.pdf/$File/shukenshi027.pdf

be notified regarding the duties that they have in sharing the weight of [responsibility for] the country.⁶⁹

In his commentary on this passage of the Rescript, Hanai has argued that this statement indicated the Emperor's determination to ensure that new laws would be created with the people in mind and that the laws would be enforced with the participation of the people.⁷⁰

While these two Rescripts certainly seem to reflect the Emperor's understanding of the importance of discussing the possibility of democratizing Japan in the future, Hanai's interpretation of these Rescripts as statements of unequivocal support for the institution of jury service appears to be exaggerated. It is likely that Hanai referred to these documents in an effort to add authority to the proposal to implement the jury system in the 1920s that he supported.⁷¹ The fact that the *Meiji* Emperor chose to discuss the issue of citizen participation in governance and in the administration of justice is doubtlessly significant, however, and reflects the fact that it was in the *Meiji* period that the seeds of the movement towards democratization that was to culminate in the first decades of the 20th century were sown.

The bureaucratic jury (*sanza*) system

The first attempt to introduce participation of persons other than court officials in the judicial proceedings in Japan dates back to 1873, when the so-called *sanza* system was first introduced in civilian courts. This system was also implemented in military tribunals, and the first *sanza* military tribunal took place in 1876. The word *sanza* consists of two characters: *san*, which means "participation", and *za*, which means "a seat" or "a position", denoting that the introduction of this system implied participation of a neutral party in the judicial hearings.⁷²

The distinctive features of the *sanza* system highlight the importance of the definition of jury service provided in the first English-Japanese dictionary that, as discussed earlier, did not mention that laypersons could serve on jury panels. Specifically, the *sanza* system, also known as the "bureaucratic jury" system (*kan'in baishin*), provided for the formation of a special jury panel that was composed of officials who were appointed by name by the Counselors of State (*Sangi*) or by the Japanese government (*seifu*) instead of laypersons.⁷³

---

69 Imperial Rescript, partially reprinted in Hanai, "Baishin Hō Ron" [The Theory [Behind] the Jury Act], p. 18.
70 Hanai, "Baishin Hō Ron" [The Theory [Behind] the Jury Act], p. 18.
71 See Chapter 3 for the discussion of the Jury Act of 1923.
72 Dimitri Vanoverbeke argues that the name for the new system – *sanza* – was the translation of the French concept of trial by jury – *Cour d'assises* (Vanoverbeke, *Juries in the Japanese Legal System*, p. 48).
73 Special jury is a jury whose members are selected for special knowledge for a case involving complicated issues (N. Vidmar, "A Historical and Comparative Perspective on the Common Law Jury", in Vidmar (ed.), 2000, *World Jury Systems*, New York: Oxford University Press, pp. 22–23). Black's Law Dictionary defines special jury as "a jury chosen from a panel that is drawn specifically for that case" and adds that "such a jury is usually empanelled at a party's request in an unusually important or complicated case" (B.A. Garner (ed.), 2004, *Black's Law Dictionary*, 8th edition, St. Paul: West Group, p. 874). England had special juries before and after the middle of the 17th century (J. Oldham, 1987,

34 *The concept of trial by jury in Japan*

In civilian courts, the number of officials on the panel was eleven during the first trial that implemented the *sanza* system and twelve in the second trial. Bureaucratic jurors made decisions regarding the question of guilt independently of the judge, and these decisions were binding on the court. The judge was responsible for determining the penalty in the event the accused was found guilty.[74] The decisions of the *sanza* panel were made based on the principle of majority.[75]

The *sanza* system was introduced on a one-time basis in trials that were deemed to be of extraordinarily complex nature. Two cases were tried with the participation of the *sanza* panels in civilian courts, while the precise number of military tribunals carried out with the participation of bureaucratic jurors is unknown. In civilian courts, separate pieces of legislation were promulgated for each *sanza* trial, outlining the rules for *sanza* participation for that particular trial. By contrast, the set of rules for *sanza* participation in military courts were meant to apply to all cases that qualified for trial by *sanza* as set forth in the rules.

The sanza *system in civilian trials*

The first *sanza* trial was the Makimura case that involved the Onos, a family of wealthy merchants doing business in Kyoto.[76] The family decided to move their residence to another city and to relocate their main store from Kyoto to Tokyo.[77] In accordance with the procedure required by law, the Onos expressed this intention to the Kyoto prefectural office, but were refused permission to leave Kyoto. The prefectural office made this decision because it expected that the relocation of the profitable business of the Onos would result in the loss of substantial revenue for Kyoto prefecture.[78] The Onos filed a complaint, and as the result of investigations, Counselor (*Sanji*) of Kyoto Prefecture Makimura and Governor of Kyoto Prefecture Nagatani became defendants in a criminal case.[79] As this case involved clashes of

---

"Special Juries in England: Nineteenth Century Usage and Reform", *Journal of Legal History*, Vol. 8, pp. 148–166; J. Oldham, 1983, "The Origins of the Special Jury", *University of Chicago Law Review*, Vol. 50, pp. 137–221). Historically there were three types of special juries: a jury of experts (members of special knowledge or expertise), a "struck jury" (principal landowners selected from a list of forty-eight names), and a jury consisting of persons from a higher class (men of high social status). The fourth type of juries that were not technically designated as special is the jury *de mediate linguae* – that is, a jury for defendants at special risk of suffering prejudice that included either only or half individuals of the same race, sex, religion, or origin (Vidmar, "A Historical and Comparative Perspective on the Common Law Jury", pp. 22–23).

74 Tokyo Asahi Shinbunsha Shakaibu [Tokyo Asahi Newspaper Company, Local News Section], 1928, *Baishin Kōza* [Lectures on the Jury [System]], Tokyo: Asahi Shinbunsha, p. 11.
75 *Id.*, p. 12.
76 *Id.*, at p. 10; M. Koyama, "*Baishin'in wa Kokka e no Bōkō*" [[Being a] Juror Is Service for the Country], in Dai Nippon Baishin Kyōkai [The Japan Jury Association], 1929, *Dai Nippon Baishin'in Kinen Roku* [The Japan Jury Commemorative Records], Tokyo: Dai Nippon Baishin Kyōkai (the original edition is not paginated); Biography Index, p. 558.
77 Osatake, *Meiji Bunka Shi toshite no Nihon Baishin Shi* [The History of Jury in Japan as [Part of] *Meiji* Cultural History], p. 31.
78 *Id.*, pp. 31–32.
79 Tokyo Asahi Shinbunsha Shakaibu, *Baishin Kōza* [Lectures on the Jury [System]], pp. 10–11; T. Hanai, 1921, "Baishin to Sanza Sei" [The Jury and Sanza Systems], *Nihon Bengoshi Kyōkai Rokuji*, Vol. 263, pp. 38–53, at p. 42. Masanao Makimura (1834–1896) and Nobuatsu Nagatani (1818–1902) were politicians of the *Edo* and *Meiji* periods (Biography Index, p. 2226 and p. 1752, respectively).

The concept of trial by jury in Japan 35

interest between the Ministry of Justice and the Ministry of Internal Affairs, the Ministry of Justice proposed that in order to preserve the fairness of proceedings it was necessary to introduce participation in the court of a neutral party.[80]

The Ministry of Justice considered introducing the jury system (*baishin*) in the Makimura case. The officials of the Ministry of Justice authored a letter to the Great Council of State discussing this possibility. The letter stated the following:

> In many countries courts provide for the jury (*baishin*) in order to certify the openness [and fairness] of trials [. . .]. [The case under consideration involves] a complaint [filed by] a citizen [against] a bureaucrat, conflicts have occurred between bureaucrats, and [this incident] has come to criminal court. [Therefore, we would like to propose that the] bureaucrats working in the Central Chamber (*Sei'in*) and the Chamber of the Left (*Sain*)[81] as well as in the Ministry of Finance and other Ministries be called upon and entrusted with the duty of jurors (*baishin*) in order to show that judicial courts are not unfair.[82]

This letter is the first official document issued by the Ministry of Justice in Japan's history where the word jury (*baishin*) was used. This document indicated that the Ministry of Justice believed that the circumstances of the Makimura incident necessitated the introduction of a neutral party that would participate in the adjudication process and add legitimacy to the verdict. It also demonstrates that the Ministry from the start had in mind the special jury of expert members rather than the layperson jury.

There is evidence that suggests, however, that the possibility of implementing the layperson jury was discussed by the officials of the Ministry of Justice. Specifically, in a statement released subsequently, the Ministry noted that as the result of deliberations it concluded that the situation and the living conditions in Japan were significantly different from those in England and France – countries that used the jury system – and that introducing the layperson jury system in a rushed manner was not beneficial for Japan.[83] The negotiations between the Great Council of State and the Ministry of Justice resulted in the decision that the administration of the Great Minister of State would draft the rules for the participation of a neutral party in the court proceedings in the Makimura case.[84] These rules were promulgated on October 9, 1873, and the word jury (*baishin*) that appeared in the letter sent by the Ministry of Justice to Great Council of State mentioned earlier was replaced in this new document with the word *sanza*. The rules stipulated the following:

---

80 The Ministry of Justice made this proposition on September 15, 1873 (Tokyo Asahi Shinbunsha Shakaibu, *Baishin Kōza* [Lectures on the Jury [System]], p. 11).
81 The Great Council of State (*Dajōkan*) was divided into three Chambers: the Central Chamber (*Seiin*), an executive body presided over by the *Dajodaijin* (the Great Minister of State); the Chamber of the Right (*Uin*), which included only the heads of administrative departments; and the Chamber of the Left (*Sain*), a legislative branch (G. M. Beckmann, 1962, *The Modernization of China and Japan*, New York: Harper & Row, p. 268).
82 A reprint of this document is available in Osatake, *Meiji Bunka Shi toshite no Nihon Baishin Shi* [The History of Jury in Japan as [Part of] *Meiji* Cultural History], pp. 50–51.
83 *Id.*, pp. 55–56.
84 *Id.*, p. 56.

The Sanza *rules*[85]

The rules concerning the operation of the *sanza* [system, implemented] in the special court (*rinji saibansho*) in order to certify the fairness of the trial are as described below.

> The Cabinet (*Naikaku*) will deliberate and appoint bureaucrats (*kan'in*) who will serve on the *sanza* [panel].[86]
>
> The *sanza* panel shall consist of nine public servants. Those public servants who cannot attend the hearings due to their public duty may be excused, and trial proceedings may take place, if six public servants are present.
>
> It shall be the responsibility of the judge to evaluate the gravity of the crime. It shall be the responsibility of the *sanza* panel to determine whether [the accused] is guilty or not guilty.
>
> Use of torture is allowed upon receiving the permission of the *sanza* panel.

On November 20, 1873, another rule was added to this list:

> If it is difficult for the *sanza* panel to reach a [unanimous] decision, the decision of the majority shall be adopted. If opinions are evenly split, this situation will be resolved by the person leading [the *sanza* deliberations] (*sekichō*).[87]

The first *sanza* trial took place with the participation of nine bureaucrats.[88] In November 1873, however, the number of persons on the *sanza* panel was increased to eleven.[89] The court found both Nagatani and Makimura guilty on December 31, 1873.[90]

---

85 Sanza Kisoku [The Sanza Rules], 1873, issued on October 9, reprinted in full in *id.*, pp. 57–58 [hereinafter Sanza Rules (1873)].
86 The Cabinet (*Naikaku*) system of government was established in Japan in 1885 (Dajōkan Tasshi [The Great Council of State Notice], No. 69 of 1885), while the Sanza Rules were drafted in 1873. Prior to 1885, the word *naikaku* was used to refer to the collegial decision-making body made up of the Counselors of State (*Sangi*) (Kokushi Daijiten Henshū Iinkai [Editorial Commission for the Encyclopedic Dictionary of Japanese History] (ed.), 1989, *Kokushi Daijiten* [The Encyclopedic Dictionary of Japanese History], Vol. 10, Tokyo: Shōgakukan, p. 499 [hereinafter The Encyclopedic Dictionary of Japanese History]). We may conclude, therefore, that the members of the *sanza* panel were appointed jointly by the Counselors of State.
87 Osatake, *Meiji Bunka Shi toshite no Nihon Baishin Shi* [The History of Jury in Japan as [Part of] *Meiji Cultural History*], p. 85.
88 The full list of the members of the *sanza* panel in the Makimura trial is available in *id.*, pp. 58–59.
89 *Id.*, p. 86.
90 *Id.*, pp. 91–93. Nagatani was sentenced to one hundred days' imprisonment with hard labor and a fine of forty yen, while Makimura was sentenced to one hundred days' imprisonment with hard labor and a fine of thirty yen (*id.*, pp. 91–93, and Hanai, "Baishin to Sanza Seido" [The Jury and Sanza Systems], p. 43).

The concept of trial by jury in Japan 37

The *sanza* system was not implemented again until 1875 when the first trial involving the case of the assassination of the Counselor of State (*Sangi*) Masaomi Hirosawa took place. Masaomi Hirosawa was found dead, stabbed thirteen times, on January 9, 1871, at his residence in Tokyo.[91] The defendants in this case were Masaichi Okida and Kane Fukui.[92] Okida admitted his guilt during police investigations that included torture,[93] but subsequently claimed that he was innocent,[94] and it was decided that this complicated case necessitated the introduction of the *sanza* system. The implementation of the *sanza* system in this case was requested by the side of the prosecution.[95] The Hirosawa trial did not use the 1873 rules for *sanza* participation that had been drafted for the Makimura case. Instead, a new detailed set of rules was written particularly for the Hirosawa trial in February 1875. These new rules stipulated the following:

Special court rules concerning the trial of the case [involving] the assassination of the late counselor Hirosawa[96]

Article 1. The court shall consist of four parties: the representative of the plaintiff (*genkokukan*), the defense representatives (*bengokan*), the *sanza* [panel members], and the judge. First, we provide a detailed [overview of]

---

91 Osatake, *Meiji Bunka Shi toshite no Nihon Baishin Shi* [The History of Jury in Japan as [Part of] *Meiji Cultural History*], p. 95. Scottish journalist and publisher John Reddie Black (1826–1880) referred to the assassination in the Hirosawa case as a "horribly cold-blooded murder" (J. R. Black, 1881, *Young Japan: Yokohama and Yedo – A Narrative of the Settlement and the City from the Signing of the Treaties in 1858 to the Close of the Year 1879 with a Glance at the Progress of Japan during a Period of Twenty-One Years*, London: Trubner, p. 299). Black stated that the assassination of Hirosawa was "supposed to be the first of an attempt to get rid of all the *Sangi*; but it did not turn out to be so" (*id.*). He did not offer any evidence to substantiate this claim. He concluded his account of the incident by noting that it "created great excitement in Tokio" (*id.*). The Ministry of Justice Museum in Tokyo holds a unique exhibit that is associated with the Hirosawa case – a doll that displays marks of Hirosawa's wounds.
92 Osatake, *Meiji Bunka Shi toshite no Nihon Baishin Shi* [The History of Jury in Japan as [Part of] *Meiji Cultural History*], p. 115; Hanai, "Baishin to Sanza Seido" [The Jury and Sanza Systems], p. 44.
93 Osatake, *Meiji Bunka Shi toshite no Nihon Baishin Shi* [The History of Jury in Japan as [Part of] *Meiji Cultural History*], pp. 102–103.
94 *Id.*, p. 103.
95 *Id.*, p. 108.
96 Hirosawa Ko Sangi Ansatsu Jiken Bekkyoku Saiban Kisoku [Special Court Rules Concerning the Trial of the Case [Involving] the Assassination of the Late Counselor Hirosawa], 1875, reprinted in Osatake, *Meiji Bunka Shi toshite no Nihon Baishin Shi* [The History of Jury in Japan as [Part of] *Meiji Cultural History*], pp. 110–114 [hereinafter Sanza Rules (1875)]. The Hirosawa assassination case of 1875 is significant in that it was especially for this case that the position of *bengokan* – the defense representative, a precursor of the position of professional defense attorney – was created for the first time in Japan's history. The *sanza* rules outlined the duties of *bengokan*. The defense representative was not allowed to argue law and was appointed by the court rather than be retained by the defendant (Sanza Rules (1875), arts. 4 and 5). See R. W. Rabinowitz, 1956, "The Historical Development of the Japanese Bar", *Harvard Law Review*, Vol. 70, No. 1, pp. 61–81, at p. 66 (discussing the role that the Hirosawa case played in the historical development of the Japanese bar).

the scope of the authority (*kengen*) of each of these parties. [It is important that none of the parties] infringe upon the scope of authority [granted to] the other parties.

Concerning the representative of the plaintiff

Article 2. The representative of the plaintiff will prepare a detailed statement concerning the circumstances [of the case] and submit it to the judge. He is also allowed to present it in the form of an oral statement.

Article 3. When all the necessary documents have been prepared, the representative of the plaintiff [shall present the case of] the party that suffered the most in the incident [on trial].

Concerning the defense representatives

Article 4. Two members shall be chosen by the Minister of Justice from the bureaucrats working at the Ministry [of Justice].

Article 5. The defense representatives are responsible for the defense of the accused, for responding to the charges filed by the representative of the plaintiff, for listening attentively as the judge conducts the inquiry, and if considered necessary for the defense of the accused, may face the [members of the] *sanza* [panel] and present their opinions to them after the hearing has been concluded. The defense representatives may not, however, discuss their understanding of whether the inquiry [conducted by the court] was good or not and of whether the defendant is guilty or not guilty, or [comment on] the appropriateness of the court's [actions]. The defense representatives are given the right to speak while the court conducts the inquiry.

Concerning the Sanza *[Panel]*

Article 6. [The *sanza* panel shall be composed of] seven members selected by the government (*seifu*). The [members of the panel] are allowed to be absent [from hearings], if their duties [preclude them from attending]. If [some members of the panel] cannot come to the hearings due to unavoidable circumstances, the trial may open in the absence of up to three public servants. In the event [a member of the *sanza* panel] falls sick or cannot attend due to other reasons, he is required to acquire a detailed understanding of the court inquiry on the day [that that member was absent] from another member of the *sanza* panel and make sure to be present [on the day when] votes are cast. If a member is absent for a long period of time due to illness or any other reason, that person may be relieved of this duty and replaced by another person selected by the government.

Article 7. As [the *sanza* panel] makes determinations regarding the presence or absence of a crime, its members are allowed to comment on whether the investigations were detailed enough, whether the inquiry [conducted by the court] was good or not, and on the appropriateness of the court's [actions]. The panel may not speak, however, prior to the time when the judge sets his questions (*monjō*).

Article 8. [The members of the *sanza* panel will] select a leader (the bureaucrat of the highest rank among them). The determination of the presence or absence of the crime will be based on the votes cast [by the *sanza* members]. Each of the members shall vote, and the leader shall see the distribution of the votes and report [the results] to the judge.

The presence or absence of the crime is determined based on the number of votes [cast for either option]. For example, in a panel of six persons, [the option for which] no less than four persons voted would be considered the majority [opinion]. If half of the panel votes "guilty" and the other votes "not guilty", the verdict should be "not guilty".

Concerning the judge

Article 9. If there is something that is difficult to understand during the statement of the plaintiff, the judge asks [clarifying] questions as many times as is necessary. In the event new information comes to light during the inquiry, the judge requests that [further] investigations be conducted by the [representative of the] plaintiff.

Article 10. When conducting an inquiry, the judge shall not assume the responsibilities of the *sanza* or the representative of the plaintiff.

Article 11. During the inquiry, it is the responsibility of the judge to decide which evidence is admissible and which is not.

Article 12. When the judge cannot attend trial hearings, he should appoint a deputy judge.

The order of trial

One day prior to the start of the hearings of this trial, the judge will notify the officials belonging to the other three parties [– that is, the representative of the plaintiff, the defense representatives, and the *sanza* –] and have a meeting with them. At the meeting, the representative of the plaintiff will state the circumstances [of the case] to the judge. After this statement, the judge, the

> representative of the plaintiff, the defense representatives, and the members of the *sanza* panel attend the trial and investigate the accused. After the investigation is completed, [the judges and the other officials] reconvene at a different place. If the defense representatives desire to do so, they may address the *sanza* panel. Upon the completion of the statement of the defense, the judge [summarizes the details of the case] from the beginning to the end and addresses the question concerning the guilt of the accused to the *sanza* panel. Then the members of the *sanza* panel move to the [location provided by one of the] Bureaus of the Ministry [of Justice] to cast their votes. The leader [of the *sanza* panel] submits [the verdict] to the judge. If [the verdict of] not guilty is decided upon, the judge immediately lets the accused go. If the verdict is guilty, the legal applications of this decision [are deliberated by the judge]. In preparation for voting [the members of the *sanza* panel] are allowed to discuss [the case] and to leave their seats.

Compared with the document stipulating the rules of conduct for the members of the *sanza* panel in the Makimura trial, the 1875 rules were much more detailed and discussed not only the rights of the members of the *sanza* panel, but also the rights of the prosecutor and of the defense. As was the case with the 1873 *sanza* rules, the draft of the 1875 rules originally included the word "jury" (*baishin*), but was subsequently amended to provide for the "bureaucratic jury" (*sanza*) panel instead.[97]

When the trial involving Masaichi Okida and Kane Fukui started, three other suspects in the Hirosawa Assassination case, Tetsugorō Aoki, Tadasu Sakaguchi, and Takashi Sakaguchi, were investigated.[98] Aoki confessed to entering Hirosawa's residence with the intention of robbing him and to killing Hirosawa after being discovered by him, while Tadasu and Takashi Sakaguchi were arrested as Aoki's conspirators.[99]

The *sanza* panel in this trial initially was to consist of seven members and to include representatives of the Ministry of Foreign Affairs and the Ministry of Finance as well as high level bureaucrats belonging to the Chambers of the Right and Left.[100] These officials were appointed to serve on the *sanza* the panel on March 3, 1875.[101]

The rules concerning the *sanza* system were amended following the appointment of the members of the *sanza* panel, on March 4, 1875. Specifically, Article 6 of the Rules was amended to read that the number of members of the *sanza* panel was to be twelve

---

97 Osatake, *Meiji Bunka Shi toshite no Nihon Baishin Shi*, p. 114.
98 *Id.*, p. 115.
99 *Id.*, p. 115.
100 *Id.*, pp. 115–116.
101 *Id.*

and that not more than five "bureaucratic jurors" could be absent during the court hearings for the trial to take place and Article 7 was amended to allow the members of the *sanza* to ask the judge to clarify certain points deemed important in the case.[102] In line with the amended rules, five new bureaucratic jury candidates including bureaucrats from the Ministry of Education and the Ministry of the Army (*Rikugun Shō*) were appointed on March 8, 1875, and on March 19, the trial opened.[103] On July 13, 1875, the *sanza* panel found the defendants not guilty.[104]

The verdict of "not guilty", however, did not signal the end of the Hirosawa Assassination case. In 1877, another suspect, Rokuzō Nakamura, was arrested.[105] On December 12, 1878, the Ministry of Justice ordered the Great Court of Judicature (*Daishin'in*) to reopen the case.[106] This case was not tried with the participation of the *sanza* panel. Instead, the number of judges was increased to twelve and each of the empanelled judges was required to vote for the verdict of guilty or not guilty.[107] New rules were drafted for this case:

Special court rules concerning the trial of the case [Involving] the assassination of the late counselor Hirosawa[108]

Article 1. This court shall consist of three parties: the representative of the plaintiff (*genkokukan*), the defense representatives (*bengokan*), and the judges. First, we provide a detailed [overview of] the scope of the authority (*kengen*) of each of these parties. [It is important that none of the parties] infringe upon the scope of authority [granted to] the other parties.

Article 2. The case on trial shall be treated as a political offence (*kokujihan*), therefore, appealing *jōkoku* is not allowed.

Concerning the representative of the plaintiff

Article 3. The representative of the plaintiff shall complete the following procedures: prepare all the necessary documents regarding the case, providing the details of the prosecution case, and submit these materials to the judge.

---

102 *Id.*, p. 116.
103 *Id.*, p. 117.
104 *Id.*, pp. 125–126.
105 *Id.*, pp. 128, 134–135.
106 *Id.*, p. 128.
107 *Id.*, p. 128.
108 Ko Hirosawa Sangi Ansatsu Jiken Bekkyoku Saiban Kisoku [Special Court Rules Concerning the Trial of the Case [Involving] the Assassination of the Late Counselor Hirosawa], 1879, reprinted in Osatake, *Meiji Bunka Shi toshite no Nihon Baishin Shi* [The History of Jury in Japan as [Part of] *Meiji* Cultural History], pp. 128–132 [hereinafter Sanza Rules (1879)].

Article 4. Those points in the dossier submitted to court that are difficult to understand may be clarified in a verbal statement. [The representative of the plaintiff] is in charge of representing the case of the plaintiff.

Concerning the defense representatives

Article 5. The Minister of Justice shall appoint two members from the bureaucrats working at the Ministry [of Justice] to [serve as defense representatives].

Article 6. The defense representatives are responsible for the defense of the accused, for responding to the charges filed by the representative of the plaintiff, for listening attentively as the judges conduct their inquiry, and if considered necessary for the defense of the accused, may face the judges and present their opinions to them after the hearing has been concluded. They may also discuss their understanding of whether the inquiry [conducted by the court] was good or not and of whether the defendant is guilty or not guilty. However, they may not speak during the time that the court conducts the inquiry.

Concerning the judges

Article 7. The Minister of Justice shall select twelve judges and appoint them for this case.

Article 8. The judge in the highest rank among them shall be selected to be the presiding judge. In the event the presiding judge cannot attend a trial hearing, a deputy judge will perform his duties.

Article 9. If a judge cannot attend the trial hearings due to illness or other unavoidable circumstances, that judge needs to ask the presiding judge regarding the deliberations at court that took place on that day in detail and is required to be present on the day when votes are cast. The trial may open in the absence of up to three judges.

Article 10. If a judge wants to address a question to the accused or to any person related to this case, he needs to obtain the permission of the presiding judge.

The order of trial

Article 11. Upon receiving the indictment materials from the representative of the plaintiff, the judges are to carefully read them and let the defense representatives read them. Once the materials have been read, the presiding judge decides the time of the meeting and notifies the other judges, the representative of the plaintiff, and the defense representatives.

Article 12. Upon the meeting of the [three] parties, those points regarding the materials provided by the representative of the plaintiff that require explanation should be explained, and those questions that the judges need to ask are to be asked.

Article 13. Once the explanations by the representative of the plaintiff are finished, the presiding judge instructs the other parties to prepare for the examination [of the case]. Prior to the start of the examination, the presiding judge explains the points of the investigation.

Article 14. After the examination of the case is finished, everyone leaves the courtroom, and the defense representatives express the points of defense to the judges.

Article 15. After the inquiry into the case has been completed, the judges express their opinions regarding the absence or presence of the crime through voting. Each judge is to vote on each point [of the investigation] and write [on the voting paper] whether he finds the defendant guilty or not guilty on each count.

Article 16. Regarding the voting procedure, the judges go to a separate room where they are allowed to discuss their opinions. No one is allowed to enter this room before all votes are cast.

Article 17. After the voting procedure has been completed, the presiding judge examines the votes cast and writes down the results of the vote.

Article 18. The verdict is based on the majority opinion regarding the presence or absence of a crime. If an equal number has been cast for the "guilty" and "not guilty" verdicts, the verdict should be "not guilty".

Article 19. If the verdict is "not guilty", the case is dismissed and the accused is let go. If the verdict is "guilty", the questions regarding the legal application are to be addressed.

The trial opened in accordance with these rules on March 12, 1880, and on March 22, 1880, the trial ended with the verdict of "not guilty".[109] Thus, despite seven years of investigation, the Hirosawa Assassination case was never resolved.

---

109 The full text of the verdict is available in Osatake, *Meiji Bunka Shi toshite no Nihon Baishin Shi* [The History of Jury in Japan as [Part of] *Meiji* Cultural History], pp. 134–135.

The sanza system in military courts

On April 13, 1876, the Navy Ministry (*Kaigun Shō*)[110] promulgated the "Provisional Rules Concerning Court Sessions" (*Saiban Kaigi Kari Kisoku*), which established the *sanza* system in Navy courts.[111] According to this document, the *sanza* system was used to adjudicate cases that involved upper rank military personnel and fitted either (1) instances when the need arose to punish an offence, but there was no article in the code formally describing that offence, or (2) instances when there was an article covering a particular offence, but the incident involved a person in the rank higher than petty officer and a crime for which the punishment was heavier than penal servitude.[112] In other words, the system was implemented in those cases that were of extraordinary nature and where there was the need to add legitimacy to the verdict.

These rules did not explicitly state if the opinions of the members of the *sanza* panel were binding on the court. They required, however, that the verdict be proclaimed in those cases when the members of the *sanza* panel agreed with the decision of the judges.[113] In case there was a difference in views regarding the verdict between the members of the *sanza* panel and the judges, the judges and *sanza* members were required to deal with the problem through deliberating further with the *sanza* members.[114]

The Ministry of the Army (*Rikugun Shō*) introduced the *sanza* system to its courts on July 27, 1872.[115] Legal historian Takeki Osatake has argued that it may be assumed that the duties of the members of the *sanza* panel were similar to those of their counterparts in the navy tribunals.[116]

The "bureaucratic jury" and the "judge-only" systems were the first experiments with the participation of a party other than court officials in trials in Japan. The possibility of implementing the layperson jury system was discussed further in the late 1870s and early 1880s in connection with the drafting of the *Meiji* Constitution and of the Code of Criminal Instruction.

The *Meiji* Constitution: the public debate

There is evidence suggesting that the possibility of introducing the layperson jury system in Japan was deliberated during the drafting of the *Meiji* Constitution. Kentarō Kaneko,[117]

---

110 Cabinet Ministry from 1872 to 1945. The Navy Ministry (*Kaigun Shō*) and the Army Ministry (*Rikugun Shō*) were established in April 1872 under the *Dajōkan* system of government to replace the Ministry of Military Affairs (*Hyōbushō*). The Navy and Army Ministries were abolished in November 1945 and replaced by the temporary Demobilization Ministry (*Fukuinshō*). Nihon Shi Kōjiten Henshū Iinkai [Editorial Committee of the Historical Dictionary of Japan] (ed.), 1997, *Nihon Shi Kōjiten* [The Historical Dictionary of Japan], Tokyo: Yamakawa Shuppan, p. 390.
111 Saiban Kaigi Kari Kisoku [Provisional Rules Concerning Court Sessions], 1876, reproduced in Osatake, *Meiji Bunka Shi toshite no Nihon Baishin Shi* [The History of Jury in Japan as [Part of] *Meiji* Cultural History], pp. 137–140 [hereinafter Provisional Rules Concerning Court Sessions (1876)].
112 Provisional Rules Concerning Court Sessions (1876), Preamble.
113 *Id.*, arts. 3–7; Osatake, *Meiji Bunka Shi toshite no Nihon Baishin Shi* [The History of Jury in Japan as [Part of] *Meiji* Cultural History], pp. 140–141.
114 *Id.*, pp. 138–141.
115 *Id.*, p. 141.
116 *Id.*, pp. 141–142.
117 Kentarō Kaneko (1853–1942) was a statesman and diplomat of *Meiji*-period Japan. He was selected to become a student member of the Iwakura Embassy and was chosen to stay in the United States to

a statesman and member of the Office for Investigation of Institutions (*Seido Torishirabe Kyoku*) – a body that was established in 1884 and was engaged in conducting research on the constitutions of Western countries – recalled that the jury system and the mechanism of impeachment were the two subjects of intense discussion over the course of deliberating the draft of Japan's Constitution (*Nippon Kokken An*) at the *Genrōin*.[118]

Kaneko stated specifically that the provisions regarding the jury were included in the government's drafts of the *Meiji* Constitution.[119] As none of the currently known drafts of the constitution contains provisions regarding the jury system,[120] it is plausible that Kaneko was referring to earlier drafts.[121] The earliest remaining draft of the constitution is dated October 1876; therefore, the version that could have included provisions regarding the institution of jury service is likely to have been written and discussed prior to 1876.[122] Legal historian Taichirō Mitani has argued that as Kaneko himself was in the United States during the period between 1871 and 1878, it is likely that he did not participate in the deliberations regarding these provisions himself, but could have heard about such deliberations from the Secretary of the *Genrōin* Sukeyuki Kawazu and Morikazu (Shūichi) Numa.[123]

Several private drafts of the constitution contained provisions regarding the institution of jury service. The draft authored by the members of the Liberty and People's Rights Group (*Ōmeisha*) society in 1879 provided for the introduction of the jury system, whose members would adjudicate crimes (*jūzai*) as well as political offences (*kokujihan*).[124] Another example was the draft of the constitution proposed by the Self-Help Society (*Risshisha*) at the end of 1880 that stipulated that the institution of jury service should be introduced in all criminal trials.[125]

---

study at Harvard University. Upon graduating from Harvard, Kaneko returned to Japan and lectured at Tokyo Imperial University. In 1880, Kaneko was appointed as secretary to the *Genrōin*, and in 1884, he became a member of the Office for Investigation of Institutions (*Seido Torishirabe Kyoku*). Kaneko became personal secretary to Hirobumi Itō when Itō assumed the post of prime minister in 1885. He also served at the House of Peers and the Imperial Diet, becoming the secretary of the latter, before assuming the post of vice minister and then minister of agriculture in 1898. In 1900, Kaneko was appointed minister of justice. He was awarded an honorary doctorate by Harvard University in 1899 in recognition of his work on the *Meiji* Constitution (Ichinose, *Major 20th Century People in Japan*, p. 726).

118 M. Itō, "Baishin Hō Iin Kaigiji Hikki" [Records of the Discussion of the Members of the Committee on the Jury Act], Session No. 17, March 10, 1921, cited in Mitani, *Seiji Seido toshite no Baishin Sei* [The Jury System as a Political System], p. 97.
119 Mitani, *Seiji Seido toshite no Baishin Sei* [The Jury System as a Political System], p. 97.
120 "Nihon Kokken An (Tekisuto): Shiryō de Miru Nihon no Kindai" [Japan National Constitution Draft (Text): Japan's Modernity as Seen through Documents], available online at http://www.ndl.go.jp/modern/img_t/022/022–002tx.html.
121 Mitani, *Seiji Seido toshite no Baishin Sei* [The Jury System as a Political System], p. 97.
122 *Id.*, p. 97.
123 *Id.*, p. 97. M. Tomasi, 2002, "Oratory in Meiji and Taishō Japan: Public Speaking and the Formation of New Written Language", *Monumenta Nipponica*, Vol. 57, No. 1, pp. 43–71, at p. 47; R. Devine, 1979, "The Way of the King. An Early Meiji Essay on Government", *Monumenta Nipponica*, Vol. 34, No. 1, pp. 49–72, at p. 53.
124 Ōmeisha Kenpō Sōan [Ōmeisha], 1879, The Judiciary, art. 8, available online at http://www.japanpen.or.jp/e-bungeikan/sovereignty/pdf/oumeisya.pdf.
125 Nihon Koku Koku Kenpō An [Draft of the Constitution of the Japanese State], art. 192, available online at http://www.cc.matsuyama-u.ac.jp/~tamura/risshisyakennpou.htm; T. Osatake, 1929, "Baishin to Fusen no Michizure [The Fellow Travelers of the Jury [System] and Universal Suffrage], *Hōsōkai Zasshi*

46 *The concept of trial by jury in Japan*

Although the enacted version of the *Meiji* Constitution did not include any provisions regarding the institution of jury service, the idea of expanding layperson participation in Japan remained in the spotlight of public debate in the 1880s and 1890s. Gen'ichirō Fukuchi, a bureaucrat and journalist, authored a piece titled "An Opinion on the Constitution of Japan" (*Kokuken Iken*) that appeared in the *Tokyo Nichi Nichi Shinbun* newspaper in 1881, in which he argued that Japan should introduce the criminal jury system and that the provisions regarding the jury system should be incorporated into the constitution.[126] Fukuchi argued that the implementation of the jury system would result in greater respect for human rights in the courtroom.[127] The jury system was also the subject of consideration by the Liberal Party (*Jiyū Tō*) in 1890. This party included the introduction of the jury system among the fifteen items on its agenda that year.[128] The debate regarding the pros and cons of the jury system was fueled further by the discussion of the drafts of the new Code of Criminal Instruction.

Boissonade's proposal: provisions concerning the jury in the draft of the Code of Criminal Instruction

Emile Gustave Boissonade de Fontarabie, a French legal scholar who was invited to Japan to advise the Japanese government, included the proposal to introduce trial by jury in his draft of the Code of Criminal Instruction that was completed in 1878.[129] The process of writing this draft began in 1877 and was done in collaboration with the members of the committee formed within the Ministry of Justice especially for that purpose.[130] Takatō Ōki[131] presided over the sessions of the committee that was headed by Kaneyasu Kishira[132] and consisted of seven members that included Boissonade and six officials of the Ministry of Justice.[133]

According to Boissonade's original draft, Japan was to introduce an all-layperson jury system that differed from the French jury system, where cases were tried by a mixed panel consisting of nine jurors and three professional judges. Boissonade proposed that crimes (*jūzai*) be adjudicated by three judges and a jury panel (*baishin*) composed of ten laypersons in district courts and courts of appeal.[134] Jurors were to be selected by lot from the list of

---

[Journal of the Law Society], Vol. 7, No. 10, pp. 445–450, at p. 447 (discussing the provisions of *Risshisha*'s draft of the constitution).

126 Osatake, "Baishin to Fusen no Michizure [The Fellow Travelers of the Jury [System] and Universal Suffrage], p. 447.
127 *Id.*, p. 447.
128 *Id.*, p. 448.
129 Mitani, *Kindai Nihon no Shihōken to Seitō* [Judicial Power in Modern Japan and Political Parties], p. 103.
130 *Id.*, p. 103.
131 Ōki Takatō (1832–1899) was a politician of the *Meiji* period. As minister of justice in 1876, he suppressed several antigovernment uprisings. In 1885 he became chairman of the *Genrōin* and in 1889 president of the Privy Council (Biography Index, p. 416).
132 Kaneyasu Kishira (1837–1883) was a judicial officer of the *Meiji* period. In 1877 he became a prosecutor at the Great Court of Judicature (*Daishin'in*) and in 1879 became the president of the Great Court of Judicature (*id.*, p. 759).
133 Mitani, *Kindai Nihon no Shihōken to Seitō* [Judicial Power in Modern Japan and Political Parties], p. 103.
134 G. E. Boissonade (translated by Y. Mori, S. Iwano), 1882, *Chizai Hō Sōan Chūshaku* [The Draft of the Code of Criminal Instruction Accompanied by a Commentary], Tokyo: Shihōsha [hereinafter Boissonade's Draft of Code of Criminal Instruction], arts. 84 and 86, cited in Mitani, *Kindai Nihon no Shihōken*

persons selected as eligible to serve as jurors. The persons whose names were on the list were to retain their status as prospective jurors and jurors in reserve for the period of one year. First, twenty jury candidates and four candidates to become jurors in reserve were to be selected.[135] These candidates were to be summoned, and the prosecutor and the defendant were to be each given the right to determine which of the twenty candidates would become jurors and form the panel. The jurors who had been selected were required to listen to the details of the case and then – after hearing the closing arguments – to come up with the answers to the questions set forth by the judge.[136] Boissonade did not provide for an indictment jury in this draft, but included a provision regarding the institution of what he called the "high jury" (*kōtō baishin*) – a ten-person jury panel that was to decide the cases tried at the High Court of Justice (*kōtō hōin*), such as offences involving the Emperor and the imperial household, instigation of internal disturbances as well as instigation of foreign aggression, and the crimes committed by the judges working at the Grand Court of Judicature (*Daishin'in*) and by the prosecutors.[137]

Boissonade argued that the implementation of trial by jury – along with other reforms, including the abolition of torture – was an important step to put the Japanese legal system on par with those of Western nations.[138]

The Code of Criminal Instruction Screening Committee (*Chizai Hō Sōan Shinsakyoku*) was set up within the *Genrōin* with the goal of examining Boissonade's draft. The committee edited Boissonade's proposal, and the revised version was submitted to the Great Minister of State (*Dajō Daijin*), Sanjō Sanetomi.[139] The provisions concerning the jury system were left intact, with only the name of the jury panel in the High Court of Justice changed from "high jury" (*kōtō baishin*) to "special jury" (*tokubetsu baishin*).[140]

---

to Seitō [Judicial Power in Modern Japan and Political Parties], p. 104. The Penal Code of 1880 adopted the French classification of offences into "crime" (*jūzai*), "délit" (*keizai*), and "contravention" (*ikeizai*).
135 Boissonade's Draft of Code of Criminal Instruction, art. 89, cited in Mitani, *Kindai Nihon no Shihōken to Seitō* [Judicial Power in Modern Japan and Political Parties], p. 104.
136 Boissonade's Draft of Code of Criminal Instruction, arts. 498, 499, 500, 501, and 502, cited in Mitani, *Kindai Nihon no Shihōken to Seitō* [Judicial Power in Modern Japan and Political Parties], pp. 104–105.
137 Boissonade's Draft of Code of Criminal Instruction, arts. 101, 98, and 99, cited in Mitani, *Kindai Nihon no Shihōken to Seitō* [Judicial Power in Modern Japan and Political Parties], p. 105.
138 Takayanagi, "A Century of Innovation", p. 21; N. Toshitani, "Tennōsei Hō Taisei to Baishin Seido Ron" [The Legal Structure of Emperor [*Tennō*] System and the Debates [Concerning the] Jury System], in Nihon Kindai Hōsei Shi Kenkyūkai (ed.), 1983, *Nihon Kindai Kokka no Hō Kōzō* [The Structure of Law in the Japanese Modern State], Tokyo: Bokutakusha, pp. 517–570, at p. 548. Boissonade's opinion statement regarding the need to abolish torture in Japan is reproduced in Hōsei Daigaku [Hosei University] (ed.), 1978, *Boissonādo Tōmonroku* [The Correspondence of Mr. Boissonade], Tokyo: Hōsei Daigaku [Hosei University], pp. 46–49. On the attitudes on the part of the members of the *Meiji*-period elite actively supporting the abolition of the use of torture in Japanese courts towards the possibility of introducing the jury system, see Toshitani, "Tennōsei Hō Taisei to Baishin Seido Ron" [The Legal Structure of Emperor [*Tennō*] System and the Debates [Concerning the] Jury System], pp. 520–532.
139 This committee was headed by Secretary of the *Genrōin* Sakimitsu Yanagiwara, and included member of the *Genrōin* Masatake Kawase, vice minister of justice (*Shihō Taifu*) and member of the *Genrōin* Seiri Tamano, general of the army and member of the *Genrōin* Izuru Tsuda, member of the *Genrōin* Junjirō Hosokawa, Prosecutor Kaneyasu Kishira, Prosecutor Akira Tsuruta, Grand Secretary at the Great Council of State Tamotsu Murata, Secretary at the Ministry of Justice Taizō Namura, and Prosecutor Chisato Sakaya as members (Mitani, *Kindai Nihon no Shihōken to Seitō* [Judicial Power in Modern Japan and Political Parties], p. 106).
140 *Id.*, p. 106.

48 *The concept of trial by jury in Japan*

The Great Council of State, however, made substantial changes to this draft, and the version resubmitted to the *Genrōin* on March 29, 1880, no longer contained any provisions regarding the jury system. Tamotsu Murata,[141] who participated in the process of making the decision to exclude the provisions concerning the jury system, commented on the reasons that led to the revision of the draft in his autobiography.[142] According to Murata, the Great Council of State concluded that because the decisions made by the members of the jury could not be influenced by the judge, it was imperative to ensure that only persons who were sufficiently educated and had a certain degree of financial stability would serve as jurors.[143] Murata stated that the provisions of Boissonade's draft did not guarantee that this would be the case.[144] Another reason for deleting the stipulations regarding jury service included the observation that as some European countries, such as Holland, did not have the jury system, it was not imperative for Japan to implement this system. Murata argued further that the view that the implementation of the jury system was not in the national interests of Japan was the third consideration that contributed to the decision to not introduce the jury system in Japan.[145]

Murata noted in his account of the discussions regarding Boissonade's draft that Kowashi Inoue,[146] who was at the time serving as a grand secretary to the Great Minister of State (*daishokikan*), played a critical role in the decision to delete the stipulations regarding the jury system. According to Murata, Inoue opposed the idea of introducing the jury system and persuaded Murata and Keigo Kiyoura[147] – another bureaucrat at the Great Council of State directly involved in the screening of the draft – to delete the provisions regarding the jury system. Inoue argued that it was possible to increase the number of associate judges in trials in the future, if deemed necessary, instead of introducing the layperson jury system.[148] It is likely that Inoue was referring to the experience of instituting the "all-judge" special jury experimented with in the latter half of the Hirosawa case.

Inoue expressed his reservations regarding the idea of introducing the layperson jury in Japan even prior to participating in the discussions of the draft of the Code of Criminal

---

141 Tamotsu Murata (1843–1925) served at the Ministry of Justice and later assumed the post of the Grand Secretary (*Daishokikan*) at the Great Council of State, the Ministry of Home Affairs (*Naimushō*), and the *Genrōin*. He was a member of the *Genrōin* and in 1890 became a member of the House of Peers (Ichinose, *Major 20th Century People in Japan*, p. 2508).
142 The reprint of the opinion voiced by Murata is available in Mitani, *Kindai Nihon no Shihōken to Seitō* [Judicial Power in Modern Japan and Political Parties], p. 107.
143 *Id.*, p. 107.
144 *Id.*, p. 107.
145 *Id.*, p. 107.
146 Kowashi Inoue (1844–1895) joined the Ministry of Justice and was sent to study in France and Germany (1872–1873). Working closely with K. F. Hermann Roesler, the government's German adviser, he prepared drafts that became the base for the Constitution of the Empire of Japan and the Imperial Household Laws. He was also one of the authors of the Imperial Rescript on Education. He was appointed to the Privy Council in 1890 and in 1893 became minister of education (Nihon Shi Kōjiten Henshū Iinkai [Editorial Committee of the Historical Dictionary of Japan], *Nihon Shi Kōjiten* [The Historical Dictionary of Japan], p. 163).
147 Keigo Kiyoura (1850–1942) joined the Ministry of Justice in 1876. In 1922, he became president of the Privy Council. In January 1924, Kiyoura formed a Cabinet and became prime minister, but was forced to resign (Ichinose, *Major 20th Century People in Japan*, p. 887).
148 Mitani, *Kindai Nihon no Shihōken to Seitō* [Judicial Power in Modern Japan and Political Parties], p. 107.

Instruction. In his "Theory of Jury" (*Baishin Ron*),[149] dated October 27, 1877, he argued against the jury system and stated that asking persons chosen randomly to represent the whole of the Japanese people was not feasible. In addition, Inoue pointed out that jurors were likely to base their decisions on public opinion, while court rulings should be free from bias. He also claimed that while in the political decision-making process it was acceptable to make decisions based on the majority opinion, this principle was not suitable for reaching decisions in a courtroom. Referring to the Anglo-American model of jury trials, Inoue argued that although jurors only decided questions of fact, while judges were to be responsible for questions of law, the questions of fact and law were interrelated and that separating the two was in reality difficult, because the law was frequently the basis for making the decisions regarding the guilt of the accused. He concluded that in the absence of legal training, laypersons were certain to make the important decisions entrusted to them based exclusively on their feelings, which he argued was not desirable. Inoue illustrated this point by noting that in the countries using the jury system, the members of the jury frequently returned verdicts that were not fair, allowing guilty persons to go free and innocent persons to be punished. Inoue concluded that in view of all these problems, Japan should not introduce the jury system.

Inoue's "Theory of Jury" attracted a lot of attention in 1877 and inspired Boissonade to write a response to defend the idea of implementing the jury system in Japan. In an article titled "A Response Concerning the Theory of Criminal Jury" (*Keiji Baishin Ron no Tōgi*), dated November 21, 1877,[150] Boissonade argued that jurors were selected to serve not to ensure that the court hearings were carried out in the presence of the representatives of the whole nation, but to guarantee that court decisions would be made by persons who were of the same status as the defendant. He also disagreed with Inoue's assessment of the quality of jurors' decisions. Boissonade argued that the judge could explain to the jurors the particulars associated with the questions of law. Regarding the claim that jurors may be biased, Boissonade argued that the bias of professional judges may be much more substantial than that of the members of the jury. He emphasized that he believed that the jurors' ability to empathize with others was not a defect of the jury system but a strength.

Despite the arguments proposed by Boissonade, Inoue remained opposed to the idea of implementing the jury system in 1880 when the draft of the Code of Criminal Instruction was being deliberated at the Great Council of State.[151] The fact that the implementation of the jury system was not perceived by the elites and by the general public in *Meiji* Japan to

---

149 K. Inoue, "Baishin Ron" [Theory of Jury], reprinted in Hanai, *Shōtei Ronsō* [Courtroom Notes], pp. 71–76; Mitani, *Kindai Nihon no Shihōken to Seitō* [Judicial Power in Modern Japan and Political Parties], pp. 108–109.

150 G. E. Boissonade, 1877, "Keiji Baishin Ron no Tōgi" [A Response Concerning the Theory of Criminal Jury], reprinted in Hanai, *Shōtei Ronsō* [Courtroom Notes], pp. 77–83; Mitani, *Kindai Nihon no Shihōken to Seitō* [Judicial Power in Modern Japan and Political Parties], pp. 109–110.

151 Inoue's firm stance and ability to persuade appear to be one of the deciding factors for deleting the provisions regarding jury service (S. Nakahara, 1989, "Meiji Kenpō Ka no Baishin Sei to Kenpō Ron" [The Jury System under the [Provisions of] the *Meiji* Constitution and Constitutional Theory], *Hōritsu Ronsō* [Law Review], Vol. 61, pp. 369–394, at p. 372, partially reprinted in Saikō Saibansho Jimu Sōkyoku Keiji Kyoku [Criminal Affairs Bureau, General Secretariat of the Supreme Court of Japan] (ed.), 1995, *Wagakuni de Okonawareta Baishin Saiban – Shōwa Shoki ni Okeru Baishin Hō no Un'yō ni tsuite* [Jury Trials That Took Place in Our Country – Regarding the Operation of the Jury Act in the Early *Shōwa* Period], Tokyo: Shihō Kyōkai, p. 10).

50 *The concept of trial by jury in Japan*

be a necessary prerequisite for the revision of unequal treaties certainly gave credence to Inoue's position.[152]

The view that Japan should not introduce the jury system was supported by Robert Brader, a British jurist and consultant of the *Meiji* government.[153] In his response to the government's inquiry on the subject of jury trials, dated December 9, 1879, Brader argued specifically that the jury was a system that had the potential of functioning effectively only in states where the freedoms of the people were protected. According to Brader, in an autocratic state such as Japan's, the jury, if introduced, would be a purely ornamental system.[154] He added that an autocratic government might choose to manipulate the jury, and if the public became aware of this, they might turn against that government. Based on his understanding of the situation in Japan, Brader recommended that the *Meiji* government not introduce the jury system. He argued that if increasing the degree of political consciousness of the Japanese people was what the Japanese government wanted, then the introduction of the jury system was not the first step to take. Brader suggested that the *Meiji* government should consider involving laypersons in local governance instead.[155]

The system allowing laypersons to participate in trial hearings was not introduced in Japan during the *Meiji* period. The arguments for and against the jury system voiced in the process of public debate triggered by Boissonade's proposal and by the private drafts of the *Meiji* Constitution became the basis for the subsequent discussion regarding the plans to introduce the jury system in Japan in the 20th century.

Evaluating the first attempts to introduce trial by jury in *Meiji*-period Japan

The attitudes on the part of the Japanese government towards the concept of jury service in the aftermath of the *Meiji* Restoration reflected the two trends that guided Japan's legal and social reforms carried out during that time: the desire to strike a balance between change and continuity and to adapt those concepts that Japan chose to adopt from the West to ensure that they fit in well with the existing environment in Japan.

The "bureaucratic jury" (*sanza*) system, implemented in Japan in 1873 and 1875, provides a powerful illustration to the Japanese government's commitment to the principle of adapting when considering adopting or transplanting a Western institution or concept.

The Makimura case, which involved members of the local government as defendants, raised the question regarding the need to provide checks for possible abuses of power during trial. The possibility of adopting the layperson jury system was considered in connection with this trial. Japan's Ministry of Justice ultimately proposed instead to implement the "bureaucratic jury", an institution providing for the participation of bureaucrats from various Ministries in the trial as jurors. The *sanza* was similar to the Anglo-American system of jury trials in that "bureaucratic jurors" selected a foreman and reached their decisions independently of the judge in a way that was similar to that of their counterparts in countries

---

152 N. Toshitani, 1981, "Jōyaku Kaisei to Baishin Seido" [Treaty Revision and the Jury System], *Shakai Kagaku Kenkyū* [The Journal of Social Science], Vol. 33, No. 5, pp. 1–32.
153 R. Brader, 1879, "Baishin Hō Iken" [Opinion Statement on the Jury Law], reprinted in Hanai, *Shōtei Ronsō* [Courtroom Notes], pp. 85–90. Vanoverbeke, *Juries in the Japanese Legal System*, p. 186.
154 Brader, "Baishin Hō Iken" [Opinion Statement on the Jury Law], pp. 87–88.
155 *Id.*, p. 90.

using the Anglo-American model of jury trials. Japan's *sanza* system had one important difference, however. Instead of laypersons chosen by lot, the *sanza* jury panel included bureaucrats appointed by name by the Counselors of State (*Sangi*) or by the Japanese government (*seifu*).

Having a jury panel consisting only of the members of the nation's cream of the crop – the highly educated bureaucratic elite – certainly made it possible to avoid the alleged weaknesses of the layperson jury systems, such as susceptibility to bias and emotions at the expense of rational judgment. Making the jury "bureaucratic" also allowed the Japanese Ministry of Justice to add authority to the verdicts in trials of an exceptionally complex nature – an objective that would arguably have been much harder to achieve if Japan chose to introduce the layperson jury system. After all, the traditional attitude of "Respect for Officials and Contempt for the People" (*kanson minpi*) was said to predispose the Japanese general public to prefer trial by professionals over trial by peers, and the implementation of the system where laypersons would make decisions regarding the fate of the accused was more likely to raise questions regarding the legitimacy of the court in complex cases than add authority to the verdict. Instituting a bureaucratic jury composed of highly respected representatives of different ministries, on the other hand, was expected to help resolve questions concerning the legitimacy of verdicts in complex cases.

The fact that the *sanza* was conceptualized as a system that was to be only implemented on a one-time basis arguably served to lessen the risk associated with the introduction of this new institution. After all, if any questions concerning the legitimacy of this trial were to arise, the system could be easily abolished and never used again. In actual fact, however, the deployment of the *sanza* panel at the 1873 Makimura trial turned out to be a successful enough idea to encourage the Ministry of Justice to resort to it again in 1875. The *sanza* system was implemented for the second time to resolve an incident that did not involve any readily apparent clashes of interest between the different branches of government, as was the case in 1873. The Hirosawa case was a complex incident that involved the assassination of a politician and featured forced confessions, and therefore necessitated extraordinary measures. The fact that the Ministry of Justice decided to resurrect the *sanza* system of bureaucratic advisors in an incident that had very different challenges to those that confronted the Makimura case appears to imply that the Ministry was satisfied with the contribution of the *sanza* panel to the resolution of the 1873 dispute.

The decision to subsequently use a panel composed of twelve professional judges instead of the *sanza* system to determine whether the final suspect in the Hirosawa case was guilty or not illustrates the willingness on the part of the Ministry of Justice to experiment when choosing to adopt the substance of a Western concept. The number of judges on this special panel of judges – twelve – may of course have been selected in an entirely arbitrary fashion. There is also the possibility, however, that the fact that the Anglo-American jury panel, as practiced in the United States and the United Kingdom, consisted of twelve laypersons played a part. If the latter is the case, then the decision to introduce the twelve all-judge panel in the Hirosawa trial may have represented an attempt on the part of the Japanese government to adapt the all-layperson model of jury trials to fit into the local environment – that is, a situation where there was a preference for professional judges.

Neither the "bureaucratic" nor the twelve-judge jury system was implemented after the Hirosawa case was concluded in civilian courts. This appears to imply that after experimenting with these two adapted models of jury trials, the Ministry of Justice concluded that the benefits that the special jury represented in the adjudication of cases did not outweigh the costs. Indeed, the implementation of the *sanza* system meant that the bureaucrats serving as jurors could not carry out their duties at their respective Ministries when engaged in adjudicating a case, while the introduction of the expanded panel of judges meant that the judges involved in the case were unavailable to resolve other disputes. The benefits of having either the *sanza* panel or the twelve judge panel in other, less complex cases were limited. After all, the decision to "bureaucratize" the jury made it impossible to make use of the positive features that layperson participation in the justice system affords. The decisions of the "bureaucratic" and "judge-only" jury remained susceptible to elite bias. In addition, the ability of both models used in the *Meiji* period to ensure fair trial was debatable. High-level bureaucrats in the Japanese government (*seifu*) and the Counselors of State (*Sangi*) appointed the members on the panel; therefore, there was the possibility that these officials could manipulate the outcome of deliberations by nominating only those members whose opinions were in line with their own.

The *sanza* system was used several times in military tribunals, and just like its counterpart in the civilian courts, this system was implemented only in those cases where there was the need to add legitimacy to verdicts. The "bureaucratic jury" system in military tribunals was not extended to all cases presumably for the same reasons as in civilian courts.

The pros and cons of either the Anglo-American or the Continental-European models of jury trials were not discussed sufficiently by either the government or the public in the course of the invention and implementation of the two adapted alternatives to the Western jury system in the 1870s. The provisions concerning the jury in Boissonade's draft of the Code of Criminal Instruction, however, served to trigger such a discussion for the first time in Japan's history.

Boissonade's proposal did not provide for the implementation of a French-style mixed-court jury system. According to this draft, Japan was to introduce an all-layperson jury system that differed from the French jury system where cases were tried by a mixed panel of nine jurors and three professional judges. While Boissonade's idea of implementing the jury system was initially approved by the *Genrōin*, the officials of the Great Council of State subsequently deleted all the provisions concerning the jury system. The reasons behind this decision were discussed by the persons taking part in the decision-making process in much greater detail than at the time when the Ministry of Justice decided to implement the *sanza* system instead of adopting the layperson jury.

The arguments against the jury system voiced in the process of public debate triggered by Boissonade's proposal and by the private drafts of the *Meiji* Constitution that included provisions introducing the jury system highlighted the concern of the Japanese government and public regarding the quality of decisions that laypersons would make in the course of the trial. They also reflected the fact that the government did not perceive there to be any significant benefits associated with the institution of jury service for Japan.

While the prestige of the exporters of the concept of jury service – the Western countries – was high during the *Meiji* period, which is an important prerequisite for the successful implementation of a transplanted institution, the fact that certain Western countries did not have the jury system was used as a justification to support the claim that the jury system was not central to the process of modernization and therefore not among the essential institutions for Japan to adopt. Furthermore, it was argued that the jury system was not a necessary prerequisite for the revision of unequal treaties. The comments made by the British advisor to the *Meiji* government, Robert Brader – who proposed that Japan should first focus on introducing the institutions of layperson participation in local governance – may have contributed to the solidification of the *Meiji* government's position that the jury system was not integral to the modernization process and that the introduction of this institution would be better discussed later, after Japan becomes a modern state. Brader's comments also highlighted the link between the institution of jury service and democratization and individual empowerment. As Brader pointed out, in an autocracy the jury system was not strictly necessary and could even be dangerous for the regime – an argument that doubtlessly added credence to the position of the opponents of the proposal to implement the jury system in the Japanese government.

Another important factor to consider when evaluating the first efforts to implement the jury system in *Meiji* Japan is the absence of the strong demand for the democratic values that the implementation of the jury system entails during the period when Japan was learning about the features of the institution of layperson participation in the judicial system. The People's Rights Movement of the 1870s and 1880s, inspired by Western ideas of liberalism and democracy, was violently suppressed by the government, and it was only in the 20th century that the movement towards democratization began in Japan in earnest. In the absence of a popular demand for the expansion of rights, the jury system was seen as an expensive and superfluous institution that did not serve any particular purpose for Japan.[156] This seems to explain why the proposal to introduce the jury system was not taken up by any significant political figures and only attracted powerful opponents, such as Kowashi Inoue. The lack of appreciation for the benefits of the jury system in the *Meiji* period also implied that neither of the actors in the legal system saw the introduction of the jury system to be in their interest. The position of defense representatives and attorneys at the time was weak, the attorneys were subordinate to the prosecutors, and the first Bar Association was yet to be formed.[157] This interest group, therefore, while potentially interested in the implementation of the jury system, as the participation of laypersons in the adjudication process may be associated with more compassionate verdicts for the accused, lacked the forum to discuss this idea and the power to promote it in the *Meiji* period. The prosecutors and the judges did not have the incentive for pushing for the change in the status quo, as the benefits of the institution of the jury system were not sufficiently highlighted in the public debate at that time. Neither did the jury system seem to be an attractive institution to the general public. After all, serving at the court – a place where torture could be and was used and where stern justice was applied – was arguably not very appealing.[158] The debate concerning the jury system remained restricted to the elite.

For the Japanese government, the jury system was just one of the many Western institutions and concepts it became acquainted with as the result of the opening up of the country. The government experimented with adapting this transplant, but in the end decided against

---

156 It should be noted that Nobuyoshi Toshitani, an authority on Japan's pre-war jury system, has argued that the *Meiji* Constitution was perceived by the elites at the time to be a document that would serve to provide a sense of stability to the nation following the suppression of the People's Rights Movement and solidify the position of the government. Given this overarching objective, including the provisions introducing a system that would allow for the participation of laypersons in the process of adjudicating trials was clearly not in the interests of the *Meiji* government (Toshitani, "Tennōsei Hō Taisei to Baishin Seido Ron" [The Legal Structure of Emperor [*Tennō*] System and the Debates [Concerning the] Jury System], p. 552).
157 The Japan Federation of Bar Associations was formed in 1896. See the section in Chapter 3, "The background to the drafting of the Jury Act", and accompanying footnotes for a discussion of the formation of the first Bar Association in Japan.
158 Vanoverbeke, *Juries in the Japanese Legal System*, p. 39.

adopting it. The costs of having the *sanza* system or the expanded judge panel outweighed the benefits, while adopting the non-adapted version of jury trials was not perceived as necessary at the time.

Conclusions

This chapter examined the history of the concept of jury service in pre-war Japan and described the first attempts to implement jury trials in the *Meiji* period. It discussed the first documents mentioning the institution of jury service, and demonstrated that while there is evidence that the concept of trial by laypersons may have reached Japan through Chinese classical texts as early as the *Nara* period, the jury as a legal institution first became known in the country following the *Meiji* Restoration.

This chapter showed that the Japanese government considered implementing the jury system in 1873 on a one-time basis in complex cases. Upon consideration, however, the Ministry of Justice decided to adapt the model of jury trials that it learned about in the West to fit into the Japanese political, cultural, and legal environment. The Ministry experimented with two alternatives to the Western concept of jury trials – the "bureaucratic" and the "judge-only" jury systems – in an attempt to adopt what it perceived to be the substance of the institution of jury service. As argued in this chapter, in all cases where the modified versions of the Western model of jury trials were implemented there was the need for added legitimacy of the court's rulings. All cases tried by *sanza* and by the twelve-judge panel involved incidents that were deemed to be of an extraordinarily complex nature. In *Meiji*-period Japan, it was the bureaucracy and the professional judges that could add legitimacy to verdicts. Laypersons, on the other hand, were not seen as sources of authority in a culture of "Respect for Officials and Contempt for the People".

The possibility of implementing such a model of jury trials that would more closely replicate the Western models of jury trials was discussed in connection with the drafting of the *Meiji* Constitution and the Code of Criminal Instruction in the late 1870 and 1880s. This chapter demonstrated that the lack of appreciation for the benefits of the layperson jury system on the part of the major actors and interest groups in the *Meiji* period was the major reason behind the lack of the idea to transplant the Western model of jury trials.

The discussion regarding the pros and cons of the layperson jury system gained new force in the early 20th century, during the period of "*Taishō* Democracy". Unlike the *Meiji*-period deliberations, in the 20th century the debate led to the implementation of the all-layperson jury system. Japan's pre-war jury system is the subject of the chapter that follows.

3 The pre-war jury system

This chapter focuses on the pre-war jury system that was introduced in mainland Japan in 1928 and suspended in 1943. It describes the details of the processes of conceptualization, promotion, implementation, functioning, and ultimately abolishment of Japan's first layperson jury system and evaluates this experience.

The chapter begins with a broad historical background that highlights the major developments in the Japanese legal system and society in the late *Meiji*, *Taishō*, and early *Shōwa* periods. It then discusses the specific developments that formed the background to the adoption of the pre-war Jury Act. The chapter proceeds to describe the drafting process of the Jury Act and the deliberations concerning this piece of legislation at the Imperial Diet and at the House of Peers. This is followed by a summary of the promulgated version of the Jury Act and a discussion of the promotion efforts carried out by the Ministry of Justice, the local Bar Associations, journalists, and various organizations. The chapter then introduces the details of two jury trials in Japan: the Oita trial and the Tokyo trial of 1928. Concluding sections discuss the amendments of the Jury Act and its suspension in 1943, analyze Japan's pre-war jury system, and summarize the findings of the chapter.

Historical background: the developments in the legal system in the late *Meiji*, *Taishō*, and early *Shōwa* periods

The processes of conceptualization, drafting, promulgation, enforcement, and suspension of the Jury Act of 1923 – the piece of legislation that provided the basis for the introduction of the jury system in pre-war Japan – encompassed three periods in Japanese history. The idea of allowing the people to play an active role in the adjudication of cases was actively discussed during the last decades of the *Meiji* period (1868–1912). Further deliberation, drafting, and finally enactment of the law that introduced the jury system in Japan took place in the *Taishō* period (1912–1926). The Jury Act was enforced in 1928, and by that time Japan had entered the *Shōwa* period (1926–1989).

Japan's experience with the institution of jury service was shaped by and reflected the major trends in the development of Japan's society during each of these three periods in Japan's history.

In the last decades of the *Meiji* period Japan found itself increasingly withdrawing inward.[1] This development was triggered first by the fact that the revision of the "unequal treaties"

---

1 B. Wakabayashi, "Introduction", in Wakabayashi (ed.), 1998, *Modern Japanese Thought, Modern Japanese Thought*, New York: Cambridge University Press, pp. 1–29, at p. 11.

was largely over by 1899, which led to a decline in the external pressure to westernize Japan.[2] Second, the *Meiji* leaders became increasingly concerned about the threats that Western liberalism and radicalism presented and focused their efforts on upholding Japan's traditional institutions. The *Meiji* Constitution of 1889 and the 1890 Imperial Rescript on Education enshrined the *kokutai* – "national essence and polity". The last ten years of the *Meiji* period were dominated by Japan's efforts to become a major imperialist power. Following its victory in the Russo-Japanese war, Japan concluded the Franco-Japanese agreement of 1907 as well as the Russo-Japanese agreements of 1907–1916, and the 1908 Takahara-Root agreement with the United States, which recognized Japan's sphere of influence in Northeast Asia. Japan annexed Korea in 1910.

The *Taishō* period has been described by historians as "an era of great possibilities".[3] It was also a time of contradictory developments. On the one hand, the end of World War I brought along the movement towards democratization, reform, and change known as "*Taishō* Democracy". On the other, this period saw a rise in the power of right-wing organizations. The adherents of the right-wing nationalist movement were alarmed by the growth of popular unrest and the spread of Western-inspired ideas and sought to reassert Japan's traditional order. This contradiction between the movement towards democratization and the reactionary movement towards nationalism and fascism was made manifest in 1925, when over the span of one year two significant pieces of legislation were promulgated. In May 1925, the Imperial Diet passed the Universal Manhood Suffrage Law, which gave the right to vote to all male citizens over twenty-five years of age, regardless of income.[4] A few weeks prior to the passage of this law, in April 1925, the same Diet passed the Peace Preservation Act, which made it illegal to criticize the *kokutai* and the system of private property – provisions directed at curtailing the activities of the Japanese Communist Party (JCP), established in 1922.[5]

One of the major features of *Taishō* Democracy was the strengthening of the position of elected bodies. In the *Meiji* period, political parties were political associations established with the goal of mobilizing the national protest movement (*Jiyū Minken Undō*) against the *hanbatsu* government rather than parties in the modern sense.[6] These "parties in preparation" (*junbi seitō*)[7] were able to speak but not act on questions of national policy.[8] With the promulgation of the *Meiji* Constitution and the establishment of the Imperial Diet, however, political parties increased in prominence. In the *Taishō* period, the power of parties was based on their control of the seats in the House of Representatives, and their ability to influence national policy was substantially increased. In 1918, when Prime Minister Takashi Hara formed his first Cabinet, the House of Representatives included almost exclusively members

---

2 *Id.*, p. 11.
3 Edwin O. Reischauer (ed.), 2003, *Japan: An Illustrated Encyclopedia*, Tokyo: Kōdansha, p. 1502.
4 Shūgiin Giin Senkyo Hō [Law Concerning Elections of Members of the House of Representatives], Law No. 73 of 1900, as amended by Law No. 47 of 1925.
5 Chian Iji Hō [Peace Preservation Act], Law No. 46 of 1925. See generally Nihon Kyōsantō [Japanese Communist Party], 1990, *Kagakuteki Shakai Shugi no 150 Nen to Nihon Kyōsantō* [150 Years of Scientific Socialism and the Japanese Communist Party], Tokyo: Shinnippon Shuppansha; G. M. Beckmann and G. Okubo, 1969, *The Japanese Communist Party: 1922–1945*, Stanford: Stanford University Press.
6 P. Duus, 1968, *Party Rivalry and Political Change in Taishō Japan*, Cambridge, MA: Harvard University Press, p. 7.
7 T. Hara, 1929, *Hara Takashi Zenshū* [Full Collection of Works by Takashi Hara], Vol. 1, Tokyo: Hara Takashi Zenshū Kankōkai, p. 337.
8 Duus, *Party Rivalry and Political Change in Taishō Japan*, p. 7.

of the Friends of Constitutional Government (*Rikken Seiyūkai*) – a party that Hara headed.⁹ This fact attracted considerable attention as the manifestation of true party government and of the decline in the power of unelected bodies, such as the *Genrōin*.¹⁰

Another prominent feature of *Taishō* Democracy was the expansion of the political involvement of the general public. In 1905, the *Hibiya* riots took place; these involved mass demonstrations protesting against the peace settlement reached after the conclusion of the Russo-Japanese war.¹¹ Another popular protest movement that was organized by the opposition parties, journalists, and businessmen in 1913 led to the overthrow of the third Cabinet of Tarō Katsura – a development known as the *Taishō* Political Crisis. This was the first time in Japan's modern history when a popular movement caused the downfall of a Cabinet. The rice riots of 1918 and the mass demonstrations held as part of the universal manhood suffrage movement¹² were further powerful manifestations of the increasing level of interest in public issues and activity on the part of the citizens of Japan.

In view of the growing involvement of the general public in political life, it does not seem surprising that during the *Taishō* period the concept of democracy became the subject of intense discussion between political thinkers. Democracy, understood as the doctrine of the people as sovereign (*minshūshugi*), contradicted the provisions of the *Meiji* Constitution, which enshrined the idea of the sovereignty of the Emperor. Therefore, a new concept and word was developed during the *Taishō* period. Democratic thinker Sakuzō Yoshino proposed the principle of government based on the people (*minponshugi*), arguing that the locus of sovereignty did not matter in Japan as long as government policy was carried out with the people's welfare in mind.¹³

The democratic developments of the *Taishō* period were countered by the movement towards fascism and nationalism that began in the years of the reign of the *Taishō* Emperor and gained prominence in the first decades of the *Shōwa* period.¹⁴ In 1924, the National Foundation Society (*Kokuhonsha*) was established. This society called upon patriots to reject foreign influences and uphold the *kokutai*. The word *kokuhon*, used in the name of the society, was presented as an antithesis to the word *minpon*, derived from Yoshino's concept of *minponshugi*. In the late 1920s, the forces of the Special Higher Police (*Tokubetsu Kōtō Keisatsu*) were increased; this was an organization established in 1911 with the goal of investigating the activities of political groups and preventing the spread of ideologies regarded by the authorities as a threat to public order. The Special Higher Police achieved greatest

---

9   Y. Itō, 1998, *Taishō Demokurashii to Seitō Seiji* [*Taishō* Democracy and Party Politics], Tokyo: Yamakawa Shuppansha, pp. 15–18.
10 Reischauer, *Japan: An Illustrated Encyclopedia*, p. 1501.
11 T. Matsuo, 2001, *Taishō Demokurashii* [Taishō Democracy], Tokyo: Iwanami Shoten, pp. 8–22.
12 T. Matsuo, "Dai Ichiji Taisengo no Fusen Undō" [The Universal Manhood Suffrage Right Movement after the First World War], in K. Inoue (ed.), 1969, *Taishōki no Seiji to Shakai* [Politics and Society in the Taishō Period], Tokyo: Iwanami Shoten, pp. 159–204 (discussing the Universal Manhood Suffrage Movement).
13 T. Sakai, 1992, *Taishō Demokurashii Taisei no Hōkai* [The Demolition of the Taishō System], Tokyo: University of Tokyo Press, pp. 8–13; S. Yoshino, 1916, "Kensei no Hongi o Toite Sono Yūshū no Bi o Nasu no Michi o Ronzu" [Explaining the Essence of the Constitution and Discussing the Ways to Preserve Its Everlasting Beauty], reprinted in T. Mitani (ed.), 1984, *Yoshino Sakuzō*, Tokyo: Chūō Kōronsha, pp. 8–135.
14 K. Shūichi, "Taishō Democracy as the Pre-stage for Japanese Militarism", in B. S. Silberman and H. D. Harootunian (eds), 1974, *Japan in Crisis: Essays on Taisho Democracy*, Princeton: Princeton University Press, pp. 217–236.

power after the promulgation of the Peace Preservation Act. In the 1930s, its forces were used to prosecute and arrest members of the Japanese Communist Party, socialists, and liberals. Japan's military took advantage of the February 26 incident – an attempted *coup d'état* during which several politicians, including the Minister of Finance Korekiyo Takahashi, were killed – to increase its political influence.[15] The Cabinet of Kōki Hirota, which was formed after the military rebellion had been suppressed, carried out policies favorable to the army and tightened censorship. Japan signed the Anti-Comintern Pact in 1936 with Fascist Germany and Italy under Hirota's Cabinet, and this pact became the predecessor of the Tripartite Pact of 1940 that was signed under the administration of Fumimaro Konoe. Japan started the Sino-Japanese War in 1937 and the Pacific War, launching an attack on Pearl Harbor in 1941.[16]

Many insights may be gained from examining the processes of deliberation of the possibility of introducing the jury system in Japan, the drafting of the Jury Act, its promulgation in 1923, enactment in 1928, and finally suspension in 1943 in connection with the corresponding developments in Japan's society and political life. Indeed, parallels between the pillar stones in the process of the establishment and subsequently suspension of the jury system on the one hand and the features of the respective periods of Japan's history on the other are numerous and striking. This chapter highlights these parallels as it addresses the questions set forth in this book.

The background to the drafting of the Jury Act

Concerted efforts aimed at introducing jury trials in Japan began in the early 20th century.[17] Unlike the attempts to implement the jury system that took place earlier in the *Meiji* period (discussed in Chapter 2), this time the idea came not from the bureaucrats at the Ministry of Justice but from attorneys who were not working for the government.

Professional defense attorneys first appeared in Japan in the 1880s. Japan's Western-inspired Criminal Code (the Old Penal Code) of 1880 contained provisions allowing defense attorneys to take part in criminal trial hearings,[18] and the Attorney Act (*Bengoshi Hō*), promulgated in 1893, outlined their responsibilities.[19] In accordance with the Attorney

---

15 B. Shillony, "The February 26 Affair: Politics of Military Insurrection", in G. M. Wilson (ed.), 1970, *Crisis Politics in Prewar Japan: Institutional and Ideological Problems of the 1930s*, Tokyo: Sophia University Press, pp. 25–50; Sakai, *Taishō Demokurashii Taisei no Hōkai* [The Demolition of the Taishō System], pp. 135–146.
16 A. Fujiwara, 1990, "The Road to Pearl Harbor", in H. Conroy and H. Wray (eds), *Pearl Harbor Reexamined: Prologue to the Pacific War*, Honolulu: University of Hawai'i Press, pp. 151–161.
17 Takayanagi, "A Century of Innovation: The Development of Japanese Law, 1868–1961", in A. T. Von Mehren (ed.), 1964, *Law in Japan: The Legal Order in a Changing Society*, Cambridge, MA: Harvard University Press, p. 21; K. Takano, "Nihon Bengoshi Kyōkai to Baishin Seido" [The Japan Bar Association and the Jury System], in Nihon Bengoshi Kyōkai [The Japan Bar Association], 1921, *Nihon Bengoshi Kyōkai Rokuji Dai 259 Gō* [Records of the 259th Meeting of the Japan Bar Association], Tokyo: Nihon Bengoshi Kyōkai, pp. 44–51, at p. 45.
18 Great Council of State Decree No. 36 of 1880, art. 360.
19 Bengoshi Hō [The Attorney Act], Law No. 7 of 1893, reprinted in Nihon Bengoshi Rengōkai [Japan Federation of Bar Associations] (ed.), 1959, *Nihon Bengoshi Enkaku Shi* [A History of the Origins of [the Profession of] Attorney in Japan], Tokyo: Nihon Bengoshi Rengōkai, pp. 54–58 [hereinafter the Attorney Act, 1893].

Act, defense attorneys were supervised by prosecutors,[20] and the court could take disciplinary action against an attorney based on a statement made by a prosecutor.[21] In 1896, attorneys established the Japan Federation of Bar Associations in an effort to improve their position through pushing for an amendment of the Attorney Act. The members of the association believed that an improvement in the status of defense lawyers would have a positive effect on the rights of the accused in Japan's courts. The introduction of the jury system was seen by some attorneys as another possible way for achieving this goal.

In 1900, Shirō Isobe[22] and Taizō Miyoshi[23] proposed that the possibility of introducing the jury system be discussed at the meeting of the Japan Federation of Bar Associations. Isobe and Miyoshi submitted a document titled "Concerning the Establishment of the Jury System" (*Baishin Seido o Mōkuru no Ken*) for consideration at the thirtieth meeting of the councilors (*hyōgiin*) of the Japan Federation of Bar Associations.[24] This document described the jury systems existing in other countries, such as England and France, and argued that a similar system should be introduced in Japan. The authors argued that there was a nascent trend towards increased public participation in all aspects of administration of power.[25] They concluded that citizen participation in the judicial system was as necessary as in all other branches of power, and that the federation should study this possibility in greater detail. This proposal was adopted at the meeting of the councilors.[26]

In 1909, the general meeting of the federation approved the idea that the jury system should be introduced in Japan, and those members of the federation who were also elected members of the House of Representatives began looking for ways to find political support for the idea.[27]

Genji Matsuda (1875–1936) was one of the members of the Japan Federation of Bar Associations also elected to the House of Representatives who supported the idea to introduce trials by jury in Japan. A member of the *Rikken Seiyūkai* (Friends of the Constitutional Government Party), Matsuda was one of the authors of the proposal concerning the establishment of the jury system in Japan (*Baishin Seido Setsuritsu ni kansuru Kengian*). In February 1910, the *Rikken Seiyūkai* submitted this proposal for deliberations in the

---

20 The Attorney Act, 1893, art. 19 (stipulating that the prosecutor of the district court was to supervise the activities of the Bar Association of that area).
21 *Id.*, arts. 31 and 32.
22 Shirō Isobe (1851–1923) was a noted politician, legal scholar, lawyer, and member of the House of Representatives and the House of Peers (T. Ichinose (ed.), 2004, *Major 20th Century People in Japan: A Biographical Dictionary*, Tokyo: Nichigai Associates, p. 222).
23 Taizō Miyoshi (1845–1908) served as a judicial officer and as the president of the Grand Court of Judicature (*Daishin'in*). M. Ueda (ed.), 1994, *Concise Japanese Biographical Dictionary*, Tokyo: Sanseidō, p. 1227.
24 S. Isobe and T. Miyoshi, 1900, "Baishin Seido o Mōkuru no Ken" [Concerning the Establishment of the Jury System], *Nihon Bengoshi Kyōkai Rokuji Dai 31 Gō* [Records of the 31st Meeting of the Japan Bar Association], reprinted in J. Iwatani, 2004, *Nihon Bengoshi Kyōkai Rokuji: Meiji Hen* [Records of the Japan Bar Associations: The Meiji Period], Vol. 6, Tokyo: Tōwa Seihon, pp. 325–368.
25 *Id.*, p. 362.
26 *Id.*, pp. 362 and 368.
27 Ichinose, *Major 20th Century People in Japan*, p. 2337; N. Toshitani, "Shihō Ni Taisuru Kokumin no Sanka: Senzen no Hōritsuka to Baishin Hō" [Lay Participation in the Judiciary: Legal Professionals in [the] Pre-war [Period] and the Jury Act], in T. Ushiomi (ed.), 1966, *Iwanami Kōza: Gendai Hō 6* [Iwanami Lectures: Contemporary Law 6], Tokyo: Iwanami Shoten, pp. 365–422, at p. 375 (discussing the drafting of the proposal concerning the establishment of the jury system in Japan).

Imperial Diet.[28] The proposal stated that lay participation in the judicial system would serve to ensure the independence of the judiciary, contribute to the impartiality of justice, and protect human rights; it urged the government to ensure that "the draft of the law that would introduce the jury system in criminal trials is prepared, and that this draft is promptly submitted to the Imperial Diet".[29]

The timing for the submission of this proposal was chosen deliberately. The Code of Criminal Procedure was being redrafted under the second administration of Prime Minister Tarō Katsura in 1910,[30] and the representatives of the *Rikken Seiyūkai* decided that it would be convenient to have the provisions regarding the jury system – if supported by the Diet – included in the new draft of the code.[31] The proposal concerning the establishment of the jury system was adopted unanimously by the House of Representatives on March 3, 1910.[32]

Why did the initiative to introduce the jury system – an idea that had been rejected outright several decades earlier, when Boissonade's 1879 draft of the Code of Criminal Instruction was considered – acquire so much support in the first decade of the 20th century? It appears that the idea became popular due to the fact that the members of the Japan Federation of Bar Associations and of the *Rikken Seiyūkai* were successful at demonstrating to the political elite of the time that the implementation of the jury system was an effective and the least radical way to achieve the goals that had come to be perceived as important by both the elites and the general public. The first of these goals was to further respect for human rights – most importantly the rights of the accused – and by doing so ameliorate those problems with Japan's judicial system that became apparent through several high profile cases that were tried during the first decade of the 20th century. The second goal was to encourage public participation in the administration of the state. The third goal was to protect the Emperor. As the cases in *Meiji*-period Japan were adjudicated in the name of the Emperor, the Emperor was indirectly responsible for all possible wrong verdicts. Having laypersons participate in the process of adjudication of cases was seen as a way to help insulate the Emperor from this responsibility.

It is clear that these goals were in fact contradictory in nature, just as the two major trends in the development of the Japanese society in the *Meiji* period were (adopting Western ideas and institutions on the one hand and ensuring that the traditions of the past were preserved). The first two goals (furthering respect for human rights and encouraging public participation) were associated with the trend towards liberalization and democratization – a trend that became even more pronounced with the start of the *Taishō* period. The third goal (protecting the Emperor) may be linked with the inclination towards conservatism, which

---

28 Toshitani, "Shihō Ni Taisuru Kokumin no Sanka" [Lay Participation in the Judiciary], p. 375.
29 T. Mitani, 2001, *Seiji Seido toshite no Baishinsei: Kindai Nihon no Shihōken to Seiji* [The Jury System as a Political Institution: The Judiciary and Modern Japanese Politics], Tokyo: University of Tokyo Press, p. 125; Shinomiya, "Nihon ni mo Baishin Seido ga Sonzai Shita" [The Jury System Existed in Japan Too], pp. 97–98.
30 The new Code of Criminal Procedure was enacted in 1922 (Law No. 75 of 1922) and became operational on January 1, 1923 (Takayanagi, "A Century of Innovation", pp. 21–23).
31 Genji Matsuda – a member of the *Rikken Seiyūkai* who was directly engaged in the submission of the proposal concerning the establishment of the jury system in Japan – explained this strategy in a statement that is reproduced in Mitani, *Seiji Seido toshite no Baishin Sei* [The Jury System as a Political System], pp. 144–145.
32 K. Hara (ed.), 1965, *Hara Takashi Nikki* [Diary of Takashi Hara] Vol. 3, Tokyo: Fukumura Shuppan, p. 12.

later became transformed into the radicalism and nationalism of the late *Taishō* and early *Shōwa* periods.

If discussed separately, none of these goals would have arguably gained unanimous support from the members of Parliament in 1910. The fact, however, that these contradictory goals that the implementation of the jury system was expected to fulfill were presented together implied that both the radicals and the liberals could find something appealing about the idea to introduce the jury system, which helps explain the overwhelming support that the *Rikken Seiyūkai*'s 1910 proposal received.

Furthering respect for human rights

On the day that the proposal concerning the establishment of the jury system in Japan was adopted by the House of Representatives, Takashi Hara – one of the leaders of the *Rikken Seiyūkai* and the politician who played an instrumental role in the introduction of the jury system in Japan – noted in his diary:

> If one considers [the fact that] not a few people receive unjust judgments in courts because of customs that are not based on respect for human rights, then [one needs to admit that] the [jury] system is necessary . . . Although the government has not yet explicitly expressed its support for or disapproval [of this idea] . . ., all members [of the House of Representatives] were in agreement [in their support of the proposal to introduce the jury system].[33]

Hara's personal enthusiasm concerning the proposal to introduce the jury system in Japan seems to have been based precisely on his understanding of the importance of furthering the respect for the rights of the accused in the courtroom.

Hara admitted that he first realized the importance of trial by jury during his two-year trip to Europe and the United States.[34] In a diary entry dated June 28, 1914, Hara recalls that what he heard and saw during this trip prompted him to consider what kind of a trial he himself would wish to have, if he were in the position of the defendant, and that this consideration prompted him to insist that Japan should introduce the jury system.[35]

Several high profile cases that were tried in the period between 1909 and 1910 served to further inspire Hara, the members of the *Rikken Seiyūkai*, and many Japanese liberal thinkers to consider whether trial by professional judges alone was the best option for Japan. The first of these cases was the scandal known as the *Nittō* incident (*Nittō Jiken*) of 1909, which made many question the reliability of public officials. This incident involved twenty-four members of the Imperial Diet representing the *Rikken Seiyūkai*, the Japan Progressive Party (*Shinpōtō*), and the Daidō Club (*Daidō Kurabu*), who were accused of accepting large sums of money from the directors of the Dai Nippon Sugar Company. The suspects were arrested and ultimately convicted in a trial that the *New York Times* correspondent referred to as one that the Americans can look at "with envious admiration".[36] While most

---

33 *Id.*, p. 12.
34 Mitani, *Seiji Seido toshite no Baishin Sei* [The Jury System as a Political System], p. 125.
35 Hara, *Hara Takashi Nikki* [Diary of Takashi Hara], Vol. 4, p. 14.
36 Anonymous, 1909, "The Grafting Legislators of the New Japan: As Revealed in Tokio Courts; 'Great Sugar Company' Has Involved Government Officials in Sum Reaching into Millions", *New York Times*, August 15, p. SM2; Anonymous, 1909, "Tokio Lawmakers Took Big Bribes; Wrecked the Dai Nippon

members of the general public agreed that the *Nittō* case demonstrated that Japan's judiciary was independent, this case also highlighted the need for providing institutional checks on the possible abuses of power by officials in general and by court officials – prosecutors and judges – in particular.

The High Treason case of 1910 (*Taigyaku Jiken*), also known as the *Kōtoku* Incident (*Kōtoku Jiken*), made the public turn its attention to the state of the justice system in Japan and to consider the ways for improving it. This case involved the uncovering of a socialist-anarchist plot to assassinate the *Meiji* Emperor. It was tried in a closed court, with Kiichirō Hiranuma serving as the prosecutor, and a group of lawyers, including Takuzō Hanai, Fusaaki Uzawa, and Shirō Isobe, defending the accused.[37] While conclusive evidence was found only against five out of the twenty-six defendants, twenty-four were sentenced to death for violating Article 73 of the Criminal Code, with the remaining defendants sentenced to eight and eleven years' imprisonment, respectively, for violation of explosives ordinances.[38] The High Treason incident had a profound impact on society. After the trial was concluded, fewer people dared to participate in the debate concerning the imperial institution, as anyone who questioned the *kokutai* was immediately put under suspicion.[39] The High Treason incident also became a subject of heated discussion between the members of the *Rikken Seiyūkai*. In a diary entry dated December 7, 1910, Hara described a conversation that he had with Makoto Egi concerning the trial. According to Hara, Egi told him that some of the defendants in this case were stating that they were innocent and that the accusations against them were groundless.[40]

The High Treason case of 1910 triggered debate regarding the state of Japan's system of justice. Many liberal thinkers and politicians who believed that the existing system of justice in Japan that allowed for pre-trial detention and where the rights of the accused were frequently ignored needed reform.[41] The arguments of the proponents of this view were expressed by member of the *Rikken Seiyūkai* and lawyer Heikichi Ogawa. He stated that Japan's system of justice was plagued by the following three problems: unreasonably rough procedures associated with arrest, equally unreasonably strict judgments of the court and heavy punishments, and the immense power of the prosecutor.[42] Hara supported this perspective, revealing in his diary that the many incidents when the police decided to arrest

---

Sugar Company, which Sought a Monopoly; Trained under Old System When the Government Bought Support of Its Policies – Diet Members Looked on Taking Bribes as a Right", *New York Times*, June 20, p. C4.

37 The defense counsel in the High Treason case of 1909 consisted of the following eleven attorneys: Takuzō Hanai, Fusaaki Uzawa, Shirō Isobe, Rikitarō Imamura, Shū Hiraide, Jirō Miyajima, San'ichirō Yoshida, Takashi Kawashima, Tatsuo Ogoshi, Kōsuke Handa, and Takematsu Yasumura (M. Shimizu, "Senzen no Hōritsuka ni tsuite no Ichi Kōsatsu" [A Study Concerning Pre-war Lawyers] in Ushiomi, *Iwanami Kōza: Gendai Hō 6* [Iwanami Lectures: Contemporary Law 6], pp. 3–43, at p. 19).

38 Reischauer, *Japan: An Illustrated Encyclopedia*, p. 532.

39 R. H. Mitchell, "The Rise of the Surveillance State 1900–1917", in R. H. Mitchell (ed.), 1983, *Censorship in Imperial Japan*, Princeton: Princeton University Press, reprinted in P. Kornicki (ed.), 1998, *Meiji Japan: Political, Economic, and Social History 1868–1912*, Vol. 4, London: Routledge, pp. 50–76, at p. 58.

40 Hara, *Hara Takashi Nikki* [Diary of Takashi Hara], Vol. 3, p. 65; Mitani, *Seiji Seido toshite no Baishin Sei* [The Jury System as a Political System], pp. 125–126.

41 Mitani, *Seiji Seido toshite no Baishin Sei* [The Jury System as a Political System], pp. 129–130.

42 H. Ogawa, "Waga Shihōbu no Konponteki Byūken" [Fundamental Fallacies of Japan's Judicial System], *Chūō Kōron*, 1914, Vol. 29, No. 8, pp. 41–42, cited in T. Mitani, 1980, *Kindai Nihon no Shihōken to Seitō: Baishin Seiritsu no Seiji Shi* [Judicial Power in Modern Japan and Political Parties: The Political History of the Creation of the Jury System], Tokyo: Hanawa Shobō, p. 152.

a member of the Diet or a member of the regional administration without any obvious reason and quickly found the arrested guilty had made him realize the importance of the jury system as a system that would help prevent arbitrary judgments from occurring.[43] Defense lawyer Fusaaki Uzawa agreed with Hara in a publication that appeared in 1910, claiming that the introduction of the jury system might help to protect the rights of the accused within the judicial system of Japan.[44]

Rikken Seiyūkai's proposal concerning the introduction of the jury system was not the only attempt to ameliorate the aforementioned problems. In 1914, a group of members of the *Rikken Kokumintō* (Constitutional Nationalist Party) that included Eitarō Takagi submitted a proposal titled "The Bill Concerning the Investigation of Crimes" (*Hanzai Sōsa ni kansuru Hōritsu An*) to the National Diet. This bill proposed to make it mandatory for the police to conduct interrogations in the presence of at least one layperson from the town, city, or village where the incident took place (the person being interrogated was allowed to request that his or her attorney be present instead). The bill stated that intimidation should not be used during interrogations (a penalty of not more than two years of penal servitude with hard labor was provided for offenders); that the prosecutor should not interrogate the suspect or persons related to the case after the suspect has been indicted (the bill provided for the penalty of not more than six months of penal servitude at hard labor, or a fine for offenders); that the laypersons or officials present during interrogation would not be allowed to share the information regarding the interrogations with anybody outside the interrogation room; and that the documents drafted during the process of pre-trial investigations would not be admissible in court as evidence.[45] This bill never became law. The proponents of "The Bill Concerning the Investigation of Crimes" tried to include sections of the bill into the draft of the new Code of Criminal Procedure, but without success.[46] Not discouraged by the failure of these attempts, Takagi subsequently became involved in the drafting of another bill, "The Bill Concerning the Protection of Human Rights",[47] which included the aforementioned provisions of "The Bill Concerning the Investigation of Crimes".[48] This new bill did not become law either, however.

Thus, *Rikken Seiyūkai*'s proposal to introduce the jury system had the distinction of being the only successful effort aimed at addressing the problems with Japan's judicial system.

Encouraging public participation

The idea of expanding citizen participation in government was a major theme in the public debate at the time that *Rikken Seiyūkai*'s proposal was drafted and after it had been passed by the Imperial Diet.

---

43 Hara, *Hara Takashi Nikki* [Diary of Takashi Hara] Vol. 3, p. 65 (entry dated December 7, 1910).
44 S. Uzawa, 1910, "*Baishin Seido ni tsuite*" [About the Jury System], *Kokka Gakkai Zasshi*, Vol. 14, No. 3, p. 69, cited in Mitani, *Kindai Nihon no Shihōken to Seitō* [Judicial Power in Modern Japan and Political Parties], p. 148.
45 Dai Nippon Teikoku Gikai Kankōkai [The Imperial Diet of Japan Press] (ed.), 1928, *Dai Nippon Teikoku Gikaishi* [Journal of the Imperial Diet of Japan], Vol. 9, Tokyo: Dai Nippon Teikoku Gikai Kankōkai, pp. 275–276; Mitani, *Seiji Seido toshite no Baishin Sei* [The Jury System as a Political System], p. 132.
46 Mitani, *Seiji Seido toshite no Baishin Sei* [The Jury System as a Political System], pp. 133–134.
47 Dai Nippon Teikoku Gikai [The Imperial Diet of Japan], *Dai Nippon Teikoku Gikaishi* [Journal of the Imperial Diet of Japan], Vol. 10, p. 589.
48 Mitani, *Seiji Seido toshite no Baishin Sei* [The Jury System as a Political System], pp. 134–135.

64 *The pre-war jury system*

Makoto Egi was one of the first lawyers and scholars to discuss the institution of jury service as a means for empowering citizens. He argued that the introduction of the jury system in Japan was not only a human rights issue, but also a political issue.[49] Egi claimed that just as Japanese citizens had the right to participate in the legislative and the administrative branches of government through electing representatives, they were entitled to participate in the judicial system.[50]

The subject of the jury system was taken up by the *Kaizō Dōmeikai* (Alliance for Reform) – one of the organizations that contributed to the realization of *Taishō* Democracy.[51] This organization, established in 1919, actively supported the introduction of the jury system as a means for democratizing the political system of Japan.[52] Etsujirō Uehara, a member of the *Kaizō Dōmeikai*, wrote in 1919 that introducing the jury system was necessary for Japan because once this system was implemented, the people would be able to "create laws, carry out laws, and control and manage laws" (*jinmin ga hō o tsukuri, hō o okonai, hō o tsukasadoru*).[53] Umeshirō Suzuki, another member of the *Kaizō Dōmeikai*, argued that the introduction of the jury system was as important a requisite of the constitutional state as universal suffrage.[54]

Takashi Hara agreed with the conceptualization of the jury system as an important vehicle for citizen empowerment and acknowledged the growing demands for the expansion of political involvement on the part of the general public that became increasingly expressed during the first decades of the 20th century. Unlike Egi and the members of the *Kaizō Dōmeikai*, however, he argued that it was too early for Japan to expand the right to vote to all male citizens of Japan regardless of income and proposed that the introduction of the jury system could be a good substitute for universal suffrage.[55] Hara saw the implementation of the jury system as a measure that would answer the need for increased participation in governance on the part of the public, but in a manner that would be safer for the preservation of the existing social order than the right to vote.[56]

Protecting the Emperor

Many liberal-minded lawyers argued that the main reason for introducing the jury system was not to empower the masses but to protect the Emperor of Japan. Makoto Egi expressed

---

49 M. Egi, 1909, *Sansō Yawa* [Window [Facing the] Mountains, Night Tales], Tokyo: Yūhikaku, pp. 52–153.
50 *Id.*, pp. 152–153.
51 The *Kaizō Dōmeikai* was organized by Tsunego Baba, Ryutarō, Seigo Nakano and several other journalists and statesmen who had attended the 1919 Paris Press Conference (Matsuo, "Dai Ichiji Taisengo no Fusen Undō" [The Universal Manhood Suffrage Right Movement after the First World War], p. 184; Duus, *Party Rivalry and Political Change in Taishō Japan*, p. 115).
52 Matsuo, "Dai Ichiji Taisengo no Fusen Undō" [The Universal Manhood Suffrage Right Movement after the First World War], p. 184.
53 E. Uehara, 1919, *Demokurashii to Nihon no Kaizō* [Democracy and Reforming Japan], Tokyo: Chūgai Insatsu Kōgyō, pp. 169–170, cited in Mitani, *Kindai Nihon no Shihōken to Seitō* [Judicial Power in Modern Japan and Political Parties], p. 162.
54 U. Suzuki, 1919, *Nihon Kaizō no Igi oyobi sono Kōryō* [The Significance of and Outline for Reforming Japan], Tokyo: Jisseikatsu Sha Shuppanbu, p. 163.
55 Mitani, *Kindai Nihon no Shihōken to Seitō* [Judicial Power in Modern Japan and Political Parties], pp. 166–167.
56 Saikō Saibansho Jimu Sōkyoku Keiji Kyoku, *Wagakuni de Okonawareta Baishin Saiban* [Jury Trials that Took Place in Our Country], pp. 16–19.

this view to Takashi Hara in connection with the High Treason case of 1910. According to Hara's description of this conversation, Egi argued that it was wrong that in Japan's courts all proceedings and decisions were carried out in the name of the Emperor, because this inadvertently made the Emperor responsible for all decisions proclaimed in a courtroom.[57] He stated that in order to ameliorate this situation it was necessary to seriously consider the possibility of introducing the jury system.[58] Hara concluded his discussion of this conversation by stating his belief that the introduction of the jury system would be an undertaking that would bring happiness to the people of Japan.[59]

The public debate

The virtues and vices of the jury system were widely discussed in the scholarly publications at the time that *Rikken Seiyūkai*'s proposal was being drafted and after it was passed by the Imperial Diet. Kichirō Hiranuma, then an official at the Ministry of Justice, opposed the idea of introducing the jury system in Japan, arguing that laypersons were likely to be swayed by emotions.[60] Kuniomi Yokota, then president of the Great Court of Judicature (*Daishin'in*), agreed that "trials based on common sense" (*jōshiki saiban*) were what Japan needed, but did not believe that the implementation of the jury system was necessary to realize such trials.[61] Another opponent of the jury system, Shinkuma Motoji, then councilor (*sanjikan*) at the Ministry of Justice, argued that in Japan, where the *Meiji* Constitution enshrined the separation of powers and provided for the independence of the judiciary, there was strictly no reason to implement the jury system.[62] Motoji also claimed that the introduction of the jury system would place a heavy burden on the shoulders of Japanese citizens.[63] Unlike Hiranuma, Yokota, and Motoji, Makoto Egi wrote extensively in support of the idea of introducing the jury system in Japan. Egi argued that as the provisions of the new Code of Criminal Procedure were influenced by the codes of France and Germany, it was important to implement the jury system in Japan to help ensure the smooth functioning of the new code, as both France and Germany used the jury system.[64]

In 1914, legal scholar and politician Shigema Ōba joined the debate regarding the pros and cons of the institution of jury service. He discussed the strengths and weaknesses of the jury systems existing in several European countries and argued that the support of the

---

57 Hara, *Hara Takashi Nikki* [Diary of Takashi Hara] Vol. 3, p. 65.
58 *Id.*, p. 65.
59 *Id.*, p. 66.
60 Hiranuma's argument against the jury system is referred to in Egi, *Sansō Yawa* [Window [Facing the] Mountains, Night Tales], p. 147; Mitani, *Seiji Seido toshite no Baishin Sei* [The Jury System as a Political System], p. 127.
61 Mitani, *Seiji Seido toshite no Baishin Sei* [The Jury System as a Political System], p. 127.
62 S. Motoji, 1910, "Baishin Seido ni tsuite" [About the Jury System], *Kokka Gakkai Zasshi*, Vol. 14, No. 3, pp. 54–55, cited in Mitani, *Kindai Nihon no Shihōken to Seitō* [Judicial Power in Modern Japan and Political Parties], p. 147.
63 Motoji, "*Baishin Seido ni tsuite*" [About the Jury System], p. 67, cited in Mitani, *Kindai Nihon no Shihōken to Seitō* [Judicial Power in Modern Japan and Political Parties], p. 148.
64 Egi, *Reikai Manpitsu* [Reikai's Scribbling], pp. 46–47. Indeed, the 1922 Code of Criminal Procedure was influenced by the German and French Criminal Codes. Takayanagi, "A Century of Innovation", pp. 22–23.

general public was critical for the successful implementation of such a system in Japan.[65] Ōba also touched upon the question of whether Japan should introduce the Continental-European model or the Anglo-American model of jury trials, and argued that the former would be preferable to the latter, claiming that the Continental-European model did not come into conflict with any stipulations of Japan's Constitution.[66]

Famous liberal thinker and author of the concept of *minponshugi* Sakuzō Yoshino argued that the common-sense judgment of the people was more precious than the formalist logic of professional judges.[67] The concept of the jury system was also popular among some of the adherents of the socialist ideology. In 1918, socialist Toshihiko Sakai listed the adoption of the jury system together with the abolition of the death penalty in the declaration of his candidacy in the popular election to the Imperial Diet in 1917.[68]

Drafting and implementation

The unanimous support that the proposal concerning the establishment of the jury system received from the members of the House of Representatives in 1910 did not result in immediate action on the part of the government. Concrete steps towards the drafting and implementation of the Jury Act were expected of the Cabinet of Kinmochi Saionji – a member of the *Rikken Seiyūkai* – that was inaugurated in 1911. The Ministry of Justice, however, argued for the postponement of the introduction of the jury system for five to seven years in view of the costs that the jury reform would entail.[69]

The political will of Takashi Hara was crucial for the beginning of the drafting process of the Jury Act. In 1919, one year after Hara became prime minister, the Extraordinary Legislative Council (*Rinji Hōsei Shingikai*) was set up within the government.[70]

The Extraordinary Legislative Council appointed ten members who were put in charge of drafting the outline of the proposal to introduce the jury system in Japan. Members included five private practice lawyers (Makoto Egi, Takuzō Hanai, Shirō Isobe, Fusaaki Uzawa, and Yoshimichi Hara); the president of the Great Court of Judicature (*Daishin'in*) Kuniomi Yokota; the head of the Imperial Accounting Inspection Bureau (*Teishitsu Kaikei Shinsakyoku*) Yūzaburō Kuratomi; president of the Tokyo Court of Appeal (*Kōsoin*) Shōtarō Tomitani; Professor of Law at Tokyo Imperial University Tatsukichi Minobe; and member of the Privy Council Kitokurō Ichiki.[71] After the first meeting, the group was joined by Itasu

---

65 S. Ōba, 1914, *Baishin Seido Ron* [On the Jury System], Tokyo: Chūō Daigaku, pp. 219–233 and 238–258. Ōba specifically argued that if the members of the general public enthusiastically receive the system and come to view being selected to serve as jurors as an honor, then the system would be a success (*id.*, p. 242).
66 *Id.*, p. 258.
67 S. Yoshino, 1919, "Baishin Seido Saiyō no Gi" [Considering the Adoption of the Jury System], *Chūō Kōron*, Vol. 34, No. 9, p. 218, cited in Mitani, *Kindai Nihon no Shihōken to Seitō* [Judicial Power in Modern Japan and Political Parties], p. 163.
68 Mitani, *Seiji Seido toshite no Baishin Sei* [The Jury System as a Political System], p. 139.
69 E. Takano, 2001, "Nihon ni okeru Baishin Hō no Shikō to Teishi: Hanseiten to Kongo ni Ikasu tame ni" [The Implementation and Suspension of Japan's Jury Act: Points for Reflection and Lessons to be Used for the Future], *Hōgaku Jānaru* [The Law Journal], No. 16, pp. 1–55, at pp. 8–9.
70 Takashi (Kei) Hara (1856–1921) served as prime minister between 1918 and 1921 (Reischauer, *Japan: An Illustrated Encyclopedia*, p. 502).
71 Mitani, *Kindai Nihon no Shihōken to Seitō* [Judicial Power in Modern Japan and Political Parties], pp. 178–179.

Matsumuro, former minister of justice and member of the House of Peers.[72] At the beginning of the work of this team, the five private practice lawyers were actively in favor of introducing the jury system in Japan, while the remaining members were less enthusiastic about the idea.[73] There is evidence that suggests that having persons actively supporting the introduction of the jury system in Japan as well as those who were initially opposed to the idea was a strategic decision on Hara's part. Sennosuke Yokota – then head of the Legislation Bureau in Hara's Cabinet – in a comment on Hara's decision to establish the Extraordinary Legislative Council has argued that Hara believed it was necessary to demonstrate to the Japanese people that the Jury Act was born as a result of deliberations between highly experienced persons who initially had different opinions regarding the usefulness of the jury system.[74]

The Japan Federation of Bar Associations expressed its support for the government's efforts aimed at introducing the jury system in 1919.[75]

The Extraordinary Legislative Council met twenty-one times over a period of one year. Regarding the question of whether the introduction of the jury system would be constitutional or not, two points were raised during the deliberations. First, Professor Minobe argued that the fact that the constitution did not provide for the institution of jury service might become a problem, if this system was introduced without a corresponding amendment to the constitution. Second, Minobe drew the attention of the members of the council to the fact that allowing laypersons to adjudicate cases would infringe upon the right of Japanese subjects to be tried by professional judges and that introducing trial by jury was therefore unconstitutional.[76] Regarding the first point raised by Minobe, Takuzō Hanai managed to persuade the members of the council that essentially the jury system was an institution, the introduction of which would need to be reflected not in the constitution but in the Code of Criminal Procedure.[77] Regarding the second point, Hanai and the other lawyers on the team argued that if the jury system were introduced, laypersons would be responsible primarily for the determination of the facts of the crime and that the decisions regarding matters of law would remain the province of the judge. The members of the council found this line of reasoning convincing.

72 At the beginning of the work of the council, the five private practice lawyers were actively in favor of introducing the jury system in Japan, while the remaining members were less enthusiastic about the idea. This difference in attitudes on the part of the members of the council was reflected in the contents of the deliberations that took place during the first meetings of the council. While Hanai and Egi were determined to start discussing the features that Japan's jury system would have, Professor Tatsukichi Minobe proposed to first consider the question of whether the introduction of the jury system would be constitutional or not (Mitani, *Seiji Seido toshite no Baishin Sei* [The Jury System as a Political System], p. 149).
73 *Id.*, pp. 149–150.
74 Osatake, *Meiji Bunka Shi toshite no Nihon Baishin Shi* [The History of Jury in Japan as [Part of] *Meiji Cultural History*], pp. 174–175.
75 Nihon Bengoshi Kyōkai [Japan Bar Association], 1921, *Nihon Bengoshi Kyōkai Rokuji Dai 259 Gō* [Records of the 259th Meeting of the Japan Bar Associations], Tokyo: Nihon Bengoshi Kyōkai, p. 3; N. Shioya, "Baishin Hō An no Kōhyō o Nozomu" [Hoping for the Announcement of the Draft of the Jury Act], in *id.*, pp. 9–11.
76 Meiji Kenpō, arts. 24, 57, 58(1). See Toshitani, "Shihō Ni Taisuru Kokumin no Sanka" [Lay Participation in the Judiciary], p. 377; and Mitani, *Seiji Seido toshite no Baishin Sei* [The Jury System as a Political System], pp. 150–151 (discussing the deliberations regarding the proposal to introduce trial by jury at the Privy Council).
77 Mitani, *Seiji Seido toshite no Baishin Sei* [The Jury System as a Political System], p. 151.

Another question that became the center of deliberation by the members of the council concerned the question of whether Japan should introduce the jury system to all trials or only to criminal trials. The members decided that at first Japan would introduce only the criminal jury system.[78] The question of whether Japan should implement the grand jury and the petit jury or only the latter became another point of intense discussion.[79] The council agreed that Japan should introduce the petit jury and postponed the discussion on the necessity of introducing the grand jury to a later date.[80] Another issue raised during deliberations concerned the range of cases that could be tried by jury. Specifically, the opinions of the members differed regarding the question of whether offences against the members of the imperial household and those involving instigation of internal disturbances should be tried by jury. Professor Yokota argued that these cases should be tried by the special jury (*tokubetsu baishin*).[81] Yokota envisaged the special jury as a panel of highly responsible persons, such as the members of the Imperial Diet – an idea that is reminiscent of the bureaucratic *sanza* system that existed in 19th-century Japan. Those members who disagreed with Yokota's proposal argued that offences against the members of the imperial household should not be eligible for jury trial at all.[82] The members of the council failed to reach an agreement regarding this point.

On April 4, 1920, the group of lawyers within the council – that is, Egi, Hanai, Hara, and Uzawa – drafted a document titled "The Main Points of the Proposal to Establish the Jury System" (*Baishin Seiritsu An Yōten*).[83] The "Main Points" were written with the goal of moving forward the discussion at the council meetings and of providing the members with a document upon which they could either vote or which they could subsequently revise.[84]

"The Main Points of the Proposal to Establish the Jury System" stipulated that Japan would introduce the jury system in criminal cases. The first article of the document stated that the jury would be responsible for coming up with the verdict (*hyōketsu*) concerning the facts of the crime. The subsequent paragraphs of the article, however, added that the judges

---

78 *Id.*, p. 154.
79 The grand jury is a selection of jurors who decide on whether or not to indict a suspect, while the petit jury decides on the verdict of guilty or not guilty during a public proceeding (J. Dressler (ed.), 2002, *Encyclopedia of Crime & Justice*, New York: Macmillan Reference USA, pp. 737–744; G. G. Coughlin and G. G. Coughlin, Jr., 1982, *Dictionary of Law*, New York: Barnes & Noble Books, p. 107).
80 Mitani, *Seiji Seido toshite no Baishin Sei* [The Jury System as a Political System], p. 155.
81 *Id.*, p. 155.
82 *Id.*, p. 155.
83 M. Egi, Y. Hara, and T. Hanai, 1920, *Baishin Seiritsu An Yōten* [The Main Points of the Proposal to Establish the Jury System], April 4, in *Hozumi Nobushige Kankei Bunsho* [Documents Related to Nobushige Hozumi], No. 1, 11–9, available on microfilm, on file with the Center for Historical Materials of Modern Japanese Law, Tokyo University, partially reprinted in Mitani, *Seiji Seido toshite no Baishin Sei* [The Jury System as a Political System], pp. 161–167 [hereinafter The Main Points of the Proposal to Establish the Jury System, 1920].
84 While some of the members of the council were displeased with this attempt to draft a document behind their backs, they subsequently agreed that "The Main Points of the Proposal to Establish the Jury System" reflected not only the position of its authors but included several concessions, which made it a good basis for further discussion. Yūzaburō Kuratomi noted in a diary entry dated April 7, 1920, that he believed it was unfair that Egi and the other lawyers prepared the draft of this document on their own (Y. Kuratomi, *Yūzaburō Kuratomi Nikki* [Diary of Yūzaburō Kuratomi], on file with the National Diet Library, Modern Japanese Political History Materials Room, partially reproduced in Mitani, *Seiji Seido toshite no Baishin Sei* [The Jury System as a Political System], p. 160).

would retain their right to determine the facts of the crime as well. The document made it mandatory for the judge to seek the verdict of the jury and stipulated that the findings of the judge had to be in agreement with that of the jury for the verdict to stand.[85] In the event the judge and the jury could not agree, the verdict of the jury would stand.[86] According to the draft, the jury would try only those cases where the possible penalty was death as well as those involving offences against the imperial family, instigation of internal disturbances, crimes related to foreign aggression, obstruction of performance of public duty, and crimes of disturbance, unless jury trial was waived by the accused.[87] Jury trial could be requested in all other cases where the penalty was more than one year's imprisonment.[88] The council added a provision that stipulated that cases involving offences against the members of the imperial household and those involving instigation of internal disturbances should be tried by the special jury (*tokubetsu baishin*)[89] that would be composed of the members of both chambers of the Imperial Diet and members of the Privy Council, as well as university professors.[90]

Based on this draft, on June 21, 1920, Kuratomi, Hanai and Egi compiled "The General Principles Concerning the Jury System" (*Baishin Seido ni kansuru Kōryō*) – a document that was unanimously supported by the council on June 28, 1920.[91]

Work on drafting the Jury Act began on the day that the Jury Act Investigation Committee (*Baishin Hō Chōsa Iinkai*) was established within the Ministry of Justice. The committee included seventeen members (some of whom had served on the Extraordinary Legislative Council): Nobushige Hozumi, Kiichirō Hiranuma, Kitokurō Ichiki, Yūzaburō Kuratomi, Kisaburō Suzuki, Shōtarō Tomitani, Naomichi Tomishima, Takuzō Hanai, Eiichi Baba, Saburō Tanida, Mastsukichi Koyama, Sōmei Uzawa, Kyōhei Iijima, Genji Matsuda, Raizaburō Hayashi, Motoji Shikuma, and Makoto Egi. The members of the committee chose eight from among themselves – Hiranuma, Kuratomi, Tomishima, Hanai, Baba, Koyama, Iijima, and Egi – to write the draft of the law introducing the jury system in Japan.[92]

The draft of the Jury Act was completed on December 4, 1920, and on January 1, 1921, the Privy Council started deliberations regarding the law. The draft was essentially a copy of "The General Principles Concerning the Jury System" (*Baishin Seido ni kansuru Kōryō*).[93] The members of the committee – established within the Privy Council with the purpose of deliberating the Jury Act – discussed this draft, and the proposal was rejected

---

85 The Main Points of the Proposal to Establish the Jury System, 1920, art. 1.
86 *Id.*, art. 11.
87 *Id.*, arts. 2 and 5.
88 *Id.*, art. 7.
89 *Id.*, art. 119.
90 Minobe argued that trial would hardly be fair, if only politicians served as special jurors, and Kitokurō Ichiki stated that university professors should also be eligible to become special jurors (*Giji Keika Yōshi* [Summary of the 18th meeting of the Extraordinary Legislative Council], *Baishin Seiritsu An Yōten* [The Main Points of the Proposal to Establish the Jury System], April 4, in *Hozumi Nobushige Kankei Bunsho* [Documents Related to Nobushige Hozumi], No. 1, 11–9, available on microfilm, on file with the Center for Historical Materials of Modern Japanese Law, Tokyo University, partially reprinted in Mitani, *Seiji Seido toshite no Baishin Sei* [The Jury System as a Political System], p. 169).
91 Toshitani, "Shihō Ni Taisuru Kokumin no Sanka" [Lay Participation in the Judiciary], p. 376.
92 Kuratomi, *Yūzaburō Kuratomi Nikki* [Diary of Yūzaburō Kuratomi], entry dated July 30, 1920, cited in Mitani, *Seiji Seido toshite no Baishin Sei* [The Jury System as a Political System], p. 172.
93 Mitani, *Seiji Seido toshite no Baishin Sei* [The Jury System as a Political System], p. 173.

on May 4, 1921.[94] Prime Minister Hara resubmitted the law for consideration at the Privy Council two more times, but without success.[95]

One of the central arguments against the draft was the claim that allowing laypersons to adjudicate cases would infringe upon the right of Japanese subjects to be tried by professional judges and that introducing trial by jury was therefore unconstitutional.[96] Another was that the introduction of the jury system implied that the integrity of Japan's legal system and social order would be compromised. Specifically, it was argued that any division in the courtroom that might result from the difference in the opinions of the judge and of the jury would undermine the fundamentals of society.[97] The third argument against the Jury Act was that it was impossible to ensure that all members of the jury would have sufficient knowledge and qualifications to make decisions regarding questions of fact.[98] Fourth, the members of the committee found that contrary to the arguments of the proponents of the introduction of the jury system in Japan, the system provided for in the draft of the Jury Act would not help protect the rights of the accused. The members of the committee concluded that as the draft of the Jury Act did not provide for a grand jury, decisions concerning indictment would remain in the province of the prosecutor, to whom the draft did not provide any incentives to conduct his investigations with greater respect for the rights of the accused.[99] Fifth, the members of the committee argued that the jury system as provided for in the draft of the Jury Act would fail to ameliorate the limitations of trial by professional judges alone, as the most important questions in a trial concerned matters of law rather than fact, and under the Jury Act the decisions regarding points of law would be decided by professional judges.[100] Furthermore, the members of the committee were not impressed with the idea to have a special jury adjudicate cases involving offences against members of the imperial household. They argued that there was a contradiction between the drafters' desire to present the Jury Act as a means for ensuring the separation of powers and freeing the judicial system from any possible pressure from other branches of power on the one hand, and the actual provisions of the draft of the Jury Act that provided for a special jury consisting of representatives of other branches of power on the other.[101]

---

94 Members of the committee included former Chief Secretary (*shokikanchō*) of the Privy Council and former Minister of Agriculture Miyoji Itō, former Secretary (*hishokan*) to the Chairman of the Privy Council and former Minister of Justice Kentarō Kaneko, former Head of the Great Court of Judicature Mikao Nanbu, former Chief Secretary (*shokikanchō*) of the Privy Council Ban'ichirō Yasuhiro, former Minister of Justice Nagamoto Okabe, Professor of Tokyo Imperial University Kitokurō Ichiki, former Chief Secretary (*shokikanchō*) of the Privy Council Seishin Hirayama, former Chief Secretary (*shokikanchō*) of the Privy Council Hideyoshi Arimatsu, and Head of the Imperial Accounting Inspection Bureau (*Teishitsu Kaikei Shinsakyoku*) Yūzaburō Kuratomi (Mitani, *Seiji Seido toshite no Baishin Sei* [The Jury System as a Political System], p. 182).

95 The second draft was rejected because it was almost entirely the same as the draft that preceded it, while the deliberations concerning the third draft that featured slight modifications in the wording of the provisions were not concluded in view of the assassination of Prime Minister Hara on November 4, 1921 (*id.*).

96 Meiji Kenpō, arts. 24, 57, 58(1). Toshitani, "Shihō Ni Taisuru Kokumin no Sanka" [Lay Participation in the Judiciary], p. 377 (discussing the deliberations regarding the proposal to introduce trial by jury at the Privy Council).

97 Toshitani, "Shihō Ni Taisuru Kokumin no Sanka" [Lay Participation in the Judiciary], p. 376.

98 Mitani, *Seiji Seido toshite no Baishin Sei* [The Jury System as a Political System], p. 185.

99 *Id.*, p. 186.

100 *Id.*, p. 186.

101 This observation was expressed by member of the committee Hideyoshi Arimatsu (H. Arimatsu, "Baishin Hōan o Ronzu", in *Arimatsu Hideyoshi Kankei Bunsho* [Materials Related to Hideyoshi Arimatsu],

The pre-war jury system 71

The revised drafts that were submitted during Hara's administration differed very little from one another. The first draft authored after the administration of Korekiyo Takahashi was inaugurated, however, involved substantial changes.[102] This draft underwent several revisions that aimed to address the criticisms that were voiced during the period of deliberations of the drafts submitted during the Hara administration.

First, the team working on the revisions, led by Miyoji Itō, produced a document containing suggestions for the revision of the draft titled "Ideas Concerning the Fundamental Principles of Revision of the Jury Act" (*Baishin Hō Shūsei Taikō Fukuan*).[103] Itō proposed to clarify that the decisions of jurors would not be binding on the court[104] and suggested that the provisions concerning the special jury be deleted and that the crimes that according to the previous drafts were supposed to be tried by the special jury be deleted from the list of offences that could be tried by jury. Following a meeting between Itō and Prime Minister Takahashi, the Cabinet and the Privy Council revised the draft of the Jury Act based on the suggestions made by Itō. Specifically, while the previous drafts stated that the members of the jury were responsible for coming up with a verdict regarding points of fact,[105] the revised draft of the Jury Act no longer contained the word "verdict". Instead, it stipulated that the jury's role was to "deliberate" points of fact[106] and answer questions submitted to it by the judge.[107] Furthermore, the provision allowing the judge to dismiss the jury was added.[108]

The Privy Council passed this draft on February 27, 1922.[109] The draft was presented to the House of Representatives by Minister of Justice Enkichi Ōki. In his speech Ōki argued that it was unnatural that in Japan – a country where citizens could participate in the legislative and the administrative branches of power – that the people were not granted the right to participate in the judicial system.[110] The fact that *Rikken Seiyūkai* was the ruling party at the time implied that the House of Representatives would most likely pass the draft of the Jury Act. Several critical points were raised during the deliberation concerning the Jury

---

No. 348, available on microfilm, on file with Center for Historical Materials of Modern Japanese Law, Tokyo University, partially reproduced in Mitani, *Seiji Seido toshite no Baishin Sei* [The Jury System as a Political System], p. 190).

102 Mitani, *Seiji Seido toshite no Baishin Sei* [The Jury System as a Political System], p. 210.
103 *Id.*, p. 221.
104 Jury Act, art. 95; Jury Act (Proposed Official Draft 1922), art. 95, reprinted in M. Egi, T. Hanai, and Y. Hara, 1923, *Baishin Hō Shingi Hen* [Compilation of [the Transcripts of] Deliberations [Regarding] the Jury Act], Tokyo: Shimizu Shoten, pp. 1–21 [hereinafter Jury Act (Proposed Official Draft 1922)].
105 Baishinsei Ritsuan Yōkō [Outline of the Draft [Concerning] the Jury System], art. 1, reprinted in Egi. Hanai, and Hara, *Baishin Hō Shingi Hen* [Compilation of [the Transcripts of] Deliberations [Regarding] the Jury Act], pp. 1–22 [hereinafter Outline of the Draft [Concerning] the Jury System].
106 Jury Act (Proposed Official Draft 1922), art. 1; Jury Act, art. 1. Also see R. Hayashi, 1928, "Nihon Baishin Hō Enkaku Shi no Issetsu" [A Paragraph in the History of Japan's Jury Act], *Hōsō Kōron*, Vol. 32, No. 9, pp. 39–43, at p. 40.
107 Jury Act (Proposed Official Draft 1922), art. 79; Jury Act, art. 79.
108 Jury Act (Proposed Official Draft 1922), art. 95; Jury Act, art. 95. Mitani, *Seiji Seido toshite no Baishin Sei* [The Jury System as a Political System], p. 230.
109 Shinomiya, "Nihon ni mo Baishin Seido ga Sonzai Shita" [The Jury System Existed in Japan Too], pp. 100–101.
110 Egi, Hanai, and Hara, *Baishin Hō Shingi Hen* [Compilation of [the Transcripts of] Deliberations [Regarding] the Jury Act], p. 22.

72 *The pre-war jury system*

Act, however. First, Member of Parliament Fujiya Suzuki raised the question concerning the absence of the provisions regarding the grand jury in the Jury Act, arguing that the grand jury was necessary to protect the rights of the accused.[111] Second, Suzuki noticed that the draft stipulated that the members of the jury would not be expected to come up with a verdict and asked why this stipulation was necessary.[112] Sennosuke Yokota, head of the Legislation Bureau, responded to this query saying that just as the judges should not be allowed to ignore the opinions of the jury, the members of the jury should not be binding the court with their opinions.[113] Several other members of the House of Representatives were openly critical of the provision that made the responses of the jury not binding on the court. Member of the House of Representatives Naohiko Seki even remarked: "The European countries and America will surely look at the Jury Act of the Japanese Empire with eyes [concealing a] cold smile."[114]

Another aspect of the Jury Act that became the subject of intense discussion among the members of the House of Representatives concerned the reasons for removing the crimes involving instigation of internal disturbances and of foreign aggression from the list of offences eligible for jury trial.[115] In response to this question, Yokota explained that the government was concerned that the implementation of the jury system might bring along problems, and that therefore it was decided that at first only the cases stipulated in the draft would be tried by the jury. He added that if it turned out that the jury system fits Japan's national character well, then "the range [of cases eligible for jury trial] might eventually be expanded."[116]

Two opposition parties in the House of Representatives – the *Kenseikai* (Constitutional Party) and the *Kokumintō* (National Party) – submitted their own proposals for revising the draft of the Jury Act. Both documents proposed that the responses of the jury should be made binding on the court and that the offences against the imperial family as well as those involving instigation of internal disturbances and foreign aggression should be made eligible for trial by jury.[117] Both proposals were rejected by the House of Representatives – a development that is understandable given the fact that the *Seiyūkai* was the ruling party and had the majority of seats in the House of Representatives at the time.[118]

The House of Representatives passed the 1922 draft of the Jury Act on March 1, 1922, and this draft was then discussed at the House of Peers.[119] During the deliberations at the House of Peers, the question of whether the opinions of jurors should be binding on the court was raised repeatedly. The proponents of the draft defended the decision to add the provisions that made the responses of jurors not binding on the court by arguing that in doing so Japan "got rid of the vices and adopted the virtues" of the Western model of

---

111 *Id.*, p. 23.
112 *Id.*, p. 25.
113 *Id.*, p. 31.
114 *Id.*, p. 34.
115 *Id.*, p. 28.
116 *Id.*, p. 32.
117 *Id.*, p. 108.
118 Takano, "Nihon ni okeru Baishin Hō no Shikō to Teishi: Hanseiten to Kongo ni Ikasu tame ni" [The Implementation and Suspension of Japan's Jury Act: Points for Reflection and Lessons to be Used for the Future], p. 17.
119 Toshitani, "Shihō Ni Taisuru Kokumin no Sanka" [Lay Participation in the Judiciary], p. 377.

the jury system[120] and adapted this model to better fit Japan's national character.[121] It was also argued that even if the responses of the members of the jury were not binding, the introduction of trials by jury as outlined in the draft of the Jury Act would allow "the will of the people [to be] injected" into court proceedings.[122] The question of whether the Jury Act should be approved was not resolved during the deliberations at the House of Peers, and the draft was not passed.

The draft of the law was again submitted to the Privy Council, which approved it on December 20, 1922. Then the draft was resubmitted to the House of Representatives. While some members of the House of Representatives repeatedly voiced their concerns regarding the provisions that made the responses of the jury not binding on the court and submitted a proposal for revising the draft in order to strengthen the position of the members of the jury and to expand the range of cases eligible for trial by jury,[123] these initiatives were not supported by the majority. The lower house of Parliament passed the draft of the Jury Act on March 2, 1923.

The deliberations at the House of Peers featured speeches in favor of and against the Jury Act. Reijirō Wakatsuki delivered the speech against the Jury Act, arguing that despite the fact that the government stated that the goal of the Jury Act was to strengthen the foundations of the constitutional state, in reality the act was being presented simply out of respect for the assassinated Prime Minister, Hara, who supported this act.[124] Another member of the House of Peers Shōtarō Tomitani argued for the adoption of the Jury Act, stating that the times have changed and that Japan needed "a new system of justice that accommodates the will of the people".[125] Upon hearing the arguments for and against the Jury Act, the House of Peers passed the act (143 votes cast for and 8 votes cast against) on March 21, 1923.[126]

The Jury Act: a summary

The enacted version of the Jury Act envisaged a jury system that on the surface appeared to be similar to the adversarial jury.[127] The Act provided for the empanelment of a

---

120 Egi, Hanai, and Hara, *Baishin Hō Shingi Hen* [Compilation of [the Transcripts of] Deliberations [Regarding] the Jury Act], p. 407. The statement quoted here was made during the deliberations at the House of Peers by Sennōsuke Yokota (1870–1925), a noted politician of the *Meiji* and *Taishō* periods. Yokota was first elected to the House of Representatives in 1909 and became secretary-general of the *Rikken Seiyūkai* in 1914. Yokota was appointed head of the Legislative Bureau of the Cabinet of Prime Minister Takeshi (Kei) Hara in 1918 and became Minister of Justice in 1924 (Ichinose, *Major 20th Century People in Japan*, p. 2711).
121 Egi, Hanai, and Hara, *Baishin Hō Shingi Hen* [Compilation of [the Transcripts of] Deliberations [Regarding] the Jury Act], p. 409.
122 *Id.*, p. 408.
123 *Id.*, pp. 712–714.
124 Dai Nippon Teikoku Gikai [The Imperial Diet of Japan], *Dai Nippon Teikoku Gikaishi* [Journal of the Imperial Diet of Japan], Vol. 14, p. 320.
125 *Id.*, p. 342. The other two speakers during the deliberations were Takuzō Hanai, who argued for the introduction of the Jury Act, and Gen Yamawaki, who opposed the implementation of the jury system in Japan (Mitani, *Kindai Nihon no Shihōken to Seitō* [Judicial Power in Modern Japan and Political Parties], p. 317).
126 Dai Nippon Teikoku Gikai [The Imperial Diet of Japan], *Dai Nippon Teikoku Gikaishi* [Journal of the Imperial Diet of Japan], Vol. 14, p. 343.
127 Jury Act [Baishin Hō], Law No. 50 of 1923, as last amended by Law No. 51 of 1929 and Law No. 62 of 1941, suspended by Law No. 88 of 1943 [hereinafter Jury Act]. One legal scholar argued that "to

twelve-layperson jury,[128] who were to deliberate the case behind closed doors without the presence of the judge.[129] Jury selection procedures resembled the methods used in the Anglo-American system at that time. Candidates for jury service had to be male citizens over thirty years of age; reside in the same city, town, or village for at least two years; pay more than three yen in national direct taxes; be literate; and possess Japanese citizenship.[130] Selection began with the compilation of a list containing the names of those individuals who satisfied the aforementioned requirements.[131] Candidates to serve on a particular case were chosen by lot from that list and summoned to appear in court.[132] The defendant and the prosecutor were then given the right to exclude those candidates that they did not wish to adjudicate the case.[133]

At the same time, the pre-war jury system had several features that distinguished it from its adversarial counterpart. Some of these features served to ensure that the judge would retain the role of the active supervisor of the proceedings, rather than assume the relatively passive role that the judge typically assumes in the adversarial system.[134] Specifically, according to the act, the members of Japan's pre-war jury were not to decide on the verdict of guilty or not guilty, but to give answers to the questions submitted to them by the judge regarding points of fact.[135] While the phrasing of the questions was up to the judge, the

---

a large degree [Japan's jury system] took after the French and the Austrian [systems], but was flavored with [elements of] the Anglo-American system, and display[ed] uniquely Japanese [characteristics]" (T. Sakamoto, 1928, "Baishin Hō no Jisshi ni Atarite" [On the [Occasion of] the Implementation of the Jury Act], *Hōsō Kōron*, Vol. 32, No. 9, pp. 57–62, at p. 58). The translation of the Jury Act made by SCAP's Legal Branch, Public Safety Division, Civil Intelligence Section, is reproduced in full in D. Vanoverbeke, 2015, *Juries in the Japanese Legal System: The Continuing Struggle for Citizen Participation and Democracy*, London: Routledge, pp. 191–214.

128 Jury Act, art. 29.
129 *Id.*, art. 82.
130 *Id.*, art. 12.
131 First, the names of those individuals who satisfied the requirements for jury service were listed by the heads of the cities, towns, and villages. The presidents of district courts then determined the number of jurors required for adjudicating cases and distributed this number between the cities, towns, and villages within the jurisdiction of that court and sent a notification to the heads of these municipalities. The list of individuals eligible for jury service was then compiled by the heads of cities, towns, and villages. This list had to be prepared no later than September 1 (Jury Act, arts. 22, 23).
132 *Id.*, art. 27.
133 *Id.*, art. 64. The prosecutor and the defendant were each allowed to excuse half of the number exceeding the number of jurors and supplementary jurors required. If the number of persons to be excused was an odd number, the additional elimination right was given to the defendant. If several defendants were tried, refusal was done jointly. In the event there was disagreement among the defendants as to which of the jury candidates was to be excused, the judge was to resolve the conflict (*id.*, art. 64). The judge put the name cards of the prospective jurors in a lottery box and informed the prosecutor and the defendant of the number jurors that were to be excused. The judge then drew the name cards out of the box and read them aloud. The prosecutor and the defendant were then to say whether they accepted or refused that candidate, with the prosecutor stating his decision first. Neither the prosecutor nor the defendant was required to explain the reasons for their decision (*id.*, art. 65). See Shinomiya, *Baishin Tebiki* [Guidebook for Jury Service], pp. 37–44 (discussing the process of jury selection and the peremptory challenge procedure in pre-war Japan).
134 N. Vidmar, "A Historical and Comparative Perspective on the Common Law Jury", in N. Vidmar (ed.), 2000, *World Jury Systems*, New York: Oxford University Press, pp. 1–52, at pp. 13–15 (discussing the differences between the adversarial and the inquisitorial systems of justice).
135 Jury Act, art. 88. After the promulgation of the Jury Act this provision was criticized by many lawyers, who argued that in order to function effectively the members of the jury in Japan should have been allowed the right to come up with the verdict of guilty or not guilty independently of the judge (H. Mikami, 1928, "Baishin Hō no Shikō o Shuku shite" [Celebrating the Enforcement of the Jury Act], *Hōsō Kōron*, Vol. 32, No. 9, pp. 49–57, at p. 50).

act distinguished between two types of questions that the judge could submit to the jury: "main questions" (*shumon*) and "supplementary questions" (*homon*).[136] Main questions concerned the presence or absence of facts constituting a crime, while supplementary questions required that the jury discuss the presence or absence of facts other than those that the defendant was initially charged with.[137] The judge could also submit "other questions" (*betsumon*) to the jury for consideration. These questions allowed the jury to deliberate the presence or absence of facts that make the establishment of the crime impossible.[138] Furthermore, the judge was given the option of disregarding the jury's responses and calling another jury.[139]

Other provisions of the Jury Act that distinguished Japan's system from the adversarial model of jury trials had in common the fact that they all served to prevent the jury system from being used often. First, the Jury Act stipulated that not all cases were eligible for jury trial. Only contested criminal cases where the maximum penalty was death or imprisonment for life were tried by jury.[140] In cases where the maximum penalty was imprisonment for greater than three years and the minimum penalty was imprisonment for not less than one year, the defendant had the right to request a jury trial.[141] Cases involving crimes committed against a member of the imperial family,[142] crimes related to instigation of internal disturbances as well as instigation of foreign aggression, crimes related to foreign relations,[143] and the election of public officials[144] were not eligible for trial by jury. The 1929 amendment of the Jury Act further limited the instances when jury trial could be requested. The provision added in 1929 stipulated that jury trial could not be requested in cases involving the

---

136 Jury Act, art. 79(1).
137 Jury Act, art. 79(2), (3). A guidebook for jury service published in 1931 provides the following example of a supplementary question: "If in the course of the trial concerning a case where the defendant is charged with attempted murder it is revealed that there is a possibility that the crime involved the infliction of bodily injury, then a supplementary question might be as follows: 'Did the accused injure the victim?'" (Shinomiya, *Baishin Tebiki* [Guidebook for Jury Service], p. 57, translated in A. Dobrovolskaia, 2008, "The Jury System in Pre-war Japan: An Annotated Translation of 'The Jury Guidebook'", *Asian-Pacific Law and Policy Journal*, Vol. 9, No. 2, pp. 231–296).
138 Jury Act, art. 79(4). The guidebook for jury service provides the following example: "['Other questions' (*betsumon*)] are relevant to cases involving the possibility that the defendant acted in self defense, or was completely drunk and therefore in an unconscious state of mind when inflicting an injury. In such cases as this when it is difficult to charge the defendant with attempted murder or with bodily injury, the following separate question may be asked: 'Did the accused inflict injury upon Mr. N in self defense?'" (Shinomiya, *Baishin Tebiki* [Guidebook for Jury Service], p. 58).
139 Jury Act, art. 95.
140 *Id.*, art. 2. These cases were referred to as "cases designated by law to be tried by jury" (*hōtei baishin jiken*). Shinomiya, *Baishin Tebiki* [Guidebook for Jury Service], pp. 18–19.
141 Jury Act, art. 3. These cases were referred to as "cases that can be tried by jury upon request" (*seikyū baishin jiken*). Shinomiya, *Baishin Tebiki* [Guidebook for Jury Service], p. 19.
142 Jury Act, art. 4(1). Violations against members of the imperial family were tried by the Great Court of Judicature (*Daishin'in*). Saibansho Kōsei Hō [Court Organization Law], Law No. 6 of 1890, art. 50.
143 Jury Act, art. 4(2). The Penal Code of Japan, Law No. 45 of 1907 [hereinafter KEIHŌ], arts. 81, 82 (enumerating Instigation of Foreign Aggression and Assistance to the Enemy, respectively), arts. 92, 93, 94 (enumerating Damage of Foreign National Flag, Preparations or Plots for Private War, and Violations of Neutrality Orders, respectively), arts. 106, 107 (enumerating Disturbance and Failure to Disperse, respectively).
144 Jury Act, art. 4(5); Shūgiin Giin Senkyo Hō [House of Representatives Members Election Act], Law No. 73 of 1900, as amended by Law No. 38 of 1902, Law No. 39 of 1902, Law No. 58 of 1908, Law No. 65 of 1910, Law No. 60 of 1919, Law No. 47 of 1925, and Law No. 81 of 1926 [hereinafter Members Election Act].

76 *The pre-war jury system*

violation of the Peace Preservation Act (*Chian Iji Hō*).[145] This amendment denied access to trial by jury to criminal defendants who adhered to communist and socialist ideologies, as crimes of political nature were outlawed by the Peace Preservation Act.[146] Second, the defendant was given the right to waive jury trial,[147] and several provisions of the Jury Act made it beneficial for the accused to exercise this right. Specifically, appealing jury decisions *kōso* on points of fact was not possible.[148] This encouraged defendants to waive jury trial in order to preserve the right to this appeal. In addition, the defendant was responsible for bearing the costs of the trial, if he or she requested trial by jury, which encouraged many to waive jury trial.[149] Third, jury trial was available only in cases that had undergone preliminary investigation (*yoshin*), which made it possible for public prosecutors to avoid trial by jury.[150]

Promotion efforts and implementation

Promotion

A period of five years separated the promulgation of the Jury Act and its enactment in 1928. During this time of preparation, the Ministry of Justice, the local Bar Associations, journalists, and a semi-governmental organization known as the Japan Jury Association actively promoted the new system.

A total of five million yen was spent on the preparations for the introduction of the jury system in Japan.[151] The fact that the country's total annual revenue in 1928, the year in which the jury system was implemented, constituted 2,005,691,105 yen demonstrates how significant that amount of money was.[152]

---

145 Jury Act, art. 4(3); Chian Iji Hō [Peace Preservation Act], Law No. 46 of 1925, as amended by Emergency Imperial Ordinance No. 129 of 1928 [hereinafter Peace Preservation Act]. It should be noted, however, that some cases that involved persons suspected of allegiance to the communist ideology were tried by jury despite this provision. These were persons who were formally accused of crimes other than those provided for by the Peace Preservation Act (see Chapter 4 for the discussion of one such case).
146 Peace Preservation Act, art. 1 (enumerating the refusal to recognize private property and formation of associations with the goal of altering the *kokutai* (National Essence)).
147 Jury Act, art. 6.
148 Jury Act, art. 101. It was possible to appeal *jōkoku* on points of law to the Great Court of Judicature (*Daishin'in*). *Id.* art. 102. The *kōso* appeal is an appeal on points of fact. In such an appeal the court considers the facts of the case as they were presented in the original trial hearing together with newly-presented materials. By contrast, in a *jōkoku* appeal, the facts established in the course of the original trial are outside the scope of consideration, with the court's task being to evaluate the correctness of the application of law (see generally Dean, *Japanese Legal System*, p. 371).
149 *Id.*, art. 107.
150 H. Kikuchi, 1959, *14 Nihon Hōritsuka Kyōkai Series: Baishin Seido ni tsuite* [14 Nihon Hōritsuka Kyōkai Series: On the Jury System], Tokyo: Japan Bar Association, p. 58; M. Urabe, 1968, *Wagakuni ni okeru Baishin Saiban no Kenkyū: Keiken Dan ni yoru Jittai Chōsa o Chūshin toshite* [Research on Jury Trials in Our Country: A Study Focusing on the Actual Experiences], Tokyo: Shihō Kenshūjo, p. 4.
151 Shinomiya, *Baishin Tebiki* [Guidebook for Jury Service], p. 14.
152 Ōkura Shō Shuzeikyoku [The Tax Bureau, Ministry of Finance], 1956, *Meiji, Taishō, Shōwa: Kuni no Sainyū Ichiran Hyō* [*Meiji, Taishō, Shōwa* – State Revenues: A Chart], Tokyo: Ōkura Shō Shuzeikyoku [The Tax Bureau, Ministry of Finance], p. 13.

The Ministry of Justice

The promotional efforts of the Ministry of Justice focused on three goals: to provide the necessary facilities for jury trials to take place, to prepare legal professionals for the introduction of the system, and to familiarize prospective jurors with their duties.

With regard to the first objective, the Ministry supervised and provided funding for the building of new courtrooms with seats for jurors and jury accommodation facilities in seventy-one district courts across Japan.[153] The building of new courtrooms began in 1926, and as it progressed, the seat layout in the jury courtroom and the relative elevation of the prosecutor's and attorney's seats became the subject of heated public discussion. Prior to the promulgation of the Jury Act, the seat of the prosecutor was put in a place that was more elevated than the seat of the defense attorney. As the result of extensive public discussion and thanks to the intervention from then Minister of Justice Yoshimichi Hara, the new jury courtrooms had the seat of the judge at the highest place in the courtroom, and the seats of the prosecutor and the defense attorney were placed at the same, lower level.[154]

The Ministry sought to achieve the second goal by carrying out several measures. First, it worked to increase the number of judges and prosecutors. Specifically, departments in charge of jury trials (*Baishin Bu*) were established in all district courts in Japan, and the Ministry decided to increase the number of staff working in these courts by 250 persons – a task that it accomplished slowly over the course of five years.[155] In 1928, the number of judges was increased by 104 persons and the number of prosecutors by 46 persons.[156] Second, the Ministry sent 36 judges, prosecutors, and other court officials abroad to study how the jury system functioned in other countries and also to observe the courtrooms with seats for jurors.[157] Third, the Ministry hosted seminars for the prosecutors and judges to prepare

---

153 Tokyo Bengoshi Kai [Tokyo Bar Association], 1992, *Baishin Saiban: Kyūbaishin no Shōgen to Kongo no Kadai* [Jury Trials: The Testimony and Implications for the Future of the Old Jury System], Tokyo: Gyōsei, p. 32. The building of the new facilities commenced in 1926. Two jury accommodation facilities were established in Tokyo and one in each city that had a district court. In addition, two jury courtrooms were built in the district courts of Tokyo, Osaka, Nagano, and Fukuoka. All other district courts were equipped with one jury courtroom (N. Ōhara, 1929, "Baishin Hō no Jisshi Junbi ni tsuite" [Regarding the Preparation for the Enforcement of the Jury Act], *Hōsōkai Zasshi* [Journal of the Law Society], Vol. 7, No. 10, pp. 309–322, at p. 314).

154 Anonymous, 1927, "Kenji to Bengoshi Zaseki wa Dōtō" [Seats of Prosecutor and Attorney to Be Equal], *Hōritsu Shinbun*, August 8, p. 17; Anonymous, "Hōtei ni okeru Kenji, Shoki narabi ni Shihō Kisha no Zaseki ni tsuite" [Concerning the Seats of the Prosecutor, the Secretary, and of the Judicial Reporters], *Hōritsu Shinbun*, August 10, 1927, p. 3; Anonymous, 1927, "Baishin Hōtei no Zaseki Mondai (2)" [The Seating Problem in Jury Courtrooms (2)], *Hōritsu Shinbun*, November 20, pp. 4–6.

155 Anonymous, 1923, "Baishin Hō Shikō Junbi" [Preparing for Enforcement of the Jury Act], *Hōritsu Shinbun*, April 3.

156 Saibansho Shokuin Teiin Reichū Kaisei no Ken [Concerning the Revision of the Number of Court Personnel], Imperial Ordinance No. 163 of 1928; Ōhara, "Baishin Hō no Jisshi Junbi ni tsuite" [Regarding the Preparation for the Enforcement of the Jury Act], pp. 313–314.

157 The numbers of prosecutors and judges sent abroad in preparation for the introduction of the jury system in Japan are as follows: 1923 (six persons), 1924 (five persons), 1925 (seven persons), 1926 (nine persons); 1927 (nine persons). Ōhara, "Baishin Hō no Jisshi Junbi ni tsuite" [Regarding the Preparation for the Enforcement of the Jury Act], pp. 319–320. For an example of publications that are based on the reports of legal professionals who were sent to observe the functioning of the jury system in other countries see Shihō Daijin Kanbō Chōsa Ka [Research Department, Minister's

78 *The pre-war jury system*

them for the introduction of the jury system.[158] These meetings took place in Tokyo in June and July 1928. Immediately prior to the enforcement of the Jury Act, the Ministry invited presidents of Japan's Bar Associations and asked for their cooperation with regard to the implementation of the new system.[159] The Ministry also published and distributed a compilation of questions concerning the Jury Act that it had received from district courts across the country and provided answers clarifying the points raised in the questions.[160]

With regard to the third goal, the Ministry supervised the organization of explanation sessions for the general public. In 1926, the Ministry issued a set of guidelines that made it mandatory for presidents of ward courts and the members of the prosecutor's office[161] to meet with heads of cities, towns, and villages to explain the importance of the Jury Act and to distribute pamphlets regarding the new system.[162] The Ministry published a total of 2,814,000 copies of two pamphlets titled "About the Jury System" (*Baishin Seido no Hanashi*) and "What Is Trial by Jury?" (*Baishin Saiban to wa Donna Mono ka?*).[163] The former was a forty-eight-page pamphlet that described the jury system that was to be implemented in Japan in great detail, contained a copy of the text of the Jury Act, and featured photographs and sketches of the jury courtrooms. The latter was an eight-page explanation of the act.[164] Presidents of ward courts and the members of the prosecutor's office were also required to organize explanation sessions for the general public regarding the importance of the Jury Act.[165]

In addition, the Ministry published 56,000 copies of the compilation of the transcripts of the speeches delivered by the vice minister of justice, the secretaries working at the Ministry of Justice, and by the president of the Tokyo Court of Appeal (*Kōsoin*) under the title of "The Points that Jurors Should Keep in Mind" (*Baishin'in Kokorogaku Beki Jikō*).[166] This compilation was distributed to candidates for jury service.[167]

The Ministry actively used advertising in newspapers as well as special programs on the radio to explain the features of the jury system and to draw the attention of the general

---

Secretariat, Ministry of Justice], 1926, *Shihō Shiryō: Baishin Seido Shisatsu Hōkokusho Shū No. 85* [Judicial Materials: A Compilation of Reports Examining the Jury System No. 85], Tokyo: Shihō Daijin Shobō Chōsa Ka.

158 Anonymous, 1928, "Baishin Jisshi Junbi no Jitsumuka Kaidō" [Meeting of Professionals in Preparation for the Implementation of the Jury Act], *Hōritsu Shinbun*, September 10, p. 1.
159 Ōhara, "Baishin Hō no Jisshi Junbi ni tsuite" [Regarding the Preparation for the Enforcement of the Jury Act], pp. 317–318.
160 Anonymous, 1928, "Baishin Mondai Shū" [Compilation of Questions Concerning the Jury [System]], *Hōritsu Shinbun*, September 18, p. 21.
161 In accordance with the Court Organization Law, all courts with the exception of civil district courts (*minji chihō saibansho*) had a prosecutor's office attached to it (Saibansho Kōsei Hō [Court Organization Law], Law No. 6 of 1890, art. 6).
162 Shihō Jikan [Vice Minister of Justice], 1926, "Baishin Hō Shikō no Junbi" [Preparing for the Enforcement of the Jury Act], Keiji No. 4015, *Commentary on Newly Promulgated Legislation*, Vol. 15, No. 5, June 4, 1926, reprinted in "Baishin Hō" [Jury Act] in Hōgaku Kenkyūkai [Society for the Study of Law], 1932, *Keiji Soshō Hō, Baishin Hō, Shōnen Hō* [Code of Penal Procedure, Jury Act, Juvenile Law], Tokyo: Jōban Shobō, pp. 1–2.
163 Ōhara, "Baishin Hō no Jisshi Junbi ni tsuite" [Regarding the Preparation for the Enforcement of the Jury Act], p. 316.
164 *Id.*, p. 316.
165 Shihō Jikan [Vice Minister of Justice], "Baishin Hō Shikō no Junbi" [Preparing for the Enforcement of the Jury Act], p. 1.
166 Ōhara, "Baishin Hō no Jisshi Junbi ni tsuite" [Regarding the Preparation for the Enforcement of the Jury Act], p. 316.
167 *Id.*, p. 316.

public to the Jury Act.[168] A total of eleven films were used by the Ministry to promote the jury system in Japan. The Ministry used the sections featuring trial by jury from American movies, including the 1920 movie starring Bert Lytell titled "Right of Way" (Japanese title: "Red-Hot Crossing" [*Sekinetsu no Jūjiro*]), distributed in the United States by Metro Pictures, and from French and Canadian motion pictures.[169] It also produced a full-feature film with the aim of advertising the jury system. The film under the title of "A Dead Body Does Not Speak" (*Kabane wa Katarazu*) was shot by the Nikkatsu Corporation in 1927.[170]

The Ministry of Justice also worked with universities and schools and organized explanation sessions for students regarding the Jury Act.

Local Bar Associations

Local Bar Associations helped the Ministry of Justice in its advertisement efforts by holding explanation sessions and mock jury trials in various districts all over Japan.[171] The first mock trial was organized by a group of lawyers in 1917, when the possibility of introducing the jury system was still being discussed.[172] After the promulgation of the Jury Act, local Bar Associations held mock trials with the goal of not only familiarizing the public with the concept of jury trials, but of preparing potential jurors for their service. The mock trials organized in 1927, for instance, had their goal in helping jury candidates get used to the atmosphere of the courtroom. In these mock trials the actors playing the roles of the judge, the prosecutor, and the defense counsel put on court clothing that was exactly like that used in real courtrooms.[173] Observers referred to mock jury trials as the most effective means of promoting the Jury Act.[174]

---

168 *Id.*, p. 317.
169 *Id.*, p. 317. Among these movies was "A Mother's Sin" [*Haha no Tsumi*] by the Pathé movie company, and a movie that was in Japanese release, "Broken Love" (D. Midori, O. Masuda, T. Katō, and K. Kontani, 2007, "Hiroshima ni okeru Baishin Saiban: Shōwa Shoki no Geibi Nichinichi Shinbun Chugoku Shinbun no Hōdō narabi ni Keiji Hanketsu Genpon o Chūshin ni shite Miru Baishin Saiban [Jury Trials in Hiroshima: Jury Trials as Seen through the Articles of the Geibi Nichinichi Shinbun, the Chugoku Shinbun as well as through the Original Criminal [Trial] Verdicts [Issued] at the beginning of the *Shōwa* Period], *Shūdō Hōgaku*, Vol. 29, No. 2, pp. 45–195, at p. 64).
170 Kurohōshi (pseudonym of Katei Watanabe), 1927, "Baishin Hō Senden to Minshū Shinri" [Promotion of the Jury Act and Popular Psychology], *Hōritsu Shinbun*, November 18, p. 3. A newspaper article reviewing this film mentioned that "A Dead Body Does Not Speak" was much easier to understand than the "foreign films" that had been shown in Japan previously, but stated that "A Dead Body Does Not Speak" had several shortcomings. First, according to the article, the film failed to emphasize the fact that most events happening in the courtroom would be scrupulously reported by newspapers and would thus be made known to the general public. Second, the subtitles had several typographical mistakes. Third, the article claimed, the prosecutor was unduly shown in a highly negative way. Fourth, the length of the section at the beginning of the film showing the Minister of Justice was much too long (Anonymous, 1927, "Baishin Hō Senden no Kansen Eiga" [Jury Act Promotional Film Endorsed by the Government], *Hōritsu Shinbun*, December 18, p. 3).
171 Anonymous, 1928, "Sendai ni okeru Mogi Baishin Saiban" [Mock Jury Trial in Sendai], *Hōritsu Shinbun*, May 20, p. 17; Anonymous, 1928, "Tokyo Bengoshikai Shusai no Mogi Baishin Saiban" [Jury Mock Trial Organized by the Tokyo Bar Association], *Hōritsu Shinbun*, August 13, p. 1; Anonymous, 1927, "Baishin Hō Mogi Saiban ni tsuite" [On Mock Jury Act Trials], *Hōritsu Shinbun*, December 28, p. 3.
172 T. Inomata, 1928, "Baishin Seido Mogi Saiban: Konjaku Monogatari (1)" [The Jury System, Mock Trials: A Story of the Present and of the Past], *Hōsō Kōron*, Vol. 32, No. 9, pp. 114–117, at p. 116.
173 Anonymous, 1927, "Baishin Hō Mogi Saiban ni tsuite" [On Mock Jury Trials], *Hōritsu Shinbun*, December 28, pp. 3–4.
174 S. Mikami, 1927, "Baishin Senden Dayori" [News Concerning Promotion of the Jury [System]], *Hōritsu Shinbun*, September 8, pp. 7–8, at p. 7.

80 *The pre-war jury system*

In addition, local Bar Associations organized the staging of plays featuring court cases tried by jury, the so-called *baishin geki*.[175] While the ability of these plays to accurately explain the features of the Jury Act has been disputed, they were certainly entertaining and attracted a lot of attention on the part of the public.[176] One such play, "Natsuko's Mother" (*Natsuko no Haha*), was staged in Yokohama in 1927. The main character of the play, the mother of a girl called Natsuko, falls in love with a villain and runs off with him to Shanghai, leaving Natsuko behind. In twelve years' time, the main character and her lover return to Japan and stay at a hotel where Natsuko – now an adult – is working. Natsuko's mother slowly realizes that the waitress working at the hotel is her daughter. The villain accuses Natsuko of theft. The following day, he is found dead. Natsuko's mother is accused of murdering him, is tried by jury, and proclaimed innocent.[177] Another play was staged in Nagoya as part of the promotion efforts organized by the Nagoya Bar Association.[178] This play was loosely based on a script written by Fuboku Kosakai – a famous detective story novelist – and opened with the scene in which a mistress of a *geisha* house, Omichi, is found dead, and three hundred yen in cash and a diamond ring are missing. The victim opened the door to her chambers thinking that her lover, Mr. Tanaka, had come to visit her and was heard saying his name out loud, but instead found herself face to face with an intruder who killed her with a knife. The knife used in the crime turned out to belong to Tanaka; this fact, together with the statements of neighbors who reported that they had heard Omichi exclaim Tanaka's name, point to Tanaka as the primary suspect. Brought to court, Tanaka denies his guilt. At the end of the trial hearing, the members of the jury respond to the question submitted to them by the judge by saying that Tanaka was not guilty. After the verdict is out, a member of the general public listening to the court proceedings accidentally notices that the person sitting not far away is holding a diamond ring in his hand. He alerts the police and gets that person arrested. The real murderer of Omichi is thus caught and brought to justice.[179] Critics have argued that the assertions made in the play were unrealistic, pointing out that in a real case Tanaka would not have been taken to court for lack of evidence.[180]

The Hōritsu Shinbun

Independent journalists and newspaper companies were also engaged in promoting the jury system. The *Hōritsu Shinbun* (the *Legal News*) was a newspaper company that not only reported on the developments associated with the implementation of the jury system in Japan, but also took the initiative in organizing explanation sessions for the benefit of the general public.[181] Lawyer Masutarō Takagi established the *Hōritsu Shinbun* in 1900

---

175 I. Ansai, 1927, "Baishin Hō Senden to Mogi Saiban" [Promotion of the Jury Act and Mock Trials], *Hōritsu Shinbun*, October 25, pp. 3–4, at p. 3.
176 One of the correspondents of the *Hōritsu Shinbun* characterized the plays as useless, because they were written primarily for entertainment reasons (Anonymous, "Baishin Hō Mogi Saiban ni tsuite" [On Mock Jury Trials], p. 3).
177 Anonymous, "Baishin Hō Mogi Saiban ni tsuite" [On Mock Jury Trials], p. 4.
178 H. Watanabe, 1927, *Mie Ken Jin Pamfuretto: Baishin Seido no Hanashi* [Pamphlet for Citizens of Mie Prefecture: About the Jury System], Nagoya: Mie Ken Jin Kai Jimusho [Office of the Society of Citizens of Mie Prefecture], pp. 1–2.
179 *Id.*, p. 2.
180 *Id.*, pp. 2–3.
181 The *Hōritsu Shinbun* was not the only newspaper company actively engaged in the promotion efforts regarding the Jury Act. The Asahi Newspaper Company also published books on the subject of the Jury Act that explained the features of Japan's jury system and compared it with those existing in other countries (Tokyo Asahi Shinbunsha Shakaibu, *Baishin Kōza* [Lectures on the Jury [System]]).

with the goal of contributing to the dissemination of information concerning legal issues for the benefit of the general public. The editors of the newspaper closely followed the intricate process of the enactment of the Jury Act and welcomed the promulgation of this new piece of legislation. Specifically, an editorial in the issue published on March 28, 1923, stated that the promulgation of the Jury Act signaled the "fulfillment of the hopes of the people" and that it represented "the most important reform in the history of [efforts aimed at] protecting human rights" in Japan.[182] The *Hōritsu Shinbun* scrupulously reported the details of mock trials that took place in various cities across Japan and discussed the progress of the building of new jury courtrooms and jury accommodation facilities.[183] It was also engaged in the organization of seminars[184] and provided a forum for free discussion regarding the prospects of the jury system to academics, lawyers, and government officials. The effect that the introduction of the jury system might have on the judicial system of Japan in general and on the practice of relying on pre-trial investigations in particular was another topic that was deliberated.[185] Following the implementation of the jury system, the newspaper provided detailed information regarding jury trials in the country and published the verdicts of these trials.[186] When the first jury trial in Japan opened in the district court of Oita prefecture on October 23, 1928,[187] the newspaper characterized this first experience as a success.[188]

The Japan Jury Association (Dai Nippon Baishin Kyōkai)

Another group that was actively involved in the promotion efforts during the period of preparation for the introduction of the jury system in Japan and after the enforcement of the

---

182 Anonymous, 1923, "Baishin Hōan no Tsūka o Shukusu" [Celebrating the Passage of the Jury Bill], *Hōritsu Shinbun*, March 28, p. 3.
183 Anonymous, 1928, "Baishin no Oshigoto ni Isogashii Tōkyō Chihō Saibansho" [Tokyo District Court Busy with Preparations for the Jury], January 1, p. 1; Anonymous, 1928, "Baishin Saiban Kunren Hajimaru" [Jury Trial Training Starts], *Hōritsu Shinbun*, March 10, p. 17; Anonymous, 1928, "Kōji o Isogitsutsu Aru Tōkyō Chihō Saibansho Baishin Hōtei" [Construction of Jury Courtroom Speeded Up at Tokyo District Court], *Hōritsu Shinbun*, April 23, p. 1.
184 Anonymous, 1923, "Baishin Hō Kōenkai Kaisai ni tsuki Shakoku" [[Newspaper] Company Announcement Regarding Jury Act Lecture], *Hōritsu Shinbun*, June 23, p. 10.
185 The general consensus was that the introduction of the jury system would not radically change the Japanese legal system. Anonymous, 1928, "Baishin Hōtei o Haikei toshite no Yoshin, Hōtei Chūshin Shugi ka Yoshin Chūshin Shugi ka" [Pre-trial Investigations against the Background of Jury Trials; Courtroom-Centered or Pre-trial Investigation-Centered Approach?], *Hōritsu Shinbun*, April 8, p. 1; Anonymous, 1928, "Baishin Hō Jō no Gigi o Ronjite, Hōsō Kakui no Kōsetsu o Motomu (1)" [Discussing the Doubts Regarding the Jury Act, Opinions of Legal Professionals Wanted (Part 1)], *Hōritsu Shinbun*, June 13, p. 3; Anonymous, 1928, "Baishin Hō Jō no Gigi o Ronjite, Hōsō Kakui no Kōsetsu o Motomu (2)" [Discussing the Doubts Regarding the Jury Act, Opinions of Legal Professionals Wanted (Part 2)], *Hōritsu Shinbun*, June 15, p. 4; Anonymous, 1928, "Baishin Hō Jō no Gigi o Ronjite, Hōsō Kakui no Kōsetsu o Motomu (3)" [Discussing the Doubts Regarding the Jury Act, Opinions of Legal Professionals Wanted (Part 3)], *Hōritsu Shinbun*, June 23, p. 3.
186 For a reprint of articles mentioning jury trial decisions that were originally published in *Hōritsu Shinbun*, see Y. Inaba, 2000, *Shiryō de Miru: Baishin Hō Hanrei Shūsei* [Looking at Archive Materials: A Collection of Jury Trial Decisions], Tokyo: Gakujutsu Sensho.
187 Anonymous, 1928, "Baishin Saiban ni Seikō Shita Ōita Chihō Saibansho" [Oita District Court Successfully [Carries Out] Jury Trial], *Hōritsu Shinbun*, November 3, p. 1; Anonymous, 1928, "Ōita Chihō Saibansho Hatsu Baishin Hanketsu" [Oita District Court's First Jury Verdict], *Hōritsu Shinbun*, November 3, p. 17.
188 Anonymous, "Baishin Saiban ni Seikō Shita Ōita Chihō Saibansho" [Oita District Court Successfully [Carries Out] Jury Trial], p. 1.

82 The pre-war jury system

Jury Act was a semi-governmental organization known as the Japan Jury Association (*Dai Nippon Baishin Kyōkai*). This organization was established in November 1928 with the goal of "educating the general public with regard to the matters related to the jury system and law in general, while explaining the beauty of the Jury Act as the law of unprecedented importance".[189] Ever since its establishment, the organization was engaged in distributing pamphlets and other materials that focused on the developments in the Japanese legal system, such as "A Quick Guide to the Constitution" (*Kenpō Hayawakari*), "A Quick Guide to Trial by Jury" (*Baishin Hayawakari*), and the Japan Jury Newspaper (*Nihon Baishin Shinbun*)[190] to its members.[191] In order to fulfill its mission, the association also arranged excursions for jury candidates to courtrooms and jury accommodation facilities as well as prisons in several cities in Japan, planned lectures, seminars, and public viewings of promotional films about the jury system, and established a permanent attorney service and provided legal consultations to members free of charge. Despite its wide range of activities, the main interest of the organization was in promoting the institution of jury service. The Japan Jury Association authored a booklet titled "The Jury Guidebook", which contained the explanation of the institution of jury service in general and the provisions of Japan's pre-war Jury Act in particular in 1931.[192]

The association was formed "under the guidance" of Vice Minister of Justice and Professor of Law On Koyama, Professor Yoshimichi Hara, and Professor Kikunosuke Makino, who served as president of the Great Court of Judicature during the period between 1921 and 1923. The association was formed "with the participation" of Professor Kiichiro Hiranuma, Professors Kisaburō Suzuki, and Takuzō Hanai, as well as "other authoritative figures in the judicial circles outside and inside the government". The association thus included members of what can be seen as opposing camps in terms of how each saw the future of Japan and of its legal system. On the one hand, Baron Kiichiro Hiranuma and Professor Kisaburō Suzuki were associated with the right-wing camp that saw its goal in combating the spread of liberal ideas. Baron Hiranuma in particular is famous for promoting the development of Japan's thought police and for establishing the *Kokuhonsha* nationalist society in 1924. Kisaburō Suzuki was a protégé of Hiranuma and his colleague at the Ministry of Justice and fellow member of the *Kokuhonsha* society. Takuzō Hanai and Yoshimichi Hara, on the other hand, were associated with the movement towards democratization that aimed to establish a court system that would serve the interests of the people.[193] As of 1931, the association was headed by Katsutarō Yokoyama[194] and included 50,000 jury candidates

---

189 Shinomiya, *Baishin Tebiki* [Guidebook for Jury Service], p. 83. The Japan Jury Association was not the only organization established to promote the jury system. Another such organization was the Organization for the Promotion of the Jury System (*Baishin Seido Fukyū Kai*), which published a booklet explaining the features of Japan's pre-war jury system (Baishin Seido Fukyū Kai, 1927, *Baishin Hō no Jissai Chishiki: Baishin'in Hikkei* [Actual Knowledge Regarding the Jury Act: A Must-Have for Jurors], Tokyo: Kōshisha Shobō).

190 This newspaper was published by Japan Jury Newspaper Company and covered the first jury trials in great detail. Several articles that appeared in the newspaper are reprinted in Saikō Saibansho Jimu Sōkyoku Keiji Kyoku, *Wagakuni de Okonawareta Baishin Saiban* [Jury Trials That Took Place in Our Country], pp. 154–184.

191 Shinomiya, *Baishin Tebiki* [Guidebook for Jury Service], pp. 83–84.

192 *Id.*

193 Shimizu, "Senzen no Hōritsuka ni tsuite no Ichi Kōsatsu" [A Study Concerning Pre-war Lawyers], pp. 18–34.

194 Katsutarō Yokoyama (1877–1931) was a lawyer and member of Parliament, representing *Rikken Minseitō* (Constitutional Democratic Party).

"from all over Japan" as its members.[195] The fate of the Japan Jury Association is not clear. We may assume, however, that as the number of jury trials in Japan decreased and as World War II progressed, the decision was most likely made at some point to suspend the activities of the association.

In general, the way in which the institution of jury service was presented in the booklets, pamphlets, and through other means of promotion in the pre-war period reflected the contradictions in the views of the politicians, lawyers, and bureaucrats that were members of the Japan Jury Association and who supported the promulgation of the Jury Act. While some promotional materials emphasized the importance of the jury system as a means to empower the general public and to allow the people to participate more actively in the administration of the judicial branch of power, other documents describing the features of Japan's jury system focused on criticizing the jury systems existing in other countries and emphasizing the superiority of the system provided for by Japan's Jury Act. Materials belonging to the latter group stated, for instance, that the American jury was susceptible to bias and claimed that Japan's jury system was better, because in Japan the judges could overturn unjust opinions of the members of the jury.[196]

Implementation

On May 28, 1927, the Ministry of Justice released several documents that provided detailed instructions for the implementation of the Jury Act.

The first of these documents was the Ordinance for Enforcement of the Jury Act, which proclaimed that the lists of persons eligible for jury service would be compiled and outlined the particulars of the jury selection process.[197] It stipulated that candidates for jury service were to be chosen by lot using a special machine, a picture of which was provided in the document.[198]

Another was a confidential circular written by the vice minister of justice and addressed to presidents of all district courts of Japan. This document stated the specific tasks that district courts had to achieve in preparation for the enforcement of the Jury Act.[199] The circular paid particular attention to the timely and accurate preparation of the lists of persons eligible for jury service.[200]

The third document was the Imperial Ordinance No. 144, which stipulated that those articles of the Jury Act that were related to the compilation of the lists of persons eligible to

---

195 Shinomiya, *Baishin Tebiki* [Guidebook for Jury Service], p. 83.
196 One promotional pamphlet referred to the American jury system as "pitiful". Watanabe, *Mie Ken Jin Pamfuretto: Baishin Seido no Hanashi* [Pamphlet for Citizens of Mie Prefecture: About the Jury System], p. 20. An explanation of the strengths of Japan's Jury Act is also provided in R. Hayashi, 1926, *Baishin Hō Shakugi* [An Explanation of the Jury Act], Tokyo: Baishin Hō Fukyūbu, pp. 2–3.
197 Baishin Hō Shikō Kisoku, Ministry of Justice Ordinance for Enforcement of the Jury Act, Ordinance No. 16 of 1927, reprinted in K. Isotani and K. Yanagawa, 1927, *Baishin no Jōshiki* [The Common Sense of the Jury], Tokyo: Hōsō Kai, pp. 25–27 [hereinafter Ministry of Justice Ordinance for Enforcement of the Jury Act]. This ordinance was supplemented by a separate ordinance issued on July 25, 1928. Baishin Hō Shikō Kisoku Tsuika, Ministry of Justice Ordinance for Enforcement of the Jury Act (An Addition), Ordinance No. 18 of 1928.
198 Ministry of Justice Ordinance for Enforcement of the Jury Act, arts. 11 and 13. See Illustration 2 in the Appendix of this book.
199 Baishin'in Shikakusha Meibo no Chōsei ni Kansuru Toriatsukai Kijun [Standards for Approaching the Preparation of the List of Individuals Eligible for Jury Service], Ministry of Justice, Vice Minister of Justice Confidential Circular No. 123 of 1927, reprinted in Isotani and Yanagawa, *Baishin no Jōshiki* [The Common Sense of the Jury], pp. 34–36 [hereinafter Confidential Circular No. 123 of 1927].
200 Confidential Circular No. 123 of 1927, art. 2.

84 The pre-war jury system

serve as jurors would be enforced on June 1, 1927.[201] A separate ordinance mandated that the provisions of the Imperial Ordinance No. 144 be applied to Karafuto – the Japanese name for Sakhalin.[202]

Imperial Ordinance No. 146 provided a clarification to Article 12(3) of the Jury Act that stipulated that persons paying not less than three yen in national direct taxes were eligible for jury service.[203] The ordinance listed the following eight types of taxes that should be considered national direct taxes: (1) land tax; (2) schedule III income tax;[204] (3) business profits tax; (4) mineral tax; (5) taxes on capital; (6) urban residential property tax; (7) mining tax; and (8) fishing tax.

The ordinances issued in the subsequent months concerned the preparation of the funds for the payment of the travelling allowance, the allowance for every day of service, the accommodation allowance for jurors,[205] and the usage of the juror accommodation facilities.[206]

The Ministry set up the Jury Act Preparatory Committee (*Baishin hō junbi iinkai*) that included the bureaucrats working at the Ministry, officials working at district courts, and attorneys.[207] The goal of this committee was to ensure the smooth implementation of the Jury Act.

---

201 Baishin Hō Chū Ichibu Shikō Kijitsu no Ken [Regarding the Enforcement Date of a Part of the Jury Act], Imperial Ordinance No. 144 of 1927, reprinted in Isotani and Yanagawa, *Baishin no Jōshiki* [The Common Sense of the Jury], p. 32 [hereinafter Imperial Ordinance No. 144 of 1927]. This ordinance proclaimed that arts. 12, 14, 17, 26, 113, and 114 of the Jury Act would be enforced on June 1, 1927.
202 Baishin Hō no Ichibu o Karafuto ni Shikō Suru no Ken [Regarding the Enforcement of a Part of the Jury Act in Karafuto], Imperial Ordinance No. 145 of 1927, reprinted in Isotani and Yanagawa, *Baishin no Jōshiki* [The Common Sense of the Jury], p. 32 [hereinafter Imperial Ordinance No. 145 of 1927]. See Chapter 4 for the analysis of the functioning of the jury system in Karafuto.
203 Baishin Hō Dai 12 Jō no Chokusetsu Kokuzei no Shurui ni Kansuru Ken [Regarding the Types of National Direct Taxes as Mentioned in Art. 12 of the Jury Act], Imperial Ordinance No. 146 of 1927, reprinted in Isotani and Yanagawa, *Baishin no Jōshiki* [The Common Sense of the Jury], p. 32 [hereinafter Imperial Ordinance No. 146 of 1927].
204 *Dai Sanshu Shotokuzei*. Scheduler income taxation was introduced in Japan in 1899, and income tax was divided into three schedules: I (corporate income, tax rate 2.5%), II (interest, tax rate 2%), and III (personal income, tax rate 1% to 5.5%). Tax Bureau (Ministry of Finance), 2006, *The Comprehensive Guidebook of Japanese Taxes*, Tokyo: Tax Bureau (Ministry of Finance), p. 2, available online at http://www.cas.go.jp/jp/seisaku/hourei/data/jt.pdf.
205 Baishin Hō Ryohi, Nittō oyobi Shishuku Ryō Kisoku [The Rules Concerning the Travelling, Daily, and Accommodation Allowances for Jurors], Ordinance No. 234 of 1928.
206 Baishin'in Shukuhaku Kitei [Accommodation Regulations for Jurors], Ministry of Justice Criminal Affairs Bureau Instructions No. 7332 of 1928; Naishin In Shukusha Kitei Dai 7 Jō ni kansuru Ken [Regarding Article 7 of the Rules Concerning Jury Accommodation Facilities], Ministry of Justice Bureau of Criminal Affairs Circular No. 7333 of 1928, cited in Ōhara, "Baishin Hō no Jisshi Junbi ni tsuite" [Regarding the Preparation for the Enforcement of the Jury Act], pp. 311–312.
207 S. Motoji, 1929, "Baishin Hō Shiren Ichi Nen no Seiseki o Kaerimiru [Looking Back at the Results of the First Trial Year of the [Functioning of the] Jury Act], *Hōsōkai Zasshi* [Journal of the Law Society], Vol. 7, No. 10, pp. 29–50, at p. 41. This committee was established in 1927 and included the following members: Naohiko Seki, Fusaaki Uzawa, Masutarō Niida, Tsunetarō Shioya, Naoyoshi Tsukasaki, Head Prosecutor at the Court of Appeal Miki, Vice President of the Great Court of Judicature Isotani, President of the Tokyo Court of Appeal Wani, President of the Tokyo District Court Imamura, Prosecutor at the Great Court of Judicature Hayashi, Chief Public Prosecutor at the Tokyo District Court Yoshimasu, Judge at the Great Court of Judicature Uno, Parliamentary Vice-Minister Hamada, Parliamentary Councilor Kurozumi, and Director-General of the Criminal Affairs Bureau Motoji (Ōhara, "Baishin Hō no Jisshi Junbi ni tsuite" [Regarding the Preparation for the Enforcement of the Jury Act], pp. 318–319).

As of September 1, 1927 – the deadline for the compilation of the list of persons eligible to serve as jurors – the number of persons who satisfied the requirements set forth by the Jury Act totaled 1,701,232 persons.[208] The district courts across Japan estimated that 54,339 persons would be necessary to serve on cases tried in 1928.[209]

In 1928, the Ministry organized seminars for persons who had been selected as jury candidates to ensure that they were aware of their duties and knew what was required of them in the event they were selected to serve as jurors.[210]

The Jury Act in its entirety was enforced on October 1, 1928. On that day Emperor *Shōwa* issued a Rescript that stated the following:

> Judicial courts uphold the social order and preserve the rights of the people and thus determine the fate of the state. Now that the Jury Act has come into force, do your duty with even greater diligence and determination.[211]

The Japanese jury in action

During the fifteen years that the jury system functioned in Japan, 484 cases were tried by jury.[212] The number of cases tried by jury peaked at 143 in 1929. Given that the Ministry of Justice had estimated that approximately 2,300 cases would be tried by jury in 1928, this number was seen as disappointing.[213] The number of cases put to juries decreased steadily afterwards. In 1942, one year before the Jury Act was suspended, only two cases were tried by jury.[214] The majority of cases adjudicated with the participation of jurors involved accusations of homicide (215 cases) and arson (214 cases).[215]

The members of the jury in the majority of cases did not accept the facts of the crime as presented by the prosecutor.[216] The effect that this fact had on the perception of the jury system by the general public was puzzling to many. Instead of raising doubts regarding the usefulness of the jury system, the news concerning the frequent clashes of opinion between jurors and the prosecutors served to increase the level of trust on the part of the general public towards the Japanese system of justice.[217] This in turn unveiled the degree of suspicion associated with the quality of work of the office of the prosecutor in pre-war Japan.[218]

---

208 I. Suehiro, 1928, *Gendai Hōgaku Zenshū* [Full Collection of Works on Contemporary Law], Vol. 24, Tokyo: Nihon Hyōronsha, p. 365.
209 *Id.*, p. 365.
210 Ōhara, "Baishin Hō no Jisshi Junbi ni tsuite" [Regarding the Preparation for the Enforcement of the Jury Act], p. 316.
211 Baishin Hō ni Saishi Shihō Bu e Chokugo [Imperial Rescript [Addressed] to the Ministry of Justice on the Occasion of the Enforcement of the Jury Act], October 1, 1928.
212 Urabe, *Wagakuni ni okeru Baishin Saiban no Kenkyū: Keiken Dan ni yoru Jittai Chōsa o Chūshin toshite* [Research on Jury Trials in Our Country: A Study Focusing on the Actual Experiences], p. 10.
213 Anonymous, 1930, "Ōkina Kitai mo Hazure Funinki na Baishin Seido" [Unpopular Jury System Disappoints Great Expectations], *Hōritsu Shinbun*, June 28, p. 17.
214 *Id.*
215 Urabe, *Wagakuni ni okeru Baishin Saiban no Kenkyū: Keiken Dan ni yoru Jittai Chōsa o Chūshin toshite* [Research on Jury Trials in Our Country: A Study Focusing on the Actual Experiences], p. 9.
216 C. Minamitani, 1929, "Bōchō Seki yori Mitaru Baishin Saiban" [Jury Trials as Seen from the Seats for the Public [in the Courtroom], *Hōsōkai Zasshi* [Journal of the Law Society], Vol. 7, No. 10, pp. 116–119, at p. 117.
217 Takano, "Nihon ni okeru Baishin Hō no Shikō to Teishi: Hanseiten to Kongo ni Ikasu tame ni" [The Implementation and Suspension of Japan's Jury Act: Points for Reflection and Lessons to be Used for the Future], p. 22.
218 *Id.*, p. 22.

The jury system therefore did appear to be contributing to the improvement of the quality of justice in Japan during the first few years of its functioning and earned the support of the public. There was even talk of establishing the indictment lay assessor (*kiso sanshin*) system – that is, a system by which members of the general public would be selected to join the prosecutor to determine together whether the accused should be indicted.[219] While this initiative was never realized, the fact that the possibility of extending layperson participation in the judicial system of Japan even beyond the jury system was discussed illustrates the fact that there was a certain degree of enthusiasm that surrounded the Jury Act during the first few years after its enforcement.

Jury candidates approached their duty diligently. The number of instances when a jury candidate failed to report to the court was minuscule.[220] There were instances when a candidate appeared in court and carried out his duty despite having a sick parent.[221] There were other situations when candidates for jury service publicly discussed their disappointment when they were excused from service. They complained that they considered it a disgrace to return to their villages not having actually served as jurors.[222]

After the enforcement of the Jury Act, the need arose for the clarification of Article 77 of the Jury Act, which stipulated that the judge had the right to give instructions to the members of the jury regarding the case after the prosecutor and the defense delivered their closing arguments and prior to the jury deliberations. In its ruling on the question, the Great Court of Judicature (*Daishin'in*) defined the scope of the instructions that the judge could give to the jury. Specifically, it stated that the goal of the judge's instructions was to enable the members of the jury to understand the legal nuances of the case and that it was not to include the judge's opinion on the case.[223]

Records of several cases tried by jury in pre-war Japan have survived to this day. Among the best documented cases are Japan's first jury trial that took place in Oita prefecture and the first case to be tried by jury in the capital of the Japanese Empire, Tokyo. These two cases attracted a significant amount of attention from the general public and journalists.

The accounts of the first jury trials that appeared in Japanese newspapers are particularly interesting because they contain not only the objective description of facts and of the details of the first jury trial procedures, the methods of questioning used by the judge during the course of the hearings, the strategies of defense and prosecution, and the attitudes of the members of the jury, but also include the subjective element: personal impressions of their authors. The impressions of the authors of the articles, in turn, provided the readers with important insights into how the jury system was perceived by the general public at the time. The *Hōritsu Shinbun* (*Legal News*) provided particularly detailed accounts of the first jury trials. This attention to detail demonstrated by the journalists of the *Hōritsu Shinbun* most

---

219 H. Hirai, 1929, "Saiban Baishin yori wa Kiso Sanshin no Seido ga Nozomashii" [Rather than Court Jury, An Indictment Lay Assessor System Is Desirable], *Hōritsu Shinbun*, January 5, p. 17. Others discussed the possibility of the implementation of the grand jury in Japan (Mikami, "Baishin Hō no Shikō o Shuku shite" [Celebrating the Enforcement of the Jury Act], pp. 56–57).
220 Motoji, "Baishin Hō Shiren Ichi Nen no Seiseki o Kaerimiru [Looking Back at the Results of the First Trial Year of the [Functioning of the] Jury Act], p. 32.
221 *Id.*, p. 32.
222 Shinomiya, *Baishin Tebiki* [Guidebook for Jury Service], p. 41.
223 Motoji, "Baishin Hō Shiren Ichi Nen no Seiseki o Kaerimiru [Looking Back at the Results of the First Trial Year of the [Functioning of the] Jury Act], pp. 44–45.

likely resulted from the journalists' keen awareness of the needs of their readership, which consisted primarily of professional lawyers and persons in other professions who were interested in the developments in Japan's legal system.

In the period between 1928 and 1930 the *Hōritsu Shinbun* printed several articles reporting in great detail on the Oita and Tokyo trials.[224] These articles provide important details that shed light on what Japan's pre-war jury trial system was like in action.

The Oita and Tokyo trials were held in 1928 – the first year of the functioning of the jury system in Japan. Both trials involved offences that were punishable by death or imprisonment for life and were therefore examples of cases "designated by law to be tried by jury" (*hōtei baishin jiken*).

The accused in the Oita case was a thirty-four-year-old man who was charged with attempted murder of his mistress.[225] The prosecution maintained that the accused tried to kill the victim with a heavy kitchen knife when he found out that his mistress no longer loved him. The defense counsel sought to prove that the defendant did not have the intention to kill the victim. During the course of the trial, the members of the jury exercised their right to question witnesses in this case.[226] At the beginning of the hearings, a juror inquired about the average amount of alcohol that the defendant was in the habit of consuming. The *Hōritsu Shinbun* correspondent reporting on this case noted that the prosecutor, the defense, and the judge made deliberate efforts to ensure that statements were easy to understand for laypersons. After completing the hour-long instructions to the jury, the judge announced the main and supplementary questions for jury deliberations. The main question was, "Did the accused have the intention to kill and [did he] fail to succeed at fulfilling this intention?" The supplementary question was, "Did the accused inflict injury without the intention to kill?" The members of the jury discussed these questions for less than half an hour and wrote down their responses, which were subsequently read out in the courtroom. The answers were "No" to the main question and "Yes" to the supplementary question, meaning that the members of the jury found that the accused did not have the intention to kill. The judge agreed with the findings of the jury and sentenced the accused in accordance with the provisions of Article 204 to six months of penal servitude. The journalist of *Hōritsu Shinbun* noted that at the end of the trial the judge stated that he was in complete agreement with the members of the jury and that he believed that there was not enough evidence to support the claim that the accused had the intention to kill.

The defendant in the Tokyo trial of 1928 was a young woman accused of attempted arson.[227] The prosecutor argued that the defendant had deliberately set her house on fire to collect insurance money, which she intended to use to rescue her family business (the family of the accused owned a confectionary store) from debts. During the course of pre-trial investigations the defendant first confessed to committing the crime, but then withdrew her confession and pleaded not guilty, claiming that she had been forced to confess by the detective in charge of investigating the case. The detailed account of the trial that appeared in the

---

224 Anonymous, 1928, "Ōita Chihō Saibansho Hatsu Baishin Hanketsu" [Oita District Court First Jury Verdict], *Hōritsu Shinbun*, November 3, p. 17; Anonymous, 1928, "Tanteiteki Kyōmi o Sosoru Tokyo no Hatsu Baishin" [Tokyo's First Jury Trial: Detective Intrigue Overflowing], *Hōritsu Shinbun*, December 30, pp. 20–22.
225 KEIHŌ, arts. 199 and 108 (enumerating Homicide and Arson of Inhabited Buildings, respectively).
226 Jury Act, art. 70(2).
227 KEIHŌ, art. 108 (enumerating Arson of Inhabited Buildings).

88 *The pre-war jury system*

Hōritsu Shinbun demonstrates how the case of the prosecution that was primarily based on the initial confession of the defendant fell apart. The accused claimed the following:

> This detective told me that if I did not confess, I would not be able to return home [. . .] He even told me what to confess to, said that I poured gasoline on a newspaper and lit it up with a match![228]

In response to the judge's question concerning these allegations, the detective stated that he never used rough methods of questioning, but had nothing to say to the following remark that was made by a member of the jury:

> The witness is simply stating that he never asked leading questions, and that what the defendant has said is not true. Unlike the statement of the defendant, which is logically organized, there is something lacking in the testimony of this witness. Can't he answer in such a way that would persuade us?[229]

When another detective who had investigated the case on trial was put on the witness stand, another member of the jury inquired: "Could you detect finger prints on the box of matches, or did you not think of looking for them?" To this question – which the *Hōritsu Shinbun* correspondent noted "sounded like one coming from a professional" – the detective replied with "a devastated look on his face": "The box was wet and it was impossible [to get fingerprints]."[230]

The members of the jury not only scrutinized the testimony of crucial witnesses, but even the question that the judge set forth for jury deliberation. The question that the judge put to the jury was: "Did the defendant at 2 AM on March 15, 1928, set the two-*tatami* size *fusuma* door in her house on fire and then together with her husband extinguish it?" Upon hearing this question, the members of the jury "stood up one after the other and fiercely protested that they could not answer this question in the form of 'yes' or 'no' ". The judge was forced to provide the following explanation to the jury: "If you answer 'no', then this means that you find the defendant not guilty, if you answer 'yes', then it will imply that you find the defendant guilty, so please bear this in mind."[231] After deliberations, the members of the jury agreed on answering "no", and thus found the defendant not guilty. The judge agreed with the findings of the jury in this case and proclaimed the defendant not guilty.[232]

The Tokyo trial was in the spotlight of the attention of not only newspaper journalists eager to report the details of this case, but also of officials of the highest ranks. The *Hōritsu Shinbun* correspondent mentioned that on the first day of this trial, several officials sat at the back of the courtroom, observing the trial hearings. Officials in attendance included

---

228 Anonymous, 1928, "Tanteiteki Kyōmi o Sosoru Tokyo no Hatsu Baishin" [Tokyo's First Jury Trial: Detective Intrigue Overflowing], *Hōritsu Shinbun*, December 30, p. 22.
229 *Id.*, p. 22.
230 *Id.*, p. 22.
231 *Id.*, p. 22.
232 For a fascinating account and analysis of the Yamafuji case in English, see D. Flaherty, "Burning Down the House: Gender and Jury in a Tokyo Courtroom", S. L. Burns and B. J. Brooks (eds), 2014, *Gender and Law in the Japanese Imperium*, Honolulu: University of Hawai'i Press, pp. 159–186.

Minister of Justice Hara,[233] President of the Great Court of Cassation Makino,[234] President of the Tokyo Court of Appeal Wani,[235] Deputy Public Prosecutor of the Great Court of Cassation Hayashi,[236] President of the Tokyo District Court Tanaka, and some high-ranking officials from the Ministry of Justice, including vice ministers and parliamentary councilors (*san'yokan*).

These two cases tried by jury demonstrate first that the members of the jury in Japan took their duty seriously and actively made use of their right to question witnesses and to address questions to the judge. Second, the accounts of both jury trials reveal that the judge retained the role of the active party, responsible for supervising the gathering of evidence and the questioning of witnesses, which is characteristic of the inquisitorial system of justice. In both trials, it was the judge who addressed most questions to the witnesses and the defendant. Third, the details of the first jury trial cases show that the members of the jury – at least in the situation where every word of theirs was in the spotlight of public attention, as was the case with the first few trials that took place in Japan – were willing to express their opinions in the courtroom and even to reprimand the detectives investigating the case and openly question their professionalism. The members of the jury could influence the decisions of the court if their initiatives were not blocked by the judges.

While these developments were hailed by the proponents of the movement towards democratization in Japan and supported by the authors of the Jury Act of 1923, they became increasingly alarming to the members of the conservative movement. As the period of *Taishō* Democracy drew to a close, the influence of the right-wing nationalist forces on the Japanese government became more pronounced. As this happened, the authorities started displaying concern regarding the possibility that adherents of ideologies that are hostile to the current regime, most notably communists, who were routinely arrested after the promulgation of the Peace Preservation Act of 1925 might use jury trials as a tactic to secure a not guilty verdict. The power of Japan's pre-war jury was certainly limited by the provisions of the Jury Act that made their answers not binding on the court. The March 15 incident (*San Ichi Go Jiken*) that took place in 1928 and involved mass arrests of suspected communists under the provisions of the Peace Preservation Act[237] made it clear to the authorities that further measures were necessary to ensure that the adherents of socialist and communist ideologies would be denied access to trial by jury. This led to the 1929 amendment of the Jury Act that refused the right to trial by jury to defendants in cases involving the violation of the Peace Preservation Act.[238] Other justifications for the 1929 amendment included the following two claims: first, that the members of the jury might not be able to come up with impartial decisions in cases filed in accordance with the Peace Preservation Act; and second,

---

233 Yoshimichi Hara (1867–1944) served as Minister of Justice between April 1927 and July 1929 (Shimizu, "Senzen no Hōritsuka ni tsuite no Ichi Kōsatsu" [A Study Concerning Pre-war Lawyers] at pp. 21–22).
234 Makino Kikunosuke (1866–1936) served as president of the Great Court of Cassation during the period between 1927 and 1931 (Ichinose, *Major 20th Century People in Japan*, p. 2292).
235 Wani Teikichi (1870–1937) served as president of the Tokyo Court of Appeal and subsequently became president of the Great Court of Cassation – a post that Wani held during the period between 1931 and 1935 (*id.*, p. 2817).
236 Hayashi Raigiburō (1878–1958) subsequently became president of the Great Court of Cassation (1935–1936) and Minister of Justice (1936–1937). *Id.*, p. 2047.
237 Reischauer, *Japan: An Illustrated Encyclopedia*, p. 923.
238 Jury Act, art. 4(3).

that the adherents of communist ideologies might use their position as defendants to spread their beliefs in the courtroom.[239]

Amendments and suspension

The limitations of Japan's pre-war jury system became the subject of criticism as early as 1929. First, it turned out that the jury system was costlier to maintain than the authorities had expected. The costs of one jury trial averaged more than 300 yen.[240] In addition, the number of cases where the defendant requested jury trials began falling, while more and more defendants in cases that had to be tried by jury in accordance with the Jury Act started waiving their right to jury trial in favor of being tried by professional judges alone.[241] Apart from the aspects stipulated in the Jury Act that made jury trial less desirable for the accused, many defendants who had the option of being tried by jury chose to waive this right in an effort to protect their privacy. Jury trials tended to attract much more attention from the press than trials by professional judges, and the names of the defendants in as jury trial were certain to appear in the newspapers.[242]

The fact that the number of jury trials began to decrease in 1930 made some journalists write articles concerning the question of whether the institution of jury service fitted Japan's national character and demand that the jury system be abolished.[243] In 1936, legal scholar and President of the Kyoto Imperial University Yukitoki Takigawa described Japan's jury as "powerless" and the participation of laypersons in the judicial system under the provisions of the Jury Act a mere "formality".[244] Takigawa stressed that the limited power of the Japanese jury included in the provisions of the Jury Act constituted one reason for the lack of popularity of the system. According to Takigawa, the fact that in Japan the institution of jury service was introduced as a top-down measure by the government, and the lack of demand for such a system on the part of the general public was another.[245] These two factors made Takigawa conclude that the future of the Jury Act was "gloomy" and that legal

---

239 S. Motoji, "Baishin Hō Chū Kaisei Hōritsu An Riyū Setsumei" [Explanation of the Reasons [for Proposing] an Amendment to the Jury Act], reprinted in Motoji, "Baishin Hō Shiren Ichi Nen no Seiseki o Kaerimiru [Looking Back at the Results of the First Trial Year of the [Functioning of the] Jury Act], pp. 29–50, at pp. 38–40.
240 Anonymous, 1929, "Baishin Hiyō Ikken Sanbyaky En Ijō" [Jury Costs More Than 300 Yen per Case], *Hōritsu Shinbun*, January 28, p. 19.
241 M. Koyama, 1929, "Baishin Hō Jisshi Go no Seiseki ni tsuite" [On the Post-enforcement Results of the Jury Act], *Hōsōkai Zasshi* [Journal of the Law Society], Vol. 7, No. 10, pp. 9–17.
242 Anonymous, 1930, "Utsunomiya Chihō Saibansho to Shin Minso Oyobi Baishin Jisshi no Seiseki" [Utsunomiya District Court and the Results of the [Implementation] of the New Civil Code and the Jury [System]], *Hōritsu Shinbun*.
243 R. Yasushi, 1931, "Baishin Hō no Kekkan" [The Defects of the Jury System], *Hōritsu Shinbun*, August 3, reprinted in Midori, Masuda, Katō, and Kontani, "Hiroshima ni okeru Baishin Saiban [Jury Trials in Hiroshima], pp. 144–150, at p. 144. For an account of a jury trial held in Sendai in 1931 and of the criticism offered of the jury trial system by Prosecutor Yamai on this case in English, see Vanoverbeke, *Juries in the Japanese Legal System*, pp. 72–73. Yamai notes specifically that one of the drawbacks of the jury system as implemented in Japan is the fact that defense lawyers made sure to excuse those jury candidates who were highly educated (Vanoverbeke, *Juries in the Japanese Legal System*, p. 75).
244 Y. Takigawa, 1936, *Baishin Hō* [The Jury Act], Tokyo: Nihon Hyōronsha, p. 42.
245 *Id.*, pp. 42 and 51. See the section in Chapter 4 titled "The Jury System in Colonial Japan: The Colonized Peoples in Japanese Jury Courts" for a discussion of the critical views of Tatsuji Fuse on the jury trial system as implemented in Japan.

scholars like himself could do nothing but "watch in sadness how the Jury Act disappears from this world".[246]

Others were less pessimistic and proposed that amending the Jury Act would raise the popularity of the system.

Amendments

The first amendment of the Jury Act was the 1929 provision that made the members of the Communist Party and those defendants who were accused of violating the Peace Preservation Act ineligible for trial by jury. This was not, however, the only amendment of the Jury Act.

In 1937, a proposal was submitted to the Imperial Diet that would make it possible for those cases that were of a particularly complex nature and involving several defendants to be tried by professional judges alone at the request of the prosecutor. The reasoning for this proposal was that complex cases would take a lot of time to adjudicate and would therefore be costly for the government.[247] The proposal was submitted in order to find a resolution for the arson case that was tried by jury in Kanagawa prefecture in 1932.[248] Japan's Bar Associations, however, opposed this amendment. Several days prior to the discussion of this proposal the Teikoku Bar Association and the Dai Ichi Tokyo Bar Association issued an opinion statement opposing this amendment.[249] While admitting that Japan's jury system needed to be improved, the members of the associations argued that in other countries complex cases with many witnesses were tried by jury, and that Japan should not be an exception.[250] In 1937 another proposal for the amendment of the Jury Act was submitted to the House of Representatives by Shizuo Makino and eight other members. This document proposed to expand the range of cases that may be tried by jury without an explicit request from the defendant to include offences punishable by imprisonment for more than three years, to allow the jury verdict to be appealed *kōso* on points of fact, to delete the provision of the Jury Act that allowed the judge to dismiss the jury and call for a retrial, and to add a provision that would make jury trial free for the accused.[251] The members of the House of Representatives voted for this proposal to be considered further.[252] Neither of the proposals discussed in 1937 resulted in amendment of the Jury Act.

---

246 *Id.*, p. 51.
247 Teikoku Gikai Shūgiin Giji Sokkiroku Dai 5 Gō [Stenography of the Proceedings of the House of Representatives, the Imperial Diet No. 5], the 71st Session, 1937, reprinted in Tokyo Daigaku Shuppan Kai (ed.), 1984, *Teikoku Gikai Shūgiin Giji Sokkiroku 69* [Stenography of the Proceedings of the House of Representatives], Tokyo: University of Tokyo Press, pp. 77–78.
248 Dai Ichi Tokyo Bar Association and Teikoku Bar Association, 1937, "Baishin Hō Chū Kaisei Hōritsu An (Seifu Teishutsu) ni Taisuru Hantai Ikensho" [Opinion Statement Opposing the Proposal for Amending the Jury Act (Submitted by the Government)], July 21, reprinted in Nihon Bengoshi Rengōkai [Japan Federation of Bar Associations], *Nihon Bengoshi Enkaku Shi* [A History of the Origins of [the Profession of] Attorney in Japan], pp. 197–201, at p. 199.
249 *Id.*, pp. 197–201.
250 *Id.*, pp. 201 and 199.
251 Teikoku Gikai Shūgiin Giji Sokkiroku Dai 7 Gō [Stenography of the Proceedings of the House of Representatives, the Imperial Diet No. 7], the 71st Session, 1937, reprinted in Shuppan Kai (ed.), *Teikoku Gikai Shūgiin Giji Sokkiroku 69* [Stenography of the Proceedings of the House of Representatives], pp. 114–115.
252 The members of the House of Representatives voted for the proposal to be considered further by a group of members especially appointed for the purpose of considering the possible amendments to the Jury Act (*Baishin Hō Chū Kaisei Hōritsu An no Iin*). *Id.*, p. 115.

In 1938, Masatake Naitō submitted a proposal that incorporated the ideas stated in Makino's draft. This proposal was passed by the House of Representatives and submitted for consideration to the House of Peers.[253] During the deliberations at the House of Representatives, it was argued that because the amendments proposed by Naitō affected the fundamentals of the Jury Act they required careful consideration, and that a special council should be set up with the goal of proposing the necessary changes to the Jury Act. Naitō's proposal was never adopted.[254]

Another proposal for amending the Jury Act was discussed in 1941. Unlike the previous efforts, this proposal was adopted. The 1941 amendment of the Jury Act consisted of a change in the frequency with which the lists of jury candidates were prepared. The provision that stated that these lists were to be drawn up every year was amended to read "once in four years".[255] The amendment was motivated by the fact that there were not as many cases tried by jury as was expected initially.

Suspension

The possibility of suspending the Jury Act became the subject of discussion in Japan's Parliament in 1943, when the government submitted the Proposal for the Suspension of the Jury Act (*Baishin Hō no Teishi ni Kansuru Hōritsu An*) to the House of Peers. Minister of Justice Michiyo Iwamura explained to the members of the House of Peers that this proposal was prepared for two reasons. First, in view of the fact that the popularity of jury trials was very low as of 1943, it was necessary to free the heads of cities, towns, and villages from the administrative duties of creating the lists of persons eligible to serve as jurors. Second, Iwamura argued that while jury trials necessitate the presence of many witnesses in court during the public hearing, becoming a witness was a burden for the citizens of a country that was at war.[256] The House of Peers did not object to the arguments of the Minister of Justice, and the proposal was submitted to the House of Representatives.

The deliberations at the House of Representatives featured arguments for and against the suspension of the Jury Act. Some speakers urged members to abolish rather than suspend the Jury Act in view of the fact that the jury system was unpopular and costly to maintain. Others argued that at times of war it was necessary to strengthen the judicial system of the country and to ensure that human rights were protected in the courtroom, and warned that if the government ignored citizens' rights, the people might turn against it.[257] Finally, the members of the House of Representatives decided that the Jury Act should be suspended during the period that Japan was at war. The Act Suspending the Jury Act

---

253 Saibansho Kōsei Hō Kaisei Hōritsu An Tokubetsu Iinkai Giji Sokkiroku Dai 2 Gō [Stenography of the Proceedings of the Special Committee on the Proposal for Amendment of the Court Organization Law], p. 1, cited in Takano, "Nihon ni okeru Baishin Hō no Shikō to Teishi: Hanseiten to Kongo ni Ikasu tame ni" [The Implementation and Suspension of Japan's Jury Act: Points for Reflection and Lessons to Be Used for the Future], p. 25.
254 *Id.*, p. 25.
255 Jury Act, art. 22.
256 *Teikoku Gikai Kizokuin Giji Sokkiroku*, 1943, p. 75.
257 *Teikoku Gikai Shūgiin Iin Kaigi Roku*, 1943, pp. 140–170.

was promulgated on April 1, 1943.[258] This Act stipulated that the jury system would be reintroduced as soon as the war was over, but did not set forth any details as to the time when this would be done.[259]

Evaluating Japan's pre-war experience with jury trials

The system provided for by the pre-war Jury Act was the first experience of Japan with layperson participation in the process of administrating justice.

Why was the layperson jury system introduced for the first time in Japan in the late *Taishō* period? As this chapter has demonstrated, a combination of several broad and specific developments produced a desire in both the general public and in the Japanese elite to push for increased rights for citizens during this period in Japan's history.

Among the broad developments that formed the background to the implementation of the jury system was the move towards democratization known as *Taishō* Democracy. This period was characterized by the strengthening of the position of elected bodies that were established in the *Meiji* period and by the expansion of the political involvement of the general public. The political parties for the first time in Japan's history had the freedom to act on questions of national policy, while the members of the general public chose to actively participate in popular movements that not only protested against certain decisions of the government (the *Hibiya* riot), but also made specific demands (the universal manhood suffrage movement).

The developments closely associated with the system of justice, on the other hand, included, first, the establishment of Japan's Federation of Bar Associations. The association's commitment to lobby for the implementation of the jury system set in motion a series of events that ultimately led to the unanimous acceptance of the proposal to introduce jury trials at the Imperial Diet in 1910. The growing disappointment with the quality of justice in Japan as administered by professional judges alone added force to the idea to implement the jury system. The *Nittō* incident of 1909 made the public question the reliability of public officials, while the High Treason case of 1910 gave rise to suspicions that the Japanese system of justice was not an independent branch of power, but one that could be used for political purposes. The public debate that followed the adjudication of these two cases highlighted the harsh conditions of the accused following arrest and the omnipotent position of the prosecutor in the Japanese justice system. The introduction of the jury system increasingly came to be seen as a way to prevent the possible abuses of power on the part of the professional judges. The importance of this debate was heightened further when the *Rikken Seiyūkai* made the proposal to introduce the jury system one of its causes. The support of this political party was critical for the transformation of the proposal to implement the jury system from an abstract idea into an item on the political agenda.

The Japanese government was initially reluctant to introduce the layperson jury system. The Ministry of Justice repeatedly proposed to postpone the discussion of the drafting of the piece of legislation that would form the basis for citizen participation in justice.

---

258 Baishin Hō no Teishi ni kansuru Hōritsu [Act on the Suspension of the Jury Act], Law No. 88 of 1943 [hereinafter Act on the Suspension of the Jury Act].
259 *Id.*, art. 3.

94 *The pre-war jury system*

The situation changed dramatically, however, with the inauguration of Takashi Hara's government. Hara's interest in the jury system and active support for the drafting of the Jury Act appears to have stemmed from two basic considerations. On the one hand, he was genuinely interested in improving the justice system in Japan and believed that the introduction of the layperson jury would enhance the position of the accused in the courtroom. On the other hand, Hara saw the jury system as the lesser of two evils, the second being universal suffrage. He supported the idea to implement the jury system in an attempt to head off the more far-reaching demands of the public in relation to universal suffrage. The political will of Takashi Hara was crucial for the drafting of the Jury Act.

Was Japan's pre-war jury system a success? As this chapter has shown, there is evidence that the pre-war jury system contributed to improving the quality of justice in Japan during the first years of its functioning by serving to broaden the perspectives of professional judges on cases. The opinions of the members of the jury could influence court decisions, provided the initiatives of the jury were not blocked by the judges. Further, as the details of the first cases tried by jury in Japan indicate, Japanese jurors took their duty seriously and, actively expressed their opinions in the courtroom. Despite this fact, however, the institution of jury service never became popular with the users of the system. After 1929, more and more defendants in cases that had to be tried by jury in accordance with the Jury Act waived their right to jury trial in favor of being tried by professional judges, while those of the accused who could request to be tried by jury chose not to do so. The situation where neither of the legal actors saw any benefits in using the jury system implied that the system was failing to function effectively.

What were the factors that led to the jury system's failure to take root in Japan? The change in the political and social situation that Japan witnessed between the Japan Federation of Bar Associations' proposal to implement the jury system in the first decade of the 20th century and the suspension of the jury system in 1943 doubtlessly played a part. At the beginning of the 20th century, Japan was moving towards democratization, while in the 1930s and 1940s democratic developments gave way to the movement towards fascism and nationalism. The aggressive politics of Japan on the international stage implied that Japan was involved in war, which provided the direct motive for the suspension of the jury system, as this institution came to be seen as superfluous and costly to maintain. The start of the war also meant that prospective jurors – men over thirty years of age – joined the army. In addition, Japan's turn to nationalism resulted in the decrease in the prestige of the West, the exporter of the concept of jury trials – a factor that also contributed to the decline in the popularity of jury trials.

While the aforementioned factors affected the jury system's ability to function effectively in Japan, it is clear that the lack of popularity of the jury system also stemmed from the nature of the provisions of the enacted version of the Jury Act.

As this chapter has demonstrated, the original draft of the pre-war Jury Act envisaged the implementation of the Anglo-American model of jury trials in Japan. As deliberations continued, however, this original model was modified. The jury system provided for by the enacted version of the Jury Act differed in several respects from its common law adversarial counterpart. The most important of these differences were that (1) the findings of the pre-war jury could be ignored by the judge and (2) the provisions of the act discouraged defendants from using the system.

What was the rationale behind adding the provisions that differentiated Japan's pre-war jury from the Anglo-American model and ultimately served to limit the popularity of jury trials by making it unbeneficial for the defendants to use trial by jury? It appears likely that the drafters made deliberate modifications to the adversarial jury with the goal of adjusting it to fit the external environment in which the system was to operate. Specifically, the drafters tried to adapt the adversarial jury system to the principles of inquisitorial procedure (through adding provisions that allowed the judge to continue to make final decisions on the guilt or innocence of the accused), to the political environment of militaristic Japan (through denying access to jury trials to the adherents of communist and socialist ideologies), and to the features of Japan's hierarchical society (through limiting the powers of the jury and magnifying the role of the judge in proceedings). In other words, Japan tried to create and introduce a jury trial system that had the "virtues" but not the "vices" of the Western model of the jury system.

Ironically, and contrary to the intentions of the drafters of the Jury Act, these modifications became the stumbling blocks that prevented the jury system from functioning effectively. In a country where citizens were said to prefer trial by professional judges to that by fellow citizens, the provisions of the Jury Act that gave the judge the right to disregard the jury's responses and call another jury could only serve to further undermine the authority of trial by jury. Criminal defendants who were interested in requesting trial by jury – adherents of the socialist and communist ideologies and those accused of violating the Peace Preservation Act – were deprived of this right by the 1929 amendment of the Jury Act, while those defendants who remained eligible for trial by jury were discouraged from requesting it by the stipulations that made it more advantageous to be tried by professional judges. The sharp decline in the popularity of jury trials that followed the 1929 amendment and the subsequent suspension of the Jury Act clearly indicate that even if Japan's pre-war system was free of the vices of the Western model of jury trial, it no longer had the virtues either.

While some scholars have argued that the jury system as implemented in pre-war Japan was incompatible with the basically inquisitorial law of criminal procedure that existed in Japan at the time of its introduction, and that this misfit was to blame for the trouble with the functioning of jury trials,[260] it appears that the opposite was true: the problem lay not in the fact that the jury system was not adapted enough to fit in with Japan's inquisitorial system of justice, but in the fact that Japan's jury was an excessively adapted version of the Anglo-American model. Similarly, the so-called cultural argument that attributes the lack of popularity of jury trials in pre-war Japan to the hierarchical nature of Japan's society – which is governed by the relative status of parties and is guided by the traditional attitude of "Respect for Officials and Contempt for the People" – fails to take into account the fact that the enacted version of the pre-war Jury Act provided for a system where the judge's position was paramount and where the opinions of laypersons could be disregarded if different from the conclusions reached by the judge. Instead of introducing a system that conflicted with or sought to change the traditional attitudes of "Respect for Officials and Contempt for the People", the Jury Act of 1923 provided for a system that was compatible with these attitudes and reinforced them.

To use Watson's terminology, the Japanese legislators adapted the transplant to ensure macro and micro fit with the Japanese environment, but in so doing they modified the imported concept in such a way that completely undermined its internal validity. This fact, in turn, doubtlessly contributed to the decrease in the motivation and enthusiasm on the part of legal actors – judges, attorneys, defendants, and government officials – with regard to the jury system. A system that was introduced with the hope that it would serve to change

---

260 Tanaka, *The Japanese Legal System*, p. 490.

Japan's justice system for the better ended up being perceived as a superfluous institution without any real power, which the excessive adaptations made it to be.

Conclusions

This chapter focused on Japan's first experience of implementing the layperson jury system.

As argued in this chapter, with regard to the first research question it was the combination of several broad developments affecting the whole of Japan's society and of specific events related exclusively to the justice system that resulted in the introduction of jury trials. The former consisted of the movement towards democratization, known as *Taishō* Democracy. The latter included the following:

(1) The establishment of the Japan Federation of Bar Associations;
(2) The occurrence of several high profile cases that cast doubt on the quality of the Japan's justice system and gave rise to the view that introducing trials by laypersons may serve to improve the process of adjudication of justice in Japan;
(3) The emergence of the *Rikken Seiyūkai* as one of the most prominent political parties and the commitment of its members to push for the implementation of jury trials;
(4) The political will of Prime Minister Hara, who considered the institution of jury service as a means to improve the quality of justice and to head off the more far-reaching demands of the public in relation to universal suffrage.

With regard to the second research question, there were two factors behind the failure of the jury system to gain popularity and take root in pre-war Japan included: the change in the political and social situation in Japan, as the country moved towards militarization, fascism, and nationalism in the 1930s and 1940s; and the problems within the Jury Act. The chapter looked at Japan's pre-war jury as a system that represented a unique cross between the Anglo-American adversarial jury and the Continental-European mixed-court jury. The features that distinguished the Japanese jury system from the Anglo-American model upon which it was originally based were added by the legislators in an effort to adjust the Anglo-American model to fit the external environment in which the system was to operate. Based on this analysis, the failure of the pre-war jury system to function effectively stemmed from excessive adaptation by the government of the concept of jury trials to fit the judicial, political, and cultural environment of Japan. The chapter concluded that instead of ensuring the smooth functioning of the imported concept, which appears to have been the intention of the drafters of the 1923 Jury Act, the modifications that made Japan's jury system unique served to undermine the internal integrity of the concept of jury trials. They transformed the jury from an institution that was originally conceptualized as a means for improving the quality of justice in Japan into one that was purely ornamental in nature. In view of these characteristics, the decision on the part of the Japanese government to suspend the jury system during war, when cutting costs and eliminating all that was seen as superfluous became a priority, appears to have been entirely justified.

Chapter 4 takes us back in time to the late 1920s and early 1930s – the first decade of the functioning of the pre-war jury system – and discusses the attempts to extend the right to be tried by jury to the colonies of the Japanese Empire.

4 Attempts to introduce the jury system in Japan's colonial possessions

This chapter discusses the attempts to introduce the institution of jury service in the colonial possessions of the Japanese Empire. Its primary focus is on two of Japan's colonies – Taiwan (where Japan's pre-war Jury Act was never enforced) and Karafuto, the Japanese name for Sakhalin, where the Jury Act functioned without any modifications until it was suspended in mainland Japan in 1943. This chapter shows that at a time when in mainland Japan the defects of the system provided for by the Jury Act started being discussed, the nationals of the colonial possessions of the empire saw the notion of trial by laypersons as a source of hope for achieving justice and greater equality with the colonizers.

The chapter begins with an overview of Japan's imperial conquests and of the country's overall strategy for administering its colonial possessions. It then discusses the case of Taiwan – Japan's first colony – where the possibility of introducing the jury trial system was discussed in the late 1920s and early 1930s. The section devoted to Taiwan opens with a brief outline of the history of the island and of its legal system prior to the start of the Japanese colonial period, proceeds to describe the political and legal developments during the years of Japanese rule, and concludes by outlining the proposals to introduce the jury system made by the members of the Taiwanese elite. The analysis of the reasons behind the failure of these proposals to lead to reform is followed by a discussion of the case of Karafuto and of the factors that lay behind the government's decision to extend the application of the pre-war Jury Act to this but not to any of Japan's other colonial territories. The chapter then discusses the position of the colonial peoples in courts in mainland Japan, noting that nationals of colonial territories found themselves in the position of criminal defendants in trials that were adjudicated with the participation of jurors in mainland Japan. This section describes the details of one such trial. The concluding sections analyze the successful and failed attempts to introduce the jury system in Japan's colonies and summarize the findings of the chapter.

Historical background: Japan and its colonies

By the time the pre-war Jury Act was enforced in Japan, the country had transformed itself into a powerful empire whose colonial possessions constituted more than three-quarters of its territory.[1] The only non-Western colonial empire, Japan acquired Taiwan in 1895, the southern part of the island of Karafuto in 1905, and Korea in 1910.[2] Japan began

---

1 Edwin O. Reischauer (ed.), 2003, *Japan: An Illustrated Encyclopedia*, Tokyo: Kōdansha, p. 214.
2 The Kingdom of Ryukyu, an island kingdom formed in 1412, lost its independence in 1872 when the *Meiji* government of Japan formed the Ryukyu *han* (feudal domain) in its place (G. H. Kerr, 2000,

administering a part of the Liadong peninsula in southern Manchuria – the Kwantung territory – in 1905 when, following the conclusion of the Treaty of Portsmouth and the Sino-Japanese Treaty, the Russian rights within the leased territory were transferred to Japan.[3] In 1914, the Japanese army established control over the Pacific Islands – the most of what constitutes Micronesia.[4]

Japan's colonial expansion implied the need to develop a strategy for ruling over the newly added territories. As Japanese historian and politician Yosaburo Takekoshi put it in 1907,

> [n]ew territory may be won by the sword, and a wide-spreading dominion may for a time be kept up by force; but unless the conquering nation possesses the qualifications necessary for the administration of its possessions, decay and dissolution inevitably follow.[5]

The Japanese government was clearly determined not to allow "decay and dissolution" to ensue, and actively sought to devise a colonial strategy that would allow the mainland to effectively rule over its new territories.

As was the case with its modernization efforts, Japan chose to examine the strategies employed by the older colonial powers, most notably Britain and France, as it sought to develop its own strategy for colonial administration. The British Empire gave a significant degree of autonomy to its colonial possessions. By contrast, France chose to follow the strategy of assimilation for its colonies – an approach that was based on the republican principles of 1789 that stipulated that all parts of the country's territory constituted an indivisible republic where the French civilization should be propagated.[6] The formulation of Japan's colonial policy involved "adopting" elements from the Western experience while making sure to "adapt" the imported notions to ensure that in their combination they would assist

---

Okinawa: The History of an Island People, Boston: Tuttle, pp. 360–371). In 1879, the Ryukyu *han* was abolished and Okinawa prefecture established. The king of the Ryukyus abdicated in the same year, marking the completion of the process of annexation of the Ryukyus to Japan. As the Ryukyus were treated as part of the Japanese mainland from the time Okinawa prefecture was established, the islands are not discussed in this chapter. See Chapter 5 for an overview of the post-war history of Okinawa and of the functioning of the jury system on the islands during the period of the U.S occupation.

3 Taiwan became Japan's first colony in 1895 by the terms of the Treaty of Shimonoseki that was concluded at the end of the Sino-Japanese war. The southern part of Karafuto and the Kwantung territory were ceded to Japan in 1905 following the Russo-Japanese war (see J. J. Stephan, 1971, *Sakhalin: A History*, Oxford: Clarendon Press, p. 86; C. W. Young, 1931, *The International Legal Status of the Kwantung Leased Territory*, Baltimore: Johns Hopkins Press, p. 50).

4 The League of Nations gave Japan the mandate to administer control over these territories that had been purchased by Germany in 1919. M. R. Peattie, 1988, *Nan'yō: The Rise and Fall of the Japanese in Micronesia, 1885–1945*, Honolulu: University of Hawai'i Press, pp. 41 and 56.

5 Y. Takekoshi (translated by G. Braithwaite), 1907, *Japanese Rule in Formosa*, London: Longmans, Green, p. 1. A member of the *Rikken Seiyūkai*, Yosaburo Takekoshi (1865–1950), is known as a vocal opponent of militarism and communism (Shakai Kagaku Daijiten Henshū Iinkai [Editorial Committee of the Encyclopedic Dictionary of the Social Sciences] (ed.), 1975, Shakai Kagaku Daijiten [The Encyclopedic Dictionary of the Social Sciences], Vol. 12, Tokyo: Kagoshima Kenkyūjo Shuppankai, p. 305).

6 *Id.*, p. 5. See also Takekoshi, *Japanese Rule in Formosa*, pp. 27 and 29–30; E. I. Chen, "The Attempt to Integrate the Empire: Legal Perspectives", in R. H. Myers and M. R. Peattie (eds), 1984, *The Japanese Colonial Empire, 1895–1945*, Princeton: Princeton University Press, pp. 240–274, at p. 240.

Japan in achieving its own objectives and reflect the unique aspects of the Japanese colonial experience.[7]

Indeed, the Japanese Empire was unlike the older empires of the West in a number of respects. First, Japan's colonial possessions were mostly acquired as a result of considerations aiming to further the country's strategic interests in an effort to contain the Western advances in the region, while security was not the primary concern for most European colonial powers.[8] Second, the majority of Japan's colonial possessions were neighboring nations with cultures that were perceived to be based on the same heritage as that of the colonizer.[9] Third, the overseas settlement of the members of the colonizing nation never became an important activity in the Japanese Empire. All of its possessions – with the exception of Karafuto – remained in essence "occupation colonies" where only a relatively small number of Japanese people lived among large groups of the native populations.[10] Finally, Japan's was an empire with a unique culture and ideology that underpinned its colonial strategy.

The careful consideration on the part of the Japanese government of these characteristics eventually resulted in the development of a model of colonial administration that was not duplicated elsewhere.[11] Japan's colonial policy placed the highest priority on furthering the economic and strategic interests of the mainland, discouraged self-rule in the colonies, and was based on a uniquely defined notion of assimilation (*dōka*).

Protecting the integrity of the empire was a consideration that was high up on the agenda of the Japanese government, given the reality that the degree of the presence of the members of the colonizing nation was limited in the absolute majority of the colonial possessions of the empire. This fact, coupled with the perceived similarity between the cultural heritage of the Japanese mainland and of its new territories, provided the rationale for the decision to implement a range of policies aimed at the eventual elimination of all differences between the colonized nations and the nation-colonizer and the ultimate absorption of the former by the latter.[12]

The notion of assimilation as used with regard to Japan's colonial efforts (*dōka*) stemmed from a different set of assumptions than that propagated by the French Empire. At the ideological level, it was based on the concept of "impartiality and equal favor" (*isshi dōjin*).[13] In accordance with this notion, the peoples of the newly added territories were expected to eventually be integrated within the "family" of the Japanese people, headed by the Emperor (*kōmin*) who would bestow equal favor to all of his subjects – those who lived in the mainland and those who were based in Japan's colonial territories.

The more liberal interpretation of the notion of *isshi dōjin* highlighted the need to ensure that the colonized had the same rights as the colonizer, while the more conservative view of this concept placed emphasis on the fact that the members of the colonized nations were to

---

7 M. R. Peattie, "Introduction", in Myers and Peattie (eds), 1984, *The Japanese Colonial Empire, 1895–1945*, pp. 3–52, at p. 6.
8 *Id.*, p. 8.
9 *Id.*, p. 7.
10 *Id.*, p. 8.
11 *Id.*, p. 6.
12 M. R. Peattie, "The Japanese Colonial Empire, 1895–1945", in P. Duus (ed.), 1988, *The Cambridge History of Japan*, Vol. 6, New York: Cambridge University Press, pp. 217–270, at p. 238. The strategy of Japan towards its colonies was not monolithic and underwent change over the course of time.
13 *Id.*, p. 241.

have the same obligations towards the state, but not the same privileges as the colonizers. Eventually, the latter view became the guiding principle for the colonization strategy that the Japanese Empire adopted.[14]

It was in the context of this broad colonization strategy that the Japanese government was making decisions regarding the pieces of legislation and institutions that it would transplant to its newly acquired territories. Herself an active recipient of legal transplants, Japan, now an empire in possession of colonial territories, found itself in the position of the "exporter" of legal concepts for the first time in history. In the process of determining which aspects of its own legal architecture to transplant to its colonies and at what time, the Japanese government was guided by the principles that had shaped its decisions when adopting foreign institutions on the one hand and by the consideration of its strategic interests in terms of keeping the empire together on the other. It evaluated the presence or absence of "fit" between the imported rule and the host environment in its colonies while being aware of the strategic importance of discouraging self-rule in its territories.

As the pros and cons of the institution of jury service were deliberated in mainland Japan prior to and following the enforcement of the Jury Act in 1928, the possibility of extending the right to be tried by jury and to serve on a jury became a subject of discussion in relation to two of Japan's colonial possessions: Karafuto and Taiwan. The application of the Jury Act was extended to Karafuto in 1927,[15] and the jury system functioned on the island until 1943 when the Jury Act was suspended in mainland Japan. By contrast, in Taiwan – Japan's first colony – the discussion of the possibility of introducing the jury system did not lead to reform.

The deliberations concerning the possibility of introducing the jury system in Taiwan and Karafuto were carried out against the background of tension created by the two opposing interpretations of the concept of "impartiality and equal favor". In Karafuto, this debate was carried out within the Japanese government and did not involve the participation of the members of the colonized peoples. In Taiwan, it took place in the context of changes that characterized Japan's colonial strategy towards ruling the island on the one hand and the transformation of the perspectives on Japanese rule on the part of the Taiwanese elite on the other.

At the point of arrival of the Japanese troops to Taiwan in 1895, the attitudes towards the prospect of becoming a colonial possession of the Japanese Empire on the island were influenced by the perceptions of the notion of foreign rule that had been formed over the course of the island's history.

Taiwan: attempts to introduce the jury system in the Japanese colonial period

Taiwan and its laws prior to Japanese colonial rule

There is no agreement among historians regarding the time when the island of Taiwan was first inhabited. Several early sources mistakenly included Taiwan in the group of islands constituting

---

14 *Id.*, p. 241.
15 Imperial Ordinance No. 145 of 1927; Takumu Daijin Kanbō Bunsho Ka [The Secretariat and Document Division of the Ministry of Colonial Affairs], 1931, *Chōsen, Taiwan, Karafuto, Kantōshū oyobi Nan'yō Guntō ni Okonawaruru Hōritsu Chō* [A List of Pieces of Legislation Enforced in Korea, Taiwan, Karafuto, Kwantung, and Micronesia], Tokyo: Takumu Daijin Kanbō Bunsho Ka [The Secretariat and Document Division of the Ministry of Colonial Affairs], p. 3.

the Ryukyu chain and thus failed to provide accurate descriptions of the origins of the inhabitants of the island.[16] It appears likely that the Taiwan aboriginal peoples who belong to the Proto-Malay group were the first group of people to permanently settle in Taiwan.[17] The *Han* Chinese arrived in Taiwan in the 12th century when the Pescadores became a part of China's Fukien province.[18] Taiwan was first discovered by the Europeans in 1544 and was named "Ilha Formosa", or "beautiful island", by the Portuguese.[19] Japanese traders who came to Taiwan from Nagasaki, Kyoto, and Sakai in 1592 named the island "Takasago", because the scenery of the island reminded them of that of Takasago in Harima province, Japan.[20]

The island's history features several periods of colonial rule that affected the legal system of the island. The Dutch Republic became the first country to colonize Taiwan when its forces arrived on the island in 1624 to establish a base for trading with China.[21] The Dutch East India Company was entrusted with the administrative, judicial, diplomatic, and other functions of sovereignty over the southern part of the island.[22] The administrative and judicial functions were carried out by the governor appointed by the Dutch East India Company and his council under the supervision of the East Indian government in Batavia.[23] Dutch rule exposed Taiwan to the notion of legal pluralism – a system under which different bodies of law are established to govern the affairs of different groups within one country.[24] During the Dutch colonial period local chiefs were entrusted with the task of adjudicating cases involving the aborigines and the *Han* Chinese residing on the island, while Dutch justice was applied to cases involving the Europeans.[25]

16 J. W. Davidson, 1903, *The Island of Formosa: Past and Present*, Taipei: SMC, p. 2; Takekoshi, *Japanese Rule in Formosa*, p. 54.
17 S. Hishida, 1907, "Formosa: Japan's First Colony", *Political Science Quarterly*, Vol. 22, No. 2, pp. 267–281, at p. 267; T. Wang, 2000, *Legal Reform in Taiwan under Japanese Colonial Rule, 1895–1945: The Reception of Western Law*, Seattle: University of Washington Press, p. 13; D. Mendel, 1970, *The Politics of Formosan Nationalism*, Los Angeles: University of California Press, p. 11; H. Mukōyama, 1983, "Nihon Tōchika ni okeru Taiwan no Hō to Seiji: Minzoku Hōgaku no Shiten ni Tatte" [Law and Politics in Taiwan under Japanese Rule: From the Standpoint of Ethnological Jurisprudence], *Kokugakuin Hōgaku*, Vol. 21, No. 2, pp. 61–106, at pp. 62–64.
18 Wang, *Legal Reform in Taiwan under Japanese Colonial Rule, 1895–1945*, pp. 13–14.
19 Davidson, *The Island of Formosa*, pp. 9–10. The names "Formosa" and "Taiwan" are used interchangeably in the English-language literature concerning the period of Japanese colonial rule over the island. This chapter refers to the island as "Taiwan".
20 Takekoshi, *Japanese Rule in Formosa*, p. 53.
21 M. Peng and Y. Ng, 1983, *Taiwan no Hōteki Chii* [The Legal Status of Taiwan], Tokyo: University of Tokyo Press, p. 6.
22 D. Angelino, 1931, *Colonial Policy*, Vol. 2, The Hague: Nijhoff, pp. 2–3; Wang, *Legal Reform in Taiwan under Japanese Colonial Rule, 1895–1945*, p. 14. It should be noted that initially the Dutch occupied only the northern part of Taiwan, but subsequently extended the territory subject to their rule to include the northern part of the island (Wang, *Legal Reform in Taiwan under Japanese Colonial Rule, 1895–1945*, p. 212).
23 Wang, *Legal Reform in Taiwan under Japanese Colonial Rule, 1895–1945*, pp. 14–15; Angelino, *Colonial Policy*, Vol. 2, p. 8. The Dutch East India Company was established in 1602 (G. Oostindie and B. Paasman, 1998, "Dutch Attitudes towards Colonial Empires, Indigenous Cultures, and Slaves", *Eighteenth-Century Studies*, Vol. 31, No. 3, pp. 349–355, at p. 349).
24 Sally E. Merry defines legal pluralism as "a situation in which two or more legal systems coexist in the same social field" (S. E. Merry, 1988, "Legal Pluralism", *Law & Society Review*, Vol. 22, No. 5, pp. 869–896, at p. 870) and as a system that involves the establishment of "different bodies of law for different groups of the population varying by ethnicity, religion, nationality, or geography" (*id.*, p. 871).
25 Wang, *Legal Reform in Taiwan under Japanese Colonial Rule, 1895–1945*, pp. 14–15; Oostindie and Paasman, "Dutch Attitudes towards Colonial Empires, Indigenous Cultures, and Slaves", p. 351.

In 1626 the northern part of Taiwan was colonized by another nation – Spain.[26] As a result, for a period of time the island found itself under the rule of three countries: the Dutch Republic had authority over the southern part of the island, Spain administered the north of Taiwan, and the Pescadores remained under the jurisdiction of *Ming* China.[27] This period in Taiwan's history came to a close with the end of Spanish colonial rule in 1642[28] and the collapse of Dutch rule in 1662, when Zheng Chenggong (known in Western sources as Koxinga) defeated the Dutch forces and forced them out of Taiwan.[29] The Zheng government sought to restore the *Ming* dynasty in China and viewed Taiwan as a base from which this goal could be achieved.[30] Martial law was established on the island during the period of Zheng's rule that continued until 1683 when the *Qing* dynasty established authority over Taiwan.[31]

During the period of *Qing* rule, no special laws were promulgated in Taiwan, with the Great *Qing* Code being used as the main source of law on the island.[32] Two provisions of the code were of particular relevance to the island. The common feature of these provisions was that they helped the administration of the island to prevent Taiwan from rebelling against the regime.[33] Specifically, the code gave government officials in Taiwan the right to execute persons guilty of committing robbery or treason and banned the manufacture of guns on the island.[34]

At the end of the 19th century, Japan began displaying an active interest in the island for the first time since the 16th and 17th centuries – a time when the links between Japan and

---

26 It should be noted that Dutch colonialism started against the background of struggle against Spain (Oostindie and Paasman, "Dutch Attitudes towards Colonial Empires, Indigenous Cultures, and Slaves", p. 349).
27 Wang, *Legal Reform in Taiwan under Japanese Colonial Rule, 1895–1945*, p. 14.
28 Hishida, "Formosa", p. 267.
29 *Id.*, p. 267. Zheng Chenggong (1624–1662) was born in Hirado, Nagasaki, Japan, and died in Taiwan. Some sources refer to Zheng as a "general" (Hishida, "Formosa", p. 267) while others call him a "pirate king" (see, for example, C. P. Fitzgerald, 1951, "Peace or War with China?", *Pacific Affairs*, Vol. 24, No. 4, pp. 339–351, at p. 341). See generally R. C. Krozier, *Koxinga and Chinese Nationalism: History, Myth, and the Hero*, Cambridge, MA: Harvard University Press, pp. 11–17 (containing a brief bibliographical account of the life of Zheng Chenggong). It should be noted that by 1662, the interest of the Dutch in Taiwan had decreased due to the fact that the volume of trade with China was declining (Angelino, *Colonial Policy*, Vol. 2, p. 5; Wang, *Legal Reform in Taiwan under Japanese Colonial Rule, 1895–1945*, p. 15).
30 Wang, *Legal Reform in Taiwan under Japanese Colonial Rule, 1895–1945*, p. 16.
31 *Id.*, p. 17.
32 *Id.*, p. 19.
33 *Id.*, p. 19.
34 *Id.*, p. 19. Local customs continued to play an important role in Taiwan (for a comprehensive account of Taiwan's customary law, see S. Okamatsu, 1902, *Provisional Report on Investigations of Laws and Customs in the Island of Formosa Compiled by Order of the Governor-General of Formosa*, Kobe: Kobe Herald, reprinted in S. Okamatsu, 1971, *Provisional Report on Investigations of Laws and Customs in the Island of Formosa, Compiled by Order of the Governor-General of Formosa*, Taipei: Ch'eng Wen), and the process of dispute resolution was based on the Chinese tradition (Wang, *Legal Reform in Taiwan under Japanese Colonial Rule, 1895–1945*, p. 24). Just as in mainland China, there was a preference for informal dispute resolution with the participation of village elders (Wang, *Legal Reform in Taiwan under Japanese Colonial Rule, 1895–1945*, pp. 24, 95). See also G. J. Chang, 1978, "The Village Elder System of the Early Ming Dynasty", *Ming Studies*, Vol. 7, pp. 53–62. For an overview of the history of Taiwan prior to the start of the Japanese colonial period, see K. Uchida, "Taiwan Tōchi Shi" [A History of the Administration of Taiwan], in H. Noyori (ed.) *Meiji Taishō Shi* [A History of the Meiji and Taisho Periods], Vol. 1, Tokyo: Meijō Taishō Shi Kankōkai, pp. 285–290.

Taiwan were initially established.[35] In 1583, Toyotomi Hideyoshi attempted to order that Taiwan submit tribute to Japan. There was no government in Taiwan at the time to receive the order, however, so Toyotomi Hideyoshi's envoys had to leave without meeting the primary objective of their visit.[36] The Tokugawa *shogunate* attempted to take the island by force in 1615 – an effort that was not successful because of a typhoon.[37] It was more than two centuries later that another chance to incorporate Taiwan into its sphere of influence presented itself. In 1874, Japan invaded the island in an attempt to respond to the murder of fifty-four Ryukyuan sailors by the Taiwanese in 1871.[38] While the primary objective for Japan in carrying out this mission was to assert its rights over the Ryukyu Islands by indicating to the international community that protecting the interests of Ryukyuans was the prerogative of the *Meiji* government rather than of the government of China, the events that transpired during the course of this mission served to deepen Japan's interest in the island as a potential colonial possession.[39] In 1895, Japan defeated China in Manchuria and Korea, and Taiwan, along with the Pescadores, was ceded to Japan.[40]

Taiwan under Japanese colonial rule

The Treaty of Shimonoseki was signed by the governments of Japan and China in May 1895. According to the terms of the treaty, China was obliged to pay reparations in the amount equivalent to twice China's national income and permanently ceded the island of Taiwan and the Pescadores to Japan.[41]

The conclusion of the Treaty of Shimonoseki presented the Japanese government with a dilemma that had to be revisited with regard to each of the colonies that Japan acquired subsequently. The dilemma consisted of the question whether the laws and the Constitution of the Empire of Japan – the *Meiji* Constitution of 1889 – were to be made applicable in the new territories of the empire.[42]

As the Japanese government had considered the French and British models of colonial rule in the course of developing its own strategy for administering its new territories generally, it was only natural that it chose to seek the advice of the French and British consultants at the Japanese Ministry of Justice in preparation for addressing this question.[43]

---

35 The island was first discovered by Japanese pirate-traders in 1560 (Wang, *Legal Reform in Taiwan under Japanese Colonial Rule, 1895–1945*, p. 13; Takekoshi, *Japanese Rule in Formosa*, p. 53).
36 Takekoshi, *Japanese Rule in Formosa*, p. 53.
37 Traders from Nagasaki came to Taiwan in 1592 (Wang, *Legal Reform in Taiwan under Japanese Colonial Rule, 1895–1945*, p. 13, and Takekoshi, *Japanese Rule in Formosa*, pp. 49–53).
38 See generally L. Gordon, 1965, "Japan's Abortive Colonial Venture in Taiwan, 1874", *Journal of Modern History*, Vol. 37, No. 2, pp. 171–185.
39 *Id.*, p. 171.
40 Treaty of Shimonoseki, 1895, full text available online at "Taiwan Documents Project", http://www.taiwandocuments.org/shimonoseki01.htm [hereinafter Treaty of Shimonoseki]. See P. Cheng, M. Letz, and J. D. Spence (eds), 1999, *The Search of Modern China: A Documentary Collection*, New York: W. W. Norton, pp. 173–177, for a transcript of the discussions held between the Chinese and the Japanese plenipotentiaries at Shimonoseki.
41 Treaty of Shimonoseki, arts. 2 and 4.
42 Chen, "The Attempt to Integrate the Empire", p. 245; M. S. Kim, *Law and Custom in Korea: Comparative Legal History*, New York: Cambridge University Press, p. 107.
43 Michel Revon (1867–1943) was a French jurist. Born in Switzerland, Revon started serving as a consultant to the Japanese government in 1888. While in Japan, Revon conducted research on Japanese culture. Upon returning to France in 1899, he taught at the University of Paris (S. Shimamoto, 1986,

Michel Revon, the French consultant to the Japanese government, argued that Taiwan should be regarded as "a prefecture of Japan in the future, if not now", and that consequently those sections of the *Meiji* Constitution that outlined the subjects' rights as well as Japan's Criminal Law should be applied in Taiwan immediately.[44] Montague Kirkwood, on the other hand, advised that Taiwan be treated as a colony and as a territory that was distinct from Japan. Kirkwood suggested that the Legislative Council be established in Taiwan and that this council should be appointed by the governor-general. He argued that the constitution of the Japanese Empire should only be applied in those territories that were a part of Japan at the time of its promulgation and that Japan should appoint local administrators and judges in Taiwan. Kirkwood's decision to recommend that Japan choose not to extend the application of its constitution to Taiwan was based on the understanding of the fact that the enforcement of the constitution would necessarily imply the extension of the right to elect the members of the Imperial Diet to the people of Taiwan – a development that, he argued, Japan was not ready for.[45] In addition, the application of the *Meiji* Constitution on the island implied that the Taiwanese would be required to pay Japanese taxes, and this, Kirkwood noted, was likely to have a negative influence on the attempts of the Japanese government to establish and maintain its rule on Taiwan.[46]

In order to determine the most appropriate course of action, in June 1895 the Taiwan Affairs Bureau was set up to deliberate the comments of the two advisors.[47] Hara Takashi, who was acting as a representative of the Ministry of Foreign Affairs at the bureau at the

---

"*Furansu ni okeru Nihon Kenkyū no Kaitakusha Misheru Rubon: Rubon Ke Tanpōki*" [Michel Revon – a Pioneer in [the Field of] Japan Studies in France: Notes of the Investigation [Concerning] Revon's Family], *Kenkyū to Hyōron* [Research and Reviews], Vol. 37, pp. 82–91; Dai Nippon Bunmei Kyōkai [The Japanese Civilization Society], 1924, *Meiji Bunka Hasshō Kinenshi* [Journal Commemorating the Birth of *Meiji* Culture], Tokyo: Dai Nippon Bunmei Kyōkai, p. 28). William Montague H. Kirkwood (1850–1926) was a noted British barrister who first came to Japan in 1874. Having served at the British legation and consulate, Kirkwood was invited to become a legal consultant to the *Meiji* government in 1885 – a position that he retained until either 1901 or 1902 (Y. Tezuka, 1947, "Shihō Shō Oyatoi Gaijin Kākuddo" [Kirkwood – A Foreign Consultant Employed by the Ministry of Justice], *Hōgaku Kenkyū*, Vol. 40, No. 3, pp. 55–65; Dai Nippon Bunmei Kyōkai [The Japanese Civilization Society], 1924, *Meiji Bunka Hasshō Kinenshi* [Journal Commemorating the Birth of *Meiji* Culture], Tokyo: Dai Nippon Bunmei Kyōkai, p. 6).

44 M. Revon, "Ryōtō oyobi Taiwan Tōchi ni kansuru Tōgi" [An Opinion Concerning the Liadong Peninsula and Taiwan], in I. Hirobumi, 1936, *Hisho Ruisan* [Classified Collection of the Private Documents of Itō Hirobumi Relating to *Meiji* Development], Vol. 18 ("Taiwan Shiryō" [Sources [Related to] Taiwan]), Tokyo: Hisho Ruisan Kankōkai, pp. 399–409; Chen, "The Attempt to Integrate the Empire", p. 249.

45 M. Kirkwood, "Shokumichi Seido" [Colonial System], in Hirobumi, *Hisho Ruisan* [Classified Collection of the Private Documents of Itō Hirobumi Relating to *Meiji* Development], Vol. 18, pp. 108–148; Chen, "The Attempt to Integrate the Empire", pp. 249–250. See also M. Kirkwood, "Taiwan Seido, Tennō no Taiken oyobi Teikoku Gikai ni kansuru Ikensho [An Opinion on the Taiwan System, the Supreme Power of the Emperor, and the Imperial Diet], available in Hirobumi, *Hisho Ruisan*, Vol. 18, pp. 78–107.

46 Chen, "The Attempt to Integrate the Empire", p. 249.

47 M. Haruyama, "Kindai Nihon no Shokuminchi Tōchi to Hara Kei" [Modern Japan's Colonial Rule and Hara Kei], in M. Haruyama and M. Wakabayashi (eds), 1980, *Nihon Shokuminchishugi no Seijiteki Tenkai, 1995–1934* [Political Evolution of Japanese Colonialism], Tokyo: Ajia Seiken Gakkkai, pp. 1–67, at p. 3. The Taiwan Affairs Bureau was an organ that consisted of nine members who represented different ministries and governmental agencies (Hirobumi Itō (Premier), Sōroku Kawakami (Vice-Chief of Staff), Miyoji Itō (Chief Cabinet Clerk), Takashi Hara (Foreign Affairs), Gentarō Kodama (Army), Gonnohyōe Yamamoto (Navy), Kenchō Suematsu (Justice), Inajirō Taijiri (Finance), and Kenjirō Den (Communications)) and was conceptualized as a central institution to oversee the administration of Taiwan (Chen, "The Attempt to Integrate the Empire", p. 250).

time, expressed support for Michel Revon's proposal to integrate Taiwan as a prefecture of Japan in view of the fact that the island was geographically close to mainland Japan and because of the many cultural similarities between Japan and Taiwan – a situation that Hara observed was substantially different from that facing European colonizers.[48] Hara argued for the extension of not only the constitution, but of as many Japanese laws as feasible to Taiwan to ensure the smooth incorporation of the island into Japan.[49]

The fierce resistance on the part of the Taiwanese towards the establishment of Japanese rule on the island made the Japanese government drop the plans aimed at integrating Taiwan as a prefecture of Japan, however. The approach favoring eventual assimilation (*dōka*) was to be adopted in relation to Taiwan subsequently, following a period of military rule and what may be referred to as the period of compromise – a time when a model allowing for a limited degree of autonomy was implemented.

During 1895 and 1896 the Japanese military ruled over Taiwan, with the military orders (*nichirei*) rather than Japan's Diet-enacted statutes (*hōritsu*) becoming the major source of law on the island.[50] The first order issued by the Japanese military on July 6, 1895, provided for the penalty of death for various resistance activities.[51] In October 1895, a military tribunal was established to adjudicate civil and criminal cases.[52] The resistance on the part of the Taiwanese was assumed to be suppressed sufficiently enough to establish a civilian government on April 1, 1896. The first civilian courts were set up in the same year, and the Japanese government began working on creating a legal framework for the island.[53]

---

48 T. Hara, "Taiwan Mondai Ni An" [Two Views on Taiwan], in Hirobumi, *Hisho Ruisan* [Classified Collection of the Private Documents of Itō Hirobumi Relating to *Meiji* Development], Vol. 18, pp. 32–34, partially reproduced in M. Haruyama, "Kindai Nihon no Shokuminchi Tōchi to Hara Kei" [Modern Japan's Colonial Rule and Hara Kei], in M. Haruyama and M. Wakabayashi (eds), 1980, *Nihon Shokuminchishugi no Seijiteki Tenkai, 1995–1934* [Political Evolution of Japanese Colonialism, 1995–1934], Tokyo: Ajia Seiken Gakkkai, pp. 1–67, at pp. 23–24.
49 Hara, "Taiwan Mondai Ni An"; M. Haruyama, "Kindai Nihon no Shokuminchi Tōchi to Hara Kei" [Modern Japan's Colonial Rule and Hara Kei], p. 24; Chen, "The Attempt to Integrate the Empire", p. 250; Wang, *Legal Reform in Taiwan under Japanese Colonial Rule, 1895–1945*, p. 37.
50 Wang, *Legal Reform in Taiwan under Japanese Colonial Rule, 1895–1945*, p. 38.
51 Taiwan Jinmin Gunjihan Shobun Rei [Order on Handling Offences [Committed on the Part of] the People of Taiwan [Against] the Japanese Army], Order of July 6, 1985 [hereinafter Order on Handling Offences [Committed on the Part of] the People of Taiwan [Against] the Japanese Army]. Article 1 of this Order provided a list of punishable offences against the Japanese army, which included the following: (1) resisting the Japanese army; (2) damaging railroads and bridges; and (3) harboring enemies or setting them free (Wang, *Legal Reform in Taiwan under Japanese Colonial Rule, 1895–1945*, p. 45 and p. 222).
52 Taiwan Sōtokufu Hōin Shokusei [The Organizational Structure of the Governor General of Taiwan Office Court], Order No. 11 of October 7, 1895 [hereinafter The Organizational Structure of the Governor General of Taiwan Office Court], reproduced in Taiwan Sōtokufu [The Office of the Governor-General of Taiwan], 1896, *Taiwan Sōtokufu Reikiruishō* [Excerpts from the Orders and Regulations of the Office of the Governor General of Taiwan], Taipei: Taiwan Sōtokufu [The Office of the Governor-General of Taiwan], pp. 8–11, on file with the National Diet Library of Japan, Tokyo; Wang, *Legal Reform in Taiwan under Japanese Colonial Rule, 1895–1945*, pp. 45 and 222.
53 Taiwan Sōtokufu Hōin Jōrei [The Governor General of Taiwan Office Court], Ordinance No. 1, 1896, available in Taiwan Sōtokufu [The Office of the Governor-General of Taiwan], *Taiwan Sōtokufu Reikiruishō* [Excerpts from the Orders and Regulations of the Office of the Governor General of Taiwan], pp. 1–3, on file with the National Diet Library of Japan, Tokyo; Wang, *Legal Reform in Taiwan under Japanese Colonial Rule, 1895–1945*, p. 223.

106 *Attempts to introduce the jury system*

In March 1896, Japan's Imperial Diet passed the Law Relating to Laws and Ordinances to Be Enforced in Taiwan, Law No. 63 (Title 63).[54] Title 63 granted the authority to issue ordinances (*ritsurei*) that had the same power in Taiwan as ordinances and statutes passed by the Imperial Diet in Japan proper to the governor-general of Taiwan.[55] The statutes enforced in Japan proper could be applied to Taiwan, but only if they were accompanied by "an ordinance for application" (*shikō chokurei*).[56] In other words, the enactment of Title 63 established Taiwan as a special territory within the Japanese Empire where the governor-general, rather than the Imperial Diet, had the supreme legislative authority.[57] This strategy of "delegated legislation" (*inin rippō*) represented a compromise between the two proposals that had been made by Revon and Kirkwood concerning the treatment of Taiwan.[58] With the promulgation of Title 63, the pieces of legislation concerning Taiwan were authored and enacted on the island rather than in mainland Japan – provisions that would have arguably been supported by Kirkwood. At the same time, Title 63 did not outlaw the extension of Japanese laws to the island and thus allowed Japan to retain the possibility of following the course of action that Revon had advocated.

Initially enforced for the duration of three years, Title 63 was extended repeatedly until 1906 when it was revised by the Law Relating to Laws and Ordinances to Be Enforced in Taiwan, Title 31.[59] Title 31 stipulated that the *ritsurei* as enforced in Taiwan should not be in conflict with those Japanese statutes that were applied in the colony, and thus signaled an attempt on the part of the colonial authorities to ensure the smooth functioning of the legal system as established on the island.[60] Title 31 was initially enforced for the period of five years, but was extended until 1921 when it was replaced by Title 3.[61]

---

54 Taiwan ni Shikō Subeki Hōrei ni kansuru Hōritsu [The Law Relating to Laws and Ordinances to Be Enforced in Taiwan], Law No. 63 of 1896 (Title 63), amended by Law No. 7 of 1899 and Law No. 20 of 1902, translated in Wang, *Legal Reform in Taiwan under Japanese Colonial Rule, 1895–1945*, pp. 192–193 [hereinafter Title 63].
55 Gaimushō Jōyakukyoku Hōkika [Ministry of Foreign Affairs, Department of Treaties, Division of Laws and Regulations], 1959, *Taiwan no Inin Rippō Seido* [Taiwan's System of Delegated Legislation], Tokyo: Gaimushō Jōyakukyoku Hōkika [Ministry of Foreign Affairs, Department of Treaties, Division of Laws and Regulations], p. 7.
56 Wang, *Legal Reform in Taiwan under Japanese Colonial Rule, 1895–1945*, pp. 38–39.
57 The governor-general was also in possession of executive and military authority in Taiwan (Wang, *Legal Reform in Taiwan under Japanese Colonial Rule, 1895–1945*, p. 39; H. C. Ts'ai, 2009, *Taiwan in Japan's Empire Building: An Institutional Approach to Colonial Engineering*, London: Routledge, p. 16).
58 Haruyama, "Kindai Nihon no Shokuminchi Tōchi to Hara Kei" [Modern Japan's Colonial Rule and Hara Kei], p. 3; Chen, "The Attempt to Integrate the Empire", p. 248; Ts'ai, *Taiwan in Japan's Empire Building*, p. 16. It should be noted that Title 63 became the subject of criticism in mainland Japan in view of the fact that it gave the governor-general of Taiwan legislative authority, which according to some participants in the debate should have remained the sole prerogative of the Imperial Diet (E. Chen, 1972, "Formosan Political Movements under Japanese Colonial Rule, 1914–1937", *Journal of Asian Studies*, Vol. 31, No. 3, pp. 477–497, at p. 482).
59 Taiwan ni Shikō Subeki Hōrei ni kansuru Hōritsu [The Law Relating to Laws and Ordinances to Be Enforced in Taiwan], Law No. 31 of 1906 (Title 31), amended by Law No. 50 of 1911 and Law No. 28 of 1916, translated in Wang, *Legal Reform in Taiwan under Japanese Colonial Rule, 1895–1945*, p. 193 [hereinafter Title 31].
60 Title 31, art. 5.
61 Taiwan ni Shikō Subeki Hōrei ni kansuru Hōritsu [The Law Relating to Laws and Ordinances to Be Enforced in Taiwan], Law No. 3 of 1921 (Title 3), translated in Wang, *Legal Reform in Taiwan under Japanese Colonial Rule, 1895–1945*, pp. 193–194 [hereinafter Title 3].

Title 3, in turn, was enacted to reflect the change in the colonial policy of Japan towards Taiwan that featured a turn towards assimilation. In a speech delivered at the session of the Imperial Diet that enacted Title 3, Prime Minister Hara indicated that his fundamental vision was to make Taiwan "the same as mainland Japan" (*naichi dōyō ni itashitai*) as soon as "conditions permit", and used the example of the Ryukyu Islands to indicate that Taiwan with its distinct culture could be assimilated into Japan.[62] Title 3 provided for the use of "ordinances for exception" (*tokurei chokurei*).[63] These ordinances were issued when a Japanese statute was to be applied in Taiwan and outlined the differences in terminology and other technical changes that were deemed necessary in order for that Japanese statute to be smoothly enforced in Taiwan. The introduction of the notion of ordinances for exception made it possible to more easily transfer Japanese statutes to Taiwan, as it was no longer necessary to request the Imperial Diet of Japan to pass supplementary provisions for the colony whenever there was the need to extend a Japanese piece of legislation to Taiwan.[64] Title 3 reemphasized the supremacy of Japanese law that was applied in the colony by stipulating that ordinances (*ritsurei*) were to be issued by the governor-general only in those instances when a corresponding Japanese statute did not exist, when promulgating a Japanese statute with the accompanying "ordinances for exception" was difficult, or when there was the need to issue an ordinance to respond to the unique circumstances in Taiwan.[65] Unlike Titles 63 and 31, Title 3 did not have a predetermined period of application and was used until the end of the period of Japan's colonial rule in 1945.[66]

A discussion of the legal framework that was established in Taiwan during the years of Japan's administration would be incomplete without mentioning several special criminal laws promulgated on the island.[67] Laws that were applied only in Taiwan included the 1898 Bandit Punishment Law, which provided for the penalty of death to two or more persons who were engaged in an act of violence, and the 1900 Taiwan Press Law that provided for strict controls on the freedom of the press in Taiwan.[68] Other Taiwanese special laws applied only to certain groups of citizens living on the island. Among the laws that were exclusively applied to Japanese citizens living in Taiwan was the 1900 Taiwan Peace Preservation Law,

---

62 K. Hara, speech at the 44th Session of the Imperial Diet, partially reproduced in Haruyama, "Kindai Nihon no Shokuminchi Tōchi to Hara Kei" [Modern Japan's Colonial Rule and Hara Kei], p. 70. Prime Minister Hara had promoted this vision for Taiwan ever since he became prime minister in 1919. Hara approved the candidacy of the first civilian governor-general in Taiwan, Kenjirō Den, as a first step towards realizing this vision (Wang, *Legal Reform in Taiwan under Japanese Colonial Rule, 1895–1945*, p. 53).
63 Title 3, arts. 1 and 2; Wang, *Legal Reform in Taiwan under Japanese Colonial Rule, 1895–1945*, p. 41.
64 This process continued being required in Korea where the equivalent of Title 31 was retained without revision (Wang, *Legal Reform in Taiwan under Japanese Colonial Rule, 1895–1945*, pp. 41–42).
65 *Id.*, p. 42.
66 Haruyama, "Kindai Nihon no Shokuminchi Tōchi to Hara Kei" [Modern Japan's Colonial Rule and Hara Kei], pp. 69–70. The years between 1921 and 1945 – the period when Title 3 was applied – therefore came to be known as "the ordinance as a main source of law" period. The period between 1895 and 1921 is referred to as "the *ritsurei* as the main source of law" period (Wang, *Legal Reform in Taiwan under Japanese Colonial Rule, 1895–1945*, p. 44).
67 Special laws are defined as pieces of legislation that are applied to a particular community or class or for particular geographical areas (H. C. Black (ed.), 1979, *Black's Law Dictionary*, St. Paul: West, p. 1253).
68 Hito Keibatsu Rei [Bandit Punishment Law], Emergency Ordinance No. 24 of 1898, translated in Wang, *Legal Reform in Taiwan under Japanese Colonial Rule, 1895–1945*, pp. 196–197 [hereinafter Bandit Punishment Law] and Taiwan Shinbunshi Jōrei [Taiwan Press Law], Ordinance No. 3 of 1900. See Wang, *Legal Reform in Taiwan under Japanese Colonial Rule, 1895–1945*, p. 47; Chen, "Formosan Political Movements under Japanese Colonial Rule, 1914–1937", p. 482.

which stipulated that those persons who had violated the laws that were in operation in Taiwan were to be expelled from the island.[69] The laws that applied only to the Taiwanese included, for example, the 1898 *Hokō* Law, which was based on the Chinese traditional *pao-chia* system that obligated all members of a *kō* (ten households) and *ho* (a group of ten *kō*) to bear responsibility for the crime committed by an individual member.[70]

The policy of assimilation that was adopted and promoted by Prime Minister Hara in relation to Taiwan and that resulted in the promulgation of Title 3 implied the gradual increase in the number of those pieces of mainland legislation and those institutions that were to be transplanted to the island. The possibility of implementing Japan's pre-war Jury Act – a law that was actively promoted by Hara – in Taiwan was discussed on several occasions during the period of Japan's colonial rule that continued until 1945 when the Republic of China (ROC) troops arrived on the island.[71]

Proposals to extend the application of Japan's pre-war Jury Act to Taiwan

The discussion concerning the possible introduction of the jury system in Taiwan took place against the background of the struggle of the people of Taiwan against Japanese rule and against the inequalities that this rule produced.

The first phase of the resistance movement against alien rule began with the establishment of the Republic of Formosa in May 1895 and concluded with the suppression of the Xilai Temple Incident (also known as the *Ta-pa-ni* incident) – the last large-scale rebellion against Japanese rule in August 1915.[72] The participants in the resistance movement during this period relied on the military means and saw their primary objective in overthrowing Japanese colonial rule.

The realization of the fact that forcibly ending Japanese domination was not a realistic objective led participants to change their strategy from military resistance to opposition through legitimate tactics. During the second phase of the movement, which lasted from 1914 to 1937, the members of the Formosan elite who had been educated in Japan and were influenced by the ideals of "*Taishō* Democracy" found themselves in the position of leadership. They created political organizations on the island in an effort to find ways to extend the rights enjoyed by the Japanese citizens on the island to the Taiwanese, thereby

---

69 Taiwan Hoan Kisoku [Taiwan Peace Preservation Regulation], Ordinance No. 21 of 1900; Wang, *Legal Reform in Taiwan under Japanese Colonial Rule, 1895–1945*, p. 48.
70 Hokō Jōrei [Hokō Law], Ordinance No. 67 of 1887. See generally H. C. Tsai, 1990, *One Kind of Control: The Hoko System in Taiwan under the Japanese Rule, 1895–1945*, PhD thesis, Columbia University; C. Chen, 1975, "The Japanese Adaptation of the Pao-Chia System in Taiwan, 1895–1945", *Journal of Asian Studies*, Vol. 34, No. 2, pp. 391–416. Other laws that applied only to the Taiwanese included the 1906 Taiwan Vagrant Discipline Regulation – a piece of legislation that gave the police the right to punish persons who were unemployed and presented a threat to the public order (Taiwan Furōsha Torishimaru Kisoku [Taiwan Vagrant Discipline Regulation], Ritsurei No. 2 of 1906) – and the 1904 Fine and Flogging Law (Bakkin oyobi Chikei Shobun Rei [Fine and Flogging Law], Ordinance No. 1 of 1904) that allowed the imposition of physical punishment for those found guilty of a crime in Taiwan (see generally Wang, *Legal Reform in Taiwan under Japanese Colonial Rule, 1895–1945*, p. 48 (discussing the contents and significance of these two pieces of legislation)).
71 J. B. Jacobs, 2012, *Democratizing Taiwan*, Boston: Brill, p. 19.
72 Chen, "Formosan Political Movements under Japanese Colonial Rule, 1914–1937", p. 477. See generally Davidson, *The Island of Formosa*, pp. 275–289 (discussing the establishment of the Republic of Formosa), and P. R. Katz, *When Valleys Turned Blood Red: The Ta-pa-ni Incident in Colonial Taiwan*, Honolulu: University of Hawai'i Press (discussing the Ta-pa-ni incident).

achieving equality with the colonizers.[73] Some of these societies embraced the notion of assimilation as they demanded equality, while others fought for the achievement of greater self-rule as a prerequisite of equality.

The first organization to be established in the second phase of the movement belonged to the former group. The Assimilation Society (*Dōkakai*) was a political society established in 1914 through the collaboration between Lin Hsien-tang, a prominent Taiwanese intellectual, and Count Taisuke Itagaki – a leader of the People's Rights Movement and an instrumental figure in the process of establishing party politics in Japan.[74] The society consisted of 44 Japanese and 532 Taiwanese members, and its declared goal was to promote "harmonious relations" between the two groups and to assist their assimilation.[75] In a speech commemorating the establishment of the society, Itagaki, who served as its president, argued that the assimilation of the two peoples was essential for resisting the attempts on the part of the "white race to dominate Asia" and argued for the promotion of equality between the Japanese and the Taiwanese.[76] This call for equality reflected the hopes of many of the Taiwanese members of the society and represented a cause for alarm for the governor-general of the island. Indeed, had the society been allowed to flourish into a prominent movement for equal rights, the privileged position of the colonizers could have been threatened.[77] After Itagaki departed from the island, the Japanese administration accused the society of the mismanagement of finances in 1915 and eventually withdrew its permit, leading to the dismantlement of the organization.[78]

It was only five years after the Assimilation Society stopped functioning that another organization aiming to further the rights of the Taiwanese was established. The New People's Society (*Shinmin Kai*) was established in 1920 by a group of Taiwanese students undergoing training at various universities in Tokyo with the goal of examining the ways of "innovating" (*kakushin*) Taiwan.[79] Under the leadership of Lin Hsien-tang, the members

---

73 Chen, "Formosan Political Movements under Japanese Colonial Rule, 1914–1937", p. 477. Some scholars have argued that the change in tactics from military resistance to political anti-colonial efforts may have been inspired by the Irish Home Rule movement (see F. Huang, S. Huang, and C. Mulvagh, 2012, "Lin Hsien-Tang's Taiwanese Home-Rule Movement as Inspired by the Irish Model", *Taiwan in Comparative Perspective*, Vol. 4, pp. 65–88).
74 Taiwan Sōtoku Fu [The Office of the Governor-General of Taiwan], 1969, *Nihon Tōchika no Minzoku Undō* [National [Liberation] Movements under Japanese Rule], Vol. 2, Tokyo: Fūrin Shobō, pp. 12–23. See generally N. Ike, 1950, *The Beginnings of Political Democracy in Japan*, Baltimore: Johns Hopkins Press.
75 T. Itagaki, 1914, "Taiwan Dōkakai Teikan" ["The Statutes of the Taiwan Assimilation Society"], art. 3, reproduced in Taiwan Sōtoku Fu [The Office of the Governor-General of Taiwan], *Nihon Tōchika no Minzoku Undō* [National [Liberation] Movements under Japanese Rule], Vol. 2, pp. 17–18. The number of the members of the society is provided in *id.*, p. 22.
76 M. Itagaki, 1969, *Itagaki Taisuke Zenshū* [A Complete Collection of the Writings of Itagaki Taisuke], Tokyo: Hara Shobō, pp. 395–412; Chen, "Formosan Political Movements under Japanese Colonial Rule, 1914–1937", p. 480; Taiwan Sōtoku Fu [The Office of the Governor-General of Taiwan], *Nihon Tōchika no Minzoku Undō* [National [Liberation] Movements under Japanese Rule], Vol. 2, p. 19.
77 Chen, "Formosan Political Movements under Japanese Colonial Rule, 1914–1937", p. 480.
78 *Id.*, p. 480. Taiwan Sōtoku Fu [The Office of the Governor-General of Taiwan], *Nihon Tōchika no Minzoku Undō* [National [Liberation] Movements under Japanese Rule], Vol. 2, p. 23.
79 "Shinmin Kai Shōtei" [Statutes of the New People's Society], art. 2, reproduced in Taiwan Sōtoku Fu [The Office of the Governor-General of Taiwan], *Nihon Tōchika no Minzoku Undō* [National [Liberation] Movements under Japanese Rule], Vol. 2, pp. 25–27 [hereinafter Statutes of the New People's Society].

of the society that was officially based in Tokyo[80] argued for the abolition of Title 63 in the hope that once this piece of legislation was repelled, a greater number of Japanese laws would be extended to the island, eventually resulting in the achievement of equal rights with the colonizers.[81] The members of the society published a monthly journal, *Taiwan Seinen* (Taiwanese Youth), during the period between 1920 and 1937, and argued for the establishment of a Parliament for Taiwan – an organ whose members would be elected by all residents of Taiwan and that would enact such laws for Taiwan that would reflect the interests of the Taiwanese.[82]

Some of the members of the New People's Society joined another organization that was actively pushing for the establishment of a Parliament in Taiwan – the League for the Establishment of the Taiwanese Parliament (*Taiwan Gikai Kisei Dōmeikai*), formed in 1923.[83]

The petition calling for the establishment of a Parliament for Taiwan was submitted to the Japanese Imperial Diet fifteen times between 1921 and 1934.[84] Out of these, the fourth to the fifteenth petitions were submitted by the League for the Establishment of the Taiwanese Parliament.[85] The proponents of the idea that a Parliament should be established in Taiwan argued that the island should be given greater prerogatives with regard to self-rule.[86] The petitions proposed that all special legislative matters concerning Taiwan be enacted by *ritsurei* in accordance with Title 3 and that the annual budget would be approved by the Parliament in Taiwan, whose members would be elected by all residents of the island – the Japanese and the Taiwanese.[87] According to the petitions, all other legislative matters were to be decided upon by the Imperial Diet of Japan.[88] All petitions were rejected by the Petition Committee of the House of Peers, and the Parliament for Taiwan was never established during the Japanese colonial period.[89]

What were some of the reasons behind the committee's reluctance to allow for the establishment of a Parliament in Taiwan? In a speech delivered at the meeting of the committee

---

80 Statutes of the New People's Society, art. 4.
81 Taiwan Sōtoku Fu [The Office of the Governor-General of Taiwan], *Nihon Tōchika no Minzoku Undō* [National [Liberation] Movements under Japanese Rule], Vol. 2, p. 27; Chen, "Formosan Political Movements under Japanese Colonial Rule, 1914–1937", p. 482.
82 Taiwan Sōtoku Fu [The Office of the Governor-General of Taiwan], *Nihon Tōchika no Minzoku Undō* [National [Liberation] Movements under Japanese Rule], Vol. 2, p. 27.
83 *Id.*, p. 355. The primary goal of the league was to promote the establishment of the Parliament in Taiwan. "Taiwan Gikai Kisei Dōmeikai Kaisoku" [The Rules for the League for the Establishment of the Taiwanese Parliament], 1923, art. 2, reproduced in Taiwan Sōtoku Fu [The Office of the Governor-General of Taiwan], *Nihon Tōchika no Minzoku Undō* [National [Liberation] Movements under Japanese Rule], Vol. 2, pp. 356–358 [hereinafter The Rules for the League for the Establishment of the Taiwanese Parliament].
84 M. Wakabayashi, 2001, *Taiwan Kōnichi Undōshi Kenkyū* [A Study of Anti-Japanese Movements in Taiwan], Kenbun Shuppan, pp. 27–26.
85 Chen, "Formosan Political Movements under Japanese Colonial Rule, 1914–1937", p. 484. The text of the first petition is reproduced in full in Taiwan Sōtoku Fu [The Office of the Governor-General of Taiwan], *Nihon Tōchika no Minzoku Undō* [National [Liberation] Movements under Japanese Rule], Vol. 2, pp. 340–341. On the fate of the first and of the subsequent petitions see *id.*, pp. 342–402.
86 *Id.*, pp. 342–402; Wang, *Legal Reform in Taiwan under Japanese Colonial Rule, 1895–1945*, p. 57.
87 Wang, *Legal Reform in Taiwan under Japanese Colonial Rule, 1895–1945*, p. 57.
88 *Id.*, p. 57.
89 It should be noted that the fact that all of the petitions were rejected by the Petition Committee implied that the Imperial Diet never got to deliberate the possibility of the establishment of a Parliament in Taiwan (Chen, "Formosan Political Movements under Japanese Colonial Rule, 1914–1937", p. 487).

in 1921 when the first petition was being deliberated, Governor-General of Taiwan Baron Kenjirō Den restated the intention of the Japanese administration that had been articulated by Hara during the parliamentary debates concerning Title 3. He argued that the ultimate goal of the Japanese administration of Taiwan was to advance the cultural standard of the Taiwanese so that the island would eventually become a part of *naichi* rather than an autonomous colony, and that the proposed plan to establish a separate Parliament for Taiwan was incompatible with this objective.[90] The argument articulated by Den doubtlessly represented a substantial enough reason for rejecting the petitions.

The colonial administration of Taiwan attempted to divert the attention of the supporters of the idea of the establishment of a Parliament for Taiwan by carrying out a reform of local administration (*chihō kaikaku*) in 1921.[91] Specifically, Governor-General Den changed the composition of the Consultative Council (*Taiwan Sōtokufu Hyōgikai*) to include not only Japanese high-ranking officials from among the bureaucrats working at the office of the governor-general, but also "persons of knowledge and experience" living on the island.[92] The latter group, of course, included not only Japanese nationals, but also the Taiwanese. Seven bureaucrats were to work alongside nine Japanese and nine Taiwanese laypersons on the council, who were appointed for the period of two years.[93] The scope of authority of the members of the council was limited to discussing the inquiries presented to them by the governor-general, however, which led many Taiwanese to dismiss the council as an organ that was ornamental in nature and lacked real decision-making power.[94]

The League for the Establishment of a Taiwanese Parliament was dissolved in 1934 amid accusations of being unpatriotic in the increasingly militaristic atmosphere of the 1930s.[95]

Yet another organization established during the second phase of the resistance movement was the Taiwan Cultural Association (*Taiwan Bunka Kyōkai*). This organization was

---

90 Hara, speech at the 44th Session of the Imperial Diet, partially reproduced in Haruyama, "Kindai Nihon no Shokuminchi Tōchi to Hara Kei" [Modern Japan's Colonial Rule and Hara Kei], p. 70; Taiwan Sōtoku Fu [The Office of the Governor-General of Taiwan], *Nihon Tōchika no Minzoku Undō* [National [Liberation] Movements under Japanese Rule], Vol. 2, p. 342; Chen, "Formosan Political Movements under Japanese Colonial Rule, 1914–1937", p. 487.
91 W. Wu, "Nihon Tōchika Taiwan ni okeru Shakaiteki Rīdā Kaisō to Gimu Kyōiku no Jisshi – Dai Ikkai Taiwan Sōtoku Fu Kyōgikaiin no Giron o Chūshin ni" [The Social Class of Leaders in Taiwan under Japanese Rule: Focusing on the First Deliberations at the Consultative Council of the Office of the Governor-General], in T. Matsuda (ed.), 2011, *Shokuminchi Teikoku Nihon ni okeru Shihai to Chiiki Shakai* [The Rule and the Local Society in the Japanese Colonial Empire], Kyoto: Kokusai Nihon Bunka Kenkyū Sentā, pp. 71–91, at p. 75.
92 Taiwan Sōtokufu Hyōgikai Kansei [The Organizational Structure of the Office of the Governor-General of Taiwan], No. 241 of 1921, art. 3, reproduced in K. Ide, 1988, *Taiwan Chiseki Shi* [The Intentions of the Administration of Taiwan], Tokyo: Seishisha, pp. 638–639 [hereinafter The Organizational Structure of the Office of the Governor-General of Taiwan].
93 K. Ide, 1988, *Taiwan Chiseki Shi* [The Intentions of the Administration of Taiwan], Tokyo: Seishisha, p. 639; The Organizational Structure of the Office of the Governor-General of Taiwan, art. 3; Chen, "Formosan Political Movements under Japanese Colonial Rule, 1914–1937", p. 487.
94 Chen, "Formosan Political Movements under Japanese Colonial Rule, 1914–1937", p. 487. The parallels with the jury trial system as implemented in pre-war Japan are hard to miss. See Chapter 3 for the discussion of the system.
95 Chen, "Formosan Political Movements under Japanese Colonial Rule, 1914–1937", p. 489; Taiwan Sōtoku Fu [The Office of the Governor-General of Taiwan], *Nihon Tōchika no Minzoku Undō* [National [Liberation] Movements under Japanese Rule], Vol. 2, p. 402.

launched in 1921 and had the promotion of Taiwan's culture as its main aim.[96] The association devoted itself to the task of furthering the process of the development of a nationalist consciousness in Taiwan to counter the effects of the cultural assimilation policies that the Japanese colonial administration adopted.[97] The association established schools (*juku*) that held classes on a variety of subjects, including Taiwanese history, and organized summer study meetings focusing on the history of the Chinese civilization.[98] Like the League for the Establishment of the Taiwanese Parliament, this organization was dissolved in the 1930s following the arrests of several of its leaders.[99]

Prior to the official closing down of the association in 1927, the organization was effectively split into two wings: one moderate and the other more radical.[100] Several moderate members of the organization, including Chiang Wei-shui – one of the founders of the Taiwanese Cultural Association – and Tsai Pei-huo[101] decided to establish an organization that became the first political party in Taiwan – the Taiwan Popular Party (*Taiwan Minshutō*).[102]

The police initially prohibited the formation of the party on the grounds that one of its proclaimed goals was the "political and financial emancipation of the Formosan people".[103] The phrase was removed from the party's statement of policy, and the governor-general sanctioned the establishment of the Taiwan Popular Party on July 10, 1927.[104] A British commentator writing about the event noted that this fact implied the recognition "for the

---

96 Taiwan Sōtoku Fu [The Office of the Governor-General of Taiwan], *Nihon Tōchika no Minzoku Undō* [National [Liberation] Movements under Japanese Rule], Vol. 2, p. 139; "Taiwan Bunka Kyōkai Shuisho" [A Prospectus of the Taiwan Cultural Association], reproduced in *id.*, pp. 138–139, at p. 139; and "Taiwan Bunka Kyōkai Kaisoku" [The Rules of the Taiwan Cultural Association], art. 2, reproduced in *id.*, pp. 140–141 [hereinafter The Rules of the Taiwan Cultural Association].
97 Chen, "Formosan Political Movements under Japanese Colonial Rule, 1914–1937", p. 490.
98 Taiwan Sōtoku Fu [The Office of the Governor-General of Taiwan], *Nihon Tōchika no Minzoku Undō* [National [Liberation] Movements under Japanese Rule], Vol. 2, pp. 148–151.
99 Born in Yilan, Chiang Wei-shui (1891–1931) was one of the key members of the resistance movement against colonial rule in Taiwan and a founder of the Taiwan Cultural Association and the Taiwan Popular Party. See generally M. Wu (translated by Y. Yokosawa), 2010, *Taiwan Shi Shō Jiten* [A Concise Dictionary of Taiwanese History], Fukuoka: Chūgoku Shoten, p. 187.
100 Chen, "Formosan Political Movements under Japanese Colonial Rule, 1914–1937", p. 491.
101 Tsai Pei-huo (1889–1983) joined the Taiwan Assimilation Society in 1914. He participated in the movements for the abolition of Title 63 and for the establishment of the Taiwanese Parliament and is known for his proposal of the romanized version of the Taiwanese language (see Wu, *Taiwan Shi Shō Jiten* [A Concise Dictionary of Taiwanese History], pp. 186–187; C. Shih, "Taiwan as East-Asia in Formation: A Subaltern Appropriation of Colonial Narratives", in G. Shubert and J. Damm (eds), 2011, *Taiwanese Identity in the 21st Century: Domestic, Regional, and Global Perspectives*, London: Routledge, pp. 237–257, at p. 247).
102 A variety of translations of the name of Taiwan's first political party are used in the materials written in English. British diplomats have translated the name of the party as "Formosan Popular Party" and as "Taiwan Democratic Party" (R. L. Jarman (ed.), 1997, *Taiwan Political and Economic Reports, 1861–1960*, Vol. 7, Oxford: Archive Editions, pp. 120 and 213). Tay-Sheng Wang, an authority on the Taiwan's legal history, translates the name of the party as the "Taiwan Popular Party" (Wang, *Legal Reform in Taiwan under Japanese Colonial Rule, 1895–1945*, p. 60), and it is this translation that this chapter uses.
103 Jarman (ed.), *Taiwan Political and Economic Reports, 1861–1960*, Vol. 7, p. 120.
104 *Id.*, p. 120; "Taiwan Minshuto Sengen" [The Declaration of the Taiwan Popular Party], July 10, reproduced in Taiwan Sōtoku Fu [The Office of the Governor-General of Taiwan], *Nihon Tōchika no Minzoku Undō* [National [Liberation] Movements under Japanese Rule], Vol. 2, pp. 428–429.

first time [of] the right of the natives to combine together for political objects" in colonial Taiwan, and argued that this "should be regarded as in the direction of progress".[105]

It was this organization that attempted to start a public debate in Taiwan regarding the possibility of introducing the jury system on the island immediately after its establishment. The finalized statement of policy of the new party contained political, economic, and social demands. The institution of jury service was mentioned in the section concerning political demands. This section contained the following demands:

(1) To secure local self-government and the right to election of members of provincial and other assemblies by popular suffrage;
(2) To secure immediate permission for Formosans to publish newspapers, and, eventually, freedom of speech, meeting, association, and publication;
(3) To secure the reform of the educational system (a) by the adoption of compulsory education; (b) by making instruction in public schools bilingual, e.g., Chinese and Japanese; (c) by introducing Chinese writing as a compulsory subject in public schools;
(4) To secure the reform of the "hook" (forced labor) system;
(5) *To secure the reform of the judicial system and the introduction of trial by jury.*[106]

In other words, the party was planning to carry out activities aimed at eliminating inequalities between the Taiwanese and the Japanese residents of the island and expanding the rights of the members of the former group. A similar list of demands was publicized by the Taiwan Popular Party in 1929 and in 1931. In both instances the demand for the introduction of the jury system appeared as one of the priorities. In the list prepared in 1929 – one year after the enactment of Japan's Jury Act – the proposal to introduce the jury system appears as item 11, and in 1931, the request for the implementation of the jury system in Taiwan appears as item 8.[107] None of the three documents provides any details as to the type of the jury system that the authors had in mind. We may assume, however, that it was the jury system as implemented in Japan that was referred to in the documents. The 1929 list in particular talks about the enforcement of the Jury Act (*Baishin Hō*) in Taiwan.[108]

What were some of the reasons behind the party's decision to discuss the possibility of implementing the jury system on the island?

Taiwanese intellectuals were, of course, well aware of the fact that the jury system was introduced on the Japanese mainland. In addition, China experimented with the institution of jury service on several occasions during the period of Japan's colonial rule over Taiwan.[109]

---

105 Jarman (ed.), *Taiwan Political and Economic Reports, 1861–1960*, Vol. 7, p. 120.
106 *Id.*, p. 120 (in English) (emphasis added); H. Mukōyama, 1987, *Nihon Tōchika ni okeru Taiwan Minzoku Undō Shi* [A History of the National Movement in Taiwan under the Japanese Rule], Tokyo: Chūō Keizai Kenkyūjo, p. 692 (in Japanese). The text of the document in Japanese is also available in Taiwan Sōtoku Fu [The Office of the Governor-General of Taiwan], *Nihon Tōchika no Minzoku Undō* [National [Liberation] Movements under Japanese Rule], Vol. 2, p. 429.
107 The full lists of demands made by the party are available in Mukōyama, *Nihon Tōchika ni okeru Taiwan Minzoku Undō Shi* [A History of the National Movement in Taiwan under the Japanese Rule], pp. 718–720 and 731–735.
108 *Id.*, p. 719. The 1931 list demands that the jury system be established in Taiwan (*id.*, p. 732).
109 The jury system was implemented on a trial basis in Shanghai under the *Qing* in the early 1910s, and a special jury system was used in Republican China to try counter-revolutionary cases during the

114 *Attempts to introduce the jury system*

Knowledge of the experiences of Japan and of China with jury trials may have played a part in the party's decision to include the provision concerning the jury system to its list of political demands.

Despite the efforts on the part of the Taiwan Popular Party to trigger a public discussion regarding the possibility of extending the Jury Act to Taiwan, however, the lists of demands did not lead to reform, and the jury system was never introduced in Taiwan. Neither were the attempts to achieve election rights successful.[110] The party itself was dissolved in 1931 by order of the police, and sixteen of its leaders were arrested for a brief period for "instigating disorder and attempting to oppose the policy" of the governor-general.[111] Prior to its dissolution, the party actively participated in the process of the organization of Taiwan's labor unions that organized strikes against Japanese factories – a movement that could not fail to alert the Japanese police to the actions of the party.[112] While the jury system was never implemented in colonial Taiwan, the right to serve on a jury and to be tried by jury was extended to another one of Japan's colonies – Karafuto – which is the subject of discussion in the section that follows.

Karafuto: the jury system on the island during the Japanese colonial period

Karafuto under Japanese colonial rule

Karafuto, the northernmost colony of the Japanese Empire, was the portion of the island of Sakhalin below the 50th parallel that was ceded to Japan by the Treaty of Portsmouth signed on September 5, 1905, upon the conclusion of the Russo-Japanese war.

According to some sources, the name "Karafuto" originally meant "land at the extremity of China", which indicates that the island, when first discovered by the Japanese, was thought to be associated with the Chinese mainland.[113] The history of the country's interest

---

period between 1929 and 1931. See generally A. Dobrovolskaia, 2014, *The Institution of Jury Service in Taiwan* (unpublished manuscript, on file with author), pp. 60–62 (discussing Imperial China's first experience with jury trials) and 76–78 (outlining the features of the special jury system used in counter-revolutionary cases in Republican China). The Provisional Act [Governing Trial] by Jury in Counter-Revolutionary Cases stipulated that the members of the six-person jury panel that was to determine the verdict independently of the judge were to be selected from the members of the Kuomintang (KMT). See Anonymous, 1930, "Jury Trial in Higher Court: Application of New Law for Trial of Counter-Revolutionaries: Jury to Be Composed of Members of Kuomintang", *North China Herald*, April 15, p. 94.

110 The reasoning behind the colonial administration's opposition to the attempts to extend the right to popular election to the island seems to have been based on the understanding that allowing the Taiwanese to vote would imply that the decisions concerning the ruling minority on the island – the Japanese – would be made by the ruled, the Taiwanese – a situation that was not in the interests of the Japanese administration (Chen, "Formosan Political Movements under Japanese Colonial Rule, 1914–1937", p. 492).
111 Jarman (ed.), *Taiwan Political and Economic Reports, 1861–1960*, Vol. 7, p. 213.
112 Chen, "Formosan Political Movements under Japanese Colonial Rule, 1914–1937", p. 492.
113 W. H. Morton-Cameron and W. Feldwick, 1919, *Present Day Impressions of Japan; The History, People, Commerce, Industries and Resources of Japan and Japan's Colonial Empire, Kwantung, Chosen, Taiwan, Karafuto*, Chicago: Globe Encyclopedia, p. 812; A. Sakaya, 1925, *Karafuto Enkakushi* [A History of Development of Karafuto], Toyohara: Karafuto Chō, p. 55. For a discussion of China's influence on the island see J. J. Stephan, 1971, *Sakhalin: A History*, Oxford: Clarendon Press, pp. 19–29.

in Karafuto dates back to as early as the 17th century. In 1651, the first expedition from Japan reached Karafuto, resulting in the drafting of the first Japanese map of the southern portion of the island.[114] The native population of the island consisted of the Gikyak, the Oroki, and the Ainu at the time Japan first reached its shores.[115]

Japan came to be directly involved in the administration of the island in the middle of the 19th century. In 1855, Russia and Japan concluded the Treaty of Shimoda that provided for the joint occupation of the island by the two powers. In 1875, the jurisdiction over the whole of the island was transferred to Russia.[116] The period of Russian rule over the whole of the island ended in 1905 with the conclusion of the Treaty of Portsmouth according to which Japan regained control over the southern portion of Sakhalin. Japan remained in control of the southern part of the island until August 1945, when the Soviet forces invaded Karafuto. It ruled over the northern part of the island between 1920 and 1925.[117] In 1945, in accordance with the Yalta agreement, the southern part of the island became a territory of the USSR.[118]

As was the case with the administration of Taiwan, Japan first established military rule over the island and then set up a local civilian administration once the island was secured. The legislation enacted to be used on the island reflected this change in strategy.

The Japanese government initially declared military rule on August 1, 1905, upon securing control over the whole of the island.[119] In less than a month, on August 28, a temporary civil administration (*Karafuto Minsei Shō*) was set up.[120] Despite the establishment of the temporary civil administration, army decrees remained the primary sources of legislation in Karafuto under Japanese rule until March 1907, when the permanent civil administration was set up.[121] During the period of military rule, criminal offences were tried by military tribunals, while civil offences were adjudicated by a civil court (*Minsei Hōin*) especially established for this purpose.[122] The first stage in the occupation of Karafuto was a time when

---

114 Morton-Cameron and Feldwick, *Present Day Impressions of Japan*, p. 898. Alternative sources place the earliest Japanese records mentioning Karafuto to a slightly later time – 1700. See generally Sakaya, *Karafuto Enkakushi* [A History of Development of Karafuto], p. 50.
115 Stephan, *Sakhalin*, p. 12.
116 On the Russian administration of the island as perceived by the Japanese see S. Takakura, 1947, *Hokkaidō Takushoku Shi* [A History of the Development of Hokkaido], Sapporo: Kashiwaba Shoin, pp. 265–272.
117 Stephan, *Sakhalin*, p. 85.
118 Yalta Agreement, 1945, art. 2(a), available online at "Birth of the Constitution of Japan", http://www.ndl.go.jp/constitution/e/etc/c04.html.
119 Sakaya, *Karafuto Enkakushi* [A History of Development of Karafuto], pp. 234–237. The provisions of the Portsmouth Treaty reduced the area that was placed under Japan's control to the southern part – the portion of the island that fell below the 50th parallel.
120 Senryōchi Minseishō no Shokuin ni kansuru Ken [Concerning the Employees of the Civil Administration of the Occupied Territories], Imperial Ordinance No. 156 of 1905, reproduced in Gaimushō Jōyaku Kyoku Hōki Ka [The Ministry of Foreign Affairs, Department of Treaties, Legislative Section], 1969, *Nihon Tōchika no Karafuto* [Karafuto under Japanese Rule], Tokyo: Ministry of Foreign Affairs, Department of Treaties, Legislative Section], pp. 105–106; Stephan, *Sakhalin*, p. 86. Sakaya, *Karafuto Enkakushi* [A History of Development of Karafuto], p. 237.
121 Stephan, *Sakhalin*, p. 86.
122 Masahisa Matsuda (Minister of Justice), 1907, speech delivered at the 23rd Session of the Imperial Diet, reproduced in full in Gaimushō Jōyaku Kyoku Hōki Ka [The Ministry of Foreign Affairs, Department of Treaties, Legislative Section], *Nihon Tōchika no Karafuto* [Karafuto under Japanese Rule], p. 85.

the Japanese administrators were primarily involved in activities associated with the repatriation of Russian citizens from the Japan-administered portion of Karafuto and the establishment of the administrative headquarters in Toyohara – originally Vladimirovka – a city that remained the capital of Karafuto from 1905 to 1945.[123]

The period of military rule ended in 1907 with the establishment of the Karafuto Agency (*Karafuto chō*).[124] The government established in Karafuto was headed by the governor (*chōkan*), who supervised the judiciary, postal, telegraph, and customs, as well as banking services in the colony, and who reported to different government agencies during different periods of the Japanese administration over the island.[125] During the periods between 1907 and 1910, and 1912 and 1917 the governor of Karafuto was responsible directly to the minister of home affairs.[126] The governor reported to the prime minister of Japan between 1910 and 1912 and between 1917 and 1929, and to the Ministry of Colonial Affairs (*Takumushō*) in the period between 1929 and 1943.[127] The Karafuto Agency originally consisted of two offices (*bu*) that handled matters relating to internal affairs (*naimu*), colonization (*takushoku*), police, and hygiene.[128] Subsequently, however, the colonization section was abolished.[129] Eventually, the work of the Agency was assisted by four supporting agencies (*shichō*), established in the main administrative centers of Karafuto.[130]

In developing a strategy for the administration of the island, the Japanese government from the start tended to treat the island of Karafuto as essentially an extension of the neighboring island of Hokkaido – a part of the Japanese mainland, or the inner lands (*naichi*) – rather than as a colony. This fact is apparent from the examination of the pieces of legislation involving the two islands. Specifically, the law concerning the use of undeveloped national land in Karafuto was highly influenced by a similar piece of legislation concerning the use of land in Hokkaido.[131] As in Hokkaido, special teams were assigned to determine the suitable

---

123 Stephan, *Sakhalin*, p. 86. As of 1909, 165 Russians lived in Karafuto (S. Ukichi, 1909, Karafuto Kaihatsusaku [The Development Policies of Karafuto], Ōtomari: Hokushindō, p. 112, cited in Stephan, *Sakhalin*, p. 86; Sakaya, *Karafuto Enkakushi* [A History of Development of Karafuto], pp. 236–237).
124 Karafuto Chō Kansei [The Organization of Karafuto Prefecture], Imperial Order (*chokurei*) No. 33 of 1907, reproduced in Gaimushō Jōyaku Kyoku Hōki Ka [The Ministry of Foreign Affairs, Department of Treaties, Legislative Section], *Nihon Tōchika no Karafuto* [Karafuto under Japanese Rule], pp. 106–107 [hereinafter The Organization of Karafuto Prefecture (1907)]. See generally S. Kusunoki, "Karafuto Sanseiken Mondai" [The Problem of Political Participation in Karafuto], in Y. Tezuka (ed.), 1990, *Kindai Nihon Shi no Shin Kenkyū* [New Research on the Modern History of Japan], Tokyo: Hokuju Shuppan, pp. 183–199, at p. 188; Sakaya, *Karafuto Enkakushi* [A History of Development of Karafuto], p. 239.
125 The Organization of Karafuto Prefecture (1907), art. 9.
126 Stephan, *Sakhalin*, p. 87; Sakaya, *Karafuto Enkakushi* [A History of Development of Karafuto], p. 239.
127 Stephan, *Sakhalin*, p. 87. The Ministry of Colonial Affairs was a Ministry that was established in 1923 and existed until 1943. The Ministry was set up to replace the Colonization Office (*Kaitakushi*) that had been established in 1910 within the Ministry of Home Affairs. The Ministry oversaw the activities of the governor-general of Taiwan and Korea as well as with those of the Agencies (*chō*) of Karafuto (*Karafuto chō*), South-Pacific Mandate (*Nan'yō chō*), and the Kwantung Lease Territory (*Kantō chō*).
128 Sakaya, *Karafuto Enkakushi* [A History of Development of Karafuto], p. 239.
129 *Id.*, p. 239.
130 Gaimushō Jōyaku Kyoku Hōki Ka [The Ministry of Foreign Affairs, Department of Treaties, Legislative Section], 1969, *Nihon Tōchika no Karafuto* [Karafuto under Japanese Rule], Tokyo: Gaimushō Jōyaku Kyoku Hōki Ka [The Ministry of Foreign Affairs, Department of Treaties, Legislative Section], p. 123.
131 Karafuto Kokuyū Mikaichi Tokubetsu Shobun Rei [Order [Concerning] the Use of Undeveloped National Land in Karafuto], Imperial Ordinance No. 290 of 1911 [hereinafter Order [Concerning] the Use of Undeveloped National Land in Karafuto]; Hokkaidō Kokuyū Mikaichi Tokubetsu Shobun

locations for agriculture and fishing. Settlers from Japan were given spots of land to work on and were asked to participate in the construction of schools and other public facilities as well as of shrines and temples for the community.[132]

It is likely that the decision to treat Karafuto as an extension of Hokkaido was based on such considerations as the geographical proximity of the two islands and the similarities in their climacteric conditions.

As should be expected given the presence of these similarities between the two islands, Karafuto became the most successful among Japan's colonies at attracting settlers from Japan.[133] As a result, Karafuto was the only colony where the Japanese population by far outnumbered that of the native citizens. As of 1930, out of the total population of Karafuto – 295,196 people – the number of Japanese citizens totaled 284,198, constituting the absolute majority of those living on the island.[134] In the same year, the Japanese population of Taiwan constituted a mere 5 per cent of the total population of the island, while that of Korea totaled less than 3 per cent of the total population.[135]

The court system in Karafuto was established immediately after military rule on the island ended; it consisted of the Karafuto District Court that was established in 1907 in Toyohara and oversaw two ward courts (*ku saibansho*), established in the same year, and four branch offices (*shucchōjo*).[136] The first of the branch offices was established in 1907, with the number of offices gradually expanded to reflect the growing needs of the growing Japanese population on the island. Another branch office was established in 1919 and the other two in 1922.[137]

In 1907, a law outlining the mechanism for the extension of mainland laws to Karafuto was promulgated.[138] This law stipulated that Japanese legislation could be made applicable

---

Rei [Act [Concerning] the Use of Undeveloped National Land], Law No. 57 of 1908 [hereinafter Law [Concerning] the Use of Undeveloped National Land in Hokkaido]. Takakura, *Hokkaido Takushoku Shi* [The History of the Development of Hokkaido], p. 276.

132 Stephan, *Sakhalin*, p. 88; Morton-Cameron and Feldwick, *Present Day Impressions of Japan*, p. 900.

133 Reischauer, *Japan: An Illustrated Encyclopedia*, p. 214. The Karafuto Agency actively promoted resettlement from the Japanese mainland through newspaper advertisements (Takakura, *Hokkaidō Takushoku Shi* [A History of the Development of Hokkaido], p. 276).

134 The 1930 population census data, cited in S. Kusunoki, "Karafuto Sanseiken Mondai" [The Problem of Political Participation in Karafuto], pp. 183–199, at p. 187.

135 *Id.*, p. 187. As of 1930, the total population of Taiwan constituted 4,592,537 people, with the Japanese population totaling 228,281, while the Japanese population of Taiwan constituted 527,016 out of the total population of 21,058,305 (*id.*, p. 187). The non-Japanese population of Karafuto included at different times Chinese, Koreans, and Russians as well as Polish settlers, while the Japanese population grew steadily over the years – from a mere 5,000 in 1905 to 189,036 in 1925 and 295,196 in 1930 (Stephan, *Sakhalin*, p. 90).

136 Karafuto Chihō Saibansho oyobi Dōkannai Ni Ku Saibansho Secchi ni Kansuru Hōritsu [Law Concerning the Establishment of the Karafuto District Court and of the Two Ward Courts within the Same Jurisdiction], Law No. 28 of 1907, reproduced in Gaimushō Jōyaku Kyoku Hōki Ka [The Ministry of Foreign Affairs, Department of Treaties, Legislative Section], *Nihon Tōchika no Karafuto* [Karafuto under Japanese Rule], p. 149 [hereinafter Law Concerning the Establishment of the Karafuto District Court and the Two Ward Courts]. Subsequently the number of ward courts was increased to three; with the number of branch offices decreased to three (see Hōsōkai [Association of Legal Professionals] (ed.), 1941, Shihō Bushokuin Roku [Records of Members of the Judiciary], Tokyo: Hōsōkai, pp. 410–412).

137 See Karafuto Chō [Karafuto Office], 1928, *Karafuto Gaiyō* [Karafuto Outline], Toyohara: Karafuto Chō [Karafuto Office], p. 299.

138 Karafuto ni Shikō Subeki Hōrei ni kansuru Hōritsu [Law Concerning the Pieces of Legislation to Be Enforced in Karafuto], Law No. 25 of 1907, reproduced in Gaimushō Jōyaku Kyoku Hōki Ka [The

in Karafuto through the issuance of imperial ordinances (*chokurei*). Imperial Ordinance No. 94 sanctioned the enforcement of more than fifty pieces of legislation concerning the judicial system functioning in mainland Japan in Karafuto.[139] Specifically, the ordinance provided for the enforcement of Japan's Court Organization Law, the Lawyer Act, the Penal Code, and the Code of Civil Procedure to Karafuto.[140] Karafuto was the only one of Japan's colonies where the Court Organization Law was extended directly by imperial ordinance. In Taiwan and Korea, this law was extended by the order of the governor-general, while in the Kwantung leased territory and Micronesia this law was extended by Court Orders.[141]

The enforcement of Japan's Court Organization Law implied that in Karafuto the court system was operating in exactly the same manner as that in Japan.[142] It should be noted that during the deliberations concerning the draft of the law concerning the establishment of the Karafuto District Court at the Imperial Diet, the need to bring the legal system on the island in accord with that of the inner lands (*naichi*) following the completion of the period of military rule was referred to repeatedly, figuring prominently in the speeches of Minister of Justice Masahisa Matsuda.[143] The arguments against this idea, voiced during the deliberations, included the claim that it might be difficult to appoint judges to work in the newly established Karafuto District Court, given the harsh climate on the island.[144] Even when discussing these possible problems, however, Karafuto was likened to the other parts of mainland Japan – namely, Naha, Okinawa, and Nemuro, Hokkaido – rather than to any of Japan's colonies.[145]

The reality that a number of significantly important pieces of legislation were extended to Karafuto immediately after the establishment of the permanent Japanese civil administration of the island implied that by the time the Japanese Jury Act was being drafted in the mainland, Karafuto was in possession of the legal and court systems that were highly similar to those of mainland Japan. This fact no doubt had a bearing on the Japanese government's decision to extend the application of Japan's pre-war Jury Act to the island.

Ministry of Foreign Affairs, Department of Treaties, Legislative Section], 1969, *Nihon Tōchika no Karafuto* [Karafuto under Japanese Rule], Tokyo: Gaimushō Jōyaku Kyoku Hōki Ka, at p. 137, and in Karafuto Chō [Karafuto Office], 1917, *Karafuto Hōrei Ruiju* [A Collection of Karafuto Legislation], Toyohara: Karafuto Chō [Karafuto Office], p. 1.

139 Shihō ni kansuru Hōritsu o Karafuto ni Shikō Suru no Ken [Concerning the Enforcement of Laws Relating to the Judiciary in Karafuto], Imperial Ordinance No. 94 of 1907 [hereinafter Ordinance Concerning the Enforcement of Laws Relating to the Judiciary in Karafuto], reproduced in Karafuto Chō [Karafuto Office], *Karafuto Hōrei Ruiyu* [A Collection of Karafuto Legislation], pp. 3–7, art. 1.

140 Ordinance Concerning the Enforcement of Laws Relating to the Judiciary in Karafuto, art.1.

141 Takumu Daijin Kanbō Bunsho Ka [The Secretariat and Document Division of the Ministry of Colonial Affairs], *Chōsen, Taiwan, Karafuto, Kantōshū oyobi Nan'yō Guntō ni Okonawaruru Hōritsu Chō* [A List of Pieces of Legislation Enforced in Korea, Taiwan, Karafuto, Kwantung, and Micronesia], p. 3.

142 Gaimushō Jōyaku Kyoku Hōki Ka [The Ministry of Foreign Affairs, Department of Treaties, Legislative Section], *Nihon Tōchika no Karafuto* [Karafuto under Japanese Rule], p. 85; Karafuto Chō [Karafuto Agency], 1929, *Karafuto Yōran* [Karafuto Outline], Toyohara: Karafuto Chō, p. 276.

143 M. Matsuda (Minister of Justice), 1907, speech delivered at the 23rd Session of the Imperial Diet, reproduced in full in Gaimushō Jōyaku Kyoku Hōki Ka [The Ministry of Foreign Affairs, Department of Treaties, Legislative Section], *Nihon Tōchika no Karafuto* [Karafuto under Japanese Rule], p. 85.

144 T. Kikuchi, 1907, speech delivered at the 23rd Session of the Imperial Diet, reproduced in full in Gaimushō Jōyaku Kyoku Hōki Ka [The Ministry of Foreign Affairs, Department of Treaties, Legislative Section], *Nihon Tōchika no Karafuto* [Karafuto under Japanese Rule], pp. 88–89, at p. 88.

145 *Id.*, p. 88.

Indeed, from the perspective of the Japanese government, the reality that many pieces of mainland legislation were being enforced in Karafuto as of 1923 implied that the institution of jury service would fit in well with the legal environment in which the system would be operating. In addition, the fact that by the start of the 1920s the Japanese population of Karafuto constituted the absolute majority of the population of the island meant that on the island, unlike Taiwan or Korea or any of Japan's other colonies, the introduction of the institution of jury service would not be seen as a reform that could be used as a stepping-stone towards achieving greater self-rule and ultimately, independence from the colonizer.

All of these factors arguably contributed to the decision on the part of the Japanese government to choose Karafuto as the only Japanese colony where the Jury Act was to be implemented. The fact that the act continued being applied in Karafuto without any disruptions until 1943, when it was suspended in mainland Japan, serves as a powerful indication that the expectations of the Japanese legislators were justified.

The jury system in Karafuto

Japan's Jury Act was extended to Karafuto by Imperial Ordinance No. 145 in 1927.[146] As in mainland Japan, the promulgation of the Jury Act was preceded by various preparations aiming to ensure the smooth functioning of the new system. The Karafuto District Court held mock trials, and the outcomes of these trials were reported on and discussed in the press and in specialist legal publications in mainland Japan. The description of one such mock trial appeared in *Hōritsu Shunjū* ("Legal Springs and Autumns") – a journal focusing on the analysis of contemporary legal issues that was published between 1926 and 1932.[147]

The mock trial featured on the pages of *Hōritsu Shunjū* took place on September 23, 1928, just days before the official enforcement of the Jury Act.[148] The mock trial took place at a newly built jury trial courtroom located within the premises of the Karafuto District Court. The case on trial involved the investigation of a case where a man was accused of murdering his thirty-two-year-old wife.[149] The trial started with jury selection and empanelment procedures, which indicates that this trial could have been perceived as one of the final opportunities to fine-tune these procedures prior to the start of the operation of the jury system.[150] The article describes the details of the case as presented by the prosecutor. The defendant was accused of murdering his wife, who had become a morphine addict and drawn her husband into financial difficulties because of her addiction.[151] The accused denied the charges.[152] In the main question, the judge sought the opinion of the members of the jury as to the intention of the actions on the part of the accused. The supplementary

---

146 Imperial Ordinance No. 145 of 1927.
147 The first issue of the journal featured the discussion of the Jury Act (see Anonymous, "Hōritsu Shunjū: Ku Gatsu Tsuitachi Zōkan" [Hōritsu Shunjū: September 1 – First Issue], in Ōkura Shō Insatsu Kyoku (ed.), 1926, *Kanpō* [Official Gazette], August 20, p. 522). Anonymous, "Karafuto Chihō Saibansho ni okeru Baishin Mogi Saiban no Jikkyō" [The Progress of the Mock Jury Trial [Held] at the Karafuto District Court], *Hōritsu Shunjū*, 1928, Vol. 3, No. 11, pp. 91–93.
148 The Jury Act was enforced on October 1, 1928.
149 Anonymous, "Karafuto Chihō Saibansho ni okeru Baishin Mogi Saiban no Jikkyō" [The Progress of the Mock Jury Trial [Held] at the Karafuto District Court], p. 91.
150 *Id.*, p. 91.
151 *Id.*, p. 92.
152 *Id.*, p. 92.

question sought to clarify whether the accused was guilty of murder that was not premeditated. The jury found the defendant guilty of murder that was not premeditated – a decision that was supported by the judge. The article concludes by mentioning that the mock trial hearing was concluded by the discussion on the part of the participants in the trial of the upcoming enforcement of the Jury Act.[153]

The first verdict in an actual jury trial to be held at the Karafuto District Court was delivered on November 6, 1928.[154] The first jury trial hearing opened a day earlier, on November 5.[155] The defendant in this case – the fifth case in Japan to be tried by jury – was a farmer who had come to Karafuto in 1926 and was accused of murdering the lover of his wife.[156] The defendant learned of his wife's affair from a letter that was authored by his brother during the time when the defendant himself was away from Karafuto and visiting his hometown. Upon his return, he confronted the lover of his wife and in a fit of anger attacked the man with a hatchet, causing five injuries to his head.[157] The defendant turned himself in after the incident, but claimed that he had not intended to kill the victim.[158] The presence or absence of the accused's intent became an important point of consideration for the court.[159] As the presiding judge observed in his instructions to the members of the jury, in the absence of witnesses of the attack, the task that the members of the jury were entrusted with was not an easy one, given the fact that the determination of facts needed to be based on the evidence presented in the course of the trial.[160] The author of an article that appeared in *Karafuto Nichi Nichi Shinbun* – a local newspaper established in 1908 – describing the trial emphasized that the members of the jury participated actively in the trial proceedings.[161] The judge urged the members of the jury to carefully consider whether this

---

153 *Id.*, p. 93.
154 Anonymous, 1928, "Karafuto Saisho no Baishin Saiban; Hikoku wa Kanpu Koroshi; Baishin'in kara mo Hikokunin ni Shitsumon ga Ari; Bōchōseki wa Asa kara Man'in Shimekiri no Seikyō" [The First Jury Trial in Karafuto; Defendant [Accused of] Killing Lover; Jurors Also Ask Defendant Questions; Observer Seats Full Since Morning; Overwhelming Success], *Karafuto Nichinichi Shinbun* [The Karafuto Daily Newspaper], November 6, p. 3. See also Shihō Shō Keijikyoku [Ministry of Justice, Criminal Affairs Bureau] (ed.), 1929, *Baishin Sesshi Shū* [A Collection of Jury Instructions], Tokyo: Shihō Shō Keijikyoku [Ministry of Justice, Criminal Affairs Bureau], p. 573.
155 Anonymous, "Karafuto Saisho no Baishin Saiban; Hikoku wa Kanpu Koroshi; Baishin'in kara mo Hikokunin ni Shitsumon ga Ari; Bōchōseki wa Asa kara Man'in Shimekiri no Seikyō" [The First Jury Trial in Karafuto; Defendant [Accused of] Killing Lover; Jurors Also Ask Defendant Questions; Observer Seats Full Since Morning; Overwhelming Success], p. 3.
156 Shihō Shō Keijikyoku [Ministry of Justice, Criminal Affairs Bureau] (ed.), 1929, *Baishin Sesshi Shū* [A Collection of Jury Instructions], Tokyo: Shihō Shō Keijikyoku [Ministry of Justice, Criminal Affairs Bureau], pp. 573–574. This was the fifth jury trial to take place in Japan (the first four jury trials took place in Oita, Mito, Nagoya, and Fukuoka, respectively (A. Yamazaki, 1929, *Baishin Saiban: Satsujin Misui ka Shōgai ka* [Jury Trials: [A Case of] Attempted Murder or Injury?], Tokyo: Hōritsu Shimpōsha, p. 309).
157 Keijikyoku [Ministry of Justice, Criminal Affairs Bureau] (ed.), *Baishin Sesshi Shū* [A Collection of Jury Instructions], p. 574.
158 *Id.*, p. 574.
159 *Id.*, p. 574.
160 *Id.*, p. 574.
161 *Karafuto Nichi Nichi Shinbun* was established in 1908 by Kumajirō Takarabe and published by the Karafuto Company (*Karafuto Nichi Nichi Shinbunsha*) until 1942 when it was merged with several other newspaper companies in Karafuto and renamed *Karafuto Shinbun*. See "Karafuto Nichinichi Shinbun" [Karafuto Daily Newspaper], available online at http://www.lib.kobe-u.ac.jp/directory/sinbun/snlist/470l.html. Anonymous, 1928, "Karafuto Saisho no Baishin Saiban; Hikoku wa Kanpu Koroshi;

was a case of premeditated murder and addressed both the main and the supplementary questions to the members of the jury.[162] The court sentenced the defendant to two years' imprisonment with hard labor.[163]

The jury system continued functioning in Karafuto until 1943, when it was suspended in mainland Japan.

The jury system in colonial Japan: the colonized peoples in Japanese jury courts

Karafuto was the only Japanese colony where the jury system was introduced and functioning during the colonial period. In mainland Japan, the reality that Japan was an empire made up of several colonies presented the Japanese judges and jurors with the challenge of having to adjudicate cases not only involving Japanese citizens, but also the members of the colonized nations.

One such case took place in 1932 and involved the investigation of the so-called Ebara Policeman Murder incident (*Ebara Keisatsushō Junsa Satsugai Jiken*) that had taken place in 1931. This well-documented case, which caused great resonance in society, has remained in the focus of interest of scholars following the publication of the verdict. The enduring interest in the case is understandable. After all, the case raised a number of important questions, including those concerning the nature of press coverage of cases in an increasingly militaristic and nationalistic environment, the existence of prejudice against the citizens of the colonized nations in Imperial Japan, as well as the significance of the exclusion of the crimes provided for in the Peace Preservation Act from the list of offences that could be tried by juries.

On January 18, 1931, Nagashige Ozawa, a member of Japan's special police force (*tokkō*) who was working in Ebara, Tokyo, was found dead.[164] The body was discovered by two Korean nationals, brothers Kim, in a room that they were renting together with brothers Ryu – Jonghwan and Nokjong (twenty-three and nineteen years old, respectively).[165] Brothers Ryu were students at an engineering school in Tokyo and were planning to return to Korea following graduation.[166] The brothers had attended a meeting commemorating the activities of Karl Marx and Rosa Luxemburg at the invitation of their friends on January 15

Baishin'in kara mo Hikokunin ni Shitsumon ga Ari; Bōchōseki wa Asa kara Man'in Shimekiri no Seikyō" [The First Jury Trial in Karafuto; Defendant [Accused of] Killing Lover; Jurors Also Ask Defendant Questions; Observer Seats Full Since Morning; Overwhelming Success], *Karafuto Nichinichi Shinbun* [The Karafuto Daily Newspaper], November 6, p. 3.

162 Keijikyoku [Ministry of Justice, Criminal Affairs Bureau] (ed.), *Baishin Sesshi Shū* [A Collection of Jury Instructions], p. 574; Yamazaki, *Baishin Saiban*, p. 309.

163 Keijikyoku [Ministry of Justice, Criminal Affairs Bureau] (ed.), *Baishin Sesshi Shū* [A Collection of Jury Instructions], p. 573.

164 Keishichō Shi Hen Iinkai [Editorial Committee of the History of the Metropolitan Police Department], 1962, *Keishichō Shi, Dai 3* [The History of the Metropolitan Police Department, No. 3], Tokyo: Keishichō Shi Hen Iinkai [Editorial Committee of the History of the Metropolitan Police Department], p. 282; T. Mori, 2010, *Fuse Tatsuji to Futari no Chōsenjin Seinen – 1931 Nen Baishin Hōtei de no Tatakai* [Tatsuji Fuse and Two Young Koreans – The 1931 Battle at the Jury Courtroom], *Hōgakkan Kenpō Kenkyūjo Hō*, Vol. 3, pp. 41–50, at p. 42.

165 Keishichō Shi Hen Iinkai [Editorial Committee of the History of the Metropolitan Police Department], *Keishichō Shi, Dai 3* [The History of the Metropolitan Police Department, No. 3], p. 282. See also T. Fuse, 1974, *Fuse Tatsuji Gaiden* [Fuse Tatsuji Biography], Tokyo: Mirai Sha, p. 182.

166 Fuse, 1974, *Fuse Tatsuji Gaiden* [Fuse Tatsuji Biography], p. 182.

were known to have read leftist press, and had attracted the interest of the police for this reason.[167] Jonghwan and Nokjong were absent from the scene of the crime and were assumed by the police to have fled.[168]

Four days after the incident, the police arrested the two brothers.[169] The fact that the brothers had come to the mainland from one of Japan's colonies (*gaichi*) and that one of the brothers had worked as a delivery man for the Proletarian Newspaper (*Musansha Shinbun*) – a newspaper established in 1925 presenting the news from a working-class perspective – immediately aroused suspicion on the part of the investigators of this case that involved the murder of a representative of the law enforcement system of Japan.[170] The first reports of the incident that appeared in *Tokyo Asahi Shinbun* seemingly ignored the fact that the trial had not yet taken place and immediately referred to the two Korean suspects as the "perpetrators" of the crime.[171] One of the articles covering the incident explained the activities of the Korean brothers as those of the extreme leftist elements who had "always called for the independence of Korea and worked to spread communism among the Koreans living in mainland Japan (*naichi*)".[172] The author of this article speculated that there was a possibility that the supposedly illegal activities of the suspects were "discovered by chance by Detective Ozawa" and that this fact forced the brothers to "strangle [the detective] to death".[173] As this interpretation of events subsequently formed the core of the case of the prosecution at the trial involving this incident, it appears likely that the primary source of information concerning the investigation of the case was the Ebara police department.[174]

---

167 *Id.*, p. 182.
168 Keishichō Shi Hen Iinkai [Editorial Committee of the History of the Metropolitan Police Department], *Keishichō Shi, Dai 3* [The History of the Metropolitan Police Department, No. 3], pp. 282–283.
169 Anonymous, 1931, "Chōsenjin no Yado de Keiji Kōsatsu Saru; Hannin wa Kyokusa Bunshi; Musansha Shinbun no Kankeisha" [Detective [Found] Strangled at Korean Home; Perpetrator an Extreme Left-Wing Element; Associated with the Proletarian Newspaper], *Tokyo Asahi Shinbun*, January 19, p. 7.
170 Keishichō Shi Hen Iinkai [Editorial Committee of the History of the Metropolitan Police Department], *Keishichō Shi, Dai 3* [The History of the Metropolitan Police Department, No. 3], p. 283. The Proletarian Newspaper (*Musansha Shinbun*) was eventually absorbed by *Sekki* – the predecessor of the post-war *Akahata*, the newspaper of the Communist Party of Japan – that was first published in 1935 (See K. Nimura, 1978, "Musansha Shinbun – Shō Shi (Jō)" [A Short History of the Proletarian Newspaper (Part One)], *Hōsei Daigaku Ōhara Shakai Mondai Kenkyūjo Shiryōshitsu Hō* [The Ohara Institute for Social Research, Hosei University Publication], No. 247, pp. 1–43; and K. Nimura, 1978, "Musansha Shinbun – Shō Shi (Jō)" [A Short History of the Proletarian Newspaper (Part One)], *Hōsei Daigaku Ōhara Shakai Mondai Kenkyūjo Shiryōshitsu Hō* [The Ohara Institute for Social Research, Hosei University Publication], No. 249, pp. 1–35, partially reproduced at "Nimura Kazuo Chōsaku Shū", available online at http://oohara.mt.tama.hosei.ac.jp/nk/mushinkaidai1.html#sokan and http://oohara.mt.tama.hosei.ac.jp/nk/mushinkaidai3.html.
171 Anonymous, "Chōsenjin no Yado de Keiji Kōsatsu Saru; Hannin wa Kyokusa Bunshi; Musansha Shinbun no Kankeisha" [Detective [Found] Strangled at Korean Home; Perpetrator an Extreme Left-Wing Element; Associated with the Proletarian Newspaper], p. 7; T. Mori, *Fuse Tatsuji to Futari no Chōsenjin Seinen – 1931 Nen Baishin Hōtei de no Tatakai* [Tatsuji Fuse and Two Young Koreans – The 1931 Battle at the Jury Courtroom], p. 42.
172 Anonymous, 1931, "Keiji Koroshi no Hannin Yokohama Shinai ni Arawareru: Keisatsu Chō, Jiken o Jyūshi" [Criminal Who Killed Policeman Appears in Yokohama: Police Focusing on Incident], *Tokyo Asahi Shinbun*, p. 2.
173 *Id.*, p. 2.
174 See K. Hasegawa, 1932, "Baishin Saiban: Keisatsukan Satsugai Jiken no Ronkoku" [Jury Trial: The Closing Statement [of the Prosecution] in the Policeman Murder Case], *Keisatsu Kyōkai Zasshi*, No. 10, pp. 12–17 (containing the details of the position of the prosecution on the case).

The determination of the investigators to treat the case on trial as that involving subversive activities on the part of a large group of suspects rather than a simple case of murder of a member of the law enforcement system is reflected in another *Tokyo Asahi Shinbun* article. This article reported that the police had called in more than sixty Koreans and retained twenty-six in custody for further questioning in connection with this incident. The article noted that there was the possibility that the murder of the detective was a part of a "grand conspiracy" (*daiinbō*) initiated by the Korean community in Japan.[175]

The information provided in the *Tokyo Asahi Shinbun* articles published prior to the commencement of the trial indicates that there was the possibility that the defendants would be charged with an offence against the provisions of the Peace Preservation Act, which outlawed communist activities in Japan. If this were to happen, brothers Ryu would have been ineligible for trial by jury.[176] This did not happen, however, with the prosecutor charging the defendants with murder.[177] As murder was an offence that entailed the possibility of the penalty of death or life imprisonment, the case was to be submitted to jury trial in accordance with the provisions of the Jury Act, unless the right to be tried by jury was waived by the accused.[178] The defendants chose not to waive their right to be tried by jury at the suggestion of their counsel.[179]

Court hearings opened on February 3, 1932, at the Tokyo District Court and continued for three days.[180] One of the defense attorneys on the case was Tatsuji Fuse – a noted defense attorney who had served on a number of high-profile cases filed against Korean defendants and those involving accusations in offences against the Peace Preservation Act.[181] Fuse himself had the experience of being the target of police investigations in response to his open expression of respect for Korea's independence movement. He acted as the defense counsel in the 1926 High Treason case against Ryul Park, the Korean independence activist,

---

175 Anonymous, "Keiji Koroshi no Hannin Yokohama Shinai ni Arawareru: Keisatsu Chō, Jiken o Jyūshi" [Criminal Who Killed Policeman Appears in Yokohama: Police Focusing on Incident], p. 2.
176 Jury Act, art. 4(3). See the section in Chapter 3 titled "The Jury Act: A Summary" and accompanying notes for the discussion of the provisions of the Peace Preservation Act. The accused continued being portrayed as communists in the press. In the introduction to the article containing the reprint of the opening statement of the prosecution that appeared in the *Journal of the Police Support Association* (*Keisatsu Kyōkai Zasshi*) – a publication established in 1900 – Prosecutor Kiyoshi Hasegawa introduces the defendants as "the natives of Korea and communists" (*chōsen umare no kyōsan shugisha*). See Hasegawa, "Baishin Saiban" [Jury Trial], No. 10, p. 12. On the *Journal of the Police Support Association*, see "Keisatsu Kyōkai" [The Police Support Association], available online at http://www.keisatukyoukai.or.jp/index.php?id=145.
177 Ōishi, *Bengoshi Fuse Tatsuji* [Lawyer Tatsuji Fuse], p. 148.
178 Jury Act, arts. 2 and 6.
179 Fuse, *Fuse Tatsuji Gaiden* [Fuse Tatsuji Biography], p. 182; Ōishi, *Bengoshi Fuse Tatsuji* [Lawyer Tatsuji Fuse], p. 149.
180 Mori, *Fuse Tatsuji to Futari no Chōsenjin Seinen – 1931 Nen Baishin Hōtei de no Tatakai* [Tatsuji Fuse and Two Young Koreans – The 1931 Battle at the Jury Courtroom], p. 44; Hasegawa, "Baishin Saiban" [Jury Trial], No. 10, pp. 12–17, at p. 12.
181 Tatsuji Fuse (1880–1953) was a noted lawyer and civil rights activist. Born in Miyagi prefecture, Fuse graduated from Meiji University in 1902 and assumed the position of probationary prosecutor at the Utsunomiya District Court. Fuse became a defense attorney in 1904. See generally S. Ōishi, 2010, *Bengoshi Fuse Tatsuji* [Lawyer Tatsuji Fuse], Tokyo: Nishida Shoten. In 1945, Tatsuji Fuse authored a proposal for constitutional reform to be implemented in post-war Japan. The proposal contained provisions concerning the jury trial system. See Chapter 5 for a discussion of this proposal.

and his wife Fumiko Kaneko, and worked on the 1927 Taiwanese Farmers' Association riot case (*nirin jiken*).[182]

The Ebara Policeman Murder incident is certain to have appealed to Fuse's sense of justice and duty for a number of reasons. First, this was a case that involved defendants who were in a particularly vulnerable position in Japan's increasingly nationalistic state. The defendants were nationals of one of Japan's colonial possessions; they were accused of murdering a member of the *tokkō* police force and were to be tried at a court in mainland Japan. In addition, they had been under police surveillance for their links with the communist circles in Japan. Second, the Ebara Policeman Murder case was to be submitted to jury trial, unless the defendants chose to waive their right to a jury.

An active proponent of universal suffrage and of the abolition of the death penalty, Fuse was one of the members of the legal profession who had actively supported the idea of the introduction of the jury system in Japan.[183] He believed that jurors were in a better position than professional judges to save the lives of innocent defendants.[184] Fuse could not conceal his disappointment when the features of the system that was envisaged by Japan's Jury Act were publicized, disagreeing particularly with the decision to endow the judges with the right to dismiss the responses of the jury. He argued that giving professional judges this right was not necessarily an effective tool for minimizing the possibility of human error that was inherent in the court proceedings, where human beings were asked to make decisions regarding the life and death of other human beings. Fuse claimed that the Japanese version of the jury system was lacking a backbone (*hone nuki*), and argued that Japan's jury system, which allowed professional judges to ignore the opinions of jurors, lacked internal consistency (*futettei*) and logic (*fugōri*).[185]

Nevertheless, Fuse did not advise the defendants in the Ebara Policeman Murder case to use their right to waive jury trial.[186] This fact clearly indicates that despite the reservations that Fuse may have had regarding the Japanese jury system and in spite of the provisions of the Jury Act that discouraged the use of trial by jury, he decided that in this case submitting the details of the case to a jury would be of benefit to the defendants.[187]

During the trial, the prosecutor argued that the facts of the case were as follows. Ozawa came to visit the home of brothers Ryu, and upon discovering leftist publications (the Proletarian Newspaper (*Musansha Shinbun*)), asked that the older brother accompany him to the police station, at which moment the younger brother – having realized that the list of subscribers to the publication had been made known to the police – murdered the policeman and fled the scene of the crime.[188] The prosecutor argued that while the defendants had claimed during the preliminary hearings that they had no intention of killing Detective Ozawa, when questioned at the police station following their arrest, they admitted that they

---

182 Ōishi, *Bengoshi Fuse Tatsuji* [Lawyer Tatsuji Fuse], pp. 113, 124–128 and 135–143 (describing the 1926 High Treason case and the Taiwanese Farmers' Association riot case (*nirin jiken*), respectively).
183 Fuse, *Fuse Tatsuji Gaiden* [Fuse Tatsuji Biography], p. 182.
184 Ōishi, *Bengoshi Fuse Tatsuji* [Lawyer Tatsuji Fuse], p. 48.
185 T. Fuse, "Baishin Seido to Kanryō Saiban" [The Jury System and the Bureaucratic Trial [System]], *Kakusei* [The Purity], Vol. 18, No. 12, pp. 7–8, at p. 7.
186 Jury Act, art. 6.
187 The barriers to the use of trial by jury included the provision that stipulated that defendants were not eligible to appeal jury verdicts *kōso* (Jury Act, art. 101).
188 Hasegawa, "Baishin Saiban" [Jury Trial], No. 10, p. 13.

did have the intention to kill the victim and that there were several indications that the case on trial was not an instance of murder that was unintended.[189]

The defendants stated at the trial that as they sought to escape, the older brother held the detective by his necktie against the wall, while the younger pressed his feet down with his hands, but claimed that they did this to flee the scene and that they did not intend to kill the detective.[190]

The prosecutor argued that it was difficult to assume that the detective, who had training in the martial arts, could have been killed in an attack that had not been carefully planned.

Fuse attempted to refute the argument of the prosecutor by stating that the fact that the detective had been trained in the martial arts implied that he could not have been easily killed by two Korean youths. Had he been attacked by the defendants, it was certain that there would have been signs of a struggle, but none were to be found. Fuse argued that the defendants accidentally pressed the victim's Adam's apple, which caused his death, and stated that he was convinced that the two brothers did not have the intention to kill the detective.[191] He continued that contrary to the assertions made by the prosecutor, the defendants were not active members of a communist group and that the perceived need to keep the addresses of the subscribers to the leftist newspaper a secret certainly did not necessitate the murder of the detective.[192]

At the end of the trial, the members of the jury were to answer the question of whether this was the case of premeditated murder.[193] The members of the jury gave a positive response to the judge's question. The court sentenced Nokjong Ryu to imprisonment for life and his elder brother to six years' imprisonment.[194]

Evaluating the attempts to introduce the jury system in Taiwan and Karafuto

After Japan became an empire, the Japanese government found itself in the position of exporter of legal concepts and institutions. As it strove to determine which aspects of its own legal system to transplant to its colonial possessions, it was guided by the principle that had guided its decisions regarding the process of importing Western institutions – that is, the need to ensure that any transplanted institution would work efficiently in the host environment. The Japanese government also carefully considered the possible long-term implications of all of the reform efforts that it chose to initiate. Legal rules and institutions were transplanted to Japan's colonies only if they were thought to be conducive to furthering the objectives of the colonizer – that is, to prioritize Japan's strategic and economic interests in the colonies and discourage the colonized nations' attempts to achieve greater self-rule.

---

189 Fuse, *Fuse Tatsuji Gaiden* [Fuse Tatsuji Biography], pp. 184–185. See also Hasegawa, "Baishin Saiban" [Jury Trial], No. 12, pp. 43–49.
190 Hasegawa, "Baishin Saiban" [Jury Trial], No. 10, pp. 13–14.
191 *Id.*, pp. 185–187.
192 *Id.*, p. 186.
193 *Id.*, p. 14. Prosecutor Hasegawa who served at the trial highlighted the attentiveness with which the members of the jury approached their duties in his opening statement at the trial (see *id.*, p. 13).
194 *Id.*, p. 284.

126 *Attempts to introduce the jury system*

Why was the Jury Act applied to Karafuto, and what were some of the reasons behind the failure of Taiwan Popular Party's proposals to implement the jury system to lead to reform in Taiwan?

Karafuto was the most integrated of Japan's colonies.[195] In 1943, Karafuto was singled out among Japan's colonies to be officially included in the *naichi* – literally "inner lands", a word used to refer to the lands constituting Japan proper.[196] The extension of the right to be tried by jury to Taiwan did not involve any risks for the empire – jury trials in Karafuto could well be expected to function in exactly the same manner as in mainland Japan, and no additional provisions were necessary to ensure that the Jury Act would function effectively in the colony.

By contrast, Taiwan remained a legally separate entity within the empire. The absolute majority of the island's population was Taiwanese. If the jury system were introduced to Taiwan, the provisions of the Jury Act would arguably need to be changed in order to accommodate for the environment in which the system would be operating – at least until the goal of complete assimilation was achieved from the perspective of the Japanese colonial administration. For instance, provisions concerning the Japanese language ability of the prospective members of the jury panel would arguably need to be added to the act to ensure that the system that it envisaged would function in a manner that was similar to that of Japan's mainland. Coming up with a plan for the necessary amendments would have required an investment of time on the part of the Japanese administration of the island – an investment that would doubtlessly have been justified, if the implementation of the system was seen as an important tool for achieving some of the objectives of the colonial regime.

As things stood in the late 1920s and early 1930s when the Taiwan Popular Party was formed and voiced its proposals, however, the primary goal of the colonial administration was to eliminate any attempts to challenge the authority of the colonizers. It appears likely that the Japanese government perceived the ultimate goal of the party's demands for the establishment of the jury system in Taiwan to be similar in nature to that of the formation of the Taiwan Popular Party – that is, to achieve the "political emancipation of the Formosan people".[197] At the time when these demands were formulated, allowing this objective to be achieved was not in the interests of the Japanese government.

Indeed, in a situation where a number of organizations and political movements were resisting colonial rule in Taiwan, introducing a system that could potentially allow the members of the colonized nation to participate in the process of making decisions concerning the presence or absence of guilt on the part of the colonizers had the potential to jeopardize the position of the colonial administration in Taiwan.

One may speculate that had Taiwan's colonial history developed in a different manner the outcome of the deliberations associated with Taiwan Popular Party's demands could have been different. As things stood, however, the demand for the introduction of the jury system in Taiwan repeated the fate of the proposal to establish Taiwan's Parliament and that of the attempts to extend universal suffrage to the island.

---

195 As of 1943, 93% of the total population of Karafuto were Japanese citizens. R. H. Myers and M. R. Peattie (eds), 1984, *The Japanese Colonial Empire, 1895–1945*, Princeton: Princeton University Press, p. 269.
196 *Id.*, p. 269.
197 Jarman (ed.), *Taiwan Political and Economic Reports, 1861–1960*, 1927, p. 120.

By contrast, in Karafuto, the external environment constituted a good fit for the institution of jury service. The court system established in this colony was essentially identical to that of Japan, while the composition of the population was similar to that of the island of Hokkaido. The combination of these distinctive features implied that the government in Tokyo did not need to concern itself with the possibility that the administration of Karafuto would attempt to demand greater autonomy.

At a time when in mainland Japan jury trials began losing popularity and the vices of the system were highlighted in the academic debate, the nationals of the colonial possessions of the empire saw the virtues of the jury trial system as an institution that could potentially make it possible for the members of the colonized nations to achieve equality with the colonizer and achieve justice in courts held in the mainland.

The Ebara Policeman Murder incident, tried by jury in the mainland, raised a number of questions that provide important insights for the understanding of the functioning of the jury system in pre-war Japan. The coverage of this case that involved the charge of murder against Korean suspects who were associated with the Communist Party in the press highlights the reality that for the majority of the time of its existence, the pre-war jury system was functioning in a society that was moving in the direction of increasing nationalism and militarism.

The details of the case highlight the reality that the ability of the pre-war jury to serve as a safeguard against potential abuses of power by the government was limited. After all, the system as provided for by Japan's pre-war Jury Act contained a mechanism that allowed the judge to dismiss jury responses.[198]

At the same time, the Ebara Policeman Murder trial also demonstrates that at a time when the jury system was starting to lose popularity and when its defects came to the forefront of debate in the Japanese mainland, it was still seen as a system that appeared to be a source of hope for justice for the nationals of the colonies of the empire accused and tried in the atmosphere of increased suspicion of the 1930s and for their attorneys.[199]

Conclusions

This chapter focused on evaluating the attempts – successful and failed – to implement the jury system in the colonial possessions of the Japanese Empire. It examined how the jury system was perceived by the representatives of colonized nations and how it was used and how it functioned in the mainland in an environment of increasing militarization and rising nationalism.

The chapter first provided an overview of the proposals to implement the jury trial system in Taiwan under Japanese colonial rule that were authored by the members of the Taiwan Popular Party – the first political party to be established in Taiwan. It concluded that the demands for the introduction of trial by jury repeated the fate of the petitions for the establishment of a Parliament in Taiwan and were never fulfilled due to the fact that by the time when they were publicized – the late 1920s to early 1930s – the Japanese government had determined that any measure aimed at the further emancipation of the Taiwanese people was not in its interests.

---

198 Dimitri Vanoverbeke argues that the pre-war jury system was essentially an instrument of control used by the militaristic state (Vanoverbeke, *Juries in the Japanese Legal System*, p. 91).
199 Yasushi, "Baishin Hō no Kekkan" [The Defects of the Jury System], *Hōritsu Shinbun*, August 3.

128 *Attempts to introduce the jury system*

The chapter then analyzed the case of Karafuto, where Japan's Jury Act was enforced without any modifications and where it continued to function until the act was suspended in mainland Japan. The fact that the legal and court systems in the colony were identical with those of Japan proper, coupled with the reality that the population of the southern part of the island – over which Japan exercised control – was highly similar to that of mainland Japan, made the transplantation of the institution of jury service relatively easy and risk-free for the Japanese authorities.

Chapter 5 explores the fate of Japan's suspended Jury Act in the immediate post-war period and describes the attempts to implement the jury trial system in occupied mainland Japan and Okinawa.

5 The occupation years
Attempts to introduce the jury system

This chapter discusses the attempts to implement the jury system in occupied Japan and Okinawa. It begins by looking at the historical background and outlining the major developments in mainland Japan and Okinawa following the conclusion of World War II, and then turns to the case of mainland Japan. This discussion first briefly describes the major legal reforms that were carried out under the Allied occupation and then outlines the proposals to introduce the jury system in post-war Japan authored by individuals and organizations, by the Japanese government, and by the lawyers working for the Supreme Commander for the Allied Powers (SCAP). The next section focuses on the experience of occupied Okinawa with jury trials. It describes the political and judicial structure established in Okinawa under the occupation and outlines the features of the civil and criminal jury systems that were implemented on the islands, followed by a summary of two cases tried by jury in Okinawa. The concluding sections analyze the experiences of Japan and Okinawa with the institution of jury service and summarize the findings of this chapter.

Historical background: the developments in the legal system in the immediate post-war period

The end of World War II signaled the start of a new period in Japan's history: the period of the Allied occupation. The occupation of mainland Japan lasted from 1945 to 1952. One of Japan's prefectures, Okinawa, remained under the rule of the United States until 1972, when the islands constituting this prefecture were reverted to Japan's control. The occupation of Japan and Okinawa resulted in sweeping legal reforms. In both mainland Japan and Okinawa the occupiers attempted to introduce the institution of jury service as part of these reforms.

The guiding principles for the occupation of mainland Japan were outlined in the Potsdam Declaration of July 26, 1945, which stipulated that the Emperor and the Japanese government would comply with any activity of SCAP aimed at achieving the following objectives: the elimination of "the authority and influence of those who have deceived and misled the people of Japan into embarking on world conquest";[1] the removal of "all obstacles to the revival and strengthening of democratic tendencies among the Japanese people";[2]

---

1 Proclamation Defining Terms for Japanese Surrender, July 26, 1945, para. 6, reprinted in E. O. Reishchauer, 1950, *The United States and Japan*, Cambridge, MA: Harvard University Press, pp. 319–320 [hereinafter Potsdam Declaration].
2 *Id.*, para. 10.

130 *The occupation years*

and the establishment of the "freedom of speech, of religion, and of thought, as well as respect for the fundamental human rights".[3]

The legal basis for the occupation of Okinawa was the San Francisco Peace Treaty, signed on September 8, 1951.[4] This document, which restored the sovereignty of mainland Japan, stipulated that the United States would "have the right to exercise all and any powers of administration, legislation, and jurisdiction over the territory and inhabitants of" Okinawa prefecture.[5]

In reforming the legal system of mainland Japan, SCAP sought to balance between introducing Anglo-American concepts and preserving Japan's pre-war traditions and between engaging the Japanese side in the reform process and handing down reforms that the occupation saw as absolutely essential for the achievement of its fundamental objectives. There is ample evidence suggesting that the occupation staff took an active interest in Japan's existing legislation and customs and involved Japanese experts in the deliberation of the reforms that the Allied forces had in mind for post-war Japan.[6] Legal reforms took into account the Continental-European character of the Japanese legal system and the strength of Japan's customs and traditions.[7] The occupation lawyers recalled that they had to "beware of any overeagerness to impose the blessings of Anglo-Saxon legal institutions upon the continental law of Japan" and argued that however "excellent these institutions may have proved at home, their adoption required conscientious scrutiny as to whether they fitted into this different system".[8] The occupation staff proclaimed their role to be that of "mentors" and "midwives" assisting Japan in its transformation rather than unilaterally imposing their own

---

3 *Id.*, para. 10. Other basic documents that lay the groundwork for the Allied occupation of Japan included the Instrument of Surrender, signed on September 2, 1945, which confirmed the acceptance by Japan of the Potsdam Declaration and stipulated the unconditional surrender of Japan's armed forces, the carrying out by Japan of all the supreme commander's orders, and stated that the Emperor and the Japanese government would be subject to the Allied commander (Instrument of Surrender, available online at "The Japanese Surrender Documents", http://www.ibiblio.org/pha/policy/1945/450729a.html#6); "United States Initial Post-surrender Policy for Japan", August 29, 1945, reprinted in Reishchauer, *The United States and Japan*, pp. 321–328); and the Moscow Declaration signed on December 27, 1945, which provided for the establishment of the Far Eastern Commission (Soviet-Anglo-American Communique, December 27, 1945, available online at "Yale Law School, Lillian Goldman Law Library: The Avalon Project; Documents in Law, History, and Diplomacy", http://avalon.law.yale.edu/20th_century/decade19.asp). See H. Borton, 1947, "United States Occupation Policies in Japan since Surrender", *Political Science Quarterly*, Vol. 62, No. 2, pp. 250–257, at p. 251.
4 Treaty of Peace with Japan, September 8, 1951 [hereinafter San Francisco Peace Treaty], reprinted in E. O. Reischauer, 1965, *The United States and Japan*, Cambridge, MA: Harvard University Press, pp. 363–378.
5 *Id.*, art. 3.
6 As early as June 1945, the Allied occupation compiled the results of its research on the Laws and Administrative Organization of Japan (GHQ/SCAP Records (RG 331, National Archives and Records Service), Box No. 1461, Folder No. 8, "Bibliography of Materials on the Laws and Administrative Organization of Japan", compiled under the direction of the Office of Provost Marshall General Military Government Division, Liaison and Studies Branch, on file with the National Diet Library (Declassified E.O. 12065 Section 3–402/NNDG No. 775011)). In Japan, SCAP ruled through the Japanese government leadership rather than directly as in Germany and South Korea (L. W. Beer, "The Present Constitutional System of Japan", in L. W. Beer (ed.), 1992, *Constitutional Systems in Late Twentieth Century Asia*, Seattle: University of Washington Press, pp. 175–223, at p. 176). The rule through the Japanese government was conducted by means of directives that SCAP issued to the government for implementation – the so-called SCAPINs (Beer, "The Present Constitutional System of Japan", p. 176).
7 A. C. Oppler, 1949, "The Reform of Japan's Legal and Judicial System under Allied Occupation", *Washington Law Review and State Bar Journal*, Vol. 24, pp. 290–324, at p. 292.
8 *Id.*, p. 292.

views.[9] Alfred C. Oppler, Chief of the Courts and Law Division of the Government Section, SCAP, and later head of the Legislation and Justice Division of the Legal Section, SCAP, has argued that the occupation staff "mostly proposed rather than imposed something" on the Japanese.[10] While the degree of freedom that the occupied nation had in its deliberations with SCAP has been the focus of debate and was probably not consistent throughout the period of occupation, the results of post-war reforms indicate that SCAP succeeded in balancing between reform and tradition – the occupation did not bring about "the wholesale Americanization of Japanese law".[11]

In Okinawa, the U.S. occupation had a different balance to achieve in its reform efforts. On the one hand, the U.S. administration of Okinawa saw its goal in providing post-war relief to the local citizens and protecting their rights. On the other hand, the long-term nature of the U.S. occupation of the islands implied that the rights of U.S. citizens stationed in Okinawa and of their dependents had to be guaranteed as well. The ambiguity of the status of the islands represented a difficulty for setting concrete goals and constrained the freedom of the U.S. administration in reforming the legal system on the islands in a more decided manner than the Allied occupation did in mainland Japan.[12] At the same time, the long-term presence of U.S. citizens in Okinawa and the need to ensure that their constitutional rights were protected implied that radical reform introducing those Anglo-American institutions that were not transplanted to mainland Japan by SCAP was necessary in Okinawa. The U.S. occupation found a remarkable compromise that allowed it to fulfill what it perceived to be its duties towards Okinawans and U.S. citizens. The occupation forces created a two-tiered system of justice and governance in Okinawa, where one tier was based on the American principles and the other tier preserved its distinctively Japanese character.

In mainland Japan and Okinawa the occupation forces tried to introduce the institution of jury service. In mainland Japan, the occupation lawyers discussed the possibility of introducing the jury system with the Japanese government on several occasions. The Japanese government was not enthusiastic about the idea, however, and the jury system was not introduced. In Okinawa, the U.S. occupation introduced the criminal jury trial system in

---

9 A. C. Oppler, 1976, *Legal Reform in Occupied Japan: A Participant Looks Back*, Princeton: Princeton University Press, pp. 37–38. Alfred Oppler – a refugee from Nazi Germany who had held various posts in the Prussian judiciary – arrived in the United States in 1939. He was posted to the Government Section of General MacArthur's Tokyo headquarters and headed the Courts and Law Division. In his memoirs Oppler argued that the occupation staff "mostly proposed rather than imposed something" (*id.*, p. 37).
10 *Id.*, p. 37.
11 M. Dean (ed.), 2002, *Japanese Legal System*, 2nd edition, London: Cavendish, p. 71.
12 Prior to the conclusion of the San Francisco Peace Treaty, various alternatives were considered as to the future disposal of Okinawa. The first proposal was to revert Okinawa to Japan's control as soon as Japan regained sovereignty. The second was to annex Okinawa to the United States as a territory taken in war, and the third was to place the islands under United Nations trusteeship. The start of the Korean War on June 25, 1950, implied that Okinawa assumed a new significance and could be used as a strategically located supply base for the U.S. forces, and it has been argued that it was with this perspective in mind that Article 3 of the San Francisco Peace Treaty was formulated (S. McCune, 1975, *The Ryukyu Islands*, Newton Abbot: David & Charles, p. 61). This article provided the following: "Japan will concur with any proposal of the United States to the United Nations to place under its trusteeship system, with the United States as the sole administering authority, Nansei Shoto south of 29 degrees north latitude (including the Ryukyu Islands and the Daito Islands), Nanpo Shoto south of Sofu Gan (including the Bonin Islands, Rosario Island, and the Volcano Islands) and Parece Vela and Marcus Island. Pending the making of such a proposal and affirmative action thereon, the United States will have the right to exercise all and any powers of administration, legislation, and jurisdiction over the territory and inhabitants of these islands, including their territorial waters" (San Francisco Peace Treaty, art. 3).

132 *The occupation years*

1963 and the civil jury in 1964. The jury system functioned successfully until Okinawa was reverted to Japan's control in 1972.

The proposals to introduce the jury system in mainland Japan under the Allied occupation

Legal reforms under the Allied occupation

Legal reforms in mainland Japan were commenced soon after the surrender of Japan.[13] SCAP began its efforts by directing the Japanese government to abolish those laws that in SCAP's assessment were oppressive of civil liberties, most notably the Peace Preservation Act.[14] The Special Higher Police was dissolved and political prisoners were released.[15]

The new constitution was promulgated on November 3, 1946, and came into effect on May 3, 1947.[16] In the process of writing the new charter for Japan, the occupation lawyers studied the *Meiji* Constitution in an effort to ensure legal and historical continuity and to understand the political philosophy of the *Meiji* period.[17] SCAP ultimately determined that the *Meiji* Constitution was irreconcilable with the political realities of the occupation – that is, the changed position of the Emperor, SCAP's desire to establish a truly representative government, and the emphasis of the Potsdam Declaration on fundamental human rights. Japan's pre-war constitution was never abrogated or suspended, however, and the new Constitution of Japan was enacted as a revision of the *Meiji* Constitution to maintain constitutional continuity.[18] In substance, however, the amendment was a completely new and different charter that sought to demilitarize, democratize, and decentralize Japan.[19] The Emperor is defined in the 1946 Constitution as the "symbol of the state and the unity of the people" whose position rests on popular will in a striking contrast to the provisions of the *Meiji* Constitution that stipulated that sovereignty rested in the Emperor.[20] In addition, the executive supremacy provided for in the *Meiji* Constitution is replaced in the new

---

13 R. B. Appleton, 1949, "Reforms in Japanese Criminal Procedure under Allied Occupation", *Washington Law Review and State Bar Journal*, Vol. 24, pp. 401–430, at p. 404.
14 Chian Iji Hō [Peace Preservation Act], Law No. 46 of 1925, abolished by Chian Iji Hō Haishi Tō no Ken [Concerning the Abolition of the Peace Preservation Act and Other [Issues]], Imperial Ordinance No. 575 of 1945, October 15; SCAPIN 93, "Removal of Restrictions on Civil and Religious Liberties", issued on October 4, 1945. SCAPIN 93 directed the Japanese government to abrogate and immediately suspend all laws, decrees, orders, ordinances, and regulations restricting political, civil, and religious liberties, to allow unrestricted discussion of the Emperor, the Imperial Institution, and the Imperial Japanese government; to remove restrictions on the collection and dissemination of information, and abolish all legal discrimination on account of race, nationality, creed, or political opinion (Oppler, "The Reform of Japan's Legal and Judicial System under Allied Occupation", p. 296).
15 Appleton, "Reforms in Japanese Criminal Procedure under Allied Occupation", p. 404.
16 The Constitution of Japan, 1946 [hereinafter Nihonkoku Kenpō (1946)].
17 Oppler, "The Reform of Japan's Legal and Judicial System under Allied Occupation", pp. 296–297.
18 *Id.*, p. 297. The 1946 Constitution was introduced as an amendment to the old constitution in accordance with Article 73 of the *Meiji* Constitution.
19 Dean (ed.), *Japanese Legal System*, p. 193.
20 Nihonkoku Kenpō (1946), art. 1. Some legal historians have argued that the Imperial institution was retained by the Americans in the new constitution because of their respect for historical continuity (Takayanagi, "A Century of Innovation: The Development of Japanese Law, 1868–1961", in A. T. Von Mehren (ed.), 1964, *Law in Japan: The Legal Order in a Changing Society*, Cambridge, MA: Harvard University Press, p. 13).

constitution by legislative supremacy.[21] According to the 1946 Constitution, the Cabinet exercises the executive power and is responsible to the Diet, which has the legislative power and is characterized in the constitution as the "highest organ of state power".[22] The 1946 Constitution proclaims the judiciary to be an independent branch of government[23] and contains an extensive Bill of Rights emphasizing individual dignity[24] and equality.[25] Article 9 of the new constitution stipulates that the people of Japan renounce war.[26]

The drafting process of the 1946 Constitution began with the notes that U.S. General Douglas MacArthur gave to the drafters. These notes, known as the "MacArthur notes", contained the basic principles that MacArthur thought were imperative for post-war Japan: the maintenance of the Emperor system, the renunciation of war, and the abolition of the aristocracy.[27] After SCAP made clear its intention to revise the constitution, the political parties and private citizens and groups prepared their own drafts for revision; the occupation forces paid close attention to these drafts, as they considered them to be expressions of the ideas of the Japanese people.[28] In July 1946, the Japanese government appointed a Provisional Legislation Investigating Committee (*Rinji Hōsei Chōsa Kai*) where the prime minister served as chairman. The committee included officials from the Ministry of Justice, Cabinet Legislative Bureau, lawyers, and legal scholars. On July 19, 1946, the Judicial System Investigation Committee (*Hōsei Shingikai*) was established by the Ministry of Justice. This committee included Ministry of Justice Officials, attorneys, law professors, and prosecutors and assisted the Provisional Legislation Investigating Committee in its work.[29] While the Cabinet Committee did not have the option of rejecting the proposal prepared by the occupation, its members could suggest specific changes, provided that the proposed change was not incompatible with the objectives of SCAP.[30] The new constitution was the result of complex negotiations between occupation lawyers and the members of the Cabinet Committee.[31]

---

21 Takayanagi, "A Century of Innovation", p. 13.
22 Nihonkoku Kenpō (1946), art. 41.
23 Prior to the promulgation of the 1946 Constitution, the judges were civil servants under the Ministry of Justice (Oppler, "The Reform of Japan's Legal and Judicial System under Allied Occupation", pp. 299–300).
24 Nihonkoku Kenpō (1946), arts. 13 and 24.
25 *Id.*, art. 14.
26 *Id.*, art. 9.
27 M. Ito, "The Modern Development of Law and Constitution in Japan", in Beer, *Constitutional Systems in Late Twentieth Century Asia*, Seattle: University of Washington Press, pp. 129–174, at p. 142.
28 *Id.*, p. 143.
29 H. Meyers, 1950, "Revisions of the Criminal Code of Japan", *Washington Law Review and State Bar Journal*, Vol. 25, pp. 104–134, at p. 107; K. Miyakawa, "Sengo no Shihō: Sono Mondaiten to Kaikaku no Shiten" [Post-war Justice: Its Problems and Perspectives on Reform], in Tokyo Bengoshi Kai [Tokyo Bar Association] (ed.), 1982, *Shihō Kaikaku no Tenbō* [Prospects of Judicial Reform], Tokyo: Yūhikaku, pp. 59–100, at p. 79.
30 Oppler, *Legal Reform in Occupied Japan*, p. 46.
31 See generally T. H. McNelly, "'Induced Revolution': The Policy and Process of Constitutional Reform in Occupied Japan", in R. E. Ward and S. Yoshikazu (ed.), 1987, *Democratizing Japan: The Allied Occupation*, Honolulu: University of Hawai'i Press, pp. 76–106 (discussing the details of the drafting process of the 1946 Constitution); R. A. Moore, and D. L. Robinson, 2002, *Partners for Democracy: Crafting the New Japanese State under MacArthur*, Tokyo: Oxford University Press (discussing the details of the drafting process of the 1946 Constitution); H. Tanaka, "The Conflict between Two Legal Traditions in Making the Constitution of Japan", in Ward and Yoshikazu (eds), 1987, *Democratizing Japan*, pp. 107–132 (discussing the details of the drafting process of the 1946 Constitution); D. E. Hellegers, 2001, *We, the*

Once the new charter was promulgated, there was the need to revise other legislation to bring the laws into harmony with the new constitutional principles.

The reform of the Civil Code was restricted to the fourth and fifth books of this piece of legislation that cover the fields of domestic relations and inheritance.[32] The code was revised to ensure compatibility with the provisions of Article 24 of the new constitution that stipulated that "with regard to choice of spouse, property rights, inheritance, choice of domicile, divorce, and other matters pertaining to marriage and the family, laws shall be enacted from the standpoint of individual dignity and the essential equality of the sexes."[33] The revisions of the Civil Code in 1947 resulted from the collaboration on the part of the Japanese with the occupation lawyers and serve as yet another example of the fact that the United States tried not to impose the Anglo-Saxon tradition on Japan. The 1947 revisions strengthened the position of Japan's civil law within the Continental-European family of law.[34] Japan's Code of Civil Procedure[35] was also amended, resulting in the simplification of Japan's appeal system.[36]

The revisions of the Criminal Code included the substantial amendment of the articles concerning crimes related to war[37] and those involving foreign relations.[38] In addition, the provisions concerning the crime of "disrespectful acts" towards the members of the imperial household,[39] outlining "offences against peace and order" (articles prohibiting the dissemination of "falsehoods with the object of confusing human minds"),[40] and the provisions concerning the crime of adultery were deleted.[41]

Japanese People: World War II and the Origins of the Japanese Constitution, Vol. 2, Stanford: Stanford University Press, pp. 518–526, 527–544 (containing the details of the drafting process within SCAP and of the discussion process with the Japanese government, respectively). The MacArthur draft of the constitution and the Japanese government draft are reprinted in Hellegers, *We, the Japanese People*, Vol. 2, pp. 673–709. It has been argued that there was a block in the cross-cultural communication between the Japanese and U.S. participants, which allowed the Japanese to make the changes that the Americans did not notice, resulting in the fact that the English and Japanese versions of the final draft of the 1946 Constitution are different in terms of emphasis and impact, with the Japanese text being much more compatible with the Japanese social and political values than the English version. See K. Inoue, 1991, *MacArthur's Japanese Constitution: A Linguistic and Cultural Study of Its Making*, Chicago: University of Chicago Press.

32 The other three books of the Civil Code were essentially left unamended, due to the fact that the occupation did not see any constitutional grounds for a revision (Oppler, "The Reform of Japan's Legal and Judicial System under Allied Occupation", p. 317).

33 Nihonkoku Kenpō (1946), art. 24, para. 2. See K. Steiner, 1950, "Postwar Changes in the Japanese Civil Code", *Washington Law Review and State Bar Journal*, Vol. 25, pp. 286–312 (containing a detailed discussion of the changes made to the Civil Code).

34 Steiner, "Postwar Changes in the Japanese Civil Code", p. 288.

35 Minji Soshō Hō [Code of Civil Procedure], Law No. 29 of 1890, as amended by Law No. 149 of 1948 [hereinafter Code of Civil Procedure]

36 See Oppler, "The Reform of Japan's Legal and Judicial System under Allied Occupation", pp. 320–321 (discussing the details of the revisions of the Code of Civil Procedure).

37 KEIHŌ, Law No. 45 of 1907, as amended by Law No. 77 of 1921, Law No. 61 of 1941, and Law No. 124 of 1947, arts. 83–89 were revoked, and arts. 81–82 were rewritten. Meyers, "Revisions of the Criminal Code of Japan", p. 112.

38 KEIHŌ, arts. 90–91 were deleted. Meyers, "Revisions of the Criminal Code of Japan", p. 118.

39 KEIHŌ, arts. 73, 74, 75, 76, and 131 were deleted. Meyers, "Revisions of the Criminal Code of Japan", p. 109.

40 KEIHŌ, art. 105 a, b, and c was deleted. Meyers, "Revisions of the Criminal Code of Japan", p. 118.

41 KEIHŌ, art. 183 was deleted. See Meyers, "Revisions of the Criminal Code of Japan", pp. 107–134 (discussing in detail the contents of the revisions of the Criminal Code under the Allied occupation).

The influence of Anglo-American law is most marked in the provisions of the new Code of Criminal Procedure.[42] Under the new code, the prosecutor and the defense counsel were given a greater role in the public trial than they previously possessed. The revised code allowed the prosecutor and the defense to request the examination of evidence, examine and cross-examine the witnesses, and raise objections regarding the examination of evidence or any depositions approved by the judge.[43] Furthermore, the new code stated that the defendant cannot be convicted on the basis of his or her confession alone.[44] The code retained some of the elements of inquisitorial procedure as well. For instance, Article 297 allowed the court to determine the scope of inquiry as well as the method of the examination of evidence.[45]

The Allied occupation also resulted in the enactment of the Habeas Corpus Act,[46] which protected citizens of Japan from illegal restraint of personal freedom. This was in line with Article 31 of the constitution, which stipulated that "no person shall be deprived of life or liberty, nor any other criminal penalty be imposed, except according to procedure established by law." During the deliberations concerning the possibility of introducing this act, the occupation lawyers did not suggest the Anglo-Saxon writ of habeas corpus as the model for Japanese legislation, as it was decided that it was "too alien to Continental law".[47] This bill was prepared in the course of collaboration between the judges of the Supreme Court, lawyers, and the members of the Diet.[48] The same Diet that enacted the Habeas Corpus Act also passed the new Juvenile Law,[49] Reformatory Law,[50] and Law Concerning Inquest of Prosecution.[51]

Proposals to introduce the jury system in post-war Japan

The possibility of introducing the jury system in post-war Japan was deliberated in connection with the most important legal reforms implemented under the Allied occupation: the drafting and enactment of the constitution, of the Court Organization Law, and of the new Code of Penal Procedure.

The interest in the institution of jury service on the part of the occupation forces and of the general public in the immediate post-war period appears to have been entirely justified. After all, the 1943 law that suspended Japan's Jury Act stipulated that the jury system would

---

42 Keiji Soshō Hō [Code of Criminal Procedure], Law No. 131 of 1948 [hereinafter Code of Criminal Procedure]; Takayanagi, "A Century of Innovation", p. 23.
43 Code of Criminal Procedure, art. 309. Appleton, "Reforms in Japanese Criminal Procedure under Allied Occupation", p. 422.
44 Code of Criminal Procedure, art. 319. Appleton, "Reforms in Japanese Criminal Procedure under Allied Occupation", pp. 423 and 407–430 (containing a detailed summary of the new Code).
45 Code of Criminal Procedure, art. 297. Oppler, *Legal Reform in Occupied Japan*, p. 142.
46 Jinshin Hogo Hō [Habeas Corpus Act], Law No. 199 of 1948.
47 Oppler, "The Reform of Japan's Legal and Judicial System under Allied Occupation", p. 320.
48 *Id.*, p. 320. The Supreme Commander expressed his support for the act by stating: "With the provision of the privilege of the writ of *Habeas Corpus*, Japan now assumes a place among those people of the world who live under positive safeguards of the sanctity of individual life, liberty and human dignity" (*id.*, p. 320).
49 Shōnen Hō [Juvenile Law], Law No. 168 of 1948. See Oppler, *Legal Reform in Occupied Japan*, pp. 149–150 (describing the contents of the Juvenile Law).
50 Shōnen In Hō [Reformatory Law], Law No. 169 of 1948.
51 Keisatsu Shinsakai Hō [Law Concerning Inquest of Prosecution], Law No. 147 of 1948.

be reintroduced as soon as the war was over.[52] In addition, several Japanese organizations and individuals saw the institution of jury service as a tool for democratizing society and included the implementation of the jury system on their agendas for deliberation in the early post-war period – a development that did not go unnoticed by the lawyers of the Allied occupation. Furthermore, the United States had a long tradition of successfully using the institution of jury service, which certainly motivated occupation lawyers to try and share their experience with their Japanese counterparts.

Proposals to include the provisions regarding jury service in the text of the new constitution (1945–1947)

At the beginning of the Allied occupation, SCAP was not planning to propose that Japan restore trial by jury. In November 1945 the Counterintelligence Corps (OCCIO)[53] sent a query to the Government Section, SCAP, regarding the position of the Section on the issue of the possible restoration of the jury system in Japan. In its response, the Government Section stated that it would not recommend that Japan implement jury trials.[54] Regarding the reasons for this decision, the note explained:

> An attempt to revive the jury system by directive of SCAP would not be desirable unless it were accompanied by a revision of Japanese court procedure. It would also require considerable retraining in common law concepts on the part of the Japanese bar and re-education of the Japanese citizenry at large as prospective jurymen.[55]

The position of SCAP changed by the beginning of 1946, however. One of the factors behind this change was the interest that several Japanese organizations and individuals expressed in the institution of jury service in the public debate concerning the provisions of the new constitution for Japan. The provisions regarding the jury system were included in a number of drafts of the constitution prepared by various organizations and individuals independently of the Japanese government. One such document, "The Outline of the Draft of the Constitution" (*Kenpō Sōan Yōkō*), was authored by the Constitution Research Group (*Kenpō Kenkyūkai*).[56] This draft of the constitution included a provision stipulating that trials at courts were to be conducted in the name of the people and in accordance with the Court Organization Law and the Jury Act. The occupation lawyers looked at "The Outline of the Draft of the Constitution" when writing their own draft of the constitution.[57] Other

---

52 Act on the Suspension of the Jury Act [Baishin Hō no Teishi ni kansuru Hōritsu], Law No. 88 of 1943, art. 3.
53 M. Itoh, 2003, *The Hatoyama Dynasty: Japanese Political Leadership through the Generations*, New York: Palgrave Macmillan, p. 98.
54 Note No. 2, Declassified E.O. 11652 Section 3(E) and 5(D) or (E) NNDG No. 775012, on file with the National Diet Library, Code: GS(B)02883.
55 *Id.*
56 Kenpō Kenkyūkai, 1945, "Kenpō Sōan Yōkō" [Outline of the Draft of the Constitution], December 27, available online at http://www.ndl.go.jp/constitution/shiryo/02/052/052tx.html#t001.
57 *Id.* N. Toshitani, "Sengo Kaikaku to Kokumin no Shihō Sanka" [Post-war Reforms and Justice [System] Participation of the People], in Tokyo Daigaku Shakai Kagaku Kenkyūjo [The University of Tokyo, Institute of Social Science], 1975, *Sengo Kaikaku* [Post-war Reforms], Vol. 4, Tokyo: Tokyo Daigaku Shuppan Kai, pp. 77–172, at p. 101 (discussing the influence of this draft on GHQ's own draft of the constitution).

drafts mentioning the right to trial by jury included Tatsuji Fuse's "Constitutional Reform Draft" (*Kenpō Kaisei Shian*)[58] and the draft prepared by the Communist Party of Japan.[59] In addition, a document jointly authored by the Japan Federation of Bar Associations and the Tokyo Bar Association urged the Japanese government to add a provision allowing the accused and his or her defense counsel to request to be tried by jury.[60] Furthermore, the virtues of the jury system as an instrument for the democratization of the society were stressed in a piece authored by the Japan Lawyers Association for Freedom (*Jiyū Hōsō Dantai*), a group of prominent Japanese lawyers. Titled "On the Democratization of the Justice System – Especially on the Political Significance of Such Reform" (*Shihō Seido no Minshuka – Toku ni Sono Seijiteki Igi ni tsuite*),[61] this document argued for the implementation of the system where laypersons would be elected by the general public to serve as jurors.[62]

The interest in the institution of jury service on the part of the aforementioned organizations and individuals was reflected in the discussions during the meetings of the committee for the Investigation of Constitutional Questions (*Kenpō Mondai Chōsa Iinkai*) – a deliberative body established on October 25, 1945, and chaired by Minister of State Jōji Matsumoto.[63] Professor Emeritus of Tokyo University Junji Nomura was one of the fierce proponents of the incorporation of the provisions regarding the jury system in the text of the new constitution during these discussions.[64] Professor Nomura discussed his position in detail in his "Position Paper Regarding Constitutional Reform" (*Kenpō Kaisei ni kansuru*

---

58 T. Fuse, 1945, "Kenpō Kaisei Shian" [Constitutional Reform Draft], December 22, art. 36 (enumerating right to trial by jury), available online at http://www.ndl.go.jp/constitution/shiryo/02/050/050tx.html#t001. The draft contains Fuse's note explaining that rather than resurrect the jury system that functioned in the pre-war period, Japan should implement a system that truly reflects the opinions of the members of the public. For a brief discussion of Fuse's life and pre-war career see Chapter 4.

59 Nihon Kyōsantō [Japanese Communist Party], 1946, "Nihon Jinmin Kyōwakoku Kenpō (Sōan)" [The Constitution of the People's Republic of Japan (A Draft)], June 26, art. 82, available online at http://www.ndl.go.jp/constitution/shiryo/02/119/119tx.html.

60 Nihon Bengoshikai, Tokyo Bengoshikai [Japan Federation of Bar Associations and the Tokyo Bar Association], 1946, "Seifu no Kenpō Kaisei An ni Taisuru Shūsei An to sono Riyū" [Proposal for Revising the Government's Constitutional Revision Draft and Reasons for Such a Revision], partially reprinted in Toshitani, "Sengo Kaikaku to Kokumin no Shihō Sanka" [Post-war Reforms and Justice [System] Participation of the People], pp. 102–103.

61 T. Okabayashi, 1946, "Shihō Seido no Minshuka – Toku ni Sono Seijiteki Igi ni tsuite" (On the Democratization of the Justice System – Especially on the Political Significance of Such Reform), *Hōritsu Jihō*, Vol. 18, No. 6, partially reprinted in Toshitani, "Sengo Kaikaku to Kokumin no Shihō Sanka" [Post-war Reforms and Justice [System] Participation of the People], pp. 103–104.

62 *Id.*

63 The possibility of adding a provision regarding either the reintroduction of Japan's pre-war jury system or the implementation of the Continental-European model of jury trials to the text of Article 60 of the *Meiji* Constitution was deliberated during the fourth meeting of the Commission, held on December 24, 1945 (Y. Naitō, 1959, *Shūsengo no Shihō Seido Kaikaku no Keika* [The Progress of Postwar Legal Reforms], Tokyo: Shihō Kenshūjo, Vol. 1, p. 16 (containing the minutes of that meeting)). In addition, the issue of jury trials was discussed in connection with the text of Article 24 of the *Meiji* Constitution that stipulated that "No Japanese subject shall be deprived of his right of being tried by the judges determined by law" (Meiji Kenpō, art. 24). Debates arose regarding the question of whether the word "judges" in the article should be replaced with the word "court" to allow for the possibility that the jury system may be introduced (T. Satō, 1962, *Nihonkoku Kenpō Seiritsu Shi* [The Formulation of the Constitution of Japan], Vol. 1, Tokyo: Yūhikaku, p. 371, cited in Toshitani, "Sengo Kaikaku to Kokumin no Shihō Sanka" [Post-war Reforms and Justice [System] Participation of the People], p. 106).

64 Toshitani, "Sengo Kaikaku to Kokumin no Shihō Sanka" [Post-war Reforms and Justice [System] Participation of the People], p. 106.

138 *The occupation years*

Ikensho), published in December 1945.[65] In this piece, Professor Nomura argued not only for the implementation of the criminal and civil petit jury systems in Japan, but also for the introduction of the grand jury that would issue indictments in cases where the possible punishment was more than six years' imprisonment. He also proposed to implement the lay assessor (*sanshinkan*) system to adjudicate criminal cases at ward courts (*ku saibansho*).[66] The final document, compiled based on the deliberations at the Constitutional Problems Research Commission, titled "The Gist of the Revision of the Constitution" (also known as the "Matsumoto Draft"), and submitted to the General Headquarters (GHQ) by the Japanese government did not incorporate any of Professor Nomura's ideas. As SCAP closely followed the deliberations at the committee, the fact that the jury system was discussed at these meetings affected SCAP's initially skeptical attitude towards the possibility of implementing the jury system in Japan.[67]

There is evidence suggesting that the GHQ considered adding a provision regarding trials by jury to its own drafts of the constitution, prepared in 1946. Specifically, among the documents associated with the GHQ's first draft of the constitution, there is a document stipulating that "[t]rial by Jury shall be accorded to anyone charged with a capital offence, and to anyone accused of a felony, at the request of the accused."[68] This provision was retained in the second draft prepared by the GHQ. The right to trial by jury was mentioned in an article (not numbered) in Chapter 4, titled "Juridical Rights".[69] It stated the following:

> Article ___ In all criminal cases the accused shall enjoy the right to a speedy and public trial by an impartial tribunal. He shall [, at his trial, be confronted with all the witnesses against him and] be permitted full opportunity to cross-examine such witnesses, and he shall have the right of compulsory process for obtaining witnesses in his favor, at public expense. At all times the accused shall have the assistance of competent counsel who shall, if the accused be unable to secure the same by his own efforts, be assigned to his use by the government.

---

65 J. Nomura, 1945, "Kenpō Kaisei ni kansuru Ikensho" [Position Paper Regarding Constitutional Reform], December 26, available online at http://www.ndl.go.jp/constitution/shiryo/02/051/051tx.html.
66 *Id.*
67 Toshitani, "Sengo Kaikaku to Kokumin no Shihō Sanka" [Post-war Reforms and Justice [System] Participation of the People], p. 107; J. Matsumoto, 1946, "Kenpō Kaisei Yōkō" [The Gist of the Revision of the Constitution], February 8 (on file with the National Diet Library, Japan), available online at http://www.ndl.go.jp/constitution/e/shiryo/03/074a/074a_001r.html. Also see Public Administration Division, Government Section, SCAP, "Charles Kades' Comments on the Document 'Gist of the Revision of the Constitution' (Matsumoto Draft)" (on file with the National Diet Library, Japan), available online at http://www.ndl.go.jp/constitution/e/shiryo/03/002_15/002_15_001r.html.
68 "Drafts of the Revised Constitution", February 1946, Hussey Papers: "24-A Draft of the 'Preamble' to the Revised Constitution" through "24-I Drafts of Chapter Ten, 'Supreme Law' of the Revised Constitution", YE-5, Roll No. 5, microformed (on file with the National Diet Library, Japan), available online at http://www.ndl.go.jp/constitution/e/shiryo/03/147shoshi.html. The page containing this provision is available online at http://www.ndl.go.jp/constitution/e/shiryo/03/002_47/002_47_117l.html.
69 "Original Drafts of Committee Reports", February 1946, SCAP Files of Commander Alfred R. Hussey, Doc. No. 8 (on file with the National Diet Library, Japan), available online at http://www.ndl.go.jp/constitution/e/shiryo/03/147shoshi.html. The section containing this provision is available online at http://www.ndl.go.jp/constitution/e/shiryo/03/147/147_019l.html.

No person shall be declared guilty of a crime except upon fair and open trial [, nor shall any person be deprived of civil rights without a trial].

[Trial by Jury shall be accorded to anyone charged with a capital offence, and to anyone accused of a felony, at the request of the accused].[70]

The provision regarding jury trials was deleted subsequently and is not to be found in the GHQ draft of the constitution dated February 12, 1946.[71] It appears likely that the occupation lawyers decided to postpone the discussion of jury trials to a later time.[72]

Meanwhile, the possibility of the introduction of the jury system in Japan featured prominently in the deliberations within the Japanese government when it was considering GHQ's draft of the constitution. As the result of these deliberations, it was decided that the text of Article 24 of the *Meiji* Constitution, which stipulated that "no Japanese subject shall be deprived of his right of being tried by the *judges* determined by law" (emphasis added), needed to be amended in such a way that would make the possible subsequent introduction of the jury system constitutional.[73] This provision was changed to read: "In all criminal cases the accused shall enjoy the right to a speedy and public trial by an *impartial tribunal*" (emphasis added); it is this wording that we find in Article 37 of the enacted version of Japan's 1946 Constitution.[74]

The prospects of introducing the jury system under the provisions of the new constitution were discussed in both Houses of the Diet during the course of the deliberations regarding the text of the new charter. At the Privy Council, the representatives of the Japanese government were asked whether they thought it was possible to introduce a truly democratic jury system under the provisions of the new constitution. The response of the government was that while the text of the new constitution did not contain any provisions directly concerning the institution of jury service, the introduction of the "American-style jury system" was more plausible under the new constitution than under the *Meiji* Constitution.[75] The government thus refrained from committing itself to introducing the jury system.

Other concrete questions were addressed to the government regarding the draft of the new constitution at the House of Representatives.[76] Specifically, Member of Parliament Shungo Abe stated that he believed that the institution of jury service was indispensable for a truly democratic country and asked Minister of Justice Tokutarō Kimura if the

---

70 Words in brackets are crossed out in the draft. See http://www.ndl.go.jp/constitution/e/shiryo/03/147/147_019l.html.
71 "Memorandum to Chief, Government Section, dated 12 February 1946", available online at http://www.ndl.go.jp/constitution/e/shiryo/03/076a_e/076a_etx.html.
72 Toshitani, "Sengo Kaikaku to Kokumin no Shihō Sanka" [Post-war Reforms and Justice [System] Participation of the People], p. 111.
73 Meiji Kenpō, art. 24. Naitō, *Shūsengo no Shihō Seido Kaikaku no Keika* [The Progress of Postwar Legal Reforms], Vol. 1, pp. 314–315; Toshitani, "Sengo Kaikaku to Kokumin no Shihō Sanka" [Post-war Reforms and Justice [System] Participation of the People], p. 112.
74 Nihonkoku Kenpō (1946), art. 37.
75 Transcript of Deliberations at the Privy Council Concerning Chapter 6 of the Draft of the New Constitution, May 13, 1945, reproduced in Naitō, *Shūsengo no Shihō Seido Kaikaku no Keika* [The Progress of Postwar Legal Reforms], Vol. 1, p. 45.
76 The possibility of the implementation of the jury system in Japan was a question that was deliberated further during the 90th Extraordinary Session of the Imperial Diet (from June 20, 1946, to October 12, 1946). Toshitani, "Sengo Kaikaku to Kokumin no Shihō Sanka" [Post-war Reforms and Justice [System] Participation of the People], p. 114.

140 *The occupation years*

Japanese government was prepared to include a provision regarding jury service in the draft of the constitution.[77] Kimura replied that he believed that in view of the lack of popularity of the pre-war Jury Act, it was necessary to carefully consider the question of whether the concept of jury service suited the Japanese national character. He added that in the post-war situation, when many buildings were destroyed, the revival of the jury system would necessitate the construction of many new facilities. He concluded by saying that the subject of the possible introduction of the jury system would be carefully studied by his Ministry.[78]

The arguments made by Minister of Justice Kimura against adding an article providing for the implementation of the jury system to the constitution were repeated on a number occasions. These included the meeting sessions of the Constitutional Draft Revision Committee, established within the House of Representatives (*Teikoku Kenpō Kaisei An Iinkai*), and the meetings of the Constitutional Draft Revision Special Committee, set up within the House of Peers (*Teikoku Kenpō Kaisei An Tokubetsu Iinkai*). All of the initiatives proposing to include an article on jury trials in the text of the constitution were blocked, and the enacted text of the constitution does not contain any provisions regarding jury service.[79]

The Ministry of Justice's proposal to introduce the jury system as part of the broad strategy of legal reforms (1945)

Simultaneously with the first deliberations concerning the text of the new constitution, the Japanese government discussed the possible expansion of layperson participation in the justice system in the course of the formulation of its broad strategy of legal reforms for post-war Japan.

---

77 Transcript of Deliberations at the House of Representatives, June 28, 1946, partially reprinted in Toshitani, "Sengo Kaikaku to Kokumin no Shihō Sanka" [Post-war Reforms and Justice [System] Participation of the People], pp. 114–115.
78 *Id.*, p. 115.
79 At the 6th meeting of the Committee on the Constitution Revision Bill, held on July 5, 1946, Toranosuke Miura, a member of the committee and a representative of the Japan Liberal Party (*Nihon Jiyūtō*), proposed to include provisions regarding the jury system in the text of the constitution, arguing that the institution of jury service was indispensable for a democratic society. The revisions proposed by Miura were not adopted, however, in view of the arguments voiced by Minister of Justice Kimura (Transcript of Deliberations at the House of Representatives, June 28, 1946, partially reprinted in Toshitani, "Sengo Kaikaku to Kokumin no Shihō Sanka" [Post-war Reforms and Justice [System] Participation of the People], pp. 114–115). At the House of Peers, Eiichi Makino pointed out the importance of considering the possibility of revising the provisions of the pre-war Jury Act to adjust it to the post-war situation in Japan (Toshitani, "Sengo Kaikaku to Kokumin no Shihō Sanka" [Post-war Reforms and Justice [System] Participation of the People], p. 117). During the 16th and the 20th sessions of the Special Committee on the Constitution Revision Bill, a member of the committee belonging to the Mutual Attainment Society (*Dōseikai*) – a peerage faction – Karoku Nomura argued that the jury trial system was the ultimate way to achieve truly democratic justice and pointed out that the jury system that existed in Japan before the war failed because of the internal problems of the pre-war Jury Act, such as the provisions that allowed the accused to waive jury trial. Minister of Justice Kimura responded by saying that he thought that ideally the jury system should be reintroduced in Japan, but that it was necessary to carefully consider the question of whether the Japanese society was ready for the implementation of this system. Kimura emphasized that the process of the reintroduction of the jury system should not be rushed in view of the difficulties of post-war reconstruction (Toshitani, "Sengo Kaikaku to Kokumin no Shihō Sanka" [Post-war Reforms and Justice [System] Participation of the People], pp. 117–119).

The Ministry of Justice established the Council for Justice System Reform (*Shihō Seido Kaisei Shingikai*) in October 1945.[80] Chaired by Minister of Justice Chūzō Iwata, this council debated the subject of layperson participation as it tried to determine what kind of specific measures Japan should implement to ensure that the rights of citizens would be protected in the post-war period.[81] The council discussed the pros and cons of introducing the all-layperson Anglo-American model and the mixed-court Continental-European lay assessor model of jury trials in Japan, and the idea to implement the lay assessor system in less complicated cases was included in a document compiled by the council in December 1945, "Tentative Draft of the Outline Concerning the Democratization of Justice" (*Shihō no Minshuka ni Kansuru Yōkō Shian*).[82] According to the Tentative Draft, Japan would introduce a mixed-court jury system where cases would be deliberated by a mixed panel consisting of professional judges and lay commissioners (*sanshinkan*) in ward courts, district courts, the court of appeal (*Kōsoin*), and the Great Court of Judicature (*Daishin'in*).[83] Lay commissioners were to have the same rights during the course of the trial as the judges. The ratio of professional judges to lay commissioners was, according to the document, to be one professional judge to two *sanshinkan* in ward courts, three judges to two *sanshinkan* in district courts, and five professional judges to four *sanshinkan* in the court of appeal and the Great Court of Judicature. Japanese citizens over thirty years of age who were educated and could obtain the recommendation of the president of the district court were to serve as lay commissioners. An eligible citizen was to be appointed by the Minister of Justice, at the request of the president of the court of appeal, to become a lay commissioner at a ward or district court, or at the court of appeal. To serve as a lay commissioner at the Great Court of Judicature, a candidate was to be appointed by the Minister of Justice at the request of the president of the Great Court of Judicature.[84]

Regarding the reasons for choosing the Continental-European model of jury trials rather than the Anglo-American model, Ken'ichi Okuno, head of the Civil Affairs Bureau of the Ministry of Justice, explained that the position of the Ministry was that implementing the *sanshinkan* system was the most sensible and "non-radical" (*onken*) way of addressing the demands for democratization of the justice system in the Japanese society.[85] Okuno added that introducing a modified version of the Anglo-American style jury system, where the opinions of the members of the jury were not binding on the court, was not an option for post-war Japan; therefore, implementing the *sanshinkan* system where the opinions of lay participants would be under the control of professional judges was a way that was most agreeable to the Ministry of Justice.[86]

---

80 *Id.*, p. 120.
81 *Id.*, p. 120.
82 Shihō Shō [Ministry of Justice], 1945, "Shihō no Minshuka ni Kansuru Yōkō Shian" [Tentative Draft of the Outline Concerning the Democratization of Justice], December 18, reprinted in Naitō, *Shūsengo no Shihō Seido Kaikaku no Keika* [The Progress of Postwar Legal Reforms], Vol. 3, pp. 503–504.
83 The word *sanshinkan* consists of two components – the word *sanshin*, which is usually translated into English as "lay assessor" (in Japanese, the lay assessor system is referred to as *sanshin seido*), and the word *kan*, which means "official". Lay participants in the Continental-European model of jury trials are called *sanshin'in* in Japanese. This chapter translates *sanshinkan* as "lay commissioners" to illustrate this difference.
84 *Id.*
85 Toshitani, "Sengo Kaikaku to Kokumin no Shihō Sanka" [Post-war Reforms and Justice [System] Participation of the People], p. 123.
86 *Id.*

During the deliberations on the Tentative Draft prepared by the Ministry of Justice, the members of the council decided against recommending that Japan implement either the Anglo-American or the Continental-European model of jury trials. Regarding the question of whether the implementation of the system envisaged in the Tentative Draft was a good idea, the council did not reach a definite conclusion and advised the Ministry of Justice to study the subject further.[87]

The new Court Organization Law and the Code of Criminal Procedure

Unlike Japan's Ministry of Justice, SCAP did not include the introduction of the jury system as an item on the list of strategically important legal reforms for Japan. The question of whether Japan should implement the jury system or not was raised by SCAP in connection with two specific reforms: the drafting of the new Court Organization Law and of the new Code of Criminal Procedure. SCAP's initiatives with regard to these two pieces of legislation included two attempts to suggest to the Japanese side to discuss the jury system. The first attempt centered around the drafts of the Court Organization Law and of the Code of Criminal Procedure that were authored by Captain Maniscalco of the Legal Section, Public Safety Division, SCAP, in 1946. The second involved the informal directives from SCAP to the Japanese government regarding the text of the new Court Organization Law that were communicated to the Japanese side by Alfred C. Oppler in 1947.

Captain Maniscalco's proposals (1946)

In 1946, two documents mentioning the possibility of implementing the jury system in Japan were prepared by the Legal Section, Public Safety Division, SCAP: the draft of the new Court Organization Law ("Proposed Revision of Law of the Constitution of the Courts of Justice") and the proposal for revision of the Code of Criminal Procedure ("Proposed Revision of Code of Criminal Procedure").

The fact that the proposals concerning two important reforms of the Japanese legal system were prepared by the Public Safety Division, Civil Intelligence Section (CIS) may appear surprising at first glance. After all, the Civil Intelligence Section was originally established as a branch that was responsible for censorship activities, conducting counterespionage, freeing political prisoners, and arresting war crimes suspects.[88] In January 1946, this section was substantially reorganized, however, and the four components that originally constituted the Section – that is, the 441 Counter Intelligence Corps, the Civil Censorship Detachment, a civil communications intelligence team, and an interrogation unit – were transferred from SCAP to the U.S. Army Forces in the Pacific (USAFPAC) Counter-Intelligence Section.[89] In place of these four subsections, the Public Safety Division was set up within the CIS.[90] This Division was put in charge of Japan's legal affairs, maritime safety, fire departments, courts, the Metropolitan Police Office, and other law enforcement agencies.[91] It was this section that initiated the reform of Japan's police system in 1946.[92]

---

87 *Id.*, p. 123.
88 E. Takemae, 2003, *The Allied Occupation of Japan*, New York: Continuum, p. 163.
89 *Id.*, pp. 163–164.
90 *Id.*, p. 164.
91 *Id.*, p. 164.
92 *Id.*, p. 297.

The occupation years 143

The two documents proposing the introduction of the jury system in Japan were authored by Captain Anthony J. Maniscalco.[93] His "Proposed Revision of Law of the Constitution of the Courts of Justice" contained the following note:

> [A]ttention is invited to the possibility that these courts may be reduced in personnel to one judge in criminal cases when the Revised Code of Criminal Procedure and the Revised Jury Act are enacted and the use of the jury becomes general.[94]

Captain Maniscalco's "Proposed Revision of Code of Criminal Procedure" included provisions implementing both the grand and the petit jury in Japan.[95] Specifically, Article 227 of the proposed revised version of Japan's Code of Criminal Procedure stipulated that

> no accused shall be made to answer (stand public action) for any crime the penalty for which may be confinement for one year or more, or for life, or an indefinite period, or death, unless an indictment or presentment made by a grand jury.[96]

This article was followed by the following note: "Rules governing selection, session etc. of grand juries should be promulgated." Article 228 read as follows: "No indictment shall be found, nor shall presentment be made, without the concurrence of at least ten jurors (of a panel of 12)."[97] A section of the proposal was devoted to stipulations regarding petit jury. Captain Maniscalco's draft suggested that Japan introduce an all-layperson criminal jury system according to which a panel of six laypersons would make decisions on the questions of fact and come up with the verdict of guilty or not guilty independently of the judge.[98] The proposal extended the right to serve on jury to all persons eligible to vote. Like the pre-war Jury Act, the proposal suggested that the jury try cases for which the maximum

---

93 Toshitani, "Sengo Kaikaku to Kokumin no Shihō Sanka" [Post-war Reforms and Justice [System] Participation of the People], pp. 124–130. Captain Maniscalco served in the Counter Intelligence Section in the Philippines prior to being posted to Japan. An internal review of his work and contribution stated that "[a]s legal officer, he at all times advised the [Public Safety] Division on revisions of laws and regulations as they affected the administration of the Japanese police, prison, and fire systems." It also points out that Captain Maniscalco "made extensive studies of the Japanese Public Safety Criminal Codes and Procedure in Japanese law" and states that the studies conducted by Captain Maniscalco "will be used as suggested material by the appropriate staff section of SCAP, which are revising Japanese jurisprudence along democratic legal lines" (Colonel C.S. Ryers, 1946, Note Addressed to Commander-in-Chief, United States Army Forces, Pacific APO 500, "Recommendation for Award of the Legion of Merit", Declassified E.O. 12065 Section 3–402/NNDG No. 775009, on file with the National Diet Library, Modern Japanese Political History Materials Room (code: G2 03783)).
94 Proposed Revision of Law of Constitution of the Courts of Justice, SCAP, art. 19.
95 Proposed Revision of Code of Criminal Procedure, not dated, Declassified E.O. 12065 Section 3–402/NNDG No. 775009, microformed on GHQ/SCAP Records General Staff II, Public Safety Division, Decimal File 1946–52, Box No. 263, Folder No. 10 (National Archives and Records Service), on file with Modern Japanese Political History Materials Room, National Diet Library (G2 01180–G2 01182), Japan [hereinafter Proposed Revision of Code of Criminal Procedure, SCAP]; Toshitani, "Sengo Kaikaku to Kokumin no Shihō Sanka" [Post-war Reforms and Justice [System] Participation of the People], p. 125 (discussing the authorship of this draft and the date when it could have been written).
96 Proposed Revision of Code of Criminal Procedure, SCAP, art. 227.
97 *Id.*, art. 228.
98 *Id.*

144 *The occupation years*

penalty is death, unless waived by the defendant.[99] It also made it possible for the accused to request trial by jury in cases involving other, less grave offences.[100] The jury was to reach its decisions based on the principle of unanimity.[101] The author of the draft appended the following note to explain why introducing the institution of jury service was important for Japan:

> In the foregoing nothing has been said of trial by jury. In Japan, a jury may be had but under the procedure as it now stands the judge can dismiss the jury if it returns a verdict with which he does not agree and continue to empanel a jury until he gets the verdict desired.
>
> It is felt that a free jury system should be incorporated in this Code and comment is desired as to whether such petit jury shall be the sole judge of the law and the facts and of the sentence or whether it should be limited to finding of the facts and the Court assesses the sentence. Also, whether the judge can comment on the facts, credibility of the witnesses etc. or not.

There is evidence suggesting that this draft was submitted to the Japanese government as a private draft prepared by Captain Maniscalco and not as the draft representing the official recommendations of SCAP.[102] This fact seems to indicate that there was a significant difference of opinions among the various sections of SCAP regarding the recommendations to give to the Japanese government on the subject of jury trials.[103] Alfred C. Oppler, Chief Officer of the Legal Unit, Governmental Powers Division, and Oppler's associate, Thomas L. Blakemore, for example, were highly critical of Maniscalco's proposals.[104] Oppler and Blakemore both expressed their concerns about imposing the Anglo-American jury trial system on Japan – a country with essentially an inquisitorial system of justice – in several internal SCAP documents written at the time of drafting of Maniscalco's proposals and subsequently admitted that there were different views regarding this subject within SCAP.[105]

As the result of the deliberations with the Japanese government and the Ministry of Justice, the provisions regarding the jury system suggested by Maniscalco were not included in the drafts of either the new Court Organization Law or the new Code of Criminal Procedure. The Ministry of Justice stated that it would "absolutely not" adopt (*tōtei*

---

99 *Id.*
100 *Id.*
101 *Id.*
102 Naitō, *Shūsengo no Shihō Seido Kaikaku no Keika* [The Progress of Postwar Legal Reforms], Vol. 2, p. 54; Toshitani, "Sengo Kaikaku to Kokumin no Shihō Sanka" [Post-war Reforms and Justice [System] Participation of the People], p. 127 (discussing this draft as prepared by Captain Maniscalco in the private capacity).
103 Toshitani, "Sengo Kaikaku to Kokumin no Shihō Sanka" [Post-war Reforms and Justice [System] Participation of the People], p. 127.
104 *Id.*, p. 158.
105 A. C. Oppler, 1946, "Memorandum for the Chief", Governmental Powers Branch, 28 March, cited in Toshitani, "Sengo Kaikaku to Kokumin no Shihō Sanka" [Post-war Reforms and Justice [System] Participation of the People], pp. 158–159; T. Yamanaka, 1975, "Oppler Hakase to no Intabyū" [An Interview with Dr. Oppler], *Hōritsu Jihō*, Vol. 47, No. 4, pp. 98–105, at p. 100; T. L. Blakemore, "Memorandum for the Chief", Government Section, Subject: Liaison with Legislative Reform Committee of the Ministry of Justice: Report #1, August 5, 1946, cited in Toshitani, "Sengo Kaikaku to Kokumin no Shihō Sanka" [Post-war Reforms and Justice [System] Participation of the People], pp. 158–159.

ukerarenai) the provisions contained in Maniscalco's "Proposed Revision of Code of Criminal Procedure".[106] The "Proposed Revision of Code of Criminal Procedure" nevertheless prompted the officials of the Japanese Ministry of Justice to reexamine the proposals voiced by the Japanese organizations and by the members of the Diet in relation to the stipulations of the new constitution and those made by the members of the Council for Justice System Reform (*Shihō Seido Kaisei Shingikai*). It also made the Japanese government reconsider the possibility of revising and reenacting Japan's pre-war Jury Act and to discuss the features of the Continental-European and Anglo-American models of jury trial.[107]

Specifically, on March 5, 1946, the Japanese government held a Cabinet meeting devoted to the issue of the possible restoration of the pre-war jury system.[108] The subject of jury trials was discussed further at the Extraordinary Judicial System Reform Preparatory Council (*Rinji Shihō Seido Kaisei Junbi Kyōgikai*) – a deliberative body established by the Ministry of Justice and consisting of representatives of the Ministry as well as the officials of the various Tokyo courts,[109] the Public Procurator's office, and the members of the Tokyo Bar Association.[110] At the meeting that was devoted to citizen participation in the justice system, the Ministry of Justice asked the members of the council to express their opinions regarding the possibility of reintroducing the institution of jury service in Japan. The idea to implement jury trials was supported by the majority of the members of the council.[111] The document "Items Determining the Attitudes of this Ministry to the Justice [System] under the New Constitution" (*Shinkenpō ni tomonai Shihō ni kanshi Honshō toshite Taido o Kessu beki Kōmoku*), which the Ministry prepared on May 29, 1946, reveals the details of the discussions held at the council.[112] According to

---

106 T. Odanaka, 1973, "Keiji Soshō Seido no Kaikaku ni tsuite" [Reforms in the Criminal Procedure System], *Shakai Kagaku Kenkyū* [Journal of Social Science], Vol. 25, No. 1, pp. 120–132, at p. 126; Toshitani, "Sengo Kaikaku to Kokumin no Shihō Sanka" [Post-war Reforms and Justice [System] Participation of the People], p. 127.
107 Toshitani, "Sengo Kaikaku to Kokumin no Shihō Sanka" [Post-war Reforms and Justice [System] Participation of the People], p. 127.
108 Anonymous, 1946, "Baishin Seido o Fukkatsu; Kakugi Kettei" [Restoration of the Jury System; Cabinet Resolution] *Asahi Shinbun*, March 6, partially reprinted in Toshitani, "Sengo Kaikaku to Kokumin no Shihō Sanka" [Post-war Reforms and Justice [System] Participation of the People], pp. 129–130.
109 That is, the Great Court of Judicature (*Daishin'in*), the court of appeal (*Kōsoin*), Tokyo District Civil Court, the Tokyo District Criminal Court, and the Administrative Court (Toshitani, "Sengo Kaikaku to Kokumin no Shihō Sanka" [Post-war Reforms and Justice [System] Participation of the People], p. 130).
110 Naitō, *Shūsengo no Shihō Seido Kaikaku no Keika* [The Progress of Postwar Legal Reforms], Vol. 3, pp. 621–637; Toshitani, "Sengo Kaikaku to Kokumin no Shihō Sanka" [Post-war Reforms and Justice [System] Participation of the People], p. 130.
111 The representatives of the Great Court of Judicature agreed with this proposal and argued that the civil jury system should also be implemented in Japan – a suggestion that the Tokyo District Court opposed. The representatives of the Bar Associations expressed their belief that the pre-war jury system should be reintroduced after adjusting its features in a way that would suit the democratic values of contemporary Japan and that the possibility of introducing the civil jury system should be studied (Naitō, *Shūsengo no Shihō Seido Kaikaku no Keika* [The Progress of Postwar Legal Reforms], Vol. 3, pp. 621–637; Toshitani, "Sengo Kaikaku to Kokumin no Shihō Sanka" [Post-war Reforms and Justice [System] Participation of the People], p. 130).
112 Ministry of Justice, 1946, "Items Determining the Attitudes of this Ministry to the Justice [System] under the New Constitution" [*Shinkenpō ni tomonai Shihō ni kanshi Honshō toshite Taido o Kessu beki Kōmoku*], May 29, partially reprinted in Toshitani, "Sengo Kaikaku to Kokumin no Shihō Sanka" [Post-war Reforms and Justice [System] Participation of the People], p. 131.

146 *The occupation years*

this document, the Ministry considered the possibility of introducing the criminal jury system that would endow the members of the jury – men and women – with the responsibility of making decisions on points of fact. The decisions of the jury would be binding on the court and could be appealed by the defendant.[113]

This tentative proposal was deliberated further at the Judicial System Reform Council (*Shihō Seido Kaisei Shingikai*) – a council that replaced the Extraordinary Judicial System Reform Preparatory Council in July 1946 and was chaired by Minister of Justice Tokutarō Kimura.[114] The Judicial System Reform Council consisted of three subcommittees (*shōiinkai*).[115] The first and third subcommittees (*Dai 1 Shōiinkai; Dai 3 Shōiinkai*) deliberated the introduction of the new system of layperson participation in Japan. The third subcommittee focused on the Anglo-American model of jury trials in its discussion, while the first subcommittee discussed the possibility of implementing the Continental-European mixed-court jury system in Japan. The conclusions of the third subcommittee were similar to those reached by the members of the Extraordinary Judicial System Reform Preparatory Council. The members tentatively agreed that the provisions regarding jury service could be included in the new Code of Penal Procedure.[116] Simultaneously, the first subcommittee looked into the features of the Continental-European jury systems existing in other countries and proposed to implement the lay assessor (*sanshin*) system in Japan.[117] The members of this subcommittee even shared ideas regarding the possible contents of the Lay Assessor Law (*Sanshin Hō*) that would formally introduce the lay assessor system in Japan.[118] According to this subcommittee's proposal, criminal defendants at district courts were to be allowed to request to be tried by a mixed-court panel consisting of one judge and three lay assessors.[119]

The aforementioned proposals regarding the introduction of both the Anglo-American jury system and the Continental-European mixed-court jury system in Japan were never realized, as during the course of subsequent discussions the members of the first and third subcommittees and the officials of the Ministry of Justice raised concerns regarding the constitutionality of layperson participation in the justice system in the capacity of jurors or lay assessors. Specifically, it was argued that implementing either the Continental-European lay assessor system or the Anglo-American jury system, where the verdicts of the members of the jury would be binding, would be in conflict with the provisions of Article 76 of the new

---

113 *Id.*
114 Toshitani, "Sengo Kaikaku to Kokumin no Shihō Sanka" [Post-war Reforms and Justice [System] Participation of the People], pp. 132–133.
115 *Id.*, pp. 132–133.
116 *Id.*, p. 135.
117 The members of the subcommittee studied the systems of layperson participation in Germany, Austria, and the Soviet Union (Naitō, *Shūsengo no Shihō Seido Kaikaku no Keika* [The Progress of Postwar Legal Reforms], Vol. 3, pp. 699–700 (containing the materials used during the deliberations of the first subcommittee); Toshitani, "Sengo Kaikaku to Kokumin no Shihō Sanka" [Post-war Reforms and Justice [System] Participation of the People], pp. 142–143).
118 Naitō, *Shūsengo no Shihō Seido Kaikaku no Keika* [The Progress of Postwar Legal Reforms], Vol. 3, pp. 967–968; Toshitani, "Sengo Kaikaku to Kokumin no Shihō Sanka" [Post-war Reforms and Justice [System] Participation of the People], pp. 139–143.
119 Naitō, *Shūsengo no Shihō Seido Kaikaku no Keika* [The Progress of Postwar Legal Reforms], Vol. 3, pp. 967–968; Toshitani, "Sengo Kaikaku to Kokumin no Shihō Sanka" [Post-war Reforms and Justice [System] Participation of the People], p. 138.

constitution, which stipulated that "all judges shall . . . be bound only by this Constitution and the laws."[120]

SCAP's directives regarding the new Court Organization Law (1947)

The possibility of implementing the jury system was next discussed by the Japanese government and the members of the GHQ at the meetings of the Extraordinary Bill Revision Committee (*Tokubetsu Hōan Kaisei Iinkai*) that were devoted to the drafting of the Court Organization Law in 1947.[121]

Maniscalco's earlier proposals regarding this piece of legislation were not discussed at this stage, but the American side again proposed to include a provision concerning the jury system in the draft of the Court Organization Law. Yorihiro Naitō, an official at the Ministry of Justice, noted in his diary in an entry dated March 9, 1947, that Alfred C. Oppler approached him suggesting that a provision stipulating that cases at higher courts and the district courts may be tried by jury should be added to the text of the law.[122] Naitō expressed his surprise at the timing of this request, as this conversation with Oppler was taking place after all the final details concerning the Court Organization Law had already been hammered out.[123] Naitō also noted in his diary that he believed that Oppler was most likely voicing this proposal not of his own accord, but that another official or officials at SCAP were likely to have come up with this idea.[124]

SCAP's recommendation articulated to Naitō by Oppler was discussed during the 5th meeting of the Revision Committee on March 10, 1947.[125] During this meeting, the Japanese side initially opposed SCAP's idea and argued that the provisions regarding the jury system should be included not in the Court Organization Law, but in those pieces of legislation that directly addressed the issue of jury trials, such as the new Jury Act, if this piece of legislation would ever be drafted.[126] In response, the representatives of SCAP explained that they did not wish to impose the jury system on Japan, but thought that it was necessary

---

120 Nihonkoku Kenpō (1946), art. 76; Naitō, *Shūsengo no Shihō Seido Kaikaku no Keika* [The Progress of Postwar Legal Reforms], Vol. 2, pp. 225 and 75–76 (containing the reprint of the minutes of the deliberations at the council devoted to the question of the constitutionality of the possible introduction of the jury or the lay assessor systems in Japan); Toshitani, "Sengo Kaikaku to Kokumin no Shihō Sanka" [Post-war Reforms and Justice [System] Participation of the People], pp. 141–142 (discussing the reasons why the proposals regarding the implementation of either the jury system or of the lay assessor system were never realized in the immediate post-war period).
121 Saibansho Kōsei Hō [Court Organization Law], Law No. 59 of 1947.
122 Naitō, *Shūsengo no Shihō Seido Kaikaku no Keika* [The Progress of Postwar Legal Reforms], Vol. 2, p. 656 (containing a reprint of the relevant section of Naitō's diary).
123 *Id.*
124 *Id.*
125 *Id.*, pp. 658–659.
126 *Id.*, pp. 658–659 (containing the minutes of this meeting). The members of the meeting included Thomas L. Blakemore, Alfred C. Oppler, Vice Minister of Justice Tanimura, Head of the Criminal Affairs Bureau (*Keiji Kyoku*) of the Ministry of Justice Sato, Civil Affairs Bureau (*Minji Kyoku*) of the Ministry of Justice Okuno, Assistant Officer (*Jimukan*) Ozawa, Director (*Kachō*) Naitō, Director (*Kachō*) Nogi, Consultant (*Shokutaku*) Kumano, Assistant Officer (*Jimukan*) Azegami, Assistant Officer (*Jimukan*) Ueda, Deputy Director of the Central Liaison Office (*Shūren Jichō*) Higuchi, Deputy Director of the Central Liaison Office (*Shūren Jichō*) Hattori, Professor Kaneko, Secretary Hirota, and Communications Assistant (*Renraku Kan*) Fujiyama (*id.*, pp. 657–658).

148　*The occupation years*

to include a provision that would open the door for the possible implementation of such a system at some point in the future.[127] At the end of the negotiations, both sides agreed that an article stipulating that "the provisions of this law shall in no way prevent the establishment by other statutes of a jury system for criminal cases" would be added to the draft of the Court Organization Law, and it is these words that may be found in the enacted version of this piece of legislation.[128]

SCAP's "Proposed Revision of the Jury Act" (not dated)

The possibility that this provision of the Court Organization Law, which was added at the insistence of the occupation lawyers and against the opposition of the Japanese side, might result in the subsequent promulgation of either the revised version of the pre-war Jury Act or of an entirely new piece of legislation providing for either the Anglo-American all-layperson jury system or the Continental-European model of mixed jury trials, was discussed at a press conference held jointly by the Government Section and the Civil Information and Education Section, SCAP, on May 3, 1947.[129] In a statement released at the conference, SCAP officials explained that the promulgation of several pieces of legislation stipulating that criminal trials in Japan would be adjudicated by judges alone did not imply that the implementation of the jury system in Japan was impossible.[130] They even asserted that a proposal for a full-fledged revision of the pre-war Jury Act was being prepared (*ima junbi saretsutsu aru*).[131]

Questions have been raised in the scholarly literature regarding the alleged draft of the revision of the pre-war Jury Act prepared by SCAP that was mentioned at the press conference in 1947.[132] The author of this book has discovered a detailed proposal for the revision of the pre-war Jury Act prepared by the Legal Branch, Public Safety Division, Civil Intelligence Section (CIS), SCAP, that fits the description made by the officials of the Government and Civil Information and Education Sections of SCAP.[133]

The Public Safety Division's "Proposed Revision of the Jury Act" is not dated. The notes accompanying the text of the proposal suggest, however, that it was written after the draft of the revised Code of Criminal Procedure was completed, but prior to the enactment of this new code. The Code of Criminal Procedure is referred to in the Draft as "the *Proposed Revised Code of Criminal Procedure*" (emphasis added).[134] Therefore, the draft may have

---

127 *Id.*, pp. 658–659 (containing the minutes of this meeting).
128 Saibansho Kōsei Hō [Court Organization Law], Law No. 59 of 1947, art. 3(3).
129 Press Statement, Government Section and Civil Information and Education Section, SCAP, "Shihō ni tsuite" [On the Judicial [System]], May 19, 1947, translated into Japanese by the Supreme Court of Japan, reprinted in Naitō, *Shūsengo no Shihō Seido Kaikaku no Keika* [The Progress of Postwar Legal Reforms], Vol. 3, pp. 878–883 (in Japanese).
130 *Id.*, p. 880.
131 *Id.*, p. 880.
132 Legal historian Nobuyoshi Toshitani has argued that finding this draft was a task for future research (Toshitani, "Sengo Kaikaku to Kokumin no Shihō Sanka" [Post-war Reforms and Justice [System] Participation of the People], p. 158).
133 Proposed Revision of the Jury Act, not dated, Declassified E.O. 12065 Section 3-402/NNDG No. 775011 GHQ/SCAP Records (RG 331, National Archives and Records Service), microformed on GHQ/SCAP Records General Staff II, Public Safety Division, General File 1945–52, Box No. 370, Folder No. 16 (National Archives and Records Service), on file with Modern Japanese Political History Materials Room, National Diet Library, Japan [hereinafter Proposed Revision of the Jury Act, SCAP].
134 *Id.*

been written sometime between 1947 and 1948 – the period when the revisions to the Code of Criminal Procedure were actively deliberated. If this document was indeed written in 1947, then it appears highly likely that it was this draft that the U.S. officials referred to during the press conference organized by the Government Section and the Civil Information and Education Section, SCAP, in May 1947.[135]

What kind of the jury system did the Public Safety Division's proposal provide for? The draft was based on the pre-war Jury Act as last amended in 1941, but provided for several radical changes that were motivated by the need to harmonize the features of the pre-war Jury Act with the provisions of the new constitution. The occupation lawyers proposed to expand the scope of cases eligible for trial by jury to include all criminal cases.[136] Furthermore, they suggested that felonies be tried by twelve jurors and misdemeanors by six jurors.[137] Eligibility requirements for jury service were changed to include women,[138] and the lists of persons eligible for jury service were to be prepared every year rather than once every four years as the 1941 amendment to the pre-war Jury Act had stipulated.[139] The majority of the articles of Chapter III Section I of the pre-war Jury Act that outlined the trial procedures were deleted because the authors of the draft expected the Proposed Revised Code of Criminal Procedure to eliminate the right of the judge to take testimony.[140]

One of the most important changes suggested by the Public Safety Division was to delete Article 95 of the pre-war Jury Act, which allowed the judge to refuse to accept the answers provided by the jury if he deemed these answers to be unreasonable, and submit the case on trial afresh to a new jury.[141] The note accompanying the proposal to make this amendment stated: "This Article must be deleted, for it makes a complete sham of the whole jury system." The draft suggested replacing this provision with the following article:

> The finding (reply) of the jury is binding and unalterable to the Court and cannot be disturbed or altered unless a trial *de novo* is guaranteed on appeal because a fundamental error of law was committed in the public trial as provided for in the Revised Code of Criminal Procedure.

Another important proposed amendment concerned the right of the accused to appeal the jury verdict. In connection with Article 101 of the pre-war Jury Act, which stipulated that it was not possible to appeal jury trial verdicts *kōso*,[142] the SCAP draft stated that "no penalty or hindrance should attach where a jury was used in the public trial," and proposed that this article be amended to read:

> There shall be no difference in the rights, methods and procedure for appeal of cases [whether] or not a jury was had in the public trial. Appeal shall lay to any proper Courts, just as in cases where no jury was had.[143]

---

135 Another possibility is that this draft was authored earlier, by Captain Maniscalco in 1945 or 1946.
136 Proposed Revision of the Jury Act, SCAP, art. 3.
137 *Id.*, art. 26.
138 *Id.*, art. 9.
139 *Id.*, art. 14.
140 Jury Act, arts. 35–56 were to be deleted according to the Proposed Revision of the Jury Act.
141 Jury Act, art. 95.
142 Jury Act, art. 101.
143 Proposed Revision of the Jury Act, SCAP, arts. 74 and 76(10).

Furthermore, the SCAP Draft made it possible to use the oral explanation and the written instructions to the jury given by the presiding judge as a basis for appeal.[144]

While the proposal prepared by SCAP suggested changing several fundamental characteristics of the pre-war jury system, some aspects of the pre-war Jury Act were left unamended. First, SCAP did not suggest introducing the civil jury system in Japan, so trial by jury was according to the draft to remain available only to criminal defendants. Second, the right of the defendant to refuse trial by jury was preserved in the proposal.[145] Third, SCAP's draft left unchanged the provision of the pre-war Jury Act that stipulated that jurors would only determine facts. The notes accompanying the proposal stated, however, that comment was invited on "whether or not the jury shall determine and fix the punishment or only be the judge of facts", so we may assume that the authors of this document were open to further discussion on this point.[146] Fourth, the occupation lawyers left intact the provisions that stipulated that the members of the jury were responsible not for coming up with the verdict of guilty or not guilty, but for coming up with the answers to the questions submitted to them by the judge.[147] In addition, the draft kept the format of the answers that the members of the jury were to provide to the judge. Just as in the pre-war Jury Act, the findings of the jury were to be phrased in the form of "Yes" or "No" answers.[148] Finally, the draft retained Article 107 of the pre-war Jury Act that made the defendant bear the costs of jury trial.[149] This provision had attracted a lot of criticism during the period of the functioning of the jury system in pre-war Japan and was blamed for the lack of the popularity of jury trials. In a note accompanying the article that contained this stipulation, the authors of the draft recommended that "a reasonable amount" be set as "a jury fee which is charged to the accused when he is convicted and that the balance of costs" should be borne by the government.

SCAP's suggested revisions to the pre-war Jury Act give credence to the argument that the Allied occupation of Japan tried not to ignore the unique features of Japan and its legislation when initiating reform. The draft of the amended Jury Act did not provide for an Anglo-American jury system. Instead, the jury system as envisaged by the SCAP draft retained some aspects of the uniqueness of Japan's Jury Act of 1923, but no longer had those features that precluded the system from being used often in pre-war Japan.

The fate of this document is unclear. Whether it was discussed with the Japanese side or not, we know that Japan did not implement the jury system in the immediate post-war period.

Why was the jury system not implemented in occupied Japan? Some of the occupation lawyers and participants in the negotiations concerning the jury system have subsequently discussed their views on this question. According to Richard B. Appleton, who worked for the Legislation and Justice Division, Legal Section, GHQ, SCAP, the expenses that the enactment of the revised Jury Act would entail were a "potent consideration for Japanese politicians struggling with the problem of balancing the budget under difficult postwar economic conditions".[150] Alfred C. Oppler, on the other hand, has argued in his memoirs that the failure of the pre-war jury system seemed to have contributed to the lack of enthusiasm

---

144 *Id.*, art. 52.
145 *Id.*, art. 4.
146 *Id.*, art. 5; Jury Act, art. 79, para. 2.
147 Jury Act, art. 79; Proposed Revision of the Jury Act, SCAP, art. 53.
148 Proposed Revision of the Jury Act, SCAP, art. 53.
149 *Id.*, art. 79 and Jury Act, art. 107.
150 Appleton, "Reforms in Japanese Criminal Procedure under Allied Occupation", p. 404.

on the part of the Japanese lawyers and politicians to have another jury experiment, even if the basis for this experiment was provided for by an amended piece of legislation.[151] Other reasons included the absence of the necessary infrastructure in the immediate post-war period that made it difficult to implement the jury system. The lack of substantial popular support for the implementation of the jury system on the part of the general public arguably also contributed to Japanese government's decision against implementing the jury system. The inability on the part of the occupation lawyers to reach consensus regarding the question of whether to insist on the introduction of the jury system in Japan also played its role. Alfred Oppler commented that the occupation lawyers "did not feel" that they "ought to adopt, against the opposition of the Japanese, institutions historically grown, after all, on a very different soil".[152] The fact that SCAP's draft was not imposed on the Japanese but became a subject of deliberation as a result of which the idea to reintroduce the jury system in Japan was dropped at the insistence of the Japanese side may be thus seen as an example of the occupation's desire to inspire change, but not to induce it by force.

The jury system in Okinawa under the U.S. occupation[153]

The political and judicial structure in Okinawa under the U.S. occupation

Military government (1945–1950)

The 10th Army of the United States landed in Okinawa on the morning of April 1, 1945, and the island was "secured" on June 21, 1945.[154] At the end of June 1945, control over the Ryukyu Islands was handed over to the military government officials.[155] The responsibility for military government was temporarily transferred to the navy (from September 21, 1945, to July 1, 1946), but then returned to the army under the deputy commander for military government, who was directly responsible to the commanding general, Ryukyus Command.[156] In August 1945, the Okinawan Advisory Council was established to aid the military government. The council consisted of fifteen people selected by the deputy

---

151 Oppler, *Legal Reform in Occupied Japan*, p. 146.
152 *Id.*, p. 147.
153 A shortened version of this section was published in the Journal of Japanese Law (A. Dobrovolskaia, 2007, "An All-Laymen Jury System Instead of the Lay Assessor (*Saiban'in*) System for Japan? Anglo-American-Style Jury Trials in Okinawa under the U.S. Occupation", *Journal of Japanese Law*, No. 24, pp. 57–80).
154 A participant in the Okinawa campaign has noted that the result of fighting was the destruction of "practically everything that was above ground". He added: "From personal observation of a greater portion of the island I would say that 90 per cent of the private dwellings on the island were destroyed, and many of the remainder were made at least temporarily uninhabitable. In addition, practically all commercial buildings, warehouses, public buildings, schools, and hospitals were destroyed. The public utilities and water supply systems in the cities were completely disrupted. The railroad and its rolling stock were completely wrecked; for a distance on the western shore not only were the tracks torn up, but all traces of the roadbed were obliterated (D. D. Karasik, 1948, "Okinawa: A Problem in Administration and Reconstruction", *Far Eastern Quarterly*, Vol. 7, No. 3, pp. 254–267, at pp. 258 and 260).
155 The terms "Ryukyu", "Ryukyu Islands", and "Okinawa" are frequently used interchangeably, and this convention is followed in this chapter.
156 Karasik, "Okinawa: A Problem in Administration and Reconstruction", p. 260; L. Weiss, 1946, "US Military Government on Okinawa", *Far Eastern Survey*, Vol. 15, No. 15, pp. 234–238.

152 The occupation years

commander and nominated by "one hundred prominent Okinawans".[157] In April 1945, the Departments of Education, Public Health, Police, Agriculture, Industry, Finance, Fisheries, Commerce, General Affairs, Postal Affairs, Judicial Affairs, and Department of Arts and Monuments were established within the council.[158] In addition, the deputy commander selected and appointed a governor whose task was to enforce the directives, orders, and policies of the military government that were issued by the deputy commander.[159]

At the beginning of the occupation, the existing laws remained in effect until the time they were either abolished or changed to conform with the U.S. policies, and the process of research and screening of the existing legal codes was carried out mostly by local lawyers.[160] During the first year of the occupation, there were allegedly no civilian tribunals in operation, as all courts were destroyed.[161] In 1948, however, municipal, local, and exceptional military courts were established throughout the Ryukyus. The responsibilities for law enforcement were gradually transferred from the military police to the newly established police department.[162] During the period of military governance of the islands, what existed was essentially a military court system consisting of a number of Superior and Summary Provost courts located throughout the islands that had jurisdiction over criminal cases involving the interests and security of the United States.[163]

U.S. Civil Administration of the Ryukyu Islands and the Government of the Ryukyu Islands (1950/1952–1972)

During the civil administration period of the U.S. governance of the Ryukyu Islands, which continued until 1972 when Okinawa was reverted to Japan's control, two principal political bodies were established.

On December 15, 1950, the U.S. Civil Administration of the Ryukyu Islands (USCAR) was set up.[164] Headed by the High Commissioner of the Ryukyu Islands, a serving lieutenant general of the U.S. Army, USCAR was the government body that replaced the U.S. military government and assumed all its powers and functions.[165] Co-existing with USCAR

---

157 *Id.*, p. 260.
158 *Id.*, p. 261.
159 Leonard Weiss, who served as economic officer in the military government of the Ryukyu Islands, has argued that the main objectives of the first period of U.S. administration of the Ryukyus were as follows: (1) the physical restoration of damaged property and facilities; (2) the continued improvement of health and sanitation; (3) the early establishment of self-governing communities; (4) the institution of a sound program of economic development of trade, industry, and agriculture; (5) the establishment of an educational program designed to assist in achieving the foregoing objectives (Weiss, "US Military Government on Okinawa", p. 234).
160 Karasik, "Okinawa", p. 261.
161 *Id.*, p. 261.
162 *Id.*, p. 261.
163 R. F. Hewett, 1965, *United States Civil Administration of the Ryukyu Islands, 1950–1960*, PhD thesis, American University, Ann Arbor: University Microfilms International, p. 56.
164 Establishment of the United States Civil Administration of the Ryukyu Islands, Civil Administration Proclamation No. 1 of 1950.
165 Hewett, *United States Civil Administration of the Ryukyu Islands, 1950–1960*, pp. 30–69 (discussing the scope of activities of USCAR). The USCAR was established with the understanding that its activities "may extend to an almost complete assumption of the authority which is normally exercised by local authorities" (United States Department of Army, 1958, *Joint Manual of Civil Affairs/Military Government, Field Manual FM 41-5, OPNAV P21-1, AFM 110-7, NAVMC 2500*, Washington: Government

was another political institution – the Government of the Ryukyu Islands (GRI) – that was established on February 29, 1952.[166] Headed by the chief executive, a Ryukyuan who was directly responsible to the USCAR High Commissioner, the GRI was to "exercise all powers of government within the Ryukyu Islands, subject however, to the Proclamations, Ordinances, and Directives of the United States Civil Administration of the Ryukyu Islands".[167] The duality of the government structure during the period of civil administration affected the judicial system established on the islands, with both USCAR and GRI maintaining their own court systems.

USCAR operated civil and criminal courts and appellate tribunals (USCAR criminal courts consisted of the Superior Court, the Sessions Court, and the Appellate Courts[168]). These courts exercised jurisdiction over those cases that were "of particular importance affecting the security, property, or interests of the United States, as determined by the High Commissioner", as well as those cases that involved:

(1) Members of the U.S. forces or those civilian persons of U.S. nationality who were employed by, serving with, or accompanying the U.S. forces in the Ryukyu Islands;
(2) Employees of the U.S. government who were U.S. nationals even though not subject to trial by courts-martial under the Uniform Code of Military Justice;
(3) Dependents of the foregoing (spouse and any child or relative by affinity, consanguinity, or adoption when dependent upon the principle for over one half of his or her support while living on the territory of the Ryukyu Islands, unless such a dependent was a Ryukyuan).[169]

The system of courts maintained by the GRI exercised jurisdiction in all other civil and criminal cases,[170] with the exception of those incidents that involved persons subject to trial under the Uniform Code of Military Justice (these cases were handled by courts-martial).[171]

Civil and criminal proceedings at GRI courts were conducted in the Japanese language, in accordance with Japanese law, and did not have juries. The courts operated by USCAR, on the other hand, used English during trial hearings and introduced jury trials.[172]

Printing, p. 3, cited in Hewett, *United States Civil Administration of the Ryukyu Islands, 1950–1960*, p. 32). Where local authorities were capable of fulfilling their functions, USCAR's activities were to "consist of nothing more than the giving of advice or the rendering of assistance" (*id.*, p. 32).
166 Establishment of the Government of the Ryukyu Islands Civil Administration Proclamation No. 13 of 1952.
167 *Id.*; Hewett, *United States Civil Administration of the Ryukyu Islands, 1950–1960*, pp. 70–109 (discussing the scope of activities of GRI).
168 Code of Penal Procedure, Civil Administration Ordinance No. 144/1955, as amended on 8 March 1963, section 1.2.1.
169 Providing for Administration of the Ryukyu Islands, Executive Order No. 10713 of 1957, section 10, para. b.
170 Providing for Administration of the Ryukyu Islands, Executive Order No. 10713 of 1957, section 10, para. a.
171 Providing for Administration of the Ryukyu Islands, Executive Order No. 10713 of 1957, section 10, para. c.
172 The validity of the dual court system established in Okinawa was deliberated in *Rose v. McNamara*, 126 U.S. App. D.C. 179. In this case, the appellant argued that President Eisenhower did not have authority to issue the executive order establishing the Ryukyuan Court System (Providing for Administration of the Ryukyu Islands, Executive Order No. 10713 of 1957). The court dismissed the claim and ruled that the "status of Okinawan court as civil administration court created by Executive Order, rather than

154 *The occupation years*

A number of features highlight the fact that the balance of power in Okinawa's legal system was heavily weighted towards the USCAR, not the GRI. For instance, any case that was initially tried in a GRI court could be transferred to the USCAR court in the event the High Commissioner deemed so appropriate. In addition, it was the USCAR that maintained the highest appellate court on the islands and had the authority to review any case, civil or criminal, tried in either (1) the inferior USCAR courts, upon appeal by any party or (2) the highest court of the GRI. Furthermore, the High Commissioner had the right to remove any judge or other judicial official working in the Ryukyuan court system "with or without stated cause, if he deems it necessary in the interests of the occupation and for the general good of the people of the Ryukyu Islands".[173]

The jury system in USCAR courts

The criminal jury (petit jury and grand jury) was introduced to the USCAR court system through two amendments issued on March 8, 1963, and effective as of March 11, 1963. The civil jury system was introduced on May 21, 1964.[174]

As a result of these amendments, any person charged with an offence before a USCAR court was given the right to indictment by a grand jury "as to any offence which may be punished by death or imprisonment for a term exceeding one year and trial by petit jury as to any offence other than petty offence".[175] The defendant also had the right to waive a petit jury trial.[176] The grand jury was summoned to work for not more than one year and consisted of not less than six and not more than nine members with an indictment found only upon the concurrence of five or more grand jurors.[177]

Procedurally, jury trials in USCAR courts closely resembled those in the United States. The names of grand and petit jurors were drawn publicly from a jury box containing the names of not less than 200 qualified persons at the time of each drawing. The jurors were selected from such areas of the Ryukyu Islands as the court directed "so as to be most favorable to an impartial trial and not to incur unnecessary expense". When the court ordered a grand or petit jury to be drawn, the clerk issued summonses for the required number of jurors.[178] The trial began with jury selection, with names randomly chosen to form a panel

---

constitutional Article III court, does not deprive it of jurisdiction of criminal prosecution of United States citizen for evading Ryukyuan income taxes" (Ruling (CA DC, March 23, 1967), reprinted in *U.S. Law Week*, October 10, 1967, p. 3133).

173 Ryukyuan Court System, Civil Administration Proclamation No. 12 of 1952, art. 6, section 7, para. b.
174 Code of Penal Procedure, Civil Administration Ordinance No. 144 of 1955, as amended on 8 March 1963, and United States Civil Administration Criminal Courts, Civil Administration Proclamation No. 8 of 1958, as amended by Civil Administration Proclamation No. 18 of 1963.
175 Code of Penal Procedure, Civil Administration Ordinance No. 144 of 1955, as amended on 8 March 1963, chapter 5, section 1.5.1.1
176 Code of Penal Procedure, Civil Administration Ordinance No. 144 of 1955, as amended on 8 March 1963, chapter 5, section 1.5.3.
177 Code of Penal Procedure, Civil Administration Ordinance No. 144 of 1955, as amended on 8 March 1963, chapter 5, section 1.5.4. The 18th amendment of the United States Civil Administration Proclamation No. 8, "United States Civil Administration Criminal Courts" (dated July 21, 1958), stated that in the Superior Court of USCAR offences punishable by death or imprisonment were to be tried before three judges in the event the defendant waived jury trial and before one judge in all other cases. See Illustration 6 in the Appendix for a photograph depicting the process of drawing names for the first jury panel in Okinawa.
178 Code of Penal Procedure, Civil Administration Ordinance No. 144 of 1955, as amended on 8 March 1963, chapter 5, sections 1.5.8 and 1.5.9.

from which the trial jury was selected. Those on the panel whose knowledge of the people or circumstances related to the case to be tried might affect their impartiality were excused by the judge. The selected jurors were then sworn to try the case. As in the United States, jury deliberations in Okinawa were carried out in a separate room, with the jurors frequently requesting material evidence to be brought in and asking the judge for clarification.[179] The judge gave instructions to the members of the jury before they retired for their deliberations. According to the jurors who participated in trials held during the U.S. occupation of Okinawa, the deliberation process involved heated discussions and all members of the jury approached their task in a highly responsible manner.[180]

On the other hand, a number of features made the jury system in Okinawa unique. First, regarding the provisions regarding qualifications for jury service in Okinawa, there was no nationality requirement, and therefore any person who had lived in the Ryukyus for at least three months and was literate (that is, could speak and read English) could be summoned for jury service.[181] This resulted in Ryukyuans, Japanese, Filipinos, Chinese, and members of other nationalities participating in trials as jurors. For example, the document "Petit Jury-SUP C-13-64", which is part of the materials related to one criminal case tried in a USCAR court – *United States of America v. Megumi Yoshihisa*, which will be referred to later in this chapter – lists jury candidates for that trial in accordance with their nationality and gender in the following way: "U.S.: 29; Ryukyuan: 13; Filipino: 5; Chinese: 2; Japanese: 1; Total: 50. Male: 34; Female: 16".[182] The fact that the petit jury in USCAR courts was not made up exclusively of U.S. citizens was used as grounds for appeal. Specifically, in *Rose v. McNamara*, the appellant argued that conviction by USCAR petit jury was invalid for this reason, and cited Title 28 of the U.S. Code, which requires that federal jurors be citizens. This claim was rejected by the court.[183]

Second, the legal framework that was put in place in Okinawa implied that cases not only involving U.S. citizens but also Japanese and Okinawans could be and were tried by

---

179 Dobrovolskaia, "An All-Laymen Jury System Instead of the Lay Assessor (*Saiban'in*) System for Japan?", pp. 76–79.
180 Japan Federation of Bar Associations, *Okinawa no Baishin Saiban* [Jury Trials in Okinawa], pp. 13–14.
181 The qualifications required of prospective jurors included the following: (1) any person who has attained the age of twenty-one, and (2) any person who has resided for a period of three months within the Ryukyu Islands with the exclusion of those persons who: (a) had been convicted of a crime punishable by imprisonment for more than one year and have not been pardoned; (b) who were illiterate (unable to speak the English language); (c) who were incapable by reason of mental or physical infirmities to render efficient jury service; (d) who served as an officer or employee of the civil administration, whether as a member of the armed forces of the United States or as a civilian. Exception from jury service could be claimed by the following persons: members of the armed forces of the United States on active duty; attorneys actively engaged in the practice of law in the Ryukyu Islands; practicing physicians, surgeons, and dentists; ministers of the gospel and clergymen of every denomination; and persons employed in police and other law enforcement activities and fire protection (Code of Penal Procedure, Civil Administration Ordinance No. 144 of 1955, as amended on 8 March 1963, chapter 5, sections 1.5.5 and 1.5.8).
182 *United States of America v. Megumi Yoshihisa* case materials. The fact that the petit jury in USCAR courts was not made up exclusively of U.S. citizens was used as grounds for appeal. Specifically, in *Rose v. McNamara*, 126 U.S. App. D.C. 179, the appellant argued that conviction by USCAR petit jury was invalid for this reason and cited Title 28 of the U.S. Code, which requires that federal jurors be citizens. This claim was rejected by the court. There is evidence that some jury trials carried out in Okinawa featured participation on the part of Korean nationals. See H. Fukurai, "Civil Jury Trials in Okinawa: Local Illustration", in M. J. Wilson, H. Fukurai, and T. Maruta (eds), *Japan and Civil Jury Trials: A Convergence of Forces*, Cheltenham: Edward Edgar, pp. 134–150, at p. 139.
183 *Rose v. McNamara*, 126 U.S. App. D.C. 179.

jurors, as the USCAR criminal and civil courts exercised jurisdiction not only over those cases that involved U.S. citizens, but also those that were "of particular importance affecting the security, property, or interests of the United States, as determined by the High Commissioner".[184]

Why did the U.S. administration of the islands decide to introduce jury trials to the USCAR courts in the 1960s? The answer to this question appears to lie in the fact that once it became clear that the American presence in Okinawa was to continue for an extended period of time, the U.S. civil administration recognized the need to ensure that the constitutional rights of U.S. citizens stationed on the islands and of their dependents were protected. Specifically, the sixth amendment of the U.S. Constitution guarantees defendants the right to "a speedy and public trial, by an impartial jury of the state and district wherein the crime shall have been committed", and, according to documentary materials remaining from the time of the occupation, American lawyers working in Okinawa repeatedly expressed the necessity of introducing the jury system on the islands.[185] However, the discussion regarding the possibility of introducing the jury system in Okinawa gained momentum as late as November 1963, when Bennet N. (Ken) Ikeda, a Hawaiian-born U.S. citizen and an executive at Empire Soap Co. of Naha, who had been found guilty of criminal fraud through false registration and mortgaging of houses, was released from Naha jail as a result of a writ of habeas corpus issued by a U.S. federal court judge in Washington, DC.[186] Ikeda claimed that he had been deprived of his constitutional rights as he had neither been indicted by grand jury nor was going to be afforded a jury trial in Okinawa. Four months later, in March 1963, the criminal jury system was introduced to the Ryukyus, and the "Ikeda case" became the first to be tried before a USCAR jury.

The first session of the jury trial opened on May 1, 1963, and the news regarding the court proceedings made the first page of *Morning Star Okinawa*, an English-language daily newspaper.[187] According to the article, the members of the jury working on the Ikeda case were "proficient in the English language" and consisted of nine men and three women.[188] Judging from the names of the members of the jury that, surprisingly, were released to the newspaper, the panel included citizens of Japanese and/or Ryukyuan nationality as well as Americans. The article directly connects the legal maneuvering of Ikeda's lawyers to the establishment of the jury system in Okinawa. It is necessary to note, however, that there were other cases of similar nature that emphasized the need of establishing a jury system in USCAR courts to protect the rights of U.S. citizens stationed in Okinawa and their dependents. For instance, in November 1963 a U.S. federal court judge in Washington, DC, reversed the decision of the USCAR criminal court that had found the wife of a U.S. serviceman guilty of beating her four-year-old child and sentenced the defendant to five years of penal servitude and deportation to the United States on the grounds that the defendant was denied trial by jury in the USCAR court.[189] The High Commissioner of the

---

184 Providing for Administration of the Ryukyu Islands, Executive Order No. 10713 of 1957, section 10, para. b.
185 Japan Federation of Bar Associations, *Okinawa no Baishin Saiban* [Jury Trials in Okinawa], pp. 8–9.
186 *Ikeda v. McNamara*, Habeas Corpus No. 416–62, D.D.C., October 19, 1962.
187 Anonymous, 1963, "Ikeda Pleads not Guilty: Okinawa's First Jury Trial Opens", *Morning Star Okinawa*, May 1.
188 *Id.*
189 Nicholson, Habeas Corpus No. 141–61, D.D.C., November 19, 1963, cited in *Rose v. McNamara*, 126 U.S. App. D.C. 179. The *Okinawa Times* reported in November 1963 that the decisions in two or three

Ryukyu Islands expressed his contentment with the introduction and functioning of the jury system in 1964, saying that the new jury system "has functioned very well, and the many objections to its institution, heard for several years prior to the establishment of the system, were found to have been illusory".[190]

The fact that GRI courts did not have trial by jury was used as a justification for not allowing U.S. military personnel accused of crimes against local citizens to be transferred from USCAR courts to GRI courts in the final phase of the occupation. In 1970, the Japan Bar Association urged the Japanese government to take steps to transfer the jurisdiction over U.S. military servicemen who committed criminal offences from USCAR to GRI courts. The background for this request was the so-called Gushikawa incident that occurred on May 30, 1970, and during which an Okinawan high school girl sustained multiple knife wounds in an attempted rape by a U.S. soldier, Herman Smith.[191] Although the GRI police carried out Smith's arrest, they were not allowed to question him.[192] The press reports at the time claimed that it was only because of the demonstrations of Okinawans in front of Smith's base and USCAR headquarters that Smith was arrested and not transferred from Okinawa.[193]

In the end, Smith's case was handled by courts-martial, with a guilty verdict announced on August 12, 1970. Smith was sentenced to dishonorable discharge, three years of confinement at hard labor, demotion to lowest enlisted grade, and forfeiture of all pay and allowances. Some Okinawan legal experts estimated that Smith would have received a sentence of at least five years' imprisonment if he were tried at a GRI court in accordance with Japanese laws.[194]

The number of jury cases tried in Okinawa after the introduction of the system and before the end of the U.S. occupation is quite small. A report prepared by the Japan Federation of Bar Associations provides the statistics for the period between 1963 and July 31, 1967, as summarized in Table 5.1.

The report specifies further that a total of 103 cases (89 criminal cases and 14 civil cases) were tried in Okinawa during the period between 1963 and July 31, 1967, and that consequently, those tried by jury represent 7.8 per cent of the total.[195] Ten is the estimated total number of cases (criminal and civil) tried before USCAR juries during the period of the system's functioning.[196]

---

cases that had been tried in Okinawa were reversed for similar reasons. This article appeared on November 22, 1963, in the *Okinawa Times* and is cited in T. Ozawa, "Ryūkyū Rettō Beikokumin Seifu Saibansho no Baishin Seido" [The Jury System in USCAR Courts], in K. Urata (ed.), 2000, *Okinawa Bei Gun Kichi Hō no Genzai* [The Present State of U.S. Military Base Law in Okinawa], Tokyo: Ichiryūsha, pp. 257–286, at p. 263.

190 High Commissioner of the Ryukyu Islands, 1964, *Civil Administration of the Ryukyu Islands: Report for Period 1 July 1963 to 30 June 1964*, Vol. 12, Naha: United States Civil Administration, p. 45. See generally Fukurai, "Civil Jury Trials in Okinawa: Local Illustration", pp. 140–141, and Vanoverbeke, *Juries in the Japanese Legal System*, pp. 102–115.

191 C. Aldous, "'Mob Rule' or Popular Activism? The Koza Riot of December 1970 and the Okinawan Search for Citizenship", in G. D. Hook and R. Siddle (eds), 2003, *Japan and Okinawa*, London: RoutledgeCurzon, pp. 148–166, at p. 150.

192 *Id.*, p. 153.

193 T. Makise, 1971, *Okinawa no Rekishi 3* (The History of Okinawa 3), Tokyo: Chobunsha, pp. 185–195, cited in Aldous, "'Mob Rule' or Popular Activism?", p. 153.

194 Aldous, "'Mob Rule' or Popular Activism?", p. 154.

195 *Id.*, p. 14.

196 Isa, *Gyakuten* [Turnaround], p. 491.

158 *The occupation years*

Table 5.1 Statistics of the number of cases tried by jury in Okinawa

Year	Number of criminal cases tried by jury	Number of civil cases tried by jury	Total number of cases (criminal and civil) tried by jury
1963	3	0	3
1964	1	1	2
1965	0	2	2
1966	0	0	0
1967 (until July 31)			1 (only grand jury sessions)

Source: Japan Federation of Bar Associations, *Okinawa no Baishin Saiban* [Jury Trials in Okinawa], p. 14.

The Okinawan jury system in action

UNITED STATES OF AMERICA V. MEGUMI YOSHIHISA (1964) – THE BEST DOCUMENTED CRIMINAL JURY TRIAL IN OKINAWA

The *United States of America v. Megumi Yoshihisa* – the fourth criminal case tried by jury in Okinawa and the only criminal case tried before jury in 1964 – is one of the best documented jury trial cases in Okinawa. Unlike other criminal cases, the details of *Megumi Yoshihisa* are available not only through official trial records but also through a literary work subsequently written by Chihiro Isa who served as a juror on it.[197]

"Turnaround: A Jury Trial in Okinawa under American Rule" (*Gyakuten: Amerika Shihaika Okinawa no Baishin Saiban*) is a detailed description of the trial – starting from the time Isa received the summons to appear in court and ending with the description of the procedures of jury deliberations and sentencing. Isa explains in this autobiographical novel that participating in a jury trial was a "life changing experience" and that his main objectives for writing down his memories of the occasion were to emphasize the virtues of the jury system, to set the record straight on the court ruling with regard to this case, and finally to show the real state of the U.S. occupation of Okinawa to contemporary readers.[198]

This case involved an incident that took place in Futenma village in Ginowan-shi. Four Ryukyuans were accused of inflicting bodily injury on two U.S. Marines by beating them and causing the death of one of them, in violation of Articles 205 (bodily injury resulting in death) and 204 (bodily injury) of the Criminal Code of Japan in effect in the Ryukyu Islands. The defendants were four "honest and sober boys", as the people living in the same village with them testified in statements that accompanied the petition supporting the defendants.[199] The villagers claimed that the U.S. Marines "were drunk, offering to fight, showing karate positions" at the time of the incident.[200] The jury on this trial, which

---

197 *Id.* Chihiro Isa was subsequently sued for tortious injury by a defendant in this case and was ordered to pay 500,000 yen in a decision that was later confirmed by the Japanese Supreme Court (Supreme Court, February 8, 1994, *Minshū* 48, 2–149, cited in Anderson and Nolan, "Lay Participation in the Japanese Justice System: A Few Preliminary Thoughts Regarding the Lay Assessor System (*saiban-in seido*) from Domestic Historical and International Psychological Perspectives", p. 958.
198 Isa, *Gyakuten* [Turnaround], pp. 471–474 and 477.
199 *United States of America v. Megumi Yoshihisa* case materials.
200 *Id.*

consisted of three Japanese or Ryukyuans and nine Americans,[201] found the defendants not guilty on the charge of murder, but guilty of inflicting bodily injury.

According to Isa's account of the jury deliberations, at the beginning of the discussion of the case the majority of jurors were in favor of proclaiming at least one of the defendants guilty of murder. It was Isa who persuaded the rest of the members of the jury to find all the defendants not guilty of violating Article 205 – hence the word "turnaround" in the title of the novel. The details of the deliberation process mentioned by Isa thus indicate that the fact that there was no citizenship requirement for prospective jurors – which allowed Americans, Ryukyuans, and Japanese to serve together as jurors – contributed to protecting the jury from being biased against either the U.S. servicemen or the Ryukyuan defendants. Based on his experience as a juror, Isa highly commends the democratic nature of the American judicial process in general and the institution of jury service in particular, emphasizing the ability of the latter to empower individuals drawn from different walks of life to strive to achieve a collective wisdom that none could achieve alone.

A favorable attitude towards the concept of jury service did not prevent Isa from arguing that the regime of occupation under which the jury system was introduced in Okinawa was essentially undemocratic and that this has resulted in the fact that the impartiality of justice on the islands was at times compromised.

Specifically, when discussing some of the problem areas of the jury system in Okinawa during the occupation, Isa notes that those witnesses who could not speak English found it difficult to adequately express their opinions at times, and that although this was apparent to Okinawans present in the courtroom, their concerns were dismissed by the court. Isa's novel features a dialogue that is interesting from this perspective. A Ryukyuan witness originally uses the word *kurasu*, which in the Okinawan dialect means "beating somebody", when describing the incident. The Japanese-English court interpreter fails to understand this word and the witness is asked to clarify the meaning of it in Japanese. Confused, the witness mistakenly rephrases the original statement using the word *korosu* (which means "to kill" in Japanese).[202]

Second, Chihiro Isa expresses concern with regard to the question of the fairness of sentencing in USCAR courts. He states that while the highest penalty for murder (Article 205) as provided by the Japanese law was twenty years' imprisonment, the punishment for this article in cases such as *Megumi Yoshihisa* (where the defendants were Ryukyuans accused of attacking U.S. Marines) was the death penalty.[203] This inconsistency led him to question the impartiality of justice in USCAR courts. Isa's view appears to reflect the perception on the part of the non-American members of the jury panel of the contradiction that existed between the democratic nature of the jury trial proceedings on the one hand and the essentially non-democratic regime of the occupation under which the judicial structure was established on the other.

---

201 *Id.*; Isa, *Gyakuten* [Turnaround], pp. 286–288.
202 Isa, *Gyakuten* [Turnaround], pp. 140–141.
203 *Id.*, p. 419. Although Isa does not explicitly say so, he appears to be referring to Code of Penal Procedure, Civil Administration Ordinance No. 144 of 1955, as amended on July 11, 1956, section 2.2.2, that states: "Any person who willfully and unlawfully kills; or who, in the course of committing a felony, causes the death of any United States Forces personnel or security guard employed by the United States of America or any agency or instrumentality thereof, while such guard is engaged in the performance of his duties as such or because of such employment, may be punished by death or such other punishment as a Civil Administration Court may order."

ROBIRDS V. FAR EAST CONSTRUCTION CO. (1964) – THE FIRST CIVIL JURY TRIAL CASE IN OKINAWA

Robirds v. Far East Construction Co. was the second of the two cases tried by jury in Okinawa in 1964.[204] It was the first civil jury trial case tried at a USCAR court.

This case involved a negligence action that resulted in the death of a former federal employee, Oren K. Robirds. This case progressed quickly and smoothly: the selection of jurors took less than an hour and jury deliberation took approximately thirteen hours.[205] The jury panel that adjudicated this case was international, consisting of six U.S. citizens, three Filipinos, and three Ryukyuans.[206]

The case on trial involved an incident that occurred on November 30, 1959, when Robirds, described in the documents as a "Department of Army Civilian", was supervising a crew engaged in repairing a broken water main on a highway in Naha, Okinawa. He was struck by the pickup truck driven by a Ryukyuan employed by Far East Construction. Robirds died immediately as a result of the injuries he sustained during the accident. Far East Construction, a contractor engaged in construction work for the U.S. forces in Okinawa, had hired the Ryukyuan employee to repair light and heavy equipment. On the day of the incident, this employee chose to work an extra shift. In the evening, he decided to go to his home to get a jacket because it was too cold to work without it. He took a vehicle for that purpose, and it was on his way back to the compound that he hit Robirds, causing his death.[207] Robirds's widow and son sued the driver and Far East Construction for a combined sum of $150,000.

The jury found against both defendants and for the widow and son of Robirds. At first, the jury assigned no damages against the driver, but assigned $65,000 against Far East Construction. This initial assignment of damages by the jury prompted the judge to instruct the jury regarding the inconsistency. As a result, the jury changed its judgment. The final decision was $5,000 against the driver and $60,000 against Far East Construction. Far East Construction appealed the verdict at the U.S. Civil Administration Appellate Court. This appeal was denied.

The opinions of the appellate court judges on this case provide several insights regarding the working of the jury system in Okinawa. For instance, the opinion of Associate Justice Abraham Black – one of the appellate court judges adjudicating this case – reveals that during the course of the trial the judge gave the members of the jury written instructions, an unusual practice for U.S. courts.[208] The opinions of appellate court judges also reveal the unique challenges that judges faced in USCAR courts. The opinion statements of all three

---

204 Several versions of the name of the company involved in this dispute appear in the materials documenting this case. While most documents refer to "Far East Construction Co.", others mention "Far East*ern* Construction Co." (emphasis added) and "Far East Construction *Services Inc.*" (emphasis added). As these materials outline the same circumstances of the case, this inconsistency is likely to have resulted from the fact that the company name was changed during the course of the trial. For the sake of consistency this chapter refers to this company as "Far East Construction Co."
205 High Commissioner of the Ryukyu Islands, *Civil Administration of the Ryukyu Islands: Report for Period 1 July 1963 to 30 June 1964*, p. 45.
206 Jury panel in the *Robirds v. Far East Construction Co.* case. This document is part of the *Robirds v. Far East Construction Co.* case materials.
207 *Robirds v. Far East Construction Co.* case materials.
208 United States Civil Administration Appellate Court, Concurring Opinion by Associate Justice Black (*Robirds v. Far East Construction Co.* case materials).

appellate court justices in the first civil case tried by jury in Okinawa make it clear that as the laws applicable to this suit were the Civil Code of Japan rather than U.S. legislation, the American judges trying this case found themselves in a unique situation of having to interpret Japanese statutes and to be conscious of the need to incorporate the Japanese legal tradition in their judgments. The opinion of Associate Justice Black, who referred extensively to precedent in Japanese courts, is particularly interesting in this regard:

> Were American substantive principles of law of vicarious liability under the doctrine of *respondeat superior* applicable in this lawsuit, I would be hard put to sustain liability on the part of the employer in this case [. . .]. [H]owever, the fact of the matter is that American principles and doctrines are not applicable to and not determining of the ultimate issue. Resort must be had to the applicable substantive Japanese law heretofore referred to and how Japanese courts have construed and applied that law. [. . .] Japanese courts appear to be more concerned with the social aspect rather than with legal principles of vicarious liability under *respondeat superior* [. . .] I am satisfied that Japanese trial courts would find liability and Appellate Courts would sustain it on the facts in the case. It is primarily for this reason that I concur in not sustaining this appeal.[209]

Furthermore, in a letter addressed to Justice Russel L. Stevens, Justice Black explained that he had discussed the case with Japanese judges and lawyers. He said that it was the fact that all the specialists that he contacted agreed that Japanese judges would find and sustain liability in this case that persuaded him to decline the appeal despite his personal "opinions and convictions".[210]

Evaluating Japan's and Okinawa's experiences with jury trials under the occupation

This chapter has focused on two case studies: the attempts to introduce the jury system in mainland Japan under the Allied occupation and the implementation of the institution of jury service in Okinawa under the U.S. occupation. These two case studies differed in terms of the results that they brought along. The efforts on the part of SCAP to transplant the jury system to Japan ended in failure, while in Okinawa Anglo-American jury trials were successfully introduced and functioned for almost a decade. The two situations described in this chapter had in common the fact that they both occurred under the circumstances of military occupation, which has provided the basis for discussing them together rather than separately.

While the two case studies presented in this chapter had the same underlying theme – the occupation – there were important differences in the nature of the military occupation

---

209 *Id.*
210 United States Civil Administration Appellate Court, Letter, February 19, 1965 (*Robirds v. Far East Construction Co.* case materials). For further details of this case and for a discussion of civil cases tried by jurors in Okinawa generally, see Fukurai, "Civil Jury Trials in Okinawa: Local Illustration", pp. 141–148. Tsuruko Robirds filed another suit upon the completion of this case against the insurers at the Home Insurance Corporation (HIC), a company based in New York, and American Foreign Insurance Corporation (AFIC). This case was tried with the participation of a jury consisting of nine Americans, one Filipino, and two Okinawan nationals (see generally Fukurai, "Civil Jury Trials in Okinawa: Local Illustration", pp. 142–144).

regimes that mainland Japan and Okinawa experienced in the post-war period. First, the length of occupation differed in the two situations described in this chapter. While mainland Japan was occupied for seven years (1945–1952), the U.S. administration of Okinawa lasted for twenty-seven years (1945–1972). Second, there were differences in the degree of clarity with regard to the terms of the occupation. In mainland Japan, the occupying forces knew from the start that their presence in Japan was temporary and that eventually Japan's sovereignty would be restored. The status of Okinawa, on the other hand, remained uncertain for many years. Third, the occupying forces in mainland Japan and Okinawa were responsible to different groups of people during the course of their administration of foreign territory. While in mainland Japan the occupation forces were responsible to the Japanese people who were the ultimate benefactors of the various reforms carried out during the occupation, in Okinawa the U.S. occupation had to fulfill its obligations not only to the local population but also to the U.S. citizens stationed on the islands.

As this chapter has demonstrated, these three factors had a profound influence on the actions of the occupying forces in mainland Japan and Okinawa and on their attitudes towards legal reform. In Japan, SCAP saw its role in aiding Japan in its transformation into a democratic state. It tried to avoid imposing the views of the Allied occupation on Japan unilaterally. The Japanese government was involved in formulating policies and in discussing which of the concepts it was willing to adopt, and its views were in most cases respected and taken into consideration by the occupation. In Okinawa, on the other hand, while the ambiguity of the status of the islands caused the United States to refrain from attempting to radically change the legal and political systems that affected local citizens by unilaterally imposing American concepts and institutions, the long-term presence of the U.S. forces on the islands implied that to protect the rights of the U.S. citizens it was nevertheless necessary to "transplant" those institutions that were integral to guaranteeing these rights. This chapter has shown that the U.S. administration in Okinawa found a way to introduce those elements that were necessary for protecting the rights of the U.S. citizens so as not to affect the citizens of Okinawa. It created a two-tiered system of justice and governance, with one tier being based on the American principles and the other preserving its distinctively Japanese character. The occupation "transplanted" the American court system to Okinawa, but this transplanted court system adjudicated only those cases that involved U.S. citizens, while the disputes between local citizens continued to be tried in accordance with Japanese laws that were left intact.

The attempts to introduce the jury system in the immediate post-war period in mainland Japan and Okinawa reflected the differences in the objectives and attitudes towards reform on the part of SCAP and the U.S. administration of Okinawa.

In mainland Japan, the possibility of introducing the jury system was discussed throughout the period of the Allied occupation. The debate began independently of the occupation forces and originated in the Japanese society. Japanese scholars and organizations first brought up the idea in connection with the drafting of the new constitution. The theme of this discussion was not suggested in any way by the occupation forces who were at the time of the debate not planning to make any recommendations to the Japanese government concerning the jury system. Both SCAP and the Japanese government took note of the public debate regarding the jury system, and the idea of implementing the jury system was incorporated in the first drafts of the constitution prepared by SCAP. The provisions mentioning trial by jury were subsequently deleted, however, and the finalized version that SCAP submitted to the Japanese government did not include any articles concerning trial by jury. Simultaneously and independently of SCAP, the Ministry of Justice began discussing the possibility of implementing the Anglo-American and the Continental-European models of jury trials as well as amending the pre-war Jury Act at various committees and councils. Like SCAP's first initiative, these discussions did not lead to any concrete measures.

SCAP and the Japanese government had the chance to jointly discuss the jury system in connection with two specific reforms: the new Court Organization Law and the Code of Criminal Procedure. During the course of these deliberations, the Japanese side opposed the drafts proposed by Captain Maniscalco that included stipulations providing for the implementation of the jury system, but conceded to SCAP's request to include an article in the text of the Court Organization Law, stating that it would be possible to implement jury trials in Japan at some point in the future. The proposal for the revision of the pre-war Jury Act drafted by SCAP in 1947–1948 was either not discussed with the Japanese government at all, or was rejected.

What were the factors that led to the failure of the numerous attempts to implement jury trials in the immediate post-war period in mainland Japan? It appears that the proposals failed because neither the Japanese government nor the public was sufficiently enthusiastic about the idea and because SCAP failed to develop a unified position on the issue. The Japanese government opposed the introduction of jury trials for several reasons. First, the jury system was seen as costly to maintain. Second, the failure of the pre-war jury system was a potent consideration that is likely to have contributed to the Japanese government's decision not to have another jury experiment. Third, in the immediate post-war period the necessary infrastructure for the implementation of the jury system was lacking, as courtrooms and other facilities needed to be rebuilt. The lack of support for the idea on the part of the general public was yet another reason for the government's decision against implementing the jury system. It appears that SCAP, on the other hand, did not see the proposal to introduce the jury system as an absolute priority and chose not to push for the adoption of the idea, which arguably served to take the pressure off the Japanese government to continue deliberating it.

The proposal to implement the jury system in post-war Japan failed to attract sufficient support of any interest groups or generate a wide base of support on the part of the society at large. While the Japan Federation of Bar Associations was in favor of the idea, it did not push for its realization in view of the arguments against jury trials presented by the government.

Neither did the proposal to introduce jury trials attract support among prominent Japanese politicians. None of the Japanese politicians chose the introduction of the jury system to be an important item on their political agenda in the immediate post-war period. This is in sharp contrast to the case of the pre-war Jury Act that was actively promoted by Prime Minister Hara. In the absence of political support, the idea was more or less destined to fail, because the occupation forces made a conscious decision not to demand that the jury system be introduced in Japan. On the side of SCAP, of course, there were individual lawyers, most notably Captain Maniscalco, who strongly believed that it was important to introduce the jury system in Japan. The strategic attitude of the occupation forces towards the issue of legal reform in general and their view that the occupation should "induce" rather than "force" reform, coupled with the fact that the transplantation of the institution of jury service was not high on SCAP's list of priorities, however, made it impossible for any individual lawyer or any single group of occupation lawyers to push for the implementation of this particular reform against the opposition of the Japanese government.

While the case of mainland Japan under the Allied occupation provides the material for discussing only the first research question – why was the jury system not introduced? – the case of Okinawa under the U.S. occupation makes it possible to address both research questions and analyze not only the factors that led to the implementation of the jury system, but also the reasons behind the success or failure of its functioning.

Why was the jury system introduced in occupied Okinawa? The reversal of several USCAR court verdicts on the grounds that the defendant had been denied the right to jury trial alerted the U.S. occupation forces to the importance of guaranteeing this constitutional right to U.S. citizens. Hesitant to transplant the institution of jury service to GRI courts that adjudicated cases involving Okinawans and Japanese in accordance with the Japanese laws, the U.S. administration of the Ryukyu Islands chose to limit the implementation of the jury system only to cases where this was absolutely necessary – that is, to those cases that involved U.S. citizens and were tried at USCAR courts.

The fact that the jury system was introduced only in USCAR courts, which carried out proceedings in a manner that was similar to that of courts in the United States, did not imply, however, that the American jury system was transferred to Okinawa without any modifications whatsoever. As argued in this chapter, in order to ensure the successful functioning of the jury system the civil administration of the islands adapted the U.S. model of jury trials to fit in with the unique environment that existed in Okinawa under the U.S. occupation. Specifically, to ensure a big enough pool of potential jurors, the nationality requirement for jury service was not included in Okinawa. The requirement for English language proficiency was added to ensure that all jurors could participate in trial hearings and deliberation. Unlike the case of Japan's experimentations with the jury system in the *Meiji* period and Japan's pre-war jury system, which involved modifications affecting the very core of the model of Anglo-American jury trials, the adaptations made to the American jury system when it was transplanted to USCAR courts did not affect the substance of the concept of trial by jury.

Thanks to these adaptations that did not disrupt the internal integrity of the American model of jury trials, the system of layperson participation in USCAR criminal and civil courts functioned smoothly. The unique situation of Okinawa presented the judges, the defense, the prosecution, and members of the jury with several challenges, however. One of these challenges concerned the fact that American judges at USCAR courts had to adjudicate cases that involved not only U.S. citizens but also Okinawans and Japanese and featured claims based on Japan's legislation. This meant that American judges had to analyze and interpret not only the applicable USCAR legislation, but also Japanese laws and precedents in reaching their decisions. Some of the judges working at USCAR courts also felt the need to ensure that their rulings would concur with those of Japanese judges. Another challenge concerned the need to provide adequate translation of all testimony delivered by non-English-speaking witnesses. Yet another difficulty concerned jury deliberations. The unique situation in Okinawa implied that the Japanese and Okinawans serving on jury in USCAR courts had to use English, which was a foreign language, and overcome the barriers of intercultural communication when participating in deliberations with non-Japanese members of the jury. The details discussed in Chihiro Isa's "Turnaround: A Jury Trial in Okinawa under American Rule" show that despite these challenges, those Japanese and Okinawan jurors who were selected for service approached their task diligently and with a great sense of responsibility. This chapter has demonstrated that the aforementioned challenges that the unique situation in Okinawa presented to the judges, the jury, the defense, and the prosecution were not powerful enough to disrupt the functioning of the jury system in USCAR courts.

To use Alan Watson's terminology, in Okinawa the United States "transplanted" not only the institution of jury service, but the whole of its legal system to USCAR courts.

The United States has a long experience of using trial by jury; therefore, the jury system was compatible with the institutional culture of the section of Okinawa's two-tiered court system where it was implemented – in USCAR courts. It is possible to speculate that the situation could have been very different were American-style jury trials implemented in GRI courts that carried out justice in accordance with Japanese laws. The proposal to transplant the institution of jury service to GRI courts could have met with resistance on the part of the Japanese legal professionals. It would have most definitely become a subject of heated debate in the same way as the proposal to implement the jury system in mainland Japan did in the early post-war period. The decision on the part of the occupation to introduce the jury system only in USCAR courts implied that there was not going to be any resistance on the part of the part of Japanese and Okinawan lawyers and judges, as the majority of them were not involved in USCAR trials and the jury reform would not affect their work in any way. For the same reason, the subject of jury trials did not figure in the public debate at all until the final years of the occupation, when it became clear that Okinawa would revert to Japan's control and when Okinawans became increasingly irritated that defendants holding U.S. citizenship and accused of committing crimes against Ryukyuans could not be tried at GRI courts – where they would have received harsher sentences than at USCAR courts. In those final years of the occupation the American side used the fact that there was no jury at GRI courts to explain why U.S. nationals could not be tried in accordance with Japanese laws.[211] For the most part of the occupation, however, the jury system was not a subject of public discussion precisely due to the fact that this system functioned only at USCAR courts. Opposition to the institution of jury service in Okinawa could arguably only have come from the prospective jurors. English-speaking Ryukyuans and Japanese citizens could have protested against the implementation of this system if they saw jury service as a burden that they did not wish to bear. The fact that the number of cases tried by jury in Okinawa was small, however, arguably served to limit the possibility of protest to a minimum, which ensured the smooth functioning of the jury system in USCAR courts.

Conclusions

This chapter examined two attempts to implement the jury system – one failed and another successful – in occupied Japan and Okinawa.

As argued in the chapter, in mainland Japan under the Allied occupation the proposal to implement the jury trial system failed because neither the Japanese government, nor the Japanese public, nor SCAP saw the introduction of the institution of jury service as a priority for Japan in the immediate post-war period. The Japanese government was concerned about carrying out post-war reconstruction and viewed the institution of jury service as a costly system to maintain. In addition, the failure of Japan's pre-war jury system to function effectively and gain popularity discouraged the Japanese government from having another jury experiment. In view of these factors, the jury proposal could not attract either political or public support. SCAP, on the other hand, did not succeed at developing a unified position on the subject of jury trials. The absence of clear recommendations from SCAP regarding the institution of jury service, in turn, took the pressure off from the Japanese government

---

211 Legal Affairs Department, 1970, "Talking Point: GRI Court Jurisdiction over U.S. Military Personnel", July 20, 1970, on file with the Okinawa Prefectural Archives (OPA), Naha, Japan.

to continue deliberating the issue. As a result, the discussion of the possibility of introducing jury trials was postponed for an indefinite period of time.

In Okinawa, under the U.S. occupation, the jury system was successfully implemented and functioned smoothly. Jury trials were introduced with the purpose of protecting the constitutional right to jury trial of the U.S. citizens stationed in Okinawa. The jury system in Okinawa functioned without any disruption due to the fact that it was introduced only in USCAR courts, which carried out trial hearings in a manner that was similar to courts in the United States that have a long tradition of jury trials.

The discussion of the possibility of implementing the jury system continued after the end of the Allied occupation of Japan. The attempts to introduce the jury system in the post-occupation period are discussed in Chapter 6.

6 The mixed-court jury (*saiban'in*) system in contemporary Japan

This chapter focuses on the attempts to introduce the jury system in the post-occupation period. It begins by outlining the historical background that focuses on the developments in Japan's legal system and society in the period between the end of the Allied occupation and contemporary times. It then discusses the efforts, led by both governmental and non-governmental organizations, to introduce the jury system in the post-occupation period. This is followed by an examination of the proposal regarding the implementation of the lay judge (*saiban'in*)[1] system prepared by the Judicial System Reform Council (JSRC) in 2001 and the discussion of the processes of drafting and enactment of the Lay Judge Act of 2004. The chapter first summarizes the provisions of this act and outlines the amendments that were made to this piece of legislation prior to its enforcement in 2009. It then focuses on the promotional efforts carried out in connection with the implementation of the *saiban'in* system in Japan, examines the points raised in the public debate regarding this new system, looks at the first case tried with the participation of lay judges in Japan, and outlines some of the preliminary conclusions regarding the first five years of the functioning of the system in contemporary Japan. This is followed by an evaluation of Japan's latest experience with jury trials and a conclusion that summarizes the findings of the chapter.

Historical background: the developments in the legal system in the post-occupation period

The Japanese society and legal system have undergone significant changes since the end of the Allied occupation. This process of transformation can be divided into two distinct stages: the reforms that took place in the first decades following the end of the occupation of Japan and the amendments that were proposed in the 1990s and in the first years of the 21st century. The reforms of the first period consisted primarily of changes to individual statutes. The changes implemented in the second period, on the other hand, aimed to revamp the whole of Japan's justice system. While the reforms that were carried out in the 1960s through the 1980s were characterized by gradualism,[2] the changes initiated in the

---

1 The word *saiban'in* consists of two components – the word *saiban*, which means court, and the word *in*, which means "member" – and has been translated in the scholarly literature in English as "lay assessor" and "lay judge". This study uses the latter translation to highlight the difference between Japan's *saiban'in* system and the Continental-European lay assessor system.
2 D. H. Foote, "Introduction and Overview", in D. H. Foote (ed.), 2007, *Law in Japan: A Turning Point*, Seattle: University of Washington Press, pp. xix–xxxix, at p. xx.

1990s and at the beginning of the new century were proposed and implemented at a speed that was unprecedented by Japanese standards.[3]

In the first decades after the end of the Allied occupation of Japan, some of the existing pieces of legislation were amended to enable the legal system to better respond to the new challenges that Japan's society found itself faced with and to adjust the legal system to the changes that the society had undergone. For example, environmental disasters, such as the Minamata disease, triggered the enactment of environmental protection measures, including the Act for the Compensation of Pollution-Related Health Injury in 1973,[4] while the greater use of automobiles in the 1960s necessitated significant reforms in the handling of traffic disputes.[5] In addition, in the early 1970s and in the 1980s, major changes were implemented in the field of labor legislation, reflecting the changes in the Japanese society, underpinned by both international and domestic influences: Japan's desire to ratify the UN Convention the Elimination of All Forms of Discrimination against Women (the Convention) by July 1985 on the one hand and the change in the attitudes towards career women in the Japanese society on the other.[6] In 1972, the Equal Employment Opportunity Law (EEOL) was enacted and substantially amended in 1985, following Japan's ratification of the Convention.[7] The oil crises of 1973 and 1974 implied that the growth of the Japanese economy declined drastically and that consequently, tax revenues decreased. This situation triggered the reforms of the tax system in 1986 and 1988 that included the adoption of the value-added tax and the modification of the income tax system.[8]

---

3 Y. Tsuchiya, 2005, *Shimin no Shihō wa Jitsugen Shita ka: Shihō Kaikaku no Zentai Zō* [Has the [Idea of] Justice for the People Been Realized? An Overview of Judicial Reforms], Tokyo: Kadensha, p. 23.
4 Kōgai Kenkō Higai no Hoshō Tō ni kansuru Hōritsu [Act for the Compensation of Pollution-Related Health Injury], Law No. 111 of 1973. See K. Fujikura, "Litigation, Administrative Relief, and Political Settlement for Pollution Victim Compensation: Minamata Mercury Poisoning after Fifty Years", in Foote (ed.), 2007, *Law in Japan*, pp. 384–403 (discussing the enactment of environmental protection measures in Japan in the 1970s and the institution of the administrative compensation system).
5 E. A. Feldman, "Law, Culture, and Conflict: Dispute Resolution in Post-war Japan", in Foote (ed.), *Law in Japan*, pp. 50–79.
6 J. S. Fan, 1999, "Recent Development: From Office Ladies to Women Warriors? The Effect of the EEOL on Japanese Women", *UCLA Women's Law Journal*, Vol. 10, pp. 103–140, at p. 115. See generally D. H. Foote, "Law as an Agent of Change? Governmental Efforts to Reduce Working Hours in Japan", in H. Baum (ed.), 1997, *Japan: Economic Success and Legal System*, New York: Walter de Gruyter, pp. 251–301 (containing a comprehensive overview of the revisions in Japan's labor legislation).
7 Koyō no Bun'ya ni okeru Danjo no Kintō na Kikai oyobi Taigū no Kakuho nado ni kansuru Hōritsu [Law on Securing, Etc. of Equal Opportunity and Treatment between Men and Women in Employment], Law No. 113 of 1972, as amended by Law No. 78 of 1983, Law No. 45 of 1985, Law No. 76 of 1991, Law No. 107 of 1995, Law No. 92 of 1997, Law No. 87 of 1999, Law No. 104 of 1999, and Law No. 160 of 1999 [hereinafter Law on Securing, Etc. of Equal Opportunity and Treatment between Men and Women in Employment], translated in The Japan Institute of Labor, 2001, *Law on Securing, Etc. of Equal Opportunity and Treatment between Men and Women in Employment*, Tokyo: The Japan Institute of Labor, available online at "Law on Securing, Etc. of Equal Opportunity and Treatment between Men and Women in Employment", http://www.jil.go.jp/english/laborinfo/library/documents/llj_law4.pdf. Other reforms in the area of labor legislation included the 1987 amendment to the Labor Standards Law, which was followed by the 1992 Temporary Measures Law Concerning Promotion of Reduction of Working Hours, and other revisions that were approved by the Diet in 1993. Foote, "Law as an Agent of Change?", pp. 251–301.
8 Foote, "Introduction and Overview", pp. xix–xx; H. Kaneko, "The Reform of the Japanese Tax System in the Latter Half of the Twentieth Century and into the Twenty-First Century", in Foote (ed.), 2007, *Law in Japan*, pp. 564–582 (providing an overview of the reforms of the reforms of the Japanese tax system in the post-war period).

At the end of the 20th century and in the first years of the 21st century, Japanese law was on the verge of a radical transformation. Concerted efforts were initiated to amend the 1946 Constitution of Japan – the world's oldest unrevised constitution.[9] In 2000, Research Commissions on the Constitution (*Kenpō Chōsa Kai*) were set up in both houses of the National Diet. Five years later, Special Committees for Research on the Constitution of Japan (*Nihon Koku Kenpō ni kansuru Chōsa Tokubetsu Iinkai*) were established.[10] The Research Commissions conducted open hearings and its members undertook overseas study missions. The results of the deliberations were compiled in a final report that was submitted to the Diet in 2005.[11] In the same year, Prime Minister Jun'ichirō Koizumi proposed an amendment to the constitution with the goal of allowing Japan's Self-Defense Forces to acquire a more active role in the international affairs.[12] The ruling Liberal Democratic Party (LDP) submitted its own proposal of constitutional revision that retained Article 9 renouncing war, but proposed to amend the second paragraph of this article to allow for a "defense force" that would defend the nation and participate in international activities.[13] The draft used the word "army" (*gun*) that was intentionally avoided in the 1946 Constitution.[14] In 2007, the Research Commissions on the Constitution in both houses of the National Diet were abolished, and in their place the Investigative Committee on the Constitution (*Kenpō Shinsa Kai*) was established in the lower house of Parliament.[15] Prime Minister Shinzō Abe pledged to push aggressively for the revision of the constitution, and the possibility of either a constitutional amendment or the creation of a completely new charter for Japan remained at the center of debate in 2015.[16]

---

9 The possibility of constitutional revision had of course been deliberated prior to the 1990s as well. It was at the end of the 20th century, however, that the idea of amending the constitution attracted the support of the ruling LDP party (R. Yoshida, 2004, "Koizumi Urges LDP-DPJ Effort to Revise Constitution", *Japan Times*, January 15, available online at http://search.japantimes.co.jp/cgi-bin/nn20040115a3.html).

10 "Research Committee on the Constitution", available online at http://www.shugiin.go.jp/index.nsf/html/index_e_kenpou.htm (in English) and http://www.shugiin.go.jp/index.nsf/html/index_kenpou.htm (in Japanese). The website of the upper house's Constitutional Research Council is available online at http://www.sangiin.go.jp/japanese/kenpou/ (in Japanese). The website of the Special Committee for Research on the Constitution of Japan in the lower house of the Diet is available online at http://www.shugiin.go.jp/index.nsf/html/index_e_kenpou.htm (in English) and at http://www.shugiin.go.jp/index.nsf/html/index_kenpou.htm (in Japanese), and the website of the upper house's Special Committee for Research on the Constitution of Japan is available online at http://wwwves.sangiin.go.jp/japanese/kenpo/index.htm (in Japanese).

11 Shūgiin Kenpō Chōsa Kai, 2005, *Shūgiin Kenpō Chōsa Kai Hōkoku Sho* [Final Report of the Research Commission on the Constitution, The House of Representatives], available online at http://www.shugiin.go.jp/index.nsf/html/index_kenpou.htm.

12 Anonymous, 2005, "Constitutional Revision: Koizumi Wants Legal Basis for Military", *Japan Times*, October 31, available online at http://search.japantimes.co.jp/cgi-bin/nn20051031a1.html.

13 Kenpō (Proposed Official Draft 2005), Jiyū Minshuto, "Shin Kenpō Sōan" [Draft of the New Constitution], available online at http://www.jimin.jp/jimin/shin_kenpou/shiryou/pdf/051122_a.pdf.

14 *Id.*, art. 9(2).

15 Kokkai Hō [The Diet Law], Law No. 79 of 1889, as last amended by Law No. 51 of 2007, art. 102(6). The Investigative Committee has not had any meetings, however, as of 2009. "Kenpō Shinsa Kai" [Investigative Committee on the Constitution], available online at http://www.shugiin.go.jp/itdb_kenpou.nsf/html/kenpou/kenpou_f.htm.

16 Anonymous, 2014, "Abe Keen to Establish New Japanese Constitution", *Japan Times*, October 18, available online at http://www.japantimes.co.jp/news/2014/10/18/national/politics-diplomacy/abe-keen-to-establish-new-japanese-constitution/#.VFw5Er4xGhQ; Anonymous, 2007, "Japan Must Change Constitution to Change Nation: Abe", *Japan Times*, May 3, available online at http://search.japantimes.co.jp/cgi-bin/nn20070503f3.htoteml.

The 1990s saw a series of fundamental reforms that sought to achieve two goals: first, to adjust the legal system to the changes that the Japanese society had undergone; second, by means of reforming the justice system, to further reshape the Japanese society. The scope of the reforms carried out in the last decade of the 21st century is impressive. Examples are diverse and include, for instance, the enactment of new pieces of legislation guaranteeing fairness and transparency (the Administrative Procedure Act in 1993[17] and the Information Disclosure Act in 1999[18]), the 1994 reform of the electoral system,[19] the 1994 implementation of the new products liability law,[20] the introduction of the revised Code of Civil Procedure in 1996,[21] and the banking and market reforms triggered by the need to address the issues highlighted during the banking crisis of the 1990s and implemented in 1997 and 1998.[22]

In addition to these seemingly isolated reforms, a comprehensive set of recommendations was proposed by the Judicial System Reform Council (*Shihō Seido Kaikaku Shingikai*; JSRC), a committee established by the Cabinet in July 1999 with the aim of debating and making recommendations regarding the possibility of legal change in Japan.[23] JSRC's proposals placed the Japanese society and legal system on a track of change that has been called "revolutionary" in the scholarly literature. Scholars have referred to this latest round of reforms in the Japanese history as "the *Heisei* transformation"[24] and have even compared it with the drastic changes that the Japanese society and legal system had undergone as the result of the *Meiji* Restoration and of the Allied occupation following the end of World War II.

17 Gyōsei Tetsuzuki Hō [Administrative Procedure Act], Law No. 88 of 1993, as last amended by Law No. 66 of 2006. See L. Ködderitzsch, 1994, "Japan's New Administrative Procedure Act: Reasons for Its Enactment and Likely Implications", *Law in Japan: An Annual*, Vol. 24, pp. 105–137 (analyzing the Administrative Procedure Act); K. Uga, "Development of the Concepts of Transparency and Accountability in Japanese Administrative Law", and T. Ginsburg, "The Politics of Transparency in Japanese Administrative Law, in Foote (ed.), 2007, *Law in Japan*, pp. 276–303 and 304–311, respectively.
18 Gyōsei Kikan no Hoyū Suru Jōhō no Kōkai ni kansuru Hōritsu [Act on Access to Information Held by Administrative Organs], Law No. 42 of 1999. See generally K. Uga, 2002, *Shin Jōhō Kōkai Hō Chikujō Kaisetsu* [New Commentary on Information Disclosure Laws], Tokyo: Yūhikaku; N. Kadomatsu, 1999, "The New Administrative Information Disclosure Law in Japan", *Journal of Japanese Law*, Vol. 4, No. 8, pp. 34–52.
19 Kōshoku Senkyo Hō, Law No. 100 of 1950, as amended by Laws No. 2, 4, 10, 47, 104, and 105 of 1994, as last amended by Law No. 86 of 2007. Arguably, the most substantial amendment of this law was Law No. 2 of 1994 that changed the electoral system from the single non-transferable vote system to the mixed-member majoritarian system. These reforms were carried out with the aim of strengthening the position of the prime minister and Cabinet. See J. O. Haley, 2005, "Heisei Renewal or Heisei Transformation: Are Legal Reforms Really Changing Japan?", *Journal of Japanese Law*, Vol. 10, No. 19, pp. 5–18, at pp. 8–10 (discussing the 1994 revisions); K. Takahashi, "Ongoing Changes in the Infrastructure of a Constitutional System: From 'Bureaucracy' to Democracy", in Foote (ed.), 2007, *Law in Japan*, pp. 237–256 (analyzing the aims and outcomes of Japan's electoral reforms).
20 Seizōbutsu Sekinin Hō [Product Liability Law], Law No. 85 of 1994.
21 Minji Soshō Hō [Code of Civil Procedure], Law No. 109 of 1996.
22 J. C. Wiley, 1999, "Will the 'Bang' Mean 'Big' Changes to Japanese Financial Laws?", *Hastings International & Comparative Law Review*, Vol. 22, pp. 379–405; Y. Miwa, "Kin'yū Seido Kaikaku no Seiji Keizai Gaku" [Political Economy of Financial System Reform], in K. Kaizuka and K. Ikeo (eds), 1992, *Kin'yū Riron to Seido Kaikaku* [Financial Theory and Institutional Reform], Tokyo: Yūhikaku, pp. 307–341; Y. Miwa and J. M. Ramseyer, "Evidence from the Deregulation of Financial Services in Japan", in Foote (ed.), 2007, *Law in Japan*, pp. 153–189.
23 The website of the Judicial Reform Council is at http://www.kantei.go.jp/foreign/judica_e.html (in English).
24 Haley, "Heisei Renewal or Heisei Transformation?", p. 5.

The mixed-court jury (saiban'in) system   171

The Judicial System Reform Council Establishment Act provided the legal basis for the establishment of the council and stated specifically that the purpose of the JSRC was to

> clarify the role to be played by justice in Japanese society in the 21st century and to examine and deliberate fundamental measures necessary for the realization of a justice system that is easy for people to utilize, measures necessary for participation by the people in the justice system, [and reforms needed to strengthen] . . . the functions of the legal profession.[25]

The committee consisted of thirteen members, including active lawyers, prosecutors, judges, legal scholars and recipients of legal services, such as organizations of corporate executives, and a novelist. The committee was empaneled for a two-year term.[26] The diversity in the backgrounds of the members of the JSRC was one of the features that set the reform effort that the committee initiated apart from previous attempts. Prior to the establishment of the JSRC, legal reform was exclusively in the province of the "three branches" of the legal profession (*hōsō sansha*)[27] – the practicing bar, the judiciary, and the procuracy – and required that consensus be reached between them before any reform was to be implemented.[28]

The ambitiousness of JSRC's recommendations is reflected in the title of the final report that the committee submitted to Prime Minister Koizumi in June 2001: "Recommendations of the Judicial System Reform Council – A Justice System to Support Japan in the Twenty-First Century".[29] In this report, which was prepared after intense deliberations and research visits to the United States, the United Kingdom, Germany, and France, the JSRC outlined the following three "pillars", or objectives, of reform. These pillars are: (1) to establish a judicial system that is easy to use, easy to understand, and reliable from the point

---

25 Shihō Seido Kaikaku Shingikai Secchi Hō [Judicial System Reform Council Establishment Act], Law No. 68 of 1999, art. 2. This article is translated in Foote, "Introduction and Overview", p. xxi.
26 The committee was chaired by Professor Kōji Satō of Kyoto University, and vice chaired by Professor Morio Takeshita of Hitotsubashi University and president of Surugadai University. Members of the committee included Professor Masahito Inoue, Tokyo University, president of Ishii Iron Works Co., Ltd.; Kitamura Keiko, dean of the Faculty of Commerce, Chūō University; writer Ayako Sono; Tsuyoshi Takagi, vice president of the Japanese Trade Union Confederation; Yasuhiko Torii, president of Keio University; Kōhei Nakabo, attorney and former president of Hiroshima High Court; and Toshiiro Mizuhara, attorney and former superintending prosecutor of Nagoya High Public Prosecutor's Office ("Members of the JSRC", available online at http://www.kantei.go.jp/foreign/judiciary/member.html). Each of the members of the council was approved by the Diet (Foote, "Introduction and Overview", p. xxi). See also D. Vanoverbeke, 2015, *Juries in the Japanese Legal System: The Continuing Struggle for Citizen Participation and Democracy*, London: Routledge, pp. 124–133 (containing a detailed overview of the discussion that took place within the JSRC).
27 Foote, "Introduction and Overview", p. xxi.
28 It should be noted, however, that while some members of the JSRC came from outside the three branches of the legal profession, the council was supported by a Secretariat whose members were drawn from these three branches (*id.*, p. xxii).
29 Shihō Seido Kaikaku Shingikai [The Judicial System Reform Council], 2001, "Shihō Seido Kaikaku Shingikai Ikensho – 21 Seiki no Nihon o Sasaeru Shihō Seido" [Recommendations of the Judicial System Reform Council – A Justice System to Support Japan in the 21st Century], June 12, available online at http://www.kantei.go.jp/jp/sihouseido/report/ikensyo/pdf-dex.html (in Japanese) and http://www.kantei.go.jp/foreign/judiciary/2001/0612report.html (in English) [hereinafter Recommendations of the Judicial System Reform Council].

of view of ordinary citizens; (2) to improve the quality of legal services in Japan (speeding up trial proceedings) and increasing the number of professionals in the field, with the aim of better responding to the needs of the general public; and (3) to provide means for increased participation of ordinary citizens in the judicial system.[30]

With regard to the first pillar of reform, the JSRC recommended the following measures: lowering filing fees, requiring losing parties to pay attorney fees and court costs, creating the litigation cost insurance, strengthening the legal aid service, providing consultation services at courts (ensuring that some courts operate nights and weekends), and offering effective relief by determining the amount of damages, with the goal of expanding access to courts.[31] JSRC's report also recommended establishing a public defense system that would be financed by public money.[32]

In connection with the second pillar of reform, the report highlighted the need to speed up the process of adjudication of both criminal and civil trial cases. JSRC members argued specifically that court sessions should be scheduled for consecutive days – an important change in a system where trials had been notoriously long.[33] In addition, the JSRC suggested measures to improve the quality of trials. The report proposed specifically that Japan's trial procedure, which is famous for its heavy reliance on documentary evidence, should be changed to allow it to be based on the principle of orality.[34] Furthermore, the report argued that Japan needed to increase the number of lawyers to enable the country's legal system to address the expected increases in the litigation rates due to the rise of global competition. JSRC's report highlighted the importance of improving the situation with the number of lawyers for solving the problem of the so-called zero-one regions – that is, areas in Japan where there were virtually no lawyers.[35] As a way to achieve this goal, the council argued for the implementation of a sweeping reform of Japan's legal education. Specifically, the JSRC proposed that graduate professional law schools (*Hōka Daigakuin*), the curriculum of which would mirror that of U.S. law schools, be established.

---

30 S. Miyazawa, "Appendix: Summary of and Comments on Recommendations of the Judicial Reform Council (2001)", in M. M. Feeley and S. Miyazawa (eds), 2002, *The Japanese Adversary System in Context: Controversies and Comparisons*, New York: Palgrave Macmillan, pp. 247–252.
31 Recommendations of the Judicial System Reform Council, Chapter 2.
32 *Id.*
33 *Id.* Although Article 37(1) of the 1946 Constitution guarantees the right to a speedy trial, many cases in Japan have been tried for a notoriously long period of time. Representative of such long cases is *Japan v. Pak*, 26 Keishū 631 (Sup. Ct., December 20, 1972) – the so-called Takada case (*Takada Jiken*). This case was left unaddressed for 15 years, and the Supreme Court found that this was in violation of Article 37(1) of the Constitution of Japan. The summary of the judgment in Japanese can be found online at http://www.courts.go.jp/search/jhsp0030?action_id=dspDetail&hanreiSrchKbn=01&hanreiNo=27015&hanreiKbn=01. The English version is available online at http://www.courts.go.jp/english/judgments/text/1972.12.20-1970.-A-.No.1700.html. JSRC's recommendations resulted in the enactment of the Act Concerning the Speeding Up of Trials in 2003 (Saiban no Jinsokuka ni kansuru Hōritsu) [Act Concerning the Speeding Up of Trials], Law No. 107 of 2003).
34 D. H. Foote, "Reflections on Japan's Cooperative Process", in Feeley and Miyazawa (eds), 2002, *The Japanese Adversary System in Context*, pp. 29–41, at p. 31 (discussing the preference of Japanese courts for written statements, prepared by prosecutors, to live testimony in the courtroom).
35 JSRC's report set targets for the number of new lawyers per year at 1,500 in 2004, at 3,000 by 2010 – roughly a threefold increase from the 2001 figure – and at 50,000 by 2018 (Recommendations of the Judicial System Reform Council, chap. 3).

JSRC's suggestions with regard to the third pillar of reform have included the introduction of the new lay judge system in Japan.[36]

JSRC's report was not the first document proposing comprehensive reform of the justice system in Japan's post-occupation history. In 1964, the Provisional Justice System Investigation Committee (*Rinji Shihō Seido Chōsa Kai*) submitted its recommendations for reform.[37] Unlike the JSRC, the Investigation Committee primarily included members of the three branches of the legal profession. Its mandate was limited to deliberating issues associated with the employment and pay of judges and prosecutors, whereas the JSRC was established with the goal of investigating a wide range of problems.[38] Some of the proposals made by the Investigation Committee were remarkably similar to those suggested by the JSRC. For example, the Investigation Committee concluded that the number of judges and lawyers needed to be increased and urged lawyers to practice in rural areas.[39] While the Investigation Committee's report appears to have had a slight impact – in 1964, more than 500 persons passed the demanding bar examination for the first time – the remainder of the committee's recommendations were not implemented.[40]

By contrast, the suggestions made by JSRC became the basis for a wide range of reforms that were carried out at an unprecedented rate. Five months after the JSRC submitted its final report, in November 2001, the Diet enacted the Act for Promotion of Judicial System Reform.[41] On December 1, 2001, one month after the enactment of this piece of legislation and in accordance with it, the Office for Promotion of Justice System Reform (*Shihō Seido Kaikaku Suishin Honbu*) was established with the goal of ensuring the implementation of JSRC's recommendations.[42] According to the Act for Promotion of Judicial System Reform, the office was to be opened within the Cabinet.[43] In actual fact, however, the office had the whole of the Cabinet as members, with Prime Minister Koizumi serving as Chair.[44] The composition of the office added legitimacy to its tasks and reflected the degree of importance that the Cabinet attached to the idea of justice system reform.[45] Almost immediately after its establishment, in December 2001, the office set up eleven Expert Advisory Committees (*kentōkai*) each of which was responsible for deliberating one of the following themes: labor, access to justice, alternative dispute resolution (ADR), arbitration, administrative litigation, the lay

---

36 *Id.*, chap. 4.
37 Rinji Shihō Seido Chōsa Kai [Provisional Justice System Investigation Committee], 1964, *Rinji Shihō Seido Chōsa Kai Ikensho* [The Opinion Statement of the Provisional Justice System Investigation Committee], Tokyo: Hōsōkai.
38 Y. Aoyama, A. Noda and S. Tanaka, 2000, "Shihō Seido Kaikaku ni Nani o Nozomu ka" [What to Expect of Judicial System Reform?], *Jurisuto*, No. 1170, pp. 2–28, at pp. 3–4.
39 Foote, "Introduction and Overview", p. xxiv.
40 *Id.*, p. xxiv.
41 Shihō Seido Kaikaku Suishin Hō [Act for Promotion of Judicial System Reform], Law No. 119 of 2001 [hereinafter Act for Promotion of Judicial System Reform].
42 *Id.*, art. 1. See "Shihō Seido Kaikaku Suishin Honbu" [Office for Promotion of Justice System Reform], available online at http://www.kantei.go.jp/jp/singi/sihou/index.html (discussing the establishment and activities of the Office in Japanese) and "Office for Promotion of Justice System Reform", available online at http://www.kantei.go.jp/foreign/policy/sihou/index_e.html (containing information on the office in English).
43 Act for Promotion of Judicial System Reform, art. 8.
44 "Members of the Office for Promotion of Justice System Reform", available online at http://www.kantei.go.jp/foreign/policy/sihou/members_e.html.
45 Foote, "Introduction and Overview", p. xxv.

judge system/criminal justice, publicly provided defense counsel system, internationalization, legal training, legal profession,[46] and intellectual property.[47] In addition, in March 2002, the office prepared the Plan for Promotion of Justice System Reform.[48] The reforms proposed in the plan were implemented swiftly. By the end of 2004, when the office was dissolved, twenty-five pieces of legislation addressing all of the major themes that had been deliberated at the Expert Advisory Committees were enacted.[49] Examples include but are not limited to the following: the Act Concerning the Speeding Up of Trials,[50] Arbitration Law,[51] an amendment of the Attorney Act,[52] amendments to the Code of Criminal Procedure[53] and to the Code of Civil Procedure,[54] the drafting and enactment of the Act Concerning Promotion of Use of Alternative Dispute Resolution,[55] the Act Partially Amending the Bar Examination Act and the Court Act,[56] the Act on Linkage between Law School Education and Bar Examination,[57] and the Act for Establishment of the Intellectual Property High Court.[58]

---

46 "Kentōkai no Kaisai ni tsuite" [Concerning the Establishment of Expert Advisory Committees], December 17, 2001, available online at http://www.kantei.go.jp/jp/singi/sihou/kentoukai/kaisai.html.
47 "Kentōkai no Kaisai ni tsuite" [Concerning the Establishment of Expert Advisory Committees], October 2, 2002, available online at http://www.kantei.go.jp/jp/singi/sihou/kentoukai/kaisai2.html.
48 "Shihō Seido Kaikaku Suishin Keikaku" [Plan for Promotion of Justice System Reform], Cabinet Resolution of March 19, 2002, available online at http://www.kantei.go.jp/jp/singi/sihou/keikaku/020319keikaku.html.
49 Only one out of the numerous proposals made by the office – the Proposal for Partial Amendment of the Law Concerning Civil Litigation Costs – was not enacted. The draft of this piece of legislation suggested allowing the parties in the civil suit to agree prior to the adjudication of the case that the party that loses will be responsible for paying the costs of the trial, including the fees of the attorneys (Minji Soshō Hiyō Tō ni kansuru Hōritsu no Ichibu o Kaisei Suru Hōritsu An [Proposal for Partial Amendment of the Law Concerning Civil Litigation Costs], submitted to the National Diet on March 4, 2003). See Shihō Seido Kaikaku Suishin Honbu [Office for Promotion of Justice System Reform], "Minji Soshō Hiyō Tō ni kansuru Hōritsu no Ichibu o Kaisei Suru Hōritsu An ni tsuite (Gaiyō)" [Concerning the Proposal for Partial Amendment of the Law Concerning Civil Litigation Costs (An Outline)], available online at http://www.kantei.go.jp/jp/singi/sihou/houan/040302/minji/gaiyou.pdf). A full list of enacted legislation is available in Tsuchiya, *Shimin no Shihō wa Jitsugen Shita ka* [Has the [Idea of] Justice for the People Been Realized?], pp. 16–20, and available online at http://www.kantei.go.jp/jp/singi/sihou/enkaku.html.
50 Saiban no Jinsokuka ni kansuru Hōritsu [Act Concerning the Speeding Up of Trials], Law No. 107 of 2003.
51 Chūsai Hō [Arbitration Law], Law No. 138 of 2003.
52 Bengoshi Hō no Ichibu o Kaisei Suru Hōritsu [Act Partially Amending the Attorney Act], Law No. 9 of 2004.
53 Keiji Soshō Hō Tō no Ichibu o Kaisei Suru Hōritsu [Act Concerning a Partial Amendment of the Code of Criminal Procedure], Law No. 62 of 2004.
54 Minji Soshō Hō Tō no Ichibu o Kaisei Suru Hōritsu [Act Concerning a Partial Amendment of the Code of Civil Procedure], Law No. 108 of 2003.
55 Saiban Gai Funsō Kaiketsu Tetsuzuki no Riyō no Sokushin ni kansuru Hōritsu [Act Concerning Promotion of Use of Alternative Dispute Resolution], Law No. 151 of 2004.
56 Shihō Shiken Hō oyobi Saibansho Hō no Ichibu o Kaisei Suru Hōritsu [Act Partially Amending the Bar Examination Act and the Court Act], Law No. 138 of 2002.
57 Hōka Dagakuin no Kyōiku to Shihō Shiken Tō to no Renkei Tō ni kansuru Hōritsu [Act on Linkage Between Law School Education and Bar Examination etc.], Law No. 139 of 2002. Japan carried out reform of legal education that resulted in the establishment of Law Schools (*Hōka Daigakuin*). See S. Miyazawa, 2001, "The Politics of Judicial Reform in Japan: The Rule of Law at Last?", *Asian-Pacific Law & Policy Journal*, Vol. 2, No. 2, pp. 89–121, at pp. 90–97 and 110–118 (discussing the reform of the National Bar Examination and the movement to introduce graduate professional law schools); J. Tamura, 2003, *Shihō Seido Kaikaku to Hōka Daigakuin: Sekai Hyōjun no Purofeshonaru Skūru Jitsugen ni Mukete* [Justice System Reform and Law Schools: Towards Realization of World-Level Professional Schools], Tokyo: Nihon Hyōronsha; K. Rokumoto, "Legal Education", in Foote (ed.), 2007, *Law in Japan*, pp. 190–236.
58 Chiteki Zaisan Kōtō Saibansho Secchi Hō [Act for Establishment of the Intellectual Property High Court], Law No. 119 of 2004.

The 2001 report prepared by the JSRC commented on the breadth of the scope of the reforms that it proposed. The authors of the report argued that the recommended reforms were a part of a larger process that has been going on in Japan, including political, administrative, economic restructuring, and the efforts aimed at decentralization.[59] The report stated that the reforms that the council promoted sought to achieve the following objectives:

(1) Transform the "excessive advance-control/adjustment type society to an after-the-fact review/remedy type society";
(2) Promote decentralization;
(3) Reform the "bloated administrative system";
(4) Improve the quality of governing ability of the political branches (Diet, Cabinet);
(5) Ensure disclosure of administrative information and accountability to the public;
(6) Improve policy assessment functions;
(7) Achieve rather transparent administration.

Through achieving these seven goals, the JSRC stated, it should become possible to reach objective eight, which was to "reinforce the transformation of the Japanese people from governed subjects to governing subjects".[60] Individual empowerment was assumed in the report to be not only an objective of reform proposals, but also a premise for their successful implementation.[61] The JSRC itself has thus attributed the breadth of the scope of the reforms that it proposed to the need to adjust the Japanese legal system to the changes that the Japanese society had undergone in the post-war period on the one hand, and to the importance of using the legal system to promote further change on the other hand.

The objectives stated in the JSRC report were closely related to the proclaimed goals of Prime Minister Koizumi's administration (April 26, 2001–September 26, 2006). After all, Prime Minister Koizumi came to power on the platform of sweeping reform, and his popularity to a large degree depended on his ability to deliver on promises to promote radical restructuring of the Japanese economy, politics, and society.[62] The first concerted efforts to conceptualize the agenda for sweeping reform, encompassing all aspects of Japan's society, go back to the activities of the administrations of Prime Ministers Obuchi (July 30, 1998–April 5, 2000) and Mori (April 5, 2000–April 26, 2001) who directly preceded Koizumi. It was Obuchi who set up the "Commission on Japan's Goals in the 21st Century" (*21 Seiki Nihon no Kōsō Kondankai*) in March 1999, four months prior to the establishment of the JSRC.[63] In January 2000 this

---

59 Recommendations of the Judicial System Reform Council, chap. 1.
60 *Id.*
61 The report stated that the "various reforms assume as a basic premise the people's transformation from governed objects to governing subjects and at the same time seek to promote such transformation" (*id.*).
62 *Economist*, 2002, "Survey: Japan; Lionheart to the Rescue?", April 18, available online at http://www.economist.com/displaystory.cfm?story_id=1076818.
63 "21 Seiki Nihon no Kōzō Kondankai [Commission on Japan's Goals in the Twenty-First Century]", available online at http://www.kantei.go.jp/jp/21century/index.html. This commission consisted of sixteen private citizens from different fields of expertise, including academics, journalists, a composer, an astronaut, an editor, and a playwright (the full list of members of the commission is available online at http://www.kantei.go.jp/jp/21century/report/htmls/1preface.html#profile). Like the members of the JSRC, the members of the commission travelled abroad in search of ideas. The commission undertook a series of consultations with intellectual leaders of Singapore, the United States, South Korea, China, and France ("21 Seiki Nihon no Kōzō Kondankai [Commission on Japan's Goals in the Twenty-First Century]", available online at http://www.kantei.go.jp/jp/21century/report/htmls/1preface.html#preface).

commission issued its final report, "The Frontier Within: Individual Empowerment and Better Governance in the New Millennium" (the Report).[64]

Just like JSRC's report, this document proclaimed individual empowerment as one of the major policy objectives. The commission's report elaborated further than the JSRC's recommendations on the changes that Japan's society had experienced in the post-war era.[65] Specifically, the report argued that in the 1990s there had been a prevailing feeling that "something about" Japan had "undergone a major shift".[66] The reasons for this shift that the report listed may be classified into the following three categories: economic (the burst of the economic bubble in the 1990s), political (undermined political order as a result of the economic turmoil), and social (changes in the value system and ethical norms at the very core of the nation).[67] The report referred to such developments in the recent Japanese history as the 1995 Great Hanshin-Awaji Earthquake and the Aum Shinrikyo nerve gas attack on the Tokyo subway in 1995, as well as rising juvenile crime, to highlight the Japanese government's inability to ensure effective crisis management, the lack of accountability in the Japanese society, and inefficiency. It concluded:

> All this left people with the impression that [the] core attributes of Japanese society on which they have prided themselves – family solidarity, the quality of education (especially primary and lower secondary education), and social stability and safety – were crumbling.[68]

The Report, just like the recommendations of JSRC, indicated that Japan needed reforms that would adjust, by means of government intervention, the legal, social, political, and economic systems in Japan to meet the changing and increasingly internationalizing environment.

This chapter focuses on one of the JSRC-inspired reforms – the introduction of the jury system in Japan.

The background to the adoption of the Lay Judge Act

In the late 1950s and 1960s, the debate regarding the possibility of expanding layperson participation in the administration of justice was restricted to the discussion of the constitutionality of the reintroduction of the jury system in Japan. For example, the commentary to the 1946 Constitution, published in 1953 by the Jurisprudence Society (*Hōgaku Kyōkai*), stated that having the court bound by the findings of the members of the jury would violate those provisions of the constitution that stipulated that judges were to be bound only by

---

64 21 Seiki Nihon no Kōzō Kondankai [Commission on Japan's Goals in the 21st Century], 2000, "Nihon no Furontia wa Nihon no Naka ni Aru: Jiritsu to Kyōchi o Kizuku Shinseiki [The Frontier Within: Individual Empowerment and Better Governance in the New Millennium], available online at http://www.kantei.go.jp/jp/21century/index.html (in Japanese) and http://www.kantei.go.jp/jp/21century/report/htmls/index.html (in English).
65 *Id.*
66 *Id.*
67 *Id.* Regarding social change, the report stated the following: "Over a long history in a meager and harsh environment, we cultivated ethical norms extolling social and organizational harmony. Socioeconomic affluence and internationalization, however, made it difficult to sustain such ethical norms unchanged. And in the 1990s, before a national consensus on the ethical framework appropriate to an affluent society could be reached, Japan experienced a major setback and slid into the age of globalization" (*id.*)
68 *Id.*

this constitution and the laws.[69] Professor Shirō Kiyomiya opposed this interpretation in a 1966 book, and argued that the fact that the constitution did not mention trial by jury did not necessarily imply that the implementation of the jury system in post-war Japan would be unconstitutional.[70] Conversely, Professor Ryūichi Hirano observed in 1958 that if the jury system was introduced, the members of the jury would be considered as part of the court and that the jury system therefore would not be in conflict with the provisions of the constitution.[71] This debate was theoretical and did not involve any concrete proposals to introduce the jury system.

The discussion of the possibility of introducing the jury system in Japan came to the forefront of public debate again in the 1980s. This time, the deliberations involved not only academics but also various citizen groups that were established especially for the purpose of deliberating the jury system. One such group was the Association for Deliberations on the Jury [System] (*Baishin o Kangaeru Kai*), formed in 1982.[72] Other groups included the Society for Advancement of Jury Trials in Niigata (*Niigata Baishin Tomo no Kai*), established in 1986 by Professor Yoshito Sawanobori of Niigata University, and the Saitama Jury [System] Forum (*Saitama Baishin Fōramu*), formed in 1988 by twelve lawyers belonging to the Saitama Bar Association.[73] The most recently formed group is the Association for the Revival of the Jury System (*Baishin Seido o Fukkatsu Suru Kai*), set up in 1995 by lawyer Chihiro Saeki, Professor Takashi Maruta of Kwansei Gakuin University and Hanako Watanabe of the Japan Judicial Interpreters Association.[74] Since their establishment, these organizations have been engaged in social research and publishing activities and have also served as organizers of public lectures on topics related to the jury system. Some have conducted mock trials in several prefectures, where volunteers were asked to participate in the deliberations regarding actual major legal cases.[75]

Some of these citizen groups authored proposals for amending the pre-war Jury Act. The Association for the Revival of the Jury System drafted one such proposal.[76] This proposal left intact the provisions of the pre-war Jury Act concerning the scope of cases eligible for trial by jury, with the exception of Article 4 of the pre-war Jury Act that denied access to trial by jury to those defendants who were accused of offences against the Peace Preservation Act. This article was of course deleted. The proposal allowed the accused to waive his or her right to be tried by jury[77] and extended the right to serve on jury to all persons eligible

---

69 Nihonkoku Kenpō (1946), art. 76 para. 3; Hōgaku Kyōkai [The Jurisprudence Society] (ed.), 1953, *Chūkai Nihonkoku Kenpō* [Annotated Constitution of Japan], Tokyo: Yūhikaku, Vol. 2, p. 1138.
70 S. Kiyomiya, 1966, *Kenpō 1* [The Constitution, 1], Tokyo: Yūhikaku, p. 283, cited in Tsuchiya, *Saiban'in Seido to Kokumin* [The Lay Judge System and the People], p. 58.
71 R. Hirano, 1958, *Keiji Soshō Hō* [Code of Criminal Procedure], Tokyo: Yūhikaku, p. 46.
72 "Baishin o Kangaeru Kai", available online at http://www.baishin.com/05baishinkai/index.htm.
73 "Saitama Baishin Fōramu", available online at http://homepage2.nifty.com/saitama-jury/soghoainai.htm.
74 "Baishin Seido o Fukkatsu Suru Kai", available online at http://www.baishin.sakura.ne.jp/.
75 The results of such trials were published and have been used by these organizations to prove that arguments regarding the alleged incompatibility of Japanese cultural values are unfounded. See Niigata Baishin Tomo no Kai (ed.), 1998, *Baishin Seido: Shimin no Te ni Saiban o* [The Jury System: Putting the Court into the Hands of the People], Tokyo: Shōgakusha; and Saitama Baishin Fōramu (ed.), 1989, *Kuni vs Itō: Baishin Seido – Sono Jissen* [State vs Ito: The Jury System in Practice], Tokyo: Equality.
76 Baishin Seido o Fukkatsu Suru Kai, Baishin Hō Kaisei An [Proposal for Amending the Jury Act], not dated, available online at http://www.baishin.sakura.ne.jp/kaiseian.html.
77 *Id.*, art. 6.

to vote.[78] Another proposal for amending the pre-war Jury Act was authored by the Jury System Research Society (*Baishin Seido Kenkyūkai*), headed by Professor Takashi Maruta.[79] This draft proposed to allow the defendant to request trial by jury.[80] It suggested that the right to serve as a juror be extended to include all persons older than twenty years of age who had lived in Japan for more than two years and had adequate command of the Japanese language.[81] The Jury System Research Society's draft proposed that the jury panel consist of ten laypersons[82] and be responsible for coming up with the verdict of guilty, not guilty, or partially guilty – a verdict that was to be binding on the court.[83] The proposals for the introduction of the jury system in Japan authored by these non-governmental organizations did not manage to win the support on the part of the government and did not lead to reform.

Despite this fact, however, the subject of jury trials came to be widely discussed in 1987, when then Supreme Court Chief Justice Kōichi Yaguchi gave the assignment to the General Secretariat of the Supreme Court (*Saikō Saibansho Jimusōkyoku*) to research the possibility of introducing the jury system in Japan.[84] As part of the activities associated with this assignment, in 1988 and 1989 Justices Hironobu Takesaki and Megumi Yamamuro were sent to the United States, and in 1990 Justice Yū Shiraki was sent to the United Kingdom. The justices were sent to study the functioning of the jury system in these two countries. The results of the studies, conducted in connection with Justice Yaguchi's assignment, were subsequently published as a series of books edited by the General Secretariat,[85] but no formal proposal for the introduction of the jury system was prepared by the Supreme Court.

At around the same time, local Bar Associations started displaying interest in the institution of jury service and sent their members to observe the functioning of the jury and of the lay assessor systems in other countries.[86] The Osaka Bar Association and the Tokyo San Bar

---

78 *Id.*, art. 12.
79 Baishin Seido Kenkyūkai [The Jury System Research Society], Shin Keiji Baishin Saiban Hōan (Risōteki Keiji Baishin Hōan) Shian [Draft of the Bill [Concerning] the New Criminal Jury Trials (The Draft of an Ideal Criminal Jury)], not dated, available online at http://www.geocities.co.jp/HeartLand-Kaede/5549/maruta/houan.htm [hereinafter The Jury System Research Society, Draft of the Bill Concerning the New Criminal Jury Trials].
80 The Jury System Research Society, Draft of the Bill Concerning the New Criminal Jury Trials, art. 3.
81 *Id.*, art. 10.
82 *Id.*, art. 20.
83 *Id.*, arts. 66, 69, and 70.
84 M. Itō, T. Ōe, and S. Katō, 1999, "Shihō Seido Kaikaku no Shiten to Kadai" [Perspectives on and Issues Surrounding the Justice System Reform], *Jurisuto*, No. 1167, pp. 52–100, at pp. 94 and 96; D. H. Foote, 1992, "From Japan's Death Row to Freedom", *Pacific Rim Law & Policy Journal*, Vol. 1, No. 1, pp. 11–103, at pp. 83–84; M. Yamamuro, "On the Introduction of the Jury System in Japan", Speech at Santa Clara University Law School, April 1990 (copy on file with author), cited in Foote, "From Japan's Death Row to Freedom", p. 84.
85 Saikō Saibansho Jimu Sōkyoku Keiji Kyoku [Criminal Affairs Bureau, General Secretariat of the Supreme Court of Japan], 1992, *Baishin, Sanshin Seido* [The Jury and Lay Assessor Systems], Tokyo: Shihō Kyōkai; Saikō Saibansho Jimu Sōkyoku Keiji Kyoku [Criminal Affairs Bureau, General Secretariat of the Supreme Court], 1996, *Baishin no Jijitsu Nintei o Chūshin toshite* [Focusing on the Jury's Fact-Finding [Ability]], Tokyo: Shihō Kyōkai.
86 See for instance, Ōsaka Bengoshi Kai [Osaka Bar Association], 1992, *Baishin Seido: Amerika Shisatsu Hōkoku* [The Jury System: A Report on the Observations [of the System's Functioning in] America], Osaka: Daiichi Hōki Shuppan; Ōsaka Bengoshi Kai [Osaka Bar Association], 1989, *Baishin Seido: Sono Kanōsei o Kangaeru* [The Jury System: Considering Its Possibilities], Osaka: Daiichi Hōki Shuppan; Tokyo Bengoshi Kai [Tokyo Bar Association], 1992, *Baishin Saiban: Kyūbaishin no Shōgen to Kongo no Kadai* [Jury Trials: The Testimony and Implications for the Future of the Old Jury System], Tokyo:

The mixed-court jury (saiban'in) system 179

Association of Tama city, a municipality in western Tokyo, established special committees to look into the possibility of reintroducing the jury system in Japan. The Committee on the Jury System of the Osaka Bar Association authored its own draft of the revised pre-war Jury Act.[87] This proposal allowed the defendant to request trial by jury in all cases where the punishment was no less than three years' imprisonment.[88] It provided for a twelve all-layperson jury whose verdict was to be binding on the court,[89] and extended the right to serve as a juror to all persons eligible to vote in Japan.[90]

What were some of the factors that reinvigorated the debate regarding the possibility of introducing the jury system among citizen groups, the Supreme Court of Japan, and the local Bar Associations in the 1980s? One factor was the growing dissatisfaction with Japan's judge-only system, which was fueled by several highly publicized verdicts by judges that included the acquittals of four death row inmates who had been serving their sentences for over twenty-five years.[91] The Menda case,[92] the Saitakawa case,[93] the Matsuyama case,[94] and the Shimada case[95] occurred over the span of seven years (the Menda incident occurred in 1948; the Saitakawa incident in 1950; the Shimada incident in 1954, and the Matsuyama case in 1955). All cases involved defendants who confessed, later withdrew their confessions, and were eventually found guilty and sentenced to death. In all four cases the court adopted the position of the prosecution in their entirety. The four defendants were not executed, however, in view of the fact that they continuously sought retrials.[96] The accused in all four cases obtained retrials, and in each case new important evidence casting doubt on the conviction was brought to light. As a result, the confessions were re-examined, and the court

---

    Gyōsei; Tokyo San Bengoshikai Baishin Seido Iinkai [Tokyo San Bengoshikai Bar Association Committee on the Jury System] (ed.), 1993, *Nyū Yōku Baishin Saiban* [The New York Jury Trial], Tokyo: Nihon Kajo Shuppan.
87 Osaka Bar Association, not dated, "Baishin Hō Kaisei Hō Shian" [Draft of the Law Amending the Jury Act], reprinted in Ōsaka Bengoshi Kai Keiji Hōsei Iinkai (ed.), 2001, *Baishin Hō Kaisei Hō Shian (Kentō Shiryō)* [Draft of the Law Amending the Jury Act], Osaka: Ōsaka Bengoshi Kai Keiji Hōsei Iinkai, pp. 4–22 [hereinafter Osaka Bar Association, Draft of the Law Amending the Jury Act].
88 Osaka Bar Association, Draft of the Law Amending the Jury Act, art. 2. This article stipulated that the defendant would be allowed to request to be tried by jury in all cases where the punishment involved death, perpetual penal servitude, perpetual imprisonment and where the punishment was three years' imprisonment or more.
89 *Id.*, arts. 71 and 72.
90 *Id.*, arts. 22 and 11, respectively.
91 Foote, "From Japan's Death Row to Freedom", pp. 14–64 (providing a detailed overview of the most important of these cases); L.W. Kiss, "Reviving the Criminal Jury in Japan", *Law and Contemporary Problems*, Vol. 62, pp. 261–283, at pp. 262–266 (summarizing the details of these cases).
92 *Japan v. Menda*, Kumamoto District Court, Yatsushiro Division, Judgment of July 15, 1983, *Hanrei Jihō*, No. 1090, p. 21. See Foote, "From Japan's Death Row to Freedom", pp. 14–30 (containing an overview of the details of this case).
93 *Japan v. Taniguchi*, Takamatsu District Court, Judgment of March 12, 1984, *Hanrei Jihō*, No. 1107, p. 13. See Foote, "From Japan's Death Row to Freedom", pp. 30–42 (containing an overview of the details of this case).
94 *Japan v. Saitō*, Sendai District Court, Judgment and Ruling of July 11, 1984, *Hanrei Jihō*, No. 1127, p. 34. See Foote, "From Japan's Death Row to Freedom", pp. 42–51 (containing an overview of the details of this case).
95 *Japan v. Akabori*, Shizuoka District Court, Judgment of January 31, 1989, *Hanrei Jihō*, No. 1316, p. 21. See Foote, "From Japan's Death Row to Freedom", pp. 51–64 (containing an overview of the details of this case).
96 Foote, "From Japan's Death Row to Freedom", pp. 64–69 (discussing the commonalities between these four cases).

180   *The mixed-court jury (saiban'in) system*

ruled that the four death row inmates had been unjustly convicted. The final rulings on the four cases were made in the 1980s.[97]

The citizen groups promoting the jury system established in the 1980s argued that the introduction of the jury system would help resolve the problem of the lack of trust on the part of the general public towards the justice system under which such erroneous verdicts were possible. The Association for the Revival of the Jury System, for instance, argued that it viewed the introduction of the jury system as a safeguard against erroneous verdicts that would help ensure that trial proceedings are based on the presumption of innocence rather than the presumption of guilt.[98] In addition, the Association for Deliberations on the Jury System stated that the lack of transparency of the Japanese court system was to blame for the horrendous errors in the administration of justice, and proposed that the implementation of the jury system would help ameliorate the situation.[99] The erroneous verdicts in the four cases discussed earlier forced the Supreme Court Chief Justice Kōichi Yaguchi to investigate the possibility of introducing jury trials.[100]

The idea of citizen participation came to the forefront of the Japanese government's agenda when the first proposals for comprehensive reform of the justice system emerged.[101]

---

97 The ruling on the Menda case was handed down in 1983, the Saitakawa and the Matsuyama cases were resolved in 1984, and the accused in the Shimada case was acquitted in 1989 (*id.*).
98 Baishin Seido o Fukkatsu Suru Kai, "Baishin Seido e no Michiyori" [The Path towards the Jury System], available online at http://www.baishin.sakura.ne.jp/kaishi.html.
99 Baishin o Kangaeru Kai, "Baishin Seido no Kiso Chishiki" [Fundamental Knowledge on the Jury System], available online at http://www.baishin.com/01kiso/index.htm.
100 Foote, "From Japan's Death Row to Freedom", pp. 83–84 (discussing the link between the erroneous verdicts and the interest of the Supreme Court of Japan in investigating the possibility of introducing jury trials). In the 1980s, the proponents of the view that the introduction of the jury system would indeed help prevent erroneous verdicts argued that the presence of jurors would lead to increased usage of live testimony as opposed to the heavy reliance of written witness statements. In addition, the introduction of the jury system would, it was claimed, lead to shorter trials, as hearings would have to be held on a continuous basis rather than be scheduled weeks apart from one another. Furthermore, allowing laypersons to adjudicate cases should make it possible for the general public to become more aware of the workings of the justice system (*id.*, p. 84).
101 The first organizations devoted to the discussion of the need for the sweeping reform of Japan's justice system were the Commission on the Basic Problems of the Legal Profession (*Hōsō Kihon Mondai Kondankai*), established in 1987, and the Council on Legal Training and Other Reforms (*Hōsō Yōsei Seido Tō Kaikaku Kyōgikai*), established in 1991. The commission and the council did not propose that Japan introduce the institution of jury service, but focused instead on the reform of Japan's legal profession. The Commission on the Basic Problems of the Legal Profession submitted an opinion statement to the Ministry of Justice in 1988 in which it argued that the legal profession in Japan was removed from the society and therefore unable to effectively address the new challenges that the society was confronting (Aoyama, Noda, and Tanaka, "Shihō Seido Kaikaku ni Nani o Nozomu ka" [What to Expect of Judicial System Reform?], p. 3; M. Ishii, 2006, "Hōsō Kyōiku o Meguru Seido to Seisaku: Hōsō Sansha no Rikigaku o Chūshin toshite" [Systems and Policies Concerning Legal Education: Focusing on the Dynamics of the Three Branches of Legal Profession], *Tōhoku Daigaku Daigakuin Kyōiku Gaku Kenkyūka Kenkyū Nenpō* [Annual Bulletin of Tohoku University Graduate School of Education], Vol. 1, No. 55, pp. 197–218, at p. 203). The authors of the statement concluded that Japan needed to reform the system of legal education to allow more persons to pass the demanding Bar Examination – a proposal that subsequently became one of the important elements of the three pillars of reform proclaimed by the JSRC. The members of the Council on Legal Training and Other Reforms reaffirmed the importance of increasing the number the lawyers, prosecutors, and judges to enable the legal profession to better serve the needs of the people (H. Gotō, 1996, "Hōsō Yōsei Seido Tō Kaikaku Kyōgikai no Kyōgi no

The first document recommending the expansion of layperson participation in the judicial system as part of a package of reforms of Japan's legal system was authored by the Japan Federation of Bar Associations. The federation issued a declaration regarding justice system reform on May 25, 1990, in which it stated that the realization of the justice system that was close to the general public should be the main objective of legal reform. This declaration argued that there was a need to ensure that the members of the general public would be allowed to participate in the administration of justice and proposed that Japan should either implement the amended version of the pre-war jury system or introduce the Continental-European model of jury trials.[102]

Another proposal suggesting the introduction of the jury system in Japan was drafted in 1994 by the Japan Association of Corporate Executives (*Keizai Dōyūkai*).[103] The proposal, titled "The Ills of Contemporary Japanese Society and the Prescriptions [to Cure Them]: Towards the Realization of a Society that Values the Individual", argued that one of the "ills" of the Japanese society was the "hypertrophy of administrative power" (*gyōsei no hidai*).[104] It stated that to overcome this problem Japan should endow the judicial system with more power and by doing so enable the judicial branch to counterbalance the excessive importance attached to administrative guidance. The report stated that the introduction of the jury system was an important step towards realizing the system of justice that would be "close to the people" (*kokumin ni mijikana shihō*).[105] The association emphasized that Japan's legal system needed sweeping reform to enable it to cope with the challenges of

---

Keii ni tsuite" [Concerning the Details of the Deliberations of the Council on Legal Training and Other Reforms], *Jurist*, No. 1084, pp. 33–37).

102 Nihon Bengoshi Rengōkai [Japan Federation of Bar Associations], 1990, "Shihō Kaikaku ni kansuru Sengen" [Declaration Concerning Justice Reform], May 25, available online at http://www.nichibenren.or.jp/ja/opinion/ga_res/1990_3.html. The recommendations made in this document were discussed further in the reports issued by the Japan Federation of Bar Associations subsequently. See Nihon Bengoshi Rengōkai [Japan Federation of Bar Associations], 1991, "Shihō Kaikaku ni kansuru Sengen (Sono 2)" [Declaration Concerning Justice Reform (2)], May 24, available online at http://www.nichibenren.or.jp/ja/opinion/ga_res/1991_4.html; Nihon Bengoshi Rengōkai [Japan Federation of Bar Associations], 1994, "Shihō Kaikaku ni kansuru Sengen (Sono 3)" [Declaration Concerning Justice Reform (3)], May 27, available online at http://www.nichibenren.or.jp/ja/opinion/ga_res/1994_3.html; Keizai Dantai Rengōkai [Japan Business Federation], 1998, "Shihō Seido Kaikaku ni tsuite no Iken" [Policy Statement Regarding Justice System Reform], May 19, available online at http://www.keidanren.or.jp/japanese/policy/pol173.html.

103 The Japan Association of Corporate Executives is a private non-profit organization that includes approximately 1,400 top executives of the 900 most successful companies in Japan. This organization, established in 1946, conducts research on subjects relevant to its activities and publishes the results in the form of policy proposals the goal of which is to influence government policy, the industry, and the general society. Research is conducted by the committees established within the organization. The proposal suggesting the introduction of the jury system in Japan was authored by the organization's Justice System Reform Committee (*Shihō Seido Kaikaku Iinkai*). See "Overview of Keizai Dōyūkai", available online at http://www.doyukai.or.jp/en/about/index.html.

104 Keizai Dōyūkai [The Japan Association of Corporate Executives], 1994, *Gendai Nihon Shakai no Byōri to Shohō: Kojin o Ikasu Shakai no Jitsugen ni Mukete* [The Ills of Contemporary Japanese Society and the Prescriptions [to Cure Them]: Towards the Realization of a Society that Values the Individual], Tokyo: Keizai Dōyūkai.

105 *Id.*

182 The mixed-court jury (saiban'in) system

globalization and to address the needs of an economy that would be increasingly led by the private sector rather than by government regulation.[106]

The ideas concerning justice system reform in general and the introduction of the jury system in particular expressed in the aforementioned reports did not go unnoticed by the ruling LDP. The party established the Special Investigative Committee on the Justice System (*Shihō Seido Tokubetsu Chōsa Kai*) in June 1997 with the goal of developing the official party position regarding the subject of legal reform. In June 1998, this committee, led by politician Yasuoka Okiharu,[107] prepared a report summarizing the details of its deliberations, which included consultations with academics as well as influential members of the Japan Business Federation, the Japan Association of Corporate Executives, the Japan Federation of Bar Associations, the Supreme Court, and the non-governmental organizations (NGOs) promoting the idea of justice system reform. In this report, "The Firm Principles of 21st Century Justice", the LDP stated that a council for the reform of the justice system should be established to deliberate the measures necessary to realize the justice system that is easy for the general public to understand and use.[108] The report emphasized that further discussion was needed regarding the question of whether Japan should introduce the jury system

---

106 Keizai Dōyūkai [The Japan Association of Corporate Executives], 1997, *Gurōbaruka ni Taiō Suru Kigyō Hōsei no Seibi o Mezashite: Minkan Shudō no Shijō Keizai ni Muketa Hō Seido to Rippō, Shihō no Kaikaku* [Aiming for Establishment of Corporate Legislation Fit to Address [The Challenges of] Globalization: A Legal System Suited for a Market Economy Led by the Private [Sector] and Justice and Legislation Reforms], Tokyo: Keizai Dōyūkai; Keizai Dōyūkai [The Japan Association of Corporate Executives], 1999, *Shihō Seido Kaikaku Shingikai ni Nozomu* [Expectations for the Judicial System Reform Council], Tokyo: Keizai Dōyūkai; Keizai Dōyūkai [The Japan Association of Corporate Executives], 2000, *Wagakuni Shihō no Jinteki Kiban Kaikaku no Bizyon to Gutai Saku: Shihō Seido Kaikaku Shingikai ni Nozomu (Dai 2 Ji)* [The Vision and Specific Policies Regarding the Reforms Concerning the Human Basis of Administration of Justice: Expectations for the Judicial System Reform Council (Part 2)], Tokyo: Keizai Dōyūkai. The importance of sweeping reform of the Japanese justice system was emphasized further in a 1998 policy statement issued by the Japan Business Federation (*Nippon Keidanren*). In this statement, the Business Federation argued that as the Japanese society moves towards becoming more firmly based on the principles of market economy as the result of administrative reforms and financial deregulation, its functioning will be based on self-responsibility to a greater extent than before. The federation predicted that the number of legal disputes is likely to rise in this situation and urged the government to implement measures to increase the number of lawyers, prosecutors, and judges and to work to ensure that cases are adjudicated faster (Keizai Dantai Rengōkai [Japan Business Federation], 1998, "Shihō Seido Kaikaku ni tsuite no Ikensho" [Policy Statement Regarding Justice System Reform], May 19, available online at http://www.keidanren.or.jp/japanese/policy/pol173.html). A policy paper written in the same year by the Twenty-First Century Public Policy Institute – a think tank established in 1997 by the Japan Business Federation – urged the government to establish a council for the reform of the justice system. These two reports emphasized the importance of judicial reform, but did not suggest introducing the jury system in Japan (21 Seiki Seisaku Kenkyūjo [The Twenty-First Century Public Policy Institute], 1998, "Minji Shihō no Kasseika ni Mukete" [Towards Revitalization of Civil Justice], December 22, available online at http://www.21ppi.org/pdf/thesis/981222.pdf; "21 Seiki Seisaku Kenkyūjo", available online at http://www.21ppi.org/english/index.html).

107 "Yasuoka Okiharu", available online at http://www.yasuoka.org/index.html.

108 The Liberal Democratic Party of Japan, 1998, "21 Seiki no Shihō no Tashikana Hōshin" [The Firm Principles of the Justice [System of the] 21st Century], June 16, available online at http://www.yasuoka.org/doc_seisaku/siho/01.htm. The NGOs mentioned among the organizations that LDP's committee consulted are the Society for Considering the Satisfying Court [System]" (*Nattoku no Iku Saiban o Kangaeru Kai*) and the Citizen Conference Demanding Open Court (*Hirakareta Saiban o Motomeru Shimin Kaigi*).

to reach this objective.[109] The JSRC, established in 1999, became the place where the proposals made by the LDP's committee, including the idea of implementing the jury system, were deliberated in greater detail.

Drafting and enactment

From the deliberations at the Judicial System Reform Council to the drafting of the Lay Judge Act

The subject of citizen participation in the administration of justice was discussed extensively during the meeting sessions of the members of the JSRC. In the first year of deliberations the members considered the possibility of introducing the Anglo-American and the Continental-European models of jury trials in Japan.[110] They concluded that it was important to approach the task of adopting the institution of jury service creatively and try to come up with a model that would best suit Japan instead of merely copying a system used in any one given country.[111]

The second year of JSRC's deliberations was devoted to hammering out the details of the jury system that would work best in Japan based on the opinions expressed by the members of the three branches of the legal profession. The 43rd meeting of the JSRC, held on January 9, 2001, was devoted to the subject of jury trials.[112] It was during that meeting that the word *saiban'in* was first used to refer to the new jury system that Japan would implement. The credit for inventing the word *saiban'in* goes to Professor Emeritus of Tokyo University Kōya Matsuo.[113] Professor Matsuo later discussed the reasons for proposing that the word

---

109 *Id.*
110 During these hearings, the representatives of the Japan Federation of Bar Associations argued for the implementation of the all-layperson jury system, while the representatives of the Ministry of Justice stated that the decision on the question of whether to introduce the Anglo-American or the Continental-European model of jury trials required further deliberations. The representatives of the Supreme Court were opposed to the introduction of the Anglo-American jury system. They argued that this system was incompatible with the principles of Japan's justice that has its goal in discovering the truth and clarifying it to the society, because in the Anglo-American jury system the members of the jury are only responsible for coming up with the verdict of guilty or not guilty and are not required to explain the reasoning behind their findings. The Supreme Court's position during the hearing was that Japan's jury system should be based on the Continental-European model and that laypersons should not be allowed to come up with verdicts independently of the judge to avoid any possible claims that this system is unconstitutional (Shihō Seido Kaikaku Shingikai [Judicial System Reform Council], 2000, *Chūkan Hōkoku* [Interim Report], November 20, available online at http://www.kantei.go.jp/jp/sihouseido/report/naka_houkoku.html; Shihō Seido Kaikaku Shingi Kai Dai 30 Kai Giji Gaiyō [Minutes of the 30th Meeting of the Judicial System Reform Council], September 12, 2000, available online at http://www.kantei.go.jp/jp/sihouseido/dai30/30gaiyou.html).
111 Shihō Seido Kaikaku Shingikai [Judicial System Reform Council], *Chūkan Hōkoku* [Interim Report].
112 Shihō Seido Kaikaku Shingi Kai Dai 43 Kai Giji Gaiyō [Minutes of the 43rd Meeting of the Judicial System Reform Council], January 9, 2001, available online at http://www.kantei.go.jp/jp/sihouseido/dai43/43gaiyou.html.
113 *Id.*; Tsuchiya, *Saiban'in Seido to Kokumin* [The Lay Judge System and the People], p. 56. In his speech at the JSRC, Professor Matsuo proposed that the system of layperson participation in Japan should be one where citizens would be invited to serve only on one case and be expected to adjudicate only contested cases, just like their counterparts in the United States and in the other countries of the Anglo-American tradition. At the same time, Matsuo argued that Japan's new system should be a mixed-court system where jurors and judges adjudicate the case together. Professor Matsuo also proposed that the accused

saiban'in be used to call the new system. He explained that he considered the difference in the way professors at national universities in Japan and their counterparts working at private universities are called in Japanese (the former are referred to as *kyōkan*, while the latter are called *kyōin*). This observation made him consider the possibility of calling Japanese jurors *saiban'in* as opposed to the word used to refer to professional judges – *saibankan*.[114] Professor Matsuo admitted that he also had in mind the fact that the word *saiban'in* was already being used to refer to the members of the Impeachment Court established within the National Diet, including members of both houses of Parliament, with the purpose of trying those judges against whom removal procedures had been instituted.[115]

The final report of the Judicial System Reform Council, published in 2001, included the following recommendations regarding the establishment of the jury system in Japan:

(1) Judges and *saiban'in* are to deliberate and make decisions both on guilt and on the sentence together. In the deliberations, *saiban'in* should possess generally an authority equivalent to that of judges; and in the hearing process, *saiban'in* should possess appropriate authority including the authority to question witnesses;

(2) The minimum requirement should be that a decision adverse to a defendant cannot be made on the basis of a majority of either the judges or the *saiban'in* alone;

(3) The jury selection pool should be made up of persons randomly chosen from among eligible voters;

(4) Applicable cases will be those of serious crime to which heavy statutory penalties attach;

(5) No distinction should be made based on whether the defendant admits or denies the charge;

(6) Defendants should not have the option of refusing trial by a judicial panel composed of professional judges and *saiban'in* (the JSRC did not specify the number of judges and *saiban'in*);

(7) The contents of judgments should be structured in the same way as those for trials by judges only;

(8) Litigants should have the right to appeal *kōso* on points of fact or on the grounds of improper sentence.[116]

Once JSRC's report was completed, the main stakeholders – the members of the three branches of the legal profession – expressed their respective positions on these proposals. The Supreme Court assumed the most conservative position and emphasized the possible problems of having untrained laypersons make decisions determining the fate of the accused. The Supreme Court argued that if the jury system was to be introduced in Japan,

---

should not be given the right to waive the right to trial by jury in contemporary Japan (*id.*, p. 56; K. Matsuo, 2001, "Kokumin no Shihō Sanka ni tsuite" [Concerning Citizen Participation in Justice], January 9, Materials Distributed during the 43rd Meeting of the Judicial System Reform Council, available online at http://www.kantei.go.jp/jp/sihouseido/dai43/43betten3.html). Professor Taichirō Mitani – an authority on Japan's pre-war jury system – also took part in the 43rd Meeting of the JSRC and briefed its members on Japan's pre-war experience with the jury system (T. Mitani, 2001, "Seiji Seido toshite no Baishin Sei: Senzen Nihon no Keiken ni Terashite" [The Jury System as a Political System: In light of Japan's Pre-war Experiences], Materials Distributed during the 43rd Meeting of the Judicial System Reform Council, available online at http://www.kantei.go.jp/jp/sihouseido/dai43/43betten2.html).

114 Tsuchiya, *Saiban'in Seido to Kokumin* [The Lay Judge System and the People], p. 56.
115 *Id.*, p. 56; Nihonkoku Kenpō (1946), art. 64.
116 Recommendations of the Judicial System Reform Council.

The mixed-court jury (saiban'in) system 185

a non-binding mixed-court jury would be preferable.[117] The practicing defense bar, on the other hand, actively promoted the idea of having an all-layperson independent jury system.[118] The Japan Federation of Bar Associations argued that the panel should consist of one judge and nine jurors.[119] The position of the Office of the Prosecutor, represented by the Ministry of Justice, was between the two aforementioned extremes. The Ministry argued that it was necessary to carefully look into the features of the Anglo-American and the Continental-European models of jury trials before making a final decision.[120]

The details of the *saiban'in* proposal were deliberated further by the Expert Advisory Committee on the *saiban'in* system that was established within the Office for Promotion of Justice System Reform.[121] The Expert Committee was chaired by Tokyo University Professor Masahito Inoue and included the representatives of the three branches of the legal profession, academics, an editorial writer at Kyodo News, and mayor of Mitaka City, Tokyo, as members.[122] On October 28, 2003, the Expert Committee compiled a list of proposals regarding the outline of the new *saiban'in* system.[123] This document proposed specifically that the mixed-court jury panels under the new system should consist of three judges and four laypersons, stipulated that for the verdict to stand the agreement of at least one judge and one juror was necessary, and that only persons older than twenty-five years of age among those eligible to vote could serve as jurors.[124] On January 29, 2004, the finalized outline was drafted.[125] The final version of the outline added to the particulars set forth

---

117 A. Gotō, S. Shinomiya, T. Nishimura, and M. Kudō, 2004, *Jitsumuka no tame no Saiban'in Hō Nyūmon* [An Introduction to the Lay Judge Act for Practitioners], Tokyo: Gendai Jinbunsha, p. 2.
118 *Id.*, p. 2.
119 Nihon Bengoshi Rengōkai [Japan Federation of Bar Associations], 2003, "Saiban'in Seido 'Tatakidai' ni taisuru Iken" [Opinion Concerning the "Sounding Board" on the Lay Judge System], May 30, available online at http://www.nichibenren.or.jp/ja/opinion/report/data/2003_23.pdf.
120 Gotō, Shinomiya, Nishimura, and Kudō, *Jitsumuka no tame no Saiban'in Hō Nyūmon* [An Introduction to the Lay Judge Act for Practitioners], p. 2.
121 The details of the deliberations at the Expert Advisory Committee are available online at "Saiban'in Seido Keiji Kentōkai" [Expert Advisory Committee on the Lay Judge (Saiban'in) System/Criminal Justice], available online at http://www.kantei.go.jp/jp/singi/sihou/kentoukai/06saibanin.html.
122 "Saiban'in Seido/Keiji Kentōkai Menbā" [Members of the Expert Advisory Committee on the Lay Judge (*Saiban'in*) System/Criminal Justice], available online at http://www.kantei.go.jp/jp/singi/sihou/kentoukai/saibanin/06meibo.html; Tsuchiya, *Saiban'in Seido to Kokumin* [The Lay Judge System and the People], pp. 60–61 (discussing the deliberations at the Expert Committee).
123 Saiban'in Seido Kenji Kentōkai [Expert Advisory Committee on the Lay Judge (Saiban'in) System/Criminal Justice], 2003, "Kangaerareru Saiban'in Seido no Gaiyō ni tsuite" [Concerning the Possible Saiban'in System Outline], October 28, available online at http://www.kantei.go.jp/jp/singi/sihou/kentoukai/saibanin/dai28/28siryou1.pdf. The drafting process of this document involved the drafting of a discussion paper outlining the preliminary details of the *saiban'in* system and the analysis of the opinions of the general public regarding this paper (Saiban'in Seido/Keiji Kentōkai [Expert Advisory Committee on the Lay Judge (*Saiban'in*) System/Criminal Justice, "Saiban'in Seido ni tsuite" [Concerning the Lay Judge (*Saiban'in*) System], March 11, 2003, available online at http://www.kantei.go.jp/jp/singi/sihou/kentoukai/saibanin/dai13/13siryou1.pdf. For a discussion of this paper in English, see Anderson and Nolan, "Lay Participation in the Japanese Justice System", pp. 940–941).
124 Saiban'in Seido Kenji Kentōkai [Expert Advisory Committee on the Lay Judge (Saiban'in) System/Criminal Justice], 2003, "Kangaerareru Saiban'in Seido no Gaiyō ni tsuite" [Concerning the Possible Saiban'in System Outline], October 28, available online at http://www.kantei.go.jp/jp/singi/sihou/kentoukai/saibanin/dai28/28siryou1.pdf.
125 Saiban'in Seido Kenji Kentōkai [Expert Advisory Committee on the Lay Judge (Saiban'in) System/Criminal Justice], 2004, "Saiban'in Seido no Gaiyō ni tsuite" [Concerning the Outline of the Saiban'in

by JSRC's report the details regarding the number of professional judges and the number of *saiban'in* to adjudicate cases, stating that they should be three and six, respectively, in contested cases and one and four, respectively, in cases where the accused admitted his or her guilt.[126] Further, unlike the October 28, 2003, proposal, this version removed the age requirement for jury service, stating that any person eligible to vote could serve.[127] The outline also stipulated that personal information regarding jurors should be protected and stated that no one could publish names or addresses of jurors without their permission. While the previous version of the outline allowed courts to reveal jurors' names, the final draft permitted only the disclosure of ages and other information that could not lead to the identification of jurors.[128] The January 29 outline also banned all media contact with acting and former jurors.[129] On the other hand, the final draft no longer contained the clause requiring media reporting on criminal cases to be conducted in such a way that would not prejudice jurors – a clause that was present in the earlier version of the outline and that prompted criticism from the Japan Newspaper Publishers and Editors' Association (*Nihon Shinbun Kyōkai*; NSK).[130]

The particulars of the finalized outline of the new jury system reflected a compromise reached by the parties of the coalition government – the Liberal Democratic Party and the New Kōmeitō – on January 26, 2004.[131] The two parties had disagreed regarding the numerical composition of the mixed panels – the LDP arguing for three judges and four laypersons, and the New Kōmeitō stating that the panel should consist of two judges and seven laypersons.[132] Based on this agreement, the government began compiling the bill introducing the *saiban'in* system, and the details included in the outline became the basis for the government's draft of the Lay Judge Act that was submitted to the National Diet on March 2, 2004.[133]

Deliberations at the National Diet and enactment

The draft was first considered by the Legal Affairs Committee of the House of Representatives (*Shūgiin Hōmu Iinkai*), which passed it on April 23, 2004. On May 20, 2004, the draft was approved by the Legal Affairs Committee of the House of Councilors (*Sangiin Hōmu*

---

ystem], January 29, available online at http://www.kantei.go.jp/jp/singi/sihou/kentoukai/saibanin/dai31/31siryou1.pdf.
126 *Id.*
127 *Id.*
128 *Id.*
129 *Id.*
130 Anonymous, 2004, "Government Unveils Draft Bill for Lay Judge Jurors – Planned Restrictions on Media Deleted", *NSK News Bulletin*, February, available online at http://www.pressnet.or.jp/newsb/0402.html; Anonymous, 2004, "2004 Prospects for Japan's Newspaper Industry", *NSK News Bulletin*, January, available online at http://www.pressnet.or.jp/newsb/.
131 Anonymous, 2004, "Parties Agree on 'Citizen Judge' Plan", *Japan Times*, January 27, available online at http://search.japantimes.co.jp/cgi-bin/nn20040127a2.html; Tsuchiya, *Saiban'in Seido to Kokumin* [The Lay Judge System and the People], p. (3) (containing a timeline of the developments regarding the drafting process of the Lay Judge Act).
132 Anonymous, "Parties Agree on 'Citizen Judge' Plan".
133 "Dai 159 Kai Kokkai 67 Saiban'in no Sanka Suru Keiji Saiban ni kansuru Hōritsu An" [The 159th Session of Parliament 69 Act Concerning Participation of Law Assessors in Criminal Trials], available online at http://www.shugiin.go.jp/itdb_gian.nsf/html/gian/keika/1D94366.htm.

Iinkai),[134] and on May 21, 2004, the National Diet passed it with a vote of 180 for and 2 against.[135]

The revisions that the bill underwent during the period when it was under consideration in Parliament in 2004 were minimal. The statement of the opposition parties requesting that the provision regarding crimes of lay judges leaking the details of deliberations be deleted[136] resulted in the amendment of Article 79, which in the government's draft stipulated that those lay judges who leaked secrets were to be punished by a "fine of 500,000 yen and/or imprisonment for up to one year". Upon revision, this provision read "a fine of 500,000 yen and/or imprisonment for up to *six months*" (emphasis added).[137] This amendment was supported by the Japan Federation of Bar Associations.[138] Another change to the government-sponsored draft that resulted from the suggestions of the Japan Federation of Bar Associations included the addition of the supplementary provisions that made it possible to review the *saiban'in* system three years after the enforcement of the Lay Judge Act.[139]

---

134 *Id.*
135 Tsuchiya, *Saiban'in Seido to Kokumin* [The Lay Judge System and the People], p. (4); H. Matsubara, 2004, "Lay Judges to Serve from 2009: Quasi-Jury System Earns Diet Approval", *Japan Times*, May 22, available online at http://www.japantimes.co.jp/cgi-bin/getarticle.pl5?nn20040522a3.htm.
136 Anonymous, 2004, "Minshutō ga Shūsei Taian 'Chōeki Sakujō' Moru Saiban'in Seido" [DPJ [Prepares] Revision Plan; Lay Judge System: To Delete Imprisonment Provision], *Asahi Shinbun*, April 14, p. 3. The proposal to delete the provisions regarding crimes of lay judges was supported by the Saitama Bar Association whose members sent recommendations to the Legal Affairs Committee of the House of Representatives. Anonymous, 2004, "Saiban'in Hō An no Shūsei Motome Seimei Saitama Bengoshi Kai" [Saitama Bar Association [Issues] Statement Demanding Revision of the Lay Judge Bill], *Asahi Shinbun*, April 22, p. 31.
137 Saiban'in no Sanka Suru Keiji Saiban ni kansuru Hōritsu An [Act Concerning Participation of Lay Judges in Criminal Trials] (Proposed Official Draft 2004), art. 79, available online at http://www.shugiin.go.jp/itdb_gian.nsf/html/gian/honbun/houan/g15905067.htm [hereinafter Lay Judge Act, Proposed Official Draft 2004)]; Saiban'in no Sanka Suru Keiji Saiban ni kansuru Hōritsu An ni kansuru Hōritsu An ni Taisuru Shūsei An [Proposed Revision of the Act Concerning Participation of Lay Judges in Criminal Trials] (Proposed Revision Draft 2004), available online at http://www.shugiin.go.jp/itdb_gian.nsf/html/gian/honbun/syuuseian/3_26F6.htm [hereinafter Lay Judge Act, Proposed Revision Draft 2004].
138 Japan Federation of Bar Associations, 2004, "Bills on Lay Judge System and Criminal Procedure Reform Clear Lower House", April 23, available online at http://www.nichibenren.or.jp/en/activities/meetings/20040423.html.
139 Article 8 states specifically the following: "Where additional investigation into the status of the law's implementation is recognized as necessary three years after the law comes into effect, based on these results the Government will create the necessary measures so that the system of lay judges' participation in criminal trials can facilitate the people's participation in justice to realize adequately its role as the foundation of our country's judicial system" (Lay Judge Act, Supplementary Provisions, art. 8). Several local Bar Associations and other organizations demanded further changes of the draft. Specifically, the Kyoto Bar Association sent a letter to Prime Minister Koizumi proposing that the number of professional judges participating in the trial be reduced to one or two (Anonymous, 2004, "Saiban'in Hō Shūsei, Kuni ni Motome Ketsugisho Kyōto Bengoshi Kai ga Sōfu" [Revision of the Lay Judge Act Demanded of Government; Kyoto Bar Association Sends [Proposal]], *Asahi Shinbun*, April 23), while other lawyers at a meeting in Tokyo discussed their concerns about the fact that the draft did not allow the accused the freedom to choose whether he or she wanted to be tried by jury, that it imposed the heavy duty on jurors of remaining silent regarding the proceedings, and that it denied the media the right to freely report on jury trials (Anonymous, 2004, "Bengoshi ra 'Saiban'in Seido' Hantai Seimei; Tokyo de Shūkai" [Lawyers [Issue] Statement Opposing Lay Judge System, Have Meeting in Tokyo], *Asahi Shinbun*, April 21). The Japan Newspaper Publishers and Editors' Association also submitted its recommendations for the revision of the bill to the Parliament (Anonymous, 2004, "Saiban'in Seifu

The Lay Judge Act: a summary

The enacted version of the Act Concerning Participation of Lay Judges in Criminal Trials (the Lay Judge Act)[140] provides for the implementation of the jury system that is a unique cross between the Continental-European and the Anglo-American models of jury trial.[141] Japan's *saiban'in* system is a mixed-court system where judges and laypersons deliberate questions of guilt and sentencing together – a feature that is characteristic of most Continental jury systems.[142] Japanese lay judges, however, are selected at random from the list of persons eligible to vote[143] and appointed to adjudicate one case rather than be nominated by local authorities to serve a fixed term.[144]

Under the *saiban'in* system, cases are adjudicated by a panel consisting of three professional judges and six laypersons.[145] There is a provision, however, for those cases where defendants plead guilty: on condition that the accused, the defense and prosecution agree, the number of judges may be reduced to one professional judge and four laypersons.[146] Lay judges participate only in criminal cases where the maximum penalty is death or an indefinite period of penal servitude.[147] A case that fits the aforementioned

---

An, Shinbun Kyōkai 'Shūsei o'" [The Japan Newspaper Publishers and Editors' Association [Demands] Revision of the Government's Draft of the Lay Judge Act], *Asahi Shinbun*, April 3). The association argued that in the situation where nothing would be known to the society about the lay judges participating in trials it would be hard for the general public to trust the decisions made by the new mixed-court panels (Anonymous, "Saiban'in Seifu An, Shinbun Kyōkai 'Shūsei o'" [The Japan Newspaper Publishers and Editors' Association [Demands] Revision of the Government's Draft of the Lay Judge Act]). These opinions were not incorporated into the final version of the Lay Judge Act.

140 Saiban'in no Sanka Suru Keiji Saiban ni kansuru Hōritsu [Act Concerning Participation of Lay Judges in Criminal Trials], Law No. 63 of 2004, as amended by Laws No. 60 and No. 124 of 2007 and Laws No. 42 and No. 37 of 2015 [hereinafter Lay Judge Act]. The text of the enacted version of the Lay Assessor Act is available online at http://www.saibanin.courts.go.jp/vcms_lf/271214saibaninhou_kaisei.pdf (in Japanese). The 2004 version of the act (the text of the act prior to the 2007 revision) is translated in Anderson and Saint, "Japan's Quasi-Jury (Saiban'in) Law". The quotations of the provisions of the Lay Judge Act that appear in this chapter use the English translation made by Professor Anderson and Ms. Emma Saint, unless stated otherwise.

141 The system provided for in the Lay Judge Act has been referred to as the "quasi-jury system" and as the "Japanese-style lay assessor system". See Anderson and Saint, "Japan's Quasi-Jury (Saiban'in) Law", p. 233; and Y. Tsuchiya, 2008, *Saiban'in Seido ga Hajimaru: Sono Kitai to Kenen* [The Lay Judge System [Is About to Start]: Expectations and Fears], Tokyo: Kadensha, p. 24.

142 Osner, Quinn, and Crown, *Criminal Justice Systems in Other Jurisdictions*, pp. 83–104 (discussing the features of criminal justice systems and the jury systems in France and Germany); Lempert, "Citizen Participation in Judicial Decision Making: Juries, Lay Judges and Japan", pp. 10–12 (discussing the differences between the mixed-court lay assessor system and the jury system).

143 According to the Lay Judge Act, any person holding Japanese citizenship and who is older than 20 years of age may be called upon to serve as a lay judge. This implies that the permanent residents in Japan, including *zainichi* Koreans, will not be eligible to become lay judges (Lay Judge Act, arts. 13 and 21(1)). Diet members, members of judicial circles, heads of local governments, members of the police and of Self Defense Forces, as well as those who have served prison terms are excluded from the selection pool (*id.*, art. 15; Kōshoku senkyo hō [Public Election Act], Law No. 100 of 1950, art. 9; Anderson and Ambler, "The Slow Birth of Japan's Quasi-Jury System (*Saiban-in Seido*)", p. 63).

144 Osner, Quinn and Crown, *Criminal Justice Systems in Other Jurisdictions*, pp. 98–99 (discussing the features of the German mixed-court jury system). The Japanese lay judge system is in this respect similar to the French jury system. French jurors are also drawn by lot from the electoral registers (*id.*, p. 88)

145 Lay Judge Act, art. 2(2).

146 *Id.*, art. 2(2) and 2(3).

147 *Id.*, art. 2(1).

classification may nevertheless be tried by professional judges alone, however, if it is determined that there are conditions that make it difficult for *saiban'in* to perform their duties because of fear of "significant violation to their peaceful existence" or fear of injury.[148] The verdict of the mixed-court panel is determined by the majority opinion, which has to include at least one judge and one *saiban'in*.[149] If the verdict is guilty, the mixed panel determines the penalty for the accused.[150] Only the professional judges on the panel interpret the law and make decisions on litigation procedure.[151] Like jurors in Japan's pre-war jury system, lay judges are given the right to question witnesses, the defendant, and the victim.[152]

If the defendant is accused of multiple crimes, he or she may be tried for each offence by a different group of lay judges, at the request of his or her counsel or the prosecutor, or based on the decision of the professional judges.[153] The three professional judges in such instances preside over all cases brought against that defendant. These judges and the different groups of *saiban'in* empaneled to try only one of the multiple offences come up with a "partial verdict" (*bubun hanketsu*) of guilty or not guilty.[154] Together with the three professional judges, the group of *saiban'in* to try the final case brought against the defendant come up with a partial verdict for that offence. Then, this mixed panel considers the partial verdicts returned by the judges and the other groups of *saiban'in* and comes up with a final, overall verdict and a sentence, if that final verdict is guilty.[155] The provisions regarding situations that involve defendants accused of multiple crimes were added because of fears that incidents

---

148 *Id.*, art. 3.
149 *Id.*, art. 67(1). The Lay Judge Act specifies that a five or six lay judge majority to acquit without a judge agreeing would result in a "not guilty" verdict, but a five or six layperson majority to convict without a judge agreeing would not result in a conviction (Anderson and Saint, "Japan's Quasi-Jury (*Saiban'in*) Law", p. 273).
150 Regarding sentencing, the Lay Judge Act stipulates the following: "Where there is a division of opinion regarding the quantum of the sentence and there is no majority opinion of the members of the judicial panel that includes both an empanelled judge and a lay judge of that opinion, then by a determination of the judicial panel, the number of opinions for the option most unfavorable to the defendant will be added to the number of opinions for the next favorable option, until a majority opinion of the members of the judicial panel which includes both an empanelled judge and a lay [judge] holding that opinion is achieved" (Lay Judge Act, art. 67(2). Anderson and Saint, "Japan's Quasi-Jury (*Saiban'in*) Law", pp. 273–274).
151 Lay Judge Act, art. 6(2). Anderson and Ambler, "The Slow Birth of Japan's Quasi-Jury System (*Saiban-in Seido*)", *Journal of Japanese Law*, p. 65.
152 *Id.*, arts. 56, 59, and 58 (enumerating the right of lay judges to question witnesses, the defendant, and the victims, respectively).
153 *Id.*, art. 71. The provisions regarding cases involving defendants accused of multiple crimes were added in 2007. See Saiban'in no Sanka Suru Keiji Saiban ni kansuru Hōritsu Tō no Ichibu o Kaisei Suru Hōritsu An [Bill Proposing Partial Amendment of the Act Concerning Participation of Lay Judges in Criminal Trials] (Proposed Official Draft 2007), available online at http://www.moj.go.jp/HOUAN/SAIBANNIN/refer02.pdf [hereinafter Bill Proposing Partial Amendment of the Lay Judge Act (Proposed Official Draft 2007)]. The list summarizing the amendments made in 2007 is available online at http://www.moj.go.jp/HOUAN/SAIBANNIN/refer04.pdf, pp. 1–32. The Bill for the Amendment of the Lay Judge Act was passed and enacted (Act Partially Amending the Act Concerning Participation of Lay Judges in Criminal Trial (Saiban'in no Sanka Suru Keiji Saiban ni kansuru Hōritsu Tō no Ichibu o Kaisei Suru Hōritsu [The Act Partially Amending the Act Concerning Participation of Lay Judges in Criminal Trials], Law No. 60 of 2007)).
154 Lay Judge Act, art. 78.
155 *Id.*, art. 86.

involving multiple crimes could take an extended period of time to resolve – a situation that might potentially make participation in trials difficult for *saiban'in*.[156]

The Lay Judge Act allows the accused to appeal jury verdicts *kōso* on points of fact in all cases with the exception of those involving defendants accused of multiple crimes who were tried by different groups of lay judges.[157]

The Lay Judge Act stipulates that in addition to acting lay judges, reserve lay judges may be selected, but that the number of *saiban'in* in reserve should not exceed the number of acting lay judges.[158] The selection procedure begins with the determination by the district courts of the number of lay judges required for the following year. The district courts are then required to communicate this number to the Election Administration Commission by September 1 of each year.[159] The municipal Election Administration Commission then prepares the proposed list of lay judge candidates.[160] Once prepared, the list is then transferred to the district courts by October 15 of that year.[161] The lists of Lay Judge candidates are prepared, and those persons who are listed receive a notification.[162] Once the date of the first trial hearing has been determined, the court sends out summonses to lay judge candidates.[163] Some candidates who have been summoned, such as students, persons aged seventy years and older, citizens with poor health, and persons engaged in child-rearing or those with nursing care responsibilities may be excused.[164]

The law provides for a penalty of up to 100,000 yen for those summoned persons who fail to appear in court without a valid reason,[165] and for a fine of up to 500,000 yen for those jury candidates who write false information in the question sheets distributed to them at the court.[166] The Lay Judge Act also provides for a fine of up to 500,000 yen or a prison sentence of up to six months for those members of the jury who leak information on the proceedings or the jury deliberations.[167] The act prohibits employers from discriminating against those of their employees who are serving as lay judges and take time off from work in order to fulfill their responsibilities as jurors.[168]

Just like the pre-war Jury Act that was enacted in 1923 and enforced in 1928, the Lay Judge Act provided for a five-year preparation period to separate the enactment of this piece of legislation and its enforcement.[169]

---

156 Reasons for Proposed Amendment of the Act Concerning Participation of Lay Judges in Criminal Trials (2007), available online at http://www.moj.go.jp/HOUAN/SAIBANNIN/refer03.pdf [hereinafter Reason for Proposed Amendment of the Lay Judge Act (2007)].
157 Lay Judge Act, art. 80.
158 *Id.*, art. 10.
159 *Id.*, art. 20.
160 *Id.*, art. 21(2). The Lay Judge Act does not specify the detailed format of these lists, but stipulates that the Proposed List of Lay Judge Candidates "may be prepared and stored on a magnetic disk" (*id.*, art. 21(3)).
161 *Id.*, art. 22.
162 *Id.*, arts. 23 and 25.
163 *Id.*, art. 27.
164 *Id.*, art. 17.
165 *Id.*, art. 112.
166 *Id.*, art. 110.
167 *Id.*, art. 108.
168 *Id.*, art. 100.
169 Lay Judge Act, Supplementary Provisions, art. 1.

Preparation for enforcement

The supplementary provisions to the Lay Judge Act state that during the five years preceding the implementation of the *saiban'in* system, the government and the Supreme Court would make adjustments necessary "to allow the smooth operation of the lay judge system".[170] These adjustments concerned the efforts aimed at the drafting and implementation of several pieces of supplementary legislation, promoting the *saiban'in* system, building new courtrooms with seats for jurors, and the provision of specialist training for judges, lawyers, and prosecutors.

Supplementary legislation

The Court Rules for cases adjudicated with the participation of lay judges were drafted by the Supreme Court, promulgated on July 5, 2007, and amended in 2008 and 2009.[171] The Court Rules provide the details regarding the provisions of the Lay Judge Act. For instance, while the Lay Judge Act stipulates that the travel, per diem, and hotel expenditures of lay judges and reserve lay judges will be reimbursed, the Court Rules specify the detailed amounts to be paid.[172]

The most important of the details provided in the Court Rules concern the particulars of the selection process of lay judges and of the deliberation process among the members of the mixed-court panel. According to the Court Rules, lay judge candidates fill out the questionnaires that contain items that will help the court determine which candidates are eligible for jury service, who may be exempted, and who may decline service.[173] Then, the candidates answer questions of the judges empaneled to try that case in the presence of the defense counsel, of the prosecutor, and of the secretary.[174] Based on these answers, the judges determine who may be excused.[175] Then the prosecutor and the defense counsel are given the opportunity to excuse several other candidates. The Court Rules do not require the prosecutor and the defense to state the reasons for their decision to excuse a candidate.[176] If the number of remaining candidates exceeds the required number of acting lay judges and *saiban'in* in reserve, then persons to serve are determined by lot.[177] The judge explains the rights and duties to the lay judges who have been selected and emphasizes that

---

170 *Id.*, Supplementary Provisions, art. 3.
171 Saiban'in no Sanka Suru Keiji Saiban ni kansuru Kisoku [Rules Concerning Criminal Trials in which Lay Judges Participate], Sup. Ct. Rule No. 7 of 2007, as amended by Sup. Ct. Rule No. 5 of 2008 and Sup. Ct. Rule No. 1 of 2009, available online at http://www.saibanin.courts.go.jp/shiryo/pdf/27.pdf [hereinafter Supreme Court Rules].
172 Lay Judge Act, art. 11 and Supreme Court Rules, arts. 7, 8, and 9 (enumerating lay judges and reserve lay judges' per diem, hotel, and travel expenditures to be reimbursed). The Rules stipulate that acting lay judges and lay judges in reserve are to be paid 10,000 yen per day, while lay judge candidates who appear and court for selection procedures, but who have not been selected are to be paid 8,000 yen for that day (Supreme Court Rules, art. 7(2)). The maximum amount of hotel expenditures that are to be reimbursed will constitute 8,700 yen in most regions and 7,800 yen in rural areas (Supreme Court Rules, art. 8(2)).
173 Supreme Court Rules, art. 22.
174 *Id.*, art. 35(1).
175 *Id.*, art. 35(2).
176 *Id.*, art. 35(3).
177 *Id.*, art. 35(4).

determination of facts needs to be based on evidence.[178] The lay judges are then required to recite an oath and to seal a document containing this oath.[179] Regarding the process of deliberations, the Court Rules stipulate that the members of the mixed-court panel are required to each state their opinions and that it is the duty of the empaneled professional judges to ensure that the discussion is fruitful.[180]

Another piece of legislation drafted during the five-year preparation period preceding the enforcement of the Lay Judge Act was a Cabinet order permitting certain persons to decline jury service. These individuals included pregnant women, women who gave birth not more than eight weeks prior to the date of the trial, persons accompanying family members for treatment of serious illness, persons whose spouse or daughter is about to give birth, and persons who live far from the court and for whom it is difficult to travel to that court.[181]

Promotion efforts

To fulfill the goals stipulated in the supplementary provisions of the Lay Judge Act concerning the need to familiarize the members of the general public with the features of the *saiban'in* system, the Lay Judge System Promotions Office (*Saiban'in Seido Kōhō Suishin Kyōgikai*) was established on August 3, 2004.[182] The Promotions Office included members of the three branches of the legal profession (the Ministry of Justice, the Supreme Court, and the Japan Federation of Bar Associations) rather than public relations professionals.[183]

When planning its activities, the Promotions Office divided the five years separating the enactment and enforcement of the Lay Judge Act into three stages.[184] The first stage, spanning from the enactment of the Lay Judge Act to the end of 2005, was devoted to explaining the features of the *saiban'in* system. The second stage, from the beginning of 2006 to the end of 2007, was focused on the promotional activities at the regional level. The final phase, from 2008 to 2009, was devoted to explaining the details of the lay judge selection and appointment procedures to prospective jurors.[185]

To achieve its objectives and explain the new system, the Promotions Office created and distributed short- and long-feature promotional films, pamphlets, flyers, and posters. It also organized consultation town meetings[186] and Lay Judge System Nationwide Forums

---

178 *Id.*, art. 36.
179 *Id.*, art. 37.
180 *Id.*, art. 50.
181 Saiban'in no Sanka Suru Keiji Saiban ni kansuru Hōritsu Dai 16 Jō Dai 8 Gō ni Kitei Suru Yamu o Enai Riyū o Sadameru Seirei [Cabinet Order Determining the Unavoidable Reasons as Stated in Article 16(8) of Act Concerning Participation of Lay Judges in Criminal Trials], Cabinet Order No. 3 of 2008, available online at http://www.saibanin.courts.go.jp/shiryo/pdf/28.pdf.
182 "Saiban'in Seido Kōhō Suishin Kyōgikai no Secchi ni tsuite" [Concerning the Establishment of the Lay Judge System Promotions Office], available online at http://www.saibanin.courts.go.jp/shiryo/pdf/22.pdf; Anderson and Ambler, "The Slow Birth of Japan's Quasi-Jury System (*Saiban-in Seido*)", p. 68.
183 Anderson and Ambler, "The Slow Birth of Japan's Quasi-Jury System (*Saiban-in Seido*)", p. 69.
184 Saiban'in Seido Kōhō Suishin Kyōgikai [The Lay Judge System Promotions Office], 2005, "Saiban'in Seido Kōhō Sukejūru (Imēji) [Schedule (Images) of the Promotion of the Lay Judge System], October 1, available online at http://www.kantei.go.jp/jp/singi/sihou/komon/dai18/18houmu4.pdf.
185 *Id.*
186 *Id.* While these town meetings were devoted to the justice system reforms in general, a significant portion of discussion concerned the new lay judge system. See for example, Koizumi Naikaku [Koizumi

(*Saiban'in Seido Zenkoku Fōramu*)[187] in cities across Japan, and advertised the new system in newspapers, journals, on television and on the Internet. To monitor the effectiveness of promotion efforts, the office conducted public opinion surveys.[188]

The Internet has been used widely as a means of distribution of the promotional materials. The Ministry of Justice,[189] the Supreme Court,[190] and the Japan Federation of Bar Associations have created websites devoted to the *saiban'in* system.[191] Each website contains explanations of the features of the new system as well as links to online versions of pamphlets and the promotional movies. In addition, the Supreme Court has sent out electronic newsletters devoted exclusively to the new jury system,[192] while the Ministry of Justice has sent out short animation features on the *saiban'in* system.[193]

The promotional movies created during the period of preparation for the implementation of the new system may be classified into three groups: (1) explanatory videos outlining the features of the new system; (2) television dramas and movies that include lay judge service as part of the plot; and (3) animations and short video clips featuring comedians that explain the details of the new system in an entertaining fashion. The videos belonging to the first group include, for example, the fifteen-minute movie titled "Criminal Trials in Which You, Too, Will Participate: The Lay Judge System Is Starting" (*Anata mo Sanka Suru Keiji Saiban: Saiban'in Seido ga Hajimarimasu*), prepared by the Supreme Court of

---

Cabinet], "Shihō Seido Kaikaku Taun Mītingu in Tokyo: Yori Mijika de Tayorigai no Aru Shihō e; Giji Yōshi" [Justice System Reform Town Meeting in Tokyo: Towards a Closer and More Reliable Justice [System]; Summary of the Proceedings], available online at http://www8.cao.go.jp/town/tokyo161218/youshi.html; Koizumi Naikaku [Koizumi Cabinet], "Shihō Seido Kaikaku Taun Mītingu in Takamatsu: Yori Mijika de Tayorigai no Aru Shihō e; Giji Yōshi" [Justice System Reform Town Meeting in Takamatsu: Towards a Closer and More Reliable Justice [System]; Summary of the Proceedings], available online at http://www8.cao.go.jp/town/takamatsu170115/youshi.html; Koizumi Naikaku [Koizumi Cabinet], "Shihō Seido Kaikaku Taun Mētingu in Utsunomiya: Yori Mijika de Tayorigai no Aru Shihō e; Giji Yōshi" [Justice System Reform Town Meeting in Utsunomiya: Towards a Closer and More Reliable Justice [System]; Summary of the Proceedings], available online at http://www8.cao.go.jp/town/utsunomiya170417/youshi.html. Also see Anderson and Ambler, "The Slow Birth of Japan's Quasi-Jury System (*Saiban-in Seido*)", pp. 69–70 (discussing the town meetings).

187 These forums were held in fifty different cities in Japan during the period between October 1, 2005, to January 29, 2006, and attracted approximately 18,000 participants (Saikō Saibansho [The Supreme Court], "Saiban'in Seido Zenkoku Fōramu" [Lay Judge System Nation-wide Forums], available online at http://www.saibanin.courts.go.jp/topics/guestionnaire.html).

188 Saiban'in Seido Kōhō Suishin Kyōgikai [The Lay Judge System Promotions Office], 2005, "Saiban'in Seido Kōhō Sukejūru (Imēji) [Schedule (Images) of the Promotion of the Lay Judge System], October 1, available online at http://www.kantei.go.jp/jp/singi/sihou/komon/dai18/18houmu4.pdf. Some of these opinion surveys were conducted during the Lay Judge System Nation-Wide Forums.

189 Hōmushō [The Ministry of Justice], "Yoroshiku Saiban'in" [The Lay Judge [System] – We Count on Your Cooperation], available online at http://www.moj.go.jp/SAIBANIN/. Saikō Saibansho [The Supreme Court], "Saiban'in Seido Zenkoku Fōramu" [The Lay Judge System Nation-Wide Forums], available online at http://www.saibanin.courts.go.jp/topics/guestionnaire.html.

190 Saikō Saibansho [The Supreme Court], "Saiban'in Seido" [The Lay Judge System], available online at http://www.saibanin.courts.go.jp/.

191 Nichibenren [The Japan Federation of Bar Associations], "Hajimarimasu. Saiban'in Seido" [The Lay Judge System Is About to Start], available online at http://www.nichibenren.or.jp/ja/citizen_judge/index.html.

192 Saikō Saibansho [The Supreme Court], "Saiban'in Seido Mēru Magazin" [E-mail Magazine on the Lay Judge System], available online at http://www.saibanin.courts.go.jp/melmaga/index.html.

193 Hōmushō [The Ministry of Justice], "Saiban'in Seido: Mitai, Manabitai" [The Lay Judge System: Want to See, Want to Learn], available online at http://www.moj.go.jp/SAIBANIN/koho/douga.html.

194 *The mixed-court jury (saiban'in) system*

Japan.[194] This short movie opens with a conversation between a man and a woman standing in front of the Tokyo District Court; they discuss the newly introduced lay judge system. The movie then explains the features of criminal procedure and shows scenes from a trial hearing, which is followed by a discussion during which the two hosts discuss their concerns and receive further explanations on the features of the new system. The movie "Lay Judges: [How We Were] Selected and What We Have Come to Understand" (*Saiban'in: Erabare, soshite Miete Kita Mono*) is an example of a promotional video belonging to the second group. This movie focuses on the experiences of six persons selected to serve as lay judges from the moment they received the summons to appear in court to the final day of service.[195] Clips featuring the popular comedy group "Nights" have been made available on DVD and the Internet by the Ministry of Justice; these are examples of the third type of promotional video.[196]

The Promotions Office designed a logo for the new *saiban'in* system and organized a catchphrase contest. The logo was revealed on June 29, 2005, and the winning catchphrase was announced on September 1, 2005.[197] The logo consists of two linked circles. One of the two circles represents the professional judges and another stands for lay judges. The fact that these two circles are linked is said to represent the cooperation between the professional and lay judges. The resemblance of these two linked circles to the symbol for infinity (∞) represents the infinite possibilities that the cooperation between judges and lay judges is expected to produce. The two circles also look like the letter "S" for *saiban'in*. The colors used in the logo are bluish-green and red, with the former color representing cool-headed judgment and the latter standing for enthusiasm and liveliness.[198] The logo is accompanied by the following catchphrase: "I will participate through my own observations, my own perceptions, and my own words" (*Watashi no Shiten, Watashi no Kankaku, Watashi no Kotoba de Sanka Shimasu*).[199] The logo has appeared on the posters, flyers, and pamphlets used to promote the new system. It also decorates the badge for lay judges that was revealed by the Supreme Court on May 29, 2009. This badge is given to lay judges and *saiban'in* in reserve at the end of their service.[200]

---

194 This video is available online at http://www.saibanin.courts.go.jp/news/video1/saibanin1_bb.html.
195 This video is available online at http://www.saibanin.courts.go.jp/news/video4.html.
196 Hōmushō [The Ministry of Justice], "YouTube Dōga" [Clips on YouTube], available online at http://www.moj.go.jp/SAIBANIN/koho/douga.html.
197 Saikō Saibansho [The Supreme Court], "Saiban'in Seido no Shinboru Māku to Katchifurēzu" [The Lay Judge System Logo and Catchphrase], available online at http://www.saibanin.courts.go.jp/symbol_catchphrase/index.html; Anderson and Ambler, "The Slow Birth of Japan's Quasi-Jury System (*Saiban-in Seido*)", pp. 71–72.
198 Saikō Saibansho [The Supreme Court], "Saiban'in Seido no Shinboru Māku no Imi" [The Meaning of the Logo for the *Saiban'in* System], available online at http://www.saibanin.courts.go.jp/symbol_catchphrase/symbol_meaning.html. This catchphrase is translated in Anderson and Ambler, "The Slow Birth of Japan's Quasi-Jury System (*Saiban-in Seido*)", p. 72.
199 This catchphrase authored by Hitomi Fujita from Tottori prefecture was chosen from among some 16,000 entries (Saikō Saibansho [The Supreme Court], "Saiban'in Seido no Shinboru Māku to Katchifurēzu" [The Lay Judge System Logo and Catchphrase], available online at http://www.saibanin.courts.go.jp/symbol_catchphrase/index.html, translated in Anderson and Ambler, "The Slow Birth of Japan's Quasi-Jury System (*Saiban-in Seido*)", at p. 72).
200 Anonymous, 2009, "Saiban'in Seido: Bajji Shisakuhin o Kōkai; Saikōsai 'Kansha Kome'" [The Lay Judge System: Model of the Badge Revealed; from the Supreme Court with Gratitude], *Mainichi Shinbun*, May 29, available online at http://mainichi.jp/photo/archive/news/2009/05/29/20090530k0000m040074000c.html.

In addition to the logo, the Promotions Office created a promotional character symbolizing the new system: a parakeet named *Saiban'inko*.[201] The fact that the Japanese for parakeet is *inko* appears to have been one of the reasons for the choice of this particular bird as the promotional character. After all, if one attaches the word *inko* to the word *saiban*, which means court, the resulting longer word sounds very similar to the word *saiban'in*, or lay judge.

The Japan Federation of Bar Associations organized symposia devoted to the new system, while district courts held seminars and lectures, organized excursions to courtrooms,[202] and created websites devoted to the particulars of the *saiban'in* system.[203]

New courtrooms and training for lawyers, prosecutors, and judges

In preparation for the implementation of the lay judge system, 170 courtrooms were reformed all over Japan to provide for seats for lay judges.[204] Unlike the pre-war jury courtrooms, where seats for jurors were located in a section separate from the seats of the judges, in contemporary Japan the professional and lay judges are seated together at a long arched desk. The seats of the judges are located in the middle of the desk with the *saiban'in* sitting to their right and left. The courtrooms are equipped with large screens where slides, graphs, and other materials are displayed. An innovative speech recognition system records the trial proceedings, saves visual images and audio data on a computer, and automatically creates transcripts of the hearings. The visual and audio data as well as the transcripts generated by this system may be referred to by the judges and *saiban'in* at any time during their deliberations.[205]

Other preparation efforts focused on providing training to the members of the three branches of the legal profession. The judges, prosecutors, and attorneys were sent to countries around the world to study various models of lay participation,[206] local Bar Associations

---

201 Hōmushō [The Ministry of Justice], "Saiban'inko no Purofīru" [Saiban'inko's Profile], available online at http://www.moj.go.jp/SAIBANIN/koho/inco.html. See Illustration 8 in the Appendix.
202 Japan Federation of Bar Associations, "Kaunto Down! Minna de Tsuchikō Saiban'in Seido" [Countdown! Let's Build the Lay Judge System Together], available online at http://www.nichibenren.or.jp/ja/event/081108.html; Saikō Saibansho [The Supreme Court], "Kakuchi no Ibento Jōhō [Information on Events Held in Different Areas]", available online at http://www.saibanin.courts.go.jp/news/announcing_to_public.html.
203 The websites of each district court are available online at Saikō Saibansho [The Supreme Court], "Kakuchi no Saiban'in Seido Kanren Jōhō' [Information regarding the Lay Judge System [Provided at District Courts] in Different Areas]", available online at http://www.saibanin.courts.go.jp/access/index.html.
204 Anonymous, 2007, "(Saiban'in Jidai) Mezase Yasashii Saibansho; Shimin ni Hairyō Shisetsu O Seibi [(The Lay Judge Era) Aiming for Courts That Are Close [to the People]; Providing Facilities that Take People's [Needs] into Consideration]", *Asahi Shinbun*, July 16.
205 Anonymous, 2009, "Saiban'in Seido: Chisai ga Setsubi o Hatsu Kōkai" [The Lay Judge System: District Court Unveils Facilities], *Mainichi Shinbun*, May 21, available online at http://mainichi.jp/area/nagano/archive/news/2009/05/12/20090512ddlk20040016000c.html.
206 Anonymous, 2004, "Saiban'in Sei Shikō Mae ni Saibankan 100 Nin o Ōbei Haken" [100 Judges Sent to Europe and the United States Before Implementation of the Lay Judge System], *Yomiuri Shinbun*, September 14, available online at http://www6.big.or.jp/~beyond/akutoku/news/2004/0914-4.html; Anderson and Ambler, "The Slow Birth of Japan's Quasi-Jury System (*Saiban-in Seido*)", p. 76).

organized training sessions in presentation skills for lawyers,[207] and prosecutors participated in seminars led by professional announcers who instructed the prosecutors on how to achieve clarity of speech and pronunciation. The prosecutors also received training in communication skills and even manners.[208] The training undergone by professional judges featured classes on how to put others at ease. The instructors of these classes reminded judges to smile frequently.[209]

Mock trials conducted at different times during the five-year preparation period served as a training opportunity for the members of the legal profession.[210] Mock trials have enabled judges, lawyers, and prosecutors to prepare for the introduction of the *saiban'in* system by providing them with the opportunity to present their cases in front of laypersons.[211]

Public debate

The virtues and vices of the Lay Judge Act and of the system that it envisages have been in the spotlight of public debate in Japan ever since the act was passed by the National Diet.

The majority of government-sponsored and independent publications that appeared during that time praised the *saiban'in* system and its potential for radically transforming Japan's legal architecture.[212] The authors of these publications stressed the democratic value of citizen participation in the justice system and argued that the introduction of the lay judge

---

207 Anonymous, 2009, "Hōtei de no Bengojutsu, Kenshūkai de Manabu, Saiban'in Seido de Bengoshi Kai" [Bar Association Preparing for Lay Judge System: [Members Learn] Court Defense Technique at a Training Session], *Asahi Shinbun*, April 6, p. 21; Anonymous, 2009, "Saiban'in Seido ni Mukete Ken Bengoshikai ga Kenshūkai" [Local Bar Association Conducts Training Sessions in Preparation for [the Introduction of the] Lay Judge System], *Nishi Nippon Shinbun*, May 2, available online at http://www.nishinippon.co.jp/nnp/feature/2009/saibanin/kiji/nagasaki/20090410/20090410_0001.shtml.
208 Anonymous, 2009, "Kenji no Hanashi Kata, Anaunsā ga Shidō; Saiban'in Seido Hikae Kenshū" [Prosecutors' Speech, An Announcer Provides Instruction at Training Session in Preparation for the Lay Judge System], *Asahi Shinbun*, April 15, available online at http://www.asahi.com/national/update/0415/OSK200904150001.html; Anonymous, 2009, "Kenji ga Manā Kenshū Saiban'in Dōnyū Hikae" [Prosecutors Get Training in Manners in Preparation for the Introduction of the Lay Judge System], *Kobe Shinbun*, June 11, available online at http://www.kobe-np.co.jp/news/shakai/0001434358.shtml.
209 Anonymous, 2009, "Saibankan ra 'Egao' Kenshū" [Judges [Have] Smile Training], *Yomiuri Shinbun*, June 6, available online at http://www.yomiuri.co.jp/e-japan/hokkaido/news/20090606-OYT8T00031.htm.
210 Anderson and Ambler, "The Slow Birth of Japan's Quasi-Jury System (*Saiban-in Seido*)", pp. 76–77 (discussing mock trials in Japan); Waseda University, "Kaitei Mogi Saiban: Anata mo Saiban'in" [Open Mock-Trial: You, too, Can Be a Lay Judge], available online at http://www.waseda.jp/law-school/topics/mogisaiban/20051027.htm (containing details of the mock trial conducted at Waseda University in 2005); Akita University, "Saiban'in Seido no Mogi Saiban" [Lay Judge Mogi Trial], available online at http://namahage.is.akita-u.ac.jp/~gpuser/mogi_saiban/ (discussing the details of the mock trial conducted at Akita University in 2008).
211 Anonymous, 2009, "Tokyo Chisai de Mogi Saiban Shūryō; Jōkyō Shōko nomi no Kēsu" [Mock Trial Concluded at Tokyo District Court; A Case of Only Circumstantial Evidence], *Sankei Nyūsu*, February 27, available online at http://sankei.jp.msn.com/affairs/trial/090227/trl0902272332006-n1.htm.
212 See for instance, T. Kobayashi, 2006, *Minna no Saiban* [Court for All], Tokyo: Kashiwa Shobō; I. Namazugoshi, 2004, *Saiban'in Seido to Kokumin no Shihō Sanka: Keiji Shihō no Daitenkan e no Michi* [The *Saiban'in* System and Public Participation in the Judiciary System: The Road towards a Great Turning Point in Criminal Justice], Tokyo: Gendai Jinbunsha; K. Ōkawa, 2009, *Saiban'in Seido no Hongi: Naze Shimin Sanka ga Hitsuyō nanoka* [The True Meaning of the Lay Judge System: Why Citizen Participation Is Important], Tokyo: Ichiyōsha.

system would lead the general public to become more assertive. Some Japanese academics supporting the new system focused their research on the likely psychological aspects and group dynamics of the deliberations of the mixed-court jury panels,[213] while others discussed the features of foreign jury systems in an attempt to assess the qualities of Japan's *saiban'in* system.[214] In addition, a wide range of guidebooks and reference materials introducing the new jury system for prospective lay judges were published.[215]

A number of contributions to the debate were critical of the system.[216] The arguments proposed in the literature belonging to this category can be divided into two groups. The first version of the anti-*saiban'in* argument, sometimes referred to in the scholarly literature as the *mochi wa mochiya de* ("every man to his trade") argument, favors trial by professional judges and rejects the idea of increasing public participation in legal proceedings beyond the existing level.[217] The second version of the anti-*saiban'in* argument, sometimes referred to as the *okazari* ("nominal" or "ornamental") argument, on the other hand, supports the government's efforts to increase lay participation in the Japanese courtroom. Proponents of this argument emphasize that this will serve to revitalize the judicial system, but claim that under the quasi-jury system that the Lay Judge Act provides for, public participation will be purely nominal in nature and will therefore fail to realize any significant change in Japan's legal architecture. They assert that instead of implementing an untested hybrid, or reintroducing the jury system that existed in the early *Shōwa* period, Japan should introduce an Anglo-American-style jury system. Some adherents of the *okazari* view reject the *saiban'in* proposal completely, while others agree to accept the mixed-court jury system as an interim measure that can be implemented to ensure a smooth transition from trials by professional judges only to an all-layperson jury.

---

213 See for instance, M. Fujita, S. Shinomiya, Y. Shiratori, T. Honjo, and S. Sugimori, 2006, "Tokushū: Saiban'in Seido – Seido no Seiritsu Katei to Hōgakuteki, Shinrigakuteki Kentō Kadai" [Special Report: The Lay Judge System – The Process of the Establishment of the System and Legal as Well as Psychological Issues to Be Studied], *Hō to Shinri* [Japanese Journal of Law and Psychology], Vol. 5, No. 1, pp. 1–25.

214 K. Itō, 2006, *Gohan o Umanai Saiban'in Seido e no Kadai: Amerika Keiji Shihō Kaikaku kara no Teigen* [Issues [to be Considered to Ensure that] the Lay Judge System Does not Produce Erroneous Verdicts: Suggestions Based on America's [Experience with] Criminal Justice Reform], Tokyo: Gendai Jinbunsha; M. Horibe, H. Ishii, Y. Sakai, O. Niikura, and K. Okura, 2004, *Keiji Shihō e no Shimin Sanka* [Citizen Participation in Criminal Justice], Tokyo: Gendai Jinbunsha.

215 See for example, Y. Fujita (ed.), 2008, *Yoku Wakaru Saiban'in Seido to Keiji Soshō no Shikumi: Heisei 21 Nen Sutāto* [Easy-to-Understand Lay Judge System and the Structure of Criminal Procedure: [The Lay Judge System] Starts in 2009], Tokyo: Sanshūsha; S. Shinomiya, T. Nishimura, and M. Kudō, 2005, *Moshi mo Saiban'in ni Erabaretara: Saiban'in Handobukku* [What If You Get Selected to Be a Lay Judge: A Handbook for Lay Judges], Tokyo: Kadensha.

216 See for instance, T. Yano, 2006, *Akireru Saiban to Saiban'in Seido: Saibankan wa naze Shin'yō Dekinai no ka?* [Repulsive Courts and the *Saiban'in* System: Why Judges Cannot Be Trusted], Tokyo: Ryokufū Shuppan; Isa, *Saiban'in Seido wa Keiji Saiban o Kaeru ka:* [Will the Lay Judge System Transform Criminal Courts]; S. Takayama, 2006, *Saiban'in Seido wa Iranai!* [We Do Not Need the Lay Judge System!], Tokyo: Kōdansha; M. Kabashima, 2005, "Saiban'in Seido, Keiji Soshōhō no Kaiaku ni Hantai Shi Baishinseido no Fukkatsu o" [Opposing the Lay Judge System and the Deterioration of the Code of Penal Procedure, Demanding Revival of the Jury System], *Gendai no Riron* [Contemporary Theory], Vol. 4, pp. 176–186; Saiban'in Seido ni Hantai Suru Kai, 2004, "Saiban'in Seido ni Hantai Suru Kai no Ikensho" [Opinion Statement of the Association for Opposing the Lay Judge System], *Hanrei Jihō* [Judicial Reports], No. 1844, pp. 3–7.

217 Isa, *Saiban'in Seido wa Keiji Saiban o Kaeru ka* [Will the Lay Judge System Transform Criminal Courts], p. 178.

Open letter prepared by the Association for Opposing the Lay Judge System (Saiban'in Seido ni Hantai Suru Kai)

One example of contributions critical of the *saiban'in* system is the open letter prepared by the non-governmental organization called the Association for Opposing the Lay Judge System (*Saiban'in Seido ni Hantai Suru Kai*), which was established in October 2003.[218] The letter, submitted to the Office for Promotion of Justice System Reform on December 16, 2003, offers a highly critical view with regard to the question of whether the lay judge system will work effectively in contemporary Japan. The group's members include former justice Tarō Ōkubo, former president of Takushoku University Shirō Odamura, lawyer Katsuhiko Takaike, and Professor Michiko Hasegawa of Saitama University. The open letter, subsequently published in *Hanrei Jihō* (*Judicial Reports*) in 2004, criticized the proposal for the reintroduction of the lay judge system and offered an alternative solution for achieving increased public participation in the legal system.[219]

The organization's criticisms are based on an analysis of the Japanese legal system and society. Specifically, the letter claims that the *saiban'in* system is unconstitutional, because it infringes on the right of an individual to a fair trial by a professional judge (Chapter 6 of the constitution) and places an unreasonable responsibility on ordinary citizens, thus affecting their right to "life, liberty, and the pursuit of happiness" – which, as Article 13 of the constitution stipulates, should be "the supreme consideration in legislation and in other governmental affairs". The authors of the letter also note that the *saiban'in* system will be costly to implement and to maintain. They warn readers that all the allowances (transportation costs for traveling to court, for instance) that will be guaranteed to lay judges will come out of the taxpayers' pockets. Admitting that the Japanese legal system needs reforms in order to minimize the effect of such limitations, as time-consuming trials and verdicts that are often too light, the authors nevertheless argue that the lay judge system is not the right way to approach these flaws. A better way, they claim, is to strengthen the existing system of *chōtei iin*, or conciliation commissioners, by allowing laypersons to participate in an advisory capacity not only in family court and civil hearings but also in criminal trials of serious nature. The letter's authors argue that unlike the *chōtei iin* system, the lay judge system is based on a radically new conception for which Japanese society is not ready, because the majority of citizens are not interested in participating directly in trials in a capacity similar to that of professional judges.

Organizations promoting the reintroduction of an all-layperson jury system in Japan

Some of the citizen groups that actively promoted the implementation of the jury system in the 1980s and 1990s opposed the implementation of the mixed-court lay judge system. After the promulgation of the Lay Judge Act, they concentrated their efforts on organizing public seminars that aim to demonstrate how an all-layperson independent jury is superior to the *saiban'in* system. For instance, in December 2004, the Association for the Revival

---

218 Anonymous, 2004, "Saiban'in Seido ni Hantai Suru Kai Hossoku" [Association for Opposing the Lay Judge System Is Established], *Kokumin Shinbun*, January 25, available online at http://www5f.biglobe.ne.jp/~kokumin-Shinbun/H16/1601/1601002devilsystem.html.
219 Saiban'in Seido ni Hantai Suru Kai, "Saiban'in Seido ni Hantai Suru Kai no Ikensho" [Opinion Statement of the Association for Opposing the Lay Judge System].

of the Jury System organized a nationwide conference, "Opposing the Lay Judge System and the Deterioration of the Code of Penal Procedure, Aiming for the Realization of the [Introduction] of the Jury System".[220]

Conference participants argued that layperson participation under the Lay Judge Act will be purely nominal in nature, as the act does not provide any incentives for discontinuing the use of pre-trial dossiers.[221] They argue that, after the implementation of the *saiban'in* system, verdicts will continue to be determined behind closed doors and prior to the public hearing, in which lay judges are to participate. Based on this analysis, the participants of the conference conclude that in order to change the criminal justice system for the better, Japan should introduce an all-layperson jury system.[222]

"Will the Lay Judge System Transform Criminal Courts? Reasons for Demanding a Jury System" (Saiban'in Seido wa Keiji Saiban o Kaeru ka: Baishin Seido o Motomeru Wake)

Another addition to the debate regarding the negative aspects associated with the *saiban'in* system was written by Chihiro Isa. In the book "Will the Lay Judge System Transform Criminal Courts? Reasons for Demanding a Jury System" (*Saiban'in Seido wa Keiji Saiban o Kaeru ka: Baishin Seido o Motomeru Wake*), Isa argues that in order to make lay participation meaningful and to give it the potential of making a positive contribution to the existing legal structure, Japan should opt for an all-layperson jury trial system.[223] According to Isa, the *saiban'in* system does not provide clear incentives to prevent those problems that have been cited as justifications for legal reform, such as the heavy reliance of Japanese courts on confessions and documentary evidence (dossiers) that prosecutors submit.[224] In the absence of such incentives, he concludes, change is unlikely to occur.

An all-layperson American-style jury, on the other hand, Isa argues, would make the transformation of the existing legal system inevitable.[225] Specifically, in the presence of an independent jury, the prosecutors will be required to demonstrate in language understandable to ordinary citizens that the defendant is guilty "beyond a reasonable doubt". Consequently, relying on the dossier or a confession alone will no longer be enough to secure a verdict, and this will result in an inevitable change in existing practices.[226] Isa also notes that jurors tend to be good fact finders and that Japanese courts would benefit immensely from the contributions of ordinary citizens who can bring in their knowledge of everyday life.[227]

Chihiro Isa became a proponent of the establishment of an American-style jury system in Japan after he had the opportunity to participate as a juror in an all-layperson system established in Okinawa under the U.S. occupation; Isa has written extensively on the subject

---

220 A summary of the discussions at the conference is available online at http://www.l-wise.co.jp/baishin/200412_zenkokukyougikai_kosshi.htm.
221 *Id.*
222 *Id.*
223 Isa, *Saiban'in Seido wa Keiji Saiban o Kaeru ka* [Will the Lay Judge System Transform Criminal Courts].
224 *Id.*, pp. 13–19.
225 *Id.*, pp. 64–91.
226 *Id.*, p. 87.
227 *Id.*, pp. 87–90.

of jury trials.[228] His 1977 autobiography, "Turnaround: A Jury Trial in Okinawa under American Rule" (*Gyakuten: Amerika Shihaika Okinawa no Baishin Saiban*), received the Ōya Sōichi Non-Fiction Literature Prize in 1978 and has since remained one of the few sources discussing Okinawa's experience with the jury system.[229] It is of no surprise, therefore, that in his latest book on the vices of the lay judge system and on the virtues of an independent jury system, the author relies heavily on his own experiences as a juror in occupied Okinawa in an effort to demonstrate that the concept of an independent jury is not incompatible with the legal consciousness of the Japanese people, and that serving on the jury panel is not as intimidating a task as many prospective lay judges in Japan tend to imagine.

"We do not need the lay judge system!" (Saiban'in Seido wa Iranai!): the book and the public movement

Another example of a recent contribution to the anti-*saiban'in* debate is the highly controversial and speculative book, "We Do Not Need the Lay Judge System!" (*Saiban'in Seido wa Iranai!*), written by Shunkichi Takayama, an attorney and member of the Tokyo Bar Association, who has criticized the lay judge proposal since its inception.[230] Takayama claims that imposing jury responsibility on a society that is not ready for such a reform is shortsighted and dangerous. Takayama even argues that jury duty is similar to general conscription service, and that speedy trials and heavy punishments that the introduction of the system is supposed to realize also are attributes seen in military tribunals. This leads him to assert that the introduction of lay judge trials might be an indication of the government's desire to militarize Japanese society. Instead of dealing with the weaknesses of Japan's judicial system, he continues, the government is attempting to place the responsibility for solving these problems on the shoulders of ordinary citizens. Based on his analysis, Takayama claims that efforts should be made to stop the establishment of the *saiban'in* system.[231]

Indeed, after the publication of Takayama's book, Kazutoshi Satō, an attorney and member of the Tokyo Bar Association, proposed starting a public movement to counter the efforts of the government, the Ministry of Justice, and the Japan Federation of Bar Associations to promote the lay judge system.[232] As possible activities of such a movement that would use

---

228 C. Isa, "Okinawa Baishin Saiban no Keiken o Fumaete" [On the Experience of Jury Trials in Okinawa], in Saitama Baishin Fōramu, *Kuni vs Itō* [State vs Ito], pp. 248–260; and C. Isa, "Watakushi to Baishin Seido" [The Jury Trial System and Me], in Niigata Baishin Tomo no Kai, *Baishin Seido* [The Jury System], pp. 175–213.
229 Isa, *Gyakuten* [Turnaround].
230 Takayama, *Saiban'in Seido wa Iranai!* [We Do Not Need the Lay Judge System!]. Also see S. Takayama, 2007, "Saiban'in Seido o Hajimesasete wa Naranai" [The Lay Judge System Should Not Be Allowed to Start], *Mō Hitotsu no Sekai e*, Vol. 8, pp. 24–26.
231 Takayama, *Saiban'in Seido wa Iranai!* [We Do Not Need the Lay Judge System!], pp. 176–195 Anonymous, 2006, "Giron naku Kokumin Sōdōin; Saiban'in Seido Hihan no Hon Shuppan Takayama Bengoshi" [General Conscription without General Discussion; Attorney Takayama Publishes a Book Criticizing the *Saiban'in* System], *Tokyo Shinbun*, October 1, available online at http://www.takayama-law.com/kiji/1221-5.gif.
232 Saiban'in Seido Haishi o Mezasu Shimin/Hōsō no Tsudoi [The Meeting of Citizens and Jurists Aiming for the Abolishment of the Lay Judge System], 2006, *Saiban'in seido haishi o mezasu shimin/hōsō no tsudoi hōkokushū* [Reports from The Meeting of Citizens and Jurists Aiming for the Abolishment of the Lay Judge System] October 20, p. 8, available online at http://www.takayama-law.com/kiji/061020.pdf.

The mixed-court jury (saiban'in) system 201

the title of Takayama's book as its name, Satō suggested organizing symposia and mock trials that would be held in order to demonstrate the inadequacy of the lay judge system.[233]

On April 26, 2007, Satō's idea was realized when a group of lawyers and academics led by Shunkichi Takayama established the movement and created an official website for it.[234] The list of the organizers includes, among others, Masakatsu Adachi, professor at Kantō Gakuin University; writer Kōsaburō Arashiyama; Muneyuki Shindō, professor at Chiba University; Takashi Yamaguchi, professor at Meiji University; and lawyer Nobuo Oda. The movement was created in order to organize anti-*saiban'in* campaigns across Japan, plan seminars, and collect signatures in support of a petition appealing to the government to stop the introduction of the lay judge system in 2009.[235]

The petition against the *saiban'in* system prepared by this movement is addressed to the speaker of Japan's House of Representatives and to the president of the House of Councilors, and gives a number of justifications for demanding the abolishment of the Lay Judge Act.[236] First, the act does not allow those citizens who oppose the concept of trials with layperson participation to be excused from lay judge duty, which the authors of the petition claim infringes on the Japanese people's right to freedom of thought and expression. Second, the burden of the responsibility to keep the details of trial hearings confidential is too great for ordinary citizens to bear. In addition, after the implementation of the Lay Judge Act, the access of the media to the courtroom will be limited to a larger extent than is currently the case, which will affect the general public's right to be informed. Furthermore, the authors of the petition argue that unlike the all-layperson jury system, where unanimous consent is necessary for a verdict to be accepted by the judge, under the *saiban'in* system cases will be determined based on the decision of the majority, and the opinions of the minority will be disregarded. The petition also refers to the results of recent public opinion polls according to which almost 80 per cent of the respondents state they do not wish to serve as lay judges.[237]

The "We Do Not Need the Lay Judge System!" movement planned a number of events aimed at winning supporters that included explanation meetings in Sendai[238] and a seminar followed by a play titled "A Lay Judge Trial" (*Saiban'in Saiban*), which highlighted the problem areas of the *saiban'in* system.[239]

---

233 *Id.*, p. 8.
234 Saiban'in Seido wa Iranai! Dai Undō, available online at http://no-saiban-in.org/index.html.
235 *Id.* This organization set up by Takayama and his supporters is not the only group demanding the abolishment of the lay judge system. Another example is the Fukuoka-based Society for Pursuing Criminal Defense for the People (*Shimin no tame no Keiji Bengo o Tomo ni Tsuikyū Suru Kai*). This group sent documents demanding the abolishment of the lay judge system to the Supreme Court on November 28, 2008, arguing that this system was unconstitutional (Anonymous, 2008, "Saiban'in Seido wa Kenpō Ihan, Shimin Dantai, Fukuoka de Haishi Uttae" [The Lay Judge System Is Unconstitutional; A Citizen Group Demands Abolishment in Fukuoka], *Asahi Shinbun*, November 29).
236 Saiban'in Seido wa Iranai! Dai Undō, "Saiban'in Hō no Haishi o Motomeru Seigansho" [Petition Demanding the Abolishment of the Lay Judge Act], available online at http://no-saiban-in.org/image/070312seigan.pdf.
237 *Id.*
238 Saiban'in Seido wa Iranai! Dai Undō, "Saiban'in Seido ni Igi Ari! Kōen Shūkai" [An Objection to the Lay Judge System! Lecture and Meeting], available online at http://no-saiban-in.org/pdf/6.16kouenkai.pdf.
239 Saiban'in Seido wa Iranai! Dai Undō, "Saiban'in Seido wa Iranai! 6.29 Shūkai" [We Do Not Need the Lay Judge System! The June 29[, 2007,] Meeting], available online at http://no-saiban-in.org/image/6.29chirashi.jpg; Anonymous, 2007, "Saiban'in Jidai: 'Chōeki no Yō na Mono', 'Jiyū ga Ii';

202 *The mixed-court jury (saiban'in) system*

The movement used posters and pamphlets to protest the introduction of the lay judge system. It also developed its own promotional character, called "*Saiban'iniranainko*" – a parakeet opposing the introduction of the *saiban'in* system and clearly an antipode of *Saiban'inko*, the character promoting the new system created by the Lay Judge System Promotions Office.[240]

On April 21, 2009, exactly one month prior to the enforcement of the Lay Judge Act the movement held a demonstration in Ginza, Tokyo, which attracted 1,850 participants despite the rain. Six days later there was another demonstration and press conference, this time in front of the National Diet.[241] During the second demonstration, the participants stated that 12,282 people had signed the movement's petition.[242] One day prior to the enactment of the Lay Judge Act, the movement had yet another demonstration that attracted 650 participants.[243]

While the movement organized by Takayama and his supporters suggested outward protest, several other recent contributions to the debate have proposed that citizens should quietly sabotage the system. These contributions urged prospective lay judges to refuse to serve by stating that their conscience does not permit them to judge others.[244] The authors of the books that put forward this argument have suggested that persons not willing to serve as lay judges may resort to Article 19 of the Constitution of Japan that guarantees every citizen's freedom of thought and conscience.[245]

Attitudes towards the system on the part of the general public

During the five years of preparation for the implementation of the Lay Judge Act, the Japanese government, the Lay Judge System Promotions Office, and major newspaper companies conducted public opinion surveys to determine the attitudes of the general public towards the new system.

One such poll, conducted in 2005, showed that while over 70 per cent of citizens knew that the new system of lay participation was to be introduced in Japan, approximately the same number (64 per cent of male respondents and 75 per cent of female respondents) did not wish to serve as lay judges.[246] The reasons behind the lack of interest on the part of the

---

Arashiyama Kōzaburō san ra, Tokyo de Shūkai" [The Era of Lay Judges: "It Is Like Penal Servitude", "It Is Better to Be Free"; Kōzaburō Arashiyama and Others Meet in Tokyo], *Asahi Shinbun*, June 30 (reporting on the meetings and play).

240 *Saiban'iniranainko* literally means a parakeet that does not need the lay judge system. Saiban'in Seido wa Iranai! Dai Undō, available online at http://no-saiban-in.org/index.html.
241 Saiban'in Seido wa Iranai! Dai Undō, available online at http://no-saiban-in.org/index.html.
242 *Id*.
243 *Id*.
244 C. Isa and T. Ikuta (eds), 2009, *Saiban'in Kyohi no Susume: Anata ga Enzai ni Katan Shinai tame* [[We] Advise [You] to Refuse Lay Judge [Service]: To Ensure that You Are Not Part to Erroneous Charges], Tokyo: Wave Shuppan; I. Kohama, 2009, *Shikei ka Muki ka Anata ga Kimeru: Saiban'in Seido o Kyohi Seyo!* [It Is Up to You to Decide between the Death Penalty and Lifetime Imprisonment: Let's Reject the Lay Judge System], Tokyo: Daiwa Shobō.
245 Kenpō, art. 19; Isa and Ikuta, *Saiban'in Kyohi no Susume* [[We] Advise [You] to Refuse Lay Judge [Service]], p. 4.
246 Naikaku Fu Daijin Kanbo Seifu Kōhōshitsu [Government Publications Office, Department of the Minister for the Cabinet Office], 2005, "Saiban'in Seido ni kan suru Yoron Chōsa" [Public Opinion Poll Concerning the Lay Judge System], available online at http://www8.cao.go.jp/survey/h16/h16-saiban/. See Anderson and Ambler, "The Slow Birth of Japan's Quasi-Jury System (*Saiban-in Seido*)", p. 69 (discussing the results of this poll).

respondents in participating in the system included the perceived difficulty of determining whether someone is guilty or not guilty and not wanting to judge others.[247] The results of opinion polls have remained rather consistent since 2005. A survey carried out by the Japanese government on February 1, 2007, showed that 78.1 per cent of respondents did not wish to serve as jurors.[248] A poll carried out in 2009 indicated, however, that despite the general lack of enthusiasm regarding the new system, 57 per cent of respondents were planning to appear in court if summoned to serve.[249]

Implementation and the first lay judge case

The criticisms of the system and the protests against its implementation did not attract a sufficient number of supporters to prevent the system from being implemented. The Lay Judge Act was enforced on May 21, 2009. Prime Minister Aso noted on this occasion that the implementation of the *saiban'in* system was "the central pillar" of the judicial reforms carried out by the government.[250] He expressed hope that the citizens of Japan would appreciate the importance of the new system and asked for their cooperation.[251]

The preparation of the list of lay judge candidates began on July 15, 2008.[252] Each of the persons on the list received a notification along with other materials that included a questionnaire that helped establish who could be excused from lay judge duty.[253] In November 2008, the Supreme Court established a call center to address the concerns of the persons whose names were placed on the list of lay judge candidates.[254]

The first case with the participation of lay judges was tried on August 3, 2009, at the Tokyo District Court.[255] The case involved Mr. Shōkichi Fujii, a 72-year-old unemployed man accused

---

247 Anonymous, 2005, "70% Don't Want to Serve on Juries in New System", *Japan Times*, April 17, available online at http://search.japantimes.co.jp/cgi-bin/nn20050417a3.html.
248 Anonymous, 2007, "Saiban'in Seido Shitteiru 81%, Sanka Shōkyokuha 78%, Tokubetsu Yoron Chōsa" [Special Opinion Poll: 81% of Respondents Know about the *Saiban'in* System, 78% Passive about Participating], *Asahi Shinbun*, February 2, p. 1.
249 Anonymous, 2009, "Saiban'in Kōhōsha ni Nattara, Yobidashi 'Iku' 57% Asahi Shinbunsha Yoron Chōsa" [If Selected as Lay Judge Candidates, 57% Will Appear [in Court as Summoned]; Asahi Newspaper Company's Opinion Poll], *Asahi Shinbun*, January 9, p. 1.
250 "Naikaku Sōridaijin no Danwa (Saiban'in Seido no Kaishi ni tsuite)" [Prime Minister's Comment (Concerning the Lay Judge System], May 21, 2009, available online at http://www.kantei.go.jp/jp/asospeech/2009/05/21danwa.html.
251 *Id.*
252 Saikō Saibansho [The Supreme Court], "Chōsa Hyō no Kaitō Jyōkyō Nado ni tsuite" [Concerning the Status of Questionnaire Responses], available online at http://www.saibanin.courts.go.jp/topics/pdf/09_03_16_cyosahyo_kaito/cyosahyo_kaito.pdf. For the first year of the functioning of the lay judge system 295,036 persons were listed (Tsuchiya, *Saiban'in Seido to Kokumin* [The Lay Judge System and the People], p. 7).
253 The forms and questionnaires that were sent out to persons listed as eligible for lay judge service are available online at Saikō Saibansho [The Supreme Court], "Saibansho kara Ookuri Suru Fūtō to Meibi Kisai Tsūchi Oyobi Sono Dōfūbutsu ni tsuite" [Concerning the Envelope, the Notification of Being Listed and Accompanying Materials], available online at http://www.saibanin.courts.go.jp/notification/envelope/index.html.
254 Saikō Saibansho [The Supreme Court], "Meibō Kisai Tsūchi ni tsuite" [Concerning Notification of [Persons Whose Names Appear] on the List of Lay Judge Candidates], available online at http://www.saibanin.courts.go.jp/notification/index.html.
255 Anonymous, "Saiban'in Saiban Hachi Gatsu Mikkka ni Seishiki Kettei, Tokyo Chisai, Josei Shisatsu Jiken de" [Lay Judge Trial Officially Set for August 3, Tokyo District Court [to Try] the Case of

of stabbing a 66-year-old woman to death on May 1, 2009.[256] The woman was a *zainichi* Korean and worked as a *seitai* therapist.[257] The defendant pleaded guilty.[258] One hundred persons from the list of persons eligible to serve as lay judges were selected by lot and summoned to appear on the first day of the trial. The selection procedures that resulted in the empanelment of six lay judges and three *saiban'in* in reserve began at 10:00 on the morning of August 3. The trial hearings started at 13:20 that same day.[259] The first day of the hearings was devoted to the opening remarks by the prosecutor and defense, followed by the testimony of an eyewitness to the incident. On August 4, the court heard from two other witnesses of the incident, from a relative of the deceased, and then from the accused. On the following day, the prosecution made its final remarks and requested the penalty for the accused (sixteen years' imprisonment). The representative of the relatives of the deceased then made a statement asking for the term of imprisonment to be extended to at least twenty years.[260] The defense delivered its closing remarks last. The attorney of the accused argued that Fujii did not have the intention to kill the victim.[261] Throughout the proceedings, the *saiban'in* exercised their right to question the accused, asking Fujii why he had a survival knife in his possession rather than a kitchen knife at the time of the quarrel between him and the victim.[262] The mixed-court panel announced the verdict of guilty on August 6, 2009, and sentenced Fujii to fifteen years in prison.[263]

By the end of December 2009, 142 cases were tried by *saiban'in*.[264] The majority of cases tried during this period (134 cases) were adjudicated within four days.[265] Deliberation time averaged 6.6 hours, according to the statistics provided by the Supreme Court of Japan.[266] Forty-two cases tried by *saiban'in* in 2009 involved the crime of robbery causing injury, thirty-three cases involved the crime of homicide, and sixteen cases dealt with the violations of the Stimulants Control Act.[267]

Female Stabbed to Death], *Japan Press Network 47 News*, available online at http://www.47news.jp/CN/200906/CN2009061201000492.html; Anonymous, 2009, "Seitaishi Shisatsu Jiken no Kōhan Kijitsu Kettei; Saiban'in Saiban Dai Ichi Gō ka" [Date of Public Hearing of the *Seitai* Therapist Stabbing Case Decided; Will This Be The First Lay Judge Trial?], June 12, *Yomiuri Online*, available online at http://www.yomiuri.co.jp/national/news/20090612-OYT1T00683.htm?from=navr.

256 Anonymous, "Seitaishi Shisatsu Jiken no Kōhan Kijitsu Kettei; Saiban'in Saiban Dai Ichi Gō ka" [Date of Public Hearing of the *Seitai* Therapist Stabbing Case Decided; Will This Be the First Lay Judge Trial?].
257 *Seitai* (literally, a properly ordered body) is a massage therapy (Nihon Iryō Seitai Gakuin [Nihon Iryo Seitai Institute], "What Is Seitai?", available online at http://www.nisg.jp/eng/index.htm).
258 S. Kamiya, 2009, "First Lay Judge Trial Kicks off in Tokyo", *Japan Times*, August 4, available online at http://search.japantimes.co.jp/cgi-bin/nn20090804a1.html. During the pre-trial hearings the defense pleaded extenuating circumstances (Anonymous, "Saiban'in Saiban Hachi Gatsu Mikkka ni Seishiki Kettei, Tokyo Chisai, Josei Shisatsu Jiken de" [Lay Judge Trial Officially Set for August 3, Tokyo District Court [to Try] the Case of Female Stabbed to Death]).
259 Kamiya, "First Lay Judge Trial Kicks off in Tokyo".
260 Anonymous, 2009, "First Lay Judges Hand Killer 15-Year Term", *Japan Times*, August 7, available online at http://search.japantimes.co.jp/cgi-bin/nn20090807a1.html.
261 *Id.*
262 *Id.*
263 *Id.*
264 Saikō Saibansho [The Supreme Court], "Saiban'in Seido no Jisshi Jōkyō ni tsuite (Sono Ichi)" [Regarding the Operation Status of the Lay Judge System (Part 1)], available online at http://www.saibanin.courts.go.jp/topics/h21_saibanin_kekka.html.
265 *Id.* Eight cases (5.6% of the total number of cases tried by *saiban'in*) took more than five days to adjudicate (*id.*).
266 *Id.*
267 *Id.* KEIHŌ, arts. 240, 199 (enumerating robbery causing death or injury and homicide, respectively) and Kakuseizai Torishimari Hō [Stimulants Control Act], Law No. 252 of 1951, as last amended

The results of polls taken among the persons who served as lay judges in 2009 immediately following the conclusion of their responsibilities indicate that 70.9 per cent of respondents found the trial that they participated in "easy to understand" – statistics that made the Supreme Court of Japan conclude that the ideal of a court system that is easy to understand has been realized.[268] In response to the question concerning the quality of citizen participation in deliberations, 75.5 per cent of respondents stated that they felt that they "could thoroughly and sufficiently deliberate the case", and only 5.9 per cent indicated that they felt that their deliberation of the case was insufficient.[269] While the majority (55.7 per cent) indicated that they had not been interested in becoming jurors prior to being summoned,[270] 96.7 per cent of respondents said that they felt that serving as lay judges was a positive experience.[271]

The first six years of the functioning of the system

At the point of writing this chapter, six years have passed since the implementation of the jury system in Japan. Six years certainly is not a sufficiently long period of time to provide us with data that would make it possible to draw any definite conclusions regarding the degree of success with which the lay judge system is functioning in contemporary Japan. Nevertheless, this period exceeds the time slot that was allotted to the preparation for the implementation of the Lay Judge Act by a year, which arguably makes 2015 a meaningful year to draw several tentative conclusions and reflect upon the information that has become available regarding the trials that have taken place with the participation of lay judges.

The statistical data for the period between the introduction of the system and October 2015 provided by the Supreme Court of Japan give support to the view that the new system has been operating successfully.[272]

During the period under review, lay judges participated in the process of determining the fate of 8,229 defendants.[273] The majority of these cases were tried within approximately

---

      by Law No. 94 of 2006. The remainder of the cases tried by *saiban'in* during the period between the date of the enforcement of the Lay Judge Act and the end of 2009 involved the following crimes: arson of inhabited buildings (eleven cases), quasi-forcible indecency causing injury (nine cases), quasi-rape leading to injury (eight cases), injury causing death (eight cases), and other crimes (fifteen cases). KEIHŌ, arts. 108, 178, 205 (enumerating arson of inhabited buildings, quasi-forcible indecency and quasi-rape, injury causing death, respectively); Saikō Saibansho [The Supreme Court], "Saiban'in Seido no Jisshi Jōkyō ni tsuite (Sono Ichi)" [Regarding the Operation Status of the Lay Judge System (Part 1)], available online at http://www.saibanin.courts.go.jp/topics/h21_saibanin_kekka.html.

268 *Id.*
269 *Id.* Other respondents either indicated that they did not know (17.3%) or chose not to answer this question (1%). Saikō Saibansho [The Supreme Court], "Saiban'in Seido no Jisshi Jōkyō ni tsuite (Sono Ichi)" [Regarding the Operation Status of the Lay Judge System (Part 1)], available online at http://www.saibanin.courts.go.jp/topics/h21_saibanin_kekka.html.
270 *Id.*
271 *Id.*
272 "Saiban'in Seido no Jisshi Jyōkyō ni tsuite: Seido Shikō-Heisei 27 Nen 10 Gatsu Matsu Sokuhō" [Concerning the Status of the Implementation of the Lay Assessor System: From the Implementation of the System to End of October, 2015 (Newsflash)], available online at http://www.saibanin.courts.go.jp/vcms_lf/h27_10_saibaninsokuhou.pdf.
273 The majority of defendants (22.21%) who were tried by lay judges were accused of murder; a roughly equal number of defendants (22.02%) were accused of robbery resulting in bodily injury. *Id.*

seven days,[274] and the time required to reach a verdict during this period was ten hours on average.[275] These figures indicate that while the average period of time required to adjudicate a case has seen an increase since 2009, trials with the participation of laypersons have been tried within a relatively short period of time. This implies that one of the objectives of the introduction of the lay judge system and of the other legal reforms envisaged by the JSRC has more or less been achieved – that is, to speed up the process of administrating justice in Japan.

The absolute majority (97.4 per cent) of trials adjudicated with the participation of *saiban'in* during the period under review have resulted in the verdict of guilty.[276]

The attitudes of persons who have had the chance to serve on the mixed lay judge panel have been consistently positive. Of respondents polled during the first eight months of 2015, 65.2 per cent indicated that the trial hearings were easy to understand, with only 2.3 per cent stating otherwise.[277] An absolute majority – 74.8 per cent – said that they were satisfied with the degree of their participation in the deliberations (only 7.4 per cent responded that they thought that their participation was insufficient).[278] As in 2009, an overwhelming majority of lay judges (96.1 per cent) assessed their experience of service as either "highly positive" or "positive".[279]

Those persons who have had the chance to serve as lay judges have shared their positive impressions not only through answering the questionnaires provided by the Supreme Court, but also through authoring blogs and acting as spokespersons for the system. Some former lay judges have participated in explanatory sessions organized by courts, sharing their thoughts and experiences with prospective lay judges,[280] while others became active members of the various groups working to promote and improve the lay judge system.[281]

---

274 *Id.*
275 *Id.*
276 *Id.*
277 "Saiban'in Seido no Un'ei Tō ni kansuru Ankēto Chōsa Kekka Hōkokusho (Heisei 27 Nen 1–8 Gatsu Bun)" [A Report on the Results of Questionnaires Concerning the Functioning of the Lay Judge System (January–August 2015)], available online at http://www.saibanin.courts.go.jp/vcms_lf/h27_ankeito_tyuukan.pdf. These figures are consistent with the responses provided by lay judges in preceding polls. In 2013, for example, 62.2% of respondents indicated that the trial hearings were easy to understand, with only 6.2% stating that they found it difficult to understand the proceedings ("Saiban'in Seido no Jisshi Jyōkyō ni tsuite" [Concerning the Status of the Implementation of the Lay Assessor System], available online at http://www.saibanin.courts.go.jp/vcms_lf/saibanin_kekka201312.pdf).
278 "Saiban'in Seido no Un'ei Tō ni kansuru Ankēto Chōsa Kekka Hōkokusho (Heisei 27 Nen 1–8 Gatsu Bun)" [A Report on the Results of Questionnaires Concerning the Functioning of the Lay Judge System (January–August 2015)], available online at http://www.saibanin.courts.go.jp/vcms_lf/h27_ankeito_tyuukan.pdf.
279 *Id.* It should be noted, however, that the numbers of candidates who are declining jury service for various reasons is on the rise. See Anonymous, 2015, "Saiban'in Seido 6 Nen Keikensha wa "Sanka Shite Yokatta' Demo Taiji Ritsu wa Zōka Keikō" [Six Years of the Functioning of the Lay Judge System; Those Who Experienced [Being Lay Judges Say that They Were] Pleased to Have Served, but Percentage of Those Who Decline Service on the Rise], *Sankei Nyūsu*, May 21, available online at http://www.sankei.com/affairs/news/150521/afr1505210004-n1.html.
280 Anonymous, 2014, "Saiban'in Seido 5 Nen; Yokohama Chisai ga Demae Kōgi de PR" [5 Years of the Lay Judge System; Yokohama District Court Promotes [System] with a Lecture [Taking Place outside the Court]], *Kanagawa Shinbun*, September 22, available online at http://www.kanaloco.jp/article/77946/cms_id/102591.
281 A. Plogstedt, 2013, "Citizen Judges in Japan: A Report Card for the Initial Three Years", *International and Comparative Law Review*, pp. 371–428, at p. 403.

One such group is the "Network of Those Who Have Served as Lay Judges" (*Saiban'in Keikensha Nettowāku*). The network was established by former lay judges, members of civil society organizations, professional lawyers, and university professors, with the goal of providing the opportunity for lay judges to share their experiences with one another and with the whole of society, and of assisting former *saiban'in* to reduce the psychological burden that their service may entail.[282] Professional lawyers work to ensure that members do not compromise their obligation to protect the secrecy of court deliberations as they participate in the activities of the network.[283]

The members of the network have repeatedly made suggestions for improving the system of support that is available to lay judges at Japanese courts.[284] When a former female lay judge was diagnosed with acute stress disorder (ASD) in April 2013, the network issued a statement calling on the Supreme Court of Japan to reconsider the emergency proposal that it had authored in 2010. This proposal incorporated several suggestions with regard to the measures that courts could take in order to reduce the psychological burden on the part of lay judges. Specifically, the network had proposed that a health support center be established at all district courts in Japan.[285] The psychological burden that lay judges have to bear in the course of their service remains an issue that is being widely discussed in the Japanese press and one that will arguably need to be considered further by the Supreme Court of Japan.[286]

Another issue that former lay judges have been successful at drawing attention to in the Japanese society is the issue of the death penalty. Twenty former lay judges have petitioned the Ministry of Justice in February 2014 to either put an immediate halt to the death penalty or provide adequate disclosure to the general public regarding the details of how the death penalty is being carried out in Japan – citing the sense of protest that they had felt about becoming "indirect murderers of (fellow) human beings".[287] This issue

---

282 See "Saiban'in Keikensha Nettowāku: Anata no Keiken to Omoi ga Kōryū no Kakehashi Desu" [Network of Those Who Have Served as Lay Judges: Your Experience and Thoughts Are Bridges to [Meaningful] Exchange], available online at http://saibanin-keiken.net. A list of supporting groups and individuals is available online at "Saiban'in Keikensha Nettowāku e no Yobikake" [A Call for [Participation] in the Network of Those Who Have Served as Lay Judges], available online at http://saibanin-keiken.net/web_005.htm. See also "Saiban'in Keikensha Nettowāku Towa" [What Is the Network of Those Who Have Served as Lay Judges?], available online at http://saibanin-keiken.net/web_002.htm.
283 "Saiban'in Keikensha Nettowāku no Omona Katsudō" [The Primary Activities of the Network of Those Who Have Served as Lay Judges], available online at http://saibanin-keiken.net/web_006.htm.
284 "Saiban'in Keikensha Nettowāku towa" [What Is the Network of Those Who Have Served as Lay Judges?], available online at http://saibanin-keiken.net/web_002.htm.
285 Saiban'in Keikensha Nettowāku [The Network of Those Who Have Served as Lay Judges], 2013, "Saiban'in no Shinriteki Futan ni tsuite' Komento", available online at http://saibanin-keiken.net/web_004.htm; "Saiban'in Keikensha Nettowāku" [The Network of Those Who Have Served as Lay Judges], 2010, "Saiban'in no Shinriteki Futan ni tsuite no Saibansho no Taiōsaku e no Kinkyū Teigen" [Emergency Proposal [Concerning] the Measures [that] Courts [May Implement] [to Alleviate] the Psychological Burden of Lay Judges], December 9, available online at http://saibanin-keiken.net/teigen20101209.pdf.
286 See Anonymous, 2014, "(Shasetsu) Saiban'in no Futan: Jittai o Tsukami Taisaku o" [(Editorial) The Burden of Lay Judges: [Coming Up with] Solutions [Aiming to] Investigate the Actual Conditions], *Asahi Shinbun*, October 4, available online at http://www.asahi.com/articles/DA3S11384501.html.
287 T. Osaki, 2014, "Provide Details on Hangings or Halt Them", *Japan Times*, February 17. The group now consists of more than seventy-five members (Vanoverbeke, *Juries in the Japanese Legal System*, p. 179).

resurfaced in 2015 when the first accused sentenced to the death penalty by lay judges was executed.[288]

The implementation of the *saiban'in* system in criminal trials has spurred discussion concerning the possibility of expanding the participation of citizens in the process of administrating justice in Japan further by making civil cases eligible for trial by lay judges.[289] While it still remains to be seen whether this reform will be implemented, the fact that this possibility is being actively discussed in Japan appears to reflect the reality that the lay judge system is widely perceived to have been functioning effectively during the first five years of its existence.

Evaluating Japan's new lay judge (*saiban'in*) system

This chapter has focused on the attempts to introduce the jury system in the post-occupation period. It has demonstrated that the idea to introduce the jury system enjoyed the spotlight of public attention three times in the post-war period: in the first post-occupation decades, in the 1980s, and then again in the 1990s.

In the immediate post-occupation period, academics discussed the constitutionality of the institution of jury service. As this debate was merely a continuation of the occupation-period deliberations and not involving any new proposals, it ultimately came to a standstill.

The institution of jury service again became the subject of debate in the 1980s when several highly publicized erroneous verdicts made the public question the reliability of judge-only justice. Unlike the discussion of the subject in the late 1950s and in the 1960s, this time the debate was not abstract. It reflected concerns about the quality of justice in Japan and

---

288 Anonymous, 2015, "Japan Hangs Two Prisoners, Including First Convicted in Lay Judge Trial", *Japan Times*, December 18; Anonymous, 2015, "Saiban'in Saiban de Hanketsu no Shikeishū Hatsu no Shikkō" [First Execution of Inmate Sentenced to the Death Penalty by Lay Judges Carried Out], *NHK NewsWeb*, December 18, available online at http://www3.nhk.or.jp/news/html/20151218/k10010344941000.html. In the first six years of the system's functioning a total of twenty-five death penalty sentencing verdicts have been delivered by *saiban'in* mixed-court panels ("Saiban'in Seido no Jisshi Jyōkyō ni tsuite: Seido Shikō-Heisei 27 Nen 10 Gatsu Matsu Sokuhō" [Concerning the Status of the Implementation of the Lay Assessor System: From the Implementation of the System to End of October, 2015 (Newsflash)], available online at http://www.saibanin.courts.go.jp/vcms_lf/h27_10_saibaninsokuhou.pdf). For an introduction of the opinions of former lay judges on the issue of the death penalty and the responsibility, see Vanoverbeke, *Juries in the Japanese Legal System*, p. 178. For an overview of the activities of the associations of former lay judges and for an introduction of the opinions of lay judges more generally, see Vanoverbeke, *Juries in the Japanese Legal System*, pp. 169–179.

289 Anonymous, 2014, "The Court Says Lay Judge System Working Well at Five-Year Mark", *Japan Times*, May 21, available online at http://www.japantimes.co.jp/news/2014/05/21/national/top-court-says-lay-judge-system-working-well-five-year-mark/#.VDJiWksxHlJ; H. Fukurai, 2013, "A Step in the Right Direction for Japan's Judicial Reform: Impact of the Justice System Reform Council Recommendations on Criminal Justice and Citizen Participation in Criminal, Civil, and Administrative Litigation", *Hastings International and Comparative Law Review*, Vol. 36, pp. 517–566, at p. 561. The text of the 2001 JSRC recommendations stated that "a new system [of layperson participation] should be introduced, *for the time being*, in criminal proceedings" (emphasis added). This phrase appears to imply that the JSRC did not exclude the possibility that the system of layperson participation could be introduced to civil trials in the future. (Recommendations of the Judicial System Reform Council; Fukurai, "A Step in the Right Direction for Japan's Judicial Reform: Impact of the Justice System Reform Council Recommendations on Criminal Justice and Citizen Participation in Criminal, Civil, and Administrative Litigation", p. 561.)

involved not only academics, but also citizen groups, Supreme Court Justices, and local Bar Associations. The debate in the 1980s resulted in the drafting of several proposals outlining the details of the new system of layperson participation that Japan could introduce. These proposals failed to attract sufficient support on the part of the general public and of politicians, however, and it was only a decade later that the possibility of implementing the jury system was discussed again.

In the 1990s, the introduction of the jury system featured not as an isolated proposal but as part of JSRC's comprehensive plan to revamp Japan's justice system. The recommendation to introduce jury trials was presented by the JSRC as the glue that bound together the other criminal justice system reforms proposed by the council, such as the realization of concentrated trials and the realization of the principles of orality.[290] While on paper Japan's criminal justice is administered in accordance with the principles of orality and concentrated trials are the goal, in reality court sessions in cases other than minor and uncontested ones have tended to be spread over months and sometimes years in the post-war period, and courts have relied on the dossiers prepared by the prosecution that contains virtually all evidence and testimony. JSRC's recommendations stated that the implementation of the lay judge system should lead to more concentrated trials, as jurors cannot be asked to participate in trial hearings that go on for too long a period of time, and that the presence of citizens in the courtroom in the capacity of lay judges should lead to greater reliance on in-court testimony rather than on the written dossiers prepared by the prosecutor. In addition, JSRC's recommendations emphasized that the *saiban'in* proposal was central to the realization of the third pillar of justice reform – the cluster of initiatives aiming to increase popular participation in Japan's justice system. In Japan, the general public has long perceived courts as places where one appears only when in serious trouble, where complicated jargon is used, and where procedures are hard to understand. The JSRC argued that the introduction of the jury system would help change this image of courts as an intimidating place.

Why did the suggestion to implement the jury system as expressed by the JSRC lead to the drafting, enactment, and finally enforcement of the Lay Judge Act, while the proposals discussed in the 1960s and 1980s did not?

It appears that one of the reasons behind the realization of JSRC's proposal to implement the jury system lay in the fact that this idea was proposed as part of a large package of reforms that in their entirety managed to acquire substantial support on the part of the business community and the LDP. This factor also accounts for the speed with which the recommendation to implement the *saiban'in* system was realized and became law. Positioned by the authors of the JSRC recommendations at the center of several important reform initiatives, the jury was seen as an idea that, if eliminated, would make the realization of other reforms that were widely perceived as necessary impossible or difficult. This is in a sharp contrast to the situation in the 1960s and 1980s, when the jury system was discussed as an isolated proposal.

What were the factors that compelled the government and the general public to agree with the idea that it was necessary for Japan to drastically reform its justice system?

The fact that several problems – most notably lawyer scarcity and lengthy trials – could not be ignored any longer was one reason for Japan's desire to start full-fledged legal reform.[291]

---

290 Foote, "Introduction and Overview", p. xxxiii.
291 *Id.*, p. xxvi.

The erroneous verdicts of the 1980s and the resulting dissatisfaction and lack of trust on the part of the general public towards the court system contributed to the feeling that Japan's system of justice was in need of reform.

Increasing internationalization that manifested itself in the growing demand for legal services and for new types of legal services (such as for example, international commercial arbitration in the area of civil justice and international justice assistance systems to facilitate the investigation of cases in the field of criminal justice) was another factor.[292] In his discussion of JSRC reform proposals, Professor Daniel H. Foote observed that in JSRC-inspired reforms, internationalization did not involve direct foreign pressure (*gaiatsu*).[293] Indeed, JSRC's recommendations reflected the desire to prepare the legal system to the new challenges that it started facing in an increasingly globalized world – a desire that was not imposed on Japan from the outside but developed within the country. Internationalization, understood in this way, served to generate business support for reform.[294] As Japanese business leaders became increasingly involved in international operations they came to appreciate the role that lawyers play in resolving disputes and in facilitating business transactions. This was in a sharp contrast with the attitudes that Japanese businesses displayed in the 1980s, for instance, when they tended to focus on the negative aspects of litigation and their potential for hampering the competitiveness of businesses.[295]

Furthermore, JSRC's goal of transforming "excessive advance-control/adjustment-type society to an after-the-fact review/remedy type society"[296] resounded with the business community and the LDP, as this objective was clearly related to the issues of deregulation and administrative reform. The goal of administrative reform was to replace administrative guidance with a system of clear and transparent rules – an idea that was welcomed by business leaders in the 1990s who saw administrative reform as a way to reduce discretion on the part of the bureaucracy. The fact that JSRC's recommendations supported the same basic principle convinced the representatives of Japan's business community to endorse justice system reform.[297]

Moreover, the change from the *Shōwa* to *Heisei* as well as the shift from the 20th to the 21st century provided the psychological incentive for reform.[298] The nuance that with the beginning of the 21st century Japan needed a fresh start was highlighted in the majority of proposals emphasizing the need to revamp Japan's system of justice in the 1990s.

Finally, the fact that the package of reforms received the support of Prime Ministers Obuchi and Koizumi added credibility to the claim that Japan's justice system needed to change. Koizumi, who assumed his post in 2001, had already achieved a reputation as a reformer, and his support certainly played an important role in the realization of JSRC's vision of reform.

What are the prospects of the system as envisaged by the Lay Judge Act to function effectively? In addressing this issue, it is possible to look at two questions. First, will the *saiban'in* system help achieve the goals stated by the JSRC – that is, serve to improve the quality of justice and empower Japanese citizens? Second, can we expect the new system to function

---

292 *Id.*, p. xxvii; Recommendations of the Judicial System Reform Council.
293 Foote, "Introduction and Overview", p. xxvii.
294 *Id.*, p. xxvii.
295 *Id.*, pp. xxvii–xxviii.
296 Recommendations of the Judicial System Reform Council.
297 Foote, "Introduction and Overview", xxviii.
298 *Id.*, pp. xxvi–xxvii.

smoothly? Both of these questions have been at the center of public debate in the years leading up to the enforcement of the Lay Judge Act.

Like the pre-war jury system, Japan's new mixed-court jury is a unique cross between the Continental-European and the Anglo-American common law jury. While Japan's pre-war jury system may be described as an Anglo-American jury system that had a number of distinctive characteristics, the *saiban'in* system as outlined in the Lay Judge Act may be looked upon as essentially a Continental-European jury system that has several unique features.

The opponents to the *saiban'in* system have argued that instead of introducing an untested hybrid, Japan should have implemented an all-layperson jury system. Indeed, it appears that the introduction of independent all-layperson jury trials would have greater potential to improve the quality of justice and empower Japanese citizens than the *saiban'in* system. An all-layperson jury would need to be persuaded that a defendant was guilty beyond a reasonable doubt and would not have the option of hearing the opinions of professional judges on the facts of the case during deliberations. In such a situation, relying on written statements alone would arguably not be enough to secure a verdict for either the prosecution or the defense. Under the mixed-court jury consisting of both judges and jurors, on the other hand, the need to drastically change the strategies in the courtroom is less pronounced. After all, if either the prosecution or defense is able to make professional judges appreciate a point, there remains a chance that this particular argument would affect the final verdict. This would not be the case were the members of the jury given the responsibility for making decisions independently of the judge. The all-layperson jury system would bestow upon jurors a greater responsibility than the *saiban'in* system, and by doing so be better positioned than any other possible model of layperson participation to serve as a means of citizen empowerment. In the Anglo-American model of jury trials, it is the sole responsibility of the members of the jury to determine the fate of the accused, while under the new *saiban'in* system this responsibility would be shared with professional judges.

On the other hand, if one refrains from comparing the *saiban'in* system with the Anglo-American model of jury trials, it becomes clear that achieving the two goals set forth by the JSRC should be easier with the introduction of the *saiban'in* system rather than without it. Indeed, the presence of laypersons in the courtroom may be expected to trigger change in the way proceedings are carried out, even if this change is not as drastic as it would have been had Japan opted for the introduction of the American model of jury trials.

How likely is the new mixed-court jury system to repeat the fate of Japan's pre-war jury? While it is too early to draw any definite conclusions, it appears that the chances of the *saiban'in* system to function smoothly in contemporary Japan are significantly higher than those of the pre-war jury system. First, the *saiban'in* system is based on the Continental-European mixed-court model of jury trials, which is more compatible with the inquisitorial elements of Japan's criminal procedure than the Anglo-American jury. Second, the elements that distinguish Japan's *saiban'in* system from the mixed-court systems used in civil law countries are not as fundamental as those aspects that differentiated Japan's pre-war jury from its adversarial counterpart. The provisions of the Lay Judge Act, which stipulate that unlike German lay assessors Japanese lay participants will be selected at random and adjudicate only one case, are unlikely to undermine the power of the Japanese jury. In fact, this modification may allow Japan's mixed-court jury system to avoid some of the limitations of European mixed trials. Specifically, it has been argued that in those systems where lay participants are appointed to serve a fixed term, jurors no longer have a fresh eye and may therefore be unable to achieve the goal of limiting elite bias and injecting common reason into court proceedings.[299] Third, the pre-war jury system functioned against the background of rising fascism and increasing militarization, a situation that is substantially different from present-day circumstances.

To what extent will the introduction of the *saiban'in* system transform Japan's criminal justice system? It appears that in rejecting the idea to implement the Anglo-American model of jury trials and in choosing to "transplant" the Continental-European model of jury trials, albeit with some minor adaptations, the Japanese government maximized the potential of the new system to function smoothly in the existing system of criminal procedure in Japan and, by doing so, simultaneously lowered the potential of the new system to radically transform Japan's justice system. The presence of laypersons on the jury panel is likely to have a long-term effect on the way evidence is presented and on the way the prosecution and the defense argue their cases, but the effect of this change will not be as dramatic. However, it could have been, if the members of the jury were given the power to make final decisions on the verdict independently of the judge.

Conclusions

This chapter has focused on Japan's new lay judge system. It discussed the reasons behind the introduction of the new system and offered some preliminary conclusions with regard to the question of whether the *saiban'in* system may be expected to fulfill the goals stipulated by the JSRC and to function smoothly in contemporary Japan.

It argued that the *saiban'in* proposal was presented as a means for realizing comprehensive reform of the criminal justice system rather than as an end in itself. It concluded that the fast adoption of JSRC's idea to implement the jury system was due to the fact that the *saiban'in* reform was presented as critically important for the success of other criminal justice reforms that were widely seen as necessary and overdue. Specifically, the introduction of layperson participation was expected to help realize more concentrated trials, ensure that proceedings are based on the principle of orality, and achieve better justice by injecting common reason and limiting the elite bias of judges, while simultaneously serving to empower citizens.

At the end of the 20th century, there was consensus among the main actors that Japan's system of justice needed reform, and that this fact explains why JSRC's proposals attracted support on the part of business leaders, the general public, the LDP, and Prime Ministers Obuchi and Koizumi. The breadth of the issues covered by JSRC recommendations implied that each of the aforementioned groups could find a proposal that it would be in its interest to support. As the *saiban'in* system was placed at the center of one of the clusters of JSRC-inspired reforms, the groups agreeing with the idea of justice system reform extended their support to the jury system proposal.

With regard to the question of whether the new system may be expected to function smoothly in contemporary Japan, the *saiban'in* system, being based on the Continental-European rather than the Anglo-American model of jury trials, has a higher chance to take root than the pre-war jury system. The chapter concluded that in rejecting the idea to implement an unadapted Anglo-American model of jury trials and in choosing to transplant the Continental-European model of jury trials with some minor adaptations the Japanese

---

299 Lempert, "Citizen Participation in Judicial Decision Making", p. 11.

government maximized the potential of the new system to function smoothly in the existing system of criminal procedure in Japan and, by doing so, simultaneously lowered the potential of the new system to radically transform Japan's justice system.

Having looked at the past and present experiences of Japan with the institution of jury service, this book next reexamines the research questions set forth in Chapter 1 and summarizes the findings of this book.

7 Conclusions

Why does legal reform happen, and what are the determinants of success and failure of a legal initiative? This book began by highlighting these two questions that are central to the ongoing academic debate regarding the origins and nature of law. It proposed to look at the various attempts – successful and failed – to implement the institution of jury service in Japan in an effort to find answers to these questions.

This book traced the history of the concept of jury service in Japan from the point of arrival of the first documents describing the features of trial by laypersons to contemporary times. It discovered that while the idea of allowing laypersons to participate in the adjudication of cases may have first reached Japan as early as the 8th century AD through Chinese classical texts, the notion of the jury as a legal institution was first introduced to the country in the middle of the 19th century when Japan turned its attention to learning from the West. This study examined a series of proposals that led to the implementation of the jury system in Japan and those that did not result in the introduction of the system of layperson participation in the judicial process.

The case studies that involved instances when the idea to implement jury trials was realized (the "bureaucratic jury" and the "all-judge jury" experiments of the *Meiji* period; the early *Shōwa*-period jury system; the jury system in Okinawa under the U.S. occupation; and the *saiban'in* system) are particularly interesting because they provide ample material not only for analyzing the factors that made particular reform possible, but also for evaluating the functioning of the systems that were introduced and for determining the reasons for the success or failure of the implemented models to take root in Japan. The proposals that suggested introducing the jury trial system in Japan at different times in history, but failed to attract sufficient support to be realized (the suggestion made by the Ministry of Justice to introduce the all-layperson jury system in the *Meiji* period that was rejected in favor of the *sanza* system; Boissonade's proposal; the numerous proposals to implement trial by jury in the immediate post-war period; and the discussion of the possibility of introducing the jury system in the 1960s and 1980s) are also important, however, because they help to broaden our understanding of the factors that need to be in place in order for a reform proposal to succeed.

This final chapter reexamines the questions set forth in Chapter 1 and summarizes the findings of the book.

Why was the jury system introduced (or not introduced) at different times in Japan's history?

This section first discusses the proposals that were realized and led to the implementation of the jury system in Japan and then examines the initiatives that were rejected.

Cases of successful implementation of the jury system in Japan (Why was the jury system introduced?)

The experimentations with the concept of jury trials in the early Meiji period

The first attempt to implement the jury system that resulted in reform in Japan was triggered by the emergence of a criminal case that involved clashes of interest between different Ministries and therefore – in the opinion of Japan's Ministry of Justice (the Ministry) – necessitated the introduction of a neutral party that would participate in the trial and add legitimacy to the verdict. The Ministry discussed the question of whether the Western layperson jury might be used to fulfill the role of such a neutral party, but ultimately decided against merely copying either the Anglo-American model or the Continental-European model of jury trials. Instead, the government tried to adapt the Western concept of jury trials to suit the political, social, and cultural environment in *Meiji*-period Japan.

This study has argued that both of the adapted models used in *Meiji* Japan – the "bureaucratic jury" (*sanza*) and the "all-judge" special jury – reflected the Ministry's perception that allowing laypersons to participate in the adjudication of difficult cases might potentially damage the legitimacy of the verdict in a culture of "Respect for Officials and Contempt for the People" (*kanson minpi*), while bureaucrats and judges, the elite of the society, were seen as a group that could add to the authority of the court. This study noted that this first successful attempt to implement the two modified versions of jury trials was led by the elites and did not involve any public discussion.

The pre-war Jury Act

MAINLAND JAPAN

The second successful attempt to introduce the jury system in Japan culminated in the promulgation of the Jury Act of 1923. This study has concluded that the jury system was introduced in Japan in the 1920s because of the following three factors. The first was the growing demand for the expansion of rights on the part of the general public and on the part of the attorneys working in the Japanese justice system – a factor that was not present in the *Meiji* period when the "bureaucratic jury" and the "all-judge jury" were introduced by the elites in two civilian trials. The second was the increasing dissatisfaction, shared by the users of the legal system and by the members of the legal profession, with the quality of justice administered by judges alone in Japan. The third factor concerned the views and attitudes of the government. The government of Prime Minister Hara saw the introduction of layperson participation in the justice system as a concession that it could make in order to ensure that the attention of the public would be swayed from demanding further expansion of political rights, most notably the right to vote. This study concluded that the Jury Act of 1923 would not have been enforced had a major political party – the *Rikken Seiyūkai* – and its leader, Prime Minister Hara, not designated jury reform as one of the important items on the political agenda.

THE PRE-WAR JURY SYSTEM IN KARAFUTO

Karafuto was the only Japanese colony where the jury system was implemented in the pre-war period. This study has concluded that the decision to extend the application of the system to this and not to any other Japanese colonial possessions stemmed from the realization that the legal system established in Karafuto was almost identical to that of mainland Japan. This was seen as a powerful indication that the jury system, if introduced on the island, would function as in mainland Japan. The fact that the composition of the population in Karafuto was very similar to that of the island of Hokkaido was interpreted to imply that the Jury Act could be enforced efficiently in Karafuto without any modifications.

Karafuto was the most integrated of all of the Japanese colonies, and this meant that the central government did not need to concern itself with the possibility of this colony attempting to achieve greater self-rule or cede from the empire. In this situation, extending the right to jury service to those persons who lived in Karafuto was not expected to lead to any consequences that could potentially be at odds with the primary objective of the colonial authorities – that is, to protect the integrity of the empire.

The jury system in Okinawa

The third instance of the implementation of the jury trial system was the case of Okinawa under the U.S. occupation. Unlike the "bureaucratic" and "all-judge" jury systems of the *Meiji* period and the pre-war jury system, the jury system in Okinawa was introduced not only in criminal trials but also in civil trials. Another difference between this case study and the ones that preceded it in Japan's history was that Okinawa's experience unfolded in the situation of the occupation. The decision to introduce the jury system originated in the U.S. Civil Administration of the Ryukyu Islands. The fact that the introduction of the jury system in Okinawa was based on the unilateral decision of the U.S. occupation forces – the ruling elite – and did not involve active deliberations in the wider society made this case study similar to the case of the *sanza* system in *Meiji* Japan. Unlike the *sanza* system, however, the jury system in Okinawa was introduced not on a one-time basis in trials of exceptional complexity, but continuously.

This study has found that the U.S. administration of Okinawa introduced the jury system solely because it recognized the need to ensure that the constitutional rights of U.S. citizens stationed on the islands and of their dependents were protected. It showed that the reversal of several USCAR court verdicts on the grounds that the defendants holding U.S. citizenship had been denied their constitutional right to be tried by jury motivated the occupation forces to implement the reform. Hesitant to "transplant" the institution of jury service to courts in the Government of the Ryukyu Islands (GRI) that adjudicated cases involving Okinawans and Japanese in accordance with the Japanese laws, the U.S. administration limited the implementation of the jury system only to cases that involved U.S. citizens and were tried at USCAR courts.

The lay judge (saiban'in) system

The latest successful attempt to expand the participation of laypersons in the judicial process in Japan is the *saiban'in* system, introduced in 2009. Unlike the previous experimentations with the concept of jury trials in Japan, this new system is based not on the Anglo-American model of jury trials, but on the Continental-European mixed-court model.

This study has argued that the proposal to introduce the *saiban'in* system was successful at attracting the support of the general public, the members of the legal profession, of the ruling Liberal Democratic Party (LDP), and of Prime Ministers Obuchi and Koizumi because it was discussed not as an isolated idea, but as a recommendation the implementation of which was presented as central to the success of a broad and ambitious plan to radically revamp Japan's system of justice.

The notion that Japan's legal system needed reform, in turn, found support in the Japanese society because of the following factors. First, the proposals by the Judicial System Reform Council (JSRC) that outlined the principles of justice system reform were published at a time when Japan's business and political circles as well as the three branches of the legal profession had reached consensus that it was necessary for Japan to drastically reform its system of justice. Second, the sense of urgency about reform was precipitated by the erroneous verdicts that were brought to light in the 1980s and the realization that in the situation of increasing internationalization that was bound to bring about new challenges that Japan had not faced previously, postponing the restructuring of Japan's legal system any further was impossible. Third, the fact that JSRC's recommendations to transform the justice system of Japan included the idea to replace the vague principles of administrative guidance with a system of clear and transparent rules served to attract the support of the business community for the idea to revamp the justice system of Japan. Fourth, the change from the *Shōwa* to the *Heisei* era and the start of the new millennium provided the psychological incentive for reform by implying that Japan needed a new start. The aforementioned factors attracted the attention of Prime Ministers Obuchi and Koizumi. The support of these two politicians and of the ruling LDP, in turn, added credibility to the claim that Japan's justice system needed change.

There are parallels to be drawn between the factors that contributed to the success of the proposal to introduce the jury system in contemporary and pre-war Japan. In both cases the general public questioned the quality of justice as administered by judges alone. In addition, both instances involved the support of charismatic politicians (Prime Minister Hara in the pre-war period and Prime Ministers Obuchi and Koizumi in contemporary times).

Cases involving proposals to introduce the jury system that were rejected (Why was the jury system not introduced?)

Boissonade's proposal: provisions concerning the jury in the draft of the Code of Criminal Instruction

The first unsuccessful attempt to introduce the jury system in *Meiji*-period Japan was initiated by the Western scholar and advisor to the *Meiji* government Emile Gustave Boissonade de Fontarabie. Boissonade's 1879 draft of Japan's Code of Criminal Instruction proposed to implement the layperson rather than "bureaucratic" or "judge-only" jury systems in Japan.

This study has argued that the lack of appreciation for the benefits of layperson participation and the general perception that the jury was not an institution that was indispensable for Japan's modernization efforts constituted one reason behind the failure of Boissonade's proposal. The inability to attract support from the political elite and from the interest groups was another. While the "prestige" of the "exporters" of the concept of jury service – the Western countries – was very high at the time when Boissonade's draft was considered, the fact that not all Western countries used the jury system was interpreted by the Meiji government to imply that the institution of jury service was not central to the process of modernization and therefore not among the essential institutions to import. In addition, the government and the general public expressed concerns regarding the quality of decisions that laypersons would make in the course of the trial, if the jury system was introduced. In the absence of the prevailing feeling of dissatisfaction regarding the quality of justice as

218 *Conclusions*

administered by judges alone, there was no incentive to push for the implementation of the layperson jury system. Furthermore, at the time when Boissonade's draft was discussed, the demand for the democratic values that the implementation of the jury system entails was very low, which contributed to the formation of the view that the jury system was merely an expensive and superfluous institution.

The proposals to implement the jury system in Taiwan

The jury system was never introduced in Taiwan during the period of Japanese colonial rule despite the attempts on the part of Taiwan's first political party – the Taiwan Popular Party (*Taiwan Minshutō*) – to start a debate concerning this possibility.

This book has argued that the jury system was never introduced in Taiwan due to a number of factors. First, unlike Karafuto, Taiwan remained a legally separate entity within the empire throughout the period of Japanese rule. Second, the majority of the island's population was non-Japanese, which implied that if the system were to be implemented on the island, its features would most likely need to be modified in order to ensure that it would function effectively in the new environment. Making such modifications would have required an investment in terms of time. In a situation where the elite on the island were demanding greater self-rule, introducing a system that could serve to empower the colonized people was not in the interest of the central government of Japan.

Post-war proposals to introduce the jury system under the Allied occupation

This study has demonstrated that the debate concerning the possibility of introducing the jury trial system in the immediate post-war period originated in the Japanese society and was later brought up by the occupation forces. This study has argued that the Japanese government opposed the idea of introducing the jury system for the following three reasons. First, the jury system was seen as a costly institution to maintain. Second, the failure of the pre-war jury system dissuaded the government from having another jury experiment. Third, in the immediate post-war period the necessary infrastructure for the implementation of the jury system was lacking. SCAP, on the other hand, did not view the introduction of the jury system as an absolute priority and chose not to impose it on the Japanese government. This study has concluded that the proposal to implement the jury system failed to attract the support of the general public and of any political figures because the factors cited by the Japanese government against the implementation of the jury trial system reflected the objective reality and were therefore convincing for the majority of the public and for the political establishment. It concluded that Japan had neither the institutional capacity nor the economic stability necessary for the implementation of the jury system in the immediate post-war period.

The discussion of the possibility of introducing the jury system in the 1960s and the 1980s

The idea to introduce the jury system enjoyed the spotlight again in the 1960s and in the 1980s. This study has found that the discussion in the 1960s was merely a continuation of the occupation-period deliberations. The debate of the 1960s ultimately came to a standstill because it did not involve any specific proposals, but was confined to the theoretical debate among academics regarding the constitutionality of the institution of jury service.

In the 1980s, the discussion was not merely theoretical, but involved several proposals outlining the details of the new system of layperson participation that Japan could introduce. These proposals failed to attract the attention of the general public and of politicians, however. This study has concluded that while at around this time the erroneous verdicts in several high profile cases came to be widely discussed, the members of the general public and the government had not yet reached the consensus that Japan's system of justice needed sweeping reform. The fact that in the 1980s the idea to implement jury trials was presented as an isolated proposal and not as a part of a broad package of reforms that were widely perceived as necessary has also contributed to the failure of the proposals. The reality that the virtues of the jury system were not widely discussed at that time in Japan also helps explain why the proposals written in the 1980s did not succeed at leading the general public to embrace the idea of citizen participation in justice.

What were the determinants of success and failure of Japan's past experiences with the jury system and how does the lay judge (*saiban'in*) system fare with regard to these parameters?

This section summarizes the findings of this study regarding the cases that involved the implementation of the jury system at different times in Japan's history.

The "bureaucratic jury" (sanza) and the "judge-only" jury systems of the Meiji period

The modified versions of jury trials used in the *Meiji* period were used in an extremely limited number of cases and on a one-time basis. This fact makes it difficult to comprehensively assess whether the "bureaucratic jury" and the "judge-only" jury systems functioned effectively or not. This study has concluded that while these models had the potential of adding legitimacy to verdicts in controversial cases, it is doubtful that they would function effectively in the long run without any adjustments.

This study has argued that the decision to "bureaucratize" the jury made it impossible to make use of the positive features that layperson participation in the justice system affords. The decisions of the "bureaucratic" and "judge-only" jury remained susceptible to elite bias. In addition, the ability of *Meiji*-period jury panels to return completely neutral verdicts was limited. It was the Ministry of Justice that appointed the members of the *sanza* and the "judge-only" panels; therefore, there was the possibility that the Ministry could manipulate the outcome of deliberations by nominating only those members whose opinions were in line with those of the Ministry. These limitations would most likely have been identified and possibly subsequently corrected had the *sanza* and the "judge-only" jury been used for a longer period of time. Regarding the decision to implement the "adapted" versions of jury trials only on a one-time basis, this study has concluded that this was most likely done to lessen the risks associated with the introduction of the new institution. Indeed, if there were any serious problems associated with the new institution, the *sanza* and the "all-judge" jury could be immediately abolished.

The pre-war jury system

This study has shown that while at the beginning of its functioning the pre-war jury system contributed to improving the quality of justice in Japan, the institution of jury service never became popular with the users of the system. After 1929, more and more defendants waived their right to jury trial, while those of the accused who could request to be tried by jury chose not to do so. Neither the legal actors nor the users of the system saw any benefits in using the jury system. This implied that the system was destined to be eventually abolished, if left unreformed.

This book concluded that there were external as well as internal factors that contributed to the demise of the pre-war jury system in Japan. The external factors concerned the changes in the political environment in Japan, while the internal factors were related to the problems within the Jury Act.

The changes in the external environment in which the jury system operated included the change from the movement towards democratization of the first decades of the 20th century to increasing militarization and fascism. As the result of its increasingly aggressive foreign policy, Japan found itself at war, which provided the direct motive for the suspension of the jury system. In the situation of war, the jury was seen as too costly to maintain and there was a lack of prospective jurors, as the overwhelming majority of men over the age of thirty holding Japanese citizenship had joined the army.

Equally important to the fate of the pre-war jury system were the problems within the Jury Act. This study has argued that the pre-war Jury Act was a modified version of the Anglo-American model of jury trials. It concluded that the drafters of the Jury Act tried to adapt the adversarial jury system to the principles of inquisitorial procedure (through adding provisions that allowed the judge to continue to make final decisions on the guilt or innocence of the accused), to the political environment of militaristic Japan (through denying access to jury trials to the adherents of communist and socialist ideologies), and to the features of Japan's hierarchical society (through limiting the powers of the jury and magnifying the role of the judge in proceedings). This study found that contrary to the intentions of the drafters of the Jury Act, these "adaptations" became the stumbling blocks that prevented the pre-war jury system from functioning effectively. The provisions allowing the judge to disregard the verdicts of the jury served to further undermine the authority of trial by laypersons, while the stipulations that did not allow criminal defendants who were most interested in being tried by jury – the adherents of the socialist and communist ideologies – to request jury trial and made trial by professional judges more advantageous for all other defendants ensured that the jury system would not be used often. This book concluded that in their effort to rid the concept of jury trials of the "vices" of the Western model of jury trials and to ensure that it functioned smoothly in Japan's political and cultural environment, the drafters of the pre-war Jury Act deprived Japan's jury system of all the "virtues" as well. In the sense that the adaptations made by the Japanese government affected the ability of the jury system to function effectively, the case study of the pre-war jury system resembled the *Meiji*-period experimentations with the jury trial system.

The jury system in Okinawa under the U.S. occupation

The jury system introduced in USCAR courts in Okinawa under the U.S. occupation is yet another example of an "adapted" model of the Anglo-American jury system.

Unlike the previous two cases – the *Meiji*-period experimentations and the pre-war Jury Act – the modifications were minimal in occupied Okinawa. The adaptations made to the jury system when it was transplanted to Okinawa included only the lifting of the nationality requirement for jury service and the addition of the requirement of English-language proficiency.

This study has argued that the limited extent of changes made to the adversarial model of jury trials was due to the fact that the jury system was introduced only in USCAR courts, which carried out proceedings in a manner that was similar to that of the courts in the United States. In Okinawa, the United States "transplanted" not only the isolated institution of jury service, but the whole of its legal system to USCAR courts. The United States has a long experience of using trial by jury, therefore, the institution of jury system was compatible with the institutional culture of the section of Okinawa's two-tiered court system where it was implemented (USCAR courts).

This study has concluded that the fact that the adaptations made to the American jury trial system upon its transplantation to USCAR courts did not affect the substance of the concept of trial by jury ensured the smooth functioning of the jury system in Okinawa.

The lay judge (saiban'in) *system*

This study has demonstrated that just like the past experiences of Japan with the institution of jury service, this latest attempt did not involve mere copying of a model already being used in other countries. As in the cases of the implementation of the *sanza* and of the "judge-only" systems of the *Meiji* period, the pre-war jury system of the late *Taishō* and early *Shōwa* periods, and the jury in Okinawa under the U.S. occupation, the *saiban'in* system featured elements of adaptation. This study has argued that like the pre-war jury system, Japan's new mixed-court jury is a unique cross between the Continental-European and the Anglo-American common law jury. Unlike the previous cases of introduction of the jury trial system in Japan, however, the new *saiban'in* system is based not on the Anglo-American but on the Continental-European model of jury trials. The inclusion of the elements that distinguish Japan's *saiban'in* mixed-court jury system from other Continental-European systems, such as asking jurors to serve on one case only rather than be nominated by the local authorities to serve a fixed term, was motivated by the desire to limit the burden of responsibility for jurors.

What do Japan's previous experiences with the institution of jury service tell us regarding the prospects of the new *saiban'in* system to function smoothly? This study has found that in the past the jury system tended to function smoothly when the adaptations made to the model of jury trials that Japan chose to adopt did not affect the core of the original model, when the political, social, and economic situations in Japan were stable, and when prospective jurors did not protest against serving. Japan's new *saiban'in* system is based on the Continental-European mixed-court model of jury trials, which is more compatible with the inquisitorial elements of Japan's criminal procedure than the Anglo-American jury. In addition, the adaptations made to the Continental-European model of jury trials are not as fundamental as to affect the quality of citizen participation. This study has argued that the provisions of Japan's Lay Judge Act that stipulate that the members of the jury will be selected at random and try only one case rather than be appointed to serve a fixed term are unlikely to undermine the power of the Japanese jury. These "adaptations" might actually serve to enable the Japanese jury to avoid some of the limitations of the Continental-European model of jury trials. While German lay assessors who are appointed to serve a fixed term have been accused of no longer having a fresh eye, due to the accumulation of their experiences in adjudicating cases together with professional judges, the members of the Japanese jury panel who serve on one case only may be in a better position to help limit elite bias of professional judges and inject common reason into proceedings.

Furthermore, unlike the situation of the pre-war Jury Act that was enforced against the background of rising fascism and militarization, the new lay judge system was introduced in a democratic society. Contemporary Japan possesses the necessary infrastructure to ensure that the new system functions smoothly. This is in sharp contrast to the immediate post-war situation – for example, when the proposal to implement trials by jury was rejected because there was the need to rebuild courtrooms and other facilities first.

Finally, this study has found that the results of polls indicate that while perspective jurors in Japan are not particularly enthusiastic about serving on *saiban'in* panels, the majority are nevertheless planning to appear in court, if summoned to serve, despite the fact that several scholars and organizations have urged citizens to boycott the new system.

This study has concluded that all of the aforementioned points seem to indicate that the new system is likely to function smoothly. At the same time, it argued that the *saiban'in* system is less likely to serve as a tool for radically transforming Japan's criminal justice system and empower Japanese citizens than the Anglo-American all-layperson jury system. Proving that the defendant is guilty beyond a reasonable doubt to a group of laypersons who would be reaching their decision independently of the judge requires a greater change in strategy on the part of the defense counsel and the prosecutor than making the same case to a mixed-court panel where professional judges participate in the deliberation process together with laypersons. After all, in the latter situation as long as the prosecution or defense succeeds at persuading professional judges of the validity of a certain argument they may expect that that point would have a bearing on the final verdict. This would not necessarily be the case, if the jury panel consisted of laypersons alone. An argument that is presented in a manner that is difficult to understand for non-professionals may be completely ignored by the all-layperson jury. In addition, the introduction of the jury system that would allow jurors to reach their decisions independently of the judge would arguably serve to empower citizens more than the implementation of the mixed-court jury system where the responsibility for making decisions would be shared with professional judges.

This study has concluded that in rejecting the idea of implementing the Anglo-American model of jury trials and in choosing to "transplant" the Continental-European model of jury trials instead, albeit with some minor adaptations, the Japanese government maximized the potential of the *saiban'in* system to function smoothly in the existing system of criminal procedure in Japan and, by doing so, simultaneously lowered the potential of the lay judge system to radically transform the way justice is administered in Japan.

A summary of findings: revisiting the two approaches to analyzing legal change

This study examined Japan's experiences with the institution of jury service through exploring two approaches to the analysis of the nature of legal change.

The first approach was based on Alan Watson's conceptualization of legal change. It proposed to look at the efforts – successful and failed – to implement the institution of jury service in Japan as examples of legal transplants. This perspective was based on the supposition that the institution of jury service would be introduced merely because of the decision of the government to "import" this institution from another country and not due to any changes that the Japanese society was undergoing. It predicted that the jury system would be successfully transplanted, if the following two conditions were satisfied. First, there had to be a "fit" between the imported institution and the host environment at the micro and macro levels – that is, the transplanted institution needed to complement the pre-existing legal infrastructure and the pre-existing institutions in the host country. Second, law reformers initially responsible for the transplant and the members of the legal profession needed to be sufficiently enthusiastic and motivated not only about the introduction of this new institution, but also about making sure that it would work well.

The socio-legal approach to analyzing legal change proposed to look at Japan's experiences with the institution of jury service from the perspective of the interaction between society and law and held that a legal reform would be successful, if it reflected the processes occurring in the society and was not in conflict with them. This approach predicted that the institution of jury service could only be expected to be introduced, if there was the demand in the society for the expansion of rights. It held that the jury system would function effectively when the society in which it operated was moving in the direction of democratization and the expansion of rights of citizens and that the system would stagnate, if the society developed in the opposite direction.

Both of these approaches provide us with unique insights regarding the questions addressed in this book.

All of Japan's experiences with the jury system involved "adopting" from foreign jurisdictions and attempting to "adapt" the imported concept to ensure that it would fit in with the pre-existing institutions. The strategy of adapting when adopting concerned not only the history of the institution of jury service in Japan, but characterized the whole process of the development of Japan's modern legal system, which the opening sections of Chapters 2 through 6 have traced. The discussion of the historical background in this study demonstrated that in the period from the *Meiji* Restoration to the contemporary times the changes in Japan's legal system involved learning about Western institutions and concepts, choosing those that were most needed to fulfill Japan's objectives at that point in time, and transforming the original models or institutions in a way that would fit the pre-existing environment and traditions of the country. The case of occupied Okinawa was unique in that the development of the legal system there was based on the decisions made by the U.S. occupation and therefore reflected the objectives of the U.S. administration rather than those of the local population. Despite this difference, however, the reforms carried out in Okinawa under the U.S. occupation also involved the transplantation of American concepts and institutions. This fact makes the framework proposed by Alan Watson highly relevant to the analysis of Japan's experiences with the institution of jury service.

The attempts to introduce the jury system in Japan – successful and failed – at different times in history support Watson's theory that for a transplanted institution to work well, it needs to complement the pre-existing legal infrastructure of the host society. Watson's theory accurately predicts that the jury system in Okinawa would function smoothly because it was essentially an Anglo-American adversarial jury operating in a system of justice that was remarkably similar to that of the United States. Being used to the institution of jury service, the American members of the legal profession working in Okinawa were in the position to ensure that this system would work smoothly, and thus satisfied the second requirement for the successful functioning of a transplanted institution.

The "legal transplant" perspective suggested that the implementation of the twelve-layperson Anglo-American model of jury trials in the pre-war period would entail difficulty because Japan at that time was using the inquisitorial system of justice. According to Watson's conceptualization of legal change, to ensure that the Anglo-American jury system would function effectively in pre-war Japan it was necessary to either reform the inquisitorial system of justice in which this jury system was to operate, or to make drastic changes to the model of jury trials that Japan "imported". This study has shown that Japan chose the latter path, but ended up excessively "adjusting" the Anglo-American model of jury trials. The jury system, as implemented in pre-war Japan, was stripped off of any power and became a purely nominal institution that added little to the process of the administration of justice in Japan. The lack of enthusiasm on the part of the government after the jury system was implemented raised further doubts regarding the prospects of the new system to function effectively. This fact gives further credence to the applicability of Alan Watson's hypothesis to the analysis of the case of the pre-war jury system in Japan.

The experimentations of Japan with the institution of jury service in the *Meiji* period (the *sanza* and the "all-judge" jury) may also be interpreted as attempts to adjust the model of jury trials to fit Japan's system of justice rather than do the opposite – that is, change the external environment to make it possible for the unadjusted model of jury trials to function smoothly. The latest attempt to implement the jury trial system – the *saiban'in* system – initially appeared to be reversing this trend. After all, the JSRC and later the Japanese government stated that the goal of the latest round of reforms was to radically change the way criminal justice was administered in the country. The introduction of the new jury system was proclaimed to be a means for reaching this aim. This study has demonstrated, however, that the *saiban'in* system may be looked upon as an "adapted" Continental-European model of jury trials that is designed to work smoothly within Japan's legal system and is therefore not as likely to produce drastic changes as the "un-adapted" Anglo-American model of jury trials. Regarding the future prospects of the *saiban'in* system, Alan Watson's theory predicts that while there are no significant clashes between the features of this new "transplant" and the legal system in which it will operate, the enthusiasm on the part of the government and of the general public will be critical for the success of this reform.

The "legal transplant" approach helps explain the seemingly puzzling fact that all of Japan's experiences with the institution of jury service involved the implementation of systems that were unique in the world. In accordance with Watson's thesis, the modifications that Japan made to either the Anglo-American or the Continental-European models of jury trials may be understood as deliberate efforts to ensure macro and micro "fit" with the host environment. The theory of legal transplants also sheds light on the reasons behind the strong opposition to implementing trial by laypersons and especially to the idea of allowing jurors to decide the fate of the accused independently of the judge that has featured prominently in the history of this institution in Japan. Japan rejected the proposals to introduce trials by laypersons in the *Meiji* period (Boissonade's proposal), during the discussions with SCAP after World War II (Captain Maniscalco's and other proposals), and during the debate regarding the possibility of implementing all-layperson trials in the 1960s and 1980s as well as during the early stages of deliberations by the JSRC when, again, the suggestion to implement independent jury trials was dismissed. The suppositions of the "legal transplant" perspective suggest that the lack of enthusiasm on the part of the Japanese government in all of the aforementioned situations stemmed from the understanding that Japan should not introduce a system that is essentially incompatible with the principles of justice that the country was using at that time.

On the other hand, this study has found that the failures and successes of Japan's past experiences with the institution of jury service cannot be explained fully by the presence or absence of "fit" between the model of jury trials that Japan tried to adopt and the institutional environment in which this system was to operate alone. The socio-legal perspective that emphasizes the importance of the developments in the society is also highly relevant to the analysis of Japan's experiences with the institution of jury service.

The conceptualization of the "bureaucratic jury" and the "judge-only jury" systems of the *Meiji* period may be understood in the context of efforts to learn about the West and try to adopt the essence of Western concepts, which was the overarching trend characterizing not only the development of Japan's legal system, but also its political and social systems during the period that followed the *Meiji* Restoration.

The socio-legal perspective sheds light on the reasons why the pre-war Jury Act was introduced and later suspended. This approach predicts that a reform may be expected to be implemented, if it reflects the development trends of the wider society. As this study has demonstrated, the realization of the idea to expand layperson participation in the justice system of pre-war Japan would have been unlikely had it not been accompanied by the movement towards democratization. After all, the proposal to introduce jury trials came to the fore of public debate in the late *Meiji*-early *Taishō* periods in connection with the Japan Federation of Bar Associations' desire to improve the rights of the accused and to add strength to the position of defense lawyers in Japan. Further, as this study has shown, the idea to introduce jury trials was deliberated and finally adopted against the background of the strengthening of the position of elected bodies in Japan and the expansion of the political involvement of the general public. The socio-legal approach to legal change helps explain why the pre-war jury system failed to function successfully and was suspended in 1943 equally well. When the pre-war Jury Act was enforced in 1928 Japan had already begun moving in the direction of increased militarization and fascism – a direction that was diametrically opposed to that of the developments of Japan during the period of "*Taishō* Democracy" that produced the reform introducing the jury system.

This approach also helps explain why the idea to introduce the *saiban'in* system was realized in contemporary Japan. As this study has demonstrated, the proposal to implement the jury system was deliberated against the background of the increasing demands for deregulation and greater citizen empowerment. Citizen empowerment through the introduction of the jury system was presented as one of the important "pillars" of the comprehensive reform of Japan's legal system. With regard to the future prospects of this latest experience of Japan with the institution of jury service, the socio-legal theories predict that in the event Japan continues on the democratic path and implements further measures aimed at promoting the transformation of the Japanese people from "governed subjects to governing subjects",[1] and if the new system is viewed upon favorably – or at least not in a strongly negative light – by prospective jurors, then the *saiban'in* system may be expected to function without disruption.

The only case study among the many examined in this book the analysis of which does not significantly benefit from the suppositions of the socio-legal approach is the experience of Okinawa. After all, in Okinawa, the jury system was implemented in the situation of the occupation, in accordance with the objectives and for their benefit of the occupying forces. The jury reform, therefore, did not reflect the developments in the Okinawan society. In all other cases discussed in this study, however, the suppositions of the socio-legal perspective find their confirmation.

This study has concluded that the socio-legal approach is applicable not only to discussing the case studies involving the implementation of jury trials in Japan, but also to analyzing the attempts to introduce the jury system that were rejected. According to socio-legal theories, the decision to reject Boissonade's proposal in the *Meiji* period reflected the fact that there

---

1 Recommendations of the Judicial System Reform Council, chap. 1.

was very weak demand for the expansion of rights in general and for the introduction of the jury system in particular among the general public, the members of the legal profession, and on the part of the Japanese government. By contrast, post-war proposals to implement the jury system in Japan (Captain Maniscalco's and other proposals) were discussed with SCAP and within the Japanese government against the backdrop of the movement towards democratization, but ended up not being implemented because the institution of jury service was not seen as an absolute priority in terms of democratizing the Japanese society by either the Allied occupation or the Japanese government. Neither did the proposals written in the 1980s lead to the introduction of the jury system, this time because the consensus on the part of the general public, the government, and the members of the legal profession regarding the necessity of such a reform had not yet been formed.

This book has concluded that in analyzing the questions set forth in this study both Alan Watson's theory of legal transplants and the socio-legal approach to legal change are indispensable and offer unique insights.

The principle findings of this book are as follows. First, the history of the institution of jury service unfolded in Japan within the context of the development of the country's modern legal system. Second, all case studies featuring the implementation of the jury system in Japan involved borrowing from other jurisdictions and adaptation of the original, borrowed concept to fit into the existing environment in Japan, with the "environment" as used here including Japan's legal system, political situation, traditions, and cultural values. Third, the proposals to introduce the jury system in Japan were rejected at different times in Japan's history because there was either a lack of understanding and appreciation of the virtues of this institution (as was the case in the *Meiji* period), or the absence of the necessary infrastructure (as in the immediate post-war period), or because the popular demand for this reform was insufficient (as in the 1980s). Fourth, the idea to implement the jury system resulted in reform in the absence of the aforementioned obstacles and in the presence of political support (Prime Minister Hara and the *Rikken Seiyūkai* in pre-war Japan and Prime Ministers Obuchi and Koizumi and the LDP in contemporary Japan) and of the consensus among the members of the general public and the legal profession that reform was necessary for fulfilling certain goals that were perceived as important (improvement of the quality of justice and expansion of rights/citizen empowerment in pre-war and contemporary Japan). Fifth, the institution of jury service tended to function smoothly when there were no significant clashes between the features of the implemented model of the jury trials and the system of justice used (the Anglo-American model of jury trials in adversarial USCAR courts in Okinawa) and when the "adaptations" made by the Japanese statesmen of either the Anglo-American or the Continental-European models of jury trials did not affect the core of these models or diminish their internal integrity (Japan's pre-war Jury Act undermined the true power of the jury by making it possible for the judge to disregard the jury's findings, and this fact contributed to the lack of popularity of jury trials).

All of these insights are relevant to the ongoing debate regarding the origins and nature of law. They shed light on the central questions of this debate: why does legal reform happen and what are the determinants of success and failure of a legal initiative? This book began by referring to these questions. It now concludes by highlighting the answers that the evidence provided by the examination of Japan's attempts – successful and failed – to implement the institution of jury service offers.

Bibliography

Primary materials

(1) *Primary materials on file with the national diet library, Tokyo, Japan:* Primary Materials Available on Microfiche:

Bibliography of Materials on the Laws and Administrative Organization of Japan Compiled under the Direction of the Office of Provost Marshall General Military Government Division, Liaison and Studies Branch, not dated, Declassified E.O. 12065 Section 3–402/NNDG No. 775011 (National Archives and Records Service), microformed on GHQ/SCAP Records (RG 331), Box No. 1461, Folder No. 8, on file with the National Diet Library (not allotted a code number).

CA Proclamation No. 12: Ryukyuan Court System, not dated, Record Group 260: Records of the US Civil Administration of the Ryukyu Islands (USCAR), Series Title: Records Set of Issuances, 1945–1972, Box No. 167 of HCRI-LN, microformed on USCAR Records, the Liaison Department, Records Set of Issuances, 1945–1972, Box No. 167, Folder No. 1, on file with the National Diet Library (code: USCAR 09135).

Colonel C. S. Ryers, 1946, Note Addressed to Commander-in-Chief, United States Army Forces, Pacific APO 500, "Recommendation for Award of the Legion of Merit", Declassified E.O. 12065 Section 3–402/NNDG No. 775009, on file with the Modern Japanese Political History Materials Room, the National Diet Library (code: G2 03783).

Japanese Court Summons to Ryukyuans, not dated, microformed on USCAR Records, the Liaison Department, 1602–03 Internal Political Activity Files, 1946–1972, Box No. 64, Folder No. 2, on file with the National Diet Library (code: USCAR 07787–0789).

Maniscalco, Anthony, not dated, Declassified E.O. 12065 Section 3–402/NNDG No. 775009 (National Archives and Records Service), microformed on GHQ/SCAP Records General Staff II, Public Safety Division, Miscellaneous File 1946–1950, Box No. 315, Folder No. 29, on file with the National Diet Library (code G2 03783).

Proposed Revision of Code of Criminal Procedure, not dated, Declassified E.O. 12065 Section 3–402/NNDG No. 775009, microformed on GHQ/SCAP Records General Staff II, Public Safety Division, Decimal File 1946–52, Box No. 263, Folder No. 10 (National Archives and Records Service), on file with the Modern Japanese Political History Materials Room, the National Diet Library (code G2 01180-G2 01182).

Proposed Revision of Law of Constitution of the Courts of Justice and Proposed Revision of the Jury Act, not dated, Declassified E.O. 12065 Section 3–402/NNDG No. 775009, microformed on HQ/SCAP Records General Staff II, Public Safety Division, General File 1946–1950, Box No. 289, Folder No. 21 (National Archives and Records Service), on file with the Modern Japanese Political History Materials Room, the National Diet Library (code: G2 02078–02079).

Proposed Revision of the Jury Act, not dated, Declassified E.O. 12065 Section 3–402/NNDG No. 775011 GHQ/SCAP Records (RG 331, National Archives and Records Service), microformed on GHQ/SCAP Records General Staff II, Public Safety Division, General File 1945–52, Box No. 370, Folder No. 16 (National Archives and Records Service), on file with the Modern Japanese Political History Materials Room, the National Diet Library (not allotted a code number).

Trials, not dated, Declassified E.O. 11652 Section 3(E) and 5(D) or (E) NNDG No. 775012, microformed on GHQ/SCAP Records (RG 331), GHQ/SCAP Records, Government Section, Central Files Branch, Summations, Documents, and Administrative Directives, 1946–1952, Box No. 2273, Folder No. 13 (National Archives and Records Service), on file with the Modern Japanese Political History Materials Room, the National Diet Library (code GS (B) 02882).

Trials, not dated, Declassified E.O. 11652 Section 3(E) and 5(D) or (E) NNDG No. 775012, microformed on GHQ/SCAP Records (RG 331), GHQ/SCAP Records, Government Section, Central Files Branch, Summations, Documents, and Administrative Directives, 1946–1952, Box No. 2273, Folder No. 13 (National Archives and Records Service), on file with the Modern Japanese Political History Materials Room, the National Diet Library (code GS (B) 02883).

Primary materials that have been scanned and made available online by the national diet library:

"Drafts of the Revised Constitution", February 1946, Hussey Papers: "24-A Draft of the 'Preamble' to the Revised Constitution" through "24-I Drafts of Chapter Ten, 'Supreme Law' of the Revised Constitution", YE-5, Roll No. 5, http://www.ndl.go.jp/constitution/e/shiryo/03/147shoshi.html.Fuse, T., 1945, "Kenpō Kaisei Shian" (Constitutional Reform Draft), December 22, http://www.ndl.go.jp/constitution/shiryo/02/050/050tx.html#t001.

Kenpō Kenkyūkai [The Constitution Research Group], 1945, "Kenpō Sōan Yōkō" [Outline of the Draft of the Constitution], December 27, http://www.ndl.go.jp/constitution/shiryo/02/052/052tx.html#t001.

Matsumoto, J., 1946, "Kenpō Kaisei Yōkō" [Gist of the Revision of the Constitution], February 8, http://www.ndl.go.jp/constitution/e/shiryo/03/074a/074a_001r.html.

"Memorandum to Chief, Government Section", 12 February, 1946, http://www.ndl.go.jp/constitution/e/shiryo/03/076a_e/076a_etx.html.Nihon Kyōsantō [Japanese Communist Party], 1946, "Nihon Jinmin Kyōwakoku Kenpō (Sōan)" [The Constitution of the People's Republic of Japan (A Draft)], June 26, http://www.ndl.go.jp/constitution/shiryo/02/119/119tx.html.

Nomura, J., 1945, "Kenpō Kaisei ni kansuru Ikensho" [Position Paper Regarding Constitutional Reform], December 26, http://www.ndl.go.jp/constitution/shiryo/02/051/051tx.html.

"Original Drafts of Committee Reports", February 1946, SCAP Files of Commander Alfred R. Hussey, Doc. No. 8, http://www.ndl.go.jp/constitution/e/shiryo/03/147shoshi.html. Public Administration Division, Government Section, SCAP, "Charles Kades' Comments on the Document 'Gist of the Revision of the Constitution' (Matsumoto Draft)", http://www.ndl.go.jp/constitution/e/shiryo/03/002_15/002_15_001r.html.

(2) Primary materials on file with the Okinawa Prefectural Archives (OPA), Naha, Japan:

Legal Affairs Department, 1970, "Talking Point: GRI Court Jurisdiction over U.S. Military Personnel", 20 July 1970 (code 0000025900).

(3) Case materials, on file with the University of the Ryukyus Library, Okinawa:

USCAR, "Civil Case 6 Far East Construction Service Inc. v. Tsuruko Robirds et al.".
USCAR, "Petit Jury for Civil Case C-1-62 Robirds v. Far Eastern Construction Co., 7–10 July 1964".
USCAR Appellate Court, "Jury Panel in the Robirds v. Far East Construction Co. Case".
USCAR Appellate Court, "Robirds v. Far East Construction Co.".
USCAR Superior Court, "Bennet Ken Ikeda v. Robert McNamara Case".
USCAR Superior Court, "Megumi Yoshihisa et al. – Homicide – 1".
USCAR Superior Court, "Megumi Yoshihisa et al. – Homicide – 2".
USCAR Superior Court, "Petit Jury for Bennett Ken Ikeda".
USCAR Superior Court, "Petit Jury for Megumi Yoshihisa Case et al. (1)".
USCAR Superior Court, "Petit Jury for Megumi Yoshihisa Case et al. (2)".
USCAR Superior Court, "Petit Jury for Megumi Yoshihisa Case et al. (3)".
USCAR Superior Court, "Petit Jury for Robirds v. [Far] East Construction Co. Case".

(4) Primary materials that have been scanned and made available online by other libraries:

The Japan P.E.N. Digital Library

Ōmeisha Kenpō Sōan [Ōmeisha's Draft of the Constitution], 1879, http://www.japanpen.or.jp/e-bungeikan/sovereignty/pdf/oumeisya.pdf.

Matsuyama University Digital Library

Nihon Koku Kenpō An [The Draft of the Constitution of the Japanese State], 1880, http://www.cc.matsuyama-u.ac.jp/~tamura/risshisyakennpou.htm.

Published works

Abramson, J., 2000, *We, the Jury: The Jury System and the Ideal of Democracy*, Cambridge: Harvard University Press.
Administrative Section Secretariat of the Legislature Government of the Ryukyu Islands, 1957, *USCAR Legislation: A Complete Collection of Outstanding Proclamations, Ordinances, and Directives with Amendments Thereto Issued by the United States Civil Administration of the Ryukyu Islands and Its Predecessors since 1945*, Naha, Okinawa: Administrative Section Secretariat of the Legislature Government of the Ryukyu Islands.
Akita, G., 1976, *Foundations of Constitutional Government in Modern Japan 1868–1900*, Cambridge: Harvard University Press.
Allott, A., 1981, "The Effectiveness of Law", *Valparaiso University Law Review*, Vol. 15, pp. 229–242.
Anderson, K., and Ambler, L., 2006, "The Slow Birth of Japan's Quasi-Jury System (*Saiban-in Seido*): Interim Report on the Road to Commencement", *Journal of Japanese Law*, Vol. 11, No. 21, pp. 55–80.
Anderson, K., and Nolan, M., 2004, "Lay Participation in the Japanese Justice System: A Few Preliminary Thoughts Regarding the Lay Assessor System (saiban-in seido) from Domestic Historical and International Psychological Perspectives", *Vanderbilt Journal of Transnational Law*, Vol. 37, pp. 966–973.

Anderson, K., and Saint, E., 2005, "Japan's Quasi-Jury (*Saiban'in*) Law: An Annotated Translation of the Act Concerning Participation of Law Assessors in Criminal Trials", *Asian-Pacific Law & Policy Journal*, Vol. 6, No. 1, pp. 233–283.

Angelino, D., 1931, *Colonial Policy*, The Hague: Nijhoff.

Anonymous, 1928, "Karafuto Chihō Saibansho ni okeru Baishin Mogi Saiban no Jikkyō" [The Progress of the Mock Jury Trial (Held) at the Karafuto District Court], *Hōritsu Shunjū*, Vol. 3, No. 11, pp. 91–93.

Anonymous, 1963, "Contemporary Practice of the United States Relating to International Law", *The American Journal of International Law*, Vol. 57, No. 4, pp. 894–919.

Anonymous, 1965, "Contemporary Practice of the United States Relating to International Law", *The American Journal of International Law*, Vol. 59, No. 4, pp. 921–926.

Anonymous, 1970, "Contemporary Practice of the United States Relating to International Law", *The American Journal of International Law*, Vol. 64, No. 3, pp. 631–652.

Aohiro, N. (ed.), 1963, *Iwanami Koza: Nihon Rekishi, Gendai-hen* [Iwanami Lectures: History of Japan, the Modern Era], Vol. 3, Tokyo: Iwanami Shoten.

Aoyama, Y., Noda, A., and Tanaka, S., 2000, "Shihō Seido Kaikaku ni Nani o Nozomu ka" [What to Expect of Judicial System Reform?], *Jurisuto*, No. 1170, pp. 2–28.

Appleton, R. B., 1949, "Reforms in Japanese Criminal Procedure under Allied Occupation", *Washington Law Review and State Bar Journal*, Vol. 24, pp. 401–430.

Aronson, B., 2014, "My Keyphrase for Understanding Japanese Law: Japan as a Normal Country . . . With Context", *Michigan State International Law Review*, Vol. 22, No. 3, pp. 816–837.

Auslin, M. R., 2004, *Negotiating with Imperialism: The Unequal Treaties and the Culture of Japanese Diplomacy*, Cambridge: Harvard University Press.

Baishin Seido Fukyū Kai [Society for the Promotion of the Jury System], 1927, *Baishin Hō no Jissai Chishiki: Baishin'in Hikkei* [Actual Knowledge Regarding the Jury Act: A Must-Have for Jurors], Tokyo: Kōshisha Shobō.

Barkan, S. E., 2009, *Law and Society: An Introduction*, Upper Saddle River, NJ: Prentice-Hall.

Baum, H., 1997, *Japan: Economic Success and Legal System*, New York: Walter de Gruyter.

Beckmann, G. M., 1962, *The Modernization of China and Japan*, New York: Harper & Row.

Beckmann, G. M., and Okubo, G., 1969, *The Japanese Communist Party: 1922–1945*, Stanford: Stanford University Press.

Beer, L. W. (ed.), 1992, *Constitutional Systems in Late Twentieth Century Asia*, Seattle: University of Washington Press.

Beer, L. W., and Itoh, H., 1996, *The Constitutional Case Law of Japan, 1970 through 1990*, Seattle: University of Washington Press.

Berenson, E., 1992, *The Trial of Madame Caillaux*, Berkeley: University of California Press.

Berkowitz, D., Pistor, K., and Richard, J., 2003, "The Transplant Effect", *American Journal of Comparative Law*, Vol. 51, pp. 163–202.

Berman, P. S. (ed.), 2005, *The Globalization of International Law*, Aldershot: Ashgate.

Black, H. C. (ed.), 1979, *Black's Law Dictionary*, St. Paul: West Publishing Co.

Black, J. R., 1881, *Young Japan: Yokohama and Yedo – A Narrative of the Settlement and the City from the Signing of the Treaties in 1858 to the Close of the Year 1879 with a Glance at the Progress of Japan During a Period of Twenty-One Years*, London: Trubner & Co.

Bloom, R. M., 2006, "Jury Trials in Japan", *Loyola of Los Angeles International & Comparative Law Review*, Vol. 28, pp. 35–68.

Bohannan, P., 1965, "The Differing Realms of the Law", *American Anthropologist*, Vol. 67, pp. 33–42.

Bohannan, P., 1967, *Law and Warfare: Studies in the Anthropology of Conflict*, New York: Natural History Press.

Boissonade, G. E. (translated by Mori, Y., and Iwano, S.), 1882, *Chizai Hō Sōan Chūshaku* [The Draft of the Code of Criminal Instruction Accompanied by a Commentary], Tokyo: Shihōsha.

Boissonade, G. E., 1882, *Projet de Code de Procedure Criminelle pour l'Empire du Japon, Accompagne d'un Commentaire* [Draft of the Code of Criminal Procedure for the Japanese Empire Accompanied by a Commentary], Tokyo: Kokubōnsha.

Bok, D. C., 1983, "A Flawed System of Law Practice and Training", *Journal of Legal Education*, Vol. 33, pp. 581–582.

Bolitho, H., 1974, *Treasures Among Men: The Fudai Daimyō in Tokugawa Japan*, New Haven: Yale University Press.

Borton, H., 1947, "United States Occupation Policies in Japan since Surrender", *Political Science Quarterly*, Vol. 62, No. 2, pp. 250–257.

Braibanti, R., 1949, "Administration of Military Government in Japan at the Prefectural Level", *The American Political Science Review*, Vol. 43, No. 2, pp. 250–274.

Braibanti, R., 1953, "The Outlook for the Ryukyus", *Far Eastern Survey*, Vol. 22, No. 7, pp. 73–78.

Braibanti, R., 1954, "The Ryukyu Islands", *The American Political Science Review*, Vol. 48, No. 4, pp. 972–998.

The Brookings Institution, 1992, *Charting a Future for the Civil Jury System: Report from an American Bar Association/Brookings Symposium*, Washington, DC: The Brookings Institution.

Chamberlain, B. H., 1895, "The Luchu Islands and Their Inhabitants: I. Introductory Remarks", *The Geographical Journal*, Vol. 5, No. 4, pp. 289–319.

Chang, G. J., 1978, "The Village Elder System of the Early Ming Dynasty", *Ming Studies*, Vol. 7, pp. 53–62.

Chen, C., 1975, "The Japanese Adaptation of the Pao-Chia System in Taiwan, 1895–1945", *The Journal of Asian Studies*, Vol. 34, No. 2, pp. 391–416.

Chen, E., 1972, "Formosan Political Movements under Japanese Colonial Rule, 1914–1937", *The Journal of Asian Studies*, Vol. 31, No. 3, pp. 477–497.

Ch'en, P. H., 1981, *The Formation of the Early Meiji Legal Order: The Japanese Code of 1871 and Its Chinese Foundation*, Oxford: Oxford University Press.

Cheng, P., Letz, M., and Spence, J. D. (eds), 1999, *The Search of Modern China: A Documentary Collection*, New York: W. W. Norton & Company.

Chesterman, M., 1999, "Criminal Trial Juries in Australia: From Penal Colonies to a Federal Democracy", *Law and Contemporary Problems*, Vol. 62, pp. 69–103.

Christy, A., 1993, "The Making of Imperial Subjects in Okinawa", *Positions*, Vol. 1, No. 3, pp. 607–639.

Conroy, H., and Wray, H. (eds), *Pearl Harbor Re-Examined: Prologue to the Pacific War*, Honolulu: University of Hawai'i Press.

Coughlin, G. G., and Coughlin, G. G. Jr., 1982, *Dictionary of Law*, New York: Barnes & Noble Books.

Dai Nippon Baishin Kyōkai [The Japan Jury Association], 1929, *Dai Nippon Baishin'in Kinen Roku* [The Japan Jury Commemorative Records], Tokyo: Dai Nippon Baishin Kyōkai.

Dai Nippon Bunmei Kyōkai [The Japanese Civilization Society], 1924, *Meiji Bunka Hasshō Kinenshi* [Journal Commemorating the Birth of *Meiji* Culture], Tokyo: Dai Nippon Bunmei Kyōkai.

Dai Nippon Teikoku Gikai Kankōkai [The Imperial Diet of Japan Press] (ed.), 1926–1930, *Dai Nippon Teikoku Gikaishi* [Journal of the Imperial Diet of Japan], Tokyo: Dai Nippon Teikoku Gikai Kankōkai.

Davidson, J. W., 1903, *The Island of Formosa: Past and Present*, Taipei: SMC Publishing.

De Tocqueville, A., 1994, *Democracy in America*, New York: David Campbell Publishers.

Dean, M. (ed.), 2002, *Japanese Legal System*, 2nd edition, London: Cavendish Publishing.

Dean, M., 1995, "Trial by Jury: A Force for Change in Japan", *International and Comparative Law Quarterly*, Vol. 44, pp. 379–404.

Devine, R., 1979, "The Way of the King. An Early Meiji Essay on Government", *Monumenta Nipponica*, Vol. 34, No. 1, pp. 49–72.

Dezalay, Y., and Garth, B. G. (eds), 2002, *Global Prescriptions: The Production, Exportation, and Importation of a New Legal Orthodoxy*, Ann Arbor: University of Michigan Press.

Dobrovolskaia, A., 2007, "An All-Laymen Jury System Instead of the Lay Assessor (*Saiban'in*) System for Japan? Anglo-American-Style Jury Trials in Okinawa under the U.S. Occupation", *Journal of Japanese Law*, No. 24, pp. 57–80.

Dobrovolskaia, A., 2008, "The Jury System in Pre-War Japan: An Annotated Translation of 'The Jury Guidebook'", *Asian-Pacific Law and Policy Journal*, Vol. 9, No. 2, pp. 231–296.

D'Oudney, K., and Spooner, L., 1999, *Trial by Jury: Its History, True Purpose and Modern Relevance*, London: Scorpio Recording Company.

Dower, J., 1996, *Japan in War and Peace*, London: Fontana Press.

Downs, A., 1957, *An Economic Theory of Democracy*, Boston: Addison-Wesley.

Dressler, J. (ed.), 2002, *Encyclopedia of Crime & Justice*, New York: Macmillan Reference USA.

Durkheim, E., 1933, *The Division of Labor in Society*, New York: Free Press.

Duus, P., 1968, *Party Rivalry and Political Change in Taishō Japan*, Cambridge: Harvard University Press.

Duus, P. (ed.), 1988, *The Cambridge History of Japan*, Vol. 6, New York: Cambridge University Press.

Dworkin, R., 1996, *Freedom's Law: The Moral Reading of the American Constitution*, New York: Oxford University Press.

Dwyer, W. L., 2002, *In the Hands of the People: The Trial Jury's Origins, Troubles, and Future in American Democracy*, New York: Thomas Dunne Books.Egi, M., 1909, *Reikai Manpitsu* [Reikai's Scribbling], Tokyo: Yūhikaku.

Egi, M., 1909, *Sansō Yawa* [Window (Facing the) Mountains, Night Tales], Tokyo: Yūhikaku.

Egi, M., Hanai, T., and Hara, Y., 1923, *Baishin Hō Shingi Hen* [Compilation of (the Transcripts of) Deliberations (Regarding) the Jury Act], Tokyo: Shimizu Shoten.

Eibun Horei Sha, Inc., 2008, *The Penal Code of Japan*, Tokyo; Heibunsha Printing, Co.

Eisenberg, T., Hannaford-Agor, P. L., Hans, V. P., Walters, N. L., Munsterman, G. T., Schwab, S. J., and Wells, M. T., 2005, "Judge-Jury Agreement in Criminal Cases: A Partial Replication of Kalven and Zeisel's *The American Jury*", *Journal of Empirical Legal Studies*, Vol. 2, pp. 171–207.

Eldridge, R. D., 2001, *The Origins of the Bilateral Okinawa Problem: Okinawa in Postwar US-Japan Relations, 1945–1952*, New York: Garland Publishing, Inc.

Ericson, S., and A. Hockley (eds), 2008, *The Treaty of Portsmouth and Its Legacies*, Hanover: Dartmouth College Press.

Evans, A. E., 1968, "Contemporary Practice of the United States Relating to International Law", *The American Journal of International Law*, Vol. 62, No. 1, pp. 189–202.

Ewald, W., 1995, "Comparative Jurisprudence (II): The Logic of Legal Transplants", *American Journal of Comparative Law*, Vol. 43, pp. 489–505.

Fairchild, E., and Dammer, H. R., 2001, *Comparative Criminal Justice Systems*, London: Wadsworth.

Fan, J. S., 1999, "Recent Development: From Office Ladies to Women Warriors? The Effect of the EEOL on Japanese Women", *UCLA Women's Law Journal*, Vol. 10, pp. 103–140.

Feeley, M. M., and Miyazawa, S. (eds), 2002, *The Japanese Adversary System in Context: Controversies and Comparisons*, New York: Palgrave Macmillan.

Feldman, E. A., 2006, "The Culture of Legal Change: A Case Study of Tobacco Control in Twenty-First Century Japan", *Michigan Journal of International Law*, Vol. 27, pp. 743–821.

Fitzgerald, C. P., 1951, "Peace or War with China?", *Pacific Affairs*, Vol. 24, No. 4, pp. 339–351.

Foote, D. H., 1992, "The Benevolent Paternalism of Japanese Criminal Justice", *California Law Review*, Vol. 80, pp. 317–390.

Foote, D. H., 1992, "From Japan's Death Row to Freedom", *Pacific Rim Law & Policy Journal*, Vol. 1 No. 1, pp. 11–103.

Foote, D. H., 2007, *Law in Japan: A Turning Point*, Seattle: University of Washington Press.

Ford, C. S., 1950, "Occupation Experiences on Okinawa", *Annals of the American Academy of Political and Social Science*, Vol. 267, pp. 175–182.
Friedman, L. M., 2002, *Law in America: A Short History*, New York: Modern Library.
Friedman, L. M., and Pérez-Perdomo, R., 2003, *Legal Culture in the Age of Globalization: Latin America and Europe*, Stanford: Stanford University Press.
Frohlich, N., Oppenheimer, J. A., and Young, O. R., 1971, *Political Leadership and Collective Goods*, Princeton: Princeton University Press.
Fujikura, K. (ed.), 1996, *Japanese Law and Legal Theory*, Aldershot: Dartmouth.
Fujita, M., 2008, *Keiji Saiban ni okeru Saibankan to Saiban'in no Ninshiki, Handan Purosesu ni Kansuru Jisshōteki Kenkyū* [An Empirical Study Concerning the Cognition and Decision-Making Processes of Judges and Lay Judges (*Saiban'in*) in Criminal Trials], Tokyo: Masahiro Fujita.
Fujita, M., 2009, *Shihō e no Shimin Sanka no Kanōsei: Nihon no Baishin Seido, Saiban'in Seido no Jisshōteki Kenkyū* [The Prospects of Citizen Participation in the Justice System of Japan: An Empirical Study of Japan's Jury System and the *Saiban'in* System], Tokyo: Yūhikaku.
Fujita, M., Shinomiya, S., Shiratori, Y., Honjo, T., and Sugimori, S., 2006, "Tokushū: Saiban'in Seido – Seido no Seiritsu Katei to Hōgakuteki, Shinrigakuteki Kentō Kadai" [Special Report: The Lay Judge System – The Process of the Establishment of the System and Legal as Well as Psychological Issues to Be Studied], *Hō to Shinri* [Japanese Journal of Law and Psychology], Vol. 5, No. 1, pp. 1–25.
Fujita, Y. (ed.), 2008, *Yoku Wakaru Saiban'in Seido to Keiji Soshō no Shikumi: Heisei 21 Nen Sutāto* [Easy-to-Understand Lay Judge System and the Structure of Criminal Procedure: (The Lay Judge System) Starts in 2009], Tokyo: Sanshūsha.
Fukurai, H., 2007, "The Rebirth of Japan's Petit Quasi-Jury and Grand Jury Systems: A Cross-National Analysis of Legal Consciousness and the Lay Participatory Experience in Japan and the U.S.", *Cornell International Law Journal*, Vol. 40, pp. 315–354.
Fukurai, H., 2013, "A Step in the Right Direction for Japan's Judicial Reform: Impact of the Justice System Reform Council Recommendations on Criminal Justice and Citizen Participation in Criminal, Civil, and Administrative Litigation", *Hastings International and Comparative Law Review*, Vol. 36, pp. 517–566.
Fukutake, T., 1989, *The Japanese Social Structure*, Tokyo: University of Tokyo Press.
Fuse, T., 1974, *Fuse Tatsuji Gaiden* [Fuse Tatsuji Biography], Tokyo: Mirai Sha.
Gaimushō Jōyaku Kyoku Hōki Ka [The Ministry of Foreign Affairs, Department of Treaties, Legislative Section], 1969, *Nihon Tōchika no Karafuto* [Karafuto under Japanese Rule], Tokyo: Gaimushō Jōyaku Kyoku Hōki Ka [The Ministry of Foreign Affairs, Department of Treaties, Legislative Section].
Gaimushō Jōyakukyoku Hōkika [Ministry of Foreign Affairs, Department of Treaties, Division of Laws and Regulations], 1959, *Taiwan no Inin Rippō Seido* [Taiwan's System of Delegated Legislation], Tokyo: Gaimushō Jōyakukyoku Hōkika.
Garner, B. A. (ed.), 2004, *Black's Law Dictionary*, 8th edition, St. Paul: West Group.
Gastil, J., Deess, E. P., and Weiser, P., 2002, "Civic Awakening in the Jury Room: A Test of the Connection between Jury Deliberation and Political Participation", *The Journal of Politics*, Vol. 64, No. 2, pp. 585–595.
Gastil, J., and Levine, P. (eds), 2005, *The Deliberative Democracy Handbook: Strategies for Effective Civic Engagement in the Twenty-First Century*, San Francisco: Jossey-Bass.
Gavin, M., and Middleton, B. (eds), 2013, *Japan and the High Treason Incident*, London: Routledge.
Gekkan Okinawa Sha, 1983, *Laws and Regulations during the US Administration of Okinawa 1945–1972*, Naha: Ikemiya Shokai.
Giddens, A., 1971, *Capitalism and Modern Social Theory: An Analysis of the Writings of Marx, Durkheim, and Weber*, London: Cambridge University Press.
Gijuku, K. (ed.), 1969, *Fukuzawa Yukichi Zenshū* (The Complete Works of Fukuzawa Yukichi), Tokyo: Iwanami Shoten.

Ginsburg, T., and Hoetker, G., 2006, "The Unreluctant Litigant? An Empirical Analysis of Japan's Turn to Litigation", *The Journal of Legal Studies*, Vol. 35, No. 1, pp. 31–59.

Green, R. K., 2002, *Democratic Virtue in the Trial and Death of Socrates: Resistance to Imperialism in Classical Athens*, New York: Peter Lang.

Green, S. W., 1955, "Applicability of American Laws to Overseas Areas Controlled by the United States", *Harvard Law Review*, Vol. 68, No. 5, pp. 781–812.

Gōtō, A., Shinomiya, S., Nishimura, T., and Kudō, M., 2004, *Jitsumuka no tame no Saiban'in Hō Nyūmon* [An Introduction to the Lay Judge Act for Practitioners], Tokyo: Gendai Jinbunsha.

Gōtō, H., 1996, "Hōsō Yōsei Seido Tō Kaikaku Kyōgikai no Kyōgi no Keii ni tsuite" [Concerning the Details of the Deliberations of the Council on Legal Training and Other Reforms], *Jurist*, No. 1084, pp. 33–37.

Hakuseki, A., 1977, *Arai Hakuseki Zenshū* [The Complete Works of Arai Hakuseki], Tokyo: Kokusho Kankōkai, pp. 193–199.

Haley, J. O., 1978, "The Myth of the Reluctant Litigant", *Journal of Japanese Studies*, Vol. 4, pp. 362–390.

Haley, J. O., 1991, *Authority Without Power: Law and the Japanese Paradox*, New York: Oxford University Press.

Haley, J. O., 1995, "Judicial Independence in Japan Revisited", *Law in Japan*, Vol. 25, pp. 1–18.

Haley, J. O., 1998, *The Spirit of Japanese Law*, Athens: University of Georgia Press.

Haley, J. O., 2005, "Heisei Renewal or Heisei Transformation: Are Legal Reforms Really Changing Japan?", *Journal of Japanese Law*, Vol. 10, No. 19, pp. 5–18.

Hanai, T., 1921, "Baishin to Sanza Sei" [The Jury and Sanza Systems], *Nihon Bengoshi Kyōkai Rokuji*, Vol. 263, pp. 38–53.

Hanai, T., 1927, *Shōtei Ronsō: Matetsu Jiken o Ronzu Fu Baishin Hō ni tsuite* [Courtroom Notes: A Discussion of the Mantetsu Incident, Includes (Notes on) the Jury Act], Tokyo: Mukenshoya.

Hans, V. P., 2007, "Introduction: Citizens as Legal Decision Makers: An International Perspective", *Cornell International Law Journal*, Vo. 40, pp. 303–314.

Hara, T., 1929, *Hara Takashi Zenshū* [Full Collection of Works by Takashi Hara], Tokyo: Hara Takashi Zenshū Kankōkai.

Harima, N., Kinoshita, S., Watanabe, H., and Wakita, Y. (eds), 2002, *Do Natte Iru?! Nihonkoku Kempo: Kempo to Shakai o Kangaeru* (The Constitution of Japan: What Has Become of It?! Thoughts on the Constitution and Society), Kyoto: Hōritsubunkasha.

Haruyama, M., and Wakabayashi, M. (eds), 1980, *Nihon Shokuminchishugi no Seijiteki Tenkai, 1995–1934* [Political Evolution of Japanese Colonialism, 1995–1934], Tokyo: Ajia Seiken Gakkkai.

Hayashi, R., 1926, *Baishin Hō Shakugi* [An Explanation of the Jury Act], Tokyo: Baishin Hō Fukyūbu.

Hayashi, R., 1928, "Nihon Baishin Hō Enkaku Shi no Issetsu" [A Paragraph in the History of Japan's Jury Act], *Hōsō Kōron*, Vol. 32, No. 9, pp. 39–43.

Hellegers, D. E., 2001, *We, the Japanese People: World War II and the Origins of the Japanese Constitution*, Stanford: Stanford University Press.

Hewett, R. F., 1965, *United States Civil Administration of the Ryukyu Islands, 1950–1960*, PhD thesis, The American University, Ann Arbor: University Microfilms International.

Higa, M., 1963, "Okinawa: Recent Political Developments", *Asian Survey*, Vol. 3, No. 9, pp. 415–426.

High Commissioner of the Ryukyu Islands, 1963, *Civil Administration of the Ryukyu Islands: Report for Period 1 July 1962 to 30 June 1963*, Vol. 11, Naha: United States Civil Administration.

High Commissioner of the Ryukyu Islands, 1964, *Civil Administration of the Ryukyu Islands: Report for Period 1 July 1963 to 30 June 1964*, Vol. 12, Naha: United States Civil Administration.

Higuchi, Y. (ed.), 2001, *Five Decades of Constitutionalism in Japanese Society*, Tokyo: University of Tokyo Press.

Hirano, R., 1958, *Keiji Soshō Hō* [Code of Criminal Procedure], Tokyo: Yūhikaku.

Hirobumi, I., 1936, *Hisho Ruisan* [Classified Collection of the Private Documents of Itō Hirobumi Relating to *Meiji* Development], Vol. 18 ("Taiwan Shiryō" [Sources (Related to) Taiwan]), Tokyo: Hisho Ruisan Kankōkai.

Hishida, S., 1907, "Formosa: Japan's First Colony", *Political Science Quarterly*, Vol. 22, No. 2, pp. 267–281.

Hōgaku Kenkyūkai [Society for the Study of Law], 1932, *Keiji Soshō Hō, Baishin Hō, Shōnen Hō* [Code of Penal Procedure, Jury Act, Juvenile Law], Tokyo: Jōban Shobō.

Hōgaku Kyōkai [The Jurisprudence Society] (ed.), 1953, *Chūkai Nihonkoku Kenpō* [Annotated Constitution of Japan], Tokyo: Yūhikaku.

Hook, G. D., 1996, *Militarization and Demilitarization of Contemporary Japan*, London: Routledge.

Hook, G. D., and McCormack, G., 2001, *Japan's Contested Constitution: Documents and Analysis*, London: Routledge.

Hook, G. D., and Siddle, R. (eds), 2003, *Japan and Okinawa: Structure and Subjectivity*, London: RoutledgeCurzon.

Hori, T., 1862, *Eiwa Taiyaku Shūchin Jisho* [A Pocket Dictionary of the English and Japanese Language], Edo: Publisher Unknown.

Horibe, M., Ishii, H., Sakai, Y., Niikura, O., Okura, K., 2004, *Keiji Shihō e no Shimin Sanka* [Citizen Participation in Criminal Justice], Tokyo: Gendai Jinbunsha.

Huang, F., Huang, S., and Mulvagh, C., 2012, "Lin Hsien-Tang's Taiwanese Home-Rule Movement as inspired by the Irish Model", *Taiwan in Comparative Perspective*, Vol. 4, pp. 65–88.

Ichinose, T. (ed.), 2004, *Major 20th Century People in Japan: A Biographical Dictionary*, Tokyo: Nichigai Associates.

Ide, K., 1988, *Taiwan Chiseki Shi* [The Intentions of the Administration of Taiwan], Tokyo: Seishisha.

Ike, N., 1950, *The Beginnings of Political Democracy in Japan*, Baltimore: The Johns Hopkins Press.

Inaba, Y., 2000, *Shiryō de Miru: Baishin Hō Hanrei Shūsei* [Looking at Archive Materials: A Collection of Jury Trial Decisions], Tokyo: Gakujutsu Sensho.

Inomata, T., 1928, "Baishin Seido Mogi Saiban: Konjaku Monogatari" [The Jury System, Mock Trials: A Story of the Present and of the Past], *Hōsō Kōron*, Vol. 32, No. 9, pp. 114–117.

Inoue, K. (ed.), 1969, *Taishōki no Seiji to Shakai* [Politics and Society in the Taishō Period], Tokyo: Iwanami Shoten.

Inoue, K., 1991, *MacArthur's Japanese Constitution: A Linguistic and Cultural Study of Its Making*, Chicago: The University of Chicago Press.

Institute of Comparative Law in Japan (ed.), 1998, *Toward Comparative Law in the 21st Century*, Tokyo: Chuo University Press.

Isa, C., 2001, *Gyakuten: Amerika Shihaika Okinawa no Baishin Saiban* [Turnaround: A Jury Trial in Okinawa under American Rule], Tokyo: Iwanami Gendai Bunko.

Isa, C., 2006, *Saiban'in Seido wa Keiji Saiban o Kaeru ka: Baishin Seido o Motomeru Wake* [Will the Lay Judge System Transform Criminal Courts? Reasons for Demanding a Jury System], Tokyo: Gendai Jinbunsha.

Isa, C., and Ikuta, T. (eds), 2009, *Saiban'in Kyohi no Susume: Anata ga Enzai ni Katan Shinai tame* [[We] Advise [You] to Refuse Lay Judge [Service]: To Ensure that You Are not Part to Erroneous Charges], Tokyo: Wave Shuppan.

Ishii, M., 2006, "Hōsō Kyōiku o Meguru Seido to Seisaku: Hōsō Sansha no Rikigaku o Chūshin toshite" [Systems and Policies Concerning Legal Education: Focusing on the Dynamics of the Three Branches of Legal Profession], *Tōhoku Daigaku Daigakuin Kyōiku Gaku Kenkyūka Kenkyū Nenpō* [Annual Bulletin of Tohoku University Graduate School of Education], No. 55, Vol. 1, pp. 197–218.

Ishii, R., 1988, *A History of Political Institutions in Japan*, Tokyo: University of Tokyo Press.

Ishikawa, M., 1997, *Uzawa Fusaaki: Sono Shōgai to Tatakai* [Uzawa Fusaaki: His Life and Fights], Tokyo: Ōzorasha.

Isotani, K., and Yanagawa, K., 1927, *Baishin no Jōshiki* [The Common Sense of the Jury], Tokyo: Hōsō Kai.

Itagaki, M., 1969, *Itagaki Taisuke Zenshū* [A Complete Collection of the Writings of Itagaki Taisuke], Tokyo: Hara Shobō.Itō, K., 2006, *Gohan o Umanai Saiban'in Seido e no Kadai: Amerika Keiji Shihō Kaikaku kara no Teigen* [Issues (to be Considered to Ensure that) the Lay Judge System Does not Produce Erroneous Verdicts: Suggestions Based on America's (Experience with) Criminal Justice Reform], Tokyo: Gendai Jinbunsha.

Itō, M., Ōe, T., and Katō, S., 1999, "Shihō Seido Kaikaku no Shiten to Kadai" [Perspectives on and Issues Surrounding the Justice System Reform], *Jurisuto*, No. 1167, pp. 52–100.

Itō, Y., 1998, *Taishō Demokurashii to Seitō Seiji* [*Taishō* Democracy and Party Politics], Tokyo: Yamakawa Shuppansha.

Itoh, M., 2003, *The Hatoyama Dynasty: Japanese Political Leadership through the Generations*, New York: Palgrave Macmillan.

Iwanami Shoten Henshūbu [The Editorial Department of Iwanami Shoten], 1981, *Seiyōjin Jinmei Jiten* [Reference Guide to Foreign Names], Tokyo: Iwanami Shoten.

Iwatani, J., 2004, *Nihon Bengoshi Kyōkai Rokuji: Meiji Hen* [Records of the Japan Federation of Bar Associations: The *Meiji* Period], Tokyo: Tōwa Seihon.

Jacob, H., Blankenberg, E., Kritzer, H. M., Provine, D. M., and Sanders, J., 1996, *Courts, Law, and Politics in Comparative Perspective*, New Haven: Yale University Press.

Jacobs, J. B., 2012, *Democratizing Taiwan*, Boston: Brill.

Jansen, M. B., 2000, *The Making of Modern Japan*, London: Harvard University Press.

Japan Civil Liberties Union, 1961, *Report on the Human Rights Problem in Okinawa*, Place of Publication Unknown: Japan Civil Liberties Union.

Japan Federation of Bar Associations (ed.), 1992, *Okinawa no Baishin Saiban: Fukkizen no Okinawa Baishinsei no Chōsa Hōkoku* [Jury Trials in Okinawa: An Investigative Report on the Jury System in Pre-reversion Okinawa], Tokyo: Takachiho Shobō.

Japan Federation of Bar Associations, Tokyo Bar Association, Daiichi Tokyo Bar Association, and Daini Tokyo Bar Association (eds), 2000, *Saiban ga Kawaru Nihon ga Kawaru: Waga Kuni Shihokaikaku no Yukue* [Changing Courts, Changing Japan: The Direction of Japan's Judicial Reform], Tokyo: Gendai Jinbunsha.

Jarman, R. L. (ed.), 1997, *Taiwan Political and Economic Reports, 1861–1960*, Oxford: Archive Editions.

Jiyū Jinken Kyōkai [Japan Civil Liberties Union] (ed.), 1989, *Baishin Saiban no Jitsugen ni Mukete: Shin Baishin Hōan (Dai Ichiji An) to sono Kaisetsu* [Towards the Realization of Jury Trials: An Annotated Draft of the New Jury Act (The First Draft)], Tokyo: Jiyū Jinken Kyōkai.

Jiyū Jinken Kyōkai [Japan Civil Liberties Union], 2003, *Tōgi Shiryō: Saiban'in Seido to Shuzai, Hōdō no Jiyu* [Materials for Deliberations: The *Saiban'in* System, Media Coverage, and Freedom of Reporting], Tokyo: Jiyū Jinken Kyōkai.

Johnson, D. T., 2002, *The Japanese Way of Justice: Prosecuting Crime in Japan*, New York: Oxford University Press.

Kabashima, M., 2005, "Saiban'in Seido, Keiji Soshōhō no Kaiaku ni Hantai Shi Baishinseido no Fukkatsu o" [Opposing the Lay Judge System and the Deterioration of the Code of Penal Procedure, Demanding Revival of the Jury System], *Gendai no Riron* [Contemporary Theory], Vol. 4, pp. 176–186.

Kadomatsu, N., 1999, "The New Administrative Information Disclosure Law in Japan", *Journal of Japanese Law*, Vol. 4, No. 8, pp. 34–52.

Kaizuka, K., and Ikeo, K., 1992, *Kin'yū Riron to Seido Kaikaku* [Financial Theory and Institutional Reform], Tokyo: Yūhikaku, pp. 307–341.

Kalven, H. Jr., and Zeisel, H., 1986, *The American Jury*, Chicago: University of Chicago Press.

Kanda, H., and Milhaupt, C. J., 2003, "Re-examining Legal Transplants: The Director's Fiduciary Duty in Japanese Corporate Law", *The American Journal of Comparative Law*, Vol. 51, pp. 887–901.

Karasik, D. D., 1948, "Okinawa: A Problem in Administration and Reconstruction", *The Far Eastern Quarterly*, Vol. 7, No. 3, pp. 254–267.

Katz, P. R., *When Valleys Turned Blood Red: The Ta-pa-ni Incident in Colonial Taiwan*, Honolulu: University of Hawai'i Press.

Kawashima, T., 1967, *Nihonjin no Hō Ishiki* [Legal Consciousness of the Japanese], Tokyo: Iwanami Shinsho.

Keishichō Shi Hen Iinkai [Editorial Committee of the History of the Metropolitan Police Department], 1962, *Keishichō Shi, Dai 3* [The History of the Metropolitan Police Department, No. 3], Tokyo: Keishichō Shi Hen Iinkai [Editorial Committee of the History of the Metropolitan Police Department].

Keizai Dōyūkai [The Japan Association of Corporate Executives], 1994, *Gendai Nihon Shakai no Byōri to Shohō: Kojin o Ikasu Shakai no Jitsugen ni Mukete* [The Ills of Contemporary Japanese Society and the Prescriptions: Towards the Realization of a Society that Values the Individual], Tokyo: Keizai Dōyūkai.

Keizai Dōyūkai [The Japan Association of Corporate Executives], 1997, *Gurōbaruka ni Taiō Suru Kigyō Hōsei no Seibi o Mezashite: Minkan Shudō no Shijō Keizai ni Muketa Hō Seido to Rippō, Shihō no Kaikaku* [Aiming for Establishment of Corporate Legislation Fit to Address (The Challenges of) Globalization: A Legal System Suited for a Market Economy Led by the Private (Sector) and Justice and Legislation Reforms], Tokyo: Keizai Dōyūkai.

Keizai Dōyūkai [The Japan Association of Corporate Executives], 1999, *Shihō Seido Kaikaku Shingikai ni Nozomu* [Expectations for the Judicial System Reform Council], Tokyo: Keizai Dōyūkai.

Keizai Dōyūkai [The Japan Association of Corporate Executives], 2000, *Wagakuni Shihō no Jinteki Kiban Kaikaku no Bizyon to Gutai Saku: Shihō Seido Kaikaku Shingikai ni Nozomu (Dai 2 Ji)* [The Vision and Specific Policies Regarding the Reforms Concerning the Human Basis of Administration of Justice: Expectations for the Judicial System Reform Council (Part 2)], Tokyo: Keizai Dōyūkai.

Kerr, G. H., 2000, *Okinawa: The History of an Island People*, Boston: Tuttle Publishing.

Kiddler, R. L., 1983, *Connecting Law and Society: An Introduction to Research and Theory*, Englewood Cliffs, NJ: Prentice-Hall.

Kikuchi, H., 1959, *14 Nihon Hōritsuka Kyōkai Series: Baishin Seido ni tsuite* [14 Nihon Hōritsuka Kyōkai Series: On the Jury System], Tokyo: Japan Bar Association.

Kim, M. S., 2012, *Law and Custom in Korea: Comparative Legal History*, New York: Cambridge University Press.

King, N. J., 1999, "The American Criminal Jury", *Law and Contemporary Problems*, Vol. 62, pp. 41–69.

Kingdon, J. W., 2001, "A Model of Agenda-Setting, with Applications", *Law Review of Michigan State University Detroit College of Law*, Vol. 2001, No. 2, pp. 331–339.

Kingdon, J. W., 2003, *Agendas, Alternatives, and Public Policies*, New York: Longman.

Kinjo, S., 1965, "Taiwan Jiken (1871–74 Nen) ni tsuite no Ichi Kōsatsu – Ryūkyū Shobun no Kiten ni tsuite" [A Study of the Taiwan Incident (1871–74) – The Starting Point of the Disposition of the Ryukyus], *Okinawa Rekishi Kenkyū*, Vol. 1, pp. 33–49.

Kiss, L. W., 1999, "Reviving the Criminal Jury in Japan", *Law and Contemporary Problems*, Vol. 62, pp. 261–283.

Kiyomiya, S., 1966, *Kenpō 1* [The Constitution, 1], Tokyo: Yūhikaku.

Klein, T. M., 1972, "The Ryukyus on the Eve of Reversion", *Pacific Affairs*, Vol. 45, No. 1, pp. 1–20.

Kobayashi, T., 2006, *Minna no Saiban* [Court for All], Tokyo: Kashiwa Shobō.

Kodner, J. J., 2003, "Reintroducing Lay Participation to Japanese Criminal Cases: An Awkward yet Necessary Step", *Washington University Global Studies Law Review*, Vol. 2, pp. 231–254.

Kohama, I., 2009, *Shikei ka Muki ka Anata ga Kimeru: Saiban'in Seido o Kyohi Seyo!* [It Is Up to You to Decide between the Death Penalty and Lifetime Imprisonment: Let's Reject the Lay Judge System], Tokyo: Daiwa Shobō.

Kokushi Daijiten Henshū Iinkai [Editorial Commission for the Encyclopedic Dictionary of Japanese History] (ed.), 1989, *Kokushi Daijiten* [The Encyclopedic Dictionary of Japanese History], Tokyo: Shōgakukan.

Komuro, N., 2002, *Nihonkoku Kempo no Mondai Ten* [Constitutional Problems of Japan], Tokyo: Shūeisha International.

Kornicki, P. (ed.), 1998, *Meiji Japan: Political, Economic, and Social History 1868–1912*, London: Routledge.

Koseki, S. (edited and translated by Moore, R. A.), 1997, *The Birth of Japan's Postwar Constitution*, Boulder, Colorado: Westview Press.

Koyama, M., 1929, "Baishin Hō Jisshi Go no Seiseki ni tsuite" [On the Post-enforcement Results of the Jury Act], *Hōsōkai Zasshi* [Journal of the Law Society], Vol. 7, No. 10, pp. 9–17.

Krozier, R. C., *Koxinga and Chinese Nationalism: History, Myth, and the Hero*, Cambridge: Harvard University Press.

Kume, K. (translated by Cobbling, A.), 2002, *The Iwakura Embassy, 1871–1873, A True Account of the Ambassador Extraordinary and Plenipotentiary's Journey of Observation through the United States of America and Europe*, Matsudo: Japan Documents.

Kuzuno, H., Sagami, Y., Ichikawa, M., and Matsumoto, K., 2002, *Atarashii Shihō o Motomete* [In Pursuit of a New Legal System], Kyoto: Ritsumeikan Daigaku Jinbun Kagaku Kenkyūjo.

Ködderitzsch, L., 1994, "Japan's New Administrative Procedure Act: Reasons for Its Enactment and Likely Implications", *Law in Japan: An Annual*, Vol. 24, pp. 105–137.

Laffont, J., and Martimort, D., 2002, *The Theory of Incentives: The Principle-Agent Model*, Princeton: Princeton University Press.

Landsman, S., and Zhang, J., 2008, "A Tale of Two Juries: Lay Participation Comes to Japanese and Chinese Courts", *UCLA Pacific Basin Law Journal*, Vol. 25, pp. 179–227.

Langbein, J. H., 1977, *Comparative Criminal Procedure: Germany*, St. Paul: West Publishing.

Lazich, M. C., 2000, *E. C. Bridgman, 1801–1861: America's First Missionary to China*, Lewiston: E. Mellen Press.

Legge, J., 1864, *Chikan Keimō* [Circle of Knowledge], Tokyo: Kondo Makoto.

Legrand, P., 1997, "The Impossibility of 'Legal Transplants'", *Maastricht Journal of European and Comparative Law*, Vol. 4, pp. 111–124.

Lehmann, J., 1982, *The Roots of Modern Japan*, Houndmills: Macmillan.

Lempert, R. O., 2001, "Citizen Participation in Judicial Decision Making: Juries, Lay Judges and Japan", *Saint Louis-Warsaw Transatlantic Law Journal*, Vol. 127, No. 16, pp. 1–14.

Lempert, R., 1992, "A Jury for Japan?", *American Journal of Comparative Law*, Vol. 40, pp. 37–71.

Levy, L. W., 1999, *The Palladium of Justice: Origins of Trial by Jury*, Chicago: Ivan R. Dee.

Lin, S., Gi, G., and Masaki, A., 1854, *Amerika Koku Sōki Wage* [Short Account of the United States of America], Place of Publication Unknown: Seiki Senhachi.

Luney, P. J., and Takahashi, K. (eds), 1993, *Japanese Constitutional Law*, Tokyo: University of Tokyo Press.

Macaulay, S., Friedman, L. M., and Stookey, J. (eds), 1995, *Law & Society: Readings on the Social Study of Law*, New York: W. W. Norton & Company.

Maine, H. M., 1986, *Ancient Law: Its Connection with the Early History of Society and Its Relation to Modern Ideas*, New York: Dorset Press.

Markovits, I., 2004, "Exporting Law Reform – But Will It Travel?", *Cornell International Law Journal*, Vol. 37, pp. 95–114.

Martin, J. (ed.), 2002, *Antonio Gramsci: Critical Assessments of Leading Political Philosophers(3)*, New York: Routledge.

Matsuda, T. (ed.), 2011, *Shokuminchi Teikoku Nihon ni okeru Shihai to Chiiki Shakai* [The Rule and the Local Society in the Japanese Colonial Empire], Kyoto: Kokusai Nihon Bunka Kenkyū Sentā.

Matsuo, T., 2001, *Taishō Demokurashii* [Taisho Democracy], Tokyo: Iwanami Shoten.

Matsushita, M. (ed.), 1988, *Japanese Business Law Guide*, Sydney: CCH Australia, Ltd.

McCune, S., 1975, *The Ryukyu Islands*, Newton Abbot: David & Charles.

McCune, S., 1989, *Intelligence on the Economic Collapse of Japan in 1945*, New York: University Press of America.

Mencius (translated by Legge, J.), 1895, *The Works of Mencius*, Oxford: Clarendon Press.

Mendel, D., 1970, *The Politics of Formosan Nationalism*, Los Angeles: University of California Press.

Merry, S. E., 1988, "Legal Pluralism", *Law & Society Review*, Vol. 22, No. 5, pp. 869–896.

Meyers, H., 1950, "Revisions of the Criminal Code of Japan", *Washington Law Review and State Bar Journal*, Vol. 25, pp. 104–134.

Midori, D., Masuda, O., Katō, T., and Kontani, K., 2007, "Hiroshima ni okeru Baishin Saiban: Shōwa Shoki no Geibi Nichinichi Shinbun Chugoku Shinbun no Hōdō narabi ni Keiji Hanketsu Genpon o Chūshin ni shite Miru Baishin Saiban" [Jury Trials in Hiroshima: Jury Trials as Seen through the Articles of the Geibi Nichinichi Shinbun, the Chugoku Shinbun as Well as through the Original Criminal (Trial) Verdicts (Issued) at the Beginning the Beginning of the *Shōwa* Period], *Shūdō Hōgaku*, Vol. 29, No. 2, pp. 45–195.

Mikami, H., 1928, "Baishin Hō no Shikō o Shuku Shite" [Celebrating the Enforcement of the Jury Act], *Hōsō Kōron*, Vol. 32, No. 9, pp. 49–57.

Milhaupt, C. J., Ramseyer, J. M., and West, M. D. (eds), 2006, *The Japanese Legal System*, New York: Foundation Press.

Milhaupt, C. J., Ramseyer, J. M., and Young, M. K. (eds), 2001, *Japanese Law in Context: Readings in Society, the Economy, and Politics*, Cambridge: Harvard University Asia Center.

Minamitani, C., 1929, "Bōchō Seki yori Mitaru Baishin Saiban" [Jury Trials as Seen from the Seats for the Public (in the Courtroom)], *Hōsōkai Zasshi* [Journal of the Law Society], Vol. 7, No. 10, pp. 116–119.

Mitani, T., 1980, *Kindai Nihon no Shihōken to Seitō: Baishin Seiritsu no Seiji Shi* (Judicial Power in Modern Japan and Political Parties: The Political History of the Creation of the Jury System), Tokyo: Hanawa Shobō.

Mitani, T. (ed.), 1984, *Yoshino Sakuzō*, Tokyo: Chūō Kōronsha.

Mitani, T., 2001, *Seiji Seido toshite no Baishinsei: Kindai Nihon no Shihoken to Seiji* [The Jury System as a Political Institution: The Judiciary and Modern Japanese Politics], Tokyo: Tokyo University Press.

Mitchell, R. H., 1983, *Censorship in Imperial Japan*, Princeton: Princeton University Press.

Miyazato, S., 1966, *Amerika no Okinawa Tōchi* (American Rule over Okinawa), Tokyo: Iwanami Shoten.

Miyazawa, S., 2001, "The Politics of Judicial Reform in Japan: The Rule of Law at Last?", *Asian-Pacific Law & Policy Journal*, Vol. 2, No. 2, pp. 89–121.

Miyazawa, S., 2006, "How Does Culture Count in Legal Change? A Review with a Proposal from a Social Movement Perspective", *Michigan Journal of International Law*, Vol. 27, pp. 917–931.

Moore, R. A., and Robinson, D. L., 2002, *Partners for Democracy: Crafting the New Japanese State Under MacArthur*, Tokyo: Oxford University Press.

Mori, T., 2010, *Fuse Tatsuji to Futari no Chōsenjin Seinen – 1931 Nen Baishin Hōtei de no Tatakai* [Tatsuji Fuse and Two Young Koreans – The 1931 Battle at the Jury Courtroom], *Hōgakkan Kenpō Kenkyūjo Hō*, Vol. 3, pp. 41–50.

Morohashi, T., 1976, *Dai Kanwa Jiten* [A Dictionary of *Kanji*], Tokyo: Taishūkan Shoten.

Morton-Cameron, W. H., and Feldwick, W., 1919, *Present Day Impressions of Japan; The History, People, Commerce, Industries and Resources of Japan and Japan's Colonial Empire, Kwantung, Chosen, Taiwan, Karafuto*, Chicago: Globe Encyclopedia Co.

240 Bibliography

Motoji, S., 1929, "Baishin Hō Shiren Ichi Nen no Seiseki o Kaerimiru [Looking Back at the Results of the First Trial Year of the (Functioning of the) Jury Act], *Hōsōkai Zasshi* [Journal of the Law Society], Vol. 7, No. 10, pp. 29–50.

Motoji, S., Uzawa, F., Hozumi, N., Makino, E., Ōba, S., Ume, K., date of publication unknown, *Baishin Seido Ron* [On the Jury System], Tokyo: Publisher Unknown.

Mukōyama, H., 1983, "Nihon Tōchika ni okeru Taiwan no Hō to Seiji: Minzoku Hōgaku no Shiten ni Tatte" [Law and Politics in Taiwan under Japanese Rule: From the Standpoint of Ethnological Jurisprudence], *Kokugakuin Hōgaku*, Vol. 21, No. 2, pp. 61–106.

Mukōyama, H., 1987, *Nihon Tōchika ni okeru Taiwan Minzoku Undō Shi* [A History of the National Movement in Taiwan under the Japanese Rule], Tokyo: Chūō Keizai Kenkyūjo.

Munger, F., 2007, "Constitutional Reform, Legal Consciousness, and Citizen Participation in Thailand", *Cornell International Law Journal*, Vol. 40, pp. 455–475.

Murakami, H., 1864, *Futsugo Meiyō* [Dictionary of the French Language], Place of Publication Unknown: Publisher Unknown.

Murdoch, J., 1996, *A History of Japan*, London: Routledge.

Muto, S., 1973, "Concerning Trial Leadership in Civil Litigation: Focusing on the Judge's Inquiry and Compromise", *Law in Japan*, Vol. 12, pp. 23–28.

Myers, D. P., 1961, "Contemporary Practice of the United States Relating to International Law", *The American Journal of International Law*, Vol. 55, No. 1, pp. 150–165.

Naitō, Y., 1959, *Shūsengo no Shihō Seido Kaikaku no Keika* [The Progress of Postwar Legal Reforms], Tokyo: Shihō Kenshūjo.

Nakahara, S., 1989, "Meiji Kenpō Ka no Baishin Sei to Kenpō Ron" [The Jury System under the (Provisions of) the *Meiji* Constitution and Constitutional Theory], *Hōritsu Ronsō* [Law Review], Vol. 61, pp. 369–394.

Nakahara, S., 2000, *Baishinsei Fukkatsu no Jōken: Kenpō to Nihon Bunka Ron no Shiten kara* [The Conditions for the Revival of the Jury System (in Japan): (An Analysis) from the Constitutional and Cultural Perspectives], Tokyo: Gendaijinbunsha.

Nakanishi, T. (ed.), 2000, *Kenpō Kaisei* [Constitutional Revision], Tokyo: Chūō Kōron Shinsha.

Nakano, I., 2005, *Beikoku Tōchika Okinawa no Shakai to Hō* [Law and Society in Okinawa under the U.S. Occupation], Tokyo: Senshū University Press.

Namazugoshi, I., 2004, *Saiban'in Seido to Kokumin no Shihō Sanka: Keiji Shihō no Daitenkan e no Michi* [The *Saiban'in* System and Public Participation in the Judicial System: The Road towards a Great Turning Point in Criminal Justice], Tokyo: Gendai Jinbunsha.

Nelken, D., and Feest, J. (eds), 2001, *Adapting Legal Cultures*, Oxford: Hart Publishing.

Nichigai Associates, Inc. (ed.), 1999, *Seiyōjin Chōsha Mei Refarensu Jiten* [Reference Guide to Foreign Author Names in Katakana], Tokyo: Nichigai Associates, Inc.

Nichigai Associates, Inc., Editorial Department (ed.), 1996, *Jinbuntsu Refarensu Jiten* [Biography Index], Tokyo: Nichigai Associates, Inc.

Nihon Bengoshi Kyōkai [Japan Bar Association], 1921, *Nihon Bengoshi Kyōkai Rokuji Dai 259 Gō* [Records of the 259th Meeting of the Japan Bar Association], Tokyo: Nihon Bengoshi Kyōkai.

Nihon Bengoshi Rengōkai [Japan Federation of Bar Associations] (ed.), 1959, *Nihon Bengoshi Enkaku Shi* [A History of the Origins of (the Profession of) Attorney in Japan], Tokyo: Nihon Bengoshi Rengōkai.

Nihon Kindai Shi Kenkyūkai [Academic Society for the Study of the Modern History of Japan], 1980, *Minponshugi no Chōryū: 1914–1923* [The Current of *Minponshugi*], Tokyo: Sanseidō.

Nihon Kokugo Daijiten Henshū Iinkai [Editorial Commission for the Encyclopedic Dictionary of the Japanese Language] (ed.), 2001, *Nihon Kokugo Jiten* [The Encyclopedic Dictionary of the Japanese Language], Tokyo: Shōgakukan.

Nihon Kyōsantō [Japanese Communist Party], 1990, *Kagakuteki Shakai Shugi no 150 Nen to Nihon Kyōsantō* [150 Years of Scientific Socialism and the Japanese Communist Party], Tokyo: Shinnippon Shuppansha.

Nihon Shi Kōjiten Henshū Iinkai [Editorial Committee of the Historical Dictionary of Japan] (ed.), 1997, *Nihon Shi Kōjiten* [The Historical Dictionary of Japan], Tokyo: Yamakawa Shuppan.

Niigata Baishin Tomo no Kai (ed.), 1998, *Baishin Seido: Shimin no Te ni Saiban o* [The Jury System: Putting the Court into the Hands of the People], Tokyo: Shōgakusha.

Niikura, O. (ed.), 2003, *Saiban'in Seido ga Yatte Kuru: Anata ga Yūzai, Muzai o Kimeru: Shimin Sanka no Saiban* [Jury System Is on Its Way: The "Guilty" or "Non-Guilty" Verdict Will Be Up to You: Trials with Public Participation], Tokyo: Gendaijinbunsha.

Noda, Y. (translated and edited by Angelo, A. H.), 1976, *Introduction to Japanese Law*, Tokyo: University of Tokyo Press.

Ōba, S., 1914, *Baishin Seido Ron* [On the Jury System], Tokyo: Chūō Daigaku.

Oda, H. (ed.), 1997, *Basic Japanese Laws*, New York: Oxford University Press.

Oda, H., 2001, *Japanese Law*, Oxford: Oxford University Press.

Odamura, S., 2003, *Konna Kenpō ni Itsumade Gaman Dekimasuka: Bōkoku no Tami to Naranai tame ni* [For How Long Can You Bear with a Constitution Like This? – In Order for Us not to Become a Ruined People], Tokyo: Meiseisha.

Odanaka, T., 1973, "Keiji Soshō Seido no Kaikaku ni tsuite" [Reforms in the Criminal Procedure System], *Shakai Kagaku Kenkyū* [Journal of Social Science], Vol. 25, No. 1, pp. 120–132.

Odanaka, T., 2001, *Shihō Kaikaku no Shisō to Ronri* [The Ideology and Logic of Judicial Reforms], Tokyo: Shinsansha.

Ode, Y., Mizuno, K., and Mura, K., 1999, *Saiban o Kaeyō: Shimin ga Tsukuru Shihō Kaikaku* [Let's Change the Court System: Citizen-led Legal Reform], Tokyo: Nihon Hyōronsha.

Office of the Comptroller, Office of the High Commissioner, 1962, *Ryukyu Islands: Facts Book*, San Francisco: United States Civil Administration of the Ryukyu Islands.

Okamatsu, S., 1971, *Provisional Report on Investigations of Laws and Customs in the Island of Formosa, Compiled by Order of the Governor-General of Formosa*, Taipei: Ch'eng Wen Publishing Company.

Okinawa Ken Bunka Shinkōkai [Okinawa Prefectural Culture Promotion Foundation], 1999, *Military Government Activities Reports*, Naha: Okinawa Prefectural Board of Education.

Oldham, J., 1983, "The Origins of the Special Jury", *The University of Chicago Law Review*, Vol. 50, pp. 137–221.

Oldham, J., 1987, "Special Juries in England: Nineteenth Century Usage and Reform", *Journal of Legal History*, Vol. 8, pp. 148–166.

Oostindie G., and Paasman, B., 1998, "Dutch Attitudes towards Colonial Empires, Indigenous Cultures, and Slaves", *Eighteenth-Century Studies*, Vol. 31, No. 3, pp. 349–355.

Oppler, A. C., 1949, "The Reform of Japan's Legal and Judicial System under Allied Occupation", *Washington Law Review and State Bar Journal*, Vol. 24, pp. 290–324.

Oppler, A. C., 1980, *Legal Reform in Occupied Japan: A Participant Looks Back*, Princeton: Princeton University Press.

Osatake, T., 1926, *Meiji Bunka Shi toshite no Nihon Baishin Shi* [The History of Jury in Japan as (Part of) *Meiji* Cultural History], Tokyo: Hōkōdō Shoten.

Osatake, T., 1929, "Baishin to Fusen no Michizure [The Fellow Travelers of the Jury (System) and Universal Suffrage], *Hōsōkai Zasshi* [Journal of the Law Society], Vol. 7, No. 10, pp. 445–450.

Osner, N., Quinn, A., and Crown, G. (eds), 1993, *Criminal Justice Systems in Other Jurisdictions*, London: HMSO.Ōhara, N., 1929, "Baishin Hō No Jisshi Junbi ni tsuite" [Regarding the Preparation for the Enforcement of the Jury Act], *Hōsōkai Zasshi* [Journal of the Law Society], Vol. 7, No. 10, pp. 309–322.

Ōishi, M., 2006, *Ōoka Tadasuke*, Tokyo: Yoshikawa Kōbunkan.

Ōishi, S., 2010, *Bengoshi Fuse Tatsuji* [Lawyer Tatsuji Fuse], Tokyo: Nishida Shoten.

Ōkawa, K. 2009, *Saiban'in Seido no Hongi: Naze Shimin Sanka ga Hitsuyō nanoka* [The True Meaning of the Lay Judge System: Why Citizen Participation Is Important], Tokyo: Ichiyōsha.

Ōkura Shō Shuzeikyoku [The Tax Bureau, Ministry of Finance], 1956, *Meiji, Taishō, Shōwa: Kuni no Sainyū Ichiran Hyō* [*Meiji, Taishō, Shōwa* – State Revenues: a Chart], Tokyo: Ōkura Shō Shuzeikyoku.

Ōsaka Bengoshi Kai Keiji Hōsei Iinkai (ed.), 2001, *Baishin Hō Kaisei Hō Shian (Kentō Shiryō)* [Draft of the Law Amending the Jury Act], Osaka: Ōsaka Bengoshi Kai Keiji Hōsei Iinkai.

Ōsaka Bengoshi Kai [Osaka Bar Association], 1989, *Baishin Seido: Sono Kanōsei o Kangaeru* [The Jury System: Considering Its Possibilities], Osaka: Daiichi Hōki Shuppan.

Ōsaka Bengoshi Kai [Osaka Bar Association], 1992, *Baishin Seido: Amerika Shisatsu Hōkoku* [The Jury System: A Report on the Observations (of the System's Functioning in) America], Osaka: Daiichi Hōki Shuppan.

Pak-Wah Leung, R., 1983, "The Quasi-War in East Asia: Japan's Expedition to Taiwan and the Ryukyu Controversy", *Modern Asian Studies*, Vol. 17, No. 2, pp. 257–281.

Parsons, S., 2005, *Rational Choice in Politics: A Critical Introduction*, London: Continuum.

Peattie, M. R., 1988, *Nan'yō: The Rise and Fall of the Japanese in Micronesia, 1885–1945*, Honolulu: University of Hawai'i Press.

Peerenboom, R., 2006, "What Have We Learned about Law and Development? Describing, Predicting, and Assessing Legal Reforms in China", *Michigan Journal of International Law*, Vol. 27, pp. 823–871.

Peng, M., and Ng, Y., 1983, *Taiwan no Hōteki Chii* [The Legal Status of Taiwan], Tokyo: Tokyo University Press.

Perez, L. G., 1999, *Japan Comes of Age: Mutsu Munemitsu and the Revision of the Unequal Treaties*, London: Associated University Presses.

Plogstedt, A., 2013, "Citizen Judges in Japan: A Report Card for the Initial Three Years", *International and Comparative Law Review*, pp. 371–428.

Poe, M., Shimizu, K., and Simpson, J., 2002, "Revising the Japanese Commercial Code: A Summary and Evaluation of the Reform Effort", *Stanford Journal of East Asian Affairs*, Vol. 2, pp. 71–95.

Porter, R. P., 2001, *Japan: The Rise of a Modern Power*, Boston: Adamant Media.

Rabson, S., 1996, "Assimilation Policy in Okinawa: Promotion, Resistance, and 'Reconstruction'", *Japan Policy Research Institute*, occasional paper No. 8, October.

Ramseyer, J. M., 1993, "Judicial (In)Dependence in Japan", *University of Chicago Law School Record*, Vol. 39, pp. 5–11.

Ramseyer, J. M., 1994, "The Puzzling (In)Dependence of Courts: A Comparative Approach", *Journal of Legal Studies*, Vol. 23, pp. 721–747.

Ramseyer, J. M., and Nakazato, M., 1989, "The Rational Litigant: Settlement Amounts and Verdict Rates in Japan", *Journal of Legal Studies*, Vol. 18, pp. 266–290.

Ramseyer, J. M., and Nakazato, M., 1999, *Japanese Law: An Economic Approach*, Chicago: University of Chicago Press.

Ramseyer, J. M., and Rasmusen, E. B., 2001, "Why Is the Japanese Conviction Rate So High?", *Journal of Legal Studies*, Vol. 30, pp. 53–88.

Ramseyer, J. M., and Rasmusen, E. B., 2003, *Measuring Judicial Independence: The Political Economy of Judging in Japan*, Chicago: University of Chicago Press.

Reasons, C. E., and Rich, R. M. (eds), 1979, *The Sociology of Law: A Conflict Perspective*, Toronto: Butterworth & Co.

Reischauer, E. O., 1965, *The United States and Japan*, Cambridge: Harvard University Press.

Reischauer, E. O. (ed.), 2003, *Japan: An Illustrated Encyclopedia*, Tokyo: Kōdansha.

Rinji Shihō Seido Chōsa Kai [Provisional Justice System Investigation Committee], 1964, *Rinji Shihō Seido Chōsa Kai Ikensho* [The Opinion Statement of the Provisional Justice System Investigation Committee], Tokyo: Hōsōkai.

Saeki, C., 1996, *Baishin Saiban no Fukkatsu* [Revival of Jury Trials], Tokyo: Daiichi Hoki Shuppan.

Saiban'in Seido ni Hantai Suru Kai, 2004, "Saiban'in Seido ni Hansuru Kai no Ikensho" [Opinion Statement of the Society for Opposing the Saiban'in System], *Hanreijihō*, No. 1844, pp. 3–7.

Saikō Saibansho Jimu Sōkyoku Keiji Kyoku [Criminal Affairs Bureau, General Secretariat of the Supreme Court of Japan] (ed.), 1992, *Baishin, Sanshin Seido* [The Jury and Lay Assessor Systems], Tokyo: Shihō Kyōkai.

Saikō Saibansho Jimu Sōkyoku Keiji Kyoku [Criminal Affairs Bureau, General Secretariat of the Supreme Court of Japan], 1995, *Wagakuni de Okonawareta Baishin Saiban – Shōwa Shoki ni Okeru Baishin Hō no Un'yō ni tsuite* [Jury Trials that Took Place in Our Country – Regarding the Operation of the Jury Act in the Early *Shōwa* Period], Tokyo: Shihō Kyōkai.

Saikō Saibansho Jimu Sōkyoku Keiji Kyoku [Criminal Affairs Bureau, General Secretariat of the Supreme Court], 1996, *Baishin no Jijitsu Nintei o Chūshin toshite* [Focusing on the Jury's Fact-Finding [Ability]], Tokyo: Shihō Kyōkai.

Saitama Baishin Fōramu (ed.), 1989, *Kuni vs Itō: Baishin Seido – Sono Jissen* [State vs Ito: The Jury System in Practice], Tokyo: Equality.

Sakai, T., 1992, *Taishō Demokurashii Taisei no Hōkai* [The Demolition of the Taishō System], Tokyo: University of Tokyo Press.

Sakamoto, T., 1928, "Baishin Hō no Jisshi ni Atarite" [On the [Occasion of] the Implementation of the Jury Act], *Hōsō Kōron*, Vol. 32, No. 9, pp. 57–62.

Sakaya, A., 1925, *Karafuto Enkakushi* [A History of Development of Karafuto], Toyohara: Karafuto Chō.

Sakihara, M., 1972, "Ryukyu's Tribute-Tax to Satsuma during the Tokugawa Period", *Modern Asian Studies*, Vol. 6, No. 3, pp. 329–335.

Sarantakes, N. E., 2000, *Keystone: The American Occupation of Okinawa and US-Japanese Relations*, College Station: Texas A & M Press.

Sato, L., 1990, "Revisionism during the Forty Years of the Constitution in Japan", *Law and Contemporary Problems*, Vol. 53, Issue 1, pp. 98–103.

Satō, T., 1962, *Nihonkoku Kenpō Seiritsu Shi* [The Formulation of the Constitution of Japan], Tokyo: Yūhikaku.

Shapiro, M., 1981, *Courts: A Comparative and Political Analysis*, Chicago: University of Chicago Press.

Shihō Daijin Kanbō Chōsa Ka [Research Department, Minister's Secretariat, Ministry of Justice] 1926, *Shihō Shiryō: Baishin Seido Shisatsu Hōkokusho Shū No. 85* [Judicial Materials: A Compilation of Reports Examining the Jury System No. 85], Tokyo: Shihō Daijin Shobō Chōsa Ka.

Shihō Raitazu Yunion, 2000, *Shihō Kaikaku Q & A: Watashitachi no tame ni Shihō ga Kawaru?!* (Q & A on Legal Reform: Judicial System to Change for Us?!), Tokyo: Gendaijinbunsha.

Shihō Shō Keijikyoku [Ministry of Justice, Criminal Affairs Bureau] (ed.), 1929, *Baishin Sesshi Shū* [A Collection of Jury Instructions], Tokyo: Shihō Shō Keijikyoku [Ministry of Justice, Criminal Affairs Bureau].

Shihō Shō Keijikyoku [Ministry of Justice, Criminal Affairs Bureau] (ed.), 1929, *Baishin Sesshi Shū* [A Collection of Jury Instructions], Tokyo: Shihō Shō Keijikyoku [Ministry of Justice, Criminal Affairs Bureau].

Shihō Shō Keijikyoku [Ministry of Justice, Criminal Affairs Bureau] (ed.), 1929, *Baishin Sesshi Shū* [A Collection of Jury Instructions], Tokyo: Shihō Shō Keijikyoku [Ministry of Justice, Criminal Affairs Bureau].

Shimabukuro, K., and Higa, Y. (eds), 1986, *Chiiki kara no Kokusai Kōryū: Ajia Taiheiyō Jidai to Okinawa* [International Exchange from the Local Level: The Asia-Pacific Era and Okinawa], Tokyo: Kenbun Shuppan.

Shimamoto, S., 1986, *"Furansu ni okeru Nihon Kenkyū no Kaitakusha Misheru Rubon: Rubon Ke Tanpōki"* [Michel Revon – a Pioneer in (the Field of) Japan Studies in France: Notes of the Investigation (Concerning) Revon's Family], *Kenkyū to Hyōron* [Research and Reviews], Vol. 37, pp. 82–91.

Shinjo, M., Mitani, S., Komori, M., and Takechi, S. (eds), 2005, *Hōgaku: Okinawa Hōritsu Jijō* [The Law: Legal Situation in Okinawa], Naha: Ryūkyū Shimpōsha.

Shinomiya, S. (ed.), 1999, *Baishin Tebiki: Hōtei San'yo Nisshi Tsuki* [The Jury Guidebook: Includes Journal of Trial Participation], Tokyo: Gendaijinbunsha.

Shinomiya, S., 2001, *Bācharu Baishin Handobukku – Moshi mo Baishin'in toshite Saibansho ni Yobaretara* [Virtual Handbook for Jury Service – If You Are Chosen to Serve on a Jury], Tokyo: Kadensha.

Shinomiya, S., Nishimura, T., Kudō, M., 2005, *Moshi mo Saiban'in ni Erabaretara: Saiban'in Handobukku* [What if You Get Selected to Be a Lay Judge: A Handbook for Lay Judges], Tokyo: Kadensha.

Shubert, G., and Damm, J. (eds), 2011, *Taiwanese Identity in the 21st Century: Domestic, Regional, and Global Perspectives*, London: Routledge.

Shūgiin Kenpō Chōsakai Jimukyoku [Office of the Research Commission on the Constitution, House of Representatives], 2003, *Meiji Kenpō to Nihonkoku Kenpō ni kansuru Kisoteki Shiryō* [Fundamental Materials Concerning the *Meiji* Constitution and the Constitution of Japan], Tokyo: Shūgiin Kenpō Chōsakai Jimukyoku.

Shwartz, R., and Millers, J., 1964, "Legal Evolution and Societal Complexity", *American Sociological Review*, Vol. 70, pp. 159–169.Siddle, R., 1998, "Colonialism and Identity in Okinawa Before 1945", *Japanese Studies*, Vol. 18, No. 2, pp. 117–133.

Silberman, B. S., and Harootunian, H. D. (eds), 1974, *Japan in Crisis: Essays on Taisho Democracy*, Princeton: Princeton University Press.

Smits, G., 1999, *Visions of Ryukyu: Identity and Ideology in Early-Modern Thought and Politics*, Honolulu: University of Hawai'i Press.

Smits, G., 2000, "Ambiguous Boundaries: Redefining Royal Authority in the Kingdom of Ryukyu", *Harvard Journal of Asiatic Studies*, Vol. 60, No. 1, pp. 89–123.

Stack, R., 2000, "Western Law in Japan: the Antimonopoly Law and Other Legal Transplants", *Manitoba Law Journal*, Vol. 27, pp. 391–414.

Steiner, K., 1950, "Postwar Changes in the Japanese Civil Code", *Washington Law Review and State Bar Journal*, Vol. 25, pp. 286–312.

Stephan, J. J., 1971, *Sakhalin: A History*, Oxford: Clarendon Press.

Stevenson, J. R., 1966, "Case Notes", *The American Journal of International Law*, Vol. 60, No. 4, pp. 858–867.

Stier, F., 1992, "What Can the American Adversary System Learn from an Inquisitorial System of Justice?", *Judicature*, Vol. 76, pp. 109–111.

Suehiro, I., 1928, *Gendai Hōgaku Zenshū* [Full Collection of Works on Contemporary Law], Vol. 24, Tokyo: Nihon Hyōronsha.

Sumner, C., 1979, *Reading Ideologies: An Investigation into the Theory of Ideology and Law*, New York: Pantheon.

Sunstein, C. R., 2001, *Designing Democracy – What Constitutions Do*, New York: Oxford University Press.

Suttles, W., 1961, "A Review of 'Okinawa: The History of an Island People'", *Pacific Affairs*, Vol. 34, No. 1, pp. 85–87.

Suzuki, U., 1919, *Nihon Kaizō no Igi Oyobi sono Kōryō* [The Significance of and Outline for Reforming Japan], Tokyo: Jisseikatsu Sha Shuppanbu.

Taiwan Sōtokufu [The Office of the Governor-General of Taiwan], 1896, *Taiwan Sōtokufu Reikiruishō* [Excerpts from the Orders and Regulations of the Office of the Governor General of Taiwan], Taipei: Taiwan Sōtokufu [The Office of the Governor-General of Taiwan].

Taiwan Sōtoku Fu [The Office of the Governor-General of Taiwan], 1969, *Nihon Tōchika no Minzoku Undō* [National (Liberation) Movements under Japanese Rule], Vol. 2, Tokyo: Fūrin Shobō.Takahashi, K., 2010, *Taishō Jidai no Chōfuken* [Government Agencies and Prefectures in the *Taishō* Period], Tokyo: Taiyō Shuppan.

Takakura, S., 1947, *Hokkaido Takushoku Shi* [The History of the Development of Hokkaido], Sapporo: Hokkaido Daigaku Toshokan Kankōkan.

Takakura, S., 1947, *Hokkaidō Takushoku Shi* [A History of the Development of Hokkaido], Sapporo: Kashiwaba Shoin.

Takano, E., 2001, "Nihon ni okeru Baishin Hō no Shikō to Teishi: Hanseiten to Kongo ni Ikasu tame ni" [The Implementation and Suspension of Japan's Jury Act: Points for Reflection and Lessons to be Used for the Future], *Hōgaku Jānaru* [The Law Journal], No. 16, pp. 1–55.

Takashio, H., 2004, *Edo Jidai no Hō to Sono Shūen: Yoshimune to Shigekata to Sadanobu to* [The Law of the Edo Period and Its Surroundings: Yoshimune, Shigekata, and Sadanobu], Tokyo: Kyūko Shoin.

Takayama, S., 2006, *Saiban'in Seido wa Iranai!* [We Do Not Need the Lay Judge System!], Tokyo: Kōdansha.

Takayama, S., 2007, "Saiban'in Seido o Hajimesasete wa Naranai" [The Lay Judge System Should Not Be Allowed to Start], *Mō Hitotsu no Sekai e*, Vol. 8, pp. 24–26.

Takayanagi, M., and Matsudaira, T., 1962, *Sengoku Jinmei Jiten* [Biographical Dictionary of the Warring States [Period]], Tokyo: Yoshikawa Kōbunkan.

Takeda, H., 1992, *Teikoku Shugi to Minponshugi* [Imperialism and *Minponshugi*], Tokyo: Shūeisha.

Takekoshi, Y. (translated by G. Braithwaite), 1907, *Japanese Rule in Formosa*, London: Longmans, Green, and Co.

Takemae, E. (ed.), 2001, *Goken, Kaiken Shiron* [A History of the Constitutional Debate: Conservative and Revisionist Perspectives], Tokyo: Shōgakukan.

Takigawa, Y., 1936, *Baishin Hō* [The Jury Act], Tokyo: Nihon Hyōronsha.

Takii, K., 2003, *Bunmei Shi no Naka no Meiji Kenpō: Kono Kuni no Katachi to Seiyō Taiken* [The *Meiji* Constitution within the History of Civilization: The Shape of this Country and Its Experience of the West], Tokyo: Kōdansha.

Takii, K. (translated by Noble, D.), 2007, *The Meiji Constitution: The Japanese Experience of the West and the Shaping of the Modern State*, Tokyo: International House of Japan.

Takizawa, M., 1971, "Okinawa: Reversion to Japan and Future Prospects", *Asian Survey*, Vol. 11, No. 5, pp. 496–505.

Takumu Daijin Kanbō Bunsho Ka [The Secretariat and Document Division of the Ministry of Colonial Affairs], 1931, *Chōsen, Taiwan, Karafuto, Kantōshū oyobi Nan'yō Guntō ni Okonawaruru Hōritsu Chō* [A List of Pieces of Legislation Enforced in Korea, Taiwan, Karafuto, Kwantung, and Micronesia], Tokyo: Takumu Daijin Kanbō Bunsho Ka [The Secretariat and Document Division of the Ministry of Colonial Affairs].

Tamura, J., 2003, *Shihō Seido Kaikaku to Hōka Daigakuin: Sekai Hyōjun no Purofeshonaru Skūru Jitsugen ni Mukete* [Justice System Reform and Law Schools: Towards Realization of World-Level Professional Schools], Tokyo: Nihon Hyōronsha.

Tanaka, H. (ed.), 1976, *The Japanese Legal System: Introductory Cases and Materials*, Tokyo: University of Tokyo Press.

Tanaka, S., 2000, *Hōgaku Nyūmon: Hō to Gendaishakai* [Introduction to Legal Studies: Law and Contemporary Society], Hōsōdaigaku Kyōikushinkōkai.

Tanase, T., 2006, "Global Markets and the Evolution of Law in China and Japan", *Michigan Journal of International Law*, Vol. 27, pp. 873–893.

Tax Bureau (Ministry of Finance), 2006, *The Comprehensive Guidebook of Japanese Taxes*, Tokyo: Tax Bureau (Ministry of Finance).

Teraoka, J. (ed.), 1981, *Meiji Shoki no Zairyū Gaijin* [Foreigners Residing in Japan in the Early *Meiji* Period], Tokyo: Teraoka Shodō.

Terasaki, O., 2008, *Jiyū Minken Undō no Kenkyū: Kyūshinteki Jiyū Minken Undōka no Kiseki* [Research on the Liberal Movement for Human Rights: The Tracks of the Radical Activists of the Movement], Tokyo: Keiyo University Press.

Tezuka, Y., 1947, "Shihō Shō Oyatoi Gaijin Kākuddo" [Kirkwood – A Foreign Consultant Employed by the Ministry of Justice], *Hōgaku Kenkyū*, Vol. 40, No. 3, pp. 55–65.

Tezuka, Y. (ed.), 1990, *Kindai Nihon Shi no Shin Kenkyū* [New Research on the Modern History of Japan], Tokyo: Hokuju Shuppan.Thaman, S. C., 1999, "Europe's New Jury Systems: The Cases of Spain and Russia", *Law and Contemporary Problems*, Vol. 62, pp. 233–261.

Tipton, E. K., 2002, *Modern Japan: A Social and Political History*, London: Routledge.

Tokyo Asahi Shinbunsha Shakaibu [Tokyo Asahi Newspaper Company, Local News Section], 1928, *Baishin Kōza* [Lectures on the Jury [System]], Tokyo: Asahi Shinbunsha.

Tokyo Bengoshi Kai [Tokyo Bar Association] (ed.), 1982, *Shihō Kaikaku no Tenbō* [Prospects of Judicial Reform], Tokyo: Yūhikaku.

Tokyo Bengoshi Kai [Tokyo Bar Association], 1992, *Baishin Saiban: Kyūbaishin no Shōgen to Kongo no Kadai* [Jury Trials: The Testimony and Implications for the Future of the Old Jury System], Tokyo: Gyōsei.

Tokyo Daigaku Shakai Kagaku Kenkyūjo [The University of Tokyo, Institute of Social Science], 1975, *Sengo Kaikaku* [Post-war Reforms], Tokyo: Tokyo Daigaku Shuppan Kai.

Tokyo Daigaku Shuppan Kai [Tokyo University Press] (ed.), 1984, *Teikoku Gikai Shūgiin Giji Sokkiroku 69* [Stenography of the Proceedings of the House of Representatives], Tokyo: Tokyo Daigaku Shuppan Kai.

Tokyo San Bengoshikai Baishin Seido Iinkai [Tokyo San Bengoshikai Bar Association Committee on the Jury System] (ed.), 1993, *Nyū Yōku Baishin Saiban* [The New York Jury Trial], Tokyo: Nihon Kajo Shuppan.

Tomasi, M., 2002, "Oratory in Meiji and Taishō Japan: Public Speaking and the Formation of New Written Language", *Monumenta Nipponica*, Vol. 57, No. 1, pp. 43–71.

Toshitani, N., 1981, "Jōyaku Kaisei to Baishin Seido" [Treaty Revision and the Jury System], *Shakai Kagaku Kenkyū* [The Journal of Social Science], Vol. 33, No. 5, pp. 1–32.

Tsai, H. C., 1990, *One Kind of Control: The Hoko System in Taiwan under the Japanese Rule, 1895–1945*, PhD Dissertation (Columbia University).

Ts'ai, H. C., 2009, *Taiwan in Japan's Empire Building: An Institutional Approach to Colonial Engineering*, London: Routledge.

Tsuchiya, Y., 2005, *Shimin no Shihō wa Jitsugen Shita ka: Shihō Kaikaku no Zentai Zō* [Has the (Idea of) Justice for the People Been Realized? An Overview of Judicial Reforms], Tokyo: Kadensha.

Tsuchiya, Y., 2008, *Saiban'in Seido ga Hajimaru: Sono Kitai to Kenen* [The Lay Judge System (Is About to Start): Expectations and Fears], Tokyo: Kadensha.

Tsuchiya, Y., 2009, *Saiban'in Seido to Kokumin: Kokuminteki Kiban wa Kakuritsu Dekiru ka* [The Lay Judge System and the People: Will the Popular Base Be Established?], Tokyo: Kadensha.

Tsuzuki, C., 2000, *The Pursuit of Power in Modern Japan: 1825–1995*, New York: Oxford University Press.

Turk, A., 1976, "Law as a Weapon in Social Conflict", *Social Problems*, Vol. 23, pp. 276–291.

Tushnet, M., 1972, "Lumber and the Legal Process", *Wisconsin Law Review*, Issue 1, pp. 114–132.

Ueda, M. (ed.), 1994, *Concise Japanese Biographical Dictionary*, Tokyo: Sanseidō.

Uehara, E., 1919, *Demokurashii to Nihon no Kaizō* [Democracy and Reforming Japan], Tokyo: Chūgai Insatsu Kōgyō.

Uga, K., 2002, *Shin Jōhō Kōkai Hō Chikujō Kaisetsu* [New Commentary on Information Disclosure Laws], Tokyo: Yūhikaku.

Ukichi, S., 1909, *Karafuto Kaihatsusaku* [The Development Policies of Karafuto], Ōtomari: Hokushindō.

United States Department of Army, 1958, *Joint Manual of Civil Affairs/Military Government, Field Manual FM 41–5, OPNAV P21–1, AFM 110–7, NAVMC 2500*, Washington: Government Printing.

Upham, F., 1987, *Law and Social Change in Postwar Japan*, Cambridge: Harvard University Press.

Urabe, M., 1968, *Wagakuni ni okeru Baishin Saiban no Kenkyū: Keiken Dan ni yoru Jittai Chōsa o Chūshin toshite* [Research on Jury Trials in Our Country: A Study Focusing on the Actual Experiences], Tokyo: Shihō Kenshūjo.

Urata, K. (ed.), 2000, *Okinawa Bei Gun Kichi Hō no Genzai* [The Present State of US Military Base Law in Okinawa], Tokyo: Ichiryūsha.

Ushiomi, T. (ed.), 1966, *Iwanami Kōza: Gendai Hō 6* [Iwanami Lectures: Contemporary Law 6], Tokyo: Iwanami Shoten.

Verwayen, F. B., 1998, "Tokugawa Translations of Dutch Legal Texts", *Monumenta Nipponica*, Vol. 53, No. 3, pp. 335–358.

Vidmar, N., 1999, "The Canadian Criminal Jury: Searching for a Middle Ground", *Law and Contemporary Problems*, Vol. 62, pp. 141–173.

Vidmar, N., 2003, *World Jury Systems*, New York: Oxford University Press.

Von Mehren, A. T. (ed.), 1963, *Law in Japan: The Legal Order in a Changing Society*, Cambridge: Harvard University Press.

Wakabayashi, B. T. (ed.), 1998, *Modern Japanese Thought*, New York: Cambridge University Press.

Wakabayashi, M., 2001, *Taiwan Kōnichi Undōshi Kenkyū* [A Study of Anti-Japanese Movements in Taiwan], Tokyo: Kenbun Shuppan.

Walpin, G., 2003, "America's Adversarial and Jury Systems: More Likely to Do Justice", *Harvard Journal of Law and Public Policy*, Vol. 26, pp. 175–186.

Wang, T., 2000, *Legal Reform in Taiwan under Japanese Colonial Rule, 1895–1945: The Reception of Western Law*, Seattle: University of Washington Press.

Ward, R. E., and Yoshikazu, S., 1987, *Democratizing Japan: The Allied Occupation*, Honolulu: University of Hawai'i Press.

Watanabe, H., 1927, *Mie Ken Jin Pamfuretto: Baishin Seido no Hanashi* [Pamphlet for Citizens of Mie Prefecture: About the Jury System], Nagoya: Mie Ken Jin Kai Jimusho.

Watson, A., 1974, *Legal Transplants: An Approach to Comparative Law*, Edinburgh: Scottish Academic Press.

Watson, A., 1977, *Society and Legal Change*, Edinburgh: Scottish Academic Press.

Watson, A., 1978, "Comparative Law and Legal Change", *Cambridge Law Journal*, Vol. 37, pp. 313–336.

Weber, M., 1968, *Economy and Society: An Outline of Interpretive Sociology*, New York: Bedminster Press.

Weiss, L., 1946, "U.S. Military Government on Okinawa", *Far Eastern Survey*, Vol. 15, No. 15, pp. 234–238.

West, M., 1992, "Prosecution Review Commissions: Japan's Answer to the Problem of Prosecutorial Discretion", *Columbia Law Review*, Vol. 92, pp. 684–724.

Wigmore, J. H., 1967–1986, *Law and Justice in Tokugawa Japan: Materials for the History of Japanese Law and Justice under the Tokugawa Shogunate 1603–1867*, Tokyo: University of Tokyo Press.

Wiley, J. C., 1999, "Will the 'Bang' Mean 'Big' Changes to Japanese Financial Laws?", *Hastings International & Comparative Law Review*, Vol. 22, pp. 379–405.

Wilson, G. M. (ed.), 1970, *Crisis Politics in Prewar Japan: Institutional and Ideological Problems of the 1930s*, Tokyo: Sophia University Press.

Wilson, M. J., 2013, "Prime Time for Japan to Take Another Step forward in Lay Participation: Exploring Expansion to Civil Trials", *Akron Law Review*, Vol. 46, pp. 641–674.

Wilson, M. J., Fukurai, H. and Maruta, T. (eds), *Japan and Civil Jury Trials: A Convergence of Forces*, Cheltenham: Edward Edgar.

Wu, M. (translated by Y. Yokosawa), 2010, *Taiwan Shi Shō Jiten* [A Concise Dictionary of Taiwanese History], Fukuoka: Chūgoku Shoten.

Yamanaka, T., 1975, "Oppler Hakase to no Intabyū" [An Interview with Dr. Oppler], *Hōritsu Jihō*, Vol. 47, No. 4, pp. 98–105.

Yamasaki, K., 1931, "The Japanese Mandate in the South Pacific", *Pacific Affairs*, Vol. 4, No. 2, pp. 95–112.

Yamauchi, M., 2004, *Sengo Okinawa Tsūka Henkan Shi: Beigun Tōchi Jidai o Chūshin ni* [The History of Reversion of Currency in Post-war Okinawa: Focusing on the Era of U.S. Military Administration], Naha: Ryūkyū Shinpōsha.

Yano, T., 2006, *Akireru Saiban to Saiban'in Seido: Saibankan wa naze Shin'yō Dekinai no ka?* [Repulsive Courts and the *Saiban'in* System: Why Judges Cannot Be Trusted], Tokyo: Ryokufū Shuppan.

Yoshida, S. (ed.), 1961, *Okinawa Shihō Seido no Kenkyū* [A Study of the Judicial System of Okinawa], Tokyo: Nampō Dōhō Engo Kai.

Young, C. W., 1931, *The International Legal Status of the Kwantung Leased Territory*, Baltimore: The Johns Hopkins Press.

Yunesuko Higashi Ajia Bunka Kenkyū Sentā [East Asia Cultural Center for UNESCO], 1975, *Oyatoi Gaikokujin* [Foreigners in Government Employ], Tokyo: Shōgakukan.

Zifcak, S. (ed.), 2005, *Globalization and the Rule of Law*, London: Routledge.

Newspaper articles and websites

Asahi Shinbun

1931, "Chōsenjin no Yado de Keiji Kōsatsu Saru; Hannin wa Kyokusa Bunshi; Musansha Shinbun no Kankeisha" [Detective (Found) Strangled at Korean Home; Perpetrator An Extreme Left-Wing Element; Associated with the Proletarian Newspaper], *Tokyo Asahi Shinbun*, January 19.

1946, "Baishin Seido o Fukkatsu; Kakugi Kettei" [Restoration of the Jury System; Cabinet Resolution], *Asahi Shinbun*, March 6.

2002, "Saiban'in Seido Dōnyū o Mae ni" [In View of the Introduction of the Jury System], *Asahi Shinbun*, June 3.

2002, "Saiban'in Seido ni Nirami, Mogi Geki de Saiban Jisshi" [In View of the (Introduction of the) Jury System, A Trial Is Shown on Stage], *Asahi Shinbun*, December 4.

2003, "Hō Shitashimi Manabō, Jūgatsu Tōka – 'Hō no Hi'" [Get Familiar with the Law: October 10 Is "Law Day"], *Asahi Shinbun*, September 5.

2003, "O Katai Basho no Heki Kaishō Kitai" [Hoping to Get Rid of the Walls Surrounding the 'Uneasy Place' [Called Court]], *Asahi Shinbun*, August 23.

2003, "Saiban'in Seido" [The Lay Judge System], *Asahi Shinbun*, September 1.

2003, "Shihō Kaikaku tte Nani? Saiban Jinsokuka, Shimin mo Sanka, Hōkadaigakuin de Jinzai Ikusei" [What Is Meant by Judicial Reform? Trials to Accelerate, Increased People's Participation, New Cadres to Be Educated in Law Schools"], *Asahi Shinbun*, September 5.

2004, "Bengoshi ra 'Saiban'in Seido' Hantai Seimei; Tokyo de Shūkai" [Lawyers [Issue] Statement Opposing Lay Judge System, Have Meeting in Tokyo], *Asahi Shinbun*, April 21.

2004, "Minshutō ga Shūsei Taian 'Chōeki Sakujo' Moru Saiban'in Seido" [DPJ [Prepares] Revision Plan; Lay Judge System: To Delete Imprisonment Provision], *Asahi Shinbun*, April 14.

2004, "Saiban'in Hō An no Shūsei Motome Seimei Saitama Bengoshi Kai" [Saitama Bar Association [Issues] Statement Demanding Revision of the Lay Judge Bill], *Asahi Shinbun*, April 22.

2004, "Saiban'in Hō Shūsei, Kuni ni Motome Ketsugisho Kyōto Bengoshi Kai ga Sōfu" [Revision of the Lay Judge Act demanded of Government; Kyoto Bar Association Sends [Proposal]], *Asahi Shinbun*, April 23.

2004, "Saiban'in Seifu An, Shinbun Kyōkai 'Shūsei o'" [The Japan Newspaper Publishers and Editors' Association (Demands) Revision of the Government's Draft of the Lay Judge Act], *Asahi Shinbun*, April 3.

2007, "Saiban'in Jidai: 'Chōeki no Yō na Mono', 'Jiyū ga Ii'; Arashiyama Kōzaburō san ra, Tokyo de Shūkai" [The Era of Lay Judges: "It Is Like Penal Servitude", "It Is Better to Be Free"; Kōzaburō Arashiyama and Others Meet in Tokyo], *Asahi Shinbun*, June 30.

2007, "(Saiban'in Jidai) Mezase Yasashii Saibansho; Shimin ni Hairyō Shisetsu O Seibi [(The Lay Judge Era) Aiming for Courts that Are Close (to the People); Providing Facilities that Take People's (Needs) into Consideration]", *Asahi Shinbun*, July 16.2007, "Saiban'in Seido Shitteiru 81%, Sanka Shōkyokuha 78%, Tokubetsu Yoron Chōsa" [Special Opinion Poll: 81% of Respondents Know about the *Saiban'in* System, 78% Passive about Participating], *Asahi Shinbun*, February 2.

2008, "Saiban'in Seido wa Kenpō Ihan, Shimin Dantai, Fukuoka de Haishi Uttae" [The Lay Judge System Is Unconstitutional; A Citizen Group Demands Abolishment in Fukuoka], *Asahi Shinbun*, November 29.

2009, "Hōtei de no Bengojutsu, Kenshūkai de Manabu, Saiban'in Seido de Bengoshi Kai" [Bar Association Preparing for Lay Judge System: (Members Learn) Court Defense Technique at a Training Session], *Asahi Shinbun*, April 6.

2009, "Kenji no Hanashi Kata, Anaunsā ga Shidō; Saiban'in Seido Hikae Kenshū" [Prosecutors' Speech, An Announcer Provides Instruction at Training Session in Preparation for the Lay Judge System], *Asahi Shinbun*, April 15.

2009, "Saiban'in Kōhōsha ni Nattara, Yobidashi 'Iku' 57% Asahi Shinbunsha Yoron Chōsa" [If Selected as Lay Judge Candidate 57% Will Go (as Summoned); Asahi Newspaper Company's Opinion Poll], *Asahi Shinbun*, January 9.

2014, "(Shasetsu) Saiban'in no Futan: Jittai o Tsukami Taisaku o" [(Editorial) The Burden of Lay Judges: (Coming up with) Solutions (Aiming to) Investigate the Actual Conditions], *Asahi Shinbun*, October 4.

Hōritsu

1923, "Baishin Hō Kōenkai Kaisai ni tsuki Shakoku" [[Newspaper] Company Announcement Regarding Jury Act Lecture], *Hōritsu Shinbun*, June 23.

1923, "Baishin Hō Shikō Junbi" [Preparing for Enforcement of the Jury Act], *Hōritsu Shinbun*, April 3.

1923, "Baishin Hōan no Tsūka o Shukusu" [Celebrating the Passage of the Jury Bill], *Hōritsu Shinbun*, March 28.

1923 "Baishin Seido Shikō Keikaku" [Plans for the Implementation of the Jury System], *Hōritsu Shinbun*, April 23.

1924, "Baishin Seido Shisatsu" [Observation of the Jury System [in Other Countries]], *Hōritsu Shinbun*, April 23.

1927, "Baishin Hō Mogi Saiban ni tsuite" [On Mock Jury Trials], *Hōritsu Shinbun*, December 28.

1927, "Baishin Hō Senden no Kansen Eiga" [Jury Act Promotional Film Endorsed by the Government], *Hōritsu Shinbun*, December 18.

1927, "Baishin Hōtei no Zaseki Mondai (2) [The Seating Problem in Jury Courtrooms (2)], *Hōritsu Shinbun*, November 20.

1927, "Baishin'in Shikakusha 6000 Nin" [6000 Persons Eligible for Jury Service], *Hōritsu Shinbun*, September 10.

1927, "Hōtei ni okeru Kenji, Shoki narabi ni Shihō Kisha no Zaseki ni tsuite" [Concerning the Seats of the Prosecutor, the Secretary, and of the Judicial Reporters], *Hōritsu Shinbun*, August 10.

1927, "Kenji to Bengoshi Zaseki wa Dōtō" [Seats of Prosecutor and Attorney to Be Equal], *Hōritsu Shinbun*, August 8.

1928, "Baishin Hō Jō no Gigi o Ronjite, Hōsō Kakui no Kōsetsu o Motomu (1)" [Discussing the Doubts Regarding the Jury Act, Opinions of Legal Professionals Wanted (Part 1)], *Hōritsu Shinbun*, June 13.

1928, "Baishin Hō Jō no Gigi o Ronjite, Hōsō Kakui no Kōsetsu o Motomu (2)" [Discussing the Doubts Regarding the Jury Act, Opinions of Legal Professionals Wanted (Part 2)], *Hōritsu Shinbun*, June 15.

1928, "Baishin Hō Jō no Gigi o Ronjite, Hōsō Kakui no Kōsetsu o Motomu (3)" [Discussing the Doubts Regarding the Jury Act, Opinions of Legal Professionals Wanted (Part 3)], *Hōritsu Shinbun*, June 23.

1928, "Baishin Hōtei o Haikei toshite no Yoshin, Hōtei Chūshin Shugi ka Yoshin Chūshin Shugi ka" [Pre-Trial Investigations Against the Background of Jury Trials; Courtroom-Centered or Pre-Trial Investigation-Centered Approach?], *Hōritsu Shinbun*, April 8.

1928, "Baishin Jisshi Junbi no Jitsumuka Kaidō" [Meeting of Professionals in Preparation for the Implementation of the Jury Act], *Hōritsu Shinbun*, September 10.

1928, "Baishin Mondai Shū" [Compilation of Questions Concerning the Jury [System]], *Hōritsu Shinbun*, September 18.

1928, "Baishin Saiban Kunren Hajimaru" [Jury Trial Training Starts], *Hōritsu Shinbun*, March 10.

1928, "Baishin Saiban ni Seikō Shita Ōita Chihō Saibansho" [Oita District Court Successfully [Carries Out] Jury Trial], *Hōritsu Shinbun*, November 3.

1928, "Baishin no Oshigoto ni Isogashii Tōkyō Chihō Saibansho" [Tokyo District Court Busy with Preparations for the Jury], January 1.

1928, "Baishin'in no Shidō Kaishi" [Guidance [Sessions] for Jurors Begin], *Hōritsu Shinbun*, January 15.

1928, "Kōji o Isogitsutsu Aru Tōkyō Chihō Saibansho Baishin Hōtei" [Construction of Jury Courtroom Speeded Up at Tokyo District Court], *Hōritsu Shinbun*, April 23.

1928, "Sendai ni okeru Mogi Baishin Saiban" [Mock Jury Trial in Sendai], *Hōritsu Shinbun*, May 20.

1928, "Tokyo Bengoshikai Shusai no Mogi Baishin Saiban" [Jury Mock Trial Organized by the Tokyo Bar Association], *Hōritsu Shinbun*, August 13.

1928, "Ōita Chihō Saibansho Hatsu Baishin Hanketsu" [Oita District Court's First Jury Verdict], *Hōritsu Shinbun*, November 3.

1929, "Baishin Hiyō Ikken Sanbyaky En Ijō" [Jury Costs More Than 300 Yen per Case], *Hōritsu Shinbun*, January 28.

1930, "Ōkina Kitai mo Hazure Funinki na Baishin Seido" [Unpopular Jury System Disappoints Great Expectations], *Hōritsu Shinbun*, June 28.

Ansai, I., 1927, "Baishin Hō Senden to Mogi Saiban" [Promotion of the Jury Act and Mock Trials], *Hōritsu Shinbun*, October 25.

Hanai, T., 1928, "Baishin Hō Ron" [The Theory (Behind) the Jury Act], *Hōritsu Shinbun*, November 8.

Hirai, H., 1929, "Saiban Baishin yori wa Kiso Sanshin no Seido ga Nozomashii" [Rather than Court Jury, An Indictment Lay Assessor System Is Desirable], *Hōritsu Shinbun*, January 5.

Kurohōshi (pseudonym of Katei Watanabe), 1927, "Baishin Hō Senden to Minshū Shinri" [Promotion of the Jury Act and Popular Psychology], *Hōritsu Shinbun*, November 12.

Mikami, S., 1927, "Baishin Senden Dayori" [News Concerning the Promotion of the Jury [System]], *Hōritsu Shinbun*, September 8.

Ōmori, K., 1927, "Baishin Seido no Konpongi" [The Fundamentals of the Jury System], *Hōritsu Shinbun*, August 28.

Uzawa, S. 1928, "Baishin Hō no Seishin" [The Spirit of the Jury Act], *Hōritsu Shinbun*, May 18.

Japan Times

2000, "Legal Experts Argue for Use of Jury System in Japan", *Japan Times*, June 5.
2002, "The Media and a Jury System", *Japan Times*, November 13.
2003, "18,000 Take Exams for New Law Schools", *Japan Times*, August 4.
2004, "Parties Agree on 'Citizen Judge' Plan", *Japan Times*, January 27.
2005, "70% Don't Want to Serve on Juries in New System", *Japan Times*, April 17.
2005, "Constitutional Revision: Koizumi Wants Legal Basis for Military", *Japan Times*, October 31.

2007, "Diet Clears Path to Referendum on Constitution; Bill's Passage Threatens to Upend War-Renouncing Article 9, Opponents Say", *Japan Times*, May 15.
2007, "Japan Must Change Constitution to Change Nation: Abe", *Japan Times*, May 3.
2011, "Lay Judge System OK: Top Court", *Japan Times*, November 18.
2012, "Lay Judge System Reviewed After Auspicious Start", *Japan Times*, May 30.
2014, "The Court Says Lay Judge System Working Well at Five-Year Mark", *Japan Times*, May 21.
2014, "Improving the Lay Judge System", *Japan Times*, May 5.2015, "Japan Hangs Two Prisoners, Including First Convicted in Lay Judge Trial", *Japan Times*, December 18.
Brasor, P., 2015, "Split Clears a Path for Constitutional Revisionists", *Japan Times*, November 21.
Hosokawa, R., 2000, "Japan Needs a New, Better Constitution", *Japan Times*, March 2.
Kamiya, S., 2009, "First Lay Judge Trial Kicks off in Tokyo", *Japan Times*, August 4.
Matsubara, H., 2003, "Prewar Democracy Bid Once Saw Jury Trials – New Law May not Give Tomorrow's Jurists Enough Freedom from Judges", *Japan Times*, January 7.
Matsubara, H., 2004, "Lay Judges to Serve from 2009: Quasi-Jury System Earns Diet Approval", *Japan Times*, May 22.
Osaki, T., 2014, "Provide Details on Hangings or Halt Them", *Japan Times*, February 17.
Shimoyachi, N., 2003, "War Veteran Questions New Law", *Japan Times*, June 8.
Takahashi, J., 2003, "Bill to Dispatch SDF to Iraq Ready for Diet – Personnel to Provide Logistic Support and Aid Under Four-Year Legislation", *Japan Times*, June 8.
Takahashi, J., 2003, "SDF-Iraq Bill Is Sent to Diet after WMD Clause Excised", *Japan Times*, June 14.
Wijers-Hasegawa, Y., 2003, "Workers Happy to Serve as Jurors as long as Trials Are Short", *Japan Times*, September 4.
Yoshida, R., 2004, "Koizumi Urges LDP-DPJ Effort to Revise Constitution", *Japan Times*, January 15.

Daily Yomiuri/Yomiuri Shinbun

2004, "70% of Pollees Don't Want to Be Lay Judges", *Daily Yomiuri*, May 27.
2004, "Saiban'in Sei Shikō Mae ni Saibankan 100 Nin o Ōbei Haken" [100 Judges Sent to Europe and the United States Before Implementation of the Lay Judge System], *Yomiuri Shinbun*, September 14.
2009, "Saibankan ra 'Egao' Kenshū" [Judges [Have] Smile Training], *Yomiuri Shinbun*, June 6.
2009, "Seitaishi Shisatsu Jiken no Kōhan Kijitsu Kettei; Saiban'in Saiban Dai Ichi Gō ka" [Date of Public Hearing of the *Seitai* Therapist Stabbing Case Decided; Will This Be the First Lay Judge Trial?], *Yomiuri Online*, June 12.

Mainichi Shinbun

2009, "Saiban'in Seido: Bajji Shisakuhin o Kōkai; Saikōsai 'Kansha Kome'" [The Lay Judge System: Model of the Badge Revealed; [From the Supreme Court "With Gratitude"], *Mainichi Shinbun*, May 29.
2009, "Saiban'in Seido: Chisai ga Setsubi o Hatsu Kōkai" [The Lay Judge System: District Court Unveils Facilities], *Mainichi Shinbun*, May 21.

New York Times

1909, "The Grafting Legislators of the New Japan: As Revealed in Tokio Courts 'Great Sugar Company' Has Involved Government Officials in Sum Reaching into Millions", *New York Times*, August 15.

1909, "Tokio Lawmakers Took Big Bribes; Wrecked the Dai Nippon Sugar Company, Which Sought a Monopoly; Trained Under Old System when the Government Bought Support of Its Policies – Diet Members Looked on Taking Bribes as a Right", *New York Times*, June 20.

Other newspapers and online publications

1928, "Karafuto Saisho no Baishin Saiban; Hikoku wa Kanpu Koroshi; Baishin'in kara mo Hikokunin ni Shitsumon ga Ari; Bōchōseki wa Asa kara Man'in Shimekiri no Seikyō" [The First Jury Trial in Karafuto; Defendant [Accused of] Killing Lover; Jurors Also Ask Defendant Questions; Observer Seats Full Since Morning; Overwhelming Success], *Karafuto Nichinichi Shinbun* [The Karafuto Daily Newspaper], November 6.

1963, "Ikeda Pleads not Guilty: Okinawa's First Jury Trial Opens", *Morning Star Okinawa*, May 1.

2002, "Survey: Japan; Lionheart to the Rescue?", *The Economist*, April 18.

2003, "Crime in Japan: Insecure", *The Economist*, October 23.

2004, "2004 Prospects for Japan's Newspaper Industry", *NSK News Bulletin*, January, http://www.pressnet.or.jp/newsb/.

2004, "Government Unveils Draft Bill for Lay Judge Jurors – Planned Restrictions on Media Deleted", *NSK News Bulletin*, February, http://www.pressnet.or.jp/newsb/0402.html.

2004, "Saiban'in Seido ni Hantai Suru Kai Hossoku" [Association for Opposing the Lay Judge System Is Established], *Kokumin Shinbun*, January 25.

2006, "Giron naku Kokumin Sōdōin; Saiban'in Seido Hihan no Hon Shuppan Takayama Bengoshi" [General Conscription without General Discussion; Attorney Takayama Publishes a Book Criticizing the *Saiban'in* System], *Tokyo Shinbun*, October 1.

2009, "Kenji ga Manā Kenshū Saiban'in Dōnyū Hikae" [Prosecutors Get Training in Manners in Preparation for the Introduction of the Lay Judge System], *Kobe Shinbun*, June 11.

2009, "Saiban'in Seido ni Mukete Ken Bengoshikai ga Kenshūkai" [Local Bar Association Conducts Training Sessions in Preparation for [the Introduction of the] Lay Judge System], *Nishi Nippon Shinbun*, May 2.

2009, "Tokyo Chisai de Mogi Saiban Shūryō; Jōkyō Shōko nomi no Kēsu" [Mock Trial Concluded at Tokyo District Court; A Case of Only Circumstantial Evidence], *Sankei Nyūsu*, February 27.

2010, "Saiban'in Saiban, 3 Bun no 2 ga Kaiken, Chisai Kainyū 29 Ken mo" [Lay Judge Trials, Two-Thirds (of Lay Judges Participate in) Press Conferences, 29 Instances of Intervention on the Part of District Courts], *Kyodo News*, February 13.

2010, "Saiban'in Saiban de Kubun Shinri, Hatsu no Bubun Hanketsu – Osaka Chisai, Taishō Gai no Gōtō, Kyōkatsu nado Yūzai" [(Case to Be Tried) Partially by Lay Judges, First Partial Verdict (Is Out) – Osaka District Court Finds [Defendant] Guilty on Counts Including Robbery and Extortion], *Nikkei Net*, March 5.

Anonymous, 2015, "Saiban'in Saiban de Hanketsu no Shikeishū Hatsu no Shikkō" [First Execution of Inmate Sentenced to the Death Penalty by Lay Judges Carried Out], *NHK NewsWeb*, December 18, http://www3.nhk.or.jp/news/html/20151218/k10010344941000.html.

Anonymous, 2015, "Saiban'in Seido 6 Nen Keikensha wa 'Sanka Shite Yokatta' Demo Taiji Ritsu wa Zōka Keikō" [Six Years of the Functioning of the Lay Judge System; Those Who Experienced (Being Lay Judges Say that They Were) Pleased to Have Served, but Percentage of Those Who Decline Service on the Rise], *Sankei Nyūsu*, May 21, available online at http://www.sankei.com/affairs/news/150521/afr1505210004-n1.html.

Websites

21 Seiki Seisaku Kenkyūjo [The 21st Century Public Policy Institute], 1998, "Minji Shihō no Kasseika ni Mukete" [Towards Revitalization of Civil Justice], December 22, http://www.21ppi.org/pdf/thesis/981222.pdf, last accessed on October 7, 2014.

'21 Seiki Nihon no Kōzō Kondankai [Commission on Japan's Goals in the 21st Century]', http://www.kantei.go.jp/jp/21century/index.html, last accessed on October 7, 2014.

'21 Seiki Seisaku Kenkyūjo', http://www.21ppi.org/english/index.html, last accessed on October 7, 2014.

'Baishin Hōtei Kaiteichū: Zembu de 3 Koto ga Shinkōchū' [Jury Trials in Session: The Total of 3 Court Hearings in Progress], http://homepage2.nifty.com/equality/houtei1.htm, last accessed on March 1, 2010.

'Baishin Sei ya Sanshin Sei to wa Chigau no desu ka' [Is (Japan's *Saiban'in* System) Different from the (Anglo-American) Jury and the (Continental-European) Lay Assessor Systems?], http://www.saibanin.courts.go.jp/qa/c8_2.html, last accessed on October 7, 2014.

'Baishin Seido Kenkyūkai [The Jury System Research Society], Shin Keiji Baishin Saiban Hōan [Risōteki Keiji Baishin Hōan] Shian [Draft of the Bill (Concerning) the New Criminal Jury Trials (The Draft of an Ideal Criminal Jury)]', http://www.geocities.co.jp/HeartLand-Kaede/5549/maruta/houan.htm, last accessed on October 7, 2014.

'Baishin Seido e no Michiyori' [The Path towards the Jury System], http://www.baishin.sakura.ne.jp/kaishi.html, last accessed on March 1, 2010.

'Baishin Seido no Kiso Chishiki' [Fundamental Knowledge on the Jury System], http://www.baishin.com/01kiso/index.htm, last accessed on October 7, 2014.

'Baishin Seido o Fukkatsu Suru Kai, Baishin Hō Kaisei An' [Proposal for Amending the Jury Act], http://www.baishin.sakura.ne.jp/kaiseian.html, last accessed on March 1, 2010.

'Baishin Seido o Fukkatsu Suru Kai' [Association for the Revival of the Jury System], http://www.l-wise.co.jp/baishin/, last accessed on March 1, 2010.

'Baishin Seido o Fukkatsu Suru Kai', http://www.baishin.sakura.ne.jp/, last accessed on March 1, 2010.

'Baishin o Kangaeru Kai', http://www.baishin.com/05baishinkai/index.htm, last accessed on October 7, 2014.

'Dai 159 Kai Kokkai 67 Saiban'in no Sanka Suru Keiji Saiban ni kansuru Hōritsu An', [The 159th Session of Parliament 69 Act Concerning Participation of Law Assessors in Criminal Trials], http://www.shugiin.go.jp/itdb_gian.nsf/html/gian/keika/1D94366.htm, last accessed on March 1, 2010.

Hōmushō [The Ministry of Justice], "Saiban'in Seido: Mitai, Manabitai" [The Lay Judge System: Want to See, Want to Learn], http://www.moj.go.jp/SAIBANIN/koho/douga.html, last accessed on March 1, 2010.

Hōmushō [The Ministry of Justice], "Saiban'inko no Purofiru" [Saiban'inko's Profile], http://www.moj.go.jp/SAIBANIN/koho/inco.html, last accessed on August 1, 2009.

Hōmushō [The Ministry of Justice], "Yoroshiku Saiban'in" [The Lay Judge (System) – We Are Counting on Your Cooperation], http://www.moj.go.jp/SAIBANIN/, last accessed on March 1, 2010.

Hōmushō [The Ministry of Justice], "YouTube Dōga" [Clips on YouTube], http://www.moj.go.jp/SAIBANIN/koho/douga.html, last accessed on March 1, 2010.

'Hōmushō: Saiban'in Seido ni kansuru Kentōkai' [Ministry of Justice: Expert Committee on the Lay Judge System], http://www.moj.go.jp/shingi1/keiji_kentoukai_saibaninseido_top.html, last accessed on October 7, 2014.

Japan Federation of Bar Associations, 2004, "Bills on Lay Judge System and Criminal Procedure Reform Clear Lower House", April 23, http://www.nichibenren.or.jp/en/activities/meetings/20040423.html, last accessed on March 1, 2010.

Japan Federation of Bar Associations, "Kaunto Down! Minna de Tsuchikō Saiban'in Seido" [Countdown! Let's Build the Lay Judge System Together], http://www.nichibenren.or.jp/ja/event/081108.html, last accessed on March 1, 2010.

'The Judicial Reform Council', http://www.kantei.go.jp/foreign/judica_e.html, last accessed on October 7, 2014.

'Kagoshima Ken Senshutsu Kokkai Giin Yasuoka Okiharu Sangiin Giin Webusaito' [The Website of Okiharu Yasuoka, Member of the House of Councilors Representing Kagoshima Prefecture], http://www.yasuoka.org/, last accessed on October 7, 2014.

254 Bibliography

'Karafuto Nichinichi Shinbun' [Karafuto Daily Newspaper], http://www.lib.kobe-u.ac.jp/directory/sinbun/snlist/470l.html, last accessed on October 7, 2014.

Keizai Dantai Rengōkai [Japan Business Federation], 1998, "Shihō Seido Kaikaku ni tsuite no Iken" [Policy Statement Regarding Justice System Reform], May 19, http://www.keidanren.or.jp/japanese/policy/pol173.html, last accessed on October 7, 2014.

'Kenpō Shinsa Kai' [Investigative Committee on the Constitution], http://www.shugiin.go.jp/itdb_kenpou.nsf/html/kenpou/kenpou_f.htm, last accessed on March 1, 2010.

'Kentōkai no Kaisai ni tsuite [Concerning the Establishment of Expert Advisory Committees], December 17, 2001, http://www.kantei.go.jp/jp/singi/sihou/kentoukai/kaisai.html, last accessed on October 7, 2014.

'Kentōkai no Kaisai ni tsuite [Concerning the Establishment of Expert Advisory Committees]', October 2, 2002, http://www.kantei.go.jp/jp/singi/sihou/kentoukai/kaisai2.html, last accessed on October 7, 2014.

Kim, Y., "Fuse Tatsuji Lived for the People and Died for the People", http://www.nahf.or.kr/Data/Newsletterlist/1305_en/sub05.html, last accessed on October 7, 2014.

Koizumi Naikaku [Koizumi Cabinet], "Shihō Seido Kaikaku Taun Mētingu in Tokyo: Yori Mijika de Tayorigai no Aru Shihō e; Giji Yōshi" [Justice System Reform Town Meeting in Tokyo: Towards a Closer and More Reliable Justice (System); A Summary of the Proceedings], http://www8.cao.go.jp/town/tokyo161218/youshi.html, last accessed on October 7, 2014.

Koizumi Naikaku [Koizumi Cabinet], "Shihō Seido Kaikaku Taun Mētingu in Takamatsu: Yori Mijika de Tayorigai no Aru Shihō e; Giji Yōshi" [Justice System Reform Town Meeting in Takamatsu: Towards a Closer and More Reliable Justice (System); Summary of the Proceedings], http://www8.cao.go.jp/town/takamatsu170115/youshi.html, last accessed on October 7, 2014.

Koizumi Naikaku [Koizumi Cabinet], "Shihō Seido Kaikaku Taun Mētingu in Utsunomiya: Yori Mijika de Tayorigai no Aru Shihō e; Giji Yōshi" [Justice System Reform Town Meeting in Utsunomiya: Towards a Closer and More Reliable Justice (System); Summary of the Proceedings], http://www8.cao.go.jp/town/utsunomiya170417/youshi.html, last accessed on October 7, 2014.

The Liberal Democratic Party of Japan, 1998, "21 Seiki no Shihō no Tashikana Hōshin" [The Firm Principles of 21st Century Justice], June 16, http://www.yasuoka.org/doc_seisaku/siho/01.htm, last accessed on March 1, 2010.

Matsuo, K., 2001, "Kokumin no Shihō Sanka ni tsuite" [Concerning Citizen Participation in Justice], January 9, Materials Distributed during the 43rd Meeting of the Judicial System Reform Council, http://www.kantei.go.jp/jp/sihouseido/dai43/43betten3.html, last accessed on October 7, 2014.'Members of the JSRC', http://www.kantei.go.jp/foreign/judiciary/member.html, last accessed on October 7, 2014.

'Members of the Office for Promotion of Justice System Reform', http://www.kantei.go.jp/foreign/policy/sihou/members_e.html, last accessed on October 7, 2014.

'Miranda no Kai' [Association for the Advancement of Miranda Rights in Japan], http://www.mirandanokai.net/, last accessed on March 1, 2010.

Mitani, T., 2001, "Seiji Seido toshite no Baishin Sei: Senzen Nihon no Keiken ni Terashite" [The Jury System as a Political System: In light of Japan's Pre-War Experiences], Materials Distributed during the 43rd Meeting of the Judicial System Reform Council, http://www.kantei.go.jp/jp/sihouseido/dai43/43betten2.html, last accessed on October 7, 2014.

Naikaku Fu Daijin Kanbō Seifu Kōhōshitsu [Government Publications Office, Department of the Minister for the Cabinet Office], 2005, "Saiban'in Seido ni kan suru Yoron Chōsa" [Public Opinion Poll Concerning the Lay Judge System], http://www8.cao.go.jp/survey/h16/h16-saiban/, last accessed on October 7, 2014.

Nichibenren [The Japan Federation of Bar Associations], "Hajimarimasu. Saiban'in Seido" [The Lay Judge System Is about to Start], http://www.nichibenren.or.jp/ja/citizen_judge/index.html, last accessed on March 1, 2010.

Nihon Bengoshi Rengōkai [Japan Federation of Bar Associations], 1990, "Shihō Kaikaku ni kansuru Sengen" [Declaration Concerning Justice Reform], May 25, http://www.nichibenren.or.jp/ja/opinion/ga_res/1990_3.html, last accessed on March 1, 2010.

Nihon Bengoshi Rengōkai [Japan Federation of Bar Associations], 1991, "Shihō Kaikaku ni kansuru Sengen (Sono 2)" [Declaration Concerning Justice Reform (2)] May 24, http://www.nichibenren.or.jp/ja/opinion/ga_res/1991_4.html, last accessed on March 1, 2010.

Nihon Bengoshi Rengōkai [Japan Federation of Bar Associations], 1994, "Shihō Kaikaku ni kansuru Sengen (Sono 3)" [Declaration Concerning Justice Reform (3)] May 27, http://www.nichibenren.or.jp/ja/opinion/ga_res/1994_3.html, last accessed on March 1, 2010.

Nihon Bengoshi Rengōkai [Japan Federation of Bar Associations], 2003, "Saiban'in Seido 'Tatakidai' ni Taisuru Iken" [Opinion Concerning the "Sounding Board" on the Lay Judge System], 30 May, http://www.nichibenren.or.jp/ja/opinion/report/data/2003_23.pdf, last accessed on March 1, 2010.

'Office for Promotion of Justice System Reform', http://www.kantei.go.jp/foreign/policy/sihou/index_e.html, last accessed on October 7, 2014.

'Reasons for Proposed Amendment of the Act Concerning Participation of Lay Judges in Criminal Trials', http://www.moj.go.jp/HOUAN/SAIBANNIN/refer03.pdf, last accessed on October 7, 2014.

'Research Committee on the Constitution', http://www.shugiin.go.jp/index.nsf/html/index_e_kenpou.htm, last accessed on March 1, 2010.

Saiban'in Seido Haishi o Mezasu Shimin/Hōsō no Tsudoi [The Meeting of Citizens and Jurists Aiming for the Abolishment of the Lay Judge System], 2006, *Saiban'in Seido Haishi o Mezasu Shimin/Hōsō no Tsudoi Hōkokushū* [Reports from The Meeting of Citizens and Jurists Aiming for the Abolishment of the Lay Judge System] October 20, http://www.takayama-law.com/kiji/061020.pdf, last accessed on October 7, 2014.

Saiban'in Seido/Keiji Kentōkai [Expert Advisory Committee on the Lay Judge (*Saiban'in*) System/Criminal Justice, "Saiban'in Seido ni tsuite" [Concerning the Lay Judge (*Saiban'in*) System], March 11, 2003, http://www.kantei.go.jp/jp/singi/sihou/kentoukai/saibanin/dai13/13siryou1.pdf, last accessed on October 7, 2014.

Saiban'in Seido, Keiji Saiban no Jūjitsu, Jinsokuka oyobi Kensatsu Shinsakai Seido ni kansuru Iken Boshū no Kekka Gaiyō', [The Outline of the Results of the Opinion Polls Concerning the Lay Judge System, the (Measures for) Improving and Speeding Up Criminal Trials, and the Prosecutorial Review System], http://www.kantei.go.jp/jp/singi/sihou/kentoukai/saibanin/dai31/31siryou4.pdf, last accessed on October 7, 2014.

'Saiban'in Seido Keiji Soshō no Kaiaku ni Hantai Shi Baishin Seido no Jitsugen o Mezasu Zenkoku Kyōgikai', http://www.l-wise.co.jp/baishin/200412_zenkokukyougikai_kosshi.htm, last accessed on March 1, 2010.

Saiban'in Seido Kenji Kentōkai [Expert Advisory Committee on the Lay Judge (Saiban'in) System/Criminal Justice], 2003, "Kangaerareru Saiban'in Seido no Gaiyō ni tsuite" [Concerning the Possible Saiban'in System Outline], October 28, http://www.kantei.go.jp/jp/singi/sihou/kentoukai/saibanin/dai28/28siryou1.pdf, last accessed on October 7, 2014.

Saiban'in Seido Kenji Kentōkai [Expert Advisory Committee on the Lay Judge (Saiban'in) System/Criminal Justice], 2004, "Saiban'in Seido no Gaiyō ni tsuite" [Concerning the Outline of the Saiban'in System], January 29, http://www.kantei.go.jp/jp/singi/sihou/kentoukai/saibanin/dai31/31siryou1.pdf, last accessed on October 7, 2014.

'Saiban'in Seido/Keiji Kentōkai' [Expert Advisory Committee on the Lay Judge (Saiban'in) System/Criminal Justice], http://www.kantei.go.jp/jp/singi/sihou/kentoukai/06saibanin.html, last accessed on October 7, 2014.

'Saiban'in Seido/Keiji Kentōkai Menbā' [Members of the Expert Advisory Committee on the Lay Judge (*Saiban'in*) System/Criminal Justice], http://www.kantei.go.jp/jp/singi/sihou/kentoukai/saibanin/06meibo.html, last accessed on October 7, 2014.

'Saiban'in Seido, Keiji Saiban no Jūjitsu, Jinsokuka oyobi Kensatsu Shinsakai Seido no Kokkaku An ni tsuite no Iken Boshū no Kekka Gaiyō', [The Outline of the Results of the Opinion Polls Concerning the Framework Concerning the Lay Judge System, the (Measures for) Improving and Speeding Up Criminal Trials, and the Prosecutorial Review System], http://www.kantei.go.jp/jp/singi/sihou/kentoukai/saibanin/siryou/0130kekka.pdf, last accessed on October 7, 2014.

Saiban'in Seido Kōhō Suishin Kyōgikai [The Lay Judge System Promotions Office], 2005, "Saiban'in Seido Kōhō Sukejūru (Imēji) [Schedule (Images) of the Promotion of the Lay Judge System], October 1, http://www.kantei.go.jp/jp/singi/sihou/komon/dai18/18houmu4.pdf, last accessed on October 7, 2014.

'Saiban'in Seido no Jisshi Jyōkyō ni tsuite' [Concerning the Status of the Implementation of the Lay Assessor System], http://www.saibanin.courts.go.jp/vcms_lf/saibanin_kekka201312.pdf, last accessed on October 7, 2014.

'Saiban'in Seido no Shinboru Māku to Katchifurēzu' [The Lay Judge System Logo and Catchphrase], http://www.saibanin.courts.go.jp/symbol_catchphrase/index.html, last accessed on October 7, 2014.

'Saiban'in Seido oyobi Kensatsu Shinsa Kai Seido ni tsuite no Iken Boshū no Kekka Gaiyō [Outline of the Results of the Opinion Polls Concerning the Lay Judge System and the Prosecutorial Review System], http://www.kantei.go.jp/jp/singi/sihou/kentoukai/saibanin/dai22/22siryou1.pdf, last accessed on October 7, 2014.

'Saiban'in Seido wa Iranai! Dai Undō', http://no-saiban-in.org/index.html, last accessed on October 7, 2014.

Saiban'in Seido wa Iranai! Dai Undō, "Saiban'in Hō no Haishi o Motomeru Seigansho" [Petition Demanding the Abolishment of the Lay Judge Act], http://no-saiban-in.org/image/070312seigan.pdf, last accessed on March 1, 2010.

Saiban'in Seido wa Iranai! Dai Undō, "Saiban'in Seido ni Igi Ari! Kōen Shūkai" [An Objection to the Lay Judge System! Lecture and Meeting], http://no-saiban-in.org/pdf/6.16kouenkai.pdf, last accessed on October 7, 2014.

Saiban'in Seido wa Iranai! Dai Undō, "Saiban'in Seido wa Iranai! 6.29 Shūkai" [We Do Not Need the Lay Judge System! The June 29[, 2007,] Meeting], http://no-saiban-in.org/image/6.29chirashi.jpg, last accessed on March 1, 2010.

"Saiban'in Saiban Hachi Gatsu Mikkka ni Seishiki Kettei, Tokyo Chisai, Josei Shisatsu Jiken de" [Lay Judge Trial Officially Set for August 3, Tokyo District Court (to Try) the Case of Female Stabbed to Death], *Japan Press Network 47 News*, http://www.47news.jp/CN/200906/CN2009061201000492.html, last accessed on October 7, 2014.

Saiban'in no Sanka Suru Keiji Saiban ni kansuru Hōritsu nado no Ichibu o Kaisei Suru Hōritsu An [Bill Proposing Partial Amendment of the Act Concerning Participation of Lay Judges in Criminal Trials] (Proposed Official Draft 2007), http://www.moj.go.jp/HOUAN/SAIBANNIN/refer02.pdf, last accessed on March 1, 2010.

Saikō Saibansho [The Supreme Court], "Chōsa Hyō no Kaitō Jyōkyō Nado ni tsuite" [Concerning the Status of Questionnaire Responses], http://www.saibanin.courts.go.jp/topics/pdf/09_03_16_cyosahyo_kaito/cyosahyo_kaito.pdf, last accessed on March 1, 2010.

Saikō Saibansho [The Supreme Court], "Kakuchi no Ibento Jōhō" [Information on Events Held in Different Areas], http://www.saibanin.courts.go.jp/news/announcing_to_public.html, last accessed on March 1, 2010.

Saikō Saibansho [The Supreme Court], "Kakuchi no Saiban'in Seido Kanren Jōhō" [Information regarding the Lay Judge System [Provided at District Courts] in Different Areas], http://www.saibanin.courts.go.jp/access/index.html, last accessed on October 7, 2014.

Saikō Saibansho [The Supreme Court], "Meibō Kisai Tsūchi ni tsuite" [Concerning Notification of (Persons Whose Names Appear) on the List of Lay Judge Candidates], http://www.saibanin.courts.go.jp/notification/index.html, last accessed on October 7, 2014.

Saikō Saibansho [The Supreme Court], "Saibansho kara Ookuri Suru Fūtō to Meibi Kisai Tsūchi Oyobi Sono Dōfūbutsu ni tsuite" [Concerning the Envelope, the Notification of Being Listed and Accompanying Materials], http://www.saibanin.courts.go.jp/notification/envelope/index.html, last accessed on October 7, 2014.

Saikō Saibansho [The Supreme Court], "Saiban'in Seido Mēru Magazin" [E-mail Magazine on the Lay Judge System], http://www.saibanin.courts.go.jp/melmaga/index.html, last accessed on October 7, 2014.

Saikō Saibansho [The Supreme Court], "Saiban'in Seido Zenkoku Fōramu" [Lay Judge System Nation-wide Forums], http://www.saibanin.courts.go.jp/topics/guestionnaire.html, last accessed on October 7, 2014.

Saikō Saibansho [The Supreme Court], "Saiban'in Seido Zenkoku Fōramu" [Lay Judge System Nation-wide Forums], http://www.saibanin.courts.go.jp/topics/guestionnaire.html, last accessed on October 7, 2014.

Saikō Saibansho [The Supreme Court], "Saiban'in Seido no Shinboru Māku to Katchifurēzu" [The Lay Judge System Logo and Catchphrase], http://www.saibanin.courts.go.jp/symbol_catchphrase/index.html, last accessed on October 7, 2014.

Saikō Saibansho [The Supreme Court], "Saiban'in Seido no Shinboru Māku no Imi", http://www.saibanin.courts.go.jp/symbol_catchphrase/symbol_meaning.html, last accessed on October 7, 2014.

Saikō Saibansho [The Supreme Court], "Saiban'in Seido" [The Lay Judge System], http://www.saibanin.courts.go.jp/, last accessed on October 7, 2014.

Saikō Saibansho [The Supreme Court], "Saiban'in Seido no Jisshi Jōkyō ni tsuite (Sono Ichi)" [Regarding the Operation Status of the Lay Judge System], http://www.saibanin.courts.go.jp/topics/h21_saibanin_kekka.html, last accessed on March 1, 2010.

Shihō Seido Kaikaku Shingi Kai Dai 30 Kai Giji Gaiyō [Minutes of the 30th Meeting of the Judicial System Reform Council], September 12, 2000, http://www.kantei.go.jp/jp/sihouseido/dai30/30gaiyou.html, last accessed on October 7, 2014.

Shihō Seido Kaikaku Shingi Kai Dai 43 Kai Giji Gaiyō [Minutes of the 43rd Meeting of the Judicial System Reform Council], January 9, 2001, http://www.kantei.go.jp/jp/sihouseido/dai43/43gaiyou.html, last accessed on October 7, 2014.

Shihō Seido Kaikaku Shingikai [Judicial System Reform Council], 2000, *Chūkan Hōkoku* [Interim Report], November 20, http://www.kantei.go.jp/jp/sihouseido/report/naka_houkoku.html, last accessed on October 7, 2014.

Shihō Seido Kaikaku Shingikai [The Judicial System Reform Council], 2001, "Shihō Seido Kaikaku Shingikai Ikensho – 21 Seiki no Nihon o Sasaeru Shihō Seido" [Recommendations of the Judicial System Reform Council – A Justice System to Support Japan in the Twenty-First Century], June 12, http://www.kantei.go.jp/jp/sihouseido/report/ikensyo/pdf-dex.html (in Japanese) and http://www.kantei.go.jp/foreign/judiciary/2001/0612report.html (in English), last accessed on October 7, 2014.

Shihō Seido Kaikaku Suishin Honbu [Office for Promotion of Justice System Reform], "Minji Soshō Hiyō Tō ni kansuru Hōritsu no Ichibu o Kaisei Suru Hōritsu An ni tsuite (Gaiyō)" [Concerning the Proposal for Partial Amendment of the Law Concerning Civil Litigation Costs (An Outline)], http://www.kantei.go.jp/jp/singi/sihou/houan/040302/minji/gaiyou.pdf, last accessed on October 7, 2014.

Shihō Seido Kaikaku Suishin Honbu Jimukyoku [Secretariat of the Office for the Promotion of Justice System Reform], "Saiban'in Seido oyobi Kensatsu Shinsa Kai Seido ni tsuite no Iken Boshū" [Invitation of Opinions regarding the Lay Judge (Saiban'in) System and the Prosecutorial Review System], http://www.kantei.go.jp/jp/singi/sihou/kentoukai/saibanin/siryou/0307kekka.html, last accessed on October 7, 2014.

Shihō Seido Kaikaku Suishin Honbu Jimukyoku [Secretariat of the Office for the Promotion of Justice System Reform], "Saiban'in Seido, Keiji Saiban no Jūjitsu, Jinsokuka oyobi Kensatsu

Shinsa Kai Seido ni tsuite no Iken Boshū" [Invitation of Opinions regarding the Lay Judge (Saiban'in) System, the Improvement and Speeding up of Criminal Trials, and the Prosecutorial Review System], http://www.kantei.go.jp/jp/singi/sihou/kentoukai/saibanin/siryou/1118kekka.html, last accessed on October 7, 2014.

Shihō Seido Kaikaku Suishin Keikaku [Plan for Promotion of Justice System Reform], Cabinet Resolution of March 19, 2002, http://www.kantei.go.jp/jp/singi/sihou/keikaku/020319keikaku.html, last accessed on October 7, 2014.

Shūgiin Kenpō Chōsa Kai, 2005, *Shūgiin Kenpō Chōsa Kai Hōkoku Sho* [Final Report of the Research Commission on the Constitution, The House of Representatives], http://www.shugiin.go.jp/index.nsf/html/index_kenpou.htm, last accessed on March 1, 2010.

'Shihō Seido Kaikaku Suishin Honbu' [Office for Promotion of Justice System Reform], http://www.kantei.go.jp/jp/singi/sihou/index.html, last accessed on October 7, 2014.

'Naikaku Sōridaijin no Danwa (Saiban'in Seido no Kaishi ni tsuite)' [Prime Minister's Comment (Concerning the Lay Judge System)], May 21, 2009, http://www.kantei.go.jp/jp/asospeech/2009/05/21danwa.html, last accessed on October 7, 2014.

'Waseda Daigaku Hyaku Nen Shi' [Hundred Years of Waseda's History], http://www.waseda.jp/archives/database/cent/1910.html, last accessed on March 1, 2010.

Waseda University, "Kaitei Mogi Saiban: Anata mo Saiban'in" [Open Mock-Trial: You, too, Can Be a Lay Judge], http://www.waseda.jp/law-school/topics/mogisaiban/20051027.htm, last accessed on October 7, 2014.

'Yale Law School, Lillian Goldman Law Library: The Avalon Project; Documents in Law, History, and Diplomacy', http://avalon.law.yale.edu/20th_century/decade19.asp, last accessed on March 1, 2010.

Appendix

I Translated documents: the *Hōritsu Shinbun* articles

(1) 1928, "Oita District Court: the first jury verdict", Hōritsu Shinbun, *November 3, p. 17*

The first jury trial in this country opened on the 23rd of last month [(October, 1928)] at the Oita District Court. The case [on trial] involved Mr. Kameji Fujioka (thirty-four years of age), a foreman at Ōura Cement and Woodenware Company ([address:] Oita Prefecture, Kita Amabe Gun, Shimoura Village, Ōaza Tokuura), who was charged with attempted murder of his mistress, Ms. Uta Kansaki (forty-one years of age), and with inflicting injury upon her with a heavy kitchen knife in a fit of rage motivated by the fact that Uta was in love with someone else.

As soon as the preliminary hearing finished behind closed doors on the 12th of last month [(October, 1928)] the summons were sent out to twenty-six [prospective] jurors. The [prospective] jurors came from across eight towns and villages of the prefecture, and six of them were at least sixty years of age, with the eldest member being seventy-one years old.

At 8:50 in the morning, the presiding judge, the associate judges, and the chief prosecutor entered the courtroom. Defendant Fujioka went in next, and then twenty-six [prospective] jurors entered the courtroom. In accordance with the set legal procedure, each [prospective] juror was asked first about whether or not he was related to the accused, and Mr. Tsuruo Fujioka along with eleven other persons was selected by the presiding judge as acting jurors, and one person was selected as a juror in reserve.

The judges and the other officials then left the courtroom, and at 10:25, the public was allowed to enter. At 10:40, everyone in the courtroom stood up, and presiding judge Kurimoto, associate judges Hasegawa and Ikeda, prosecutor Endō and others entered and took their seats. After letting the members of the jury rest for about five minutes, presiding judge Kurimoto asked them to rise and read out the following oath of jurors: "I solemnly swear to follow my conscience and to conduct my duty fairly." [The judge then had] the members of the jury place their personal seals on [the document containing] this oath, and submit it, and the trial hearing finally began. As is customary, the judge began by confirming the identity of accused Fujioka. When prosecutor Endō questioned the accused regarding the facts constituting the offence charged, the defendant replied so quietly that his response could not be heard, and the members of the jury showed signs of impatience. As the time devoted to questioning [of the accused] was about to come up to one hour, the interest of the members of the jury started to weaken.

Most of the questioning procedures were finished by 11:15. The presiding judge then addressed the jury [and summarized what had been said] in such a way that even the defendant would agree was not disadvantageous to him. Juror Kiichiro Andō then asked, "What is the amount of alcohol that the defendant is in the habit of consuming on average?" This first question asked by a member of the jury prompted the judge to ask further questions in order to clarify the amount of alcohol the defendant was consuming on average and the amount he consumed on the day of the crime. Then the judge turned to the juror and asked if the answers obtained were sufficient, and Mr. Andō replied, "Yes," and nodded affirmatively. Next, [juror] Yūta Ōe asked another question, which was followed by the examination of evidence.

The judge took a sketch into his hands and showed it to the members of the jury, saying: "This is a sketch depicting the scene of the crime. The members of the jury must look very carefully at all pieces of evidence and acquire a good understanding of each." While saying these words, the judge unfolded the sketch and showed it to the members of the jury. Next, a heavy kitchen knife, which was the weapon [used in the crime], was handed over to the accused, and he was asked to first demonstrate how he held that knife prior to going to see his mistress and then to show how he was holding the knife when he stabbed his mistress so that the members of the jury could see. The weapon was then given to the members of the jury so that they could examine it. This was followed by the display of a blood-stained *yukata* that was worn by the victim, and at noon the court went into recess until 13:00.

The trial proceeded with the examination of witnesses, but not a single juror had any questions to ask the witnesses. The witnesses included a beautiful woman of mature years and a *geisha* who looked bewitching even in the stern atmosphere of the courtroom.

The court went again into recess and the hearings re-opened at 15:00. Electric lights were turned on, and chief prosecutor Endō delivered his closing arguments glancing in the direction of the jurors' seats and [making an effort] to ensure that [his speech] was easy to understand for the members of the jury. The prosecutor concluded his speech with the following statement: "[Regarding the question of] whether the accused had the intention to kill, you have to carefully consider this." The prosecutor thus refrained from making a recommendation for punishment. Then, defense counsel Satō argued that there was no intent to kill on the part of the defendant and requested a decisive reduction in penalty and the suspension of the sentence. The hearing was adjourned at 17:45.

On the following day, [October] 24, the twelve members of the jury who had started the day at a special accommodation facility settled down in their seats at 9:00, and the trial re-opened at 9:15. Presiding judge Kurimoto turned to the jury and delivered his instructions, in which he discussed for an hour how the trial had developed during the course of the previous day. Then, [the judge issued the main and supplementary questions. T]he main question was: "Did the accused have the intention to kill and [did he] fail to succeed at fulfilling this intention?" The supplementary question was: "Did the accused inflict injury without the intention to kill?"

The court then went into recess at 10:25. At that time, the members of the jury proceeded to the deliberation room where they first elected the [jury] foreman by mutual vote and then began deliberations during which each member stated his opinion. The [agreed-upon] answers of the jury were compiled into a response sheet that was then sealed with the personal seal of the jury foreman. The response sheet was prepared within twenty minutes, and the jury then notified the judge. At 11:00 the court session re-opened.

The judge asked the secretary to read out the responses of the jury, which were: "'Main question': 'No'; 'Supplementary question': 'Yes.'" [Thus, the jury] found that the accused did not have the intention to kill. The judge thanked the members of the jury for their service and the hearing was adjourned. On the day when sentencing took place – [October]

25 – the hearings started at 9:30 and the jurors were not present. Sentencing began immediately after the hearings started. Presiding judge Kurimoto sentenced the accused in accordance with [the provisions of] Article 204 of the Penal Code to six months of penal servitude, in line with the prosecutor's request. After the sentence was announced, the judge stated that his opinion was in agreement with that of the jurors and that he found that there was not enough evidence to support the claim that the accused had the intention to kill and that [he thought that] this was a case of injury.

(2) 1928, "Tokyo's first jury trial: detective intrigue overflowing", Hōritsu Shinbun, December 30, p. 20

The first jury trial to be held at Tokyo District Court opened at Jury Courtroom Number 2 as the year drew to a close, on December 17. The accused was a young woman. The preliminary investigation had resulted in an acquittal, and the case was brought to the public hearing only because the prosecutor appealed that verdict, so the prospects for the defendant were bright. On the [first] day of the trial, there were members of the public in the courtroom eager to listen to the proceedings as early as 5:30 in the morning. By 8:00 the number of people present in the courtroom significantly exceeded the number of available seats.

After the jury panel had been formed, the trial opened at 11:20. Minister of Justice Hara,[1] President of the Great Court of Cassation Makino,[2] President of the Tokyo Court of Appeal Wani,[3] Deputy Public Prosecutor of the Great Court of Cassation Hayashi,[4] President of the Tokyo District Court Tanaka and some high-ranking officials from the Ministry of Justice, including Vice Ministers and Parliamentary Councilors (san'yokan), sat down in a row at the back of the courtroom.

Finally, the wooden plates were struck on wooden boards – that moment was exactly like the beginning of a play[5] – and Justice Dōun Toyomizu who would be presiding over that day's hearings appeared from behind the curtains and settled down in his seat in front of the courtroom that was filled with people who were all standing. A look at the jury panel revealed that many members were either gray-haired or bald elderly gentlemen. The oldest juror on the panel was 65 years old. All members of the jury had very dutiful faces, and three jurors appeared to be representatives of the *intelligentsia*, while some looked as if they might be in government service.

The judge turned towards the jurors while remaining in his seat and said with a deliberate air, "Members of the Jury!" The judge continued that serving as jurors on the first jury trial to open in Tokyo was a great honor and talked in detail about the rules for jury service as

---

1 Yoshimichi Hara (1867–1944) served as minister of justice between April 1927 and July 1929 (Shimizu, "Senzen no Hōritsuka ni tsuite no Hito Kōsatsu" [A Study of Legal Professionals in the Pre-war Period], pp. 21–22).
2 Makino Kikunosuke (1866–1936) served as president of the Great Court of Cassation during the period between 1927 and 1931 (T. Ichinose (ed.), 2004, *Major 20th Century People in Japan: A Biographical Dictionary*, Tokyo: Nichigai Associates, p. 2292).
3 Wani Teikichi (1870–1937) served as president of the Tokyo Court of Appeals and subsequently became president of the Great Court of Cassation – a post that Wani held during the period between 1931 and 1935 (*id.*, p. 2817).
4 Hayashi Raigiburō (1878–1958) subsequently became president of the Great Court of Cassation (1935–1936) and minister of justice (1936–1937). *Id.*, p. 2047.
5 The reference here is to the sound that signals the beginning of a Kabuki play (Edwin O. Reischauer (ed.), 2003, *Japan: An Illustrated Encyclopedia*, Tokyo: Kōdansha, pp. 701–706).

well as the importance of this duty. This was followed by an explanation of the order of the proceedings for adjudicating the case. While this explanation that took more than twenty minutes and sounded like a lecture covered all points that were important, your correspondent felt that it was excessively detailed and long. The judge probably decided to proceed in this manner because this was the first jury trial [to take place in Tokyo]. The jurors made their oath, and the trial started. Prosecutor Hōjō's statement regarding the facts constituting the crime was also the longest that your correspondent has had the opportunity to hear in a courtroom. The prosecutor made explanations using a wall chart, and his round face was puffed up during his speech, which made him look like a globefish while he was making his detailed statement.

[According to the prosecutor,] the facts constituting the crime were in short as follows. On July 10, 1927, Uichi Yamafuji, husband of the defendant, Kanko [Yamafuji], bought a confectionary store ([address:] Tokyo, Magome Machi, Shimizukubo 3532) together with all the products contained therein from Mitsuo Ikeda for 5,000 yen and began selling confectionary at retail. It was there that the incident occurred. Business did not go well. Debts rose, and by March 1928, the amount owed to suppliers reached 900 yen. The [defendant's] husband, Uichi, had not participated in the business from the start and was indifferent as to the debts that were being accumulated, so Kanko was despairing over the situation on her own. When Kanko [was about to conclude that] nothing could be done to rectify the situation the thought of fire insurance suddenly came to her. The shop was insured by the Imperial Insurance Company for 3,000 yen and by the Chiyoda Insurance Company for 5,000 yen (property insurance in both cases), and [the defendant] thought that if she could collect insurance money, her torment would be over. It was in this way that the thought of setting the store on fire crept into her mind. So on March 14, 1928, she gave coins worth 15 *sen* to her seventeen-year-old maid and told her go to the Ōokayama Drug Store to buy some gasoline. The bottle containing the gasoline that was left after [the defendant] finished cleaning her *tegara* ribbon[6] with it was placed on a shelf near the bathtub. The defendant went to bed at 23:00, but could not sleep. She got up at 2:00 in the morning and alone went to the shop counter. There she took two newspapers and poured gasoline over them. She then lit the papers up with a match that she took from near the stove and stuck the burning papers in a hole in a two-*tatami* size[7] *fusuma* door.[8] The defendant then lay down. Upon hearing the fire crackling she became frightened and together with family members tried to put the fire out. This is the gist of what was said [by the prosecutor]. In response to the judge's question [that followed this description], the defendant said, "All [that has been said] is completely untrue!" The defendant thus completely denied the story [presented by the prosecutor].

"The two *fusuma* doors were not burnt in your house on March 15 at 2 in the morning then?" – it was with this [question] that the hearing started. The details regarding the location [of the rooms] were clarified one by one using a wall chart. [It was also clarified that] the fire was discovered by Kanko first and that she discovered it because her child started crying and as she fed the child she started wondering about where the cracking sound might

---

6 *Tegara* is a ribbon for Japanese hairstyling (The Encyclopedic Dictionary of the Japanese Language, Vol. 9, p. 601).
7 One *tatami* measures 1.76 by 0.88 meters in the Tokyo area (Reischauer, *Japan: An Illustrated Encyclopedia*, p. 1530).
8 In Japanese architecture, *fusuma* are vertical rectangles which can slide from side to side to redefine spaces within a room, or act as doors (*id.*, p. 48).

be coming from and thought that it might be a fire. The maid woke up next and the two women together tried to wake the head of the family up. As he would not wake up, they had to shake him to make sure that he was awake. The maid was told to carry the child on her back, but who had given the child to her she could not remember. Together with the husband the two women poured water over the fire and finally succeeded at putting it out. There was a very strong smell of gasoline in the room. They went back to bed without checking whether the front door was properly closed at around 2:30, but could not sleep until the morning. The judge asked questions regarding the process of extinguishing the fire, the way the doors were closed and what they talked about once they lay down to sleep and other details to the extent that seemed excessive. Next, the trial clarified the following past events: the fact that the two-*tatami* size *fusuma* door had been burnt last September and the fact that one week prior to the date that the incident [under current investigation] took place, on the evening of March 8, a wainscoting panel that was located very close [to the place of this year's fire] was burned. The defendant was asked if she believed that the fire [in these incidents] had been initiated by her husband and was asked about the statements that she had made during the preliminary investigation. Kanko stated that although she used to think that her husband might have been responsible, she no longer thought so.

The statements that followed highlighted the fact that when Kanko decided to report the fire to the police the following morning, Uichi tried to stop her, which planted the seeds of doubt among the listeners. The defendant then talked about how the detectives and other officials from the Ōmori Police Department came [to the house] and carried out their investigation, about being taken to the police station, and about how Detective Masubuchi started pressuring her, saying, "If you tell us that you did it and apologize, we will let you go home," and that she ended up saying things that she knew were not the truth. When saying these words, the defendant took out a handkerchief and started crying. The judge reprimanded Kanko for admitting that it was she who did it in front of the prosecutor and of the magistrate.

Very detailed questions followed, but accused Kanko answered these questions with such clarity that one could hear people in the audience whisper, "What a [capable and] reliable woman!" The court had a short recess from 14:10, and at 15:00 the curtain went up again for the testimony of twenty-six witnesses. Kanko's husband, Uichi, was the first to testify. He appeared [in the courtroom] wearing a crested kimono and *hakama*.[9] The questions that he was asked slowly moved from those concerning the details of his everyday life to those concerning the details of the incident. In response to the question, "Who was the first to know that there was a fire?" he answered, "The defendant and the maid, what remained after the fire smelled of gasoline, and the defendant looked dazed." He pointed his finger at Kanko and referred to his wife sometimes as "the defendant" and sometimes as "Kanko". The members of the jury smiled every time [he talked about his wife]. Uichi's testimony continued for two hours, and he gave clear answers. During this testimony, the prosecutor showed pieces of burned newspaper to the members of the jury, asking them to look at them closely. Next to testify was Tomi Kansawa (seventeen years of age) who was working for Kanko as a maidservant at the time of the incident. She only said, "I found out about the fire when the mistress woke me up," and replied, "I forgot," or "I do not know," to all other questions, which made all members of the jury feel impatient. However, when the time came for the display of the bottle of gasoline the maid's attitude changed. According to the prosecutor, this bottle was used by Kanko to start the fire, while Kanko insisted that she only used the

---

9 Formal traditional Japanese attire for a man, consisting of a long pleated skirt (*id.*, p. 490).

gasoline to clean a red *tegara* ribbon. When asked about who told her to buy the gasoline, the maid said that she had been asked to buy it by the mistress one day before the fire. When asked, "What was the amount of gasoline in the bottle at the time when you made the purchase?" after repeating several times that she did not remember she finally said, "This much." She then made marks on the bottle using ink, indicating that about one *sun*[10] of gasoline had been used [since the purchase]. Then, the members of the defense panel stood up one after the other saying, "Didn't the witness state at the preliminary investigation that one fifth of the bottle's contents was missing? Which [statement] is true then?" With these words the members of the defense panel came close to the witness stand. At that moment, all members of the jury looked as if they had been sprinkled with cold water as they looked intently at the lovely girl, trying to interpret the expression on her face.

"Now it seems that more from the bottle was missing than at the time of the preliminary investigation," Tomi said finally and burst into tears. The prosecutor then stood up and said, "Try making a mark with ink on the bottle and show us the amount that you thought was missing at the time of the pre-trial investigations." With these words the examination of evidence by the prosecutor and the defense that reminded one of the sparkles of fireworks began. This was followed by a triangular hard-fought struggle between the judge, the defense counsel, and the prosecutor regarding the fact that although at the preliminary hearing Tomi testified that she was not aware of what that gasoline was used for, at the public trial hearing she stated that she actually remembered seeing Kanko cleaning her *tegara* ribbon with it. Next, Mr. Manzō Miyada (thirty-four years of age), engaged in the production of Western-style clothes ([address:] Kanda, Minami Kōka-machi 8), the owner of the house that the Yamafujis were renting, was called to testify. He described the house in detail, and when his testimony was finished, the presiding judge said that that day's hearings would be adjourned and that the hearing would be continued on the following day with the testimony of the remaining witnesses. It was at 19:15 that the members of the jury were allowed to finally leave the courtroom. Before they departed, the judge thanked them for that day's service and said:

> In order to ensure that the fairness of the jury trial is not compromised, even at the risk of causing you inconvenience, we would like you to stay at the jury accommodation facility and not have any interactions with outsiders. If you absolutely have to have such an interaction, you must receive permission from the court, and only meetings in the presence of the clerk on night duty will be allowed.

After these words of strict warning the hearing was adjourned.

On the second day of the trial, December 18, trial hearings began on time – shortly after 10 in the morning – despite the fact that two or three witnesses and members of the defense panel were missing. The trial was to continue with the testimonies of witnesses who were to determine whether the deepening mystery would be solved or not, so the courtroom was even fuller than on the first day of the trial, and some of the members of the public who had been present on the previous day were [again in the courtroom]. The faces of the members of the jury no longer displayed the tiredness of the previous day, but were glowing with renewed energy and interest. The jurors settled down again in their seats. Their faces and general demeanor seemed relaxed, probably due to the fact that they had become used to being in the courtroom. Defendant Kanko also seemed quite relaxed as she could even be seen swinging her legs when seated in her chair. The first witness called to the stand that day

---

10 One *sun* equals 3.03 cm (The Encyclopedic Dictionary of the Japanese Language, Vol. 7, p. 1110).

was Mr. Yoshikazu Hiroi, a salesperson working for Chiyoda Insurance Company. Mr. Hiroi spoke smoothly about the insurance contract that Uichi and Kanko concluded with his firm for the amount of 5,000 yen shortly before the day that the fire took place at their house (March 15, last year [1927]). Whether it was the Yamafujis or Hiroi himself who proposed the amount of 5,000 yen first he initially could not recall, but then he added, "I think it was I." After several simple exchanges this witness left the courtroom. Next, Mr. Midori [Kōro],[11] a representative of "Echigoya", a confectionary located in Ōmori-machi, Minami Hara 463, that had business with the shop owned by the Yamafujis, took the witness stand. He testified that [the store] had approximately 300 yen-worth of transactions with the Yamafujis' store monthly and that the payment of bills by the Yamafujis slowed down one or two months prior to the incident. Upon hearing the next question – "What was the amount of accounts receivable as of March 15?" – the witness started looking for something in his pocket and it seemed that he was going to produce an object with notes on it. The judge said, "Do not look [for any papers], it is fine if you give us a rough estimate." As the judge scolded [the witness], the faces of the members of the jury glittered in an unusual way. The defense then addressed the following question to the witness: "Look at your notes and tell us precisely." At that moment Justice Toyomizu exclaimed: "Without the permission of the judge!" Little by little [everyone in the courtroom] became animated again. When the permission was being requested, the members of the jury had a tense expression on their faces. Next, the owners of other confectionaries that did business with the defendant's shop, Mr. Yahachi Hara (forty-three years of age), Mr. Miyoshi Machida (forty-nine years of age), Mr. Tōzō Mamoriya (twenty-eight years of age), and several others, gave straightforward answers with regard to the questions concerning the detailed amounts of money transactions between their shops and that of the defendant in the months prior to the fire and the amounts of accounts receivables. Nothing significantly affecting the development of the case was brought up in these testimonies, so these testimonies turned out to be favorable to the defendant. The court had a recess that started at 12:50. The hearing re-opened at 14:15, and the questioning of witnesses continued. Before the hearings started, the judge said to the members of the jury, "The questioning of witnesses will most likely take all of tomorrow, so I would like to request you to participate in the hearings until the day after tomorrow." The jurors were thus [notified that they would be] "conserved" [at the jury accommodation facility] for yet another night. The next witness was Mr. Manbei Sawada, the older brother of the defendant. The judge said to him, "You may refuse to testify." After glancing in the direction of his sister, Sawada said, "With your permission then I refuse [to testify]," and hurriedly left the courtroom. This was followed by the testimony of the mother of the defendant's husband, Mrs. Oyoku Fujiyama, who had been summoned to court from a faraway village in Toyama. This testimony was favorable to the witness. Next, the owner of yet another confectionary wearing a *shirushibanten*[12] was questioned, which was followed by the testimony of the older sister of the defendant, Ms. Kiyoko Miura. The judge put the notorious red *tegara* ribbon on display, and Miura said, "That is precisely the ribbon that I gave to Kanko and the one that I told her to clean with gasoline." "What? You are saying that you told her to clean this with gasoline?" The judge and the prosecutor fervently pursued the subject further by asking if she had told Kanko [to clean the *tegara* ribbon] simply as a word [of advice] to accompany the gift, or because the *tegara* was dirty. This was followed

---

11 Illegible in the original.
12 A traditional Japanese coat worn by workmen (The Encyclopedic Dictionary of the Japanese Language, Vol. 7, p. 481).

266 *Appendix*

by a minor clash of opinions between the prosecutor and the members of the defense panel. The trial re-opened at 16:20, after a recess. The testimony of Mr. Kōkichi Takahira from Togoshi, Tokyo, was followed by that of the defendant's father, Mr. Kiemon Sawada, an elderly gentleman. When he took the stand he said, "Kanko has never told me that she was troubled by loans." This testimony was favorable to the defendant. Defense attorney Tsukasaki then asked, "On the day that followed the day of the incident when Kanko was retained by the police, the sixteenth, you were at the Yamafujis' house. How did you spend the day there?" The father replied, "That night . . . My wife and I . . . We hugged our grandchild and spent the whole night crying." Upon hearing this answer that was uttered in a tearful voice, Kanko threw herself on the floor and started sobbing, and all the grief that she had obviously been trying to control started flowing out. Upon hearing these sobs, the elderly father leaned his head on the wooden edge of the witness box and broke down in bitter tears. The dealer of *konnyaku* jelly[13] and the *soba*[14] merchant sitting in the jury box were deeply moved and tearful. The judge proclaimed that the hearings for that day were adjourned. It was 17:20. The defendant continued crying and screamed, "Let me see my child!" The prison guard tried to put a braided straw hat (*amigasa*)[15] on the defendant, but she threw the hat away and acted like a madwoman. The elderly father again broke down in tears.

On the third day of the trial, December 19, the trial hearing opened at 10:05 and witness testimonies continued. Mr. Jinsaku Takei who lived in the second floor of the house where the Yamafujis were staying described the state of affairs at the house when fire was discovered on March 15. He stated that the fire that occurred at the house last September appeared to have been the work of the hands of an outsider. Takei testified further that the lock of the gate was taken off and that *tabi*[16] footprints were discovered in the close proximity to the house. He described the incident when the wainscoting panel outside the house got burned on March 8 this year. [Your correspondent wondered] what the judge was thinking about as he was listening to this faltering explanation. When asked, "Haven't you, the witness, ever gone downstairs by the side of the roof when debt-collectors came?" the witness said, "This sometimes happened," thus making everyone aware of his disgraceful behavior and making everyone in the courtroom burst out in laughter. Next, a contractor, Mr. Kamekichi Nogami, who employed Takei as a laborer took the witness stand and was asked to talk about the character of Takei. This was followed by the testimony of Mr. Morio Kubo who used to serve as a clerk for the Yamafujis. He appeared in the courtroom wearing a *shirushibanten*. Kubo talked about how he had been held for twenty days at the Ōmori Police Station as a suspect in the incident of fire that occurred on March 8 and described the events of the time when there was a fire in September last year. Pressured by the defense counsel regarding the lock of the garden gate, he said, making it apparent that he found these questions tiresome, "[Taking the lock out of the door] was someone else's doing, so I do not remember all the details," and became passive [in his further answers]. Next, a confectionary workman, Mr. Daisaku Wakui, talked about the strange gossips concerning the defendant and Mr. Taizō Kawase and stated that their relationship did not seem to

---

13 A gelatinous food made from devil's-tongue starch (Reischauer, *Japan: An Illustrated Encyclopedia*, p. 825).
14 *Soba* is a type of noodle principally made from buckwheat flour, with wheat flour, yam, or egg white serving as a thickener (*id.*, p. 1436).
15 *Amigasa* is a braided straw hat that is usually flat on top and has sides to cover the face (The Encyclopedic Dictionary of the Japanese Language, Vol. 1, p. 558).
16 *Tabi* is a sock worn with traditional Japanese clothing (Reischauer, *Japan: An Illustrated Encyclopedia*, p. 1493).

be a particularly deep one. When he said, "After all, Kanko was only fifteen-sixteen then and maybe she was just trying to imitate what she had seen in the movies," the courtroom became abuzz with conversations and laughter. Defendant Kanko was also chuckling while looking at the ground. Upon the request of the prosecutor, witness Mitsuo Ikeda was questioned, after which the trial went into recess at 13:00. The hearings were resumed at 13:20 and began with the appearance of Mr. Sakae Tajima (thirty-two years of age), a policeman in charge of photographing [the scene of the crime]. He was asked about the time when the photographing of the scene of the incident took place. Then Policeman at the Shimizukobo Police Station, Mr. Kumao Tamura (thirty-five years of age), testified that he immediately went to inspect the scene of the incident before filing the suit and that he discovered that the frames of the *fusuma* were intact and that the paper was burned. He then went on to state that when he examined the glass door, he found it locked and that no footprints could be detected outside. Upon hearing this, Kanko shrieked, "That is not the truth, all lies!" and started crying. The judge gently soothed her. The next witness was Detective Kin'ichirō Masubuchi (thirty-one years of age). He stated that "at the scene, a match box was found and the remains of scraps of paper and traces of a match that had been lit," and described in detail [the scene of the crime]. "Based on these findings, we questioned Kanko, and she could not conceal the truth any longer and in the end confessed to committing the crime." In response to that, the judge asked, "Did you question her particularly violently at the police station?", and detective Masubuchi replied that they never would do such a thing and that they never raise their voices. The judge then said that raising voices was not the same as using rough methods of questioning and that even if their voices were soft this did not necessarily imply that rough methods were not being used and addressed hard questions to this witness. Then Kanko raised her voice, started crying, stood up from her seat, and said:

> This detective told me that if I did not confess, I would not be able to return home, that I was to say everything and that what I had said before was all untrue. He even told me what to confess to, said that I poured gasoline on a newspaper and lit it up with a match!

At that moment, juror Aizō Satō (sixty-five years of age) broke his silence for the first time and – his face displaying deep emotion and in an oratorical tone – said, "The witness is simply stating that he never asked leading questions, and that what the defendant has said is not true. Unlike the statement of the defendant, which is logically organized, there is something lacking in the testimony of this witness. Can't he answer in such a way that would persuade us?" The juror thus let the first arrow of questions fly, but after the warning from the judge the witness stepped down. The public was overjoyed, and at 18:00 the court had a short recess. At 18:20 the hearings were resumed. Following the testimony of the defendant's brother-in-law, Mr. Yoshio Sawada (twenty-four years of age; [address:] Ebara-Machi, Tokyo), who was in the confectionery business and rushed to the scene on the day of the fire, the head of the judicial department at the Ōmori Police Station, Mr. Zenkichi Satō (forty-eight years of age), gave testimony that was more or less in agreement with that of Detective Masubuchi. The judge reprimanded Satō saying, "Nobody will call you to account simply because you are the person in charge of the judicial department [at that police station], stop talking nonsense!" The testimony went back and forth, and juror Jutarō Koizumi asked, "Could you detect finger prints on the box of matches, or did you not think of looking for them?" To this question that sounded like one coming from a professional, Satō replied with a devastated look on his face, "The box was wet and it was impossible [to get fingerprints]." With this phrase witness testimonies that had continued for three days were concluded, and at 20:00 the hearing was adjourned.

On the fourth day of the trial, as all witness testimonies had been concluded, the judge started his explanation of the evidence. This explanation was so detailed that all listening to it felt as if they were given the chance to hold each piece of evidence in their own hands. The prosecutor and the defense counsel had a clash of opinions regarding the reading out of the report of the investigation of the suspect. At 14:00, the closing remarks of prosecutor Hōjō that were as forceful as a fervent fire began. During the closing remarks that were decidedly sharp, the prosecutor linked the evidence one by one to the [established] facts. At certain times [during this speech] defendant Kanko would bend down on her chair and start crying. The prosecutor noticed this but went on, saying "You should better not cry. I am almost finished."

When the [prosecutor] finished his closing remarks that continued for more than two hours the court went into recess, which was followed by the passionate closing remarks delivered by attorney Tsukasaki and two other members of the defense panel. These remarks were finished at 21:30.

On the last day of jury [duty] trial hearings began at 10:20. The judge started his instructions [to the jury]. This was preceded by the prosecutor's [attempt to] refute two or three points stated by the defense counsel in the closing remarks the day before. The judge then explained the evidence. He began by explaining the rules of the admissibility of evidence, proceeded to the explanation of the credibility of evidence, and then touched upon the evidence in the case on trial, paying particular attention to the issues concerning confessions. In the middle of this explanation, at around 13:20, the members of the jury asked two or three questions. Your correspondent thought that the instructions of the judge were much too long and verbose. It should be possible to make these explanations in a more simple and efficient way.

Finally, [the judge set] the questions [for jury deliberations]. [The first] question was read out and was as follows: "Did the defendant at 2 AM on March 15, 1928, set the two-*tatami* size *fusuma* door in her house on fire and then together with her husband extinguish it?" When the defense stated their concern that the phrasing of the question might result in misunderstandings, the members of the jury stood up one after the other and fiercely protested that they could not answer this question in the form of "yes" or "no", thus giving the judge a hard time and making all people in the courtroom groan. The position of the court was that the case on trial was a case of attempted arson, therefore, it was imperative to ask the question of whether the fire was subsequently extinguished [by the defendant], and that if the jury believed that the defendant did extinguish the fire, then they would answer in no way other than "yes" to this question. Finally, after a recess, the trial re-opened at 14:10, and the judge explained to the jurors, "If you answer 'no', then this means that you find the defendant not guilty, if you answer 'yes', then it will imply that you find the defendant guilty, so please bear this in mind." After receiving this explanation, both sides agreed on this compromise and the members of the jury proceeded to the deliberation room at 14:20, and behind the curtains and with entry closed to all outsiders and to all those who were not supposed to know anything about the process the deliberations continued for two hours. At 16:20, the trial was re-opened. Darkness enveloped the courtroom – due to a power outage the electricity went out – and the light of candles made everything in the courtroom look different. The faces of the jurors were beaming and reflected a feeling of relief after carrying out their heavy responsibility as they were settling down in their seats. The responses of the jury were handed to the judge by the clerk. The courtroom was filled with such an incredible sense of tension that it was difficult to breathe when the judge briefly looked over the responses and handed them over to the secretary who then raised his voice and read out: "Response [of the jury]: 'No.'" Everyone in the courtroom released a sigh of relief. The Judge thanked the members of the jury for their service. Juror Yasushi Muraoka stood up and eloquently expressed his gratitude to everyone present for making it possible for the members of the jury to carry out their important responsibility in the first jury trial in Tokyo in a manner befitting such a beautiful occasion. Finally, after further consultations the defendant was proclaimed categorically not guilty.

(3) 1928, "The accused members of the Communist Party to request trial by jury", Hōritsu Shinbun, December 28, p. 19

The number of members of the underground Communist Party who have been persecuted in district courts across Japan has reached 300. In addition, 196 members are currently undergoing pre-trial investigations in Tokyo. Out of the forty-six party members who studied at the Communist University [of the Toilers of the East] in [Soviet] Russia, approximately half have returned to Japan and started new activities [in the country]. The arrests of remaining members of the party are continuing, so the number of persons being investigated has exceeded 500 as of the end of this year.

Even if arrests are temporarily discontinued, the verdicts of the preliminary hearings will be out no sooner than May or June next year, while public trial hearings on these cases should open in November–December. Among those cases that are being tried in Tokyo alone, about twenty defendants may be sentenced to lifetime imprisonment or death, which means that these cases will be tried by jury. The view that as a matter of strategy [. . .][17] almost half of the defendants who are members of the Communist Party will be requesting trial by jury has become predominant. The judicial authorities look upon this as a serious problem and are currently in the process of developing an appropriate response.

(4) 1930, "Violation of the Jury Act", Hōritsu Shinbun, March 13, p. 18

Article 109 section 1 of the Jury Act stipulates that in the event a juror leaks information regarding the contents of jury deliberations or the distribution of votes during jury deliberations the penalty of not more than 1,000 yen is applied. Section 2 of the same article stipulates that in the event a newspaper publishes this information the publisher of that newspaper and the editor are also to be held responsible and are to be required to pay the penalty of not more than 2,000 yen. The first violation [of article 109 of the Jury Act] in this country occurred in Miyagi Prefecture and is currently being investigated by the Sendai District Court and prosecutor's office. The incident involved a murder case that was tried at the Sendai District Court on February 25 and 26. Mr. Tokuzō Kimura (forty-eight years of age; [employee of] a restaurant; [address:] Ishimaki-chō, Ishimaki Nakanose 3) was elected as the jury foreman. [Upon completing his duty] Mr. Kimura returned home and was approached by a reporter of a certain newspaper and told that reporter about the contents of the deliberations and about the distribution of votes. This information was subsequently published by the said newspaper. This constitutes the first violation of the Jury Act in our country since the introduction of the jury system and is therefore looked upon as an incident of extreme importance by the Court and the prosecutor's office. It was taken up by Prosecutor Ichikawa who summoned jury foreman Tokuzō Kimura for questioning on the afternoon of March 5.

---

17 Illegible in the original.

II Illustrations

Illustration 1a The front page of the issue of *Hōritsu Shinbun* (*Legal News*) reporting on the first jury trial in Japan (Ōita District Court)

Source: Anonymous, 1928, "Baishin Saiban ni Seikō Shita Ōita Chihō Saibansho" [Oita District Court Successfully [Carries Out] Jury Trial], *Hōritsu Shinbun*, November 3, p. 1.

Illustration 1b The front page of the issue of *Hōritsu Shinbun* (*Legal News*) reporting on the first jury trial in Tokyo

Source: Anonymous, 1928, "Tokyo ni okeru Hatsu Baishin" [Tokyo's First Jury Trial], *Hōritsu Shinbun*, December 30, p. 1.

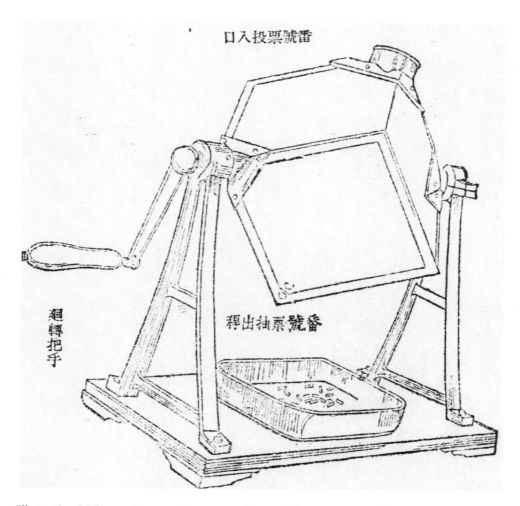

Illustration 2 The machine used in pre-war Japan to determine who would become candidates for jury service

Source: K. Isotani and K. Yanagawa, 1927, *Baishin no Jōshiki* [The Common Sense of the Jury], Tokyo: Hōsō Kai, p. 31.

Illustration 3 A photograph taken during a mock trial held in 1928

Source: Anonymous, 1928, "Daiichi Tokyo Bengoshi Kai Shusai Mogi Baishin Saiban" [Mock Jury Trial Organized by the Daiichi Tokyo Bar Association], *Hōritsu Shinbun*, September 23, p. 1.

Illustration 4 Court clothing

Source: Anonymous, 1927, Cover Page Photograph, *Hōritsu Shinbun*, August 25, p. 1.

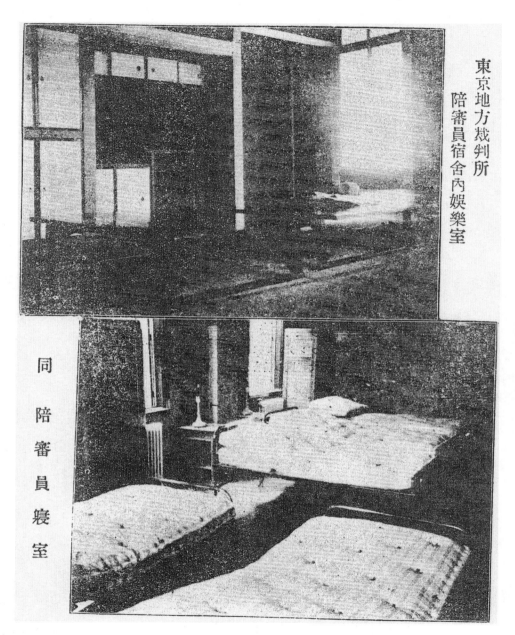

Illustration 5 Photographs taken inside the jury accommodation facility at the Tokyo District Court (1928)

Source: Anonymous, 1928, "Tokyo Chihō Saibansho" [Tokyo District Court], *Hōritsu Shinbun*, October 5, p. 1.

Illustration 6 Drawing names for the first jury panel in Okinawa
Source: High Commissioner of the Ryukyu Islands, 1963, *Civil Administration of the Ryukyu Islands: Report for Period 1 July 1962 to 30 June 1963*, Vol. 11, Naha: United States Civil Administration, p. 40.

Illustration 7 The logo of the lay judge system
Source: Saikō Saibansho [The Supreme Court of Japan], http://www.saibanin.courts.go.jp/.

Illustration 8 Promotional character *Saiban'inko*
Source: Hōmushō [The Ministry of Justice], "Saiban'inko no Purofīru" [Saiban'inko's Profile], http://www.moj.go.jp/SAIBANIN/koho/inco.html.

Illustration 9 Posters prepared by the "We Do Not Need the Lay Judge System!" movement
For the Abolishment of the Lay Judge System! The Lay Judge System: A Nuisance!
Source: "Saiban'in Seido wa Iranai! Dai Undō" [We Do Not Need the Lay Judge System! Movement], http://no-saiban-in.org/index.html.

Illustration 10 Promotional character *Saiban'iniranainko*

Source: "Saiban'in Seido wa Iranai! Dai Undō" [We Do Not Need the Lay Judge System! Movement], http://no-saiban-in.org/index.html.

Index

Note: Page numbers in bold indicate a table on the corresponding page.

Abe, Shinzō 169
Abe, Shungo 139
Act Concerning Participation of Lay Judges in Criminal Trials 7; *see also* Lay Judge Act
Act for the Compensation of Pollution-Related Health Injury (1973) 168
acute stress disorder (ASD) 207
Adachi, Masakatsu 201
adversarial system of justice 3, 3n13
Allied occupation of Japan 130n3, 130n6
all-layperson independent jury 198–9
alternative dispute resolution (ADR) 173
amendments to Jury Act 90–3
Anglo-American model of jury systems: conclusion 220–2; influence of 135, 141–2, 146, 164; introduction 3–6, 8; Jury Act and 94; Jury Act selection *vs.* 74; in Okinawa 161; *saiban'in* system *vs.* 18n84; trial by jury concept 50–1
anti-*saiban'in* argument 197, 200–2
Appleton, Richard B. 150
assimilation notion 99, 108, 109
Association for Deliberations on the Jury System 177
Association for Opposing the Lay Judge System (*Saiban'in Seido ni Hantai Suru Kai*) 198
Association for the Revival of the Jury System 177, 180, 198–9
Attorney Act (1893) 58–9

baishin, defined 29–30
Black, Abraham 160–1
Blakemore, Thomas L. 144
Bohannan, Paul 11
Boissonade de Fontarabie, Emile Gustave: Code of Criminal Instruction 46–50, 52; conclusions 217–18; introduction 7; trial by jury concept 24, 24n26
Brader, Robert 50, 52–3

Bridgman, Elijah Coleman 28–9
bureaucratic jury (*sanza*) system: in civilian trials 34–5; Code of Criminal Instruction 46–50; conceptualization of 225; conclusion 54, 219; historical background 55–8; introduction 6–8; *Meiji* Constitution 44–6; in military courts 44; overview 33–4; rules 36–43; trial by jury attempts 50–4

Charter Oath of Five Articles 20–1
Chiang Wei-shui 112
Chinese classical texts 26–8
Civil Code reform 134
Civil Intelligence Section (CIS) 142
"closed country" (*sakoku*) 21n6
Code of Civil Procedure 170
Code of Criminal Instruction 46–50, 54, 60, 142, 217
Code of Criminal Instruction Screening Committee 47–9
Code of Penal Procedure 146
colonialism 97–110
Constitutional Draft Revision Special Committee 140
Constitution of Japan 169
Continental-European model of jury systems 3–9, 221
Council for Justice System Reform 141
Council of Elders (Genrōin) 24
Counterintelligence Corps (OCCIO) 136, 137n63
Court Organization Law 135, 142, 147–8

Daidō Club 61
Dai Ichi Tokyo Bar Association 91
Dai Nippon Sugar Company 61
Dajōkan 21n5
death penalty rulings 207
defense representative rules 38, 42
Deliberative Councils 21n3

Den, Kenjirō 111
Durkheim, Émile 11
Dutch East India Company 101

Ebara Policeman Murder incident 121–7
Election Administration Commission 190
Equal Employment Opportunity Law (EEOL) 168
Expert Advisory Committees 173–4
Expert Committee on the Lay Judge System 208
Extraordinary Judicial System Reform Preparatory Council 145
Extraordinary Legislative Council 66–8

Feldman, Eric A. 13
"fit": macro and micro 16
Foote, Daniel H. 211
Freedom and People's Rights Movement 25
French Civil Code 23–5
French Criminal Code 23
French-Japanese dictionary 29
French jury system 31, 46
Friedman, L.M. 10
Friends of Constitutional Government 57
Fujii, Shōkichi 203
Fukui, Kane 37
Fusaaki Uzawa 27
Fuse, Tatsuji 123–4, 123n181

General Headquarters (GHQ) 138–9
German Civil Code 25
Gneist, Rudolf von 25
Government of the Ryukyu Islands (GRI) 152–4, 165, 216
Grand Court of Judicature 47
Great Council of State (*Dajōkan*) 35, 48–9
Great Court of Judicature 86, 141, 145n111
Great Hanshin-Awaji Earthquake 176
Gushikawa incident 157

Habeas Corpus Act 135
Haley, John O. 14, 15
Hanai, Takuzō 32–3, 67
Han Chinese 101
Hara, Takashi: drafting of Jury Act 94; extension of Constitution 105; pre-war jury 61, 64–5, 67, 71; vision for Taiwan 107
Hara, Yoshimichi 82
Hideyoshi, Toyotomi 103
High Court of Justice 47
High Treason case (1910) 62, 62n37
Hiranuma, Kiichiro 82
Hirosawa, Masaomi 37
Hirosawa case 51
Hoetker, Glenn 15
Hokō Law (1898) 108

Hōritsu Shinbun newspaper company 80–1, 80n181, 86–8
human rights concerns 61–3

Ikeda, Bennet N. (Ken) 156
Imperial Diet: establishment of a Parliament for Taiwan 110; introduction 2; Jury Act and 59–60; as major law 105–6; *Nittō* incident 61–2; pre-war jury system 55; Universal Manhood Suffrage Law 56
indictment lay assessor system 86
Inoue, Kowashi 48–9, 53
Inoue, Masahito 185
inquisitorial system of justice 3, 3n15
Isa, Chihiro 158–9, 158n197, 159n203, 164, 199
Isobe, Shirō 59
isshi dōjin notion 99
Itagaki, Taisuke 109
Itakura, Shigemune 27, 27n40
Itō, Miyoji 71
Iwata, Chūzō 141

Japan Association of Corporate Executives 181–2, 181n103
Japanese Communist Party 58
Japanese exceptionalism 14
Japanese legal consciousness 14
Japan Federation of Bar Associations: mixed-court system 181–2, 183n110, 185, 195; occupation years 137, 157; pre-war jury system 59–60, 96; reforms 208n292; trial by jury concept 53n157
Japan Jury Association 81–3
Japan Lawyers Association for Freedom 137
Japan Newspaper Publishers and Editors' Association 186
Japan Progressive Party 61
Japan's Bar Association 78, 157
Japan's Court Organization Law 118
judge-only jury 6–8, 225
judge rules 39, 42
Judicial System Reform Council (JSRC): conclusions 217; introduction 1–2; mixed-court jury 167, 170–1, 175–6, 183–6; occupation years 146
Judicial System Reform Council Establishment Act 171
Jurisprudence Society 176
Jury Act (1923): in action 85–90; amendments 90–3; conclusions 96; courtrooms and lawyer training 195–6; drafting of 58–66; encouraging public participation 63–4; extension to Taiwan 108–14; implementation of 66–73; introduction 55; local Bar Associations 79–80; Ministry of Justice 77–9;

promotion efforts 76–85, 192–5; promulgation of 76; proposed revisions 148–51; public debate over 65–6; quasi-jury system under 197; respect for human rights 61–3; summary of 73–6; supplementary legislation 191–2; suspensions 90–1, 92–3; *see also* mixed-court jury (*saiban'in*) system
Jury Act Investigation Committee 69
Jury Act Preparatory Committee 84
Jury Guidebook 82
jury plays (*baishin geki*) 80, 201
jury selection in Japan: pre-war jury 74; in the *saiban'in* system 190; at USCAR courts 154
jury service in Japan: Chinese classical texts 26–8; concept of 26–33; documents describing 28–32; introduction 1–9; legal reform and Japanese law 14–16; past and present experiences 16–18; pre-war experiences 93–6; rescripts of *Meiji* Emperor 32–3; theories of legal change 9–13; *see also* bureaucratic jury (*sanza*) system
jury system, in colonial possessions: conclusions 127–8; evaluation of attempts to introduce 125–7; historical background 97–100; introduction 97; Japanese jury courts and 121–5; Taiwan 100–14
jury system, occupation years: conclusions 165–6; evaluating experiences of 161–5; historical background 129–32; introduction 129; legal reform strategies with 140–2, 140n79; proposals to introduce 132–51, 218–19; under U.S. occupation 151–61, **158**
Jury System Research Society 178

Kaizō Dōmeikai (Alliance for Reform) 64, 64n51
Kanda, Hideki 16
Kaneko, Kentarō 44–5
Karafuto: historical background 97; under Japanese rule 114–19; jury system in 119–21; pre-war jury system in 215–17
Karafuto Agency 116
Karafuto District Court 117
Katō, Hiroyuki 30
Kawashima, Takeyoshi 14
Kimura, Tokutarō 139
Kirkwood, Montegue 104
Kisaburō, Suzuki 82
Kishira, Kaneyasu 46
Kiyomiya, Shirō 177
Kiyoura, Keigo 48
Kokuhonsha nationalist society 82

Kosakai, Fuboku 80
Kume, Kunitake 30–1

Law Concerning the Procedures of Revising the Constitution of Japan 2
Lay Judge Act (2004): mixed-court system 176–83; preparation for enforcement 191–6; summary 188–90, 188n143; *see also* mixed-court jury (*saiban'in*) system
layperson participation 4
League for the Establishment of a Taiwanese Parliament 111–12
Legal Affairs Committee of the House of Councilors 186–7
Legal Affairs Committee of the House of Representatives 186
legal culture 13
legal reform: introduction 1–2; Japanese law and 14–16; thematic classification 13n63; two approaches 222–6
legal transplant 9–10
Liberal Democratic Party (LDP) 15, 169, 186, 210–11, 216
Lin Hsien-tang 109
local Bar Associations 79–80, 195–6
Lohr, Steve 14

MacArthur, Douglas 133
main questions for jurors (*shumon*) 75
Makimura case 35, 50–1
Makino, Shizuo 91
Maniscalco, Anthony J. 143, 143n93
Masutarō, Takagi 80–1
Matsuda, Genji 59
Matsuda, Masahisa 118
Matsuo, Kōya 183–4
Meiji Constitution (1889): applicability in new territories 103; bureaucratic jury (*sanza*) system 44–6; drafting of 25, 52; introduction 1
Meiji Emperor 32–3
Meiji Restoration (1868): historical background of pre-war jury 20–6; introduction 1, 6; societal trends 60–1; trial by jury attempts 50–4, 93–6, 215
"micro-fit" concerns 16
Milhaupt, Curtis J. 16
military courts 44
Ming dynasty 102
Ministry of Economy, Trade, and Industry (METI) 15
Ministry of Justice 77–9
Mitani, Taichirō 45
Mitsukuri, Rinshō 23
mixed-court jury (*saiban'in*) system: all-layperson independent jury 198–9; Anglo-American system *vs.* 18n84;

anti-*saiban'in* argument 197, 200–2; conclusions 213, 216; drafting and enactment 183–7; evaluation of 209–13; example of contributions 198; first years of 205–9; historical background 167–76; implementation 203–5; introduction 8, 17–18, 167; negative aspects of 199–200; occupation years 141; public debate 196–203; *see also* Lay Judge Act
Miyazawa, Setsuo 13
Miyoshi, Taizō 59
mock trials 79–81, 119–20, 177, 196n210
Morning Star Okinawa 156
Mosse, Albert 25
Murata, Tamotsu 48

Naichi (inner lands) 6
Naitō, Masatake 92
Nakazato, Minoru 15
National Foundation Society 57
national isolation policy 21n6
New Kōmeitō 186
New People's Society 109
Nittō incident 61–2, 93
Nomura, Junji 137
Nottage, Luke 16

Ōba, Shigema 65–6
Ogawa, Heikichi 62
Oita trial 87–9
Okida, Masaichi 37
Okiharu, Yasuoka 182
Okinawa jury system **158**, 158–61, 216
Okinawan Advisory Council 151–2
Okinawa occupation *see* U.S. occupation of Okinawa
Okuno, Ken'ichi 141
Onos family 34
Ōoka, Echizennokami 27, 27n41
Oppler, Alfred C. 131, 144, 144n105, 150–1
order of trial 39–41, 42–3
Osaka Bar Association 178–9
Ozawa, Nagashige 121–2, 124–25

Peace Preservation Act: accusations against 123; laws applied to 107–8; offenses against 177; overview 132n14; pre-war jury system 58, 76, 89, 95
Pearl Harbor attack 58
Peerenboom, Randall 13
People's Rights Movement 109
Pescadores 101
plaintiff rules 38, 42
Potsdam Declaration (1945) 129
pre-war jury system: conclusions 219–20; drafting of Jury Act 58–66; existing literature on 18n83; historical background 20–6; introduction 8, 20, 55; mainland Japan 215
principal-agent theorists 11–12
Privy Council 71–3, 139
promotion efforts: pre-war jury 76–83; *saiban'in* system 192–5
Provisional Justice System Investigation Committee 173
Provisional Legislation Investigating Committee 133

Qing dynasty 102

Ramseyer, J. Mark 15
Republic of China (ROC) 108
Research Commissions on the Constitution 2, 169
Revon, Michael 104–5
Rikken Seiyūkai 62–3, 65
ritsuryō system of government 21
Robirds, Oren K. 160–1
Robirds v. Far East Construction Co. (1964) 160–1
Roesler, Hermann 25
Russo-Japanese war 56, 114
Ryukyu Islands administration 152–4

saiban'in system *see* mixed-court jury (*saiban'in*) system
San Francisco Peace Treaty (1951) 6, 130, 131n12
sanshinkan, defined 141n83
Santetomi, Sanjō 47
sanza system *see* bureaucratic jury (*sanza*) system
Satō, Kazutoshi 200
Seki, Naohiko 72
Self-Help Society 45
Shiraki, Yū 178
Shōwa Constitution (1946) 1
Shōwa period (1926–1989) 55
Smith, Herman 157
socio-legal approaches to the study of Japanese law: main schools 14–16
socio-legal theories 11, 17, 224
Special Committees for Research on the Constitution of Japan 2
Special Higher Police 57–8
special jury 33n73
Stein, Lorenz von 25
Stevens, Russel L. 161
Stimulants Control Act 204
success notion in legal reforms 9n34
supplementary questions for jurors (*homon*) 75, 75n137
Supreme Commander for the Allied Powers (SCAP): Court Organization Law directives

147–8; Jury Act, proposed revisions 148–51; jury service in Constitution text 136–40; jury system, occupation years 162–3, 226; legal reforms under Allied occupation 132–5; overview 129–30
Supreme Court of Japan 179
suspensions of Jury Act 90–1, 92–3
Suzuki, Fujiya 72
Suzuki, Umeshirō 64

Taishō period/democracy (1912–1926) 55–7, 64, 93, 108, 225
Taiwan: historical background 97, 98n3; Jury Act, extension to 108–14; laws prior to Japanese rule 100–3; laws under Japanese rule 103–5; proposals to implement jury system 218
Taiwan Affairs Bureau 104
Taiwan Cultural Association 111–12
Taiwan Popular Party 113–14, 126
Taiwan Press Law (1900) 107
Taiwan Seinen (Taiwanese Youth) 110
Takekoshi, Yosaburo 98
Takesaki, Hironobu 178
Takigawa, Yukitoki 90
Tanase, Takao 13
Teikoku Bar Association 91, 178–9
Tocqueville, Alexis de 4
Tokugawa, Yoshimune 22
Tokyo District Court 123
Tokyo trial 86–9
Toshitani, Nobuyoshi 53n156
Treaty of Portsmouth 114–15
Treaty of Shimoda 115
Treaty of Shimonoseki 103
Tripartite Pact (1940) 58
Tsai Pei-huo 112, 112n101

Uehara, Etsujirō 64
UN Convention the Elimination of All Forms of Discrimination against Women 168
unequal treaties 21–2
Uniform Code of Military Justice 153
United States of America v. Megumi Yoshihisa (1964) 155, 155n182, 158–9
Universal Manhood Suffrage Law 56
U.S. Army Forces in the Pacific (USAFPAC) Counter-Intelligence Section 142
U.S. Civil Administration Appellate Court 160
U.S. Civil Administration of the Ryukyu Islands (USCAR) 7–8, 152–7, 165, 216, 221
U.S. Constitution 156
U.S. occupation of Okinawa: jury system under 151–61, **158**, 218; military government 151–2; Okinawa jury system **158**, 158–61, 220–1; Ryukyu Islands administration 152–4; USCAR jury system 154–7
Uzawa, Fusaaki 27n42

Vanoverbeke, Dimitri 18

Watson, Alan 14, 16, 164–5, 222
Weber, Max 12

Yaguchi, Kōichi 178, 180
Yamaguchi, Takashi 201
Yamamuro, Megumi 178
Yokota, Kuniomi 65
Yokota, Sennosuke 67–8, 72
Yoshino, Sakuzō 57, 66

Zheng Chenggong 102, 102n29